New Lights from Old Truths

Living the Signs of the Times

History of the Sisters of Providence
of Saint Mary-of-the-Woods, Indiana

Volume IV
1926-1966

Sister Maureen Abbott, SP

Saint Mary-of-the-Woods, Indiana

Cover designed by Christina Blust
Edited by Sister Janet Gilligan, SP
Packaged by Wish Publishing

Printed in the United States of America
10 9 8 7 6 5 4 3 2

You expect, my dear children,
that I now have many new things to say to you,
which have been collected in my travels;
that I can now give you many new lights.
This indeed I should desire much to be able to do;
but be not disappointed to find
that they will radiate from the same old truths
which you have heard repeatedly.
Close not the eyes of your soul to them,
for you will see many things in new lights
if you give the Holy Spirit free access to your minds and hearts.

Mother Theodore Guerin,
Instructions to the sisters

Sisters of Providence History Series

New Lights from Old Truths: Living the Signs of the Times
History of the Sisters of Providence, Volume IV, 1926-1966
Sister Maureen Abbott, SP

A Path Marked Out: History of the Sisters of Providence, Volume III, 1890-1926
Sister Mary Roger Madden, SP

Against All Odds: Sisters of Providence Mission to the Chinese, 1920-1990
Sister Ann Colette Wolf, SP

History of the Sisters of Providence, Volume II, 1856-1890
Sister Eugenia Logan, SP

History of the Sisters of Providence, Volume I, 1840-1856
Sister Mary Borromeo Brown, SP

In God's Acre
Sister Mary Theodosia Mug, SP, Editor

Life and Letters of Sister St. Francis Xavier
Clémentine de la Corbinière

Letters and Journals of Mother Theodore Guérin
Sister Mary Theodosia Mug, SP, Editor

Life and Life-Works of Mother Theodore Guérin
Sister Mary Theodosia Mug, SP

☙Table of Contents

&

List of Tables

❧Foreword

The reader who leafs through these pages may be smiling as he or she views the photographs. "That looks just like my classroom!" "Is that Sister So-and-So?" Fourth in the series chronicling the history of the Congregation of the Sisters of Providence of Saint Mary-of-the-Woods, Indiana, the volume covers the period of expansion between 1926 and 1966, a period when hundreds of thousands of children were the beneficiaries of the Catholic school system in the United States. Many will be able to identify with the educational setting I have tried to describe in these pages. At times the students and graduates may have wondered what life was like for the women in the front of the classroom. The photos, memoirs, diaries and correspondence in our archives which I drew upon to assemble this narrative will enable the reader to understand and appreciate religious life from the perspective of those who lived it during these years.

Since my previous writing assignments did not include training in historical research, I adopted the approach recommended by D'Ann Campbell: "The task of the historian is to:

- Discover what did happen,
- Explain why it happened, and
- Relate that explanation to the values, resources, and constraints of the people at the time."

In order to accomplish this objective, it seemed important to provide twenty-first century readers with a more detailed description of the lifestyle of the sisters during this era. For this reason, the book is organized to feature several chapters which provide the necessary background to understand the events themselves.

- The Prologue: Summarizes the 1840-1926 history of the Sisters of Providence.
- Chapter 1: Introduces the context and culture of religious life in the twentieth century.
- Chapter 2: Describes the hierarchal organization of the congregation during this period.
- Chapters 3-4: Begins the chronological narrative, 1926-1938.

- Chapter 5: Analyzes how and why an early reorganization attempt failed.
- Chapter 6: Explains the process through which new members were incorporated.
- Chapters 7-16: Continue the chronological narrative, 1938-1966.

The wider picture of how congregations of women religious function within the Catholic Church emerges through descriptions of dealings with officials in Rome and with bishops in the United States, as well as with the network of various Catholic organizations such as the National Catholic Education Association. In addition to the sisters themselves, the reader will meet the men and women whose generous contributions of time, money and contacts were essential to the success of the educational mission. Side by side with the administrative and organizational work of the superiors that provides the backbone of the narrative are stories of daily life. Inspired by the photo of five young women who joined the Congregation in 1929, I took creative liberty in describing actual incidents from their lives to illustrate comparable events in the lives of many others. After all, as playwright Edward Albee observed, "Fiction is fact distilled into truth."

The rich biographical material of the archives provided ample material for sketches which portray the careers of the talented women whose interior calling to a deep spiritual life within the structure and support of a community found an outlet in their lively classrooms from Boston to California. Due to major changes in convent life over the decades, I felt it was important to explain for contemporary readers the systems of governance and formation operative during this era with separate chapters on those topics. Likewise the abundance of archival material on the unique contributions of the Congregation to the field of education prompted a chapter devoted to why the work of education was truly a ministry as well as a profession.

As the chronological narrative describes the expansion of the missions, it reveals the process by which those charged with governance determined how the "new lights" offered by the ever-shifting circumstances of American society illuminated the path marked out by the "old truths" of the founding spirit. It was this process that guided the council's decisions to sustain and strengthen the educational institutions already established and also to undertake new missions. Along the way realities of day-by-day community life demanded adaptation of governance structures from the top-down system of earlier times to the more egalitarian model of today.

The reader is invited to pick and choose chapters and topics of interest or read the book chapter by chapter. Some may prefer to skip footnotes entirely while others will savor small details or want to follow leads to related literature. Those who are closely associated with the Sisters of Providence will understand the centrality of the motherhouse as "Home" and enjoy the tidbits relating campus developments while others may simply skim by the infrastructure details. The map of the property will enable readers who have not had the opportunity to visit Saint Mary-of-the-Woods to have a way to understand the layout of the places mentioned, including the significance of the contiguous facilities of the motherhouse and Saint Mary-of-the-Woods College.

As one of a number of histories of religious congregations which have been published in recent years, I am hopeful that the book will not only add to the historical record of the contributions of women religious to the American church, but also lead to a deeper understanding of the underlying causes for what may have appeared to outsiders as sudden changes of long-standing patterns. As someone who began religious life during the era described and has continued to live it during an era of continuing change, it is my hope that the reader will come away with a clearer understanding of the remarkably fulfilling lifestyle of Catholic sisters.

— Sister Maureen Abbott, SP

❧Acknowledgments

While I must claim the responsibility of authorship, the book would never have arrived at publication without the assistance of many others. Due to the fact that during the nine years of research and writing I was living in Portland, Oregon, and working part-time, much of that assistance required extra effort on the part of all concerned. The wonderful hospitality of Sister Mary Ryan, director of our congregation archives, made my time in archives a pleasure. There I enjoyed the assistance of her staff, Sisters Donna Butler, Marianne Mader, Marie Esther Sivertsen and Regina Shaughnessy. Special credit must go to archives staffer Sister Marie Grace Molloy, who was ever at my beck and call via email requests for fact checking and searches. As the months and years of the project dragged on, I owe Sister Rosemary Borntrager a huge debt of thanks for her enthusiastic reception of the first drafts of each chapter; her cogent comments in offering a preliminary critique inevitably revived my flagging energies. In addition, it was her suggestion, together with her artistic talent and rigorous research that led to the inclusion of the historical map of the properties. Sister Janet Gilligan gladly took up the tedious work of editing the manuscript; her hours of labor and numerous phone consultations assured a professional result. Careful reading on the part of the other editorial board members, Sisters Ann Casper, Rosemary Borntrager, Mary Ryan, Rosemary Schmalz and Lisa Stallings corrected many details. I am especially grateful to three editorial board members who provided unique perspectives from their professional fields: corporate historian Patricia Abbott Ashton, historian Father James Connelly, CSC, PhD, and organizational consultant Tracy Schier, PA, PhD.

Thanks to the efforts of graphic artist Sister Pat Linehan the photographs, maps and timeline are sharp and clear. My ever-lurking worries about formatting were put to rest by the competent services of our publishing expert at Wish Publishing, Holly Kondras. Knowing that readers are lured to pick up a book by an attractive cover, heartfelt thanks go to the talented graphic artist on staff with our Office of Congregational

Advancement, Christina Blust, for her design. I am particularly grateful to a generous bequest from the estate of James B. and Betty Ryan that has covered publication costs, making the volume free of charge to the sisters whose lives are described in these pages.

As the fourth writer in this series, I learned much from the work of those who authored the previous volumes, Sisters Mary Borromeo Brown, Eugenia Logan and Mary Roger Madden. I am especially indebted to Sister Mary Roger for her generous advice and encouragement. Her extensive work of conducting many oral histories has made it possible to include first-person anecdotes in the narrative. Special thanks go to the sisters at Owens Hall during these years who welcomed me as a frequent guest and whose lively stories of their life experiences during the era described in this book stimulated my curiosity and desire to communicate the joys and challenges of the calling we share. A word of thanks is also in order for my Portland housemate, Sister Jeremy Gallet, who kept the home fires burning during my many research absences.

More and more as I delved into the files and boxes of our archives, my appreciation for the hundreds of sisters whose lives created this community and inspired this volume has grown and sharpened. With strong roots in our woodland home, truly we are a Providence.

— Sister Maureen Abbott, SP

Note: *The first time the name of a Sister of Providence appears in a chapter, her last name is given. Thereafter it is omitted in that chapter. If a sister's name has changed, the name indicated is her name at the time, with her earlier or later name in parentheses.*

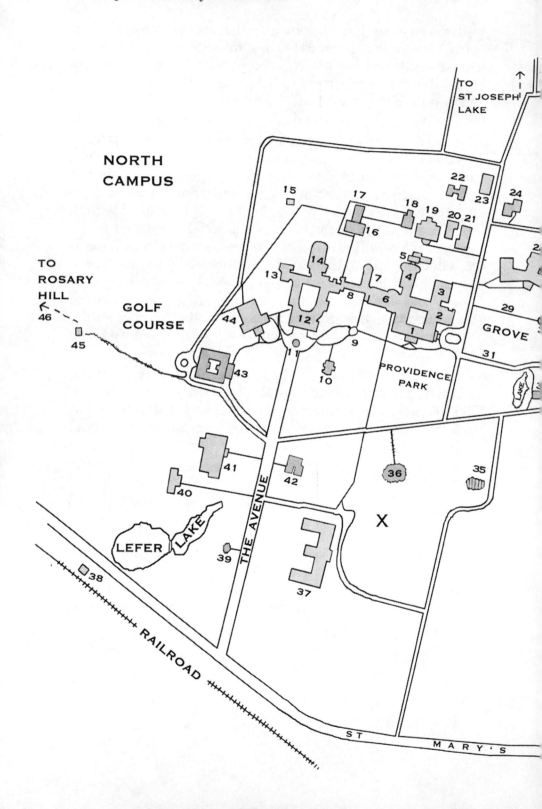

Map of Saint Mary-of-the-Woods, 1926 to 1966

#	NAME	DATE

Names of razed buildings are in italics.

01. Providence Convent — 1890
02. Express Hall
03. *Novitiate (old)* — *1904-1986*
04. Lourdes Infirmary — 1922
05. *Our Lady of Lourdes wing* — *1941-2001*
06. Church of the Im. Conception — 1891
07. Blessed Sacrament Chapel — 1924
08. St. Rita / St. Agatha Halls (corridor) — 1902
09. Our Lady of the Campus (statue) — 1904
10. Chaplain's Residence — 1888
11. Fountain — 1914-1930; 1930
12. *Foley Hall* — *1860-1989*
13. *Museum*
14. Foley Dining Hall (O'Shaughnessy) — 1920
15. Lodge — 1940
16. Gymnasium — 1909
17. Pool — 1923
18. Water Plant — 1919
19. Power House/ Carpenter Shop — 1892
20. Laundry — 1948
21. *Cannery / Bakery* — *1910-2012*
    Print Shop (2nd floor) — *1913/1988*
22. *Greenhouse (new)* — *1953-2011*
23. Garage — 1919
24. Marian Cottage — 1954
25. *Men's House*
26. Stables — 1925
27. *Dairy barn* — *1923-1972*
28. Novitiate (new) — 1960

29. Shrine Path
30. Sacred Heart Shrine
31. Stations of the Cross   1937
32. St. Anne Shell Chapel   1844, 1876
33. Cemetery   1861
34. *Coal Tipple*   *1892-2013*
35. *Greenhouses (old)*   *1919-1953*
36. Grotto of Our Lady of Lourdes   1928
37. Le Fer Hall   1924
38. *Railroad Station*   *1855-1958*
39. Our Lady of Fatima Shrine   1954
40. Guest House (faculty residence)   1964
41. Library   1965
42. Woodland Inn   1894
43. Guerin Hall   1913
44. Conservatory of Music   1913
45. Post Office   1928
46. Rosary Hill   1908
X. Site of future Science building   1964

❧ Prologue

❧ A Look Back 1840-1926

Hark! On the windswept Breton shores . . .

Sung as part of the 1940 Centennial celebration, this stirring hymn[1] would become the annual anthem to celebrate tshe October 22, 1840, Foundation Day when six Sisters of Providence from Ruillé-sur-Loir, France, arrived at Saint Mary-of-the-Woods, Indiana. It is to these Breton shores that we look for our story's beginnings, for it was from the small village of Etables perched upon the bluffs overlooking the Atlantic Ocean that Anne-Thérèse Guérin responded to the call to serve God as a Sister of Providence. Mother Theodore Guérin was canonized as a saint in October 2006, and her story, which has become part of American Catholic heritage, is well told elsewhere.[2] How the Sisters of Providence of Saint Mary-of-the-Woods have carried forward this remarkable woman's legacy, the charism of Providence, is detailed in the three previous books of this series.[3]

Before continuing the Congregation's mid-twentieth century story in this volume, a look back at the major events detailed in the earlier works will set the stage for the reader.[4]

The Founding Years

Beginnings

When the pioneer bishop of Vincennes, Indiana, Bishop Simon Gabriel Bruté, sent his vicar general Father Celestin de la Hailandière to France in 1838 in search of priests, sisters and brothers to serve his frontier diocese, Bruté was already in his final illness. Named as Bruté's successor, Bishop de la Hailandière returned to his native Brittany where there were vigorous efforts to revitalize the church's life after the ravages of the French Revolution. It was here that Father Jacques-François Dujarié had first gathered a few followers in 1806 to assist his pastoral ministry. By 1834, the tiny group of women at Ruillé-sur-Loir had grown to more than 255 professed sisters in fifty-eight houses of the Sisters of Providence.[5] In 1835, his Brothers of St. Joseph had been placed under the direction of Reverend Basile Moreau, who joined the congregation of Brothers with his previously formed community of Auxiliary Priests of Le Mans to form the Congregation of Holy Cross.

Anne-Thérèse Guérin had heard of the good work of the Sisters of Providence and followed her heart's call to give herself to God by joining this Congregation in 1823. Because she had remained at home to care for her mother and younger sister, at age twenty-five she was more mature than most candidates, so she was appointed local superior of the difficult mission of Notre Dame, Rennes, in 1826. It was here, in the rough and ready neighborhood surrounding the school, that the Providence spirituality which had captured her imagination bore fruit in service to a generation caught in the midst of cultural change. During her ten-year term there, the scholarly Bishop John Baptist Bouvier of Le Mans had in 1835 provided a Rule for the community.[6] Sister Theodore was quick to grasp that following this Rule would channel the energies of the young sisters under her care to enable them to grow spiritually through their ministry of teaching.[7] In 1834 she was sent to the small village of Soulaines where in addition to teaching she educated herself to serve the sick.

A missionary spirit was sweeping France at this time,[8] giving the invitation to minister in foreign lands a compelling appeal. When Bishop de la Hailandière approached Bishop Bouvier and Mother Mary Lecor, Superior of the Sisters of Providence, seeking sisters for Indiana, Sister Theodore was an obvious choice to lead such a group. Doubting her own ability, she was initially reluctant to volunteer, but after reflecting on the Rule's admonition that "The Sisters must be disposed to go to any part of the world," she agreed to lead the small band of six missionaries to America.

Other volunteers were not lacking, however. News of the plan to send sisters to the foreign missions brought three new recruits to the Congregation.[9] Bishop de la Hailandière's visit with the Le Fer de la Motte family impressed Irma Le Fer so profoundly that she entered the Congregation as Sister St. Francis Xavier at age twenty-three, but her poor health delayed her departure for another year. Sister Mary Xavier Lerée, age twenty-seven, and Sister Mary Liguori Tiercin, age twenty-two, were accepted as novices specifically for the American

Mother Theodore Guérin

mission. In addition to Sister Theodore, age forty-one, Mother Mary designated Sister St. Vincent Ferrer Gagé, also an experienced superior at age forty, as her assistant. The talented Sister Basilide Sénéschal, age twenty-eight, had not volunteered, but when assured that an eventual return to France was not out of the question, she agreed to go. Sister Olympiade Boyer, a thirty-four-year-old novice who had served with Sister Theodore at Soulaines, petitioned the bishop for permission to be included in the band.

In spite of their steadfast missionary intention, departure was heart-wrenching, since they knew they might never see their homeland again. At Havre, aboard the ship, Sister Theodore described her feelings "when I felt the vessel beginning to move and I realized that I was no longer in France. It seemed as if my soul were being torn from my body."[10]

The Years of Sorrow

An exhausting six-week journey from New York followed the forty-day ocean voyage. Almost immediately upon their arrival at the tiny frontier settlement of Saint Mary-of-the-Woods in the Indiana forest, they realized they faced two major obstacles. First, the isolation of the place chosen for their ministry made them question its suitability for a school. Second, the fickle nature of their ecclesiastical superior, Bishop de la Hailandière, soon became apparent. While the young country's sense of "manifest destiny" would spark the population growth that gradually provided pupils and support for their fledgling Academy, the second difficulty was a greater trial to the sensitive foundress. To whom did she owe obedience? On whom could she rely for support?

As she welcomed and formed the women who joined the community, she relied on the Rule for guidance, instructing them by example in practices of prayer, charity, pedagogy and the daily duties of common life. As the immigrant sisters learned the language, customs and business systems of a

strange country, they had ample practical opportunity to practice their reliance on Providence when they faced a series of
calamitous events: bank failure; the undermining of their superior's authority by their chaplain, Father Stanislaus Buteux;
a fire that destroyed their first crop; and Mother Theodore's
serious illnesses.

Leaving the tiny community and struggling Academy in
the charge of Sister St. Francis Xavier Le Fer, in April 1843
Mother Theodore took the promising novice Sister Mary Cecilia Bailly as her companion and journeyed to France in search
of support. While there, she conferred with Bishop Bouvier
and Mother Mary to establish basic principles for clarifying
mutual obligations between the community and Bishop de la
Hailandière. To her great sorrow, her superiors reiterated the
decision "that the Community in Indiana had to be separated
from the Motherhouse at Ruillé-sur-Loir." [11] Meanwhile, during her absence of almost ten months, Bishop de la Hailandière had taken the opportunity to step in and manage the
community's affairs, opening new missions and assigning the
sisters as well as accepting their vows and even holding an
election in a failed attempt to replace her as superior. Having
achieved some success in soliciting financial support, notably
from France's Queen Amelia as well as from sympathetic bishops, Mother Theodore hastened home but was struck with a
serious illness which kept her in New Orleans for six more
weeks.

When she did return to Saint Mary-of-the-Woods, it was
clear that the Bishop was convinced that the sisters had severely damaged his reputation and that he was determined to
establish his authority. The community had grown to the point
that it was more financially independent and its numbers
warranted electing a council to assist Mother Theodore. What
it needed from the Bishop was both his approval of the Rule
and the deed to the Saint Mary-of-the-Woods property. There
followed a contest of wills, much prayer and a series of confrontations. Sister Mary Borromeo Brown describes one such
encounter before the Bishop left for France on November 4,
1844: "She knelt humbly before His Lordship to beg his blessing. Then she rose, and the two dark-eyed Bretons faced each
other. She lifted her glance without flinching to the frowning

eyes which in his nephew's words 'made everybody quail.' They proceeded at once to business."[12]

The business was never amicably concluded. In fact, it was not only the Sisters of Providence who were forced to negotiate the bishop's unpredictable moods. Many priests had left the diocese and even their loved chaplain and intermediary, Father John Corbe, contemplated this course of action. Father Edward Sorin, CSC, who had accompanied Sister St. Francis on her voyage from France, migrated with his Holy Cross community to the far northern reaches of the diocese and wrote to her from their settlement at Notre Dame, Indiana, of his concern.

By 1845, with Mother Theodore's health gravely impaired, the council was seriously investigating arrangements for moving to Detroit or New Orleans. Although the Sixth Provincial Council of Baltimore in May 1846 accepted Bishop de la Hailandière's resignation, its recommendation to Rome was not published, resulting in rumors and anxiety as the decision worked its way through ecclesiastical channels. In spite of this uncertainty and the Bishop's vacillation of favor, the sisters continued to serve and even accepted a new mission in Fort Wayne. At their final confrontation in Vincennes in May 1847, Bishop de la Haliendière deposed Mother Theodore, who fell seriously ill for several weeks while the sisters made plans to leave. The June 5, 1847, announcement that Bishop John Bazin would succeed Bishop de la Hailandière finally ended the "years of sorrow."

The Years of Peace

Two significant December events must have made the Advent season of 1847 seem to be the advent of a new era for Mother Theodore. The most important was Bishop Bazin's consecration, which led to a confirmation of the Congregation's role in the diocese, with Mother Theodore as superior general. In addition, the opening of a bridge across the Wabash River eased the relative isolation of Saint Mary-of-the-Woods and allowed access to Terre Haute and from there to the wider world. With his advice to, "Bury the past and never think of it, save to bless the Providence of God,"[13] Bishop Bazin signaled strong support by approving the Rule and by giving over the deed to the property at Saint Mary-of-the-Woods, paving the way for major improvements. His untimely death after only six months was deeply mourned, but the appointment of their longtime friend, Father Maurice Saint-Palais, as the Bishop of Vincennes ensured continued backing and encouragement.

When in 1852 the First Plenary Council of Baltimore decreed that each parish should have a school, the evangelizing role of the sisters was clear.[14] They had earned the respect of the clergy, and Mother Theodore astutely designed a format for a contract that would ensure harmonious relations between pastors and superiors as several new missions were opened.

It was mainly from these parishes and the thriving Academy that the Congregation attracted new members.[15] Due to both the frontier culture and the minimal education of the young women who entered, the formation period at the motherhouse was extended to three years, also preparing them as teachers.[16] Her re-election during the August 1848 retreat had assured Mother Theodore of the affection and loyalty of the rapidly growing community. With the larger numbers, more responsibility was given to her two-member council—Sister St. Francis as novice mistress and Sister Mary Cecilia as first assistant and superior of the Academy. Having delegated these responsibilities, she devoted herself to building projects and visitation of the now several missions.

Because the Rule relied greatly on experienced local superiors, she bemoaned the American culture's low expectations of women, whose limited education did not prepare them well for this duty.[17] As the American sisters gained experience, they gradually took more responsibility for continuing the formation of newer members through mission experience, helping fledgling teachers gain skills and nourishing their sense of mission. The spirit of prayer and unity so evident during the "years of our trials" was reinforced when the sisters gathered each August for the annual retreat, and Mother Theodore could now rely upon a seasoned core of members to accept additional missions.[18] Her spiritual leadership remained strong through her daily five o'clock conference,[19] her letters and her yearly visitations to acquaint herself with the various ministry situations in which the sisters labored. Her guiding axiom was "The Rule, gently," with frequent admonitions for adequate food, rest and time for prayer, as well as allowance for human frailty.

The 1852 motherhouse (top left) superseded the oft-expanded Thralls farmhouse shown in the foreground.

The sisters' Saint Mary-of-the-Woods convent home, a farm-house purchased from the Thralls family to accommodate ten members, had been continually remodeled and enlarged and by 1849 housed twenty-seven professed sisters, six novices and fourteen postulants. The need for construction of a new and larger motherhouse was urgent.[20] After months of planning and overseeing the construction, one can only imagine Moth-er Theodore's feelings when they moved to the new and spa-cious convent. As always, she saw beyond the externals. She notes in the community diary on August 7, 1852, the day on which the chapel of the new building was dedicated: "O my God, grant that all who dwell in this house may love thee much, may love one another, and may they never forget why they came here."[21]

As she conducted her annual visitations, Mother Theodore enjoyed the gradual improvements in transportation in the Wabash Valley. A raised road was constructed over the treach-erous Wabash River bottoms; the National Road linking Indi-ana to the East Coast continued to be improved; railroad lines extended both east and west, north and south, replacing the canals. Steamboats on the Ohio and Wabash Rivers were still available.

Due to her active involvement with the construction of St. Vincent Academy in Terre Haute, in-town accommodations were now available for easy connections. With her purchase of railroad stock, she was instrumental in having the line extended to a station on Saint Mary-of-the-Woods' property by October 1855. Over the years, her ministry was hampered by frequent illnesses which often sidelined her for months at a time. Her final illness occurred during Holy Week of 1856, and she died on May 14, 1856.

The Formative Years

Mother Mary Cecilia Bailly 1856-68

As its grief gradually subsided, the community realized it had arrived at a milestone.[22] Of the original six French sisters, only four remained, and they had also lost Sister St. Francis, whom many regarded as among the group of foundresses. Nonetheless, a significant number of the early entrants, both the Americans and several Frenchwomen who had come later, had been formed by Mother Theodore and Sister St. Francis and had then gone on to positions of responsibility as local superiors. Several had been close to Mother Theodore and had shared the burden of her worries and dilemmas during the "years of our sorrows." Of the forty-seven sisters who gathered for the retreat in August 1856, the ten who, as members of the General Council, had the responsibility of electing her successor for a three-year term were confident that the community was well established. All of them realized that no one among them approached the stature of their beloved foundress, but they ensured continuity by electing her assistants Sister Mary Cecilia as superior general and Sister Anastasie Brown as first assistant, and the French foundresses Sister Basilide as econome[23] and Sister Mary Joseph Le Fer as mistress of novices.

The next twelve years marked a momentous time for the United States as the issue of slavery drove the states apart and into the Civil War. Although the southern counties of Indiana were sympathetic to the South, the state's population had shifted northward with the growth of the railroads and commerce. Regardless of their own leanings, as women without a vote, the sisters were relegated to the sidelines. This situation changed when in May 1861 the community accepted the challenge of supervising and nursing the sick and wounded at the military hospital in Indianapolis. For a short period in 1861-1862 they also ran a military hospital in Vincennes, Indiana, and after the war sponsored a hostel for veterans until 1871.

Mother Mary Cecilia's aptitude for business was put to good use during the twelve years she served as superior general. Although there had been some question about the stability of the land at Saint Mary-of-the-Woods, in 1860 the Council made the decision to retain the motherhouse at its founding site. The Academy, now known as Saint Mary's Institute, was greatly enlarged with the construction of a three-wing building. A wing designated for the novitiate was added to the new convent, and a separate chapel building was erected. Purchases of adjoining property greatly increased the motherhouse acreage. News of the approval of the Ruillé Rule provided the occasion for Sisters Basilide and Mary Joseph to visit their homeland to obtain copies so the American branch could better understand the requirements for eventual canonical approval of its *Constitutions*.

Mother Anastasie Brown
1868-1874

When the Congregation gathered for the August 1868 retreat and elections, the selection of Sister Anastasie Brown to replace Mother Mary Cecilia caused a sharp split in the community.[24] Daughter of pioneer Aloysius Brown, and one of the first graduates of the Academy, her affable and optimistic spirit had enabled her to give years of competent service as superior of the Academy and a member of the council. Now she and that same council had the difficult task of moving forward as a new administration in the face of Mother Mary Cecilia's obvious distress at being passed over for a fourth term. They authorized a mission in northern Indiana so as to utilize the Bailly family's property there to establish a school, although they were fearful that the disaffected former superior general would influence her disgruntled sympathizers to split off and use the site to begin a new community. This dispute required intervention on the part of both Bishop Saint-

Palais and Bishop Joseph Dwenger of Fort Wayne and proved disheartening through both of Mother Anastasie's terms.[25] However, with the approbation of the Rule in 1870 and the approval of the English edition in 1871, there could be no doubt of the strength of the Congregation's foundation.

The Catholic Church itself was in difficulty, both in Rome, where Pope Pius IX watched the dissolution of the Papal States even as the First Vatican Council convened, and also in the United States, where the bishops worked to reunite the faithful who had so recently followed different flags. Unfortunately, Mother Anastasie's ambitious projects coincided with the financial failures associated with the Reconstruction period following the Civil War. Property purchased in Indianapolis was unable to be used as planned; it was later sold to the Little Sisters of the Poor. A well-situated and beautiful new building was erected for Saint John Academy in Indianapolis at considerable expense. The purchase and renovation of a hotel in Madison, Indiana, to expand Holy Angels Academy was unsuccessful and the property became a liability. In Terre Haute, philanthropist Chauncey Rose helped finance purchase of the property and construction of Providence Hospital, but religious prejudice among the citizens prevented its success and necessitated its closure in 1875. St. Vincent's Academy in Terre Haute suffered when political negotiations required the sisters to move from its original site, only to be forced to buy back the property at a loss in 1876.

Mother Mary Ephrem Glenn 1874-1883

When the twenty-member Chapter now required by the Rule assembled in August 1874, an understandable mood of uneasiness prevailed. Their governance deliberations resulted in the election of thirty-eight-year-old Sister Mary Ephrem Glenn as superior general while retaining most of the experienced council. [26] All agreed that the financial situation should not impede the mission. The ill-fated Providence Hospital was purchased by Bishop Saint-Palais to accommodate

the orphans who were moved from the aging Vincennes institution. He also agreed that it was time for the community to go beyond Indiana to accept missions in Saginaw, Marshall, Kalamazoo and Port Huron in Michigan and Galesburg and Lockport in Illinois. Indiana was not neglected, however, with the opening of several missions: three in Terre Haute and two in Indianapolis, as well as in Peru, Washington, Evansville and Columbus.

However, Bishop Saint-Palais' years of service were numbered, and the sisters mourned the death of their long-time friend in 1878. It was indeed a season of loss as one by one the sisters so influential from the French founding days went to their eternal reward: Sister St. Vincent Ferrer Gagé in 1874, Sister Basilide Sénéschal in 1878, Sister Mary Theodore Le Touzè (Mother Theodore's niece) in 1879, and Sister Mary Joseph Le Fer in 1881.

The naming of Father Silas Chatard, rector of the North American Academy in Rome, as bishop, and the relocation of the bishop's residence to the state capital of Indianapolis were to mark a new era of cooperation between the Diocese of Indianapolis and the Congregation of the Sisters of Providence. With his scholarly background and great interest in education, Bishop Chatard would become a regular visitor and interested adviser at Saint Mary-of-the-Woods. As the financial situation of the community improved, additional adjacent parcels of land were purchased and a new novitiate wing was added to Providence Convent.

Mother Euphrasie Hinkle
1883-1889

As Bishop Chatard was unwilling to allow a dispensation for a fourth term for Mother Mary Ephrem, the Chapter elected as superior general her thirty-seven-year-old second assistant, Sister Euphrasie Hinkle, who had become a convert during her years as a student at Saint Mary's Institute.[27] From the previous council, only the mistress of novices, Sister Mary Cleophas Foley, was returned to office, resulting in a major change in the community's leadership and setting the stage for significant challenges. In response to continued requests for sisters, smaller missions in Indiana, Michigan and Illinois were accepted, while in 1886 Mother Euphrasie accompanied the sisters opening St. Philip (later St Mel) in Chicago, with the two nearby missions of Our Lady of Sorrows and Our Lady of Providence Academy opening the following year. In 1886, the cornerstone for a new and larger chapel at the motherhouse was laid, and the following year the community rejoiced when word was received that the Rule had received final approval.

The implementation of the new *Constitutions* required a fresh start. Only a year after the 1886 election, a new General Chapter was convened in August 1887. Mother Euphrasie was re-elected along with her same council, including longtime Mistress of Novices Sister Mary Cleophas, now in the role of first assistant. Due to the continued growth of the Congregation in conjunction with the expansion of the country's railroads, the council decided to accept the far-away missions of Chelsea, Massachusetts, South Omaha, Nebraska, and Kansas City, Missouri.

In the light of these exciting events, no one could have anticipated the tragedy which struck on February 7, 1889, when fire destroyed the motherhouse convent, barely sparing the chapel construction site. The enlarged Academy building was able to accommodate the sisters, novices and postulants, but no homecoming or retreat was possible that summer. To compound their sorrow, the sisters learned of the untimely death of Mother Euphrasie on August 27, 1889, at the age of forty-three. Rather than attempting a Chapter immediately, Bishop Chatard recommended that Sister Mary Cleophas manage the Congregation's affairs until the next scheduled chapter in July of the following year.

The Years of Expansion: Mother Mary Cleophas Foley 1890-1926

The next thirty-six years form a unique period in the history of the Congregation of the Sisters of Providence, who flourished during this long period under the leadership of a single superior, Mother Mary Cleophas.[28] "The history of this one woman, seemingly so ordinary in its origins, is, in fact, the history of the community from 1890-1926."[29] In 1862, in the

midst of the Civil War, at the age of seventeen, she had followed her older sister, Sister Aloysia, to the community. After a year of formation, she taught for four years, completing her preparation for vows under the guidance of Sister Aloysia just prior to her sister's untimely death in 1866. She herself suffered from poor health, but the Chapter of 1868 elected the twenty-three-year-old Sister Mary Cleophas to the post of mistress of novices. Sister Mary Joseph Le Fer had served in this role during Mother Mary Cecilia's administration, carrying forward the legacy of her own formation under Mother Theodore and her own sister, Sister St. Francis Xavier. She generously mentored her young successor as the two were re-elected four times to serve side-by-side on the 1868-1883 councils. Sister Mary Cleophas continued in this role of forming new members until she herself was elected first assistant in Mother Euphrasie's second term. Since she had shouldered the responsibilities of superior general after the calamitous fire and Mother Euphrasie's death, the community naturally turned to her for continued leadership in the Chapter of 1890, providing experienced assistance by returning to the council two former superiors, Mother Anastasie and Mother Mary Ephrem. The many significant events of her extended administration can be considered in two phases.

Initial Phase 1890-1908

Rebuilding Providence Convent was the first priority. Completion of the Church of the Immaculate Conception was to follow immediately, and then development of plans for the addition of the façade and a fourth floor to the Academy building, all within seven years. Soon after, construction began on a wing to connect the Academy with the church and convent as well as on a completely separate novitiate building. With the Catholic population shifting to urban areas, the community gradually withdrew from Michigan and from small rural schools,[30] opening five missions in Indianapolis, ten in Chicago and three in the northern Indiana industrial suburbs of

This 1904 sketch shows Foley Hall, the Church of the Immaculate Conception and Providence Convent, with the chaplain's residence in the right foreground.

Chicago. A new area of influence opened with the establishment of an academy and parish school in the nation's capital, Washington, D.C.

The community's horizons widened considerably when Mother Mary Cleophas and Third Assistant Sister Mary Alma Ryan traveled to Europe in 1902, renewing the ties with Ruillé as well as visiting England, Lourdes and Rome, where they had an audience with Pope Leo XIII. En route home they stopped in Boston and Washington, D.C. The contacts and ideas and purchases of artwork gleaned during this pilgrimage had lasting and visible effects during subsequent years.

Bishop Francis Chatard's support and encouragement were invaluable to the community during this time. When Mother Theodore's remains were transferred to the crypt of the church in 1907, he encouraged the opening of the Cause for her canonization. He was active in efforts to establish procedures and norms for certification of the sisters as teachers by the community's Board of Examiners as they developed standardized guides for teaching the subjects in the various grades, and he readily approved sisters studying at secular universities and abroad to prepare them for teaching higher education. Summer school included nationally recognized lecturers and the sisters were expected to pass examinations to demonstrate teaching competence.

Second Phase 1908-1926

When Bishop Chatard approved the council's request that a dispensation be given to allow Mother Mary Cleophas to serve an unprecedented fourth term, she accepted after the Vatican's Sacred Congregation ruled that it was permissible. At age sixty-three, she continued to exhibit the spiritual and physical energy necessary to lead the growing Congregation and was delighted that the first order of business was the dedication of the beautifully appointed Church of the Immaculate Conception. Construction of several support buildings—the gymnasium, the combined print shop, bakery, and cannery, as well as the statue of Our Lady of the Campus soon followed. The construction of two magnificent buildings, Guerin Hall and the Conservatory of Music, greatly expanded the prestige and program of Saint Mary's Institute, which by 1913 had evolved into the fully accredited Saint Mary-of-the-Woods College.

Content with this steady and peaceful development, the 1914 Chapter retained Mother Mary Cleophas at the helm. However, as members of an apostolic Congregation, the sisters felt the impact of events in the wider world, especially World War I and the influenza epidemic, which slowed the pace of the Congregation's growth. It was during this time that the community withdrew from orphanages because alternate strategies for such care were now considered preferable. During the more prosperous postwar years, the policy of accepting schools near to those already established continued: six in Chicago and five in the Chicago environs; four in Indianapolis; twelve in southern Indiana; two in the Boston area; and two in the Washington, D.C., area. In spite of her protests and declining health, Mother Mary Cleophas was prevailed upon to accept a sixth term. Amazingly, she continued to think in global terms and accepted the challenge of sending a band of volunteers to establish a mission in China in 1920.[31] In 1922 the eighty-seven-year-old general superior again traveled to Rome, this time on behalf of the canonization process for Mother Theodore.

She and her competent council continued major improvements of the motherhouse grounds, building a new infirmary, water plant, garage, greenhouse and dairy barn. The expansion of Saint Mary-of-the-Woods College continued as a spacious dining hall was attached to the main building, an indoor swimming pool was added to the gymnasium, and the elaborate Le Fer Hall was built along "the Avenue." Two projects dear to Mother Mary Cleophas' heart were the construction of the Blessed Sacrament Chapel and the renovation of a large farmhouse at Rosary Hill as a residence for retired sisters. While this latter innovation was not readily accepted by the sisters, the beautifully appointed Blessed Sacrament Chapel continues to foster the strong Eucharistic spirituality deeply engrained from the founding days.

From Mother Mary Cleophas' perspective, the growth which was most significant was to be found in the spiritual foundation of the Congregation, what she described as "the path marked out for us by Divine Providence, the path wherein our holy founders and those who have preceded us have walked with so much courage and generosity."[32] She had rejoiced to see so many of those she had formed in their novitiate days go on to positions of responsibility, and she continued to give instructions to the entire community gathered each summer for classes and the Jesuit-preached retreat. She was able to get to know the younger members through giving their thirty-day retreat when they returned home for the six-month "Second Novitiate" prescribed by the Rule in preparation for perpetual vows. When the community became too large for her to retain the custom of an annual interview with each individual, she assigned sisters to one of her councilors, so that in addition to her local superior, each sister had a "home superior" with whom she could discuss her physical and spiritual well-being.[33] The end of Mother Mary Cleophas' administration was truly the end of an era.

The table on the following page summarizes the statistical growth of the Congregation during these years.

TABLE 1: *Growth of the Congregation, 1840-1926*

Year	Professed sisters	Sister of Providence schools					Catholics in U.S.
		Indiana	Illinois/ Chicago	East Coast	Other	Total	
1840	4	1				1	
1856	67	16				16	
1890	451	36	5	1	8[a]	50	
1896	522	39	7	1	6	53	
1902	610	43	11	1	6	61	
1908	685	42	16	4	2	64	14,210,755[b]
1914	806	49	20	7		75	15,721,815[c]
1920	935	40	23	6		69	17,735,533
1926	1092	40	23	8	1 (China)	72	18,605,003

[a] 6 in Michigan; 1 in Kansas City, Missouri (closed 1894); 1 in South Omaha, Nebraska (closed 1907)

[b] 1906

[c] 1916

Source: Sister of Providence data from Superior Generals' reports to General Chapter, SMWA. Catholic population data from *The Official Catholic Directory.* New York: P. J. Kenedy & Sons. Annual editions as indicated

❧ Part I: 1926-1949

✑ Chapter 1
Why They Came

Five young women from St. Rose, Chelsea, meet at the Boston train station in 1929 to travel together to enter the novitiate of the Sisters of Providence. They are, from left to right, Marie O'Kane, Catherine Dunne, Bertha Tobin, Frances Conlin and Eileen Carroll.[1]

The joy and exuberance of five young women setting out on a journey captures the spirit of the Twenties when our story begins. It was a time of ever-expanding horizons, and their lively confidence as they stride into the future bespeaks a Boston upbringing that had accustomed them to look forward to opportunity and success. What sparked their enthusiasm? The smiling onlookers might have been surprised to know the destination on their tickets, a small village in rural Indiana, Saint Mary-of-the-Woods. With all the prospects this thriving Eastern seaport city had to offer, what was the attraction of such a humble faraway location? What was the future they were choosing to pursue?

The story that follows is centered in that very village at the motherhouse of the Sisters of Providence. When the much altered house used by the original group of sisters had been replaced in 1852 by the structure built to serve as a true motherhouse, Mother Theodore had penned the prayer, "O my God, grant that all who dwell in this house may love thee much, may love one another, and may never forget why they came here."[2] Seventy-seven years later these five and others like them were coming to join their lives to the enterprise she had founded. This volume explores why they came and what they accomplished during the forty year period of 1926-1966.

It was an era in which the spirit of the times was often at variance with the spirit of the Sisters of Providence. As always, the challenge for these women was to ponder old truths in order to gain the new lights they needed to heed the signs of the times and live their call with fidelity and joy.

The Spirit of the Times

Cultural Shifts

Writing in the 1970s, historian Sidney Ahlstrom describes the decade in which these young women grew up. "The decade of the twenties is the most sharply defined decade in American history. Modern technocratic America came of age and began to be conscious of its newly released potentiality. The United States became an urban nation not only in statistical fact but in its dominant mood."[3] In peoples' daily lives, two major technological breakthroughs contributed to an increasingly active lifestyle: electricity and the automobile.[4] As new homes were wired, all manner of appliances like vacuum cleaners and washing machines not only made life more comfortable, but, together with indoor plumbing, also raised standards of cleanliness. A bright electric lamp by a chair in the living room made it easy to read a book, the newspaper, the *Saturday Evening Post* or another of the many magazines now available to expand personal horizons. Since those same living rooms were now usually furnished with a radio, the family could gather to listen to music, the news, political commentary, sports events and, of course, advertising.

Social historian Dorothy Brown describes the times this way: "It was Coolidge prosperity, or the 'Golden Glow,' that was the central reality of the decade."[5] With a concentration of the population in urban centers, streetcars and interurban trains invited exploration beyond the immediate neighborhood. More and more families owned automobiles, while the supportive infrastructure of roads, gas stations, dealerships, factories and restaurants created a network of employment opportunities. Radio and cinema established national audiences and spawned a celebrity culture. Traditional social values became more relaxed, with less discipline for children and more freedom for youth. Progressive educational methods stressed experience rather than rote learning. With improved food processing methods, more dietary choices were available through brands and chain stores.

It was possible to speak of a national culture. When the five young women arrived at Saint Mary's and met their counterparts from Chicago and southern Indiana, most of whom came from similar middle class Catholic backgrounds, despite their strong personal ethnic heritages they would have had much in common with their new companions.

Demographic and Political Shifts

A great deal of the decade's energy flowed from the immigrants who had accounted for the growth in population and contributed significantly to the expanding economy. David Kyvig points out that by the end of World War I, "Almost 45 percent of the white population had either come to the United States themselves or were the children of immigrants."[6] Charles Morris highlights the importance of Catholics within this group.

> At the century's turn, with 12 million American Catholics, Catholicism was not only the country's largest religious denomination by a substantial margin but, with a massive new influx of Catholic immigrants and a high Catholic birth rate, was by far the fastest growing. The number of American Catholics quadrupled between 1860 and 1900, and, despite a slowdown in Catholic immigration by World War I, kept growing to almost 20 million in the 1920s. Catholicism was first of all an urban phenomenon. ... Altogether, almost half of all Catholics were concentrated in the Northeast, with another 30 percent in the upper Midwest above the Ohio River.[7]

The Catholic population was gradually finding its voice in the political arena, but not without struggle. The relocation of domestic energies following World War I led to strikes and a severe recession in 1921. Following the 1917 revolution in Russia, the rise of worldwide communism led to a "Red Scare," with arrests of foreigners and suspected anarchists. Immigrants and their children in ethnic urban neighborhoods suffered the sting of renewed prejudice. Among those who considered themselves "natives," the patriotism generated by the war strengthened their American identity and their determination to step back from world involvements and restrict further diversification. A series of laws restricting immigration to quotas of the existing population was, in Sidney Ahlstrom's view, "a Nordic victory—and it brought a long, colorful epoch in American history to a close. The country had somehow lost confidence in its assimilative powers."[8]

Immigration quotas were not the only reactionary response, as Ahlstrom points out:

> More ominous still was the rapidly expanding activity of the Ku Klux Klan. It had been revived in 1915 ... retaining the anti-Negro aims of the old Klan but soon broadened its scope to include anti-Catholicism and anti-Semitism. The Klan thus became a distinctly Protestant organization with chaplains and specially adapted hymns.[9]

Because its clandestine membership was drawn from the respectable ranks of churchgoing community leaders, it carried considerable clout in politics. This influence of the Klan was especially strong in Indiana. When the 1920 passage of the Nineteenth Amendment gave women the right to vote, the sisters registered in force for the 1924 elections as a means of counteracting anti-Catholic policies. The Congregation chronicler proudly noted that, "It is the first time in the history of Saint Mary-of-the-Woods that our Sisters have ever voted here though some have voted before on the missions ... All have voted before noon."[10]

However, this act of civic responsibility was augmented by increased attention to spiritual duties. All-day exposition of the Blessed Sacrament brought the sisters to the chapel as well as to the voting booth. Election returns, as well, were evaluated by the chronicler from a spiritual perspective.

> Today our fears are confirmed as to the election in Indiana—almost entirely republican, and pro K.K.K. Dear Mother [Mary Cleophas] tells us, however, that since Providence has brought about such results, God has His designs in all. We must respect

those whom He has placed in authority and pray much for them.[11]

Local politics in the cities was another story, for political machines often favored Catholic interests. The nomination by New York's Tammany Hall of Al Smith as the Democratic candidate for the presidency in 1928 gave Catholics the sense that they had arrived. In fact, he garnered large majorities in northern cities, but was crushed nationally, largely because he was Catholic. Morris notes a significant byproduct of this event:

> The outcome of the Smith campaign greatly reinforced the Catholic separatist impulse, as did the perceived inequities of the educational system, the antireligiosity of mainstream secular culture, the commercial glorification of sin and sexual permissiveness. Without wavering in their patriotism or hypernationalism, Catholics executed a remarkable emotional withdrawal from secular America.[12]

This self-imposed Catholic isolationism created an environment highly conducive to the mission of the Sisters of Providence.

Catholic Identity

For Catholics, the parish was central to their identity. Providing not only spiritual nourishment through liturgy and devotions, the block-size plant also afforded facilities for education and a vibrant social network for all ages. For several generations it was self-perpetuating, since priests and sisters became role models for youth looking for their place in the world. The priesthood was an appealing career path for upwardly mobile sons of immigrants and attracted the best and the brightest to seminaries. For girls whose dreams went beyond the domestic roles of housewife and mother, a teaching career as "Sister" offered an alternative path. To marshal all these activities, the pastor's role was key, and as Morris astutely observes, for the pastor, "the schools were an unrivaled pastoral window."[13] When Father Michael Scanlon, pastor of St. Rose in Chelsea, Massachusetts, was asked to provide a recommendation for the five young women in the photo, he was easily able to pen such phrases as "She comes from an exemplary family," and "only 16 but quite responsible with an excellent mind."[14]

In many ways the parish school served as the engine of Catholic identity. Although the 1884 Baltimore Council's mandate that every child be placed in a Catholic school was never fully implemented, bishops and priests alike understood its central role. Not only did the school serve a catechetical function, but the upward mobility of its graduates attracted the favorable attention of civic leaders. As Morris observes, "The Church's constant emphasis on discipline, order, and family responsibilities ensured steady, if unspectacular, economic progress."[15] Recognizing the fertile field for their ministry of education, religious congregations such as the Sisters of Providence had established an unquestioned role in staffing parish schools. As can be seen from Table 2, during the following decades this role would continue to grow.

TABLE 2: *United States population by decades, 1920-1970*

Year	Total population	Catholic population		Sisters (Statistic first published 1946)	Parishes with schools
			% of Total		
1920	106,521,537	17, 735,553	17.0%		5,852
1930	123,188,000	20,203,702	16.4%		7,225
1940	132,122,446	21,403,136	16.2%		7,597
1950	152,684,417	27,766,241	18.2%	147,310	7,914
1960	180,671,158	40,871,302	22.6%	168,527	9,814
1970	205,052,174	47,872,089	23.2%	167,167	10,406

Sources: http://www.npg.org/facts/us_historical_pops.htm; *The Official Catholic Directory.* New York: P. J. Kenedy & Sons. Annual editions as indicated.

The leadership of a handful of colorful bishops who later became cardinals wielding considerable clout in America's largest cities was calculated to foster Catholics' sense of identity. Morris describes the strategy:

> The goal was to make it possible for an American Catholic to carry out almost every activity of life—education, health care, marriage and social life, union membership, retirement and old age care—within a distinctly Catholic environment.[16]

A Catholic subculture provided a well-rounded alternative to popular culture. National organizations for professionals had become popular, so Catholics founded their own Physicians' Guild, Press Association, Knights of Columbus, National Catholic Educational Association and so on. Anyone who wanted a Catholic viewpoint only needed to pick up the *Catholic Digest*, join a Catholic book club, or listen to "The Catholic Hour" on the radio.

Those living in cities with large Catholic populations were able to further strengthen their sense of Catholic identity through major events that generated bursts of public fervor. Historian Jay Dolan describes one such event, the 1926 Eucharistic Congress.

> Catholics from all parts of the country traveled to Chicago to take part in it. For five days they put on an unparalleled display of devotion and faith; an open-air Mass at Soldier Field attracted an estimated 150,000 people. ... The main event of the congress was the procession of the Eucharist on the last day ... while the magnificent pageantry of their Mother Church was unfolded before them. This was Catholic triumphalism, Catholic big, at its best.[17]

The Changing Role of Women

Within this Catholic subculture, what was the role of women? In the larger society, since the turn of the century, the "Gibson Girl" had given way to "the flapper." Social historian Joshua Zeitz characterizes the influence of the upstart stereotype:

> By the early 1920s it seemed that every social ill in America could be attributed to the 'flapper'—the notorious character type. ... She was the envy of teenage girls everywhere and the scourge of good character and morals. Nobody could escape the intense dialogue over the flapper.[18]

However, another image of women had begun to emerge, for the Progressive Era had in fact ushered in many reforms which significantly expanded opportunities for women to become involved in public life. The women's suffrage movement had gained increased visibility through its support of the 1919

Eighteenth Amendment which prohibited the making, selling or transporting of alcohol. The leaders' main objective was achieved the following year when the Nineteenth Amendment gave women the vote. The women who stepped forward to take leadership in the movement claimed the title of "New Woman."

Of course there were many women who could not identify themselves either as a flapper or as a New Woman. Perfectly comfortable and agreeably occupied with the multiple tasks of domestic management and enjoying the status of being the center of the family, they embraced their traditional role. Kathleen Sprows Cummings describes the attraction of this position.

> The New Woman stood in stark contrast to the Catholic "True woman," the model whom all Catholic women were supposed to emulate. ... God had created the True Woman to be more spiritual than her male counterpart. Her highest calling was to motherhood, if not in the physical sense, then at least in the spiritual one. The home was her "God-appointed sphere" and the place where she could remain except for attending church or performing acts of charity. Characterized by generosity, self-abnegation, and a penchant for self-sacrifice, the Catholic True Woman exercised power only through her influence over men.[19]

Generally speaking, most Catholic women adopted this ideal. As the demand for women in secretarial positions increased, most who took such jobs viewed them as temporary until they would marry and begin their own families. Those who did desire more active roles in society often aspired to a teaching career. When this desire was prompted by a deeper spiritual call, such a young woman need look no farther than the ever present role model of the sisters who taught them.

In reflecting on her own decision to become a Sister of Providence, Sister Marceline Mattingly, who entered the Congregation in 1933, recalled that it came at a very early age. Her mother had pointed out the sisters who sat up in the front of church.

> She told me, "Now you go and listen to sister and then come home and tell me everything she said." So, that's what I did. I went in, sat down and sister was teaching catechism. ... So, I listened to everything, and I just thought, oh, I thought it was so wonderful. I decided right then and there I was going to be a sister. ... And the day I made my first communion I promised

Jesus, I said to Jesus, "Now I want to be a sister. So please help me be a sister." I wanted to teach the children. And I'm five or six years old, I wanted to teach the children.[20]

Sister Marceline also notes that, "In 1925-26, lay Catholics weren't very active in their church," but becoming a sister was an obvious option for women who wanted to have an active role in the church. Her intention did not waver. Because her family moved several times, during her grade school years she was taught by sisters of three different congregations, providing ample opportunity to assess the possibility of each one. Here she explains the rationale for her actual choice.

> But when I went to Reitz Memorial [in Evansville, Indiana] as a freshman and we were there a week or so, I can remember saying, "Now this is the community, these are the ones I really want to go to." And for a long time I was afraid to tell anybody why because I didn't think it was a proper reason. But [laughs] the reason I liked them so much, they had more fun than those other sisters did [laughs]. So that was the reason I was going to enter them. But, of course, my motives changed quite a bit before I finally made it.[21]

As with many women of her cohort, it was the spirit of the sisters that proved to be what attracted Elizabeth Mattingly to pursue her dream and go on to become Sister Marceline.

The Spirit of the Sisters

Apostolic congregations of women had come into being for this very purpose of channeling the desire to serve God through service to one's neighbor. It was this same impulse that brought Anne-Thérèse Guérin to join the Sisters of Providence in France and to found the Congregation in the United States in 1840. During the founding years her example and instructions had inspired a legacy of zeal, piety and community which her daughters carried on in the spirit of Providence.

A Spirit of Zeal

Mother Theodore clearly understood the intimate connection between the two aspects of the call. She counseled the sisters in her instructions: "Piety is only a name for devotion; and what is devotion but zeal?"[22] The Rule itself enshrined such a spirit and she often directed the sisters to derive their inspiration from the Rule.

You expect, my dear children, that I now have many new things to say to you, which have been collected in my travels; that I can now give you many new lights. This indeed, I should desire much to be able to do; but be not disappointed to find that they will radiate from the same old truths which you have heard repeatedly. Close not the eyes of your soul to them, for you will see many things in new lights if you give the Holy Spirit free access to your minds and hearts. Oh, who can measure the dignity Our Lord has conferred upon us by admitting us to a life in which we share divine honors, associating us with Himself in the salvation of souls! The means are pointed out in our *Constitutions*—instructing others and advancing ourselves in perfection. Solid virtue—perfection—implies a life of prayer.[23]

The Rule which had inspired Mother Theodore had been revised over the years, yet in the first half of the twentieth century, Sister Mary Borromeo Brown noted that its regulations retained "to this day the original wording of their venerated author, Bishop Bouvier."[24] The Rule, officially known as the *Constitutions*, succinctly describes the inspiration for taking up life as a Sister of Providence: "The spirit of the Congregation is a great zeal for the glory of God, an ardent desire to acquire perfection, and to contribute to the sanctification of our neighbor."[25] Such zeal is truly the "why" of "why they have come here."

While their students would not have been aware that Sisters of Providence aimed at this lofty goal, they had multiple opportunities to experience that spirit of zeal. Within their parochial lives, sisters played a prominent role. Pupils came to know "Sister" on an individual personal level not only by following her directions and instruction for six hours a day in the classroom and on the playground, but also by volunteering to clean the blackboards after school, when there was opportunity for more relaxed conversation. At Mass, the silent file of sisters, eyes down and hands clasped beneath voluminous extended sleeves, gave witness to a deeper level of prayer. The popular media has taken liberties with these images, leaving interested persons to wonder what life was really like behind convent walls during this era. The brief sketch which follows provides a sense of the lifestyle of the Sisters of Providence and sets the stage for the remaining chapters.

The blend of active service to the needs of society with the pursuit of a deeper spiritual life was the warp and woof of community life. Over the years since its foundation, the members of the community had developed a core of practices to "deepen, energize and form the fundamental contour of [their] lives."[26] The daily schedule, or *horarium*, provided the structure to attend to both spiritual and active aspects.[27] From the rising bell at ten minutes to five in the morning to lights out at nine thirty at night, each sister knew exactly where she was to be and what she was to be doing. Two significant sections of the day were set aside for prayer: an hour and a half in the morning before breakfast and then another hour in the evening before supper.

As for active service to the needs of society, the Rule offered a high ideal and wide scope: "The end proposed by this Congregation is to honor Divine Providence, and to promote God's merciful designs upon mankind, by devoting itself to works of charity, as will be explained elsewhere."[28] While such works included care of the sick and the relief of the unfortunate,[29] the Rule goes on to specify that "the principal end of the Congregation, as regards our neighbor, is the education of young girls and their training in virtue."[30] The benefits of education for the rapidly expanding Catholic populations were already clear as the next generation of immigrants became increasingly qualified for better paying and more influential positions. For example, a girl in the 1922 class of Providence High School in Chicago later expressed her gratitude for her Catholic education in a letter: "Because of Sister Francis Joseph's after-school coaching, I scored 96 in my entrance exam for the Teachers' College."[31]

A Spirit of Piety

When young women of the time made a conscious decision to focus on what they knew to be a spiritual call to a life of prayer and service, what Mother Mary Cecilia Bailly said of Mother Theodore Guérin in a completely different time and place could also be said of most of them: "It is needless to mention that she was brought up in piety; everything in connection with her infers that her life from her childhood was under the influence of religion. Her habits, her affections and every principle of action in her, were all guided by motives of piety."[32] Almost all the young women who sought entrance to the Congregation during this era, many of them teenage girls, were reared in Catholic families. This often meant that they were also part of a large and extended family with a father who worked and a mother who ran the household. They played with many brothers and sisters as well as the Catholic children in the neighborhood. They walked with them to the parish school where they were taught by sisters, made their First Communion in the parish church, sang in the choir, attended devotions and participated in social gatherings. Many watched brothers leave for the seminary. Yes, they too were raised in piety.

Their insular Catholic environment provided much to nourish that piety. Although the church sanctuary was the prerogative of ordained men and altar boys, women drawn to spiritual matters could choose from an array of Catholic publications designed to assist silent and devout participation. Small pamphlets could be carried in purse or pocket and used to while away the time on a streetcar ride by reflecting on "Thoughts from the Following of Christ," such as "Whence will your patience be crowned, if you meet with no adversity?"[33] A gift for a particularly devout girl might be Father Lasance's prayer book, a fully indexed 890 page compilation of prayers and spiritual reading with a highly attractive aim.

> In thought and tendency, MY PRAYER-BOOK purposes to be the embodiment of Christian optimism and altruism; the exponent of all that is helpful and invigorating in the Christian life—of whatever is calculated to promote man's temporal and eternal welfare; it lays stress upon the fact that while the short cut to happiness is by way of self-renunciation, self-denial, self-conquest, self-control, in the following of Christ, nevertheless good cheer, heartfelt joy, and genuine happiness, far from being incompatible with the practice of the Catholic faith in particular, are really the concomitant or rather the outgrowth and efflorescence of a virtuous Christian life.[34]

Proud of their religion, most families would have in a prominent place a large Bible with pages for inscribing the names of relatives on a family tree, but except for lavish illustrations that might entertain younger children, the Bible was seldom consulted. More popular were small lives of Christ in which scripture was combined with devotion.

Since attendance at Sunday Mass was a given, after the 1935 revival of the "dialogue Mass," which invited congregations to speak aloud the Latin responses, almost indispensible was the Sunday Missal with the "pulpit text of all Epistles and Gospels," drawings and juxtaposed Latin/English prayers to assist "active participation."[35] Surrounded by such a rich background of Christian formation, many found the transition to religious life to be almost seamless.

Community Life: A Spirit of "Sisterliness"

Integral to the active and contemplative aspects of the sisters' lives was what Sister Angelyn Dries, OSF, has felicitously described as the inner role of "'sister'—to one another and to other women as well. Cleaning and laundering, the development of maternal instincts in care for children and fostering greater quality of life for those in their care all nurtured home, hearth, and traditional feminine values."[36] For Sisters of Providence such "sisterliness" was a cherished undergirding value, a "practice of hospitality to one another."[37] Visits and correspondence with family were limited. To help sisters pursue a life of prayer, interactions with seculars were restricted by rules and customs. Sisters were cautioned against being drawn into controversies and encouraged to adopt manners consonant with the habit they wore as a sort of personal cloister. Such restrictions on external contacts had the effect of weaving a rich social tapestry within the community itself.

Among themselves, the practice of silence limited conversations outside of the socializing recreation time to occasions of "necessity, charity, or politeness," thus putting the focus on worthwhile exchanges that fostered close friendships. Of course, not all communication depended on words. Status and duties were distributed according to length of time in community, but the various household chores and activities provided ample opportunity for mutual service and interaction. Newspapers spread to protect freshly mopped floors often yielded snippets of news from the outside world. Permission to work together on school projects allowed for fun and creativity. Listening to Saturday opera broadcasts or occasional political events could spark later conversations. At times a sense of mischief lightened an otherwise dull evening recreation of sewing basket mending. Superiors who saw the benefit of an occasional treat were known to provide ice cream bars as a snack or "collation" on a hot summer afternoon, or to suggest to a young professed sister showing signs of stress that an after-school walk to pick up apples from the corner store would help the cook. Serving as a companion for someone with an after-school dental appointment provided a welcome diversion.

While mission life provided many natural occasions for sisterly bonding, none matched the opportunities of summer for Sisters of Providence, when members would return to Saint Mary-of-the-Woods for the traditional "Homecoming."[38] As teachers, the sisters expected to use the summer vacation for enhancing their own education by taking the classes needed for certification and degrees which were scheduled at Saint Mary-of-the-Woods College summer sessions. But the main attraction was the time together with friends. After supper in the evenings, long walks around the campus were marked by pleasant conversation and restful stops on park benches, as well as encounters with novices, postulants and younger members walking in large groups. Those with talent for performance would meet to plan the entertainment for the singing, skits, speeches and orchestra performance that made up the several programs presented in the Conservatory in honor of those celebrating their Golden Jubilee or Mother's feast. The publication of the summer newsletter, *Woodland Echoes*, provided practical outlet for high school English teachers.[39] "Sisterliness" was literal for the many who had siblings in the community, as they were allowed to share the same room and often signed each other up for projects which allowed for more time together.

A Spirit of Providence

While the horarium was uniform from one convent to the next, the circumstances in which the sisters lived it out were anything but uniform. The main variables were both physical and human: physical in the sense of the neighborhood and size of the house itself and human in the person of the local superior and, for parish schools, the pastor.[40]

Each year on August 15, when the annual retreat ended, the sisters would gather in the Church of the Immaculate Conception at Saint Mary-of-the-Woods for the reception and profession ceremonies. At the conclusion of these lengthy ceremonies, they would kneel to listen to the bishop read the "Obedience List." Starting with the name of the local superior, the bishop would read the names of the sisters assigned to each mission. Hearing her own name was the signal for each sister to sit down. Sometimes, her "obedience" would be the same as the previous year, but sometimes she would find herself assigned to a new, unfamiliar mission, and the moment would spark feelings of anticipation or anxiety.

During the previous eight days of retreat, each sister would have packed all her belongings in preparation for the next day's departure for the mission assignment she had just received. The Ignatian retreat, with its call to complete dedication, coupled with the ceremonies just witnessed, would have focused her attention on her vocation, her desire to be an instrument of Providence. Every sister had at one point knelt in the sanctuary and pronounced vows of poverty, chastity and obedience in a spirit of offering herself for service. The sisters trusted that the superiors had reasons for their placement decisions, and so they accepted their assignment as God's Providence for them during the coming year.

Possible tears and upset notwithstanding, the next day they found their way to the designated departure place along the railroad tracks just beyond the front gate and joined their companions for the journey. The high school teachers might find themselves headed to one of the academies or high schools owned by the community or to a combined elementary/secondary parish school. An elementary teacher could be among the thirty-six others in the huge St. Mel Convent in Chicago, or one of only three at nearby St. Peter's in Linton, Indiana. No matter. Wherever it might take them, they felt that they shared in God's work. Scattered though they would be, the daily practice of reciting the Congregation's prayer of Reunion[41] would remind them of their shared commitment to works of love, mercy and justice.

Achieving this union of spirit required a delicate balance of the natural tension between the ever shifting American cultural and political milieu and the legacy of Mother Theodore. As noted above, their venerated foundress had cautioned the sisters not to expect "new things" based on her travels, but rather to notice that her words would simply radiate from "the same old truths." Those who had been chosen to succeed her as superiors general had followed her example in traveling to seek out new things which would expand the mission, but had not wavered in inviting the Holy Spirit to help them "see many things in new lights." Over the eighty-six years since the foundation hundreds of women had glimpsed the spirit of the sisters, been welcomed into membership, internalized its possibilities and taken on the responsibility of fostering the union of spirit prayed for in the Reunion.[41] When Mother Mary Cecilia Bailly took up her duties in 1856, sixty-seven sisters were available for the mission. As this book takes up the Congregation's story in June 1926, Mother Mary Raphael Slattery was "mother" to 1,092 sisters. Before setting out to follow the events of the next forty years until 1966, it will be helpful to understand the system of governance which had evolved to direct the growing Congregation's multiple activities.

Although the five women introduced at the beginning of this chapter provide a tiny sample of the hundreds who made up the Congregation during this time, incidents from their lives will be featured in sidebars to illustrate how the day-to-day lives of the sisters at large were affected by the decisions of those chosen to govern. It is to that system of governance that we now turn our attention.

❧ Chapter 2
Governance

This 1937 photo of the sisters gathering at Marywood in Anaheim, California, provides a glimpse of the hierarchical status within the community which the habit otherwise concealed. In the center of the row of seated sisters is Mother Mary Raphael Slattery. At her right is Fifth Councilor and Supervisor of Schools Sister Francis Joseph Elbreg. Seated at Mother Mary Raphael's left is Sister Regina Clare Carlos, provincial superior of the West. Also seated are three local superiors: first on the far left is Sister Marion Loretta Sullivan from Hawthorne; on the far right is Sister Bernard Marie Crowley from Alhambra; to her right is Sister Mary Dorothea Magrady from Van Nuys. Standing behind Mother Mary Raphael is Sister Margaret Rose Brennan, superior of Marywood.

"Good morning, Mother." Startled at the sound of the voice, the old woman in the chair beside the window turned from her gaze across the ravine to the Academy building beyond and smiled up at her visitor.

"Good morning, Mother," she replied. "Come in."

If such a conversation had occurred at Providence Convent in late June 1926, it would have been the first time in the eight years since Mother Anastasie Brown died that two living Sisters of Providence had borne the title of "Mother." When the newly retired Mother Mary Cleophas Foley welcomed her successor, the newly elected Mother Mary Raphael Slattery, they would have had much to discuss. The two sisters had known each other well for many years in many capacities since the days when, as novice mistress, Sister Mary Cleophas welcomed the first young women to join the Congregation from the recently established St. Joseph Academy in Galesburg, Illinois. Though half the age of her superior, Mary Elizabeth Slattery, the future Mother Mary Raphael, had grown up in the same type of devout Irish immigrant family. She quickly adapted to the novitiate's disciplined regimen of spiritual formation and teacher training, proving an eager and able student.

Having demonstrated unusual ability as principal and local superior in several large houses, Sister Mary Raphael had been elected in 1902 as the Congregation's treasurer. From 1902 to 1926, serving in Mother Mary Cleophas' energetic administration, she had been of major assistance with her frequent trips to the missions and contacts with banking and business men. After the delegates to the 1926 Chapter heard her financial report, they had unanimously expressed "satisfaction at the excellent management of the funds and the prosper-

Sister Mary Raphael Slattery, c. 1902

ous condition of the temporalities of the Community."[1] This recognition of her twenty-four years of diligent service coupled with her reputation for faithful observance of the Rule made her their choice to succeed the revered eighty-three-year-old superior general.[2]

In order to appreciate the extent of her new responsibilities, the reader needs to understand the organization of the Congregation. In some respects the governance structure was very much the same as that of other women's congregations. In other respects it was unique. To understand the difference, it's necessary to trace its roots in the gradual emergence of a ministerial lifestyle which was both recognized by Catholic legal structures and greatly prized by the Catholic faithful. Readers who are familiar with the way in which the Congregation was governed during these years may prefer to bypass this section entirely and turn to page 53, where the members of the 1926 council are introduced.

Evolution of Governance Structure

Apostolic Religious Congregations

For centuries the church had provided support and protection for women's monastic communities. While men's congregations such as the Jesuits adapted monastic and mendicant structures to support active roles in society, women were restricted to the cloister, and convents proliferated to accommodate the many who followed a contemplative calling. During the decades following the Reformation, the war-weary people of France had experienced a religious revival, prompting the desire on the part of many devout women to combine their devotion with social activism. Rather than joining existing congregations, they gathered on their own by living as *dévotes* in prayer communities from which they acted as *charités* in service to the poor. Historian Elizabeth Rapley notes the cultural resistance to the flourishing of this movement of religiously inclined women.

> But success brought its own problems. The more they entered the big cities, the more visible they became, and the more the question of their half-nun status began to surface. The old adage was still in force, *aut murus aut maritus* (either a convent wall or a husband). Women at large were women in peril. The hierarchy had to be anxious, since any contravention of church law and/or public morality would certainly be laid at their door. Fathers and mothers had to worry that their daughters might lose their reputations.[3]

Nonetheless, society needed services and the women needed an outlet for their spiritual energies. One solution was a mitigated cloister where free schools sponsored by wealthy *dévotes* were housed within convent walls. Vincent de Paul was successful with a more original approach, enlisting the talent of the wealthy widow Louse de Marillac to train Marguerite Naseau and other young peasant women to form the

Daughters of Charity. Another cleric who in 1662 sought the support of women was Friar Nicolas Barré in Rouen, whose group of prosperous bourgeoisie auxiliaries were adept at instructing women and children. Within a few years the group grew into a community and over the next decades they spread across France. Rapley observes that, "Attitudes had changed over the years, and these women would not be pressed into the cloister. ... They also served as a model for numerous other women's teaching congregations across France."[4] Little by little the church's attitude changed as well. These were women of the church, and as one foundress after another presented her desire for formal recognition to Rome, the need for a change of church law from the cloister-only approach to an alternate structure for apostolic religious life for women became clear.[5]

A similar innovation in the lifestyle of men who felt called to religious service also demanded changes in church law. Jean-Baptiste de La Salle saw the need of education for the working poor, but he saw no need for those who joined him to become priests. Their shared vocation to provide education for boys of the working class was reason enough to form a community—the Brothers of the Christian Schools. Little by little the communities of women and men that were formed to give service attracted more followers than the monastic foundations. Rapley comments on the significance of this change:

> The age of mysticism was giving way to the age of Descartes and the scientific revolution. More and more, as the century went on, people in power came to rate religious institutions according to their "utility."... A new source of talent and energy—bourgeois talent and bourgeois energy—poured into the service of the Church.

> And this, seen from the vantage point of social history, was one of the great contributions of the religious orders to the modernization of society. They created a bridge over which people of modest background could pass to positions of influence.[6]

The skeptical attitudes of the Enlightenment paved the way for the attempts of the French Revolution to suppress religion. Yet even Napoleon sensed the strong undercurrent of religion among the people. The sheer utility of the apostolic congregations motivated him to permit a limited re-emergence. After his overthrow and the return of the monarchy, a religious revival took hold that would sustain the rapid growth of such

congregations. It was in this atmosphere that another generation arose to reclaim the heritage of apostolic religious life begun a century earlier. Rapley summarizes:

> France was several decades ahead of the rest [of Europe] in the
> way it opened up to what was in fact a major women's move-
> ment. Whereas in much of the Continent the female religious
> life continued to mean enclosure, in France it swiftly evolved to
> mean community life combined with active service of one kind
> or another. ... Before the end of the century, 400 new active-life
> congregations would join those already in existence.[7]

The Sisters of Providence was one of these congregations.

The Rule as a Support to the Apostolic Lifestyle

When Father Jacques François Dujarié, like many priests
in France, gathered a group of women to assist his pastoral
ministry in 1806 rural France, his efforts to catechize a lost
generation of children drew immediate support from Breton
women. By the time Anne-Thérèse Guérin entered in 1823,
the community had fifty sisters in twenty houses, and eleven
years later it had grown to 255 professed sisters in fifty-eight
houses. The bishop of Le Mans, Jean-Baptiste Bouvier, was
among the visionary bishops who recognized the value of
women's contributions to the life of the church. With his advice the fledgling group separated from Father Dujarié's brothers, formed a corporation and opened more establishments.
Because of his scholarly background, Bishop Bouvier was able
to further this growth by providing a Rule.[8] This 1835 Rule
drew on the community's thirty years of experience in living
an apostolic religious life and provided an inspirational charter for future growth. In her position as superior at Rouen,
Sister St. Theodore internalized its call to sanctity through service. It was this same Rule which later gave her the confidence to stand up to Bishop de la Hailandière to protect the
integrity of the American foundation.

Nonetheless, once separated from Ruillé, since the
Congregation's Rule was specific to the Diocese of Le Mans in
France, and she was now accountable to the Bishop of
Vincennes in the United States, there was reason to question
its binding force. Mother Theodore found herself caught between the two bishops as they sparred over who had authority over the Congregation.[9] In fact, it would not be until several
years after her death that the Rule would be one of many sub-

mitted for papal approbation during the nineteenth century. Once approved by Rome, the Congregation would be accountable to a papal congregation rather than a local bishop. Given the high regard Bishop Bouvier commanded in Rome,[10] and the fact that his chancellor, Canon Lottin, went to Rome in 1861 to work for papal approbation of the French Rule, it is likely that this Rule would have been a model for the norms for apostolic congregations issued by Pope Pius IX in the 1862 decree *Ad universalis*. In her study of these developments, Lynn Jarrell, OSU, points out that since it stipulated that the superior general must be elected from among the members, this decree was the first of a series of church laws that enabled communities of women religious to maintain their internal organizational structures across dioceses.[11]

In 1857, when the Vincennes diocese was divided to create the diocese of Fort Wayne, the American Sisters of Providence found themselves in two dioceses. Their acceptance of missions in Michigan in 1875 brought them into the Detroit diocese. Undoubtedly, the memory of Mother Theodore's experience sharpened their appreciation of the value of papal approbation in order to ensure that their own superiors—not three different bishops—had authority over their internal affairs. When Bishop Silas Chatard became Ordinary of Indianapolis in 1878, because of his years as rector of the North American College in Rome and his connections there, his assistance was invaluable in securing the Decree of Praise for the American Rule in 1887.[12] Always alert to multiple avenues for the success of her goals, Mother Mary Cleophas sought legal advice from Edward Higgins, SJ, to prepare the correct form of the documents.[13] With the 1887 Decree of Praise, the Congregation achieved the status of a Pontifical Congregation, and as such, enjoyed the benefits of church laws supporting apostolic life. The Congregation was now well positioned to expand its educational apostolate in cooperation with the hierarchy with the assurance that individual bishops could not interfere with its internal affairs.[14]

Governance According to the Sisters of Providence *Constitutions*

Jarrell points out that when the Sacred Congregation for Religious issued the decree *Normae* in 1901, it "sought to make use of its years of experience in working with these new foundations to instruct bishops."[15] Because *Normae* provided an outline of an ideal institute of simple vows, it had the positive effect of making it easier for the many congregations developing at that time to gain approval. However, it also had the negative effect of a cookie cutter approach which dissipated the energy of the founding charism. The Rules of religious congregations were to be divided into two parts: a section of fundamental codes subject to canonical approval and a section that developed these codes in accordance with the charism of the founder. Each version of the Rule of the Sisters of Providence had different titles for these sections: 1872, Constitutions and Rules; 1897, Part I and Part II; 1919, Constitutions and Duties of the Sisters. For the Sisters of Providence, the 1919 revision with the separation of the required canonical stipulations into "Part I: Constitutions" from practices that retained the imprint of the founders in "Part II: Duties of the Sisters" had a significant effect. Changes were required for the first section, but the second section, written by Bishop Bouvier and referred to as the Rules, required little revision.

Commenting in 1949 on the revisions required for the 1862 edition, historian Sister Mary Borromeo Brown notes, "The Constitutions show much more revision than the Rules proper, many of which retain to this day the original wording of their venerated author, Bishop Bouvier."[16] Consequently the second section, rich with scriptural references and exhortations, formed a bedrock of spirituality. Because it set such a high standard for life as a Sister of Providence, superiors often selected quotes from this document as anchors for exhortation and encouragement in the "letters circular" sent twice a year to the sisters. This volume will refer to the entire document as the *Constitutions* or the Rule. In later years, the *Constitutions* would require further revision, but the following discussions will explain the basics of the governance structure operative throughout the period of time covered in this volume.

Superiors

The Local Superior

The keystone to the entire governmental structure of the Congregation was the local superior. In professing membership in the Congregation, each sister pronounced vows of poverty, chastity and obedience. The Rule explains the significance of the third vow: "The vow of Obedience, the bond and essence of the religious life, imposes the obligation to obey the Holy See, the General Chapter, and the Superior General, and all other legitimate Superiors in all that is conformable to the letter and the spirit of the *Constitutions*."[17] On a day-to day basis, sisters on the missions looked to their local superior as the mediator of their obligations of obedience. Part II of the 1929 *Constitutions* explained in detail the duties associated with these obligations, including the dispositions of hating their own will, resolving to do God's will and respecting in superiors "the Authority with which God has invested them."[18]

In the section "Duties of the Sisters toward the Local Superior,"[19] sisters were exhorted to cultivate a polite, obliging and respectful attitude and never criticize her, but rather consult her about the pupils and utilize her advice in their teaching. In all except the very largest houses, the same sister was both principal of the school and the superior in charge of the convent, so there were frequent opportunities for interaction between the sisters and the local superior.

On their part, the sisters appointed as superiors had to be thirty years old and to have made final vows. The age requirement put many women who entered at age twenty or above on a "fast track" since most entrants were in their teens. While an appointment was for three years with only one additional three-year appointment allowed, it was common to assign successful superiors to another mission at the end of six years. For local superiors who took to heart the Rule's admonition to be "a model of modesty, regularity, and piety, [and to treat the sisters] with mildness, affability, and kindness, and give freely to each one according to her needs, in sickness or in health,"[20] the role became an avenue for growth in their own spiritual lives.

In 1932, facing the need to find ninety-three such women among their number who could be appointed in this capacity to lead each house, Mother Mary Raphael admonished her council:

> The Community is placed under the supervision of the Superiors and it is incumbent upon them to look after the interests of the Community in general and each Sister in particular. The spiritual side must always come first. Subjects look to Superi-

ors with confidence and trust. It is necessary therefore, that Sisters be selected in whom virtues—prudence, kindness, forbearance, patience, etc.—predominate. The purpose of this session is to name such Sisters, putting aside personal feelings and all favoritism, and selecting for Superiors those whom, the members feel before God, are most competent.

The mission lists were then examined, and after discussing the pros and cons, the following names were submitted.[21]

From house to house, each local community followed the *Constitutions* regarding the "Employment of the Day," which prescribed not only the activities but also the schedule. "The Sisters shall rise, in all seasons, at five o'clock. ... All the Sisters should be in bed by half-past nine o'clock."[22] From pre-dawn till dark each sister knew her duties, but it fell to the local superior to assign the various responsibilities or "employments" such as purchasing supplies, preparing and serving food, cleaning various areas of the house, answering the doorbell and phone, etc. By direction and example she would oversee the observance of communal spiritual practices such as silence and the monthly retreat Sunday, as well as interaction with the outside world, providing petty cash and giving permissions for medical appointments and assigning a companion. She was the official intermediary with the pastor and his assistants, as well as any lay employees. When newly professed sisters were assigned to the house, she continued their formation with instructions on community customs, religious decorum and proper etiquette.

Their role as principals of the schools enabled many local superiors who were known for being school women to mentor young teachers who aspired to excellence. Some teacher training was incorporated into classes for the novices, but serious practice teaching was a trial by fire when inexperienced teachers were expected to assume full responsibility in whatever grade and classroom was assigned. Saturday morning study hour was a time for sitting down with the "young professed" and drawing up lesson plans for the next week, so it was presumed that the superior was familiar with the entire curriculum. Her style of approach had a great deal of influence on the success of these fledgling teachers and on their future lives as Sisters of Providence, as Sister Rosalie Hussey gratefully described:

Sister Berchmans was the most motherly superior I ever had. I feel I owe everything to her, for she was my first superior and gave me my first training in mission life. She was such a woman herself and tried to train the young Sisters and novices to be womanly. She did it in such a kind, motherly way that it would make one want to do as she wished. If she corrected you for something, it was firmly but kindly. You could go back to her in just a few minutes after and you would never know that she had ever given you a correction. I mean her manner was just as if nothing had ever happened. She has been my model in many ways in the past.[23]

Of course, not every sister who was appointed to serve as a local superior possessed the natural human qualities which were compatible with this role. Another sister who served in this era also reported negative experiences, such as crying in her pillow at night after a public reprimand. To provide a modicum of training for the local superiors, during the summer weeks when the sisters were at Saint Mary-of-the-Woods the superior general would gather the local superiors for "instructions," such as these samples from undated handwritten notes:

- Pray a great deal to ask our Lord to give us the grace and light to bring out the good in each Sister.

- Be exact yourself to little things, then require it of your Sisters.

- Never talk about the faults of your Sisters.

- If you are with seculars, pray much that you may not disedify them.

- Try to improve your Sisters—culture, bearing, intellectually.[24]

The Home Superior

Although the term "home superior" does not appear in the *Constitutions*, it had become customary for each sister to be assigned to one of the assistants, as the *Constitutions* designated the six sisters elected to the general council. The practice begun by Mother Theodore of meeting with each sister during their time of rest and relaxation at Saint Mary-of-the-Woods during the summer had been continued by the superiors general until during Mother Mary Cleophas' time, the Congregation had become too large.

She assigned the younger sisters to one or the other of her councilors, while she herself continued to see each of the older professed sisters. In this annual visit, the "Home Superior" would
inquire into the physical and spiritual well-being of the sister
and give her counsel and encouragement in her ministry. This
practice, which continued into the period following Vatican
Council II, served to bond the sister to the congregation in the
person of the general officer and provided her with a councilor
and advocate in time of trial.[25]

During the years of temporary profession, sisters were enjoined to write once a month to their home superiors on retreat Sunday, while all sisters who "belonged" to the home
superior were expected to schedule an appointment during
the annual retreat. On their part, council members were directed by Rule to reward any confidences with "charity, prudence, and discretion, neither flattering nor discouraging them.
… They shall observe an inviolable secrecy upon what has been
confided to them."[26] Because the placement of each sister was
arranged by the council, these letters and conferences provided
the means for communicating difficulties and desires. While
the major criterion for placement was to fill teaching positions
for the school, with due consideration to observations gleaned
from visitations, this relationship often provided a personal
touch to assignment decisions.

The term "home superior" also had a literal meaning, in
that each assistant was given specific duties at the motherhouse.
For example, on the 1938-1944 council, Sister Helen Clare
Freiburger was in charge of arranging the schedule for priests
and divine services, while Sister Eileen Walker was to take
care of ordering the car, supervising the clothing department,
arranging employments by assigning sisters at the motherhouse
to specific tasks and responsibilities and presiding in the large
dining room. Secretary Sister Marie Stanislaus Curran's responsibility for travel arrangements would require a close fa-
miliarity with train schedules, fares and passes. When home,
the assistants were expected to be models of attendance in
chapel, refectory (dining room) and at recreation, as well as
being available in their offices after breakfast. When emergencies incapacitated local superiors, the assistants were often sent
as a substitute for short periods.

The Superior General

This chapter began with the intention of explaining the responsibilities of the superior general, but as the preceding discussion indicates, her interactions with most of the sisters were limited. Nonetheless, the Rule stressed a personal relationship, noting that, "she bears the title of Mother and she should have the feelings of a Mother for all the Sisters, regarding them as her beloved daughters."[27] Hers was the duty of having the *Constitutions* observed, first by her own lived demonstration of their spirit and practice, and secondly by exercising her authority for the common good. As will become evident in the following chapters, the personality and spirituality of the woman who occupied this post would greatly affect the fortunes of the Congregation during her term of office.

In canonical terms, it was the superior general who was invested with the authority of a major superior.[28] In practical terms, she depended greatly on her council to guide the Congregation's affairs. The Rule provided direction for the needed cooperation between "Mother and her council":

> They shall be closely united by the bonds of charity and confidence, having nothing hidden from the Superior, always speaking to her with respect, but, at the same time, with candor, having with her but one heart and one soul, as they participate in the same authority.[29]

The *Constitutions* stipulated not only the duties of the assistants, but also designated roles for a general secretary, who during this time was one of the councilors, as well as a treasurer and a *procuratrix* or econome responsible for the operations of the motherhouse, including purchasing, maintenance, the farms and employees.

All of the councilors had offices in "Tile Hall" along the front hallway of Providence Convent. While the *Constitutions* stated that "the Sisters shall not inquire curiously among themselves what the Superior General and her council are about to do or ought to do, in what concerns the government of the Congregation,"[30] all were well aware that decisions that "came from Tile Hall" were to be obeyed. The council met on a regular basis, often on Sunday mornings in the tiny council room adjacent to the secretary's office. Major responsibilities at the motherhouse, such as care of the sick, were parceled out among the councilors. Normally each of them participated in the visi-

tation of the houses on the missions to assure the exact observance of the Rule and also to ascertain the needs of the mission. A "Visitation Report" form provided specific points to be
noted regarding spiritual exercises, observance of rule, convent regulations and school regulations, as well as general conditions of the building, finances, health and spirit of the sisters.
During the intensive meetings devoted to compiling the annual Obedience List of each sister's placement for the following year, these forms provided data to guide the decisions.

The General Chapter

At this point the question becomes: who were the persons
who filled the roles of the superior general and her assistants,
and how were they chosen for these positions? To answer that
question we must go to the very first article of the *Constitutions*:

> The Sisters of Providence of Saint Mary-of-the-Woods, in the
> diocese of Indianapolis, Indiana, form a Congregation of Sis-
> ters, who, bound by simple vows, are under the authority of a
> General Chapter and of a Superior General, assisted by her
> Council.[31]

This article makes it clear that the highest authority of the
Congregation is the General Chapter. The Chapter was a representative body which met every six years in order to examine the report of the previous administration, elect a new one
and "transact the more important affairs of the Congregation."[32]

Membership

The 1926 Chapter had, in fact, marked a major change in
the makeup of this authoritative body. The Congregation had
doubled in size during the thirty-six years of Mother Mary
Cleophas' administration, growing from 522 professed sisters
to 1,092. In order to represent the entire Congregation, the
membership of the Chapter included both ex-officio and elected
delegates. The superior general and her council were delegates
"by right" or ex-officio. According to the 1887 *Constitutions*,
sisters who had been appointed as local superiors of houses of
ten or more sisters were also ex-officio, and an equal number
of private sisters (those not superiors) were elected. With the
policy of accepting schools in larger cities rather than smaller
towns, the number of houses with more than ten sisters had

greatly increased. Consequently, the membership of the 1914 Chapter had swollen to ninety-nine members. Burdened by a similar size, the 1920 Chapter called for a change, limiting ex-officio local superiors to those with twenty or more sisters, plus an equal number of elected private sisters.[33]

The need for changes within the Congregation of the Sisters of Providence coincided with the promulgation of the 1917 Code of Canon Law. The recently promulgated code would require concomitant changes in the Congregation's *Constitutions*, in addition to the change requested for Chapter membership. Although the code was recent, due to her years of experience Mother Mary Cleophas was familiar with church law and understood the need for clear guidelines. In addition, her two visits to Rome had acquainted her with the importance of personal contacts with influential hierarchy.[34]

After the Congregation's Cardinal Protector[35] Diomede Falconio, OFM, died, Father Alexis Henry Lépicier, OSM, prior general of the Servites and rector of their college in Rome, assumed this position. Because Our Lady of Sorrows School in Chicago, staffed by the Servites, was one of the first missions of the community in Chicago, the two religious communities enjoyed a long-standing relationship.[36] In 1919, Father Lépicier was in Chicago for the Servite Chapter, a timely opportunity for Mother Mary Cleophas to meet with him. In recording the topics of the meeting, secretary Sister Mary Alma noted:

> In all the matters he was consulted about the V. Rev Father proved himself the saintly humble religious, the experienced Superior, the learned theologian, and this interview was a special grace at this particular time when so many are ready to quote Canon Law in defense of their opinions. [37]

Mother Mary Cleophas and her council realized that a complete revision of the *Constitutions* would require additional time, but that the question of Chapter membership needed immediate attention. She petitioned the Sacred Congregation for Religious that the number of delegates to the General Chapter be fixed permanently at thirty-two, including the superior general, the treasurer, six councilors and twenty-four elected delegates. This request was granted in a February 28, 1924, rescript, so that from 1926 on, this became the norm for General Chapter membership.

Election of Delegates

The process of electing these delegates was a meticulously choreographed affair. Although the Rule stated that "The General Chapter represents the entire Congregation," not every sister had the right to vote for its members. The Rule retained the distinction between "choir" sisters, who were bound to the daily recitation of the Little Office of the Blessed Virgin, and "sisters *coadjutrix*," who were exempt from choir in order to attend to meal preparation and household tasks. Only choir sisters who were perpetually professed were eligible to vote. In addition to these restrictions, further emphasis on the importance of the charge of electing delegates was given by the exhortation in the superior general's letter circular convening the upcoming Chapter.

> The selection of those who are to be members of the General Chapter is a serious matter, and each of you, my dear Sisters, should feel the responsibility of your part in a duty of such grave importance to the Community. Hence, the need of seeking light from above by fervent, humble prayer, and of following the dictates of conscience without regard to one's personal feelings. You should call to mind the necessity of selecting a Sister who can worthily discharge the duties of a delegate; that is, one whose character combines virtue, sound judgment, prudence, and loyalty to the best interests of the Community.[38]

The letter went on to prescribe a ritual to be conducted in the community room of each house on the same date and time for each house. In preparation for this ritual, the sixth assistant, the secretary, had the complex task of preparing several lists at the motherhouse. First she drew up a list of all the houses with the number of sisters residing in each. The next step was crucial but complicated: crucial because the Rule prescribed twelve sections; complicated because each section had to be composed of houses within the same diocese as much as possible, with all sections relatively the same size.

While not exactly "gerrymandering," the 1936 grouping exemplifies the creative arrangements which ensued. One of the twelve sections consisted of just four Chicago houses with a total of ninety-four sisters, while another section grouped six California, one Oklahoma and three Illinois houses to a total of sixty-seven sisters in these ten "nearby" houses. After these sections had been determined, the secretary turned her attention to preparing four sub-lists from each section: 1) co-adjutrix sisters and 2) temporarily professed sisters (thus identifying the sisters ineligible to participate); 3) perpetually professed choir sisters who could vote, but could not be delegates; 4) choir sisters who were professed for five years and therefore could vote and were also eligible to receive votes. It was this final list that she typed as a ballot for each section. She then needed to stuff individual small envelopes with a ballot and a small blank slip and an even smaller envelope, preparing sufficient envelopes for each perpetually professed choir sister in each house in that section. The last step was counting out and packaging sets for each house.

As for the actual voting, on the designated day at the designated hour the eligible sisters assembled in the community room for the ceremony; they recited the "Veni Sancte Spiritus" and "Oremus," then listened as the local superior read the official letter circular with its admonitions and specific instructions. The superior then distributed the small envelopes to each sister. This would be the first time the sister knew those for whom she could cast a ballot. Within the next few minutes she must decide "who she thinks before God best fitted as a delegate or member of the General Chapter." She might or might not know all those sisters whose names appeared on the typed slip, but over the years of postulancy, novitiate, temporary vows, second novitiate and several missions, she would have come to know a good many. One of her votes must go to a local superior, the first name on each convent's list. A sister looking at a Chicago section list would have four names from which to choose. Her own local superior would be better known to her, and perhaps deemed worthy of her vote, but she could also be passed over. She would then turn her attention to the remaining sixty or more names, from which she could choose only one.

After a few minutes of reflection, each sister would kneel and write her two choices on the *billet*[39] in ink, place it in the small envelope with her list, seal it and hand it to the local superior. The superior in turn would place all the small envelopes in a large envelope and seal it. All were enjoined to regard their choice as a sacred confidence, so there was no sharing of who had voted for whom, but rather a redoubling of prayer that the sisters who would be elected as delegates through this process would have the wisdom to elect those best qualified as superiors for the next six years. For the vast majority of the Congregation, this single moment every six years was their entire participation in the general government.

The numbers from the 1926 elections further emphasize the limited participation of the sisters at large. Of the 1,092 professed sisters, 754 were finally professed choir sisters eligible to vote. Of this number, although 546 were eligible to be elected, twelve of the delegates were to be chosen from the pool of ninety local superiors, while the other twelve would be chosen from the much larger pool of 456 private sisters. Given these odds, it is not surprising that sisters who were assigned to positions of responsibility such as superiors of large houses (who were also principals of the attached school or academy) or former superiors were usually elected to be delegates. Because their election showed the confidence the membership had in the Chapter members, it was usually from among themselves that the superior general and her council were chosen.

The Chapter of Elections

After the local election ceremony, the superior would mail the large envelopes to the sixth assistant, the secretary. On a designated day, the council would meet to count the ballots and identify the delegates who were duly elected. In June, about a week before the Chapter, those who had been elected delegates would receive a letter advising them to appear.[40] In the Chapter their duties were brief and conducted in a manner that ensured the utmost confidentiality. As required by the *Constitutions*, the bishop presided at the election.[41] Several sisters were assigned to keep watch outside the doors. The business session was minimal, including a financial report presented by the treasurer with perhaps a vote to authorize upcoming major expenditures for building projects. From time to time, delegates would raise items from the floor, although no agenda was circulated in advance. The main business was the election, with members exhorted to consult their consciences with the good of the community uppermost in their minds. Immediately following the counting of the ballots, the newly elected superiors, if present, took the oath of office. Anyone not present was summoned. By noon or that afternoon the General Chapter was concluded.

The Chapter was generally scheduled to conclude on Homecoming Day in June, when the sisters returned to Saint Mary-of-the-Woods from their missions for the six-week summer school followed by retreat. House diaries of the time indicate the perception of the role of the Chapter as electors, noting that sisters elected as delegates left their missions early to return to Saint Mary-of-the-Woods in order to "assist at the election of a Superior General and her council."[42] The excitement of Homecoming was heightened by the news of who had been elected and the opportunity to greet the superior general and her council in person, as this 1926 Diary entry records:

> The elections are over at 11:30, but the Installation takes place only at 3 P.M. After Benediction the Community meets in the Community room to greet the newly elected Superiors. As our dear Missionaries are arriving at almost every hour the greetings and welcomes are continuous until 5:30 when supper is served. Beads and Office had been said at 1:30, so the evening was one of gala recreation. The Chicago special with its 300 Missionaries did not arrive until 5:15. Rev. Mother and Mother Mary Cleophas met them in the Tile Hall.[43]

The 1926-1932 Council

We conclude this chapter by imagining ourselves among the arriving crowd, eager to congratulate the newly elected Mother and her council as we meet the women who played significant roles in this period of the Congregation's history.

Mother Mary Raphael Slattery 1861-1940

Mary Elizabeth Slattery's parents, Patrick and Johannah Slattery, had immigrated from Limerick, Ireland, to Galesburg, Illinois, in 1861. Born in 1863, she was the oldest of five girls, one of whom died in infancy. When the Sisters of Providence arrived in Galesburg in 1878 to open St. Joseph Academy, she enrolled to complete her high school education, graduating in 1881. She entered in 1882, one of the first to enjoy the newly completed novitiate building with Sister Mary Cleophas Foley as mistress of novices.

As Sister Mary Raphael, she returned to her home state and taught at Sacred Heart, Lockport, for a year and then at St. John, Loogootee, Indiana, but her poor health required her to return to Saint Mary-of-the-Woods mid-year. Strong again, she was named superior at Valparaiso at age twenty-five. From

there she was sent to Chicago as superior at the recently established Our Lady of Sorrows before returning to Saint Mary-of-the-Woods in 1894-1895 for second novitiate, during which time she assisted the secretary general. She was then named superior of St. Agnes Academy in Indianapolis. In the role of superior she was regarded as amiable, with a mild and gentle firmness in managing house and school. Well-grounded by these varied mission experiences, she was elected in 1902 at age thirty-nine to serve as sixth assistant and treasurer. The 1906 Chapter separated the role of treasurer from the council, but her services were greatly appreciated and she was appointed treasurer for the next three terms, assisting Mother Mary Cleophas for twenty-four years during the period of the Congregation's major expansion.

Sister Mary Bernard Laughlin 1876-1948

Mary Laughlin was the first of twelve children born to Irish immigrant Michael and his Ohio-born wife Mary in Fort Wayne, Indiana, in 1876. She first met the Sisters of Providence as a pupil at St. Peter and went on to graduate from St. Augustine Academy. Her mother's health was poor, so Mary stayed home to help with her younger siblings, also working, attending daily Mass and helping out with parish activities. She maintained contact with the sisters and was finally able to follow her heart and enter the Congregation in 1905 at age twenty-nine. After she spent a year as an eighth-grade boys' teacher, her talents and life experience were recognized when she was appointed superior of St. Joseph, Indianapolis, while still under temporary vows. During 1915-1926 she served as superior of three large Chicago houses: St. Agnes with seventeen sisters, St. Andrew with nineteen sisters and then at the combined Our Lady of Sorrows/Providence High School convent with eighty-two sisters. Known for kindness, wit and organizational ability, at age fifty she was elected as a delegate to the 1926 Chapter, which in turn chose her as first assistant to Mother Mary Raphael.

Sister Berchmans Collins 1873-1942

Mary Anne Collins was born in 1873 in Ontario, Canada. After her father died, her mother moved with her only child to Chicago. It was there that she met the Sisters of Providence, although she did not enter the community until 1897 when she was twenty-four. As a music teacher, she was sent where she was needed, moving almost every year from mission to mission in Indiana and Chicago. After being appointed a local superior at age thirty-seven, she taught upper grades for ten years before being appointed econome at the motherhouse in 1920. However, she served in this capacity for only a year before returning to another series of appointments as local superior. Although she was not herself a delegate to the 1926 Chapter, its members elected her as second assistant. As a local superior, she was regarded as kind, strict and prayerful and at age fifty-three, her recent experience in this role would prove most beneficial to the council.

Sister Gertrude Clare Owens 1887-1963

Genevieve was the first child born to Margaret and Michael Haughan in Chicago in 1887. After her father died in an accident, her mother married Michael Owens, and the family grew with the births of two younger sisters and a brother. Genevieve felt called to serve the sick and suffering, so she planned to enter the St. Joseph Sisters of Concordia, Kansas. During her formative years the Sisters of Providence moved into their new St. Andrew Convent across the street from the family home, beginning a relationship which led to her entering the novi-

tiate in 1904 at age seventeen. Two years later, as newly professed Sister Gertrude Clare, she took the train west to St. Agnes in South Omaha, Nebraska, during the last year of its operation under the Sisters of Providence. That same year her younger sister Rose entered the novitiate. Rose, whose religious name was Sister Genevieve Therese, contracted tuberculosis and died in 1910 at age twenty-one.

Perhaps as a comfort to her and their parents, Sister Gertrude Clare was sent to Chicago to work among the Italian immigrants at St. Columbkille, returning there as superior after her second novitiate. Her sound practical judgment and initiative were soon evident, and at age thirty-one she was made superior at the recently established Marywood Academy in Evanston. A chronicle of the time describes her two years there as "lighthearted." She had a quiet ability to delegate and to encourage the talented seventeen-sister household, several of whom went on to positions of authority in subsequent years.

As a superior, she was among the ex-officio delegates who had assembled for the 1920 General Chapter, which elected her second assistant at age thirty-three. She proved to be invaluable to Mother Mary Cleophas in this role, taking on extra duties of visiting the sick and also replacing the ailing superior general in giving the thirty-day retreat meditations for those making their second novitiate. In 1926, with the almost clean sweep of the 1920 council, she was one of only two home superiors to be re-elected to continue her duties as third assistant. Sister Gertrude Clare would go on to many years of service as a member of the council, eventually being elected superior general.[44]

Sister Mary Ignatia Hanson 1879-1933

Born in 1879, Joanna Hanson grew up in Chicago and prepared herself for a teaching career, graduating from Chicago Teacher's College in 1901. She then taught in the Chicago public schools before entering the community in 1904 at age twenty-five. After five years at St. Agnes Academy, Indianapolis, she was one of the eight Sisters of Providence sent to the first summer school for women religious at Catholic University in 1911, becoming one of the first to receive a BA degree from that institution in 1912. Her 1914 MA thesis, "The Cultural Value of Religion in the Development of the Child," put forth the philosophy of a truly Catholic education. She then went on to teach in many of the

Congregation's academy/boarding schools, mentoring younger sister teachers. While at St. Rose, Chelsea, she was elected a delegate to the 1926 General Chapter, which chose her to be fourth assistant at age forty-seven.

Sister Francis Joseph Elbreg 1895-1986

Beatrice Elbreg was the first of two daughters born to Frederick and Emma Elbreg in Indianapolis in 1895. The family was closely connected to the Sisters of Providence, since her mother had graduated from St. John Academy in Indianapolis and her aunt, Sister Mary Gabriel, had joined the Congregation in 1885. After graduating from St. John Academy in 1911 at age sixteen, she entered the

novitiate that same year. As she proved a quick and eager student, she was soon qualified to teach such diverse subjects as Latin and physics at Providence High School in Chicago and St. Augustine in Fort Wayne. During this time she completed her college degree and was then sent to Indiana University to study for a Master's degree in education. With the backing of Sister Basilissa Heiner, the council member in charge of schools, she designed a master's thesis based on a questionnaire which was sent to 102 sisters, all of whom returned them for her analysis, an effort which made her widely known across

the Congregation. When Sister Basilissa died in 1923, Sister
Francis Joseph was well-prepared to step into her shoes and
was appointed at age twenty-eight to finish out her mentor's
term as fifth assistant. Consequently, in spite of her relative
youth, the 1926 Chapter elected her to continue this post.

Sister Geraldine Mullen 1870-1945

Eva Mullen was born in Savanna,
Illinois, in 1870 and met the Sisters
of Providence in her early teens when
they arrived to establish a mission in
that small town on the upper Mississippi River in 1884, returning with
them to the motherhouse three years
later to enter the Congregation at age
seventeen. She began her high school
teaching career at the recently opened
faraway mission of St. Rose, Chelsea,
and after a year at St. Joseph,
Hammond, Indiana, spent five years
at Saint Mary-of-the-Woods Acad-
emy. After a year at St. Agnes Academy in Indianapolis, she
served as principal of St. Leo School in Chicago before returning to Saint Mary-of-the-Woods for sixteen years as instructor, prefect of studies and secretary during the years of its
gradual evolution into a fully accredited Catholic liberal arts
college.[45] Known for her tireless service and willingness to take
the initiative in strengthening the college programs, her gracious and affable manner endeared her to both faculty and
students. She was elected a delegate to the 1926 Chapter, which
in turn elected her at age forty-six to the Council as sixth assistant and secretary.

We can only imagine the animated conversations which
took place on that balmy summer evening as the missionaries
settled into their summer routine. Each sister picked up an
envelope with small slips of paper identifying her dormitory
at the new Le Fer Hall, or Guerin or Foley Hall, her place in
chapel at Sacred Heart Chapel in Foley Hall or in "the Big
Church," the classes she was to take toward her degree and

certification, her meal employment as server or scullery assistant and her table assignment in Foley Dining Hall. If in temporary vows, she would also learn which superior had been designated to supervise her evening recreation when she could look forward to gathering with her novitiate peers, strolling the grounds as they chatted about their activities during the previous year. And in the midst of the lighthearted reunions, each one would be on the lookout for any sisters who might have information to satisfy her curiosity about the new superiors.

❧ Chapter 3
Expansion of the
Mission 1926-1938

Sisters from Galesburg pose at the Golden Jubilee of St. Joseph, Galesburg,
June 16-18, 1929. Two of the group play a major role in this book's story:
standing third from the left is Sister (later Mother) Marie Helene Franey and
fifth from the left is Mother Mary Raphael Slattery, whose administration is
described in this chapter.

The 1926 Council

"Good morning, Sisters." As the six sisters sitting around
the long table in the small council room on July 20, 1926, mur-
mured "Good morning, Mother," in response, Mother Mary
Raphael couldn't help smiling. She herself had occupied one
of those chairs when she had first moved to the motherhouse
in 1902 after being elected to serve as treasurer general. During the first six years of her twenty-four years in that role, her
responsibilities had been that of an assistant as well as treasurer; however, the duties of the treasurer had become so demanding that the role of treasurer had been separated from
the role of assistant and made an appointed office. The business and financial tasks suited her well, and she had been appointed for each of the intervening three terms, attending
council meetings only when summoned to report on finances

or the numerous building projects underway during Mother Mary Cleophas' administration. On this day, it had taken great effort on her part to walk to the head of the table and seat herself in the chair so long occupied by her much admired mentor. How would she be able to meet the expectations of the sisters? How would her well-honed skills of making columns of figures come out even and negotiating contracts help her be truly a mother to more than one thousand women religious? Yet she smiled.

Looking around the table at the familiar faces, she felt that God was indeed responding to her prayer at Lauds that morning: "*Deus, in adjutorium meum intende.*" Surely God was inclining to her aid by making available such a talented group of assistants. First Assistant Sister Mary Bernard Laughlin's years of experience as local superior at large houses in Indianapolis and Chicago would compensate for her own lack of recent mission experience. With experience at sixteen missions, including a year as econome at Saint Mary-of-the-Woods, Sister Berchmans Collins would be adaptable to any assignment. Sister Gertrude Clare Owens was a steady and familiar presence, having already served as second assistant during the previous term. Sister Mary Ignatia Hanson's brilliant academic credentials would ensure continuity at the Academy during its planned transition from the campus.[1] In spite of her youth, Sister Francis Joseph Elbreg, after being appointed to fill out the remaining three years of Sister Basilissa's term as supervisor of schools, had already become familiar with the Congregation's fifty-six schools. After sixteen years dealing with the various publics at the Academy and College, Sister Geraldine Mullen would find it easy to move into her new role as secretary. As for her own former role as treasurer, Mother took comfort in knowing that she had trained the successor she had appointed, Sister Adelaide O'Brien. The appointment of Sister Aloyse Hennessy as mistress of novices the previous year, after three different sisters in that position within four years, assured her of stability in the novitiate.

As they bowed their heads for the prayer which began their meeting, no one of these women could have foreseen the challenges which lay ahead. Nonetheless, the tasks at hand were clear because major projects were already underway. Foremost would be the establishment of provinces, first by selecting and establishing new missions from coast to coast, and then by altering the long-established governmental structures. This first task was the one most familiar to Mother Mary Raphael and she quickly turned her attention to its implementation. This chronicle of the events of her administration will begin by first tracing the geographic expansion of the missions and then go back to examine the many factors that inhibited the realization of the hoped-for goals.

The Mission of Education

"The principal end of the Congregation, as regards our neighbor, is the education of young girls and their training in virtue."[2] This mission statement for the Sisters of Providence meshed well with the needs of the times in the United States. Just as Mother Theodore had understood her vocation as integral to the church's mission, her successors had continued to fulfill the mission by serving in two types of schools: private academies for girls and parish elementary schools. During the early years of the foundation, the establishment of girls' academies fit well with what historian Jay Dolan describes as the "prevailing concept of woman as the moral guardian of the family and chief domestic educator."[3] Side by side with academy-style education was cooperation with the bishop to staff parochial schools.[4] The 1884 Third Plenary Council of Baltimore had mandated parish schools, creating a demand for sister-teachers which in turn greatly expanded mission opportunities for the Congregation.[5]

In this context one might ask what a parish would need to offer in order to obtain the services of the Sisters of Providence to staff its school. The policies regulating such arrangements are clear from the standard contract used at the time:

Made and entered into by and between _____, Superior General of the Sisters of Providence, Saint Mary-of-the-Woods, Indiana, of the first part, and _____ (Pastor, Parish, City, State), of the second part.

Witnesseth: The party of the first part agrees to furnish the number of Sisters that may be required to teach the School attached to said church five days each week during the scholastic year which will commence in September and terminate in June; and should the Reverend

Pastor so desire, to take charge of the pupils on Sundays and Holy Days of Obligation at Mass, Vespers, and Religious Instructions, and of the Young Ladies Sodalities and of the school Sodalities. The Sisters are not permitted to teach large boys; that is, those boys who have completed the Eighth Grade or their fourteenth year.

The party of the second part agrees for and in consideration of the above mentioned to pay to the party of the first part an annual salary of ____ for each Sister engaged in the school. Should any circumstance beyond control necessitate the temporary employment of a lay teacher, the expense thereof is to be borne by the party of the second part. The party of the second part also agrees to provide for the Sisters a suitable residence properly furnished and to provide schoolrooms also furnished according to the requirements of the time, well heated and ventilated and otherwise conducive to the success of the school. Furthermore to furnish fuel and light and water for said buildings and keep them in repair; also to provide some one to do the work of a janitor.

The party of the second part further agrees to permit the Sisters to teach and govern the school according to the customs established in their Community as far as the customs of the country will permit; to teach music and to retain all compensation for the same; he also agrees to attend to the spiritual wants of the Sisters according to the requirements of their Rule; that is, Mass, daily Communion, and weekly Confession.

In witness whereof, we have hereto set our hand and seal this __ day of ___ Anno Domini 19__. [6]

Several provisions of this contract are worthy of notice. Last mentioned but first in importance was the clause ensuring that the sisters' spiritual lives would receive the sacramental support required by the Rule. Within Catholic circles, teaching was thought of as a vocation, with heartfelt acknowledgment that any young woman's desire to be a sister included a desire for union with God. There would be no question on the part of the parish that provision must be made for the sisters' spiritual lives so that the taproot of deep spirituality would nourish their teaching and example.

Basic as well was the provision for remuneration. The dollar amount of the salary would fluctuate over the years, but the situation of the Catholic schools was similar to that of public schools, where teaching had become in large part a female occupation, and women were typically paid one-third to one-half the salary given to males.[7] As for "a suitable residence," judging from the observation made by Sister Agnella Hyde concerning her experience of the housing of the time, considerable leeway was allowed in the actual application of this clause. "So-called convents were actually just neighborhood houses with the convent in front and the school tacked on the back."[8] In Chicago in 1927 the situation was brought to the attention of the Archdiocesan School Board, which undertook a survey to make recommendations for improving convent facilities.[9] Depression-era conditions also modified the degree to which expectations could be met, and allowances were made for economic conditions of particular locations.

The very word contract implies negotiation and the word negotiation acknowledges pressure. Correspondence between the superior general and bishops and priests as well as the discussions of the council reveal a great deal of pressure as prevailing norms shifted. As we shall see, one clause of this contract would succumb to such pressure: the longstanding provision that "the Sisters are not permitted to teach large boys." By the 1920s, two factors would greatly influence the context in which the Sisters of Providence would carry out their mission: 1) the institutional response of the American Catholic church to Progressive Era reforms; and 2) the personalities and styles of the bishops of the dioceses in which the Congregation had schools.

The Context of the Mission of Education

American Catholics and Progressive Era Reforms

During the nineteenth century, Catholic secondary education in the United States had flourished.[10] Based on the ideals brought by immigrant educational religious congregations such as the Sisters of Providence, academies for girls and "colleges" for boys served families with the means to educate their children beyond the elementary grades. The establishment of The Catholic University of America by the hierarchy in 1889 had been hailed as a way to recognize the unique contribution of Catholic thought as the underpinning for a classical education. However, rapid technological advances had created concurrent academic specializations at other private and state colleges and universities. New subjects were introduced into the secondary curriculum to prepare students for either immediate entry into the work force or for higher education. By 1900 students' acceptance into college depended on their graduation from accredited high schools. Accreditation was now a necessity for Catholic secondary schools.

An 1899 conference of Catholic college rectors in Chicago led to the formation of the Catholic Education Association (CEA). Rev. James A. Burns, CSC, president of Notre Dame University, spearheaded the Association's efforts to establish high school graduation requirements for Catholic secondary schools. Catholic high school curricula would now be expressed in "units" and their programs would be expected to meet accreditation requirements. This would enable their graduates to meet the admission standards accepted and enforced by regional accrediting agencies such as the North Central Association of Colleges and Secondary Schools. In 1923 the CEA formally adopted the standards set by the American Council on Education, setting the stage for re-negotiating arrangements for the educational mission. Philip Gleason points out how this change would affect the Sisters of Providence.

> The key to the plan was the central Catholic high school—an institution operating under episcopal authority but drawing on more than one parish and being staffed by members of one or more religious communities ... building directly on the base of parochial education.[11]

But how could the quality of traditional Catholic education be safeguarded? How could small Catholic girls' academies such as those sponsored by the Sisters of Providence meet such standards? The need for national leadership to combine and focus the efforts of the hierarchy together with religious congregations with strong educational experience was clear. Since the United States bishops had decided to retain the national office they had created during the First World War, now known as the National Catholic Welfare Council (NCWC), its committee structure became an appropriate vehicle for hierarchical input. A friendly collaboration of religious congregation educators working through the CEA and the bishops' NCWC's education department was the solution.

Together these groups worked to develop recommendations for educational programs and organizational structures. The 1920 appointment of Rev. James H. Ryan, a senior faculty member of Saint Mary-of-the-Woods College, as head of the NCWC's education department certainly paved the way for the Congregation to capitalize on emerging policies. Meanwhile, in 1905 The Catholic University had begun degree programs to train diocesan superintendents of Catholic schools. In 1927 the CEA added "National" to its title and, now known as the NCEA, became the active forum for strengthening Catholic education at all levels through its several departments. To maintain quality, centralization was an idea whose time had come.

Role of the Hierarchy in Implementing Educational Standards

The internal structure dictated by the 1917 Code of Canon Law placed authority for education in the hands of the local bishop. However the code offered no specific educational guidelines, leaving considerable leeway for each bishop as to how to go about using the available expertise. Despite strong support for Catholic parochial education, the haphazard growth of schools which had already taken place presented a daunting challenge for any bishop bent on centralization. In Chicago, for example, local pastors such as Arnold Damen, SJ, a longtime supporter of the Sisters of Providence,[12] functioned as one of what James W. Sanders baldly labels as "superintendents of virtually independent parish systems."[13] By 1915 more than forty religious congregations operated schools in Chicago. Sanders goes on to describe the somewhat dysfunctional system of the time.

> Each order had its own organization, usually independent of the bishop, and extending beyond diocesan borders. Little communication took place between the different religious communities. ... Each religious order thought of its schools as a system in itself.[14]

Adapting to Revised Secondary Accreditation Standards

The Sisters of Providence certainly operated in this self-regulated manner. By 1926 the congregation staffed seventy-three secondary and elementary schools across six dioceses: Indianapolis and Fort Wayne in Indiana; Chicago and Peoria in Illinois; Boston and Baltimore on the East Coast. By far the largest number of schools was in the Diocese of Indianapolis, with thirty-eight, and the Archdiocese of Chicago, with twenty-two. As Mother Mary Raphael contemplated her expansion plans, she would also have to maintain strong relationships with the six bishops of these dioceses. The changing secondary requirements would prove especially challenging for the historic small academies established in the nineteenth century. The following discussion examines how this challenge played out in the three dioceses of Indianapolis, Fort Wayne and Chicago.

The Diocese of Indianapolis

Indianapolis, Indiana

The Sisters of Providence had been quick to recognize the trends regarding accreditation and had decided to accentuate the status of Saint Mary-of-the-Woods College as an accredited institution of higher education by discontinuing secondary education on the campus. Rather than completely terminating the historic Academy, the decision was made to transplant it to a more urban location. During the final year of Mother Mary Cleophas' administration, with the assistance of members of the College Endowment Board, the Congregation located a unique property northeast of Indianapolis. In 1916 the prominent banker Stoughton Fletcher had built an elaborate 40,000 square-foot residence along a ridge overlooking Fall Creek in the style of an English manor home and named it Laurel Hall. When his fortunes took a turn for the worse, he was forced to declare bankruptcy and sell the estate. The Congregation was able to purchase the 220 acre site, complete with a power house and garage, a greenhouse, three stucco houses, five cottages and a laundry for $588,800.[15]

In September 1926, Ladywood School for Girls opened in the renovated Fletcher mansion on extensive grounds in a growing section of Indianapolis, with fourteen girls in grades nine and ten forming the nucleus of the plan to gradually expand into a college preparatory high school. On September 28, 1926, Bishop Chartrand and twenty-two priests took part in the solemn high Mass for the formal opening. Father Henry Dugan was appointed as chaplain and instructor. With the addition of third and fourth years, plans went forward for the construction of Loretto Hall to provide additional space for resident students and classrooms, science laboratories and an art studio, ensuring full accreditation in 1928. Promotional literature featured photographs of the students enjoying riding the bridle paths on the wooded campus, studying in the paneled library with its stained glass windows and praying in a chapel made by renovating the former ballroom. Over the ensuing years the new establishment gradually attracted a stable enrollment of both day and resident students.

Together with St. John Academy and St. Agnes Academy, the Congregation now staffed three girls' high schools in the state capital. In other parts of the diocese, the situation developed differently.

Evansville, Indiana

In 1853 Mother Theodore herself established two missions in the city of Evansville, Assumption and Holy Trinity. In 1912 Mother Mary Cleophas sent sisters to expand Assumption to include a girls' academy. By 1925 Bishop Chartrand decided to implement the central Catholic high school model by combining Assumption Academy and Boys' Catholic High School to form Reitz Memorial High School, a co-institutional school with separate classes for boys and girls in one building. The boys occupied the first floor of the building with Holy Cross Brothers as principal and faculty while the girls occupied the second floor with Sisters of Providence as principal and faculty. Still both schools continued to be listed with the state of Indiana as separate institutions. In 1941 the two libraries were combined to serve both schools, but it was not until 1947 when a furor erupted over the distribution of tickets to basketball finals based on separate listings that it was agreed that the two schools would become a single co-institution.[16] At that point the male head of the boys' division was listed as principal and the Sister of Providence head of the girls' division was listed as assistant principal even though each administrator continued as head of a separate faculty. Meanwhile, when nearby Holy Trinity grade school closed, the building was used as an "annex" for the ninth grade students.

Washington, Indiana

In 1857 Mother Mary Cecilia built a small school in the bustling southern Indiana town of Washington where the Holy Cross Brothers were already teaching boys. In 1870 Mother Anastasie had constructed a beautiful building to serve as St. Simon Academy for Girls. The Sisters of Providence also provided sisters for the parish school, St. Simon, and for some years they also taught at nearby St. Mary School. In 1919 Bishop Chartrand authorized the establishment of a central high school for the boys and girls of Washington and vicinity. When the co-institutional Washington Catholic High School opened in 1920, the Brothers of the Sacred Heart were in charge of the boys' department and St. Simon Academy for Girls became the girls' department.

Washington was hard hit by the Great Depression with many layoffs, making it impossible to pay the faculty salaries. Although the brothers had done excellent work for over ten years and gained many vocations for their work in Africa, their superiors decided to withdraw in 1932. The convent diarist explained the circumstances; "The brothers' salary was much greater than the Sisters. ... They deeply regretted leaving and many people also appreciated the Brothers. The Sisters were much underpaid but the school had to carry on."[17] However, it was almost more significant than the financial sacrifices entailed that the situation forced the first major challenge to the Congregation's longstanding policy of not teaching older boys.

With the brothers gone, the pastor had dismissed the high school boys, so the 1933-1934 school year included only the grade school and high school girls, much to the dismay of the parents. In response to the pastor's pleading letters, Mother Mary Raphael told him that she had consulted with Bishop Chartrand, who had encouraged the sisters to take the boys but did not command it. Finally the council relented, and Mother relayed their decision to Father O'Hara. "We have decided to take the boys for one year, and then only until you can replace us by Brothers or other teachers capable of teaching the young men."[18] Freshman boys were admitted for the 1934-1935 school year, but with still no brothers available, despite the stress on the faculty as evidenced by frequent replacements, the sisters could not bring themselves to turn the boys away and accepted another freshman group for 1935-1936.

The occasion of the school's centennial celebration in 1937 brought the new bishop, Bishop Joseph Ritter, to Washington and, impressed by the devotion of the people and doubtless also by what the house diary described as, "Sister St. Sophia's splendid orchestra," he and the pastor made plans to make Washington Catholic a coeducational high school. The Sisters of Providence would provide the principal and some of the teaching faculty, with the parish priests teaching religion and lay men and women also serving on the faculty. This strong episcopal support, combined with the improved economy, plant modifications and male faculty led to an increase in enrollment and positioned the now coeducational high school for a successful future.

Terre Haute, Indiana

Not all the cross-city consolidations involved coeducation. Mother Theodore herself had brought the Sisters of Providence across the Wabash River to Terre Haute with the construction of St. Vincent Academy, which opened in 1849 and was later renamed St. Joseph Academy.[19] The Franciscan Fathers had begun a boys' high school, St. Bonaventure Lyceum, in 1872, but it did not thrive and closed in 1876.[20] In 1882 the Congregation purchased a lot and built St. Patrick School and convent next to that Terre Haute parish.[21] Both schools combined coeducational grade schools with girls' high schools and each high school had loyal alumnae. However, by 1937 the declining enrollment and the poor condition of the building at St. Joseph led Mother Mary Raphael to bring the matter to the bishop's attention as another situation which would benefit from combination. He replied that nothing would please him more than to undertake a central high school in Terre Haute, "but that cannot be done now."[22] However, after a change in pastors, he ordered a merger of the two schools—St. Joseph and St. Patrick—to form Central Catholic High School for Girls, which opened in 1938.[23] A final Mass was celebrated in the historic building at St. Joseph on October 10, 1939, after which it was torn down. The property was sold the following year when a new convent was built. Provision for boys would not take place for another decade.

Vincennes, Indiana

In 1843 the Sisters of Providence began teaching in Vincennes, including care of orphans and a free school for girls which in time became the highly regarded St. Rose Academy.[24] In 1872 a boys' school was opened nearby, staffed by the Brothers of the Sacred Heart and later by the Brothers of Holy Cross, although it closed in 1886. The Congregation constructed a new building for St. Rose in 1884 but it was not until 1924 that Gibault High School for Boys was built nearby and staffed by the Brothers of the Sacred Heart. When the Brothers withdrew in 1938, the Gibault building was used for the grade school children. At that point, a later local historian recorded that St. Rose Academy "has become the central Catholic High School of the city, drawing girls equally from all the parishes."[25] As will be seen in Chapter 4, financing of the Vincennes Catholic schools became a serious issue during the Great Depression.

The Diocese of Fort Wayne

Lake County Schools

Mother Theodore had ventured to the city of Fort Wayne in Indiana's northeastern region in 1846 to found St. Augustine Academy, and two years later the sisters began teaching at Cathedral's grade school. Even after the diocese of Fort Wayne was created the following year, strong ties continued, and in 1891 the sisters accepted another parish school, St. Patrick, which in 1903 expanded to include a girls' high school, St. Catherine. Over the years these schools were the seedbed of numerous vocations to the Sisters of Providence.[26] In the northwest corner of the diocese, the Sisters of Providence staffed four parish schools in Lake County on the outskirts of Chicago—St. Joseph and All Saints in Hammond and Sacred Heart and St. John the Baptist in Whiting. Beginning in 1910 All Saints included a small high school offering both classical and commercial classes, but in 1921 Catholic Central High School opened nearby and with its continued expansion, the All Saints high school department closed in 1930.

When John F. Noll was named bishop of the Diocese of Fort Wayne in 1925, his extraordinary resumé alerted the Congregation to expect renewed activity. From his earliest years as a priest he had devoted his life to evangelization. In order to combat anti-Catholic propaganda he had authored and published Catholic pamphlets, an enterprise which had become the nation's first national Catholic weekly newspaper, *Our Sunday Visitor*. He was instrumental in founding the Catholic Press Association, served on the board of the Catholic Extension Society and sponsored the catechist society of Victory Noll sisters in Huntington.[27] Now, as bishop, he set his sights on upgrading the Catholic presence in the city of Fort Wayne.

Central Catholic High School, Fort Wayne

Bishop Noll purchased a large tract of land in order to establish a new parish, St. Jude, with the intention of first building the school and later the church and other buildings. He wrote to Mother Mary Raphael to point out that at St. Augustine Academy, situated cheek to jowl with the cathedral on downtown's "Cathedral Square," quarters were cramped and that the community might want to purchase some of the recently acquired acreage with the plan of eventually moving the historic academy to that location. He was also desirous of utilizing some of the St. Augustine property, as it was adjacent to the cathedral, and he pressed the issue. From Mother Mary Raphael's perspective, undertaking the construction of a new building was out of the question and negotiations dragged on for several years.

By 1938 Bishop Noll felt the time was ripe to build a central Catholic high school for both boys and girls, envisioning it rising near the cathedral. To accomplish this aim he needed to persuade the Sisters of Providence not only to incorporate their two academies, St. Augustine and St. Catherine, into this plan but also to allow a portion of the Congregation's property to be used as part of the site of the new high school. By this time he had become active in national affairs as secretary of the United States Catholic Welfare Conference and had launched both the Catholic News Service and the radio program "The Catholic Hour." Without doubt, the Sisters of Providence found he was a bishop to be reckoned with. Moreover, because his sister Evelyn had professed vows as a Sister of Providence in 1915 as Sister Rose Beatrice, he could count on family connections to reinforce his cause.

Once he had obtained reluctant agreement from Mother Mary Raphael, in 1937 he invited the sisters to inspect the blueprints which showed a three-story building with the boys on one side and the girls on the other. However Bishop Noll had polled the priests and reported that they favored a coeducational school, with the expectation that the sisters would teach the boys. So entrenched was the policy of not teaching older boys that Bishop Noll pushed the issue by suggesting that perhaps the Holy Cross sisters might be willing to undertake the project. He also pointed out that his long-range plans included construction of a convent for the sister faculty. Once again, the sisters did agree to teach freshman boys. Another congregation of sisters was engaged to teach the coed upper grade classes. As for male faculty, the plan was for the Holy Cross brothers, who had served for eighty years in Fort Wayne, to withdraw and be replaced by diocesan priests specially trained for education. Salary was another point of negotiations, as Mother Mary Raphael insisted on maintaining the standard of $50 per month for each sister.[28]

In order to assure a good beginning for the new centralized school, some sisters took time from their 1937 summer classes to go to Fort Wayne to assist with registering their students. They were rewarded with a "phenomenal" enrollment of over 1,000 students, a wonderful response from the Fort Wayne Catholic community.[29] However, since the new building was not ready by September, the two academies opened as usual in the fall of 1937 until the move was completed the following year.

The Archdiocese of Chicago

The Chicago Archdiocese had long been a fertile field for the educational mission of the Sisters of Providence. Mother Mary Cleophas had continued the direction of her predecessor, Mother Euphrasie, in establishing schools in the city and its near environs, so by the time Archbishop George Mundelein began his energetic administration of the rapidly expanding metropolitan area in 1916, the Sisters of Providence staffed seventeen schools there. To supply better educated workers for the rapidly expanding economy of Chicago, compulsory public education was extended through high school. Unwilling to abandon his young flock to the public schools, Archbishop Mundelein developed a master plan for providing Catholic secondary education on a regional basis with easy availability to all parishes.[30] Rather than using the approach of building diocesan central high schools for feeder parish schools, he chose instead to both encourage the expansion of strategically located small parish high schools and also to enlist the resources of religious congregations in building their own high schools to serve multiple parishes. He called upon the Sisters of Providence to assist with both aims.

Parish High Schools in Chicago

In 1918 Archbishop Mundelein prevailed upon the Sisters of Providence to take over the tiny parish high school at Saint Mary Parish in suburban Joliet.[31] After considerable retrofitting of the buildings it was renamed Providence High School, offering both academic and commercial programs to girls from many parishes. Meanwhile, two of the Congregation's small high schools for girls attached to the Chicago parishes of St. Agnes and St. Leo were closed, with the students directed to attend the regional Mercy High School, which opened in 1924.[32] For the people of Chicago, the conferring of the red hat of a cardinal on their archbishop that same year signaled Vatican approval of his firm administrative style.

Providence High School

Another long-established Sister of Providence school lent itself to Cardinal Mundelein's master plans for comprehensive high schools with both commercial and college preparatory curricula.[33] Our Lady of Providence Academy had opened in 1897 when the small upper classes at nearby Our Lady of Sorrows had outgrown that facility.[34] As the enrollment had far exceeded the building's capacity, shortly after her election in 1926, Mother Mary Raphael met with Cardinal Mundelein and began ambitious plans for expansion as a regional high school. After the purchase of several properties on Central Park Avenue at Monroe, an architect was engaged to draw up plans for a magnificent new building and construction went forward. In March 1929, the entire faculty of thirty-seven sisters with the student body of 725 girls moved to the spacious and well-equipped facility of Providence High School, which was dedicated by Cardinal Mundelein on May 9, 1929.[35]

PHS, as it was popularly known, would go on to be immortalized by 1939 graduate Jane Trahey as the setting of her humorous best seller, *Life With Mother Superior*, later made into the movie *The Trouble with Angels.* Its graduates will appear often in the following pages, since many went on to enter the

Providence High School, Chicago

Congregation and many of these members would assume positions of responsibility as principals and superiors. When the school celebrated its golden jubilee, the program listed the names of 180 Sister of Providence graduates and twelve novices as well as some twenty-nine graduates who were members of other congregations.[36]

Meanwhile, the boys were not neglected. St. Philip High School (later re-named St. Mel), built on the Our Lady of Sorrows property in 1910 by the Servite Fathers, whose American Province was headquartered there, had constructed a new annex in 1924 to house a splendid athletic facility. In 1938 a new wing was added to the high school, and in 1945 a football stadium was constructed.[37]

This model of what Sanders characterizes as "the private Catholic high school owned by religious orders, not the Diocese,"[38] prevailed in Chicago. With no restrictions based on geographical boundaries, students could and did come from anywhere. Over the years to come, Providence High School would attract girls not only from nearby schools, but also from other Sister of Providence grade schools across the city and would prove to be an outstanding educational institution for generations of Chicago's young Catholic women, as well as a training ground for young sister teachers and future principals and superiors.

Parish Schools in Indiana

Requests came regularly to the council to send sisters to staff schools all across the country,[39] but the council was alert to rumors that the Indianapolis priests felt "that we favor the Chicago schools and send our best teachers to that city. In consequence they will not send subjects to our community."[40] When possible, and often to strengthen ties with long-standing missions, preference was given to Indiana locations. In August 1926 two sisters were sent to open a tiny school at St. Ann Parish in the Mars Hill neighborhood of Indianapolis, living at nearby St. Anthony with the priest's housekeeper providing commuter service in her automobile.

When Bishop Chartrand requested that the Sisters of Providence take charge of the school at Annunciation in the town of Brazil which the Oldenburg Franciscans were leaving, Mother felt the Sisters of Providence could not refuse because Brazil was so close to the motherhouse. Three sisters were assigned, arriving on August 16, 1932, to begin long years of service at the welcoming parish.

In the Fort Wayne Diocese, Bishop Noll had purchased a large tract of land to establish a new parish. The grade school building, originally named The Sharon Terrace School, opened in March 1929 with the sisters commuting from St. Augustine. By the following year, classrooms in the school were partitioned to provide living quarters for the sisters on site, but as each year additional space was needed for another grade, in 1949 a house was purchased to serve as a convent. As the parish became established, the school came to be known as St. Jude School. Despite the Depression, Fort Wayne was growing and Bishop Noll developed a similar plan of establishing another parish starting with the school, with living quarters for the sisters within the school building. Barely completed, St. John the Baptist opened in September 1930 with five sisters.

Establishments on the West Coast

The lure of California had long fascinated Americans attuned to the idea that it was America's "manifest destiny" to expand westward, and Sisters of Providence were no exception. As early as the turn of the century Jesuits from the San Francisco area wrote to Mother Mary Cleophas inviting her to send sisters to staff a school in Los Gatos, noting that it was "considered one of the best health resorts in California."[41] However, they also recommended investigating Los Angeles, and in 1916 she did so,[42] but the Congregation was overextended and unable to implement such a plan.[43] The following year Bishop John Cantwell was appointed to lead the diocese of Monterey-Los Angeles, which at that time encompassed the entire state south of San Francisco. Realizing the task before him and the need for Catholic education, he almost immediately set out on a trip back east to recruit teaching sisters, with a stop at Saint Mary-of-the-Woods in 1921. His follow-up letter praised the quality of the Catholic education he had observed at Saint Mary-of-the-Woods. The beautiful new perpetual adoration chapel also caught his attention as a testament to the spirit of the Congregation.[44]

Parish Schools

When Father John Ford became pastor of St. Joseph, Hawthorne, in 1924, he remembered his former teachers from Chicago and also came calling.[45] With stories of Mother Mary Cleophas' 1916 trip fresh in memory, and envisioning provinces from coast to coast, Mother Mary Raphael felt the time was ripe to accept a mission in California. She and Sister Berchmans traveled to Los Angeles in January 1928 to meet with Bishop Cantwell. Father Ford arranged to include his friend Father Edmund Keohan, pastor at St. Elisabeth, Van Nuys, in the interview. With both pastors agreeing to provide convents and to cover the cost of railroad tickets for the sisters, the council agreed to open missions at both parishes in the fall.

The nine Sisters of Providence who opened the first two missions were part of an influx of people to Los Angeles, whose population doubled in the decade, reaching 1,238,048 by 1930.[46] The newcomers were spread out over 450 square miles in scattered centers linked by streetcars. The founding sisters described Van Nuys in 1928 as "a small country village" and Hawthorne as "a country place."[47] About the only buildings in the town were a bank, a five-and-ten-cent store and a grocery store."[48] Warmly welcomed by the parishioners, the sisters soon felt very much at home, even so far from their Saint Mary-of-the-Woods "Home." In fact, the following year, Mother Mary Raphael herself, suffering from poor health, took advantage of the mild climate and country atmosphere of the Van Nuys convent for an extended medical leave.[49]

Bishop Cantwell had continued to be of great assistance in establishing the Sisters of Providence in the sprawling diocese so as to assure future growth.[50] He wrote in support of the request of the pastor at St. Therese, Alhambra, and was delighted when five sisters were sent to staff that school in August 1930. While Mother Mary Raphael was in California on medical leave in 1928, the pastor of St. Ambrose, Hollywood, asked her to furnish teachers for his proposed school. Although he had not received a favorable reply, he again pressed the issue and four sisters were assigned to St. Ambrose in September 1935; the beautiful new church was dedicated by Bishop Cantwell that November.

Marywood High School and the Western Province

Although Bishop Cantwell agreed to the plan approved in 1932 for a province in the Los Angeles Diocese, with a temporary arrangement for a provincial house at St. Joseph Convent, Hawthorne, he was on the lookout for property where a West Coast provincial house could be established. When the congregation of Dominican Sisters from Cuba at St. Joseph Academy in Anaheim held their chapter of elections in 1934, he discovered both the precarious financial situation of the school and also the internal dissension in that community. Superintendent of Schools Father Martin McNicholas further advised him that the school did not meet accreditation standards.

Mother Mary Raphael and Sixth Assistant Sister Eugenia Clare Cullity traveled to California in April 1934 to conclude the negotiations with Bishop Cantwell for a Sister of Providence sponsored high school with boarders. On-site inspection revealed that the Anaheim location was ideal. In addition to the school itself, the adjacent compound built around a lovely patio contained a dormitory for students, parlors, a chapel and a complete novitiate. The land boom of the twenties and cooperative marketing of the fruit from the surrounding orange groves had made the region economically sustainable even during the depression, and nearby St. Boniface Parish would provide sacramental assistance.

Nonetheless, finances proved daunting. Mother Mary Raphael felt strongly that God would provide, so she negotiated arrangements for assuming the debt and consulted with both Bishop Cantwell and Bishop Ritter to secure their advice before recommending purchase to the council. Bishop Ritter, acutely aware of the Congregation's finances, strongly advised caution. However, when Bishop Cantwell agreed to sign notes for a significant portion of the cost and prematurely announced that a central girls' high school would open in the fall, the council agreed, deciding on the name of Marywood. Exhausted from the pressure of overseeing so many projects, Mother Mary Raphael spent the summer of 1934 at Ladywood in Indianapolis.

The Sisters of Providence took possession of the facility on July 2, 1934, with sisters from the convents at Alhambra, Hawthorne and Van Nuys inaugurating their summer home by cleaning and organizing the building. The recently named provincial superior, Sister Regina Clare Carlos, assumed the duties of novice mistress and welcomed four postulants. A faculty of seven sisters with a housekeeper was assigned to open the high school. When Bishop Cantwell visited on October 31, 1934, fourteen boarders and fifty-two day students were enrolled in grades nine to eleven, with twelve girls in four lower grades.

Because travel from the motherhouse to the West Coast was both expensive and time-consuming, until such time as local vocations would be able to staff the missions, a rotation schedule of returning to the motherhouse every four years was established. Marywood became the summer home for sisters missioned in California. Classes were arranged on site for some

Marywood in Anaheim, California

sisters while others took classes at Immaculate Heart College or Loyola. Others were responsible for summer catechism classes for Mexican immigrant children in the area and for these sisters, these "home missions" were a welcome challenge. Though they successfully achieved their goal of catechizing the children and providing them with prayer booklets, they themselves were learners, with practically the whole summer community participating in the concluding event, a procession and fiesta.[51] Commenting on the enthusiastic involvement of entire families, Sister Mary Adele Miller wrote, "Their Church seems to be the center of their interest and their lives. It was a procession such as we had never seen before!"[52]

The Home Missions

Oklahoma

Establishing a beachhead for a West Coast province in California was not the only criterion for deciding which requests for new missions should be accepted. After having taken on the foreign mission of Kaifeng, China, in 1920, the entire Congregation had become "mission-minded." In fact, a memoir of the times states: "Shortly after the opening of our California missions, someone very wisely coined the expression, 'next-door to China,' in references to these Western Missions."[53] The traditional practice of using the term "mission" to describe the schools to which each Sister was assigned indicates the attitude of evangelization that undergirded their efforts,[54] but certain locations stimulated special zeal.

The Catholic Extension Society had been founded in Chicago in 1905 by Father Francis Clement Kelley to serve the "home missions," that is, parishes in rural and isolated parts of the country. Father Kelley was in residence at St. Francis Xavier parish in Wilmette, Illinois, when the Sisters of Providence opened the school in 1909. He and the talented priests he recruited for his office conveyed their enthusiasm for this cause to the sisters, and when he was appointed bishop of the Diocese of Oklahoma City, which at that time included the entire state, he turned to the Congregation for sisters to serve there. Since Oklahoma City was a stop on the Santa Fe Railroad route, Mother Mary Raphael had the opportunity to stop off on her return from California in February of 1928 in order to examine a parish school that Bishop Kelley thought could later be expanded to include an academy. Noting the healthful climate as well as the poverty of the people, she set plans in motion which brought five sisters to Corpus Christi Parish in Oklahoma City the next August.

North Carolina

In April 1931, Bishop William J. Hafey of the Diocese of Raleigh, which at that time comprised the entire state of North Carolina, came to Saint Mary-of-the-Woods to ask for sisters. Undaunted at finding that Mother Mary Raphael was in Chicago, he traveled by train to meet with her there and begged her to send three sisters to a small school at St. Therese in the town of Wilson. The Congregation's friend at the Extension Office, Father Eugene J. McGuinness, encouraged the move. He stressed the potential for genuine missionary work, as described by Extension literature. "North Carolina was called 'the China of North America' and this for two reasons: First, because of its small percentage of Catholic population, namely one third of 1%. The Second, the fields are white for the harvest."[55] From the Congregation's point of view, establishing an outpost at Wilson, with a location relatively close to Washington, D.C., would expand the small eastern province. The four sisters who arrived in September 1931 found a tiny enrollment of twenty from the twelve Catholic families in a town of 10,000, yet made a brave beginning.

Four years later, three sisters were sent to open another tiny school, "strictly of a missionary type," at Blessed Sacrament in the town of Burlington. They found that only fifteen of the twenty-five pupils in grades kindergarten through five were Catholic. Apparently the expectation of better education outweighed any prejudice because by the following year the numbers had grown to sixteen Catholics and twenty-eight non-Catholics.

In 1937 a third North Carolina mission was opened at St. Patrick, Fayetteville. The house diarist recorded the 1937 route to the new mission, stating that the pastor "motored to the Immaculata"[56] to transport the sisters who had arrived by train from Saint Mary-of-the-Woods. Four of the sisters stayed at Burlington until their convent was ready, then went on another ninety-six miles to Fayetteville. The climate was hot and humid, but the town was steeped in history, and the house adapted for the convent offered a taste of southern living. Adjacent to Fort Bragg, the parish included military families, affording a unique window into military life during the war years. The sisters at the three North Carolina missions were delighted when, after eighteen years at Extension, Father McGuinness was made Bishop of Raleigh in 1937 and made a practice of stopping in at the convent to visit the sisters.[57]

Expansion of East Coast Missions

Mother Mary Raphael's immediate priority in September of 1926 was to visit the well-established East Coast missions— in the Northeast, St. Rose, Chelsea, founded in 1889, Sacred Heart, Malden, in 1908, and St. Patrick, Stoneham, in 1910. From there she traveled to the Mideast where in Washington, D.C., the Congregation had opened Immaculata and St. Ann in 1905 and Dunblane in 1913. The nearby Hyattsville, Maryland, property had been purchased in 1912 with a view to establishing a provincial house at the site; an adjacent twenty-six acres had been purchased the following year.[58] The community chronicler described the new establishment, which had been named Maryhurst: "On the summit of the elevation was a tract of sixteen acres on which were a fine large residence of sixteen rooms and spacious halls, a tenant's house, barn, carriage house, pump house, ice house, etc."[59]

Historian David Kennedy helps us understand why a country estate rather than a location in the capital city was chosen to serve as an administrative center.

> Washington in 1933 was still a spacious, unhurried city with a distinctly southern flavor. As yet unjacketed by suburbs, it slept dreamily amid the gently undulating Virginia and Maryland woodlands, its slow rhythms exemplified by the World War 'temporary' buildings that were scattered about town and by the unfinished columns of what would eventually be the Department of Labor. It was not yet an imperial city, the vibrant center of political and economic command that Roosevelt was to make it.[60]

The ensuing growth of Washington's environs was the reason the Congregation established a wider presence with the acceptance of three parish schools in the vicinity. Maryhurst had been opened in 1920 and in 1925 a small school was begun there. Already in 1925 the pastor of the neighboring parish, St. Clement, Lansdowne, planned to open a school and

approached the superior, Sister Angela Therese Brillon, to inquire whether the Sisters of Providence would consider staffing it when it would open in September 1927. She and Sister
Mary Cyril Kilroy, superior at Immaculata, were instructed to
visit the parish, after which Sister Mary Cyril wrote to Mother
Mary Raphael:

> The prospects are such as almost to compel acceptance. The
> place is closer to Baltimore than The Immaculata is to Wash-
> ington—about eleven minutes ride. It is a developing center,
> judging from recent accomplishments. The priest is a man of
> God, full of zeal and good sense. When I first met the Arch-
> bishop (M. J. Curley) he thought the Sisters of Providence did
> not want parish schools. I made him understand the contrary.
> When parting with him that day he said to me, "The next time
> there is an opening for a school, I will remember you." No doubt
> his suggesting to Father Kenny to apply for us is in fulfillment
> of the promise made. Please do not refuse this offer. To do so
> would be disastrous to our future in the Archdiocese. To accept
> is to draw further missions in the vicinity.[61]

This report received prompt attention in the form of an
agreement to accept the school. The five sisters who arrived at
St. Clement in August, 1927, found "a beautiful little convent,
immaculately clean, comfortably furnished and everything
taken care of for the welfare of the sisters."[62] During her visit
that fall Mother Mary Raphael's positive assessment of the situations was marred only by her falling and breaking her arm.

It wasn't long before Sister Mary Cyril's prediction proved
true. The pastor of Ascension Parish in Halethorpe, a town
only two miles away, invited the sisters to open his newly built
and well-appointed school. Although there was yet no convent, he would supply daily car service and they could live at
St. Clement, an arrangement that was inaugurated with the
opening of the school in September 1929. However, only one
year later he was able to raise funds to build a convent on site.

Meanwhile, the sisters continued to conduct a school in
the Maryhurst building for the children of neighboring Holy
Redeemer Parish. Using funds given to him as a personal gift,
the pastor constructed a school building on the parish grounds,
and in 1931 the sisters began a daily commute from Maryhurst,
often in the same school bus that picked up the children. In
1941 a nearby home was purchased and remodeled as a convent for the sisters. With the growth of the federal government

during the Great Depression, the suburbs of Washington, D.C., continued to grow, and with it, the Catholic Church. On July 22, 1939, Pope Pius XII established the Archdiocese of Washington with the Most Reverend Michael J. Curley as the first Archbishop.

Missions in Illinois

As the waves of immigrants to Chicago had gradually been assimilated, the next generation took advantage of the city's expanded transit systems to relocate in the northern suburbs. After accepting St. Francis Xavier in Wilmette in 1909, Mother Mary Cleophas had established in 1915 Marywood School for Girls, a boarding and day high school, in nearby Evanston[63] and then agreed to staff St. Athanasius in 1923. As described in the Book of Establishments, this parish school "was for a few years an 'out school'; meaning that the sisters resided at Marywood and went out each day to the school,"[64] but by October 1927 the growing prosperity of the area enabled the pastor to rent "a small house—very small indeed,"[65] for a convent adjacent to the school

As we have seen, Mother Mary Raphael had made it a priority to accept new missions well beyond Chicago in order to prepare the way for provinces by strengthening the East and West Coast establishments. When the pastor of St. Joseph, Downers Grove, wrote to Mother Mary Raphael asking for six sisters to staff his school, the council was not entirely favorable. However, a major advantage of the location of the village of Downers Grove was the fact that it was nineteen miles from Chicago on the Burlington line of the network of railroad tracks snaking out from the city. Convenient westward connections linked it to the missions of Aurora and Galesburg. Since they were hard put to find sufficient sisters to fulfill current obligations, Mother Mary Raphael actually called for a secret ballot to decide the question. After examining the premises, the council did decide to accept the school for September 1931.

Early Efforts at Racial Integration

Chicago

Already the growth of Chicago's Catholic population indicated demographic shifts which later blossomed into the city's western suburbs, while the neighborhoods these families vacated were being occupied by internal migrants rather than foreign immigrants. The need for urban workers had drawn many African-Americans to Chicago during World War I and the economic woes of the Great Depression forced more and more blacks from the south to move to Chicago in search of jobs. These demographic shifts were being felt at St. Anselm School at Sixtieth and South Michigan Avenue where the Sisters of Providence had served since 1910, and by the 1920s they found themselves entwined in Cardinal Mundelein's efforts to meet this challenge.[66]

The 1884 Third Plenary Council of Baltimore had decreed that in order to provide pastoral care for African-Americans, dioceses should designate a parish whose mission would be specifically designed for their needs. Black Catholics were to register at these parishes, have their children baptized there, and attend school there, but they were welcome to attend Mass at any parish they wished. As Jay Dolan points out, "Like the national-parish concept, both people and clergy viewed this arrangement as appropriate at that time. But racism hardened the line separating black and white Catholics."[67] Though they were but a tiny percentage of Chicago Catholics, African-Americans had formed a worshipping community as early as 1888 and by 1892 they had built St. Monica Church, a mission of nearby St. Elizabeth Parish, which in turn was adjacent to St. Anselm. By 1912 school facilities were provided at St. Monica's where African-American students were taught by the Sisters of the Blessed Sacrament, an order founded by Mother Katherine Drexel to work among Native-Americans and African-Americans.

Expansion of the elevated train lines and the upward mobility of immigrant Catholics were already causing population shifts, but most white parishes did not welcome the black newcomers. Although Archbishop Mundelein had gradually decreased the number of ethnic parishes in favor of territorial parishes, he believed that evangelization of blacks was most effective from a strong parish base and in 1917 he decreed that nearby St. Monica would serve as "the Negro parish." Sanders comments:

> The evidence suggests that Mundelein's motives were mixed;
> he acted partly to placate whites opposed to Negroes in their
> parishes, partly to facilitate what he considered the best means
> of promoting the growth of Negro Catholicism in Chicago. …
> Refusing to take a stand on "the justice or injustice" of the
> racial situation, he confessed himself "quite powerless to change
> it."[68]

Although the vigorous protests on the part of the black
community were ignored by the Archbishop, he actively pursued his evangelization goal by seeking the assistance of the
Divine Word congregation to supply a zealous pastor. After
the energetic Father Joseph S. Eckert, SVD, arrived in 1921, St.
Monica's flourished to the point that in 1924, since nearby St.
Elizabeth had become an entirely black neighborhood, the
parish and its mission were consolidated in the spacious St.
Elizabeth plant.

During this time St. Anselm struggled to maintain its own
ethnic heritage, with Celtic crosses and stone shamrocks adorn-
ing the beautiful Romanesque church proudly dedicated in
1925.[69] In 1919 the convent diarist thought it important to note
that one of their eighth grade boys had won "the First State
Prize for having the best composition in the Irish History Essay Contest."[70] However, as early as 1911 St. Anselm pastor
Father M. P. Gilmartin had written to Mother Mary Cleophas
that real estate agents had told him that "the best people are
moving north."[71] Families continued to move away, causing
the school enrollment to dwindle from 495 in 1923-1924 to
165 at the end of the 1930-1931 school year. The Catholic children among the new black residents could not take their places
since they could only register at St. Elizabeth, which was overcrowded. The situation came to a head when in January 1930
St. Elizabeth Church burned to the ground.

Superiors had visited regularly to discuss the situation with
Father Gilmartin so they were not surprised to learn that St.
Elizabeth would now merge with St. Anselm, with Father
Eckert as pastor of the combined congregations. The convent
diarist records the outcome.

> He [Father Gilmartin] told us that St. Anselm's was to be hence-
> forth devoted to the colored people. In September 1932 the col-
> ored children are to be admitted for the first time into St. Anselm
> School. As soon as the white people of the parish heard this,

they were loud and unanimous in voicing their determination not to allow their children to return to the school. Word came from Reverend Mother Mary Raphael on June 5, 1932, stating that the Sisters of Providence would withdraw because it was clearly understood that the Sisters of the Blessed Sacrament were not only willing but anxious to replace us; and because of their special training for missionary work of this kind it was believed that the change of Sisters would be of benefit to all concerned.[72]

According to the Book of Establishments, the sisters concluded that "St. Anselm was for the colored obviously in God's designs."[73]

Indianapolis

America's shifting racial landscape soon provided other opportunities for the Sisters of Providence. In the Indianapolis Diocese, St. Rita Church had been established in 1919 as the African-American parish. During the years when immigrants from Europe were flooding into the country, teaching orders had tended to focus on particular ethnic minorities and this practice had been applied to African-American schools as well. Recognizing that education should take cultural differences into account, the Congregation preferred to do as they had at St. Anselm—defer to congregations whose training better prepared them for such situations.[74] However, because no specially trained sisters were available and the school was small, in 1929 the Sisters of Providence had accepted the tiny St. Rita School. When Bishop Ritter took the helm of the diocese in 1934, care for this portion of his flock would become a priority. During his visit to the parish he noticed that the building was completely inadequate and set plans in motion for improvement by combining the facilities with nearby St. Bridget.[75] In 1936 he persuaded the Franciscan Sisters to give their St. Bridget property to the diocese, including the renovated convent onsite.

That same year, the appointment of Father Bernard Strange as pastor of St. Rita was to have a profound effect on the parish and indeed the entire neighborhood. To enlist invigorated support from the teaching sisters, Father Strange penned an impassioned plea to Mother Mary Raphael:

The school is the right arm of this mission. In it lies our future great colored parishes in Indianapolis. It is the road to the hearts

Pupils at St. Rita (Bridget) School, c. 1936

of the parents. … These people are truly God's poor. God still loves the humble, the downtrodden, the poor, those who are looked down upon by the rest of men. The church is their only hope. … These people have just left their churches because of immorality among their leaders. They do not find the church by its Four Marks. They judge it by its leaders.[76]

After the superiors inspected the newly available building with the school on one side and a convent on the other, an additional sister was added to the faculty. Other Sister of Providence schools in the city staged a "St. Rita Day" to collect school supplies to donate. On September 14, 1936, the bus from St. Rita Church arrived with sixty-one eager black children, few of whom were Catholic. The children, as superior Sister Clare Mitchell wrote to Mother Mary Raphael, "formed ranks at once and marched to Saint Bridget Church."[77] When he visited the following Sunday, Bishop Ritter expressed his satisfaction at the situation.

Father Strange had high hopes that continuing their education into Catholic high schools would prepare St. Rita graduates for successful careers and more influential positions in society.[78] He solicited Bishop Ritter's support and made arrangements with the principals of three girls' academies (two operated by the Sisters of Providence, St. Agnes and St. John, and the Franciscan St. Mary Academy) for each school to accept two girls who had graduated from eighth grade in 1937. With the blessing of Mother Mary Raphael, Sister Mary Joan Kirchner, principal of St. John Academy, met with the freshman homeroom teachers and planned to ensure that the new girls would be welcomed by their classmates. Much to her surprise, five girls arrived on registration morning. Father Strange explained that the other schools had backed out and one of the six girls had said she preferred public school if that was the attitude of Catholic schools. Sister Mary Joan tells how she dealt with the situation:

> I hastily called all the Sisters to the office and presented the problem to them. Here were five girls in place of the two we expected. What should we do? The immediate and unanimous decision of the Sisters was, "Let's take all five of them."

> After the girls left I sat at the telephone all afternoon and evening to receive a succession of calls of protest. Not one person identified himself or herself. I refused to discuss the matter on the phone but told each caller that if he/she would come to the academy I would be glad to explain the whole matter. No one accepted my invitation. We lost only five or six girls to St. Agnes Academy. I was never told why both St. Agnes and St. Mary's withdrew their agreement.[79]

Doubtless due to the attitudes of the sister-faculty and the norms they established, the white students accepted their new classmates. However, the St. John Alumnae Association, which had recently contributed to the refurbishing of their alma mater, did raise some concerns. Association President Helen O'Gara wrote to Bishop Ritter to point out the negative effect on the enrollment because of the failure of St. Agnes and St. Mary to accept the students.

> We, as an organization and as individuals, are proud to think our school was the first to do what is expected of any Catholic school in assuming responsibility for the education of the Catholic negro girls in Indianapolis. But, we feel if the other schools had accepted them, as we understood was agreed, we would not be paying such a high price to give to them what is their God-given right—a Catholic education.[80]

Miss O'Gara also wrote to Mother Mary Raphael, enclosing a copy of this letter. After expressing the pride of the alumnae in the decision, she pointed out that even though the sisters on the faculty could be changed to another assignment, St. John would remain and needed the "cooperation from the other Catholic academies of Indianapolis."[81]

It must be acknowledged that the decision to accept the students had been based on phone conversations rather than formal negotiations and written agreements. Even though the bishop supported Father Strange's request he had some concern as to whether or not this bold move would succeed.[82] There is no record of why St. Agnes did not accept any of the St. Rita applicants that year, but two years later its 1939 graduating class included an African-American student who had only enrolled for her senior year.[83]

Meanwhile Sister Mary Joan scheduled an Open House at St. John's to show off the recently refurbished building and began sending monthly newsletters with notices of awards won by students. These public relations efforts were rewarded in the spring when eighty-five girls registered for September's freshman class, double the number of the previous year. As she later recalled, "From then on, a mixed enrollment was just taken for granted."[84]

St. Mary-of-the-Woods

The Juniorate

When "Rosary Hill," the large farmhouse which had been renovated in 1921 for use as a residence for senior sisters, was vacated in 1927,[85] the council considered using it for a boarding school because "In places where there are no Catholic high schools girls who have vocations to the religious life are lost to us, Rosary Hill would make an ideal school for such prospects. This did not carry because the school could not be accredited."[86] However, plans were underway to relocate the Saint Mary-of-the-Woods secondary school boarding program to what was to become Ladywood School in Indianapolis. By 1931, the final class would have graduated and space for a new and separate preparatory high school for candidates to the religious life would become available in Foley Hall. However, Providence intervened to arrange an earlier start for this innovative program.

In August 1930, Agnes Schafer was preparing to join two other girls from St. Charles, Bloomington, to enter the novitiate. [87] Her eighth grade teacher, Sister Theresa Marie Cannon, not realizing that Agnes had skipped a grade, was astonished to discover that she was only twelve years old. In later years, the heroine of this tale describes how this dilemma was resolved not only in her favor but how it advanced the projected plan for a preparatory school.

Concerned about disappointing the prospective religious, Sister explained the situation to the pastor, Rev. Paul V. Deery, who called on the Superior General and presented the problem to her. Mother Mary Raphael told Father that for some time she had desired to begin an Aspirancy, and that if Agnes still wished to come when she learned she would not be permitted to enter the Novitiate at once, and if others could be found to join her, the Aspirancy would be opened in the fall.[88]

Agnes did indeed wish to come and, sure enough, others did join her. She arrived on August 21, 1930, and by the eighth of September, five girls—two freshmen and three sophomores— occupied a row of beds in the dormitory area of Foley Hall and began using various other rooms for classes, dining and recreation. As a form of preparation for novitiate entry, the arrangement was named the juniorate. Mistress of novices Sister Aloyse was in overall charge of the tiny group of students, now known as "candidates," while supervisory and instructional duties were added to the responsibilities of sisters with academy, college, novitiate and even infirmary assignments. Classes were already organized for postulants and scholastic novices in need of high school credits, so the candidates simply slipped into desks next to them. Academy students passed them in the hall and continued to occupy their usual quarters and continue their studies. Their graduation in June 1931 ended the storied days of the Academy at Saint Mary-of-the-Woods as planned and opened the way for the full-fledged operation of Providence Juniorate.

Meanwhile, in April 1930, the council gave official approval to the opening of a juniorate, or school for prospective postulants, giving a heartfelt, if tardy, blessing to its tiny de facto existence.[89] The hope was to support girls' vocational aspirations and spiritual development, yet delay their actual entrance until they had completed high school. Letters were sent to the local superiors asking them to invite prospective candidates from the eighth grade. By September 1931, there were sixteen candidates and several postulants in the high school classes. By 1932, twenty-three freshmen were enrolled with only candidates—no novices or postulants—making up the student body.[90] Clearly, this was an idea whose time had come.

Saint Mary-of-the-Woods College

Over the years, as educational standards continued to evolve, the institution begun by Mother Theodore as "The Academy" in 1840 had changed considerably.[91] Upon receiving its charter as a college in 1901, its name had been changed to the College of Saint Mary-of-the-Woods. After its affiliation with Catholic University in 1913, it received recognition from several accrediting institutions.[92] In keeping with the contemporary belief that Catholic identity required strict separation from the hostile prevailing culture, and that men and women should be educated separately, the demand for higher education for Catholic women sparked a growth of such institutions.[93]

Philip Gleason points out two significant reasons for the growth of Catholic women's colleges at this time: the first was the professionalization of education.

> The professionalization of education and the rapid growth of employment opportunities in that field were the most important of the social factors affecting the place of women in Catholic higher education … [since] … the rising expectations as to the credentials expected of teachers would require academic preparation.[94]

Secondly, there was a strong feeling within the Catholic community that a firm grounding in ethics, philosophy and religion was the foundation necessary for a proper integration of practical knowledge. As Gleason notes, the prevailing view was that "a Catholic college should serve as the nucleus for the building of a Catholic culture."[95]

Responsive to the needs of the times, the Congregation continued its efforts to be in the forefront of higher education for women.[96] Attuned by her experience as treasurer to the need for secure legal and financial underpinnings, as superior general Mother Mary Raphael carried forward the administrative arrangements begun under Mother Mary Cleophas. The 1846 Charter empowering the Congregation to conduct schools of higher education, hospitals and orphan asylum did not differentiate between the Congregation and its educational institutions. A visitor to the grounds could immediately recognize the distinction between the two simply from the buildings, with Providence Convent as the headquarters for the Congregation and the impressive College campus with the three recently constructed buildings, Le Fer Hall, Guerin Hall and the Conservatory of Music flanking the original Saint Mary-of-the-Woods Institute building. The time had come to clarify the legal relationship between the two entities.

Certainly the 1927 plans for two major construction projects, Providence High School in Chicago and a classroom building at Ladywood put increased strain on the Congregation's resources. With a view to completing the accreditation requirements of the North Central Association, that year the council made two significant decisions: separating the finances of the Congregation from those of the College[97] and ensuring strong leadership for the College with the appointment of an exceptionally talented sister as dean, Sister Eugenia Logan.

Sister Eugenia Logan 1889-1983

Agnes Logan was the youngest of ten children born to William and Mary Ann Logan, both children of pioneer Fort Wayne families. Father Benoit had said Mass at her grandfather's house and officiated at the marriage of her parents. Her mother emigrated from Ireland as a small child during the famine and had attended St. Augustine Academy, one of the young pupils who met Mother Theodore when she visited in 1856. Agnes also graduated from St. Augustine in 1906, completing both commercial and academic tracks, and then worked as a secretary in a legal office until she entered the community in 1908. Demonstrating an aptitude for languages, she studied Greek, Latin, French, German and Spanish, so was a welcome addition to the faculties of several academies, teaching four years at St. Agnes Academy, three years at Providence High School in Chicago, and four at Marywood, Evanston, before going to Immaculata in Washington, D.C., for five years as Dean of the Junior College. The principals at these schools were among the community's most respected, giving her multiple hands-on opportunities to learn the well-developed Sister of Providence educational system from both administrative and teaching perspectives. During summers she took additional courses at Loyola and De Paul in Chicago and earned her MA at Indiana University in 1925. Under her capable leadership, working closely with the general council, the College entered a period of expansion that continued through the difficult Depression and war years. In addition to her administrative duties, Sister Eugenia's scholarly and literary output, accompanied by her involvement in numerous civic and Congregation activities, was remarkable. Due to her subsequent 1950 appointments as supervisor of congregation high schools and later as archivist, historian and author of the second book of this series, she will appear frequently in these pages.

When Mother Mary Raphael returned from her trip to California in January 1928 she put in place a reorganized governing structure for the College. On February 19, 1928, the original 1846 Charter was amended to allow the College to operate as a separate entity from the Congregation's other educational institutions. This business model allowed the Congregation's council (the superior general and her six councilors) to continue to regulate the affairs of the College through the formation of two civil corporations. The corporation for the Congregation would be managed by a Board whose original membership consisted of Mother Mary Cleophas (likely an honorific appointment) and three council members: Sisters Berchmans Collins, Gertrude Clare Owens and Mary Ignatia Hanson, together with treasurer general Sister Adelaide O'Brien. The corporation for the College would be managed by a Board of Trustees consisting of a combination of three council members—Sisters Mary Bernard Laughlin, Francis Joseph Elbreg and Geraldine Mullen—and five College administrators: Sisters Eugenia Logan (dean), Celeste Miller (registrar), Mary Viola Burke (admissions secretary), Francis Raphael Donlon (treasurer) and Teresa Lucile Zeller (secretary).[98] The working relationship between the two entities was spelled out through Articles of Agreement specifying that the buildings and estate remained the property of the Congregation and were leased to the College, while the College would retain ownership of equipment and pay the Congregation for services of maintenance and labor.

Even prior to these developments, with an eye to complying with the accreditation requirements of the North Central Association, initiatives of the various College departments had been successful in meeting fourteen of the fifteen criteria. In 1923, when the North Central Association had established the requirement of an endowment fund, the loyal Alumnae Association had formed a National Executive Committee with plans to raise the necessary money. However they were unable to reach their goal of one million dollars.[99] To expand the scope of support, in 1926 an Associate Board of Trustees was established, including not only three Sisters of Providence (including council member Sister Francis Joseph) and three alumnae, but eight area businessmen, resulting in considerable expansion of fund-raising efforts in Terre Haute and Indianapolis.[100] Although the ambitious monetary goal was not realized, a change in North Central accreditation standards which acknowledged the financial impact of contributed services (with which the College was well endowed with so many Sisters on the faculty) ensured compliance. Because the Associate Board of Trustees (also known as the Endowment Board) had proved so beneficial, sisters on the two governing Boards continued to forge relationships with men active in the wider community who could provide not only monetary support but also advice and contacts. The March 1929 council minutes note that "Mr. Cooper, President of the Terre Haute Trust Company, is nominated to succeed Mr. Royce on the Board of Trustees for our Endowment Fund."[101] The women in Alumnae Association along with the men in the Associate Board of Trustees assured the College of two active auxiliary fund-raising organizations. In this series of astute moves, Mother Mary Raphael established a structure which met civil society's expectation that the Congregation and College were accountable for their fiduciary responsibilities. At the same time the two-board governing structure, with council members holding key positions on both the Congregation Board and the College Board of Trustees, made it possible for her to fulfill her obligation as superior general of managing the temporal affairs of the Congregation. In actual practice, matters concerning the College could be decided during regular council meetings. The dean and College faculty members on the College Board of Trustee were readily available for consultation on an informal basis as they came and went for meals and prayers. This system of governance would serve Saint Mary-of-the-Woods College well for many years.

Other significant moves to consolidate the academic standing of the College included ensuring a well-rounded faculty and expanding curricular offerings. As early as 1915 efforts had been made to diversify the universities where the sisters assigned to the College were sent to study for degrees, including non-Catholic institutions such as the University of Wisconsin, Indiana University, Columbia University and The University of Chicago.[102] Faculty members began to travel to foreign countries in the summers to pursue special studies in their fields. In June 1926, Sister Mary Joseph Pomeroy, who was herself a graduate of the College, was the first faculty member to receive a doctoral degree from Columbia, and just three years later Sisters Gertrude Smith and Amata McGlynn received doctorates from Indiana University and Sister Mary Borromeo Brown earned a doctoral degree from Fordham. By the 1926-1927 academic year, of the forty-three faculty members of Saint Mary-of-the-Woods College, twenty-five were Sisters of Providence, with eleven lay women, three lay men and four priests rounding out a diverse faculty.[103]

The curriculum offerings assured the young women graduates of certain employment as educators. A major by-product of this policy was that courses could be both taught in the novitiate and adapted for the summer session to provide young sisters with the two-year academic preparation required for teacher certification. The arts offerings were extensive, with five possible music tracks and several art majors, as well as speech and drama. In 1928 Saint Mary-of-the-Woods became the first Catholic college in the country to offer a journalism major. Certainly the liberal arts offerings of literature and history reinforced the contributions of the College's Catholic culture. Active participation in the Sodality and Catholic Students Mission Crusade, various devotions and attendance at Sunday High Mass in the Convent Church of the Immaculate Conception in cap and gown complemented academics with opportunities for personal faith experiences.

On October 1, 1928, a United States Post Office opened in neighboring Saint Mary-of-the-Woods' village, a testimony to increased activity on the campus. In 1929 the College qualified to be admitted to the American Association of University Women. The illumination of the statue of Our Lady of the Campus in December of that same year seemed to confer an additional blessing. In 1930 the United States Bureau of Immigration approved the College for foreign students, making it possible to bring three postulants from China to study.

Perhaps when Mother Mary Raphael looked over at Our Lady's statue as she closed her shutters at night she breathed a prayer to Mary for all the sisters she had sent to the newly opened missions. As Chapter 4 will reveal, many other ongoing programs also demanded her heartfelt prayer as well as her administrative attention.

❧ Chapter 4 Difficulties and Obstacles 1926-1938

First Communion recessional at St. Ann Church, Washington, D.C. (undated photo) Despite major difficulties associated with the Great Depression, the celebration of their pupils' religious events was always a highlight for Sisters of Providence.

In order to focus on the Sister of Providence mission, the preceding chapter traced its expansion from 1926 to 1938 by describing the opening of new establishments and the invigorating of existing commitments. Without a doubt the "Spirit of Zeal" was a major characteristic of the Sisters of Providence during this time. Yet there are many clues from this narrative that the "Spirit of the Times" had undergone major changes. An examination of the events of Mother Mary Raphael's two consecutive terms reveals that the changes affecting the country had serious repercussions for the Congregation.

Changing Times

Social historian David Kyvic calls attention to a significant reality:

> The apparent prosperity of the twenties was, in fact, unevenly distributed. A small elite lived very well and a comfortable middle class expanded, while a large working class dependent on wages maintained a somewhat insecure existence. Rural communities, largely reliant on a sagging agricultural sector, fared even worse.[1]

As noted in the Prologue, the Sisters of Providence had decided to concentrate their educational mission in urban areas, but at times they were confronted with the poverty of rural America. When two sisters from Marywood in Anaheim, California, undertook to teach a "Vacation School" in 1934 to prepare children in nearby Placentia for First Communion, Sister Mary Adele Miller records the shock they felt at the poverty they found tucked amid the orange groves.

> Only a fifteen-minute ride and we found ourselves in—what seemed to me—a 'slum district', except that there were no large tenement houses, but very small, one-story 'shacks' in each of which there were, however, either many families, or one family with many, MANY children.[2]

The pace of economic growth stuttered unevenly and then collapsed in grand fashion when the largely unregulated banking system failed, taking many businesses down with it. Even large corporations felt political pressures on their international trade arrangements and cut back their operations. Layoffs multiplied. Although President Herbert Hoover worked hard to stabilize the economy, the demoralizing effect of so many willing workers unable to find employment had a powerful political effect. By 1932 Americans were eager for the New Deal promised by Democrat Franklin D. Roosevelt.

However, even after Roosevelt became president in March 1933 and put his brain trust to work in the first Hundred Days, the alphabet soup of government agencies was barely able to stem the rising tide of poverty and gloom. All of these events had an impact on the Sisters of Providence. To reduce expenses at the motherhouse, only sisters needing classes to keep up certification were allowed to come home for the summer.[3] When a severe drought gripped the nation's midsection from 1933-1936, creating a dust bowl that forced farmers off their land and drove up food prices, a summer newsletter sent to the sisters unable to come to Saint Mary-of-the-Woods told of the impact of the weather pattern at the motherhouse. "We need rain very badly. For the last three weeks or more, even when the sky darkens we are not even sprinkled. We are still praying for rain with confidence, as Sisters of Providence."[4] Fortunately, the investment of the previous decades in the farm infrastructure provided insulation for the food supply.[5] At Saint Mary-of-the-Woods, the poultry farm, greenhouse and orchards were a mainstay for the College and motherhouse.

With the New Deal failing to restore prosperity, many Americans worried that fascism or communism would replace democracy. News of the advance of militaristic regimes of Japan and Germany continued to appear. Fervent prayer was regarded as the strongest weapon against the evils of the time. Portraying the disasters of the times as a chastisement for the offenses of atheism and irreligion, Mother Mary Raphael urged the sisters to acts of self-denial and reparation. Echoing the hierarchy's concern about the success of communism in Spain and Russia, rosary bands were formed in 1936. Basic needs such as finding a job or the success of a family business led people to special devotions. The sisters missioned at Our Lady of Sorrows in Chicago witnessed thousands of working class people attending the novena in honor of Our Sorrowful Mother begun by the Servites in 1937.[6]

Many of the dispirited populace turned to religion to sustain their faith. The strong anti-Catholic bias which had contributed to the defeat of Al Smith's bid for the presidency in 1928 gradually lessened. The "radio priest" Father Charles Coughlin gained an audience with a mellow voice that adapted the church's social teaching to the problems of the day, especially attacking the evils of communism.[7] Sidney Ahlstrom notes that even after Coughlin's anti-Semitic tone led to his being silenced by his bishop in 1940,[8] the popularity of Monsignor Fulton J. Sheen, who began broadcasting on the Catholic Hour in 1930, sustained the presence of a Catholic voice in the media.[9] Charles Morris notes that other indications of the Catholic Church's growing influence on the country were in the air. The formation of the Legion of Decency to impose moral guidelines on motion pictures through a rating system had a major effect on attendance. In 1934 Protestants and Jews also took the pledge to attend only decent movies.[10] Occasional headlines featured cardinals and bishops socializing with presidents, such as a 1935 photo of Cardinal Mundelein with President Roosevelt receiving an honorary degree from Notre Dame University.[11]

Meanwhile, with the gradual escalation of hostilities in Europe and Asia, accompanied by heated discussion about the extent of American involvement, a somber mood continued throughout the decade of the thirties. Having established a mission in China in 1920, the Congregation had a narrow window into events unfolding across the Pacific.

The China Mission

Early Struggles

By 1926, the Sisters of Providence had been laboring in Kaifeng, China, for six years,[12] When Bishop Joseph Tacconi, a member of the Italian congregation known as the Pontifical Institute for Foreign Missions, had pleaded for sisters to teach women in his diocese in Honan Province, the missionary spirit was so strong that three hundred sisters had volunteered for the mission. The six sisters who arrived in Kaifeng on November 24, 1920, were shocked at the overwhelming poverty of the situation in which they found themselves. They worked hard to study Chinese and cope with the extremes of heat and cold, but not all agreed as to the main focus of the mission. Some were so distressed by the suffering of the people that they wanted to devote themselves to direct outreach, while others insisted that education would equip women to help themselves. In addition to these internal disagreements, the superior, Sister Marie Gratia Luking, struggled to get Bishop

Tacconi to comply with his contractual obligations. When Sister Mary Elise Renauldt died of smallpox while nursing victims of the illness barely five months after their arrival, their sense of isolation intensified. An exchange of letters to the motherhouse via train and ship could take up to eight weeks, and all their pleas for a superior to visit in order to understand their situation went unheard.[13] Sister Marie Gratia went so far as to request that she be replaced as superior of the mission.

At home, letters from the sisters were interpreted as a need for stronger leadership for the distant mission. When Sister Marie Gratia's term expired, Sister Joseph Henry Boyle was appointed to succeed her, with Sister Mary Margaretta Grusinger appointed as the other new missionary. When the two sisters arrived in 1923, the situation in Kaifeng had turned even worse due to the civil war which was raging nearby. Hua Mei, the small school for girls that the Sisters had opened in 1921, closed, and the sisters' compound was overcrowded with refugees as civil war intensified. Nationalist feelings were strong, but loyalties shifted among warlords competing for regional power. Foreigners were suspect, especially missionaries, making the sisters' situation precarious.

Shortly after Mother Mary Raphael was elected, Bishop Tacconi was in Chicago en route back to China from his visit to Italy, providing the opportunity for him to meet with her in October 1926 and to provide an in-depth update for her regarding the situation of the missionary sisters. However, just months later the political situation worsened to the point that in the summer of 1927 evacuation from Kaifeng was necessary. At that time, Sister Eugene Marie Howard's brother, Archbishop Edward Howard of Portland, Oregon, asked that she be allowed to return to the United States due to their mother's poor health. In July, he arranged for passage to Seattle for her and her companion, Sister Winifred Patrice O'Donovan. At the same time, Mother Mary Raphael recalled Sister Joseph Henry and her companion, Sister Clare Mitchell. The remaining missionaries, Sisters Marie Gratia, Marie Patricia Shortall and Mary Margaretta Grussinger sought refuge in Korea, and the following April they went on to Darien, Manchuria, where they could better support themselves while continuing to study Chinese.

By 1929, as circumstances in Kaifeng had improved, it was clear that Sister Marie Gratia was capable of assuming leadership of the China mission, and she was again appointed superior.[14] Inspired by the work of the sisters, young Chinese women were asking to become sisters themselves. Three promising "probationers" were accepted in 1930 with a view to their being sent to the novitiate at Saint Mary-of-the-Woods. The College had recently been approved to admit foreign students, so although the Chinese Exclusion Act remained in force and would prevent them from remaining in the United States, it would be possible for them to earn a degree before returning to China. Sister Marie Gratia arranged for their passports and travel, and they arrived at Saint Mary-of-the-Woods on May 12, 1930. Given the restrictions on Chinese immigration, in November 1930 the council decided to support the formation of a local diocesan institute, the Providence Sister-Catechists, in order to provide an avenue for native vocations. The Congregation would assist the new institute by providing a Sister of Providence to serve as novice mistress in China. The Catechist Society will be discussed in more detail in Chapter 6.

In October 1931, Third Assistant Sister Berchmans Collins traveled to China for visitation, bringing three additional sisters to serve there. Sister Agatha McFadden proved invaluable for her work with the orphans at Holy Childhood School, but she would die of cancer after only five years. Sisters Carmel Baker and Monica Marie Rigoni adapted quickly to the work and became mainstays of the Providence mission. Indeed, when Sister Berchmans returned to the United States with a Chinese postulant, Mary Ma, her personal experience of the remarkable work being accomplished in the face of such overwhelming odds resulted in an upsurge of support from the motherhouse. Although the Congregation's financial situation prevented Mother Mary Raphael from contributing to the construction of the long-planned-for middle school, the indefatigable Sister Marie Gratia was able to arrange a loan and Ching I School opened its doors on September 12, 1932. Indeed, the significance of the role of this extraordinary woman for the China mission requires a more in-depth introduction.

Sister Marie Gratia Luking 1885-1964

Josephine Luking was born on May 10, 1885, to Mary and Henry Luking of Connersville, Indiana, where she and her brother William and two sisters, Kathleen and Mae, received their early education from the Sisters of Providence at St. Gabriel School. Because of her father's early death in an accident, after secondary education at an Indianapolis business school she went to work in an office where her diligence earned regular promotions. When she was twenty-one, her family circumstances had improved to the point that she was able to follow her desire for religious life, entering the novitiate in 1906. After her profession, her work experience was put to good use in her assignment to teach in the commercial department at St. Columbkille in Chicago. Following final profession she was appointed superior at St. Mary, Richmond, Indiana, and then at two of the major Sister of Providence academies, Our Lady of Providence in Chicago and St. Augustine in Fort Wayne. When sisters were asked to volunteer for a life commitment for the new China mission in 1920, she did so and was appointed to lead the group of six missionaries.

For Sister Marie Gratia, the mission cross she received on September 29, 1920, was indeed indicative of the trials she would bear over the next forty-four years of missionary work. Quick to learn not only the language but also the Chinese culture and worldview, she also possessed an innate ability to rise above crushing setbacks. Because of the difficulties of communication with the motherhouse, her leadership abilities were questioned and she was replaced as superior after only one three-year term, but she was reappointed in 1929. Always obedient to her faraway superiors, she was nevertheless not hesitant to suggest adaptations, as well to take the initiative in meeting a never-ending set of challenges. In spite of the ongoing Chinese civil war, she became adept at negotiations with church and government officials and was instrumental in beginning a congregation of Chinese Providence Sister-Catechists, then providing formation and leadership during its nascent years. When new sister missionaries arrived from the United States, she arranged for their training and placement in order to maintain an orphanage and two schools, then with them survived internship under Japanese occupation. When the Communists gained control in 1948 and most American missionaries returned home, she moved the entire Providence in China mission to Taiwan. There she continued the mission of educating Chinese women by founding Providence College. During all these years, she only returned to the United States once in 1956 to celebrate her Golden Jubilee. In 1960 she was honored by the Taiwan Ministry of Education for her forty years of service to China, In 1961 the Congregation honored her with the honorary title of Mother. Mother Marie Gratia died on October 29, 1964, and after an elaborate funeral befitting her remarkable achievements, was buried in Taichung.

Support for the Missions

The twenties were a time when the missionary impulse gained strength in the American Catholic Church. Evangelism had always been a distinguishing feature of Protestant churches and the revivals led by Dwight L. Moody during the late nineteenth century had generated a wave of enthusiasm in college students who pledged to become foreign missionaries.[15] Recognizing the importance of gaining the support of Catholics for foreign missions, in 1918 Father Clifford J. King, a seminarian at Divine Word in Techny, Illinois, had launched a comparable movement, the Catholic Students Mission Crusade.[16] Like so many other Catholic colleges, Saint Mary-of-the-Woods established a chapter of the organization. In 1921 the journalism department launched the publication of *The Bugle Call*, a monthly newsletter devoted to informing Catholic students about missionary efforts and providing an avenue for channeling donations. Distributed in bundles of ten for a twenty-five-cent yearly subscription to students in all Sister of Providence schools, the magazine was a window into another world. Over the years the sisters who were missioned in China supplied photos and stories which continued to sustain interest and support. Elementary and secondary schools throughout the country caught their teachers' missionary spirit and eagerly compared their contributions to those of other schools in the lists published each month.

In Kaifeng, under Sister Marie Gratia's leadership, the Providence Sister-Catechists continued to flourish in their nearby Nan Kuan convent. Those who took vows were assigned to mission and, just as at St. Mary-of-the-Woods, returned to the Kaifeng "motherhouse" in the summer for retreat. However, the arrangements for the three young women joining the Sisters of Providence and making their novitiate at St. Mary-of-the-Woods did not go as smoothly. Sister Providence, the former Therese Ying, who joined the congregation in 1930, stated that it was inappropriate for her to associate with Sister Agnes Joan Li because she considered her to be from a lower caste, and she left the community.[17] Both Sister Agnes Joan and Sister Marie Stella (Adalina Bonizzon, Bishop Tacconi's Italian protégé) experienced indications of prejudice from some of the sisters. This eventually caused Adalina to return to Italy.[18] The arrival of Mary Ma (later Sister Bernadette) at Saint Mary-of-the-Woods in March 1931 provided some companionship for Sister Agnes Joan, and in 1937 they returned to China together.[19]

The frequency with which the China mission appears in the council minutes indicates the council's concern for the missionary sisters and the responsibility they felt for their welfare. Distance and danger notwithstanding, the superior general was indeed responsible.

Affairs of Administration

The *Constitutions* left no doubt about the extent of Mother Mary Raphael's responsibility: "All affairs of administration are under the authority of the Superior General assisted by her Council."[20]

First among these affairs as she began her administration in 1926 was the need to finalize the work of bringing these *Constitutions* into harmony with the recently promulgated Code of Canon Law. Sister Mary Ignatia Hanson's scholarly talents were put to excellent use as she prepared for the council's consideration drafts of a revised *Constitution* based on the advice of the Congregation's canonical consultant, Father George M. Sauvage, CSC. After final approval from the Vatican, a new edition of the small black Rule book was published in 1929. For Mother Mary Raphael, observance of these *Constitutions* took pride of place. During the first years of her administration her letters and instructions were often exhortations to take to heart the Rule's direction as a sure path to sanctity. The long-standing practice of sending a letter circular at Christmas and again in the spring to call the sisters "Home" for retreat provided regular opportunities for reminders that the apostolic life was only effective when it flowed from a strong spiritual foundation.

When the sisters gathered at the motherhouse for their summer studies prior to retreat, it was customary to assemble in the Conservatory's auditorium for Mother's instructions, providing an opportunity for her to personally urge close observance of the religious decorum associated with the unique identity of a Sister of Providence of Saint Mary-of-the-Woods. In some respects it is difficult to gauge the reaction of the sisters to Mother Mary Raphael. Historian Sister Angelyn Dries, OSF, points out that in a certain sense, the spirit of the times was having an unexpected influence within religious congregations.

> In parallel fashion with the business world around her, increasing bureaucracy brought a shift in leadership style. Authority rested in the office of the head of the community rather than in her person. Losing some of the immediacy of a family approach to running the institute, congregations emphasized the organization as a source of power. [21]

Although her stern appearance created the impression that she lacked humor, and the council minutes describe complaints from "difficult" sisters, other reactions of the sisters indicate that they appreciated her role in their lives. For example, on the occasion of her first official visitation at Immaculata in Washington, D.C., the house diarist noted that Mother "gave one of her inspiring talks."[22]

Working with the Council

With regard to other major responsibilities, the *Constitutions* provided direction for Mother herself. "The Superior General shares her authority and her administration with the Council in a manner more or less extended, according to the nature and importance of the affairs."[23] Specific situations required the council's involvement and insured that consultation would occur. Simple common sense was given legal language: "It is of the highest importance that there exist perfect union between the Superior General and her Council, for upon this union depends in a great measure the prosperity of the Congregation."[24] A review of the 1926-1938 council minutes indicates that the combination of Mother Mary Raphael's personality and the difficult economic times fostered an unintentional drift in emphasis to organizational goals rather than personal concern for the sisters.

Given Mother Mary Raphael's lack of recent council experience, as well as a similar lack for four of the six council members, they certainly had some difficult moments. Since they were elected in June, the council's first responsibility was to use their summer meetings to draw up the sisters' appointments for the 1926-1927 scholastic year. Unfortunately their inexperience and lack of knowledge regarding the sisters and the various convent situations was soon apparent. Almost immediately after the Obedience List was read on August 15 and the sisters departed for mission, calls came regarding needed changes, a process that continued throughout the year. By September the council minutes report that "this information ... concerning the dismissal of Sisters, brought pressure to bear upon the division of the Council."[25]

At times the minutes record that the council invoked the option of utilizing a secret vote to settle an issue.[26] Periodically, Mother Mary Raphael, possibly sensitive to criticism, came close to assuming a scolding tone as she exhorted her council to strict observance. Given that her assistants were well-known for such fidelity and that Sister Mary Ignatia had prepared a new edition of the "Book of Customs" and edited Mother Mary Cleophas' instructions for local superiors, the council members might have had reason to question her tact. Yet at other times she was effusive in her praise of their support, especially since her periodic medical leaves required them to take on extra duties.[27] It is a tribute to these intrepid women that they were able not only to work through these problems, but also to accomplish so much. Certainly they appreciated Mother Mary Raphael's experience for the constant backdrop to their discussions—finances.

The Great Depression and Finances

Of all the dates chronicled for the Great Depression, the one which surely leaps out at the reader would be the October 29, 1929, "Black Tuesday" stock market crash. Significant as that event was, the country's economy encompassed much more than the market, as historian David M. Kennedy explains:

> Much mythology surrounds these dramatic events in the autumn of 1929. Perhaps the most imperishable misconception portrays the Crash as the cause. ... Legend to the contrary, the average American—a description that in this case encompasses at least 97.5 percent of the population—owned no stock in 1929.[28]

Such was certainly the case for the Sisters of Providence. Rather, the Congregation's investments were very heavily in real estate tied to the brick and mortar associated with providing the infrastructure for the educational apostolate.

Even in 1929, with the 1921 recession fresh in memory, many pundits regarded the crash as a business cycle downturn. The real crisis emerged the following year when banks in the Midwest began to fail,[29] and "on December 11, 1930, it struck close to the central nervous system of American capitalism when New York City's Bank of United States closed its doors."[30] With the sisters' business affairs so intertwined with banks, there was major cause for concern.

The system of money management for the Sisters of Providence was relatively simple. The Rule provided for two business officers: the treasurer to take care of revenue—deposits and disbursements — and a procuratrix who took care of "temporalities," mainly arranging for provisions and the payment for these. In the smaller houses, the local superior had these responsibilities, while in the larger houses, duties would be delegated. Each house was expected to cover its own expenses and send any surplus revenue to the motherhouse, where the central fund was administered by the elected treasurer general and by the procuratrix or econome. During her twenty-six years in the role of treasurer, Mother Mary Raphael had established definite procedures and accounting practices for handling Congregation finances.

When Providence Convent had been constructed in 1890, the building included three walk-in vaults with fire-protected doors and combination locks.[31] The first-floor vault was off of the secretary's office while directly above it another vault formed part of the treasurer's back office. A third vault directly below in the basement contained older documents. The treasurer's vault held all manner of items, ranging from precious chalices to specifications and plans for the various buildings to bank documents and payroll records. The College funds were handled there as well, with faculty members depositing money collected for various functions and the College treasurer coming once a week to write necessary checks. Special cupboards were built to house the bound ledgers used to record the detailed accounts of receipts and expenditures. Invoices and checks were carefully filed for convenient reference. Bills were filed according to payment date, with discounts noted.[32] Monthly balance sheets showing the assets were prepared and carefully copied into the ledgers. Lay employees were paid weekly in cash, since most didn't have bank accounts. The econome figured the hours on Thursday and prepared individual payroll envelopes with the name, the needed amount and a receipt. The treasurer went to town on Friday morning to get the cash and took it into the bedroom adjacent to her office to apportion it for distribution at the end of the day.

It was all very business-like. However, the business of the Congregation was basically education, which is not known for profitability. It was a business whose name was Providence, so some aspects of the treasurer's office were designed to express that reality. When a large payment was due on a debt or a note from the bank, the record was placed behind the statue of St. Joseph on the mantel. Every day prayers were said to St. Joseph that the money would be found to pay the amount needed.[33] While more practical persons might scoff at such an apparently naïve approach to fund-raising, a visit to the well-ordered campus bore witness to the power of prayer.

Financial Obligations

So where did the money come from? The income that the motherhouse depended on was the sisters' stipends and the music teachers' fees. The need for music teachers was legendary since their classes were independent of the parish and therefore the fees came free and clear to the community. Low stipends were also legendary. A survey of the times shows a range of $600-$1200 per teacher per a ten-month year, or $9,530-$19,060 in 2010 dollars.[34] Parishes usually provided housing and utilities, but food, clothing, transportation, health care and education were paid for by the sisters. At the Congregation-owned academies, maintenance and improvements would be additional expenses. At the end of the year, any surplus was "sent home" to the motherhouse, so when funds were low, two or three times a year, the treasurer took the train to Indianapolis and Chicago to make the rounds to collect sufficient cash to cover motherhouse expenses. Any donations and patrimony (inheritances which came to the sisters) were welcome supplements.

And where had the money gone? Over the years since its foundation, the Congregation had consistently invested in its academies and from time to time had agreed to assume the costs of some parish schools. As seen in Chapter 3, the legal separation of the finances of the Congregation from those of the College in 1928 allowed flexibility in managing resources. In addition to the combined College-motherhouse campus at Saint Mary-of-the-Woods, by 1928, the sisters owned some

TABLE 3: *Real estate holdings, 1935*

School	City	Founded	1928 Worth	1935 Worth
St. Joseph Academy	Terre Haute, IN	1843	$30,000	$27,902
St. Rose Academy	Vincennes, IN	1843	$45,000[a]	$16,793
St. Augustine Academy	Fort Wayne, IN	1846	$30,000	$45,000
St. Simon Academy	Washington, IN	1857	$27,110[b]	$12,110
Holy Trinity School	New Albany, IN	1857	$10,000	$5,806
St. John Academy	Indianapolis, IN	1859	$407,500	$412,349
St. Ignatius Academy	Lafayette, IN	1861	$20,000	$25,000
Providence High School [c]	Chicago, IL	1866	$463,648	$1,269,234
Our Lady of Sorrows Convent	Chicago, IL	1866		$350,000
St. Patrick School	Indianapolis, IN	1875	$12,000	$10,595
St. Joseph School	Indianapolis, IN	1877	$20,000	$19,802
St. Patrick School	Terre Haute, IN	1882	$25,000	$10,509
St. Agnes Academy	Indianapolis, IN	1893	$606,440	$623,502
Holy Cross School	Indianapolis, IN	1896	$17,700	$12,365
Immaculata Seminary	Washington, D.C.	1905	$779,205	$801,913
St. Philip Neri School	Indianapolis, IN	1909	$23,401	
Marywood School	Evanston, IL	1915	$921,611	$997,493
Maryhurst Convent	Hyattsville, MD	1919		$84,473
Ladywood School	Indianapolis, IN	1926	$658,749	$833,319
St. Jude	Fort Wayne, IN	1928	$12,534	$22,123

Source: Data from financial records, SMWA. a. 1884 building, b. 1870 building, c. Originally built as part of Our Lady of Sorrows, a new building was constructed in 1929.

twenty properties, whose worth fluctuated with the times, as shown in table 3.

Statements of assets and liabilities were mainly calculated on these properties, since the accounts receivable and cash on hand were kept at a minimum. The Congregation was fortunate to have the help of seasoned businessmen such as Mr. Neil J. Gleason, Sister Mary Neil's father, who kindly accepted an invitation to come to the campus during this period to provide advice and assistance regarding best practices for handling the debt.[35] Due to the continuous investment in new properties, loans and notes based on current holdings were a constant worry, especially in light of the bank panics, as the data in table 4 indicates, since liabilities were rising faster than assets at this time.

TABLE 4: *Finacial fluctuations*

Year	Assets	Liabilities
1924	$7,630,632.89	$1,034,557.33
1932	$11,165,936.36	$2,541,715.00
1933	$11,092,145.21	$2,513,393.04
1934	$11,009,549.27	$2,427,691.52
1935	$10,832,868.71	$2,366,697.42
1939	$10,802,395.00	$1,201,014.09
1940	$10,840,506.99	$1,117,149.61

Various measures were taken to cope with the financial difficulties. Prayer was paramount. The novices frequently formed rosary bands to pray earnestly that money would be found, and when large amounts were due, novenas preceded the due dates. Often it was necessary to borrow money from one bank to pay a loan due at another bank. Circular letters to the missions begging for prayers and/or money were a last resort. Fortunately, the prayers for continued strong enrollment were heard, since a solid number of paying students in

Congregation-owned institutions ensured regular income simply to stay afloat. Requests for major maintenance needs were put on hold. To reduce the Congregation's expenses, the 1933 summer school at Saint-Mary-of-the-Woods was originally cancelled, then restricted to those needing certification. The constant stress wore down the stamina of the treasurer general, Sister Adelaide O'Brien, who was ordered to take medical leave in 1935. Sister Mary Cyril Kilroy was appointed in her stead to carry forward loan negotiations which were underway with banks in Wisconsin and Chicago.

Mother Mary Raphael's Health Challenges

Similar financial difficulties had been Mother Mary Raphael's daily occupation for many years. During her forty-one years of service as teacher, superior and treasurer she had always accepted her assignments from her superiors as God's will for her. Nervous though she might feel as the community assembled in the church to hear the announcement of her election by the 1926 General Chapter and the sisters came forward one by one to express their support, she knew she could rely on God's help to fulfill those responsibilities. Little did she realize at that point how the physical and psychological reserves which rested on that strong spiritual foundation would be tested in the years ahead.

Barely had Mother Mary Raphael's term begun when, on her first visitation trip to the houses on the East Coast in September 1926, she fell and broke her arm while at Immaculata in Washington, D.C. As she gradually adapted to her new duties, she relied on her longtime mentor, Mother Mary Cleophas. Pleased to share how her predecessor's plans were moving forward, Mother Mary Raphael was saddened to witness how Mother Mary Cleophas' strength seemed to decline with each visit. Her own energies seemed to diminish as well, and by October 1928 her doctor prescribed total rest at a sanitarium in nearby Alton, Illinois. When Mother Mary Cleophas died on December 27, 1928, Mother Mary Raphael returned for the funeral. This sad event seemed to inhibit her recovery. Although she expressed her gratitude to the council for the excellent care she had received, it was clear that she was not able to resume her duties.

In January 1929 she wrote to the sisters, "I have been strongly advised by the doctors and others to go away for a while."[36] She met with the council to allocate responsibilities among them as she left for a protracted stay in California at St. Elisabeth, Van Nuys. By April, the council's concerns had increased to the point that they discussed the situation with Bishop Chartrand and dispatched Sister Berchmans to California to ascertain her progress. It was not until after the August retreat when the sisters departed for their mission assignments that Mother Mary Raphael was able to return to Saint Mary-of-the-Woods and take up her duties again in September.

The timing of this leave of absence was providential, because she certainly needed all her strength when, the month after her return, the stock market crash of October 29, 1929, dramatized the unstable economic conditions in which the Congregation's business was enmeshed. Stress certainly took its toll on her ability to perform her duties, but her reputation for business acumen probably influenced her election to a second term in 1932. Her Golden Jubilee celebration that summer was a reminder that she was a sixty-nine-year-old, so it was not surprising that after the sisters returned to the missions she left for a fortnight's rest.

The General Chapter of 1932

A Desire for Change

When perpetually professed Sisters of Providence gathered in their various chapels on the evening of December 21, 1931, they were doubtless oblivious to the contrast between two photos in that week's issue of *Time* magazine—the cover showing Hitler waving his clenched fists during a speech and another in the back pages of Mahatma Gandhi seated over his spinning as he led a non-violent civil disobedience struggle.[37] For the sisters, it was the feast of St. John and their moment during a restful Christmas break to participate prayerfully in the election of Chapter delegates. This internal Congregation election lacked the political drama soon to play out during the 1932 campaign, which would oust President Hoover and sweep Franklin D. Roosevelt into office the following November. However, when the envelopes sealed that evening were opened weeks later at Saint Mary-of-the-Woods, a similar de-

sire for change seemed to prevail. Seventeen of the twenty-
five sisters chosen had never before been Chapter delegates.

When the elected delegates assembled on June 23, 1932,
and Bishop Chartrand opened the proceedings by inviting
questions from the floor, the minutes record that two of these
sisters did indeed take the occasion to rise to bring into the
open topics which had been brought to their attention.

> Sister Eugenia Clare [Cullity] recommended that the educa-
> tional program of the Order be conducted on a more liberal
> basis, and that the organization of this program be put in the
> care of more than one person, preferably in the care of a com-
> mittee similar to the one formerly in charge of educational mat-
> ters.

> Sister Catherine Marie [Daly] asked for information regarding
> the formation of provinces. His Excellency announced that four
> provinces would be formed; namely one in the West, one in the
> East, one in Indiana, and one in Illinois.[38]

As there was no printed agenda and neither precedent nor
protocol for discussion, these questions simply hung in the air.
Perhaps some of the delegates in their role as teachers had
come to understand the rules of parliamentary procedure, but
there was no formal motion. It would appear that the role of
the delegates was only to elect a new council and to use this
opportunity to raise issues which they expected the council to
take up later. Bishop Chartrand simply moved to the usual
order of business, calling upon Mother Mary Raphael to present
her report.

Despite her frequent absences due to poor health and the
difficult financial situation later detailed by Treasurer Sister
Adelaide, Mother Mary Raphael was able to list impressive
accomplishments in her report. Membership had increased by
116 to a total of 1,208. Fifteen new houses had been opened,
and numerous sisters had earned degrees: five PhD's, seven
MAs, four MAs in Music, and fifty-four BAs, while 259 had
received Indiana State Teachers Licenses. A high school
juniorate had been initiated and sixty-six novices and twenty-
five postulants were in the novitiate, bringing the total of young
women who had joined the community during the six years
to 284. Thanks to the support of students in schools in the
United States, the China mission was flourishing, with three
Chinese postulants actually on campus. In addition, a Cat-

echist Society had been established there, with twenty novices and fifteen postulants already having entered.

Nonetheless, a desire for change was evidenced in the voting for the superior general and her councilors, with not a single ballot tally showing a unanimous choice. Despite her well-received report and her staunch manner, Mother Mary Raphael must have experienced a worrisome soul-searching as she heard the name of First Assistant Sister Mary Bernard Laughlin read ten times in the count of votes for superior general; nonetheless Mother Mary Raphael was re-elected on the first ballot. Apparently Sister Eugenia Clare's recommendation concerning education was welcome, for she was elected to replace Sister Francis Joseph Elbreg as fifth assistant and director of education. Two newly elected councilors, both local superiors, had to be summoned: Sister Helen Clare Freiburger from the church, and Sister Marie Stanislaus Curran all the way from Chelsea, Massachusetts. According to established custom, the Chapter delegates' lips were sealed, so none of the discussion or voting or the feelings of the delegates would have been topics for later conversation. All these events were regarded as the work of Providence and simply commended to prayer.

Re-elected to serve as councilors during Mother Mary Raphael's second term were First Assistant Sister Mary Bernard and Third Assistant Sister Gertrude Clare. Sister Adelaide was re-elected as treasurer, a position that was not part of the council. The change motif was carried forward with four new council members, introduced below.

The 1932-1938 Council

Sister Helen Clare Freiburger 1887-1977

Born in 1887 in Sheldon, Indiana, near Valparaiso, Mary Freiburger enrolled at Saint Mary-of-the-Woods Academy for her high school education. After graduating in 1904, she entered the novitiate at age seventeen, receiving her early formation under Sister Manetto Quigley. She taught middle and upper grades for twenty years at only two schools in Chicago, St. Mel and St. Leo, before being appointed superior at St. Agnes, Chicago, for one year and then returning to St. Mel for a three-year stint as superior of the thirty-five-member house. In 1930 she traveled to California to open St. Therese, Alhambra, and had just returned for the summer when, at age forty-five the 1932 Chapter elected her as second assistant to Mother Mary Raphael. She would go on to serve seventeen years as a member of the general council before returning to parochial school for nine years.

Sister Eileen Walker 1887-1977

Muriel Walker was born in 1887 in Loogootee, a small town in southern Indiana where the Sisters of Providence had been a presence since 1862. She delayed entrance until 1919, when she was twenty-three. Most of her teaching experience was as a middle and upper grade teacher in seven Chicago schools under nine superiors over twelve years. She was then appointed superior at four houses over seven years. Clearly able to adapt to a variety of circumstances, she was known for her alert, interested manner and ready smile. She was among the delegates of the 1932 Chapter who elected her as fourth assistant to Mother Mary Raphael. She would be re-elected to a second term in the 1938 council and then return to parish schools as local superior and middle grade teacher before retiring to the infirmary in 1964.

Sister Eugenia Clare Cullity 1881-1948

Hattie Cullity was twenty-one when she arrived at Saint Mary-of-the-Woods as a postulant in 1905. Oldest of ten children, she had graduated from St. John, Indianapolis. Three years later, her younger sister Josephine followed her to community, receiving the name of Sister St. Philomene. After her novitiate, she taught in two of the large and long-established Sister of Providence academies, St. Augustine in Fort Wayne and Providence in Chicago. She was among the first sisters to attend DePaul University when the summer school was opened to women in 1911. The following year she was assigned to study for an MA at Catholic University, one of the three sisters living at St. Mary's Cottage on campus in 1912 as part of Mother Mary Cleophas' short-lived experiment.[39] During her second novitiate in 1914, she was assigned to assist the secretary general, Sister Mary Alma Ryan. She then returned to Washington, D.C., to teach at Immaculata. She was one of the founding members of Marywood, Evanston, in 1915, and taught at Saint Mary-of-the-Woods College for three years before returning to high school, where as senior teacher, she was of great assistance in training younger sisters as teachers. Doubtless due to her strong academic background and reputation as an educator, at age fifty-one she was elected as fifth assistant for education. Her duties in that regard were as assistant dean of the College, since Sister Francis Joseph was appointed supervisor of schools. Her academic background would prove to be a valuable asset in drafting the necessary adaptations to the *Constitutions* for discussion as the Congregation moved into provincial structures. She was not re-elected in 1938 and after five years as local superior and teacher in Burlington, North Carolina, went on to serve as superior at Immaculata during the war years and devote her energy and vision to increasing its reputation and enrollment. Her untimely death at age sixty-six was a great loss.

Sister Marie Stanislaus Curran
1884-1977

Margaret Curran entered community in 1907 at age sixteen in the middle of her senior year at Saint Mary-of-the-Woods. She had a great variety of mission experience, teaching at ten missions in Chicago, Connersville and Indianapolis. She was then appointed superior at two missions before returning to the classroom as a commercial teacher for three years and then was appointed superior and supervisor at St. Rose, Chelsea. She had not yet boarded the train to return to St. Mary-of-the-Woods for the summer in 1932 when she received word that she had been elected as sixth assistant and secretary general, a post she would fill for the next twelve years. In her later years she filled the post of registrar at Immaculata under Sister Eugenia Clare and then alternated between middle grade classrooms and the role of local superior in the East and in Chicago and environs, finally returning to the motherhouse in 1970.

Bogged down by seemingly never-ending financial preoccupations, as well as the arrangements to distribute responsibilities to provincial superiors, Mother Mary Raphael's second term was marked by the need for frequent periods of rest. She spent the summer of 1934 at Ladywood, and after the 1935 summer session and retreat, required a hospital-based month-long respite. She was confined to the infirmary in January 1936 but continued to work from there. While conducting visitation of the East in May 1936, she again fell and broke her arm. The following year she spent the month of March at Marywood, Evanston, telling the council she hoped her hiatus would not be advertised.[40] In September 1937, after the sisters returned to the missions, she entered a hospital for a rest. Considering all these physical setbacks with probable psychological side effects, it is remarkable that she was able to accomplish so much. Again in her second term, she owed much to her capable councilors.

Working with the Local Ordinary

Within the Church, any affairs of administration required cultivating cordial relationships with the bishop of each diocese in which there were houses. Although the Congregation's mission had expanded well beyond the Indianapolis Diocese, because the motherhouse was located within it, close association with the ordinary (the bishop appointed to exercise ordinary executive power over the diocese) was required by canon law. Over the course of years, this association had come to be marked by mutual respect and warm relationships.[41] However, circumstances of the times tested the quality of the necessary interactions between chancery and motherhouse. Bishop Joseph Chartrand, as coadjutor to Bishop Chatard since 1910 and ordinary since 1918, was very familiar with the operations of the Congregation and available for consultations regarding canonical questions such as the establishment of the Catechist Society in China or the dismissal of sisters. However, in certain instances, such as taking over the boys' high school in Washington, Indiana, for the fall semester of 1932 and allowing the lay sisters to vote for General Chapter delegates, he insisted on making the decision.[42]

The economic conditions of the Great Depression had a profound effect on the diocese and other religious congregations in Indiana. In 1933, the banks' seizure of St. Viator College in Illinois brought home to the Sisters of Providence the realization that they were not immune from a similar fate. News came that other congregations were on the verge of bankruptcy.[43] Parishes had trouble paying even the meager stipends. In September 1933, Mother Mary Raphael wrote to the pastors concerning "the perplexing and delicate financial question," asking that full salaries be paid, or if that was impossible, a promissory note be signed for the balance.[44]

After Bishop Chartrand's death December 8, 1933, these economic circumstances brought special challenges to forming a cordial working relationship with his successor. The new ordinary, Joseph Elmer Ritter, was born July 20, 1892, in New Albany and received his elementary education at St. Mary School. He entered St. Meinrad Seminary for high school, college and seminary studies, graduating summa cum laude. After his 1917 ordination, his hopes for pursuing doctoral studies in Rome were dashed by the hostilities of the World War.[45] Assigned to the Cathedral to assist Bishop Chartrand, he soon proved himself so capable that he was named rector at age thirty-three. Observing his talent for business as he raised funds for Cathedral High School and served on influential priests' consultation committees, Bishop Chartrand gave him more and more responsibility. He was named vicar general and was made auxiliary bishop in February 1933. Only ten months later, Bishop Chartrand, age sixty-three, suffered a heart attack at the rectory, receiving the last sacraments from his loyal long-time associate. With years of administrative experience under his mentor's tutelage, after he was consecrated as ordinary of the Indianapolis Diocese in an impressive ceremony at the Cathedral on April 24, 1934, Bishop Ritter lost no time in putting his own stamp on the diocese.

A major goal was, as his biographer emphasizes, "putting diocesan finances back in shape."[46] To this end, he established forward-looking policies for parish reporting and insisted on full payment of diocesan assessments. Noting that the diocese was verging on bankruptcy, he decreed that those who had loaned money to the diocese simply cancel the debt, or at least the interest payments. Mother Mary Raphael was shocked when in May 1934 Bishop Ritter asked that the community simply forgive the $50,000 loan made to his predecessor, Bishop Chartrand. He expressed his demands in unapologetic terms:

> Am I not justified, then, in asking the same of St. Mary's-of-the-Woods? I am afraid St. Mary's feels that the Diocese is for St. Mary's, but not St. Mary's for the Diocese. As I told you before St. Mary's should be happy to accede to this request in part payment for all that Bishop Chartrand did for it.[47]

Since the sisters were in no position to comply, yet frequently needed to consult with the bishop on other matters, it was an awkward situation. The council minutes describe a temporary solution. "In view of the intended visitation and the necessity to be in His Excellency's good graces, it was decided to be patient about our debt."[48] The following year, the Congregation donated a parcel of the Ladywood property to Bishop Ritter as a site for his house. Meanwhile the tension surrounding this obligation dragged on. The country was still wallowing in the sludge of the Depression despite three years of New Deal legislative efforts to bring relief, and these conditions certainly provide the background for the tone of the bishop's letter. Nonetheless, coming so soon in his administration, the disagreement did not augur well for pleasant relationships. From time to time over the next several years the subject was broached, but it was not until April 1937 that the loan was repaid by the diocese, with $30,000 of it immediately spent to pay for new boilers at the motherhouse.

The long-standing practice of pastors and sisters taking their grievances to the bishop prompted Bishop Ritter to express additional forthright opinions over the years. He did not always agree regarding individual's requests for dispensations.[49] He interceded for those who felt partiality was shown in giving permission to visit dying parents.[50] On the other hand, he was most supportive of pursuing the Cause of sainthood for Mother Theodore, releasing Father Kilfoil from parish duties to serve as postulator, with the hope that "nothing will be left undone on our part."[51] He was supportive of the work being done toward reorganizing the community into provinces and generous with helpful critiques and suggestions, as shall be seen in the next chapter. Like most of his contemporaries in the hierarchy, he was strong in his support for Catholic education and felt it was appropriate to serve as spokesperson when pastors' or sisters' concerns were brought to his attention. Pastors with complaints about poorly prepared principals or frequent turnover of classroom teachers could expect his backing.

In a tradition dating back to his predecessors, the sisters also looked to him as a mediator, and felt free to bring matters to his attention when they felt that they had not had a just hearing from their superiors. As Mother Mary Raphael's second term neared its close, Bishop Ritter forwarded to her and to Supervisor of Schools Sister Francis Joseph a copy of a severely critical letter he had received from a sister who wrote to him because "none of us has the courage to come out in the open for fear of consequences; for if an individual does protest, she is given to understand that she is not a good religious."[52] The bishop noted that the letter was "a good sample of others that have come to my office and of frequent complaints that I receive from the Sisters."[53] The writer enumerates complaints concerning the quality of local superiors who are appointed over and over, partiality for no apparent reason, the excuse of "we are so many" for lack of response to problems, as well as noting that the method of electing delegates to the General Chapter did not allow for the sisters to express their wishes. Although receiving such negative criticism from one of their own through the channel of their bishop must have been demoralizing, the council not only discussed the issue but recorded each complaint point by point in the minutes.[54] Once past these difficult times, over the years to come, Bishop Ritter would develop a strong working relationship with the sisters and come to regard them as friends and colleagues for the mission.

The Supervisor of Schools

The concerns about educational supervision that Sister Eugenia Clare had voiced during the 1932 Chapter seemed based on some confusion stemming from a new and innovative addition to the recently published 1929 edition of the *Constitutions*, Chapter XXXIX, The Supervisor of Schools. In a procedure similar to selection to the office of general procuratrix, the supervisor was to be appointed by the superior general with the advice of her council. Since charge of the schools had always been in the care of one of the assistants, this was a major change. Very likely the increasing professionalization of Catholic education and the concomitant need to continue the high educational standards of the Congregation had led to this change.[55]

The 1929 *Constitutions* describe the supervisor's role:

> To oversee the teaching in the schools, to plan and direct the studies of the Sisters, and to see that the methods employed are conformed to the best usage, as well as to the particular needs and circumstances of the place.

> She shall visit as directed by the Superior General the various houses, examine the classes, and when necessary, show the Sisters, especially the young and inexperienced, how to conduct the work of the school room.

> She shall see that the program approved by the Superior General is carried out and shall assign the Sisters the studies and special work to be pursued.[56]

Although Sister Francis Joseph's relative youth and lack of experience would later lead to the problems communicated to Bishop Ritter, her natural abilities combined with her academic preparation and the experience of being a member of the 1926-1932 council made her an appropriate candidate for the position. Not surprisingly, she was appointed. No longer a home superior with an office in Tile Hall, she turned her attention to designing and equipping an Office of Education in Foley Hall, described in the chatty newsletter sent to the sisters who were unable to come to Saint Mary-of-the-Woods in the summer of 1933:

> No doubt you know about Sister Francis Joseph's new Education Department at Foley Hall. Besides the main office, which is the former Academy Principal's office, there are five little rooms along the hall leading from the main office. The main room is especially attractive. A very lovely counter separates the section where Sister's desk is from the rest of the office. ... It serves another purpose as a wonderful desk file. On its inner side are arranged a series of filing drawers. ... Those Sisters who have made a special trip to see the office] seemed not a little surprised to find everything so well organized.[57]

With the passing of the years, it's likely that almost every teaching Sister of Providence would visit this office to consult about her own file, as its cumulative record of her academic credits gradually documented the path Sister Francis Joseph patiently plotted to enable her to achieve teaching credentials, college diplomas and graduate degrees. Due to its immense importance for the core mission of the Congregation, this topic will return in a later chapter.

Southern Indiana Parish Schools

The educational mission of the Sisters of Providence had had its beginnings in southern Indiana and it was these historic establishments which now provided a short burst of unexpected financial assistance to the Congregation. However, this came about only because several of them were threatened with closure. Local politics led to different developments in a cluster of four cities: Jasper (Dubois County), Vincennes (Knox County), Washington (Daviess County) and Loogootee (Martin County). The unique circumstances of each school caused considerable concern and extensive negotiations for the council over the decade of the thirties.

Jasper

The Congregation's first mission was St. Joseph in Jasper, which Mother Theodore fondly referred to as "our eldest daughter."[58] The dynamic Father Joseph Kundek had arrived in 1838 from Croatia, a province of the Austrian-Hugarian Empire, to pastor the tiny settlement. When he saw the potential of the hardwood forest and fertile soil, he advertised in German newspapers and encouraged an influx of Catholic immigration. By 1841 he had built a substantial brick church and a rudimentary school building with accommodations for sisters. As the founder of the town, he was also heavily involved in early civic affairs, which led to the arrangement described in the St. Joseph Convent diary:

> From 1824 on, the State of Indiana had provided in its law that there should be three trustees for each township, and in 1843 Father Kundek decided that the township or county trustees should take over the financial end of the school.
>
> The contract included this clause: "On these conditions they will receive gratis the children of the county. The county will pay you."[59]

The original contract drawn up between Father Kundek and Mother Theodore provided for a cash payment of $100 per year and food staples and housing. After Father Kundek's negotiations with the state, St. Joseph operated as a public school with the Congregation supplying teachers who met certification standards, including faculty who were proficient in German. An elected county superintendent assured compliance with state regulations and the continuing close harmony with Dubois County officials assured regular income for the Congregation. As the years went on, the city of Jasper became known for the making of excellent furniture and the small community grew and prospered. A new school was built in 1927. The combination of agriculture and manufacturing proved to be an economic buffer for the thrifty citizens during the difficult Depression times, ensuring continued public support for the school.

Vincennes

Northwest of Jasper in Knox County the city of Vincennes, originally the major city of the diocese during the days when the economy had flourished from Wabash River traffic, was now feeling the economic pinch. Pastors of the three parishes applied to the state of Indiana for financial aid from the state relief fund. In addition to the three parish schools—St. Francis Xavier, St. John, (both staffed by Sisters of Providence) and Sacred Heart (staffed by the Benedictine Sisters)—they interceded for St. Rose Academy for girls and Gibault High School for boys. Faced with the prospect of an influx of students should the Catholic schools close, local public school officials supported the request. They reasoned that it would be more economical to let the parishes finance the maintenance of existing school buildings while public funds were used to pay the salaries of the religious faculty. The decision was made for the state to pay the minimum salary for all the sisters and brothers teaching in the Vincennes schools during the 1934-1935 school year.[60] The $800 for elementary teachers and $1000 for high school teachers for the year was a windfall for the religious faculty during such hard times.

Politically unpopular, this decision was immediately contested, with the result that only grades one through six were funded the following year. This compromise was based on the argument that the Catholic schools did not have adequate facilities for the required curricular offerings for the upper grades. The salaries of the grade school teachers had to be stretched to take care of the unpaid upper grade sisters. During this time public school officials supervised the teaching and programs in all three schools. Since the sisters' credentials were on a par with other teachers in the system, the curriculum followed state guidelines and enrollment remained stable, the arrangement proved satisfactory to school officials.

Nonetheless, a determined opposition filed a lawsuit protesting the use of public funds for private and religious education. The case dragged on in the local court and had to be moved to neighboring Daviess County, with further delays. Although a trial date was finally set, the school board cut off payments during the 1938-1939 school year pending a decision. Finally on September 23, 1940, the judge ruled that since the schools had continued to be clearly Catholic, not public, the state constitution prohibited paying the salaries of faculty.[61] Since the school board members had acted in good faith, back payment was authorized, but the practice could not continue. Fortunately, by that time the economy had recovered to the point that parents were able to pay tuition.

Washington

The trial described above had been held in the Daviess County seat of Washington, where years of negotiations with the Congregation had ensured that the parishes had supported Catholic education. Financial stresses had caused the Sacred Heart Brothers to withdraw, but when the Sisters of Providence agreed to teach high school boys, parishioners also supported the co-institutional central Catholic high school for children of both parish schools. No public assistance was sought. Though spared civic embroilments, the sisters at St. Simon did suffer greatly from the uncertainty caused by the somewhat bitter negotiations between the bishop and pastor and the council over the issue of taking on coeducational secondary education.

Loogootee

Meanwhile, at St. John, Loogootee, only a few miles farther east in Martin County, a situation similar to that in Vincennes prevailed. Founded in 1862, the parish school had expanded to include a small girls' high school. By 1932 the financial situation was such that the pastor followed the lead of his Vincennes colleagues and sought public assistance. Once again the state's obligation to educate the 310 elementary school pupils would have led to overcrowding. In January 1932, St.

John began operation as a public school with the grade school sisters being paid through the state relief fund.[62] Even when the $800 salary paid to each of the grade school teachers was extended to support the three high school teachers, a considerable surplus was available to send to the motherhouse.

The situation was of course threatened by the Vincennes lawsuit. In all likelihood St. John's parishioners traveled to the Daviess County Courthouse to hear the arguments. However, specific instructions from the state had made it possible for the Loogootee supervisor to manage teacher and pupil building assignments which satisfied all citizens. The ruling from the Indiana Supreme Court that qualified teachers could be paid from public funds was interpreted to mean that the status quo was satisfactory.[63] A later local historian describes the decision: "From that time on St. John Grade School was a public-parochial school, officially known as Elementary #2. The Sisters were retained as teachers. The public school corporation rented the St. John building and paid the teachers' salaries and other bills pertaining to the school."[64]

It seems strange to find four very different funding solutions in four adjoining counties, all in the same state. Perhaps the only explanation is the oft quoted maxim that all politics is local.

Convent Life during Hard Times

Undoubtedly this difficult period affected the daily lives of the sisters, certainly in terms of the frequent requests for prayers. A brief excerpt from the house diary of St. Simon Convent in Washington, Indiana, provides a poignant note of realism regarding the extent of the stress felt in many places. The music teacher "broke down, was taken home to build up, broke down again, then left for the remainder of the year. No one replaced her. Sister [X] gave out in April."[65] The sidebar on page 127 describes how one of the young women met in the opening pages of Chapter 1 found herself in the midst of this stressful situation.

Because of the normal practices of poverty, the sisters were accustomed to the relatively Spartan food and accommodations which many Americans were finding to be their lot, albeit not by choice. Occasional news from family letters would

The Life:

Sister Mary Patricia Carroll

Sister Berchmans rang the bell at her place at head table in the Foley Hall dining room and uttered the long-awaited words, "Benedicamus Domino!"

"Deo Gratias!" erupted the joyful response from the hundreds of sisters thus released from eight days of silence. It was August 15, 1934, and they had just heard their assignments for the following year as Bishop Chartrand read the Obedience List.

"Oh, Philip!" cried Sister Mary Patricia, hugging her friend, "I get to stay!"

At the conclusion of their novitiate days in March 1932, both Sister Mary Patricia Carroll and Sister Philip Conlin had been assigned to Our Lady of Sorrows in Chicago, but the following August Sister Mary Patricia had been changed to St. Joseph in Terre Haute. Then, after only three months teaching seventh grade, she was transferred to finish the year teaching first grade at St. Catherine in Indianapolis. On August 15, 1933, she was called for St. Simon in Washington, Indiana, to teach a combined fifth and sixth grade class. What a relief to know that the next year she would return to a familiar setting!

The situation was not unusual. The Congregation was responsible for supplying the entire faculty for each of its schools and when someone became ill, a replacement had to be found. Each sister was under obedience to accept her assignment and indeed, wanted to go where her superiors felt she was most needed. Although the horarium and curriculum were the same from one house to another, it was unusual for one so young to be switched among different grades.

Fortunately for Sister Mary Patricia, the superior carefully selected for St. Simon that year was the gentle and much experienced Sister Mary Stanislaus Graffe, former mistress of novices and later a provincial superior.

doubtless have apprised some sisters of the serious problems loved ones were facing, but such matters were not spoken of among themselves.[66] Because the parish was such a center of Catholic social life they would certainly have been aware of charitable outreach efforts and at times they were even able to be a part of these. For example, the superior at St. Sylvester in Chicago, Sister Rose Genevieve Flaherty, arranged to have hot coffee served in the warm furnace room at the convent to the unemployed who lined up outside in the winter.[67] The Sisters of Providence could count themselves lucky to have useful employment, sufficient food and adequate shelter.

The China Situation

Three new missionaries went to China in 1934 to strengthen the Ching I faculty—experienced high school teachers Sisters St. Francis Schultz and Francis de Sales Russell and music teacher Sister Elizabeth Cecile Harbison. Due to the success of its graduates in gaining admission to the university, enrollment at Ching I grew steadily in spite of increased political unrest. Several members of the Ying family had joined the faculty and when one of them, Ying Chen Li, became principal, they decided to play upon the patriotic impulses of the students to oust the foreign sisters and take control of the school. The following incident provides insight into the tensions of mission life.

For several years after its outright takeover of Manchuria, Japan had been extending its influence southward both by military means and by infiltration. By 1936 some Japanese held official posts in Kaifeng and on their visits to Ching I had taken an interest in the outdated *National Geographic* map Sister Francis de Sales had posted on her classroom wall, asking her to teach them the English names of the countries. During her explanation, she had used crayola to highlight China but had innocently left Manchuria the same color as Japan, causing some Chinese students to feel she was acknowledging that Manchuria belonged to the Japanese. Incensed by such insensitivity on the part of the foreign sisters and egged on by the rebellious faculty, a group of students seized the map and drew up a document demanding that Sister Marie Gratia turn over the school to the clique. Sister St. Francis recounts the confrontation:

Sister, astute woman that she was, calmly looked the paper up and down, turned it over, then said to the ring-leader: "This paper bears no chop (seal). Who is the responsible party? No person in China, you know as well as I, ever notices a paper that does not bear a seal."The day was won.The student leader lost face and departed in tears, packed her things, and left.[68]

In October 1936 Sisters Agnes Loyola Wolf and Mary Liguori Hartigan arrived to lend their energies to the mission. It was now possible to accept a new mission in Hsinhsiang. In 1937, two additional Americans, Sisters Mary Evangela O'Neill and Theodata Haggerty accompanied the returning Chinese Sisters of Providence, Sisters Agnes Joan and Bernadette, just as the Japanese invasion began in earnest. On their arrival they found Shanghai in shambles from the bombing and street fighting. Meanwhile Sister Mary Evangela's health had declined to the point that she needed to return home. She and Sister Elizabeth Cecile had barely departed for the United States when Kaifeng fell to the Japanese on June 6, 1938. The missionaries now had to carry on their work under Japanese army occupation, a situation to which we will return in Chapter 7.

Promotion of Mother Theodore's Cause

A key aspect of Mother Mary Raphael's spiritual leadership was her personal devotion to Mother Theodore. Two years after she came to Saint Mary-of-the-Woods to take up her duties as treasurer, Sister Mary Theodosia Mug's book, *The Life and Lifework of Mother Theodore Guérin*, was published, enabling her to become familiar with the foundress' counsels.[69] Residing at the motherhouse, she had a front seat as significant events played out during the following decade. She was present for the impressive services held when, on December 3, 1907, Mother Theodore's remains were transferred from the cemetery to the crypt of the recently dedicated Church of the Immaculate Conception. She participated in the excitement surrounding the news that part of Mother Theodore's brain had been preserved intact. Since she lived with Sister Mary Theodosia in Providence Convent, she no doubt observed her colleague's numerous health problems, so she was probably one of the first to notice Sister's renewed appetite and vigor after the October 30, 1908, healing, later certified as a miraculous cure. Very likely she sat among the sisters in the crypt on September 8, 1909, for the session opening the process for

Mother Theodore's canonization. Conversations with Mother Mary Cleophas about her experiences during her 1913 journey to Rome would certainly have enhanced Mother Mary Raphael's own respect and devotion to the foundress.

When in 1921 Father Emmanuel Ledvina, a priest of the Indianapolis Diocese who had served with the Extension Society for many years, was named as bishop of Corpus Christi, Texas, he asked to have his episcopal consecration take place at Saint Mary-of-the-Woods. Among the many distinguished prelates attending the impressive ceremony and banquet was Bishop Van de Ven of Alexandria, Louisiana. The occasion made him realize the importance of his diocesan archives' collection of correspondence between Bishop Martin and Mother Theodore, and he sent them on to Sister Mary Theodosia.[70]

As a close witness to all of these experiences, Mother Mary Raphael's own spirituality deepened, and six months after her election as superior general, she called for a novena of prayers for the Cause, exhorting the sisters to the charity which she felt would bring about the needed miracles.[71] In July, 1927, it was her privilege to receive confirmation from the Congregation for the Causes of Saints that the writings had been approved.

Shortly after she began her second term she called the attention of the council to the fact that the twenty-fifth anniversary of the transfer of the remains of Mother Theodore and Sisters St. Francis Xavier and Mary Joseph from the cemetery to vaults in the crypt of the Church of the Immaculate Conception was "a propitious time to reawaken in the hearts of our sisters a lively faith and devotion for the speedy canonization of our venerated foundress."[72] She actively used her contacts with the hierarchy to further the Cause. In November 1934, Cardinal Mundelein and other prelates signed the official petition supporting the Cause.[73] At her urging, in 1936 Bishop Ritter released Father Thomas Kilfoil to serve as postulator to undertake the necessary research in France. Mother Mary Raphael also authorized the continuation of Sister Mary Theodosia's editing work, resulting in the 1937 publication of the *Journals and Letters of Mother Theodore Guérin*. Not only did the volume provide excellent documentation for the upcoming centenary celebration, but generations of Sisters of Providence would be able to steep themselves in their foundress' remarkable spirit.

Another small volume printed for private circulation within the Congregation, *Biographical Sketches*, volume I, told the stories of the four succeeding superiors general. Three sisters had been commissioned to prepare the brief biographies: Sister Anita Cotter for Mother Mary Cecilia Bailly and Mother Mary Ephrem Glenn, Sister Francis Cecile Miller for Mother Anastasie Brown and Sister St. Cosmas Gallagher for Mother Euphrasie Hinkle. In her September 1937 letter introducing the work, Mother Mary Raphael stated her hope that, "This record will strengthen the bond of union between the past and present, so that as the present builds into the future we shall not be separated in affection from the Sisters who prepared the way for us."[74]

Home Improvements

The twelve years of Mother Mary Raphael's administration were hard times for the country as a whole, with widespread unemployment and the scrambling of political leaders to implement the reforms of the New Deal. By way of contrast, the first impression of anyone arriving on the motherhouse campus of Saint Mary-of-the-Woods would have been one of prosperity because of the major building projects and improvements that had gone forward during Mother Mary Cleophas' terms. Economic conditions certainly curtailed further projects, but several projects dear to the hearts of the sisters came to fruition during these years.

A little beyond the motherhouse itself, the senior residence at Rosary Hill was vacated on June 10, 1927, and eventually came to be used as a residence for motherhouse employees. The following year, on February 11, 1928, the Grotto of Our Lady of Lourdes was dedicated. In October of 1928 Saint Mary-of-the-Woods Village opened its very own United States Post Office, a short walk across the campus. The year 1929 saw the installation of an elevator in the infirmary and the illumination of the statue of Our Lady of the Campus.

A radio placed in the community room in 1926 made it possible to take vicarious part in events such as the International Eucharistic Congress held in Chicago. Radios gradually became part of the local houses in order to provide for cultural programs such as the Saturday opera broadcasts. During the summer of 1931 large portraits of each of the five former superiors general were unveiled in a presentation which included the reading of a short sketch of each one's life. After the sisters had departed for the missions, the campus became the site of the annual priests' retreat, with the many altars in the crypt used for their individual Masses. Less exciting but noteworthy was news that chickens from the poultry farm brought home prizes from the state fair that year.

Since 1909 a small Print Shop had been included within the various auxiliary buildings on campus, and in 1926 it was greatly expanded to provide for the printing of curriculum guides as well as event programs and pamphlets. From its presses the first edition of the beloved *Woodland Echoes*, a printed journal of summer events sent to the sisters on mission, was published on August 4, 1932. The column "Fifty Years Ago" provided details of one of the year's jubilarians— Mother Mary Raphael herself—as she entertained the sisters with tales of her travels from Galesburg in 1882.[75] Publication credits for the first edition list two sisters who would later rise to prominence: Sister Rose Angela Horan as editor-in-chief and Sister Theresa Aloyse Mount as associate editor. Coming "home" for summer school and retreat was so significant for the sisters that when economic conditions forced curtailment of the publication in 1933, an informal newsletter replaced it.

It would seem that Providence smiled on this enterprise when Sister Cecile Morse answered the call to religious life in 1935 at age twenty-six. She had learned the printer's trade in her father's shop and had pursued a career in the field before entering. From 1937 on she was assigned to the Print Shop, where her skills and talent were a true gift to the Congregation, making possible the label of "Providence Press" on many publications authored by Sisters of Providence.

Budget constraints prevented further campus improvements, one exception being the council's approval of Sister Catherine Miriam Butler's long-pursued dream of erecting outdoor Stations of the Cross along the driveway to the cemetery in 1937.

While the grounds themselves seemed little changed to the twenty-eight sisters arriving on June 24, 1938, for the General Chapter, Mother Mary Raphael's report would show that much indeed had changed. At age seventy-five, after twelve years marked by so many challenges, it was time for her to step down from the responsibilities of office.

The reader who is eager to know how the Congregation overcame the difficulties and obstacles described in this chapter will want to bypass Chapter 5 and Chapter 6 and go directly to Chapter 7. The reader who is curious about the underlying organic developments which prepared the members for changes yet to come will take a detour to answer two questions. First, how did the Congregation adapt the governance structure to manage the coast-to-coast expansion and growth spurt? Chapter 5 will explore in detail the efforts begun during Mother Mary Raphael's administration to implement the proposed plan of reorganizing the traditional home-based governance system into a regional-based system of provinces. Second, how were new members prepared to commit themselves to a life of spiritual growth and dedicated service? Chapter 6 explains the formation system of the times. At that point, Chapter 7 will pick up the thread of ongoing events beginning with the Chapter of 1938.

❧ Chapter 5
Attempts at Provinces
1933-1949

Sisters set out for their missions from the Saint Mary-of-the-Woods train station, August, 1940.

Long-Range Plans

The chronicle of the development of the Congregation during the first half of the twentieth century in the previous chapters has made periodic reference to provinces. A closer look at the efforts to incorporate an intermediate administrative structure provides insight into the spirit that animated the Congregation. Its steady growth during Mother Mary Cleophas' 1890-1926 administrations had stretched the capacity of the council to sustain the personal style of governance which had characterized its early years.[1] It was increasingly clear that decentralization would have two major benefits. The proximity of a provincial superior would make her more available to the sisters and help restore the warm founding spirit of Mother Theodore. At the same time, continuing the practice of regu-

larly returning to Saint Mary-of-the-Woods for study and retreat would sustain the tradition of the motherhouse as the
heart of the Congregation.[2] The canonical solution was to reorganize into provinces. The Sisters of Providence solution
would prove to be quite different.

On the cusp of the new century, Mother Mary Cleophas
undertook to use the evolving canonical structures to support
the growth of the Congregation by setting the wheels in motion to decentralize its administration.

Geographic Expansion

Toward this end, the frequent requests from priests to staff
schools were prioritized so as to establish the necessary geographical spread to support such a venture. During Mother
Mary Cleophas' second term, the Congregation gradually withdrew from the Michigan foundations and looked to the East
Coast for new fields. In Massachusetts, the Sisters of Providence presence begun at St. Rose, Chelsea, in 1899 was
strengthened by the addition of the two missions of Sacred
Heart, Malden (1908), and St. Patrick, Stoneham (1912). A
1902 invitation to open an academy in Washington, D.C., the
nation's capital and the site of the newly established Catholic
University of America, was most welcome. Lengthy negotiations resulted in the opening of St. Ann, Holy Trinity and
Immaculata in 1905, followed by Dunblane in 1913.[3]

The minutes of the 1914 General Chapter show that Mother
Mary Cleophas sought and received confirmation from the
delegates as to the necessity of this eventual change. "The rapid
growth of the community makes it evident that this may be
necessary within a few years. All the members of the Chapter
signified their entire approval and consent."[4] The Book of Important Events describes how she followed up with the 1919
purchase of extensive property "with a fine large residence ...
for a Provincial Motherhouse" in Hyattsville, Maryland.[5]
Named Maryhurst, it opened as a residence for sister students
at Catholic University in 1920 and as an elementary school
the following year.

Requests had also come from the West Coast. When Mother
Mary Cleophas and Sister Mary Alma Ryan traveled to California in 1916 as guests of Frances Wilhoit Hampton, a graduate of the college, they perceived the ministerial possibilities as

well as the health-related advantages of the mild climate. Although they were unable to accept several offers of parish schools, when Bishop John Cantwell visited St. Mary-of-the-Woods in 1921 to solicit assistance, his guarantee of episcopal support reinforced their desire to expand the mission from coast to coast.

Beginnings of Provincial Structure

Legal Advice

Although the 1870 First Vatican Council had called for a total update of the vast body of church law which had evolved in bits and pieces over the centuries, due to the political upheaval in Europe that culminated in World War I, the work suffered many delays. Created in 1904, Cardinal Gaspari's Commission for Canon Law spanned two pontificates before the remarkably comprehensive compendium it compiled was promulgated as the 1917 Code of Canon Law. The norms regarding religious congregations, which had been published separately, were incorporated into the code. Although a revised translation of the 1897 Sisters of Providence *Constitutions* had appeared in 1915, a complete updating to bring it in conformity with the new code was needed. To assist with this project, the community engaged the services of Father George M. Sauvage, CSC, who would be an active liaison with the Congregation for Religious for the implementation of the plan for provinces.

Born in France, after service in the French army Father Sauvage joined the Congregation of Holy Cross in 1895 just at the time the French government was severely restricting religious congregations. General Superior Father Gilbert Français had closed down the French province, bringing most of its members to the United States, so the young seminarian was sent to Rome for his studies. After his ordination in 1899, Father Sauvage completed advanced studies and then was assigned to teach at Holy Cross College in Washington, D.C., from 1903 to 1914, where he may have made the acquaintance of the Sisters of Providence. Since he was a French citizen, he was recalled during World War I to service in the French army as an interpreter for the British Expeditionary Force.[6]

The organization of the Congregation of Holy Cross was typical of many religious congregations whose members were spread not only across several dioceses, but also across different countries. For them, the provincial structure was ideal. The generalate office in Rome was a central administrative heart with a general superior and council elected from across the membership. The geographic provinces each had their own administration in the persons of a provincial superior and council to direct all the activities of that area, including its charitable works, property, finances and novitiate. Each province contributed money and staff personnel to the general administration. Even though he was a member of the American province, after the war, because of his expertise, Father Sauvage was appointed procurator general at the Holy Cross Congregation's generalate office in Rome.

During his time there, he also served as a consultant to the Congregation of Religious. Given the close association of the Congregation of the Holy Cross with the Sisters of Providence, since both groups traced their roots to Father Dujarié's foundation, he was an ideal choice to provide canonical assistance. It was for this purpose that he came to Saint Mary-of-the-Woods in June 1926 just prior to the Chapter that elected Mother Mary Raphael. Although the intention of the new council was to begin the provinces right away, he advised them to first concentrate on updating the existing *Constitutions*. After returning to Rome, he wrote to Mother Mary Raphael:

> Will you allow me the liberty, since you are preparing the division of your Congregation into Provinces, to advise you to examine this question with all its aspects and most carefully. It is such an important stage in the life of a Congregation and it is so difficult to correct successfully an organization, after it has already been in operation![7]

His advice was accepted and indeed would prove prophetic. The consultations on the necessary revisions to the Rule gradually went forward and were approved on June 2, 1928. As we saw in Chapter 4, the amended edition of the Sister of Providence Rules and *Constitutions* was printed and issued in 1929. This gradual approach to provinces allowed time both for geographic expansion and also for study and experimentation of the best ways to implement an intermediate level of government.

Internal Delays

No one could have predicted the other major events that would eventually derail the project, but in fact the Congregation's existing structure and practices would become obstacles to its success. Certainly the transition to a new superior general for the first time in thirty-six years complicated matters. Much more the steady and serious worker than the visionary leader, Mother Mary Raphael carried forward Mother Mary Cleophas' initiatives, but especially after the death of her friend and long-time mentor in December 1928, her poor health further diminished the possibility of immediate change.

The most significant obstacle was the sheer weight of normal administrative duties. The *Constitutions* clearly stated that the major responsibility of the superior general and her council was to further the mission of the Congregation: "to honor Divine Providence, and to promote God's merciful designs upon mankind, by devoting itself to works of charity."[8] Over the years, "works of charity" had focused on education, partly to found and staff female academies, and partly, in cooperation with the hierarchy, to staff parish schools. The major resource for carrying out this mission was the sisters themselves. This fact required forming and educating new members, arranging for their certification as teachers and caring for their health. Arrangements for appropriate placement of sisters to fit the specialized needs of each mission had become an annual manipulation of the pieces of a gigantic jigsaw puzzle. Personal correspondence was voluminous. "Temporalities," or the funding, building and maintenance of properties, consumed a tremendous amount of time.

Little time and energy remained for the creative thinking needed to realign the administrative structure. In addition, the stable economic infrastructure established during the twenties suffered the initial shock and then the ongoing dislocations of the Great Depression. When Mother Mary Raphael met with her council after Mass in January 1929, her discouragement was apparent. She had recently returned from a sick leave only to be overwhelmed again, commenting, "The community is now too large to reach and care for the individual Sisters."[9] The following month she was encouraged to go to Van Nuys, California, for an extended leave of absence from her duties.

Tentative Plans

It was not until 1930 that the matter of provinces received attention. Writing to Cardinal Lèpicier in May, Mother Mary Raphael pleaded, "As we are now 1,148 members, it is growing more and more impossible to reach all according to our desire."[10] The council discussed the location of the future provincial houses, but Bishop Chartrand did not feel the time was ripe. Mother Mary Raphael was convinced that smaller geographic areas would ease the strain on finances and on her assistants, so she pressed the issue. In August she wrote to Bishop Chartrand, noting that the Holy Cross Sisters' move into provinces could be interpreted to mean that the Fort Wayne Diocese was ahead of the Indianapolis Diocese.[11] This suggestion of lesser status apparently had the desired effect because the very next day he replied, asking for a map of the proposed division indicating the territories of the proposed provinces.

Table 5 showing the allocation of houses according to the proposed plan indicates a very uneven distribution.

TABLE 5: *Distribution of establishments by province, 1931*

Province	Houses		Location of provincial house
	By state	Total	
Indiana	Indiana 38 Oklahoma 1	39	St. Mary-of-the-Woods, Diocese of Indianapolis
Illinois	Illinois 24	24	Marywood, Evanston Archdiocese of Chicago
Eastern	Massachusetts 3 Maryland 3 District of Columbia 1 North Carolina 1	8	Maryhurst, Hyattsville, Archdiocese of Baltimore
Western	California	3	St. Joseph, Hawthorne, Diocese of Los Angeles

Finally, in August 1931, a formal request for the division of the Congregation into provinces together with a letter from Bishop Chartrand was sent to their old friend and cardinal protector, Cardinal Alexis Lépicier, who was also Prefect of the Congregation for Religious.[12] An official rescript from the Sacred Congregation of Religious dated February 15, 1932, authorized the division of the Congregation into four provinces, with the long range plan of eventually establishing a fifth province in China.

In June 1932 the General Chapter convened, no doubt expecting to enact the long-anticipated government restructuring. Although Fourth Assistant Sister Mary Ignatia Hanson had worked hard to prepare a preliminary proposal of how the arrangement would affect Congregation operations, because of the press of other business and the fact that her health had declined, the Chapter members received no report. It is not surprising that Sister Catherine Marie Daly asked about the matter. Based on previous consultations Bishop Chartrand was able to announce that there would indeed be four provinces: one in the West, one in the East, one in Indiana, and one in Illinois, but neither he nor the council elaborated with specific details. Frustrated on this front and concerned about her health, the delegates almost unseated Mother Mary Raphael, and they did elect several new councilors.

Thus alerted to the community's concerns and the need to move forward, the following month Bishop Chartrand urged Mother Mary Raphael:

> Since some provisional rule has to be established to regulate provincial matters I have undertaken to sketch what that rule is to be…. Changes can be suggested that experience seems to dictate. In that way an actual provincial law of a provisional nature can be worked out during the next few years.[13]

He also advised consultation with the Holy Cross Sisters who had made similar arrangements two years previously. Excellent though this advice was, its legal language simply did not resonate with Mother Mary Raphael's assessment of the signs of the times. Money and morale were her chief concerns. Nonetheless, the gradually building momentum could not be resisted.

Initiation of Provinces

Eager to follow up on the agreement to establish a province in California, Bishop Cantwell issued a press release describing the new headquarters of the Sisters of Providence at Hawthorne. Having had no official notice from the motherhouse, the California sisters learned of the plan in May 1933 through the diocesan newspaper, *The Tidings*.[14] It was necessary to move quickly. However, Mother Mary Raphael's hastily devised plan to announce and implement the move to provinces was met with resistance on the part of the council. Since it had already been decided that only a limited number of sisters could come home that summer, she reasoned that grouping many of the sisters in four Chicago houses would help these sisters to begin to establish regional bonds. Her immediate concern was the savings which would be effected, but she had not given thought to the fact that many of those sisters needed essential classes for certification. The entire carefully constructed summer assignment list had to be completely changed to accommodate this need.

Her letter circular of June 15, 1933, rather than setting out a clear course of action for separating the whole Congregation into four distinct provinces, retained the focus of a call to summer assignments and retreat. It was a back door approach in which she touched upon one of the major difficulties inherent in the plan, the deep-seated attachment of all the sisters to the motherhouse.

> This surrender [God] expects from you, particularly, in whatever His decision may be concerning the division of the Community and your place in them. This separation may be a costly sacrifice, as it certainly will be a sacrifice for those who are not to come to their loved Home this summer. ... They are not severing the ties which have so long bound them to this loved spot, round which their fondest recollections cling. No, they will have their turn; some next year, others the year following.[15]

Thus it was clear from the beginning that the sisters could expect to retain their ties to Saint Mary's. However, little else was clear. From Mother Mary Raphael's point of view, one of the major benefits of the plan would be easing the stress on the central administration by supplying a major superior closer to the sisters on the missions. The next step in the gradual transition to a formal provincial government was to begin to have the sisters relate to a provincial superior. Appointment to the office would establish the role; later the sisters in each province would elect their own superior. For these first appointments, when the council took up the topic in July 1933, it became clear that Mother Mary Raphael thought of the provincial superior as having delegated authority rather than authority flowing from the office itself.[16] The council minutes list the qualities she would look for in a candidate. She stated that a provincial should be "humble and dependent . . . one that will do nothing without consulting Home Superiors."[17]

What was their role to be? Some preliminary work on the provincial structures had been done during the 1926-1932 term by Fourth Assistant Sister Mary Ignatia, who had compiled interim rules for provinces drawn from canon law and other religious communities. After modifications, the relevant sections were published in a small booklet, "Rules for Provincial Superiors," indicating their responsibility to "govern and watch over the respective Provinces assigned to them, under the authority and surveillance of the Superior General. By exemplary behavior and annual visitation of the houses, she shall spare nothing to render the Sisters happy in their vocation."[18] Apparently the audience for the booklet was the superiors themselves, but not the sisters, since there is no indication that it was published to the Congregation at large.

How were the sisters informed of the expectations inherent in the new structure? A letter from Mother Mary Raphael to local superiors told them to keep in close communication with the provincial superior, who could now grant most permissions. In a letter to the sisters she explained the line of command. "In fact, the Sisters are advised to take their difficulties to the Home Superiors only when the Local Superior or the Provincial Superior cannot or will not adjust these difficulties."[19] In the same letter the local superiors were told that "The Sister Provincial will visit each mission at least once a year; see the Sisters, and visit the school."[20]

Appointment of Provincial Superiors

And who were these provincial superiors? While the council didn't wholeheartedly endorse Mother Mary Raphael's choices, they clearly saw the importance of selecting women who would quickly gain the confidence of the sisters. All were well known and respected throughout the community as school women and local superiors. Because of its size, an assistant provincial was appointed for the Illinois province.

The East: Sister Aloyse Hennessey
1879-1952

Mary Hennessey became acquainted with the Sisters of Providence as a pupil at St. Patrick School in Indianapolis and three years after graduation entered the novitiate at age nineteen. Novice Mistress Sister Basilissa Heiner quickly spotted her wonderful combination of academic potential and easy disposition. After profession, Sister Aloyse taught at seven missions in seven years before going to Immaculata in Washington, D.C., in 1908. She taught at Immaculata while taking classes at Catholic University, earning a master's degree in 1914 as well as the appellation, "a round peg to fit in any hole." In 1914 at age thirty-five, she was elected sixth councilor during Mother Mary Cleophas' fourth term, serving alongside her mentor, Sister Basilissa, and assisting her in the duties of supervisor of schools. She was reelected to the council for the 1920-1926 term, after which she served as mistress of novices from 1926 to1933. Mother Mary Raphael chose her to serve as the first provincial superior of the East at Maryhurst from 1933 to1939. In 1947 she returned to the East for her final assignment as mistress of novices from 1947 until the novitiate closed in 1949.

The West: Sister Regina Clare Carlos
1889-1955

Born in Connersville, Indiana, Mary Carlos attended high school at the Academy at Saint Mary-of-the-Woods, entering the community in 1907 at age eighteen. She taught high school at Providence in Chicago and Cheverus in Malden, Massachusetts, for fifteen years before being appointed superior at St. Simon, Washington, Indiana, at age thirty-one. She went on to serve in the same capacity at Cheverus, St. Joseph, Hammond, St. John, Loogootee, and St.

John Academy, Indianapolis. She was appointed provincial for the West in 1933 at age forty-four. When her appointment ended in 1939, she returned to high school teaching.

Indiana: Sister Mary Rose Cummings 1885-1966

Born in Alton, Illinois, Helen Cummings was educated by the Sisters of Providence and at age twenty-three followed her sister, Sister Josetta Marie, to the Congregation. She taught middle and upper grades at four different missions before being named local superior of St. Mary, Aurora, at age thirty-seven, going on to serve in this capacity at St. Leo and St. Andrew in Chicago, Sacred Heart in Evansville, and St. Patrick in Indianapolis. She was appointed Indiana Provincial at age forty-eight, but did not complete the term because the 1938 Chapter elected her fourth assistant to Mother Mary Bernard. She then served as a local superior in Chicago until her 1946-1949 appointment as Illinois provincial, after which she returned to elementary classrooms until her retirement.[21]

Illinois: Sister Francis Borgia Brophy 1867-1934

Catherine Brophy followed her two older sisters across the Wabash River from Terre Haute to the novitiate at Saint Mary-of-the-Woods in 1886 at age nineteen. She spent her early years as a teacher at St. Rose, Chelsea. After a year at St. Columbkille in Chicago she was named superior at Our Lady of Sorrows, then at Sacred Heart in Malden, St. Rose in Chelea and St. Mel in Chicago before returning to St. Columbkille's for ten years. As an eighth grade boys' teacher, she was known as firm and stern, but always kind-hearted and prayerful. Appointed in 1933 as the first provincial in the Illinois province, when she became extremely ill that year, her assistant, Sister Carita, took over her duties. She died a year later at age sixty-seven.

Sister Carita Kiley 1893-1959

Ann Kiley and her two sisters lived in Our Lady of Sorrows Parish, were educated by the Sisters of Providence at Our Lady of Providence Academy and went on to enter the novitiate at Saint Mary-of-the-Woods. Ann entered in 1912 at age nineteen, her sister Kathleen (Sister Annunciata) followed two years later and their younger sister Frances (Sister Robert) entered in 1928. After her profession, Sister Carita's first assignment was under Sister Gertrude Clare at Marywood, Evanston. In 1920 she lived at Maryhurst, Hyattsville, and studied at Catholic University She earned her MA from Fordham in 1928, then returned to Marywood as superior and principal until assuming the duties of assistant, then provincial superior of the Illinois province in 1933. When her term ended, she served as dean of women at Saint Mary-of-the-Woods College until her appointment as provincial superior of the West from 1945-1949. After six years as superior at Ladywood, Indianapolis, she returned to the classroom until her death.

ॐ

Announcement and Implementation

The official announcement of the division of the Congregation into provinces was made to the sisters during the August 1933 retreat. At the same time, a news release through the National Catholic Welfare Conference was published in diocesan newspapers announcing the names of the provincial superiors and the locations of the provincial houses. At Marywood, Evanston, the house diary simply records the new arrangement with no elaboration: "Marywood was appointed the provincial house of Illinois, with Sister Francis Borgia as Provincial and Sister Carita the Assistant Provincial and Local Superior."[22] Although the Indiana province was to be headquartered at Saint Mary-of-the-Woods, no note is made of its beginning or the location of an office for Sister Mary Rose. The only province to have an independent house also had the only formal inaugural statement; the Maryhurst, Hyattsville, diarist wrote: "From Immaculata, Sister Aloyse went to Maryhurst, which with her arrival became the Provincial House of the Eastern Province."[23]

In fact, once the words of blessing and encouragement following the August retreat had died away and the four women arrived at their new domiciles, they must have felt considerable trepidation. An earlier anonymous historian of the provinces provides this account:

> The effect of this communication [the letter to local superiors] was to cause great perplexity to the Provincials whose powers had not yet been defined by Constitutions, and to the Sisters who had been accustomed to an exact definition of what they might do, and to whom they should address themselves for permissions of varying importance.
>
> Further confusion was caused by the fact that the Provincials, some of whom had not been specially trained for supervision, were empowered to visit the schools and, implicitly also, to suggest changes. This power was further complicated by the fact that the General Election of 1932 had removed the Supervisor of Schools [Sister Francis Joseph Elbreg] from the General Council, although she still retained the office and the duties of General Supervisor. One member of the Council [Sister Eugenia Clare Cullity] was assigned to the work of Councilor on Education, and further misunderstandings resulted.[24]

The rationale for subdividing the community was most evident on the East and West Coasts due to the distance involved. The train trip to Boston or Washington, D.C., took one and a half days, while to reach southern California, travelers could expect to spend a day and a half and two nights on the train. Telephones had become more common and more reliable, but were more useful for messages rather than real conversation. Rather than sending a home superior to assist a local community which was experiencing great difficulty, having a provincial nearer at hand would be most helpful and this role often proved a boon to the home superiors.

The East Coast, with a large house on extensive wooded acreage near to the nation's capital and an experienced superior familiar with the area, was well equipped for the change. However, on the West Coast, one of the first responsibilities of the newly appointed provincial superior, Sister Regina Clare, was to locate and purchase a suitable property. Bishop Cantwell recommended taking over a small girls' school in Anaheim and, after lengthy negotiations, this was arranged.[25]

The ambitious goal of starting up the new high school with a new faculty in the fall of 1934 at the same time as the move of the provincial house from Hawthorne to Anaheim and the start-up of a novitiate was daunting.

The appropriate lines of authority were very confusing. The property at Anaheim included schoolrooms, a dormitory and cafeteria for boarders and a convent area which could accommodate postulants and novices. The previous school had not established a strong reputation and the Congregation was new to the area. The sister appointed as local superior and principal was an experienced academy teacher, Sister St. Philomene Cullity. However, she came to this task after ten years at the premier academy of Marywood, Evanston, and, at age forty-seven, she had never been a principal or superior. At the same time, Sister Regina Clare moved her provincial office into the convent and had the responsibility of setting up facilities for a novitiate; in fact she had also been appointed to be mistress of novices, a double appointment, which was not permitted by Canon Law.

Although Sister Regina Clare did have experience as a superior and principal, the council wanted the fledgling West Coast high school to get off to a good start, so Fifth Assistant and Director of Education Sister Eugenia Clare Cullity was sent to assist with the organization required for the opening of Marywood High School, Anaheim. There were now three superiors: a home superior, a provincial superior and a local superior. Not only that, but two of these superiors, Sister St. Philomene Cullity and Sister Eugenia Clare Cullity were blood sisters. Who was in charge of what? Letters went back and forth between Mother Mary Raphael, Sister Regina Clare and Sister St. Philomene as these difficulties were gradually sorted out.

Having appointed the provincials and sent them off, further work on the provinces on the part of the council was not a major priority. Decisions regarding necessary adaptations were made on an ad hoc basis by the superior general and her council. The council minutes provide an example of how questions which came up were handled.

> It is thought that the Supervisor's [of schools] work from now on will be in Indiana and Illinois. The Western and Eastern Provincials will take care of their own supervision. It is de-

cided not to duplicate names in the Community. The aspirants from the various Provinces will come Home to make their Second Novitiate.[26]

The untimely death of Bishop Chartrand in December 1933, followed by the installation of his auxiliary Bishop Joseph Ritter as his successor in March 1934, further delayed substantial planning. In June 1936 the death of Cardinal Lèpicier, the community's long-time friend and cardinal protector in Rome, left an additional gap in the hierarchical chain of command. However, with the next General Chapter only two years away, there was an urgent need to prepare specific proposals regarding the provinces for its consideration. Mother Mary Raphael wrote to Bishop Ritter "to ask that your Excellency will grant permission to have the four Provincials declared members of the General chapter *ex officio*."[27] His reply noted certain restrictions: "This permission is granted, however, for the time being only and subject to any change or modification that the Holy See may make in approving the proposed Rules for Provinces."[28]

While the sisters' day-to-day lives experienced minor alterations, as shown in the sidebar featuring Sister Philip Conlin, it was the task of the council to provide the required canonical format. Fifth Assistant Sister Eugenia Clare was given the responsibility of preparing a draft of a revision of the Rules to present to the 1938 chapter. When this draft was given to Bishop Ritter in July 1936, he quickly noted the "very little independence given to the provinces," which he felt "would nullify the very purpose you are striving to achieve, namely to keep the order from becoming unwieldy in its management and government."[29] He recommended consultation with the canonist who had assisted with the 1929 *Constitutions*. In November 1936, Mother Mary Raphael sent the draft to Father Sauvage to solicit his advice. His reply provided much for her and the council to ponder:

> I have read this draft. There is much that is good in it. However, many modifications and additions will be required to put it in harmony with Canon Law and with the jurisdiction of the Sacred Congregation.
>
> You must also realize that the establishment of Provinces implies modifications which affect more or less directly and seriously other parts of the Constitutions, as for example, the admission to Novitiate and to Profession, the composition of

The Life:

Sister Philip Conlin

Kneeling among her band members in the crypt chapel in March 1937, Sister Philip slipped her right hand down to feel the crucifix on the chaplet hanging from her waistband.

Yes, it was really in a new place, hanging below the circle of beads to indicate that she was now finally professed. Listening to Sister Gertrude Clare's beautiful meditations and reflecting prayerfully on their meaning during the thirty day retreat had prepared her to add a vigorous "forever!" to the vows she had pronounced the previous day. Now, at the end of her second novitiate, she awaited her new assignment. Unlike her four Boston companions, she had been assigned to only one mission during her time of temporary profession. On this day she smiled broadly as she sat when she heard, "Sister Philip, St. Clement, Lansdowne." After eleven years in the Midwest, she was returning to the East Coast.

Once the provincial structure was begun in 1933, placements were gradually being arranged to assign sisters to their "home" areas. Leaving the thirty-plus sister Our Lady of Sorrows convent in Chicago for the small Washington, D.C., suburban parish school would be a big change, but she would continue to teach first and second graders. Although she didn't know her local superior, Sister St. Cyrilla, perhaps the smaller size of the eastern province would make it easier to consult the provincial superior if she had need. Indeed, Sister Aloyse would certainly remember her from novitiate days.

Sister Philip would go on to experience the provincial structure from the viewpoint of the East. Two years later she was assigned to teach at her home parish, St. Rose in Chelsea, probably teaching the children of her former classmates.

the General Chapter, the relations of the Provinces with the general administration, etc.... As you know, of course, this last point is one of the most delicate in the life of a Community and so should be determined with great prudence and precision.

To tell the whole truth, it seems to me extremely difficult the work may be done satisfactorily, unless it be done by a collaboration of the Consultor in charge with you and your council. There are many points which may be decided in various ways, but in fact, cannot be decided in the way more consonant with your tradition and spirit, unless you have the opportunity to present your own views and reasons.[30]

Clearly, Father Sauvage's years of association with the Sisters of Providence had sensitized him to their unique needs and he understood the importance of taking the time for an in-depth conversation in order to be of real assistance. He stated his intention of going to Notre Dame in the spring and of meeting with the council then. If such an arrangement would unduly delay matters, he proposed that the council could submit the draft to the Sacred Congregation and appoint another consultant. Rather than lose the benefit of his experience, Mother Mary Raphael readily agreed to meet with him when he came to Indiana, but unfortunately his plans fell through. It was not until August 1937 that he was able to send a redaction of the draft, aligning its articles with the requirements of law.

Father Sauvage advised that this revised draft be presented to the 1938 chapter for any modifications they might suggest. Although he did come to Notre Dame in the summer of 1938, his obligations to the Holy Cross General Chapter there prevented him from coming to Saint Mary-of-the-Woods to assist with preparation of the materials for the sisters' Chapter. Nonetheless, Mother Vincentia, CSC, urged Mother Mary Raphael not to miss the opportunity for a personal consultation. "He is so learned, so gracious and so insistent on the type of religious discipline that you and I approve that I know a talk with him would be comforting to you."[31]

The General Chapter of 1938

Unfortunately, the 1938 General Chapter of the Sisters of Providence was already in session when Mother Vincentia's letter arrived, precluding any such meeting. At age seventy-five, after thirty-six years in general administration, Mother Mary Raphael was happy to pass the responsibility of leading the Congregation to her loyal assistant of the previous years, Sister Mary Bernard Laughlin, who was elected superior general on the first ballot. After these elections, the Chapter went on to consider the major agenda item of incorporating into the *Constitutions* the amendments and new sections relative to provinces. Copies of the revised *Constitutions* were provided, but none of the delegates except the ex-officio council members had seen and studied them previously.[32] In order to expedite the business, Bishop Ritter suggested that the *Constitutions* be read aloud. Delegates expressed concern about fairness of representation from the smaller provinces, as well as reducing the visitation of home superiors in favor of provincials. The minutes state:"The General Chapter then accepted the proposed plan for Provincial *Constitutions* with the modifications above stated, with the understanding that further revisions may be made, if found desirable, at the next meeting of the General Chapter." The session devoted to this discussion opened at 1:30 p.m. and adjourned at 3:45 p.m.

The following month Bishop Ritter, who had spoken with Father Sauvage at Notre Dame, wrote to Mother Mary Bernard to urge her to take the opportunity to visit with the consultant, whom he described as "about the most capable person, experience and knowledge, as well as interested, that you could possibly have to take up these matters with."[33] Applying his episcopal perspective to the situation of the Sisters of Providence Congregation, the bishop stated his concerns strongly:

> [Father Sauvage] expressed himself so definitely as to the importance of these constitutions and also of you coming personally to take up the matter with him that of my own accord I told him I would write you to this effect. ...After all, the future of Providence community lies in these constitutions—if they are not wisely drawn up it may in the end mean the alienation and possible separation of the provinces.[34]

The very next week Mother Mary Bernard and her newly elected Fourth Assistant Sister Mary Rose (recently the Indiana provincial), together with Sister Eugenia Clare (who had not been re-elected, but had drawn up the draft of the *Constitutions* to incorporate provinces) traveled to Notre Dame to meet with Father Sauvage on August 8-9, 1938. The Book of Important Events chronicles the results of this meeting. Father Sauvage "read our rules page by page and commented on it.

The changes were few. He wanted to have our work completed on the *Constitutions* in order to take them with him when he leaves for Rome in September. Mother M. Bernard thinks this cannot be done."[35] Again, canonical corrections took a back seat to the practical realities facing a new administration.

When Mother Mary Bernard reported to the council as to topics about which the council had been doubtful, the focus of her remarks was not on moving the experimentation to a new level by giving the provincial superiors the actual power of that office, but rather on incidental yet more immediate items such as the formula for the vows or the fact that the College would be part of the Indiana Province. She noted that the draft of the revised *Constitutions* stated clearly that "The Provincial Superior has the immediate authority over all the houses and sisters of her Province,"[36] but made no comment as to the effect this extremely significant change would have on her own role as superior general. Despite Bishop Ritter's hopes that a face-to-face meeting between Father Sauvage and the new council would help the Congregation to better utilize the model of provinces described in canon law to advance its mission, it is very unclear as to what mutual understanding was arrived at through this consultation. The one person most competent to carry forward the work, Sister Eugenia Clare, was on her way to a new assignment.

By November, the required documents were sufficiently organized to take to Bishop Ritter in preparation for his trip to Rome the following year. It was to be only a few months after that, on August 4, 1939, that news would reach them of Father Sauvage's incapacitating stroke. Mother Mary Bernard was content to have the revisions remain words on paper while continuing the policies and practices of her predecessor. She did take Bishop Ritter's suggestion that a sister be sent to study canon law, assigning Sister Eugenia Logan for a summer course at St. Louis University in 1941.[37] The superior general and the home superiors continued to conduct visitations and assign the sisters to their missions, but they also relied on the provincials to provide reports based on their visitations and to troubleshoot local emergencies.

1939 Provincial Appointments

In August, when the provincials' six-year terms expired, replacements were appointed. Again, care was taken to ensure that all of those appointed had the confidence of the sisters, as each of the appointees had been elected as a delegate to one or more General Chapters.

East: Sister St. Eugenia McBarron 1874-1966

When Maud McBarron's mother was widowed, their uncle, Father Eugene McBarron, was appointed the guardian for her and her three sisters. They grew up in New Albany, Indiana, where they were educated by the Sisters of Providence. Maud entered the community in 1890 at age sixteen, receiving the name Sister St. Eugenia. Her younger sister Anna later followed her, receiving the name of Sister Frances Helen. Sister St. Eugenia's first mission was Our Lady of Sorrows in Chicago where her superior, Sister Mary Raphael, got her off to a good start as a middle grade teacher. After teaching for seventeen years at six schools, including six years with the "minims" at the Academy at Saint Mary-of-the-Woods, she was appointed superior to open St. Francis Xavier in Wilmette in 1912. After assignments at nine schools in thirteen years, she was again appointed superior at three schools within four years before finding a secure niche as superior at Providence High School, 1933-1939. Although she was somewhat frail and delicate, her innate dignity, deeply pious nature and gentle humor served her well in these duties. One sister described her as "so exact that one could tell the time by her coming." At age sixty-five she was appointed provincial of the East, serving from 1939 to1945. After three years as local superior she was again appointed as provincial of Indiana, 1948-1949, retiring shortly thereafter.

West: Sister Mary Stanislaus Graffe 1878-1971

Amelia Graffe was born into the pioneer Fort Wayne family of George and Mary Graffe in 1878. When she was sixteen she and her sister Mary (later Sister Clare Marie) entered the community. After professing vows in 1898 she went west to teach high school at Savannah, Illinois, and Omaha, Nebraska,

and then in Chicago. Described as naturally reserved and deeply pious, she was also considered "affable and approachable" and a fine choice to be appointed as mistress of novices at age thirty, a position she filled from 1908 to 1914. She then went on to a series of appointments as local superior, including opening Marywood, Evanston, and Ladywood, Indianapolis. In 1938 at age sixty she was appointed mistress of novices at Marywood, Anaheim. The following year she went on to serve as provincial of the West 1939-1945. After two additional terms as local superior, she retired to the motherhouse.

Illinois: Sister Margaret Donelan 1874-1949

Martha Donelan came to the novitiate in 1895 at age twenty, following her aunt, Sister Mary Ellen Donelan, to the community. After gaining experience as an upper grade teacher she was appointed local superior at St. Mel, Chicago, immediately after her final profession. Except for two one-year teaching assignments she continued to serve as local superior at thirteen schools from 1912 to1940, including six years at St. Vincent Orphanage in Vincennes and eleven years in separate terms at Reitz Memorial in Evansville. Over the years she gained a reputation as a strong advocate of community life, setting the example by her competence and willingness to help, so her opinion and advice were valued. At age sixty-five she was appointed Illinois provincial, serving from 1939 to1944. After an additional term as local superior, she retired to the motherhouse.

Indiana

Although little is recorded as to the duties of the Indiana provincial, this post had considerable turnover. Because the first Indiana provincial, Sister Mary Rose, had been elected to the General Council in 1938, Sister St. Louise Bordenet had filled in at the post after fifteen years as econome at the motherhouse. Her death a year later at age seventy-three led to the appointment of Sister Berchmans Collins, who had also served briefly as econome at St. Mary-of-the-Woods in 1920, as well as having been elected second assistant on the General Council during Mother Mary Raphael's first term.[38] She too died in office and was replaced in 1942 by Sister Aloysius Clare Wilkinson.

By the time Mother Mary Bernard began her administration, the advantages of having an intermediate level of government working closely with the general administration were evident. However, the additional effort needed to formally erect four independent government units, each with its own offices and personnel, loomed as an impossible burden. A suggestion to investigate the use of vicariates, a system in which the intermediate superior acts as an agent of the superior general, a model used by the Society of the Sacred Heart, was not followed up. Financial worries persisted as the Great Depression lengthened. Strict economy was required to eliminate the debt. The situation of war in China created considerable concern for the safety of the sisters there. In the midst of these difficulties, the 1940 Centenary of the Congregation's foundation in Indiana, with its outburst of major celebrations at the motherhouse, inhibited any momentum on the provincial fronts.

The very next year, national and international events completely disrupted life for all Americans, including the Sisters of Providence. The December 8, 1941, Japanese attack on Pearl Harbor swept the country into a state of war, with serious side effects on the resources of the Congregation. With the United States at war with Italy, access to the Vatican was handled through the NCWC in Washington, D.C., and restricted to high priority topics. The Maryhurst property was requisitioned for housing purposes and purchased by the government in 1941. Temporary arrangements were made to place the provincial house at Lady Isle in Portsmouth, New Hampshire. An alternate property in Rockville, Maryland, was purchased in 1944, but could not be occupied until the summer of 1945.

The General Chapter of 1944

Meanwhile, as the 1944 General Chapter approached, attention was once again given to the preparation of a revised draft of the *Constitutions*. During January 1943, correspondence was begun with another canonical consultant, the Very Reverend Joseph Gallen, SJ, at Woodstock College in Woodstock, Maryland, on the matter of provinces. Father Gallen advised a study of other congregations' constitutions newly-approved by Rome and gave a list of those who could be contacted, agreeing to help with the work of the commission on revision.[39]

Bishop Ritter advised that so long as the *Constitutions* were in tentative form, experimentation could continue on the working plan and agreed that extending the trial period for the provincial structure would be beneficial in the long run. Rather than following the 1938 Chapter's recommendation to conduct a complete review, the 1944 General Chapter simply authorized continuing the status quo. The superior general, her council and the provincials were to oversee ongoing adjustments to the provinces during the interval between the 1944 and 1950 Chapters.[40] As in the 1938 Chapter, in 1944 the provincials participated as ex-officio members.

New Provincials Appointed

Events the following year enabled the Congregation to return to a more normal footing. The end of the war in 1945, the evacuation of the sisters from China to safety and a new mission in Formosa (present-day Taiwan) and the improved economic situation opened new horizons. These events also revived an interest in the possibilities inherent in a provincial structure. Experienced leadership was desirable, so three of the sisters appointed as provincials in 1946 had previously served in this role: in Indiana, Sister St. Eugenia McBarron (Eastern provincial, 1939-1944); in Illinois, Sister Mary Rose Cummings (Indiana provincial, 1933-38, as well as fourth assistant, 1938-1944); and in the West, Sister Carita Kiley (Illinois provincial, 1934-38). The provincial named for the East, Sister St. Philomene Cullity, had successfully led the establishment of Marywood, Anaheim, and had taught at and then become president of Immaculata Junior College in Washington, D.C.; she was to live at the new Maryhurst in Rockville and continue as president of the junior college.[41]

Changes of episcopal leadership in Indiana during these years would also affect the Congregation's operations and create a need to form working relationships with new incumbents. In 1944 the creation of the Diocese of Evansville brought the missions in the southern portion of the state under the jurisdiction of Bishop Henry Grimmelsman. At the same time, the Fort Wayne Diocese was split to form the Diocese of Lafayette under the leadership of Bishop John Bennett, and Indianapolis became an archdiocese. In 1946 Archbishop Ritter was appointed to head the St. Louis Archdiocese, with Bishop Paul Schulte of Leavenworth, Kansas, named as his successor.

End of Provinces

As another year passed, the health problems Mother Mary Bernard had suffered during her first term returned. In 1948 she again became ill, resulting in her death on October 6, 1948, at age seventy-two. After consultation with canonist Father James O'Connor, SJ, confirmed the necessity of providing for a Chapter of Elections within six months, arrangements were made to convene the Chapter on March 25, 1949. Once again, in addition to the twenty-four elected delegates, the six assistants, treasurer general and provincial superiors would be ex-officio delegates. It fell to First Assistant Sister Helen Clare to arrange not only for the funeral for the highly regarded Mother Mary Bernard, but also to attend to the detailed requirements for the Chapter.

As this would be Bishop Schulte's first time to preside, based on his experience with other congregations of religious women in the Leavenworth Diocese, he asked his canonist for the Indianapolis Archdiocese, Father Charles Ross, to research the section of the Code of Canon Law on Religious so as to be well-prepared. One of the sisters, either in writing prior to the election or in personal conversation, asked the bishop if the provincials had the right to vote since their names were not mentioned in the Rule. When he and Father Ross arrived and noted that the four provincials were included among the delegates, they realized that since the necessary amendments to the *Constitutions* had never received approbation, the four sisters were ineligible to participate. To be certain, they placed a long-distance call to Father Adam Ellis, SJ, a professor of canon law and coauthor of a standard text on the subject,[42] who confirmed this opinion.[43]

When the delegates assembled in the chapter room at the appointed time, the provincials were asked to step into the bishop's parlor in Tile Hall. After about twenty minutes, Bishop Schulte and Father Ross came into the chapter room to make an astonishing announcement, as described in the minutes of the 1949 Chapter.

> He said that he had asked the provincials to withdraw because a question had arisen as to their right to vote in the Chapter since our Rules and *Constitutions* did not give them this right. He asked if they had enjoyed the right of voting in previous elections, and when answered in the affirmative, he said that the community had extended this right through a canonical error, and that while the elections in which they took part would not be invalidated through this canonical error, nevertheless the error could not be permitted to continue.

> He reviewed briefly the history of the provinces, saying that in 1932, the permission had been asked to erect provinces, and that this permission was given. The chapter of 1938 adopted the provincial constitutions on a tentative and experimental basis, but no further report was filed with the Holy See regarding the operation of the provinces, and no request had been made to confirm the existence of these provinces. Therefore as far as Rome is concerned, the provinces have no document confirming their existence, and they would not be regarded as established until the confirmation of Rome was given. If they had been approved and canonically established then the Rule would have been amended to acknowledge their existence, and the constitutions would have binding force, having been confirmed and become operative. Since this was not done, the constitutions of the provinces have no binding force, and the provincials of these provinces would not be allowed to vote.[44]

The four provincials, Sister St. Eugenia (Indiana), Sister Mary Rose (Illinois), Sister St. Philomene (East) and Sister Carita (West) were invited in for the session during which the reports were given, but they did not return for the eleven o'clock morning session when the elections were held in the crypt. One can only imagine the ruffled feathers beneath the well-disciplined countenances of the assembly as it went about its business. With the focus on elections, the agenda did not include discussion of the apparently never-ending topic of provinces.

It fell to the newly elected council to take official action to formally end the experiment with provincial structures, for which task they assembled the very next morning. Three of the six sisters seated around the table had not yet been in office for twenty-four hours.[45] During the years 1926-1949, when the community had attempted to reorganize into provinces, each of the six had had a different experience of that form of government. Mother Marie Helene had taught at the College from 1926 until her 1938 election as general secretary. Like her, Sister Rose Dolores had served the previous term on the council, after fourteen years at Ladywood. It is highly doubtful that they ever had much contact with the Indiana provincial while on mission during 1933-1938. Sister Gertrude Clare had just been elected to the council for the sixth time, so she was the only member who had never had a provincial superior over her. All three had likely had working contacts with the appointed provincials during their time as home superiors. The three new members, Sisters Rose Genevieve Flaherty, Catherine Celine Brocksmith (both former local superiors) and Loretta Therese O'Leary, had all been missioned in both Chicago and Indianapolis, where encounters with provincial superiors would have been more likely.

Having served as secretary for the previous council, the newly elected superior general, Mother Marie Helene, understood the required protocol. She wasted no time in clarifying the effect the bishop's decision would have on the council's responsibilities. The council minutes make it clear that the matter was handled with dispatch. Given that "the Provinces in actuality did not exist, [she called the question]: Shall our Community be divided into Provinces as was suggested in 1932? The vote was affirmative 0; Negative 6. The decision stands, therefore, that the Community will not have Provinces"[46] The decision was quick and unanimous. Rather than rubber-stamping the bishop's assessment, the council members were undoubtedly affirming the feeling of the entire community that the canonical structure of provinces simply didn't fit the Sisters of Providence style or spirit. The benefits of clear-cut canonical distinctions were evident in a hierarchical culture and the benefits of a business model of chain of command were well accepted in American culture, but such benefits had not emerged from their sixteen years of experience with this model. It was time to move on.

Mother Marie Helene immediately sent to all the houses a letter alluding to the feelings engendered by the sudden change and explaining the situation:

> We cannot explain the plan of God; all we can do is to accept and then endeavor to follow with sincerity of purpose His leadings. Surely this is the one great strengthening thought behind everything—the belief that God is with us at all times and that personally He guides and directs the happenings of our lives.

Her letter then gives details of Archbishop Schulte's information and actions and concludes with the following information:

> You will see from this, dear Sisters, that there is need of considerable adjustment and this adjustment will be made within the coming months. We earnestly solicit your prayers that the members of the council will be guided by the light of the Holy Spirit in their decision. In the meantime we have delegated to the Provincials the same powers which they have held previously and this will continue at least until the summer.[47]

Little by little the provincial structures disappeared. The novices and postulants in the East were brought home from Maryhurst the following week and the Rockville property was sold that summer. The provincial superiors were quickly assigned to posts as local superiors on the August Obedience List. The one exception was the West, where distance warranted continuing intermediate assistance. Because her experience in establishing Marywood, Anaheim, during 1934-1937 had made her familiar with the California situation, Sister St. Philomene was given delegated authority as the "Western Representative" in addition to her assignment as principal at Marywood.

Thus ended the sixteen-year attempt at provinces. In recording the events in the Maryhurst diary, the charitable chronicler writes: "The Sister [who expressed her concerns to the bishop] no doubt did not know what a momentous question she was raising."[48] Perhaps she did. Perhaps this nameless sister was less the naïve innocent than the astute diplomat exerting influence for change. On this topic, the archives yield no clue.

ૐ Chapter 6
Formation

Novices and Postulants, 1921

Vocations

We now return to the questions posed in Chapter 1: "What was the attraction of the life of a vowed religious that continued to draw so many young women? Indeed, how were they lifted out of the rapidly changing culture and transformed into 'Sister'?" A glance at the photo above provides insight into the sheer scope of this endeavor. With a six-month postulancy, a new group of young women entered the novitiate each winter and each summer, while the group that had completed the two-year novitiate period professed vows and left for mission. Grouped as "bands" by the twice yearly entrance dates, at any given time approximately 130 postulants and novices resided in the novitiate building. During Mother Mary Raphael's first term, the winter band averaged thirty individuals, while the summer band averaged eighteen. A number of factors influenced the motivations of the 294 young women who presented themselves at Saint Mary-of-the-Woods in the six years between 1926 and 1932 with the desire of becoming Sisters of Providence.

External Motivational Factors

The twenties were a time when the role of women was uncertain. Those who favored a more active role for women in society had found that by volunteering, especially in church work, they could challenge the middle class myth that "true womanhood" belonged within domestic confines. As social historian Wendy Kaminer observes, "By playing her woman's role outside the home, she would begin to change it."[1] Settlement houses such as the famous Hull House in Chicago provided venues for women to use their talents to exert influence in society. This idea was not, however, a novel one, as Chicago historian Suellen Hoy notes: "To live as neighbors among poor migrants and work on their behalf would hardly have been considered new to Chicagoans who had witnessed or benefited from the labors of the Sisters of Mercy or other religious communities of women."[2] In addition to charitable work, employment opportunities gradually expanded for women. During the nineteenth century women were usually employed in factories or domestic service, but with the growth of business and the standardization of the typewriter more and more women entered the work force through office occupations. Moreover, in the early twentieth century, the teaching profession came to be dominated by women.

As discussed in Chapter 1, by and large Catholics maintained an insular society that fostered a strong religious identity. Hoy identifies the appeal of the woman religious as a role model in this setting:

> Young women saw that religious life offered them a way to do necessary work and feel important. Defining themselves in terms other than those imposed by having husbands and children, Catholic sisters quietly challenged the "cult of true womanhood." In short, they acted "in the world to a greater degree than was permitted to most women or was pursued by most men" by voluntarily linking their "individual identity to a larger corporate identity." The Sisters of Mercy were not only free to walk the streets of Chicago without male escorts, they were also educated and self-supporting, held top administrative posts, and owned substantial amounts of property.[3]

It is highly doubtful that holding a top administrative post was a major motivating factor for any of the applicants at Saint Mary-of-the-Woods. For those who did think of their decision as a career path, other considerations, such as limited opportunities, were more likely to play a central role, as pointed out by historian Charles Morris: "Still, convents were turning away an onslaught of applicants, a comment, perhaps, on the power of faith, but also on the bleak prospects facing so many working-class girls of the time."[4] This more realistic assessment is borne out by the decline in the number of applicants during the war years when more opportunities opened for women. The superior general's report to the General Chapter of 1938 counted ninety-eight novices and postulants while by the 1944 report the number had dropped to sixty-one.[5]

To be sure, "the power of faith" did place the option of religious life squarely in the minds of young women. The topic of vocations was often raised by priests and sisters in Catholic schools, where rapid expansion increased staffing needs. Kathleen Sprows Cummings highlights the major reason the hierarchy strongly supported recruitment of women:

> [Superintendents and] Catholic educators followed a similar trajectory. Once they settled on women religious as the most convenient and the least expensive solution to this problem, they realized that continuing to attract a sufficient number of young Catholic women to religious life would be a key factor in ensuring the permanency of the parochial system.[6]

Bishops and priests used the pulpit and their considerable influence in parish communities not only to invite young men to consider the priesthood but also to extend a parallel invitation to young women to become sisters.

The sisters themselves often set the goal of "replacing themselves," and were on the lookout for girls who showed interest. Sister Marie William Hoerner recalls her own perceptions of what attracted her to religious life while she was a student at St. Augustine Academy in Fort Wayne:

> As a religious, she [Sister Eugenia Clare Cullity] is the one I feel who exemplified for us with others there, and in our grade school, too, what the religious life was. They didn't talk vocations to us. They lived. It was with a sense of our needs and of needs out there that they dealt with us, they guided us. But it wasn't just in word they were doing things with us. And that is what made us want to be around. And the more we were around the more we saw their loving attitude toward one another. We saw their fun and their teasing. I know I came to the Novitiate without ever having thought or talked about vows of poverty, chastity and obedience, ever. I saw how they lived—the simplicity of their lives. ... [At school] we had a spirit that made us come early and stay late. We loved to be around the sisters. ... They would throw us out and we would hang around to hear them begin the chanting. It sounded so wonderful, so mysteri-

ous. ... It was all of this that said to us, "This is a beautiful life and it's open to us." [7]

Internal Motivating Factors

Even taking such external factors into account, the consistently recurring reason given by the sisters themselves for entering the convent was the strong feeling of being called by God. Many grew up in families where Dad would get up early and leave the house fasting in order to attend Mass and receive Communion on his way to work. In the evening, he would gather the family to say the rosary together. Growing up in such an environment made religious practices a significant part of daily life. For many youngsters such example and experiences were not just family routines, but also launch pads for their own spiritual lives. For them, the usual sacramental milestones of First Confession, First Communion and Confirmation had an additional effect. Gradually, they came to understand that they had a vocation to religious life. It was the most natural thing in the world to set their sights on entering the convent, and they could be sure their parents would support their choice as a blessing.[8] It was not unusual for two or more girls from the same family to follow one another to Saint Mary-of-the-Woods.

Conditions for Admission

Naturally, an individual's desire to become a sister had to be accompanied by qualifications that would make the Congregation desire to have her as a member. These qualifications, drawn from Canon Law, were generically described in the *Constitutions:*

> Those who seek admission to the Congregation should be the offspring of legitimate marriage, be of a respectable family, of moral integrity, and in good health. They should be prompted by a right intention, have only supernatural aims, and be fit to discharge the duties of the religious life.[9]

A letter from the young woman's pastor, together with certificates of baptism and confirmation, would satisfy these requirements and verify that the applicant was at least fifteen years of age. Additional stipulations from the Code of Canon Law were listed, but rarely applicable for most candidates, though anyone "afflicted with a heredity disease" was enjoined to declare it. As for psychological suitability, the *Constitutions* listed certain qualities:

> It is necessary that those who desire to embrace this holy Institute should not be inclined to melancholy or levity. They must have a good spirit and an upright mind, with a disposition candid and submissive to the will of Superiors. They should be amiable and conciliatory, so as to live with others in union of heart and mind. They must be judged capable of instructing youth or of taking care of the sick; or, at least, they must show an aptitude for acquiring what they do not possess.[10]

Simply due to their upbringing, applicants of the time would usually have no trouble identifying with Mary Pipher's description of parental expectations:

> Early in the century, parents wanted children to work hard, complain little, cooperate with others, and respect authority. ... In a Middletown study of Muncie, Indiana, in 1924 parents were asked what quality they most desired in their children. At the top of the list were obedience and conformity.[11]

Certainly not all applicants fit this bill. Some came from situations in which choosing religious life meant defying the attitudes of those who regarded it as an inferior social state. For example, when the parents of Sister Ann Louise (Doris) Healy died, she became a ward of her aunt and uncle who sent her as a boarder to Dunblane and then Immaculata in Washington, D.C. There she was surrounded by classmates who were daughters of military and diplomatic families, regardless of religion. Though her friends thought entering the convent was foolish, as a sophomore in college she had the strength to follow her convictions: "I really thought God wanted me to be a sister and I was going to be a sister."[12] Whatever her background, the conviction that she had a vocation—a call from God to be a Sister—was the most significant motivator.

Providence Juniorate

As noted above, one of the canonical requirements was age. Girls were required to present a baptismal certificate on which the birth date would indicate that they "had at least fifteen years completed."[13] In a time when most Americans regarded eighth grade graduation as sufficient education, it was common for working-class people to end their schooling at that point in order to go to work. For girls who reached this milestone, it was time to set plans in motion for their future. Evidence of this need to set the course of one's future early in life can be can be seen in the fact that in 1929, six of the forty-seven entrants were fifteen years of age. After completing their novitiate and professing vows at age eighteen, they would be sent out to teach. However, after Progressive Era reforms led to the passage of laws strengthening teacher credential requirements, novitiate training was woefully insufficient to meet the more stringent standards.

Corresponding educational reforms extended compulsory education through high school in many locations, postponing the need for career choices. Since the laws varied from state to state, postulants arrived at the novitiate with a great range of age and previous education. This situation created major hurdles for those charged with ensuring that novices would complete the novitiate with not only sufficient credits for high school diplomas, but Normal Teachers' certification as well.[14] It is not surprising that during the decade from 1914 to1924, seven different sisters were appointed mistress of novices. It was not until Sister Aloyse Hennessy took the helm in 1925 and held this position for eight successive years that a more suitable system for the "one-room schoolhouse" approach was introduced and stabilized.

A major step in that direction was the establishment of a juniorate, a high school for prospective postulants, as described in Chapter 3. In September 1931, Providence Juniorate, under the direction of Sister Annunciata Kiley, opened in Foley Hall with seventeen students and its own faculty of qualified postulants, novices and professed sisters. Although at first the student body of first, second and third year students was made up of a mixed group of novices, postulants and candidates, within a few years, when high school graduation became a prerequisite for entrance to the Congregation, postulants and novices had phased out of the classes. Wearing their distinctive uniform, the high school students known as candidates enjoyed a program that included the usual secondary school curriculum, as well as music, drama, athletics, a student newspaper and sodality. They attended daily Mass and Benediction with the motherhouse community and had their own time for spiritual reading and meditation.

A long-time faculty member, Sister Marie William, relates that, "At first I didn't believe in the juniorate—girls leaving home at that age—but I became a convert when I saw how they matured."[15] She attributed this result to the well-rounded program. In addition to classes, each girl learned to play a musical instrument and participated in many activities, such as Sodality, Catholic Student Mission Crusade, Holy Week retreats, sports, recreation and parties. They went home for Christmas and the summer vacation. A later description of the school adds: "Eventually the Providence Juniorate became a fully accredited college preparatory high school and was also licensed to provide practice teaching experience for college students enrolled in secondary education courses."[16] By 1938, Mother Mary Raphael was able to report to the General Chapter that since its inception in 1930, Providence Juniorate had enrolled 187 girls and thirty-eight had already entered the postulancy.

The Novitiate

The 1917 Code of Canon Law gave considerable attention to the formation of religious, and much of this legislation was incorporated into the 1929 edition of the *Constitutions*. While the legal structure provided clear guidance to ensure a solid initial formation, the true heart of the process was to be found in a living tradition begun by Mother Theodore.[17] Almost her first act had been to purchase the Thralls farmhouse to ensure the seclusion the postulants awaiting her needed in order to devote their entire attention to their formation. She enclosed the porch and converted it to a chapel with the Blessed Sacrament available day and night.

As the Congregation grew, she delegated the role of mistress of novices to her dear friend, the saintly Sister Saint Francis Xavier Le Fer. Upon Sister Saint Francis Xavier's untimely death, Mother Theodore assigned the role to Sister Mary Joseph Le Fer, whose musical talent infused the spirituality of the formation program with chant and hymns. Sister Mary Joseph's successor, Sister Mary Cleophas, with the able assistance of the scholarly Bishop Chatard, fresh from his position as rector of the North American College in Rome, expanded the program to include theology and normal school classes for teacher certification. Between 1890 and 1914, three highly respected mistresses of novices, Sisters Basilissa Heiner, Manetto

Quigley and Mary Stanislaus Graffe, further solidified the novitiate program.

The importance of the role of the mistress of novices was clearly highlighted in the *Constitutions:* "The welfare of the Congregation and the good it is designed to accomplish depend in great measure upon the manner in which the subjects are formed."[18] Specific directives were given as to what the program entailed and how the mistress should go about it, with provision made for sisters to assist her. The process unfolded in three phases: six months of postulancy, a year of "canonical" novitiate and a year of "scholastic" novitiate. During the time period covered in Part I of this volume, the Congregation was blessed with a sister extremely well endowed to fill this key role, Sister Rose Berchmans.

The Postulancy

The *Constitutions* are clear about the purpose of the first phase of formation. "The object of the Postulate is the examination of the vocation and the first formation of the candidate."[20] Many of the young women who discussed their plans for entrance felt so strongly that they were called to be sisters that they felt no need to examine their vocation. Nonetheless, the process itself involved a mutual discernment, however unarticulated. When the young woman brought up the subject with a favorite sister, if that sister saw potential, she took on the role of sponsor, assisting her with making the necessary arrangements. After further discussion with the girl's parents and her local superior, the sponsor would provide a list of items to be brought, a list that would bring home to her the stark simplicity of the life she had chosen—black shoes and stockings, unscented soap and plain cotton underwear. Next came the question of how she could adjust to her initial regimen of formation in the novitiate.

When a young woman arrived at the door of Providence Convent to begin her training, she was paired with a "guardian angel," a novice assigned to show her around and introduce her to the daily routine. She would change from her secular clothing, don the postulant uniform and then return to the parlor to bid farewell to her family, knowing her future contacts would be greatly limited. There would be periodic mail, of course, and regular visiting days during the novitiate,

Sister Rose Berchmans Patterson 1894-1970

Rose Ellen Patterson was born in Loogootee, Indiana, an only child. After completing her elementary education with the Sisters of Providence at her parish school, St. John, she went on to attend high school at the Academy at Saint Mary-of-the-Woods and then entered the novitiate in 1912. She spent nine years teaching grades five through eight at St. Mel, Chicago, under three different superiors before being assigned as an assistant in the novitiate in 1923 at age twenty-nine. Working alongside Novice Mistress Sister Aloyse Hennessey was a formative experience for her. She was well prepared to succeed her mentor as mistress in 1933 when Sister Aloyse was appointed provincial of the East. Blessed with a sense of humor and an appreciation of the human condition, she went on to serve in this role for eighteen years under three superiors general. In a 1947 article, she described her role as helping "the splendid young girls who have felt the irresistible appeal of Christ ... each one bringing her own particular personality, her own distinctive gifts of mind and heart and asking but to be taught how to give all to His Work."[19] She would fill this role until 1951, and after years of service as a local superior, she again took up formation duties with the junior sisters when the Congregation began its Sister Formation Program in 1958.

but later family contacts would be very dependent on the location of her assignments. The entire experience was designed to pare down life's comforts to the base essentials in order to focus on the spiritual foundation of the life for which she was testing herself.

The three-story novitiate building became her new home, where she was given a bed in a dormitory, with a modicum of privacy afforded by curtains drawn about it at night, a cigar box for storage of toilet articles, a box called a commode for clean laundry, a desk in the study hall and a prie-dieu, a designated pew in the chapel.

Strictly speaking, the postulants were segregated from the novices in terms of their daily schedule. There was a period of instructions on the basics of their chosen life, training in chanting the Little Office of the Blessed Virgin Mary and lessons on proper decorum, as well as formal classes for college credit. In actual practice, both postulants and novices followed the same regimen of rising, prayers, Mass, breakfast, an "employment" or domestic chore, instructions, classes, a short period of prayer to examine one's conscience, dinner, recreation, the rosary (noon beads), classes and study, prayer and spiritual reading, supper, recreation, night prayer and preparing for bed and lights out. It was an intensive introduction to the common life.

Two of the practices designed to deepen the postulant's spiritual life bear elaboration. First, silence. Almost every activity of the day was carried out without conversation, although when necessity, charity, or politeness required verbal communication, beckoning someone to a doorway to exchange a message was permissible. Lest nonverbal communication mar the tranquil atmosphere which was desired, postulants were instructed to keep their eyes cast down in order to foster recollection. As might be expected, silence did not come easily to lively and energetic young women. In spite of the best of intentions, there were times when suppressed merriment burst forth. Nonetheless, a gradual appreciation of silence as "the parent of prayer and the foundation of religious life"[21] repaid the effort required

A stricter regimen of silence called profound silence was observed from the time the bell was rung for night prayers until after Mass the next morning. It was a time for recollection and prayer.

The second practice needing elaboration is the examen.[22] Personal goal setting and self-discipline were integral to the formation process. The midday prayer of examen was a time for each one to pull out a small black book to place pencil marks indicating how well or poorly she had observed practices that would help her internalize the virtues of charity, recollection, promptness and discipline. Each postulant and novice wore a small set of beads hidden beneath the cape called "perfection beads." These could be pulled down each time there was a slip in the behavior being monitored, with a prayer of thanksgiving as the desired good habit became easier. Daily instructions given by the mistress of postulants provided guidance and direction as to what was expected and provided the stimulus for focusing attention on spiritual motivation for exterior behavior.

Additional assistance was provided both by the example of the novices and corrections from the sharp-eyed novitiate sisters. Periodically the bands assembled at a "Chapter of Faults" to announce aloud individual failings. Those who sought additional penance could request to take a meal kneeling. Periodic conferences with the mistress provided individualized assistance. Weekly confession built in the opportunity for mentioning points of confusion to a priest. Periodic retreats provided time for more intensive reflection and formulating resolutions which would become the basis for future "examens."

When they gathered after the noon and evening meals for recreation, simply talking with band members (the group who had entered at the same time) helped to deepen friendships and a sense of community. When weather permitted, the entire group went for walks around the grounds, providing an outlet for the energy and spirit of youth. Even sitting together in the community room and chatting over a sewing basket led to the formation of close bonds. Wednesday afternoon walks around the grounds and the sharing of sweets and snacks offered a welcome mid-week break. Working together to accomplish the routine tasks which benefited from many hands, such as peeling apples in the cannery or passing the freshly laundered clothes to boxes in the laundry, engendered a strong sense of community.

As with any initiation, rites had evolved to indicate progress. Midway through the six-month postulancy, each postulant submitted three names by which she wanted to be known as a religious. Gathered for a special ceremony, each postulant knelt before the superior general, who placed on her head a black cap and pronounced the name the superiors had chosen for her. Now came a time for increased scrutiny by the novitiate sisters, because the mistress of novices had to recommend each postulant prior to formal admission into the novitiate. Although her desire for a total commitment to God sustained each postulant's efforts, there was always the possibility of being sent home if it was determined that she did not have a religious vocation. At times, someone might go to her place in chapel only to discover that the belongings of the person sharing her prie-dieu had been removed. No explanation was offered and no one spoke of the fact that a decision for departure had been made, nor if the decision had come from the individual or from on high. She could only breathe a deep sigh and pray that she herself would respond to the grace of vocation. Of course, anyone who realized that this was not the life for her was free to leave, but she was instructed to say nothing to the others.

As the day of reception drew near, each one made many trips to the sewing room. A long-standing tradition had evolved that dramatized the interior commitment of choosing to be a bride of Christ by the exterior act of wearing a wedding gown for the reception ceremony. Some postulants' families provided gowns, while those previously used and donated were available for others. Fitting sessions alternated between the elaborate silks and satins of the gowns and the black serge of the habit itself. The frothy white bridal veil would be put aside while the *serre-tete*, the tight fitting headpiece, was placed over the hair and pulled tightly back. The stiffly starched cap with the white cotton novice's veil would then be pinned to it. The contrast between the bridal attire and the religious habit could provide additional insight into the decision she was making.

The decision was not hers alone. Based on regular reports from the mistress of novices, the superior general with a vote of her council would make the actual determination as to who would receive the religious habit. Those who, in the opinion of the council, had "not shown the proper attitude toward religious life," or "who had no vocation as was evident from her conduct,"[23] were dismissed. Individual interviews with the superior general herself were scheduled for each postulant, providing at least a brief and awkward opportunity for personal conversation. Yet another interview, this time with the bishop or his appointed representative, was required by canon law;[24] although it was more of a formality than an in-depth conversation, the arrangement afforded an external opportunity to raise any complaint. An eight-day retreat immediately preceding the ceremony of reception concluded the postulancy.

The Canonical Year of Novitiate

Canon law required all religious communities to designate one full year during which "it is forbidden to employ the novices in the external charges of the institute, or in the ministry or in studies properly so called."[25] To emphasize the unique nature of a year with an intense focus on spiritual formation the first year of novitiate was referred to as canonical year. Courses in religion and community history were included and the instructions for living religious life begun during the postulancy were continued. Each novice was given an employment or work assignment that usually changed several times over the year, varying manual labor with other tasks. The intent was training in work habits and high standards of cleanliness, but the large numbers of novices also provided a greatly appreciated labor force at the motherhouse. The horarium, or daily schedule, was very much the same as that to which they had become accustomed during the postulancy.

With the goal of preparing the novice to profess the vows of poverty, chastity and obedience, instructions covered general topics. There might be practical tips for religious decorum such as "Watch guard of the eyes" or advice for fostering inner attitudes to support it such as "Maintain a quiet, peaceful spirit."[26] Admonitions such as "Begin the day with perfect promptitude in rising" might be accompanied by a statement recognizing that keeping up daily effort wouldn't be easy, yet "Have confidence during trials and difficulties because we know that God has deep care of us." It was up to each one to determine how to apply the guidance to her own situation, again with periodic conferences with the mistress.

The well-stocked library provided a good selection of spiritual reading. Those whose successful auditions had gained them membership in the choir spent many hours in rehearsal. The arts of caring for starched caps and neckerchiefs so as to present a tidy appearance in the habit and of walking with appropriate religious decorum were ongoing learning experiences. A periodic window into the wider world occurred during the academic year, when postulants and novices could file into the balcony of the Conservatory to attend performances and speakers scheduled by the College as cultural events. Regular writing of letters home provided a means of helping loved ones understand the gradual process of adapting to the chosen lifestyle.

Fun was not lacking as the friendships begun during postulancy continued. With two entrance dates each year, the recreation group now included another band and novices were encouraged to "be general" and vary their companions. On Sunday evenings the entire novitiate recreated together. Special occasions called forth talent in creating and putting on skits and programs. Summer was a special time when the sisters, home from the missions, could occasionally visit. Friday evening picnics in the grove and the annual St. Anne procession provided welcome variety to the usual schedule.

The Scholastic Year of Novitiate

Although the second year of novitiate did allow for novices to "be employed in the various works of the Institute … first place must be given to their spiritual formation."[27] For most, the time was devoted to normal school or college classes to prepare them for teaching. Some who had already completed college were assigned to teach classes themselves. However, Mother Mary Raphael was insistent that "no novice may be sent on mission before the expiration of two full years."[28]

Novice class with Professor Sister Mary Borromeo Brown

The Coadjutrix Sisters

It must not be thought that all of the young women who sought to become members of the Congregation wished to become teachers. Even among the founding group of six sisters we find a *coadjutrix* sister, the Latin term used in the *Constitutions* to describe those women who wished to assist the mission with the auxiliary services so necessary to life in those days. Sister Mary Borromeo Brown uses the example of Sister Olympiade Boyer to illustrate the important role of these members. Arriving at Saint Mary-of-the-Woods with Mother Theodore at age thirty-four and still a novice, she "was an excellent cook and skilled in all sorts of household work and in the care of the sick, having had some hospital work before entering the novitiate at Ruillé. She proved to be a distinct asset to the Community."[29] One of the postulants awaiting the 1840 arrival of the sisters was Catherine Guthnek, who became a cook. The purpose of the foundation was education, but mid-nineteenth century circumstances were such that many behind-the-scenes tasks were needed to provide such education. Fortunately, the call to religious life was heard by many women who wanted to serve in this capacity.

With the nineteenth-century proliferation of congregations of women engaged in active ministry, the legal descriptors of canon law simply borrowed from the monastic tradition which required dowries for those aspiring to become "choir sisters." Those with little or no money might qualify as "lay sisters" who took vows with the intention of doing the domestic chores while the choir sisters prayed the Divine Office. As one of the early foundresses of an apostolic congregation, Mother Catherine McCauley was among those who expanded the concept of membership beyond those who wished to devote themselves to apostolic service, as explained by Suellen Hoy.

> She did not initially provide for lay sisters in her Institute of Mercy. But she was finally persuaded to do so by some industrious and pious women who had "neither fortune nor education" and were thus unable to seek admission into any of the religious communities then in Ireland. ...
>
> The lot of lay religious may have no appeal today, but there is little doubt that some women of working-class families saw in it an opportunity to better their lives. ... They were probably attracted to a community of educated and religious women,

where they would receive regular meals, a full night's sleep, periods of recreation each day, and care when they became ill or old.[30]

When Mother Theodore arrived in America she encountered a similar situation, as described by Sister Mary Borromeo Brown:

> At first there was no question of lay Sisters, but before long the Bishop [de la Hailandière] began to receive applications from so many estimable young girls, who for lack of early opportunities could never hope to function as teachers, that he proposed their reception as lay Sisters. "I think it very probable that you could have lay Sisters by changing the name," he wrote [to Mother Mary.] Most of the pioneer women were illiterate. … The immigrants, too, deprived for centuries of educational facilities in their native land, were not better educated.[31]

However, the American ethic of equality was often at odds with the inherent class distinctions of the lay and professional occupations of the sisters. The wording of the French Rule exhorted the sisters coadjutrix to virtues of "modesty, recollection, mildness, exactitude, and activity in their employments; also, by their good-will and unlimited devotion."[32] At the same time, it fostered somewhat degrading distinctions.

> For their spiritual advancement they shall keep themselves mindful of their lowliness, honor the Sisters as belonging to an order above them, and serve them with love, as the well-beloved spouses of Jesus Christ. …
>
> They shall not read any book without the permission of the Superior, who will give them those she deems most suitable to their state, and they cannot apply themselves to learn anything without her permission. They shall regard as a dangerous temptation the thought of raising themselves any higher.[33]

When Mother Euphrasie prepared to send the American edition of the *Constitutions* to Rome for approval in 1886, in addition to consulting Bishop Chatard she solicited the opinion of Fort Wayne's Bishop Dwenger, who responded:

> In the beginning you once mention "Coadjutrix Sisters" meaning evidently "Lay Sisters" … [but] you have no distinction between "choir" and Lay Sisters and if you had it would be wise to abolish this distinction. I know several communities who had this distinction in Europe but were forced to abolish it in this country. Would it not be better to omit the allusion to CS altogether?[34]

His wise suggestion arrived too late to be considered. Because it was during this time that canon law regarding religious women was in a transitional stage, this item passed unnoticed by those charged with approving the document. Consequently the 1887 edition of the Rule retained this unfortunate wording.

During the 1927 consultation for the revision of the *Constitutions* canonist Father Sauvage suggested replacing the term coadjutrix with lay sisters, but the council disagreed, sending him this explanation:

> We prefer to retain the title "sisters *Coadjutrix*" rather than "Lay Sisters," as this latter is very distasteful to our American Sisters, and will no doubt cause some little disturbance should the change be made. We try to make as little distinction as possible in the Community, and feel that the term "coadjutrix" would be very much more acceptable than the term "Lay."
>
> We have rewritten Chapter L [50] concerning the Coadjutrix Sisters, omitting what was applicable only to conditions as they existed in the French community.[35]

The 1929 *Constitutions* did eliminate class status references such as "lowliness" and "an order above them" while retaining the caution about ambition or changing employments, as well as a differentiation in the habit to be worn. However, clearly more remained to be done toward true equality. Only ten years later, this topic was revisited by the General Chapter of 1938.

> It was stated by Sister Marie Stanislaus [Graffe] that the Sisters employed in domestic work feel that a distinction was made between them and the other Sisters, especially so since the Rule treated of them so definitely.
>
> Discussion followed in which it was stated that a greater charity would be effected by the elimination of these Rules, and a spirit more in accord with the prevailing custom of the country.[36]

Noting that all the sisters took the same vows, the Chapter members voted to remove the entire section on coadjutrix sisters from the *Constitutions*. The hard times of the Depression had sharpened dissatisfaction with distinctions between classes in the country, and it's possible that these cultural attitudes were carried into community life.[37] However, this resolution was taken at the same time as the many resolutions regarding provincial structures, and the Congregation had not had sufficient experience with provinces to justify submitting resolutions about them for Rome's approval. With so much unfinished business, as well as the severe restrictions in communication with the Vatican during the war years, it would not be until 1954 that the copy of the *Constitutions* in the sisters' hands reflected the change mandated by the 1938 Chapter.

Apart from such discussion, there was no doubt that the talents of these devoted women were needed for the time-consuming tasks necessary for simply maintaining a household as well as for the specialized health-related services often provided as outreach to parishioners. The significant factor in deciding to admit candidates as coadjutrix sisters was their suitability for religious life. The program of postulancy and novitiate training could be adapted to each one's fitness for future service.[38] The details of how their formation was adapted are not clear, but it is likely that after the canonical year they were sent on mission. At times, classes pertinent to their duties were provided.[39]

The policy of welcoming auxiliaries certainly proved beneficial for many years,[40] However, as societal conditions changed, the number of women entering for this purpose formed a dwindling percentage of each year's applicants. During the decade of 1840-1849, 30 percent of those entering took this path toward profession, but by the 1900-1909 decade the number had declined to only 7 percent. This number dropped to only 3 percent during the twenties when laws greatly restricted immigration, indicating that many of the earlier applicants had come from recent arrivals to the country. Age was certainly another factor which influenced these vocations. Generally speaking, over the first hundred years of the Congregation's history, the age range of each entrance group hovered between sixteen and thirty-nine. Most women who entered with the intent to become teachers were quite young, with a median age of eighteen, while the median age of those interested in auxiliary service was around twenty-two, even including women who were in their thirties and forties.

Certainly as electricity and labor-saving devices became widely available there was less need for in-house domestic assistance. Compulsory educational standards and more job opportunities provided attractive alternatives for single women and would also account for fewer applicants for the auxiliary role in the Congregation. By mid-century the services of sister cooks were relatively rare and greatly valued and the sisters themselves are held in fond memory by those who lived with them.[41]

Novitiates in the Provinces

With the inauguration of provinces in August 1933, the plan included opening novitiates in the East and the West with the hope that the prospect of being closer to home would encourage vocations.[42] Aspirants from the Midwest would continue to enter at Saint Mary-of-the-Woods. The situation in the East was ripe for this enterprise, while much remained to be done in the West. In both locations the leadership of this enterprise fell to the newly appointed provincials who also served as mistresses of novices for the initial phase of establishment.

The Eastern Novitiate

Sister Aloyse Hennessey, the newly appointed provincial superior for the East, having just completed eight years as mistress of novices, was in an excellent position to organize a novitiate. Another major advantage was the fact that the site, Maryhurst in Hyattsville, Maryland, had been opened and in operation since 1920. The large building, situated on spacious grounds outside the city center, yet convenient to the excellent resources of the Catholic University of America and Immaculata, was ideal for the purpose. Professors from The Catholic University taught theology classes to the novices and postulants, who took the same exams as the university students. Sisters of Providence studying for graduate degrees were also called upon to teach. The extensive grounds allowed for the traditional outdoor activities held at Saint Mary-of-the-Woods, such as the annual Saint Anne Procession. The well-established schools in the Boston and Washington, D.C., areas had given the Sisters of Providence a high profile as a teaching community, with graduates likely to consider entrance. Almost immediately, a small and steady stream of applicants fully realized the hopes for the enterprise.

Mother Mary Raphael and First Assistant Sister Mary Bernard Laughlin's arrived at Maryhurst to witness on September 26, 1934, the first fruits of the long-cherished dream, as described by the Maryhurst diarist. "Today for the first time two postulants received the Holy Habit at a place other than St. Mary-of-the-Woods. The Right Rev. Bishop McNamara officiated, assisted by 13 priests—Benedictines, Oblates, Dominicans, and Diocesan clergy. The Immaculata choir sang for the ceremonies."[43] The reception and profession ceremonies were the same as those at the motherhouse. In March 1937, the Apostolic Delegate, Archbishop Amleto Giovanni Cicognani, presided when six novices made their profession.

During the war years, after the Hyattsville estate was sold to the government in 1942, the novices at Maryhurst were sent to the central novitiate at Saint Mary-of-the-Woods. Postulants continued to be received at the remodeled Loretto House across from Immaculata, though this facility was crowded and not at all ideal. The Maryhurst chronicler describes an intriguing contrast, noting that the nearby campus of American University was the site of barracks for the newly established women's branch of the navy known as the WAVES: "There were at times over 3,000 women there and there was constant passing to and fro in front of Loretto."[44] In 1945, a new site was purchased in Rockville, Maryland, allowing the eastern novitiate to accommodate postulants and canonical novices at the new Maryhurst in Rockville, which was a beautifully landscaped and wooded estate near the White Fathers' property.

Of the seventy-three women who entered during the 1934-1949 years of the eastern novitiate's existence, fifty-two nov-

Rogation Day Procession Maryhurst, Hyattsville, 1936

Postulants at Maryhurst Convent, Rockville, Maryland. Top row: Sisters John Michael Holbrook, Ignatius (Joan) Mathews, Ann Loyola (Ann) Scott; front row: Ann Francis Hammersley, Ann Richard Cronin.

ices professed vows. The cessation of the province itself was the reason for the novitiate's closure. Its success can be attributed not only to the well-established Catholic communities which provided vocations and the beautiful setting which lent itself to the same program as at Saint Mary-of-the-Woods, but also in large part to the steady leadership of Sister Mary Dominica Adamson. She served as mistress of novices from 1937 to 1947 and was then replaced by the much experienced Sister Aloyse Hennessey for the final two years.

The Western Novitiate

On the West Coast, the situation was entirely different. The three houses forming the tiny western province at its inception had only been opened for five years and none was really suitable for a novitiate. The provincial, Sister Regina Clare Carlos, had considerable experience as a local superior but none as a novitiate sister. Nonetheless, shortly after her arrival in 1933 at St. Joseph, Hawthorne, three young women entered as postulants there. The need for better accommodations certainly intensified the negotiations for the purchase of Marywood in Anaheim, making the July 1934 move most welcome. The location and setting amid the orange groves on the sparsely settled southern California rolling hills were delightful, and the existing convent/high school compound was readily adapted for the novitiate.

In spite of the fact that the Congregation had only recently been established in southern California, various personal contacts spread the news of the nearby novitiate and a small but steady stream of applicants continued to arrive. On February 12, 1937, Bishop John Cantwell presided as two young women pronounced vows and three received the habit. The twenty-three priests who witnessed the ceremony could return to their parishes and continue to spread the word that the Congregation was putting down roots. As they completed their training, the newly professed were assigned to the California missions, so the first they saw of the motherhouse was when they arrived several years later for the period before final profession called second novitiate. Their numbers remained small, and over an eleven year period, five different sisters were appointed mistress of novices. Of the twenty-two postulants who entered, sixteen went on to profess vows. After Pearl Harbor was bombed in 1941, the two canonical novices were sent to Saint Mary-of-the-Woods in January 1942. With few entrants during the war years, the western novitiate was discontinued in 1945.

China: Providence Sister-Catechists

Although Sister Marie Gratia Luking greatly desired to begin a novitiate in China, both the distance and the precarious political situation deterred the council from authorizing the admission of candidates there. During the missionaries' enforced 1927-1929 exile from Kaifeng due to the civil war, travels to Peking, Korea and Manchuria had convinced Sister Marie Gratia that the mission would be greatly strengthened by employing the talents and energies of Chinese women themselves. In Korea she visited the novitiate the Maryknoll Sisters had set up to train native sisters and took careful note of their procedures. In February 1929, shortly after she was reappointed superior of the mission and returned to Kaifeng, she outlined for the council the details of a plan she had developed with the Kaifeng vicariate to establish a society of religious women who would be trained to undertake work in catechumenates for women and children, primary schools, health care dispensaries and sodalities for care of churches.[45] This project received approval from the council and on May 1, 1929, three young women were accepted as probationers for one year.

But the question remained: probationers for what? Were the women to be Sisters of Providence of Saint Mary-of-the-Woods or were they to belong to an as-yet-to-be-established congregation? This question was decided by vote of the council in favor of establishing a diocesan congregation which could be more effectively directed according to local Chinese needs and customs.[46] As additional candidates arrived, the probationers became postulants and Sister Mary Patricia Shorthall was appointed as novice mistress. On March 19, 1931, the first postulants received a modified holy habit, a grey uniform dress of Chinese style and fabric and a white veil. Meanwhile Sister Marie Gratia worked diligently to prepare a set of *Constitutions* to guide their formation and by that summer was able to send an English copy to Mother Mary Raphael, stating that it was "taken from our own holy rule with a few changes to suit conditions. The Bishop asked that it be very brief, and I tried to make it so."[47] Bishop Tacconi sent these *Constitutions* to Rome and on January 19, 1932, the Providence Sister-Catechist Society received official Vatican approval.

By the time Second Assistant Sister Berchmans Collins visited the mission in October 1932, two groups of postulants had progressed to novice status. There still remained an ambivalence regarding accepting Chinese women into the Sisters of Providence novitiate in the United States. However, apparently Sister Marie Gratia took advantage of Sister Berchmans' on-site visit to demonstrate the value of having native Chinese Sisters of Providence as members of the Ching I senior school faculty, because when Sister Berchmans left, probationer Mary Ma traveled with her and entered the novitiate at St. Mary-of-the-Woods. Although many factors militated against a continuation of this policy, its wisdom would be abundantly demonstrated when the American sisters were interned during the war. The presence of Chinese sisters allowed Ching I to remain open in the hands of Sisters Agnes Joan Li and Bernadette Ma. It would not be until 1953 that another Chinese candidate, Madeline Fu, a Ching I student who had fled to Taiwan to escape Communism, would enter the novitiate at Saint Mary-of-the-Woods and later profess vows as Sister Donna Marie Fu.

By December 1933, a separate novitiate building for the Providence Sister-Catechists was ready for occupancy in Nan

Kuan on the outskirts of Kaifeng. The formation program for the Providence Sister-Catechists was similar to that of the Sisters of Providence, though perhaps somewhat stricter. The Chinese novices learned Latin hymns as well as many of the devotions dear to the Sisters of Providence, such as processions for rogation days and the feast of St. Anne. They began and ended their day with the Chinese morning and night prayers commonly used by Christians who gathered at the outlying missions. Priests from the seminary came for classes in Christian doctrine to prepare the women for their work in the parishes. Sister Marie Gratia provided retreats and special instructions. In 1937 when recently arrived Sister Mary Liguori Hartigan was sent to assist newly appointed novice mistress Sister Monica Marie Rigoni, she observed, "The whole spirit of the novitiate was one of recollection."[48]

In addition to her duties as superior of the American Sisters of Providence, Sister Marie Gratia acted as superior for the Providence Sister-Catechists, often taking one with her as a companion on her various travels, working with the vicar general to identify suitable mission opportunities for newly professed sisters and arranging an annual summer retreat for the community. Already by 1932 she was able to report: "Now Providence Sister-Catechists have entered the ranks, and from now on, every six months others will follow."[49] Her confidence was well founded because by the time the sisters had to abandon the Kaifeng mission in 1947, the Society counted forty professed sisters serving on sixteen missions, with eight novices and sixteen postulants in the novitiate. Their story will continue to be followed in future chapters.

Ceremonies and Milestones

The two dates of January 23 and August 15 were much anticipated in the novitiate as the semi-annual occasions for the ceremonies of reception and profession. The weeks leading up to the retreats which would prepare the postulants and profession novices spiritually for the definitive step they were taking were filled with expectation. On Sunday evenings, when the entire group recreated together, the novice mistress would often ring her bell and ask if the profession novices would like to sing their song. With alacrity the band that was completing the final two months of their scholastic year would gather as a

Reception Ceremony, August 15, 1962

group near the piano where a prospective music teacher would lead them in the "Profession Song."

> Profession! The day of triumph, when we pledge our all to Him.
>
> Giving and yet receiving joy that only God can give.
>
> God-like the call he sent us, seeking hearts that will be true.
>
> Queen-like must be our answer: Yes, my God, my all for you.[50]

It was an emotional moment which heightened the anticipation of pronouncing their vows and embarking on mission life. At recreation, as they watched the novitiate sisters weave the black cords for the ivory cross they would receive together with the black veil during the upcoming ceremony, the profession novices were touchingly reminded that the long-awaited goal was close at hand. Sixty days before their reception into the Congregation, the postulants were encouraged with another traditional song that began "Oh cherished little sisters."

For many years, the final preparations and rituals for reception and profession followed precisely the same order. Eight days prior to the actual day, the atmosphere throughout the building was hushed in the silence of the profession novice and postulant retreats. On the eve of the great day, both groups were called to the parlor to meet the bishop for the formal questions that would certify their readiness.

On the morning of the ceremony, all rose as usual at 4:50 a.m. and received communion at the early Mass, with the postulants leaving the chapel for breakfast at 7:00 a.m. and then dressing as brides.[51] At 8:30 the entire novitiate gathered to sing to the brides as they went to the parlors to visit with relatives. By 8:45 the entire community assembled in the church to watch the file of postulants walking slowly up the aisle while the novice's choir sang the Litany of Loretto, invoking Our Lady's protection. At 9:00 the bishop and attendants entered the sanctuary and intoned the "Veni Creator." This invocation to the Holy Spirit was taken up by the choir as the postulants filed into the sanctuary. In solemn voice they asked "for the Holy Habit of the Sisters of Providence and for the favor of admission into their novitiate."[52] After responding to the bishop's questions and prayers, each one came forward to receive the blessed habit and then left the church to exchange her bridal finery for the black serge habit and white veil.

The bishop then blessed the chaplets, the large rosaries worn as part of the habit, and the black veils to be given to the profession novices. Next the chaplain assured the bishop that the profession novices were prepared "insofar as human frailty may know" to pronounce their vows and they filed into the sanctuary as the Litany of the Saints was chanted by the choir. The bishop then directed the novices to declare their intention, and after doing so they knelt and together recited the long-anticipated vow formula. Next, each one went forward to kiss the Book of Gospels and seal her consecration with the oath, "So help me God, and His Holy Gospels." As the bishop placed the black veil over each one's cap, he prayed, "Accept this veil which marks you as a spouse of Jesus Christ and shields you from the world." At that moment one of the superiors whisked away the white novice veil beneath the new black veil while the choir reverently sang the "Suscipe Domine": "Take, Lord, and receive all my liberty, my memory, my understanding and my entire will. ... Give me only your love and your grace. That is enough for me."

Next the choir sang the hymn "Tota Pulchra Es," asking Mary's intercession as the newly robed novices re-entered the church to receive their chaplets. As they departed the sanctuary, the aspirants, the sisters who had completed their six-month second novitiate, entered the sanctuary to pronounce their perpetual vows. After their declaration of freedom and desire, a hush fell over the assembly as they knelt on the marble floor. Together they recited the vow formula, consecrating themselves with an emphatic "Forever!" to the life of a Sister of Providence. As each one went forward to swear an oath on the Bible and sign her vow card, the choir burst into "Veni, Sponsa Christi," "Come, Spouse of Christ!" The group then knelt together in the sanctuary to receive a solemn blessing. The only external indication of their new status was the placement of the crucifix on the chaplet, moved from alongside the beads to full view suspended below it. The ceremonies concluded with a Solemn High Mass.

Continuing Formation

Because the Congregation's spirit was to be characterized by "an ardent desire to acquire perfection,"[53] the structure of the life itself included multiple opportunities designed to motivate each sister to build upon her initial formation.

Mission Life

The goal of the novitiate had been to prepare the novice to profess vows, and the coda to the ceremony was the giving of an "obedience," her mission assignment. The classes she had taken as a scholastic novice had been chosen to prepare her for a teaching position, and the classes themselves would have indicated primary, elementary, secondary education or music as the likely teaching objective. But since ordinarily there was only a single year of preparation, many may have felt uncertain about undertaking the challenging teaching duties that awaited them. The size of the houses to which they might be assigned varied considerably, from the small town parish schools with three or five sisters to a large city parish or a Congregation-owned academy. True, each house followed the same horarium, but size and location had a great deal to do with how the "young professed" adapted to mission life. Especially significant would be three influential groups: the home superiors, the local superiors and the older sisters who served as mentors.

The Home Superior

Each sister was assigned to one of the six assistants on the superior general's council. One of the activities of the monthly retreat Sunday was to write a letter to this sister.[54] It was an opportunity simply to give an account of how things were going or to express concerns. The quality of this relationship varied widely, since each superior would have a large number of sisters under temporary vows sending such letters as well as numerous finally professed sisters who also had the option to call on her for assistance. During the summer retreat, each sister was expected to make an appointment with her home superior for a conference. The usefulness of this arrangement for continuing formation depended greatly on the personality and disposition of both the superior and the individual sister. With minimal formal training in counseling or spiritual direction, each superior developed her own style of handling this aspect of her responsibilities. Sister Rose Dolores Thuis is a home superior who is warmly remembered for the spiritual assistance she provided by means of written meditations she prepared and sent to "her" sisters.[55]

The Local Superior

While the *Constitutions* highlighted the role of the local superior as a model and listed her duties of leadership, the personality and style of each superior greatly affected how helpful this relationship was for those under her care. Each year, as the council pored over the assignments for each house, their chief concern was naming the person to head the list since so much of community life depended on her ability to convey a healthy religious spirit. Special instructions for superiors were held during the summer, but while the advice and suggestions were well-intentioned, the circumstances of the moment during the year called forth the best and the worst in those who were named to that office. Superiors who had developed a deep spirituality and integrated the spirit of the Rule into their own lives and practices were greatly appreciated.

Older Sisters as Mentors

As much as possible, newly professed sisters were assigned to missions where they could be paired with experienced teachers who would assist the local superior by explaining the routine to the new teachers and helping them with lesson plans.

What the novice had learned in theory she now saw in action, and such personal example inspired her as she set her own goals. The influence of these mentors can be seen in this tribute to Sister St. Philomene Cullity:

> She always had time and gave it willingly and without stint, to any of us younger Sisters who needed help. She showed us how to take care of papers in the quickest way and how to avoid loading ourselves with papers we would never find time to correct. When she was the infirmarian, she showed us how to prepare a tray to take to someone who was sick. She would go to the basement to pump hot water and bring it up to wash the patient. She was always a lady, and always true to the principles she taught.[56]

Retreats

Integral to the formation process was the retreat. During the novitiate, eight-day retreats were included as preparation for transitional events such as reception and profession of vows. As had been done from the earliest days of the Congregation's foundation, each year the superior general sent a letter circular calling the sisters to the annual retreat:

> During the Retreat, the Sisters shall examine themselves seriously on what they should have been, what they have been, and what they must be in the future; they shall make a review from the date of their last Annual Retreat, revive in themselves the spirit of piety, and draw thence additional strength to perform their duties with greater perfection.[57]

Over the years, Jesuits had been called upon to preach the annual retreat using the Ignatian Spiritual Exercises. The annual retreat was scheduled for August 6-15 and culminated on the feast of the Assumption with the ceremonies of reception and profession, followed by the reading of the Obedience List. Due to numbers, three retreats were given simultaneously in three locations, the novitiate chapel, Sacred Heart Chapel in Foley Hall, and the Church of the Immaculate Conception, with three talks or meditations and a conference each day as well as time for personal reflection.

A retreat master of the times recorded his approach, appealing to the best in each sister:

> God exercised divine power in order to prove to me, personally and individually, that He has a personal and individual love for me. I want you to keep this thought before your mind during

the whole retreat. God loves me, not because I am a member of the human race, but He loves me as an individual. ... "I have loved you with an everlasting love; therefore have I called thee." ... God is going to be very generous with you during these days. Be generous, therefore with Him.[58]

Realizing that, as the *Constitutions* warned, "Zeal the most active will diminish if not kept up and renewed,"[59] the first Sunday of the month was set aside for the monthly retreat, when the schedule was adjusted to allow time to revive the spiritual fervor of the annual retreat. A booklet of suggested prayers provided a structure for the day's reflections, including a "preparation for death" with a detailed examination of conscience.[60]

Second Novitiate

In many respects, what might be considered the crown jewel in the formation process for the Sisters of Providence was "second novitiate." Envisioned by the *Constitutions* as a "school of spirituality,"[61] it had been incorporated into the Rule in 1887 following the Decree of Praise which approved the pontifical status of the Congregation. The 1917 Code of Canon Law prescribed that perpetual vows should be taken after three years of temporary vows, with the option of three additional years if needed.[62] Since the community's custom had been to allow eight years, a special request was made to extend the time of temporary profession to five years

> in order that the young religious have a longer period of trial to prove their stability, and that the Second Novitiate which the rule provides as a preparation for the profession of perpetual vows may take place not earlier than the last or fifth year of temporary vows.[63]

This request was granted, ensuring the continuation of the time-honored practice so beneficial to the individual and the entire community. As a complement to the arrangement of two entrance dates each year, the time of the second novitiate had been set at six months. Those who were eligible were to be replaced on their mission assignment and brought home. They took up residence in a special dormitory in Providence Convent and resumed a schedule similar to the one they had known in the novitiate, under the direction of Third Assistant Sister Gertrude Clare Owens. The key element of the formation was a thirty-day retreat which followed the complete Ignatian Spiritual Exercises as adapted for the Sisters of Providence. A room in Tile Hall was designated for the second novitiate community room and here the sisters known as aspirants gathered for the points of meditation as well as special instructions. After having tested their vocation through active service and mission life, this time of renewal served as the capstone of their initial formation and prepared them to profess their vows once more, this time "Forever!"

Departures

Despite all the opportunities for spiritual development, it cannot be supposed that the program was suited for all who came to test their vocation, as can be seen in the table on page 192. Indeed, the following chapters will explain the changes in society and within the congregation which completely altered the formation program.

The novitiate served as an effective screening process in determining suitability for the life. The mistress of novices met regularly with the council to provide observations. Comments from the council minutes such as "has not shown the proper attitude towards the religious life," "self-willed," "vain and worldly," and "duplicity" were heeded when decisions were made regarding reception of the habit or profession of vows. At other times, possible health issues were deemed less significant than the fact that the novice "has manifested a really religious spirit."[64] Indeed, many who left did so because they themselves discerned that their call was to the married or single life and continued to "manifest a really religious spirit" in the next phase of their lives.

Once the sister professed vows, as a member of the Congregation with rights defined by canon law, decisions regarding departure, if not mutual, could cause considerable controversy. When individuals protested their assignments, efforts were usually made to accommodate them, but when the situation repeated itself, there was reason to doubt the authenticity of a vocation. In one such instance, "This Sister is declared incorrigible. The Secretary is directed to draw up the required formula for dismissal; that is, a request to the Ordinary for a dispensation from Perpetual Vows."[65] In such cases, the safeguard for the sister was to appeal to the bishop, and in the rare instances of such situations, lengthy negotiations were

TABLE 6: *Perseverance of entrants in final years of decades, 1929-1969*

Year	Entrances	Departures						Persevered
	Total	Dismissed		Left			Total	
			During novitiate	Temporary Vows		Perpetual dispensed		
				Left at End	Dispensed			
1929	47	4	6	2	0	2	12	33
1939	42	0	5	2	1	3	11	31
1949	47	1	11	1	0	8	21	26
1959	50	3	12	8	16	5	44	6
1969	7	0	3	2	0	0	5	2

needed to effect reconciliation. When questions arose regarding vow renewal, usually the situation could be handled internally, as when the council minutes state that, "it was decided to bring sister home that efforts may be made to correct her."[66] However, council minutes also indicate that the decision could also be at the individual's initiative: "Sister felt she was out of place in community and withdraws."[67]

In other instances where a sister's disobedient behavior was obvious to others, the situation could escalate. Though unusual, such "defections" did occur, as in an instance described in detail by the Book of Important Events.

> Sister allowed herself to be influenced by her sister's complaints [another Sister of Providence] and by her mother's constant interference in what she considered the welfare of her daughter. She was eager for self-improvement and frequently expressed her surprise that she was not given advantages as were

other sisters. ... The building in which she taught was apart from the school; hence she was mistress of her realm and certainly exercised the liberty it afforded her. [A former pupil acted as an intermediary to mail letters to her sister and mother in which they made secret plans to use their mother's inheritance to go to Arizona or even to found their own community. When this was discovered,] Rev. Mother called both sisters to St. Mary's that they might make their application for dispensations and leave in the proper manner. ...The next morning they laid aside their holy Habits, put on secular garb, and left with their mother.[68]

Most departure situations were considerably more prosaic, as noted in the community diary: "Today at ten o'clock, Sister N., whose vows expired, left for her home."[69]

For middle-class Americans who had become accustomed to ongoing improvements in living standards, the stresses of the Great Depression and war years gradually took a toll which expressed itself in the Congregation by individual requests for exemptions from rules, customs and even the life itself. Based on a flurry of reasonably legitimate complaints coming to the superiors, it is clear that the stamina of more and more Sisters of Providence was also diminished. The council minutes indicate that some were simply "unable to take the stairs" while others went so far as to ask for dispensations due to "the strain of religious life."[70] This combination of two factors—the normal physical diminishments of age which made it impossible to continue in the schoolroom and situations of sisters wavering in their vocations—greatly complicated the annual process of assigning sisters to missions where their professional and spiritual formation could best be continued.

For the vast majority, as the processes outlined here demonstrate, the Congregation had over the years taken to heart Mother Theodore's admonition to "never forget why they came here" by developing tried and true methods of formation. Clearly most of the women drawn to religious life found proven paths to self-fulfillment, to a deep and life-giving spirituality and a commitment to service to God's people in the opportunities for formation provided by the Sisters of Providence.

❧ Chapter 7
Celebration, Expansion and War 1938-1949

The White Cross of Gladness - *Centenary Program of Saint Mary-of-the-Woods College*

A Time of Transition

As Mother Mary Raphael began the final year of her twelve years of office, she and her council seemed as uncertain as the rest of the country regarding the best way forward. By May of 1937 it was obvious that President Roosevelt's New Deal had done its utmost to revitalize the economy but had proved insufficient. More and more layoffs continued through the summer, the stock market plunged again in September, and the 1938 midterm elections eroded support for his program. As we have seen, it was during this time of unrest that even loyal Sisters of Providence felt the need to take their complaints to Bishop Ritter.

International events did little to boost morale as diplomatic maneuvers failed to deflect Hitler's militaristic expansion of Germany's borders, while the Vatican's support of Franco in Spain as an opponent of atheistic communism blurred Catholics' perceptions of fascist alliances.[1] For Sisters of Providence, it was Japan's 1937 invasion of China and the welfare of the mission there that was of greatest concern as intermittent letters brought news of the bombings and the sisters' care of the wounded soldiers at Kaifeng. Even while preparations went forward for the 1938 General Chapter, it was clear that, despite the Rule's injunction to remain aloof from worldly affairs, the world's affairs would inevitably have a greater and greater impact on their lives.

The General Chapter of 1938

When Bishop Joseph Ritter called the Chapter to order at 9:00 a.m. on Friday morning, June 24, 1938, thirty-seven women responded to the roll call of delegates. Of this number, thirteen were ex-officio members. How could this be when the *Constitutions* named only the superior general and her six assistants, plus the treasurer general as ex officio delegates? A great deal of study had gone into preparing a draft of the changes needed in the *Constitutions* once the provincial structure was approved and, of course, four provincial superiors had already been appointed. As seen in Chapter 4, Mother Mary Raphael had written to Bishop Ritter asking that the provincials be included as members of the Chapter, and he replied that the permission was granted "for the time being only." With twenty-four members elected at large and eight general officers and now four provincials the total would have been thirty-six. Who was the thirty-seventh member?[2]

When the 1932 Chapter elected Sister Eugenia Clare Cullity as fifth assistant and director of education, Sister Francis Joseph Elbreg had continued in the role of supervisor but was not on the council. Was she entitled to be a member of the Chapter? Although there is no record of any discussion of this question, she in fact was the thirty-seventh member.[3] In light of Bishop Ritter's role the previous October in forwarding complaints from the sisters about "the supervisor of schools being autocratic," perhaps he raised an eyebrow, but he didn't raise an objection.

Despite the difficult Depression years of her second term, Mother Mary Raphael had a great deal of good news in her report. In addition to the China mission, the Congregation now had houses coast to coast. The long-anticipated intermediate level of government had actually been in operation for four years. Providence Juniorate had been established, and a small but steady stream of applicants arrived twice yearly at the novitiates newly established in Maryland and California as well as at the novitiate at Saint Mary-of-the-Woods, bringing the total membership to 1,240. Six new missions had been opened, with sisters now teaching in ninety-three schools, a day nursery and the College as well as doing catechetical work in many parishes. In addition to the 482 who had received teacher licenses, eighty had earned bachelor's degrees and eighteen had achieved master's degrees. In China, the catechist society continued to grow and the schools to operate in spite of the civil war situation.

The treasurer's report was equally encouraging in that it represented a balanced budget, although loans had been negotiated to cover major expenses associated with the College, Ladywood in Indianapolis, Providence in Chicago and the western and eastern provincial houses. Due to Sister Adelaide O'Brien's continuing poor health, Sister Francis Raphael Donlon had been appointed to fill out her term and she presented the report.

Mother Mary Bernard Laughlin

The elections reflected a certain satisfaction with the status quo. At age seventy-five, with poor health and thirty-six years of service, Mother Mary Raphael was clearly not a candidate. She graciously accepted the gratitude and appreciation of the delegates. Her first assistant, Sister Mary Bernard Laughlin, was elected as superior general on the first ballot, and Bishop Ritter immediately administered the oath of office. Almost all the assistants were re-elected: Sisters Gertrude Clare Owens and Marie Stanislaus Curran retained their positions as third assistant and sixth assistant/secretary, while Sister Helen Clare Freiburger moved up to first assistant, and Sister Eileen Walker to second assistant. The office of fourth assistant required two ballots, with Indiana Provincial Sister Mary Rose Cummings being elected. The voting for office of fifth assistant and director of education revealed some division in preference. Sister Eugenia Clare had been given many behind-the-scenes projects, such as preparing the revised draft of the *Constitutions* and assisting with the College administration, while Sister Francis Joseph had been more visible to the sisters as she visited the schools, and this seemed to tip the balance. Slightly more than half of the votes, the required absolute majority, went to Sister Francis Joseph on the first ballot, signaling the desire of the delegates that the role of supervisor of schools should have the status of a council member. Sister Francis Raphael was handily elected to continue her appointed role as treasurer general.

Unlike many previous Chapters, the business at hand included not simply elections, but an agenda—discussion of the proposed revisions to the *Constitutions*, which would move the transitional phase of the provincial government into the canonically approved form. This would have been the first opportunity for sisters beyond the inner circle of the council to have seen the specifics laid out. The long-term effects of creating four semi-independent governmental units were immediately apparent to the delegates. Contemplating the domino effect of shifting responsibilities for local superiors, school supervision, finances, visitation and placement prompted each delegate to think hard about how her own life would be affected. Once each province had separate chapters and election procedures, what would happen to the existing network of relationships that had brought this General Chapter group together? Doubtless sensitive to the imbalance of representation already evident within their own membership, this topic brought delegates to their feet to begin a lively discussion. Guided by parliamentary procedure, a series of motions, seconds and voting eventually led to the approval of the proposed plan. The Chapter minutes are careful to add "with the understanding that further revisions may be made, if found desirable, at the next meeting of the General Chapter."[4] Breathing space was ensured.

Another topic of significant import was also on the agenda—the sisters coadjutrix. As we have seen in Chapter 6, by 1938, less than ten years after the 1929 *Constitutions* had moderated the French Rule, the non-teaching auxiliaries already felt that references to them in the *Constitutions* were demeaning.[5] Apparently their complaints were heard and the Chapter members dealt with the issue with the intention of fostering greater charity. They voted to remove from the *Constitutions* the sections pertaining to the sisters coadjutrix, charging the superior general with inserting alternate clauses excusing sisters responsible for domestic work from spiritual exercises.

When the 1938 Chapter adjourned at 3:47 p.m. that afternoon, the delegates must have come away with a sense of accomplishment. In a mere two and a quarter hours they had conducted a true Chapter of Affairs. The sisters arriving for homecoming might have been disappointed at seeing no new faces in Tile Hall, but in uneasy times it was with a sense of security that they learned that the familiar and comforting presence of Sister Mary Bernard was the woman they would now address as Mother. And Mother Mary Bernard could move into her new role with confidence since she knew the strengths of her experienced assistants. Unemployment might be the fate of most of those who lost jobs in 1938, but such a status was unknown within the Congregation. Outgoing Fifth Assistant Sister Eugenia Clare was immediately assigned a new challenge as superior of Blessed Sacrament in North Carolina. Sister Francis Raphael, whose interim appointment had been resoundingly approved when she was elected by the Chapter to continue in the post of treasurer, though not a member of the council, requires a brief introduction.

Sister Francis Raphael Donlon 1894-1981

Elizabeth (Bess) Donlon was born in Chicago in 1894, one of six children of John and Margaret Donlon. She was educated by the Sisters of Providence at St. Mel and at Providence High School and then studied at De Paul University. She joined the work force before entering the novitiate in 1921 at age twenty-six. After her profession in 1923, she spent a semester as the treasurer of Immaculata in Washington, D.C., before returning to Saint Mary-of-the-Woods where she worked under Sister Mary Raphael during her final two years as treasurer. This firm grounding in the Congregation's finance system made her an ideal liaison with the College when she was appointed to build up its endowment. Due to the poor health of Treasurer General Sister Adelaide, she had proved to be the mainstay in the smooth functioning of the office and was well-positioned to take over full responsibility for this key office. She would serve in this role for twenty-eight more years through four subsequent administrations, retiring in 1966. She offered volunteer service at three missions before returning to the motherhouse in 1971, where she died on November 6, 1981.

When Mother Mary Bernard moved to her new place at the head of the council table in June 1938, she was well aware of the challenges facing the Congregation. Given that the council members were the same sisters with whom she had worked so closely during the previous six years, she must have felt she could continue with confidence on the same path as her predecessors. By now the experimental plan of provincial government was familiar to all, and she could count on the assistance of provincial superiors to be close to situations in the far-flung local communities. Already on the horizon was the celebration of the Congregation's one-hundredth anniversary of its foundation, an event which would be a catalyst for the sisters' expressions of their animating spirit in visible and creative ways.

Centenary Celebration

Planning

After being elected to her second term in 1932, Mother Mary Raphael had set the wheels in motion for a major celebration by asking Fifth Assistant Sister Eugenia Clare to begin planning for the 1940 commemorative events. Sister Eugenia Clare lost little time in utilizing that unmatched vehicle for accomplishing a task—forming a committee. Having been missioned at Providence High School in Chicago with Sister Eugenia Logan and having taught at the College, she was quick to see the advantage of utilizing her friend's position as dean of the College to focus its conveniently located and excellent resources on this goal.

Under their leadership the committee met at least yearly from 1932 to1936 and generated ideas and plans which would involve the members in highlighting the history and works of the Congregation.[6] Fortunately, there was a great deal of material readily available. Mother Theodore had ever been mindful of taking note of her surroundings and had kept a journal of her travels; such chronicling had become second nature in the community. During Mother Euphrasie Hinkle's 1883-1886 administration, a formal collection and administration of the early documents had been begun. Sister Mary Theodosia Mug had utilized these for her 1904 biography of Mother Theodore.[7] During her tenure as curator she edited them further in order to publish the *Journals and Letters of Mother Theodore Guerin* in 1937, making the founding history widely available to the sisters and the public.[8]

The College Library, located in Foley Hall, housed a Community Historical Section that included a museum with artifacts and documents from the founding times. The director of the museum, Sister Ignatia Braheny, brought forth the idea of preparing a visual depiction of significant moments of the Congregation's history through the medium of dioramas. Miniature three-dimensional scenes in domed cases could be viewed through a glass window by pushing a button activating both an interior light and a recorded explanation. When diorama artist Henri Marchaud executed a sample based on sketches from the times, the lasting value of such an eye-catching display was clear. Mr. Gregory Kamke was engaged to create additional scenes depicting the chronology of key historical events beginning with the storm at sea on the voyage from France to the United States, featuring such events as the first graduation ceremony at the Academy and concluding with the 1886 laying of the foundation of the church.[9]

The tremendous talent available in the sister faculty of the College music and art departments made possible the presentation of an historical pageant. Materials would be prepared to be sent out to the Sister of Providence schools in order to provide background for an essay contest and the preparation of a memorial booklet. Lest any avenue of talent might go unexplored, the sisters were invited to contribute original literary or musical compositions. With the 1938 change of administration and the loss of Sister Eugenia Clare, Mother Mary Bernard continued to encourage the plans. She appointed Sister Mary Joseph Pomeroy, one of the first graduates of the College and now a member of the College faculty, chair of the committee and assigned her an office in Foley Hall. Sister Francis Joseph recruited the assistance of primary teachers Sisters Anne Clementine Lee and Bernadetta Ryan to write and Sister Anne Clementine to illustrate a child's version of Mother Theodore's early life, which was published as *Anne Therese* in 1939.

In preparation for the Centenary celebration, efforts were made to spruce up the grounds. In March 1938 a tree specialist was engaged to look after the preservation of the campus trees, many of which were showing signs of decay.[10] The long-awaited outdoor stations along the road leading to the cemetery were blessed on November 2, 1938. Plans were drawn up to expand and landscape the cemetery. The statue group depicting Calvary at its far end was refurbished, a large stone Celtic cross was placed over Mother Theodore's original grave and a tablet listing the names of sisters who were buried in other locations was placed on a large stone marker. With the death of Chaplain Monsignor Augustine Rawlinson on December 10, 1939, it was decided to designate a special section of the cemetery for chaplains who expressed a wish to be buried there.[11] The large Sacred Heart Chapel in Foley Hall was renovated and new pews were installed. Landscaping of a traffic circle created a graceful transition from the Avenue to the beautiful Italian Renaissance façade of Foley Hall, and a historical marker was placed in its courtyard to mark the site of the first chapel.

The extravagant events of this year-long celebration provide a unique perspective on the scope and influence of the Congregation, as well as the achievements of many sisters, and justify an extended digression. The investment in the members' education over the years now bore abundant fruit as they deftly carried on scores of behind-the-scenes activities. Public performances for the opening and closing events showcased the talents of students, alumnae and friends. Only among themselves during the summer did the sisters come forth to stand in the spotlight as they shared their enthusiastic enjoyment of their joint heritage with one another.

Centenary Events

Opening of the Centenary

The year-long celebration officially opened in conjunction with the January 23, 1940, reception and profession ceremonies. On the eve of the ceremony the College glee club, verse-speaking choir and orchestra combined to present the pageant *The White Cross of Gladness* in Cecilian Auditorium, with Bishop Ritter and his party occupying one of the boxes. Using the white crucifix worn as part of the habit as a symbol of the Christian faith in triumph over pain, Sister Teresa Aloyse Mount's composition dramatically summarized significant events in the Congregation's history. History professor Monsignor Joseph Kempf used the occasion to announce the winners of the essay contest from Sister of Providence schools from coast to coast.

Early the next morning a solemn procession from the library in Providence Convent through the hall to the main door of the church was led by members of the College faculty in academic regalia, followed by the postulants in bridal attire. Then came the clergy, many in habits of their orders and others in "new and brilliant vestments," including Bishop Ritter wearing the elegant *cappa magna*, the ceremonial mantle which required an assistant dressed in scarlet and black to walk behind him carrying its long train.[12] A combined choir of novices and College students sang plain chant for the High Mass, traditional pieces such as the "Ecce Sacerdos" for the processional and the "Suscipe" to accompany the profession ceremony. A banquet for the guests followed in the College dining hall, with speeches from civic leaders. Guests were invited to stop by the Alumnae Office to view the scale models of the various Sister of Providence schools which had been built locally and shipped with pride from near and far. They could also purchase rosaries made by Sister Baptista Courcier or other souvenirs. The following week the College hosted a dinner for Terre Haute businessmen.[13]

Summer Celebrations

May 30, 1940, Memorial Day, was the occasion for a wide ranging celebration. It began with a field Mass in the cemetery. This was followed by a ceremonial decorating with flags of the graves of the sister Civil War nurses. The ceremony was accompanied by a volley fired by the Fort Benjamin Harrison Post of the American Legion and a bugle rendition of taps. The assembly then marched to the music of Chicago's forty-eight-member Providence High School band to bless each of the three historical markers of the first convent, chapel and

Top row, left to right: Sisters Alma Therese Klee, Jane Maher, Alexa Suelzer, Francis Borgia Van Hoy, Edward Clare (Rita) Lerner, Rita Marie Frawley, Daniel Ahlfeld, Denise Dillon, Francis Eugene Bussing. Bottom row, left to right: Sisters Cecilia Ann Miller, Ann Marguerite Frye, Ann Bernice Kuper, Ann Mary Dietz, Patricia Louise Quinn and two unidentified postulants.

motherhouse, and then went on to the new flagpole in front of Le Fer Hall for a culminating flag-raising ceremony.

The usual summer gathering at the motherhouse was marked by a series of events by and for the sisters themselves. On June 27 the sisters assembled in groups led by Mother Mary Bernard and the council members for pilgrimages to the cemetery. On July 16 the Jubilee celebration featured a play written by Sister Francis Cecile Miller based on the life of Mother Theodore and performed by the novices and postulants. The annual St. Anne procession on July 25 was followed the next day on the feast itself by a concert of original compositions which the program described as arranged "in the form of a musical travelogue through Saint Mary-of-the-Woods."[14] On August 5, although the chronicler carefully notes that it was only "after the examinations were over,"[15] the entire day was given over to recreation. A small parade sparked the celebration, with a drum and bugle corps leading a group of novices and postulants dressed in authentic historical garb from the founding days to the present.

Closing Celebration

As invitations went out for the grand closing celebration on the actual anniversary date, October 22, 1940, the response was overwhelming. So many clergy planned to attend that the council minutes record that Fourth Assistant Sister Mary Rose was dispatched to the Indianapolis chancery to consult "as to what is needed for the proper care of the hierarchy."[16] Arrangements were made with Sister Rose Dolores' brother, Father John Thuis, OSB, to bring from St. Meinrad Archabbey ten portable altars as well as sacred vessels and vestments to place in Le Fer Hall to accommodate the many priests who would offer Mass.[17]

On October 14 the entire Congregation began spiritual preparation with a novena. At Saint Mary-of-the-Woods the three-day celebration began the weekend of October 19 and the transportation committee was kept busy meeting alumnae and friends at the train station.[18] The College students had given up their rooms in Le Fer Hall and doubled up in Guerin Hall to accommodate overnight guests attending the 9:00 a.m. High Mass on Sunday, October 20. Some simply enjoyed visits to favorite campus places before departing for their work week, but many had arranged the time so as to be present for Monday's Alumnae Day. Following the High Mass in Sacred Heart Chapel in Foley Hall, the alumnae in a body visited Mother Theodore's tomb in the crypt of the church and later enjoyed a luncheon in the College dining hall.

Meanwhile, behind the scenes, clergy were arriving for the big events of the next day. By afternoon Archbishop McNicolas of Cincinnati and Bishop Ritter had arrived and were greeted in the Blue Parlor of Le Fer Hall by Mother Mary Bernard and her council, who remained to receive the alumnae and guests. Special guests were presented with a bound souvenir program containing an abbreviated history of the Congregation complete with photographs of the three provincial houses in Anaheim, California, Evanston, Illinois, and Hyattsville, Maryland. Throughout the afternoon the College riding master, Captain Lancaster, led students on horseback in several colorful miniparades down the Avenue. A carillion concert followed a dinner served to the guests. That evening a musical was presented by the alumnae, and a College glee club serenade concluded the day. The chronicler commends the enthusiastic spirit of the alumnae, commenting, "The loyalty and love of the 'old girls' was remarked. To have been a former student seemed to be the greatest point of interest today."[19]

Tuesday, October 22, 1940, dawned bright, clear and warm, an ideal "Indian summer" day. The various masters of ceremonies busily assembled the procession at Le Fer Hall. Promptly at 9:45 a.m. the cross-bearer led the alumnae, students in cap and gown, visiting university presidents in academic regalia, priests, monsignors, abbots and bishops with Archbishop McNicolas in full *cappa magna* as they solemnly proceeded along the sidewalk to the Church. As the sisters' and novices' choir sang, the congregation was able to follow the ceremony with specially printed souvenir Mass programs. Bishop James Hugh Ryan of Omaha, who had played an influential role as administrator and professor at Saint Mary-of-the-Woods College, preached the sermon.[20] He used the occasion to pay glowing tribute to the sacrifice and prayer of the Congregation's leaders and members.

A banquet catered by the Terre Haute House was then served to the guests, followed by speeches from the hierarchy, members of the College endowment board and a distinguished alumna. In the afternoon the guests returned to the church to enjoy the performance of a cantata composed specifically for the occasion by Sister Cecilia Clare Bocard, with words by Sister Eugenia Logan. Entitled *Queen of Heaven,* the life of Mary as expressed through the joyful, sorrowful and glorious mysteries of the rosary, it was sung by the sisters' and novices' choir and several sister soloists. Sung Vespers concluded the concert, with supper then served to the guests. A 7:00 p.m. carillon concert was then followed by an elaborate staging of the pageant, *The White Cross of Gladness,* featuring music by the Terre Haute Civic and State Teachers College Symphony Orchestra.

The chronicler concludes: "Thus ends the day – our centenary celebration."[21]

Yes, the events were concluded, but the lives of the sisters had been profoundly touched. The legacy of Mother Theodore was now preserved in literary form in the published *Letters and Journals,* which were taken up in conversation and repeated reading. Sisters entertained their Saint Mary-of-the-Woods visitors with tours of the dioramas and after the 1949 publication of volume one of the community history, they could expound at length on the scenes depicted. In coming to appreciate the unique heritage of the Sisters of Providence, each sister had the opportunity to reflect on her own vocation and the story of why she had come and become part of the larger story.

Expansion of the Mission

The events described in the previous section bear witness to the energy and talent of the sisters. Clearly the abilities they displayed had been developed through their work as educators, a work which had continued to find new venues during this time. Rather than the strategic selection of missions which had characterized her predecessor's terms, Mother Mary Bernard gave priority to requests from bishops and priests with long-standing ties to the Congregation. Nonetheless, the designs of Providence led her along some unexpected paths.

The West

Unplanned and unexpected but certainly welcome was the invitation to open St. Anthony School in Gardena, California. It was already August 1940 when the pastor requested sisters for his newly constructed school. Sister Mary Stanislaus Graffe had barely arrived in Anaheim to begin her term as provincial superior. After an immediate consultation with the diocesan supervisor of schools and a visit to the parish, she wired the motherhouse urging immediate acceptance. Worried that a refusal might prevent future invitations, in her follow-up letter she urged, "Surely you can't refuse when we are trying to gain a foothold in this big California field."[22] Since school was to start the following week and the sisters had already arrived at their assigned missions, three sisters from nearby missions and one from Illinois were reassigned. Undaunted by these last-minute arrangements, the small band of pioneers was welcomed to their comfortable convent and in turn prepared their classrooms to welcome the pupils on opening day. Already the policy of local recruitment was bearing fruit, for the first California postulant, Sister Angela Clare Gorman, was one of the four sisters assigned to the new mission.

Academies Phased into Diocesan High Schools

As described in earlier sections, the professionalization of education had led to the establishment of diocesan offices of education in order to ensure coordination of efforts and high standards.[23] This reallocation of administrative authority had an impact on longstanding policies and practices of the Sisters of Providence. Gradual adaptation was inevitable, but it was not without some painful adjustments.

Fort Wayne, Indiana

Plans and negotiations that had gone forward during Mother Mary Raphael's term culminated with the opening of the newly constructed Central Catholic High School in Fort Wayne in 1938. Because plans for housing for the sister faculty were still in progress, the Sisters of Providence who formed the faculty continued to live in the two previous academies' convents. Some of the sisters lived next door at St. Augustine Convent, while others had to commute from St. Catherine Convent. Each house had its own superior, but only the St. Augustine superior retained the title and responsibilities of principal. Both groups took their main meal during the lunch period at St. Augustine, but the "out-sisters" were charged for the meal. A certain amount of friction inevitably occurred and complaints were sent to the motherhouse, requiring visits from the home superiors and changes of local superiors.

Another source of discontent was the fact that, since the Congregation did not teach "large boys," another congregation of sisters had been engaged for this purpose. This arrangement of two congregations with differing policies yet sharing faculty responsibilities proved unsatisfactory. It was decided that the sisters would teach boys in the upper level classes the following year, and the other congregation would withdraw. Meanwhile there began a long series of renovations and moves of the buildings around "Cathedral Square." The old St. Augustine convent was torn down and a new chancery was built on the site. The old chancery was renovated to provide faculty housing, and in 1949 the thirty-six sisters on the high school faculty took up residence in the renamed Providence Convent.[24] Next door was the parish rectory, with the brothers' former residence next to it. In 1951 this residence was remodeled to house the grade school sisters and renamed Cathedral Convent, with some of the downstairs rooms given over as a family residence for the parish custodian.[25]

Evansville, Indiana

A similar situation prevailed in the Indianapolis diocese at Reitz Memorial High School in the city of Evansville, where it took several years to work out a housing plan for the sisters. The sisters on the faculty had lived at Assumption Convent and relied on transportation by auto, but when a new priest was assigned to Assumption Parish he questioned this expense. Superintendent Father John Holloran organized a nine-parish committee in 1938 to raise funds to purchase a home and renovate it as a convent for the sister faculty. Even then, the growth of enrollment and need for increased faculty required the addition of an entire story to the house, and it was not until November 1939 that the twelve sisters had their own convent.

Parish Schools

Indiana

In the single year of 1941 three new schools were opened in the Diocese of Indianapolis. One provided the occasion for the Sisters of Providence to continue efforts toward racial integration. In the city of Evansville along the Ohio River, the African-American population was increasing.[26] The black Catholic community was served by Assumption Parish, with the sisters there teaching catechism to the children on Sundays. In 1941 Bishop Ritter decided that African-American Catholics should have their own parish, and he established St. John Church, asking the Sisters of Providence to serve as faculty for its two-room school. Both a record of success at St. Rita in Indianapolis and the proximity of the Assumption convent motivated the decision to comply with his request. Two sisters were assigned to live at Assumption and commute to teach at the fifty-pupil school. Bishop Ritter dedicated the church[27] in May and expressed satisfaction when he visited the school in October 1942.[28] Later, during the war years, when the sisters could not return to the motherhouse, two sisters conducted a summer school. In 1945 the parish supplied a two-story house with a chapel behind the school to serve as a convent for the three sisters then assigned.

To provide Catholic education for his small St. John the Baptist parish in the town of Newburgh on the Ohio River near Evansville, Father Francis Mellon requested the services of the Congregation. Beginning in 1941 two sisters lived at Assumption Convent in Evansville and commuted to

Newburgh, leaving on the seven o'clock bus and returning home on the five o'clock bus each day. Every pastor's desire for a Catholic school at that time is well expressed in his assessment of their work. "The two splendid nuns you sent have all the qualifications to transform our children into real honest-to-goodness Catholics."[29] As his circumstances improved, his gratitude took concrete form when he purchased a home for the sisters in 1947, and three years later he provided an even larger house next to the rectory.

That same year the superiors visited the recently established parish of St. Thomas Aquinas in Indianapolis and found it to be what the Book of Establishments described as a "splendid location and many wooded spaces where homes may be built ... and where the parishioners realized the benefit that comes to a parish when the Sisters are an integral part of it."[30] When St. Thomas Aquinas School opened in 1941 the first band of sisters lived at St. Agnes and commuted by taxi until in 1947 the rectory was renovated to serve as a convent home.

Chicago

During the fifty-five years that Sisters of Providence had served in Chicago, the city had changed around them. The sisters at St. Mel School could only chuckle at the account of the band of twelve who had alighted from the train in 1886 and traveled "the rough and muddy roads on the open prairies with goats and wild geese running about"[31] to arrive at the parish then known as St. Philip. By 1931 the archdiocesan newspaper, *The New World*, described the area as "a neighborhood of spacious thoroughfares and substantial houses."[32] It was also a very Catholic neighborhood, for by 1941 it was necessary to split St. Mel Parish and form Holy Ghost Parish, with its own school. St. Mel's pastor, Msgr. Francis A. Purcell, was named administrator of Holy Ghost. A later parish chronicler explained that to manage this assignment, "it was the wish of Msgr. Purcell that the two schools be considered as one, hence the name St. Mel-Holy Ghost School given to Holy Ghost School."[33]

Even at that the St. Mel parish plant was of staggering size, for it included the all boys' St. Mel High School with a 1945 enrollment of 1,500 and the elementary school, including a kindergarten, with some 1,000 pupils.[34] By 1942 the former rectory was converted to become the convent, but by 1945 it was necessary to construct an addition to house the twenty sisters in residence. During this time, as their numbers increased, the sisters moved from one part of the building to another with construction constantly going on around them. It was not until 1947 that Holy Ghost finally became a separate school with distinct faculties named on the Obedience List.

Not far from St. Mel's, Our Lady of Sorrows School had also been continuously staffed by the Sisters of Providence since they had built the combined Providence Academy/Our Lady of Sorrows in 1887. In the early days the convent and school were both in the single building. However, when the Congregation built Providence High School nearby and the high school sisters moved to its convent quarters in 1929, the original building was remodeled to serve as the convent for the parish school faculty as well as the music department and kindergarten. By that time it was expected that the parish would provide both school and convent buildings, so in 1944 the Congregation offered to sell the building to the Servite Fathers who staffed the parish, but they declined the offer. Only three years later, two unanticipated events forced the issue. First, a fire badly damaged the convent in 1947 (see Chapter 8). Second the neighborhood was undergoing drastic change due to both to the construction of the Congress Expressway (later named the Eisenhower) a few blocks from the property,[35] and also to demographic shifts which would completely alter the complexion of the area in a few short years. During the negotiations following the fire the Servite Fathers agreed to purchase the entire property from the Sisters of Providence with a plan to use part of the west wing of the renovated building as offices of the American province of the Servants of Mary.[36]

The East – Lady Isle

On the East Coast, an entirely unexpected event led to a unique establishment. The story of the Sisters of Providence is intertwined with those who became close to the sisters and caught the spirit of Providence, often maintaining ties over the years and contributing in many ways to the mission. An early example of such partnership is the story of Elizabeth Marable Brennan.[37] After the death of her mother, although eleven-year-old Elizabeth was not Catholic, she was enrolled as a boarder at St. John Academy in Indianapolis, where her music studies with Sister Marie Besner continued until her graduation.[38] Elizabeth found her music teacher's kindness a great comfort, especially when sister suggested that Mary, the Mother of God, would always be Elizabeth's mother as well. After her marriage to Phillip A. Brennan, Elizabeth converted to the Catholic faith and became active in Catholic social circles and organizations. She attributed her work of founding "Mary's Day" in 1928, an annual celebration of the motherhood of Mary on the Saturday before Mother's Day, to the influence of Sister Marie. Her devotion expanded to a worldwide vision as she arranged for several shrines under the title of Mary, Mother of Mankind, including the donation of a specially sculpted statue to her alma mater.[39]

In 1940, after Judge Brennan retired from his position on the Supreme Court of New York and Mrs. Brennan's health declined, the couple expressed their desire to give their summer home, Belle Isle, in Portsmouth, New Hampshire, to the Sisters of Providence. Mother Mary Bernard's illness prevented an immediate response, but in July 1941 she and Sister Marie visited Mrs. Brennan at Belle Isle. They were amazed at the beauty of the site—an actual island complete with an estate house and outbuildings. The council decided to accept the of-

Lady Isle, Portsmouth, New Hampshire

fer and to use the facility as a summer home for sisters and for retreats for ladies during the school year, naming it Lady Isle and placing it under the patronage of Mary, Mother of Mankind. In September 1941, Mother Mary Bernard and Sister Francis Raphael met with the Brennans at the Isle to sign the transfer of property.

The Book of Establishments describes the magnificent site as including not only the thirteen-room estate house with all its furnishings, kitchen ware, linens and so on, but also a caretaker's house, two completely furnished cottages, a tool shed and greenhouse, boat house, bathing house, fire house, large barn and a garage with a five passenger Chevrolet car.[40] Mother Mary Bernard had written to the provincial of the East, Sister St. Eugenia McBarron, to come from Maryhurst to Lady Isle. We are indebted to her for this forthright account of her new appointment:

> We got there on Saturday and Mother took us all over the Isle. I couldn't quite understand the way Mother was talking. When she showed us the barn, she said, "This would make a wonderful residence hall, wouldn't it?" Of course I answered, "yes." On the first floor, she said, "it would be nice to have boxes here for the Sisters' clothes, don't you think so?" I looked at her and wondered, "Just what is all this coming to?" We went to Mass at Portsmouth, and then afterwards Mother had a talk with all of us. She said to me, "Sister, I will be going in the morning— I'm going to St. Mary's—and you take over." Just like that—you take over! Then she asked, "How much money have you?" I told her I had $96, and she answered, "Bank it." And so we started on $96. That was the year the war broke out in December. ... All during the winter we lived in a blackout. There was a Navy yard just across the street from us—one of the largest in the world. Although we had a boat, we couldn't use it for the waters were dangerous—everyone was fearful of mines.[41]

During the negotiations for the transfer of the property, Bishop John B. Patterson had invited the Congregation to assume charge of the small school being vacated by the Sisters of Mercy in nearby Rochester, New Hampshire. Three sisters arrived there in September 1942 to take up residence in the comfortable convent, walking about a mile to a converted barn which served as school, with grades one through four in one classroom and grades five through eight in the other.

Sisters pose for photo after their annual retreat at Lady Isle.

Lady Isle proved to be a great asset and much-beloved re-treat and vacation site for the Congregation over the years. Gradually the buildings were remodeled to provide a chapel and dormitories. With the cooperation of the missions in the nearby Boston vicinity, Sister St. Eugenia initiated a series of weekend retreats for young women. In all likelihood the stress of the war years was a significant motivator, as each regis-trant was reminded through her letter of acceptance: "Only a limited number have the coveted privilege of these days of peace and restfulness, separated from the troubles, distractions, and enjoyments of the world, in the peaceful atmosphere of the Sisters' home."[42]

Upon arrival, each retreatant received a manual of devo-tions and a white veil to be worn during the conferences given by the Jesuit priest engaged as retreat master. The retreat min-istry was short-lived however, lasting only from 1946-1951. Meanwhile, renovation of the facilities, including the widen-ing of the entrance, strengthening of the sea wall and convert-ing the barn into classrooms, made it possible to open a school in September 1947. This building, named Marian Hall, could be adapted in the summer to accommodate the sisters missioned in the Northeast during their annual retreat. Begin-ning in 1945, the month of July was always scheduled as va-cation for these sisters since they only went to Saint Mary-of-the-Woods every other year.

In 1945, Mrs. Brennan offered to give her Brooklyn home to the Congregation with the stipulation that two sisters would live there and continue her work with the Mary's Day movement, but this offer was declined.[43]

Saint Mary-of-the-Woods College

At the beginning of her administration, Mother Mary Bernard took the time to meet with individual sister faculty at Saint Mary-of-the-Woods College in order to become better acquainted with the College's workings and needs. Although the finances of the Congregation and the College had been legally separated in 1928, the Board which administered the College was composed entirely of Sisters of Providence, some from the council and others from the faculty. To ensure that its programs would attract students, priority was given to raising the College's local profile by encouraging an active presence in the Terre Haute community. Sisters often visited prospective students as part of the admission process.[44] In addition to advertising and personal recruitment, a key strategy was ensuring that the curriculum would meet or excel accreditation requirements.

As they returned from study for advanced degrees and attendance at professional conferences, the sister faculty distinguished themselves among their peers. Under the leadership of Sister Esther Newport, in October 1937 a meeting of thirty-six sisters representing various colleges gave birth to the Catholic College Arts Association.[45] Sister Esther's paintings were often exhibited, and her illustrations were published in a Bible history textbook for grade schools.[46] The Conservatory of Music's music department, under the leadership of Sister Marion Cecile Spencer, was remarkable for both its size and the breadth of its offerings.[47] When Sister Mary Lourdes Mackey joined the faculty in 1936 as orchestral instructor, she not only taught at the College but also visited music classes in the schools. Sisters Cecilia Clare Bocard and Florence Therese Fitzgerald received commendatory reviews in scholarly journals for their published compositions.[48] In 1946 the College qualified to be accepted into the Association of American Universities.[49] When a representative of the American Association of University Women visited in 1948, she was amazed that a Catholic women's college could be so similar to Bryn Mawr.[50]

The Catholic identity of the College was strengthened not only with the appointment of priests with advanced degrees to faculty positions[51] but also by students attending Sunday Mass in cap and gown, ecclesiastical speakers on timely Catholic topics and involvement of sodality members in outreach catechetical instruction in neighboring towns.

The College also responded to changes in social norms and to the needs of the Congregation. As smoking became more common for women, a lodge was constructed on the north campus to provide for this. The summer sessions provided courses which provided sister-teachers with continuing education courses toward their bachelor degrees.

The Country at War

Looming large over all these events was the state of the country and indeed the state of the world. As the 1938 school year got underway, the sisters were attentive to Pope Pius XI's call for prayers for peace as European leaders met in Munich. They rejoiced in the belief that their prayers had been answered when a pact was signed which relieved international tensions for the moment. When the Nazi blitzkrieg beginning in September 1939 extended the boundaries of the Third Reich from the Atlantic to the North Sea, they again formed rosary bands to pray for peace. However, the general American mood of isolationism and the interlude of the so-called "Phony War" allowed an exuberant launch to the Centenary celebration. Even as the sisters celebrated, the men and women who found jobs in the factories which were beginning to supply ships and planes to a beleaguered Britain also had cause for optimism.

China, of course, was another story. In spite of sporadic on-site reports from their sisters there, the community at large had little understanding of the scope of the hostilities in Asia. Following the surprise strategy of the Japanese attack on Pearl Harbor, the sisters were as shocked as the rest of the country to learn that they were now at war. The chronicler at Saint Mary-of-the-Woods records the bald facts of the new situation: "December 8, 1941 – Today, the feast of the Immaculate Conception, the Japs fire on Pearl Harbor. President Roosevelt declares War at 11:00 a.m. today. It is confirmed by the Senate and Congress. A State of War is officially declared on December 9, 1941."[52] Both the missionary sisters and those on the home front would soon feel the effects of war.

Japanese Occupation of China

As seen in Chapter 4, the China mission had undergone many trials due to the civil war that raged during the thirties.[53] The city of Kaifeng where the high school, Ching I, the orphanage and the Catechist Society novitiate were located had fallen to invading Japanese troops on June 6, 1938, just as Mother Mary Bernard began her term. Because Japan and Italy were allies, the fact that the mission's sponsor, Bishop Tacconi, was Italian made it possible for the ten Sisters of Providence to continue their work with the refugees who crowded their small dispensary. The Japanese authorities made adjustments to the curriculum but allowed the school to open in the fall as usual. Students were doubtless startled to see two Chinese Sisters of Providence as faculty for the first time—Sisters Agnes Joan Li and Bernadette Ma, recently returned from their studies at Saint Mary-of-the-Woods College.

Distance and occupation did not prevent the Kaifeng community from celebrating the Centenary. The student mission association at Providence High School in Chicago had taken on the project of raising money for a chapel for their sister school in Kaifeng. The beautiful new building was blessed on January 22, 1940, with a High Mass celebrated the next day to open the Centenary year. In spite of increased tensions, in early October, when the United States consul advised that Americans who were not "engaged in work" should evacuate, the Chinese community celebrated Foundation Day with a three-act play on the life of Mother Theodore. The audience included diocesan priests who were making their retreat in Kaifeng as well as newly appointed Bishop Antonio Barosi who had replaced Bishop Tacconi on his retirement.[54]

As 1941 began, Sister Mary Gratia became very ill with pneumonia and did not recover until April. When news came that she had relapsed, to forestall any confusion in the event that she might not recover, Sister St. Francis Schultz was appointed as her first assistant with the right of succession,[55] but by September the seasoned superior was better. This was fortunate indeed when a sudden visit from Japanese army officers on December 8 brought the shocking news that a state of war existed between Japan and the United States. The sisters were ordered to move immediately to a nearby Baptist mission house where they remained for nineteen days, crowded together with eight Benedictine sisters and four Protestant missionary women. On Christmas they were told they could return home, but for an entire week they lived in high tension as conflicting orders were brought from army and church officials. Attempts to communicate with Saint Mary-of-the-Woods through the Red Cross were unsuccessful.

Finally, the thoroughly frightened sisters were told to move to the newly built and relatively roomy Benedictine convent in Kaifeng, where the Benedictine sisters welcomed them. Rumors swirled about killings of missionaries by Communists and the probable ultimatum of repatriation. Their house arrest and worries were somewhat relieved by the relative freedom of the Italian priests who were able to negotiate some financial support, for Mother Mary Bernard's relief check had failed to reach them.

By March of 1943 the tides of war were turning against the Japanese, and the occupation army ordered all enemy foreigners to be concentrated in camps. On March 21, the two Chinese sisters and the Providence Sister-Catechists stood disconsolately on the platform as the train with the eight American sisters chugged out of the Kaifeng station headed for Weihsien in Shantung Province. There, at a Presbyterian mission compound, they were interned with about 2,000 enemy aliens from Britain, Europe and the United States, including many Catholic clergy, sisters and lay people.[56] The internees organized themselves into committees and parceled out the space, with the Sisters of Providence occupying what had been a classroom. In addition to their housekeeping duties they were able to maintain their schedule of spiritual exercises and join in the various activities devised to provide relaxation.

In August they were delighted to learn that negotiations through the apostolic delegate would allow them to go to Peiping (now Beijing), where they were housed together with forty other American sisters of various congregations and thirty-two Belgian sisters in the large Christ the King Convent compound of the Spanish Daughters of Jesus. On September 9, 1943, they sent a cablegram to Saint Mary-of-the-Woods: "Peiping like heaven after purgatory."[57] In this relative sanctuary Sister Marie Gratia used the opportunity to consult with the other missionaries to develop long-range plans. In the twenty-three years she had been in China she had learned not only the language but had come to understand the political structure of the country. She had gained the confidence of the sisters by her ability to place them where their talents could best be utilized and had often incorporated their advice into her decisions. She had been able to strike a balance between the requirements of the Rule and the adjustments needed for the mission For example, during the very cold winters she had the sisters adopt the padded layers worn by the Chinese as a layer of the habit. During the stifling hot summer, when the sisters had worked long hours among the wounded soldiers and refugees, she had allowed the sisters to dispense with the cap and wear the veil directly on the *serre-tete*. Moreover, she had successfully justified these decisions to her superiors.

Now in Peiping she gathered the sisters in council to discuss plans for when the war would end. Although Sister Bernadette had fallen ill and had come to Peiping for care, Sister Agnes Joan had remained in Kaifeng and kept the school open. Despite the difficulty of her imposed responsibility, she recalled the consideration of the occupiers: "The Japanese are a very religious people. I used to go teach in the novitiate to teach math. Every afternoon I used to go. The Japanese just let me go. They had respect for the habit. The rest [of the visitors] they used to check."[58]

The wisdom of incorporating native Chinese sisters within the Congregation of the Sisters of Providence was obvious and it heightened Sister Marie Gratia's desire to establish a novitiate. She was able to identify potential candidates among the Ching I graduates who went on to university, and she would have liked to be able to encourage them to become Sisters of Providence rather than joining the Catechist Society. Her earlier request to establish a novitiate in China had been refused,[59] but now, noting the upcoming twenty-fifth anniversary of the Chinese foundation, she again pleaded that the time was ripe.

> There will be a great revival of all missionary works after the war. We want to do our part in the reconstruction work for the honor and glory of our Holy Mother the Church, and also for the cause of our own beloved community, and our Venerable Mother Theodore's cause.[60]

She intended to establish a house in the capital city where promising candidates could study at university and sisters could come for periodic medical attention. This never happened.

The Home Front

Writing to the sisters on January 6, 1942, Mother Mary Bernard was quick to echo the posture of the Catholic bishops in urging the sisters to patriotic service and devotion.

> Our Holy Rule cautions us against engaging in controversial topics especially of a political nature. Many of us, as part of our duties of instruction, must teach political and historical events and their significance, but we must all realize the great duty and obligation of loyalty to our President and to our Government. ...The topics that in times of peace might be subjects of debate are not so now in this time of national emergency when unity is the great aim to be achieved. Let us not discuss the whys and wherefores of governmental decision and directions, but insofar as they relate to our lives let us try to carry them out to the best of our ability.[61]

She used the occasion to urge simplicity and frugality of living by adopting a uniform size for the "winter box," the specially constructed trunk in which each sister kept all her clothing and personal possessions.[62]

An unanticipated call to cooperate with the government came when Sister St. Philomene Cullity, superior at Immaculata in Washington, D.C., notified Mother Mary Bernard that she had been approached regarding the use of the building. Further investigation revealed that the Federal Bureau of Investigation wanted to negotiate a ten-year lease, but this arrangement was considered unacceptable. Within weeks another offer was received from the government to purchase the original Maryhurst property in Maryland. After preliminary trips on the part of the Congregation's lawyers, Mother Mary Bernard and Treasurer Sister Francis Raphael traveled to the nation's capital to investigate the options in person. The Maryhurst diarist records its impending fate.

> All windows have to be blacked out at night, the street lights dimmed. Berwyn now has its own convent. What a gap at Maryhurst! First the Provincial moved, and now the Sisters. We have been crowded for many years, and now are lost in the big house. ... Word that our beloved Maryhurst may be sold. There have been hundreds and hundreds of small houses built in the near neighborhood which will in time depreciate the

property at Maryhurst, and it is for the best, although hard on human nature.[63]

Sure enough, on May 18, 1942, Mother Mary Bernard's letter to the sisters informed them that the provincial house in the East had been relocated to Lady Isle and the novitiate had temporarily closed, with the novices coming to Saint Mary-of-the-Woods and the postulants moved to a house across from Immaculata. A fortunate by-product of this negotiation was the use of the $100,000 purchase price to pay off a large outstanding bank loan. On the West Coast, the two novices in California were brought home to the motherhouse to complete their formation, effectively closing the western novitiate.

When the time came for the June letter circular with its usual invitation to the motherhouse for summer classes and retreat, it was clear that there had been some doubt about whether "homecoming" would even be possible. However, with the warning that everyone must be ready to suffer inconveniences and hardships, the summer of 1942 proceeded in the usual fashion. Mother Mary Bernard's 1942 December letter circular counseled the sisters to accept the war's privations in a spirit of love and penance, and by May 1943 she confirmed their fears that the difficulties of traveling and food rationing would not allow the beloved gathering at Saint Mary-of-the-Woods that summer. Letters were sent to local superiors where houses were to remain open asking them to remind the sisters that the arrangement was a contribution to the defense of the country. Suggestions were made that teaching summer school might bring in some income, or produce from a victory garden could be canned, but a caveat was given to "not require this from Sisters who are not willing."[64] Although "little surprises" such as picnic suppers were encouraged, it would be important "to impress the sisters not to infringe on religious culture."[65]

Those spending the summer in the Indianapolis diocese would likely have attended the special parish Masses on Independence Day mandated by Bishop Ritter, who noted that "millions of motives suggest themselves as we recall the roster of our boys in military training and at the battle front."[66] Of course many of the sisters had fathers and brothers in uniform. Between military red tape and community strictures about correspondence, news about the safety of family members was often slow to reach them For example, Sister Agnes

Farrell's father and brother were both stationed at Pearl Harbor on December 7, but it was not until Christmas that she learned that they were both safe.[67] The practice of the sisters not discussing family likely contributed to considerable private heartbreak, but there would be no records of such incidents.

The situation on the missions during the war varied considerably depending on location. In Fayetteville, North Carolina, the expansion of adjacent Fort Bragg with the call-up of reserve officers ballooned the population of both the base and the town. The sisters had the added burden of catechetical instruction for the families, but they also had the added benefit of having their convent renovated and extra deliveries of rationed items such as sugar and flour and sometimes even steak because of the interventions of the army chaplain.[68] In Washington, D.C., some markets actually closed for lack of meat to sell, and the scarcity of gas ration cards made it very difficult to maintain a car.[69] The sisters in Oklahoma remained on the mission for two summers, suffering temperatures of 106 degrees and canning snap beans in the school kitchen to supplement scarce groceries. Their German-speaking pastor was given a gas-ration card for his trips to say Mass for the young German soldiers interned at the prisoner of war camp in nearby McAlester, and he shared its use with the sisters for their trips to Guthrie to take exams from the Benedictines who were providing them with correspondence courses.[70]

Life at Saint Mary-of-the-Woods went on much as usual, with some noteworthy changes. On May 29, 1942, the first blackout went off according to plan. Routine maintenance tasks often had to be put on hold due to the shortage of help. In spite of rationing, a good supply of meat and poultry was still available because of the farm. The golf course behind Guerin Hall was converted to farmland with plantings of soybeans and winter wheat. In May 1943, due to a strike across the country, the Government took over operation of the coal mine on the property. This small coal mine had been in operation since 1895. After a 1920 fire a new shaft and equipment had made it possible to mine sixty tons of coal a day. The coal was brought via a small rail trolley across the campus to fuel the dynamos which supplied electricity for the entire campus. Although it was a non-commercial mine and its union workers had not joined the strike, its operation came under the executive order, and the American flag flew over the mine to indicate its compliance with national security requirements. As noted earlier, Sister Ignatia Braheny was appointed as postmaster at the Saint Mary-of-the-Woods Village post office, serving from 1942 to 1944. With a General Chapter scheduled for 1944, and the need for certification classes, most of the sisters were able to come to the motherhouse that summer, with those from the larger houses asked to bring supplemental food.[71] A weekly newsletter was sent to those remaining on the missions.

By 1945 train travel had been severely cut back, requiring the cancellation of the Easter holiday at the College. On April 12, the country absorbed the shock of President Roosevelt's death. Less than a month later the news of Germany's surrender on May 8, V-E Day, brought heartfelt prayers of gratitude. To observe the day of prayer called for by President Truman for the following Sunday, a special 2:00 p.m. service was held in the church, attended by students, lay faculty, workmen and their wives; it was followed by a parade down the Avenue. Although packages had been sent to the sisters in Ruille, France, all through the war, it was only now that news was received from them that four of the French Sisters of Providence had been killed during the conflict.

The news of Japan's surrender came on the final day of the August retreat, making the usual festivities of August 15 jubilant indeed. On September 30, 1945, the clocks were set back one hour as the "war time" established by executive order to save light and fuel throughout the country was lifted.[72] Along with the rest of the war-weary country, the sisters could now resume more normal lives.

As we have seen, Maryhurst, the eastern provincial house in Maryland, had been sold during the war. Sister St. Eugenia had divided her time between Lady Isle and the provincial house at Maryhurst until it was sold, with Lady Isle serving as the province headquarters from 1941-1945. Meanwhile, in 1944 another location had been found to serve as provincial headquarters. It was near the nation's capital, a twenty minute drive from Immaculata. The Maryhurst chronicler describes it in this manner:

It is a large house surrounded by 13 5/8 acres on Rockville Highway, near Rockville, and also near Georgetown Prep School and the new Holy Cross property—the old Corby Estate. It is an ideal spot. The house sets back from the highway about a quarter of a mile and is approached by a fine driveway. The grounds immediately around the house are beautifully landscaped, but the outlying parts are real woods.[73]

In July 1945 newly appointed Provincial Superior Sister Mary Rose Cummings took possession of the new Maryhurst, and the eastern novitiate once again resumed operations when the four postulants moved to Maryhurst from their cramped location at Loretto House across from Immaculata.

Governance

Relationships with the Vatican

In February 1939, together with all Catholics in the United States, the sisters had mourned the death of Pope Pius XI. Just ten years earlier they had rejoiced with him when the Lateran Treaty had re-established the political independence and diplomatic standing of the Catholic Church that had been lost in 1870 when Italian unification had led to the creation of the Vatican State. During the years of Russia's Communist expansion and the worrisome Nazi military buildup in Europe, they had responded wholeheartedly to the pope's calls for prayer. Once again on March 2, 1939, the sisters' radios were tuned to news of the conclave. The chronicler recorded that when they heard that white smoke announced the election of Eugenio Cardinal Pacelli, it was with "joy that filled our hearts" that the black bunting was removed, bells were rung and the novices' choir sang the "Te Deum" in honor of their new pope, to be known as Pope Pius XII.[74]

As we have seen, during the war the Congregation's integral connection with the universal church was keenly appreciated. Even though the United States was at war with Italy, as head of the neutral Vatican City State, Pope Pius XII was able to carry on limited administrative connections throughout the world through apostolic delegates. In China, Archbishop Mario Zanin was instrumental in negotiating the release of missionaries from internment in 1943 and in sending messages to Mother Mary Bernard through Archbishop Amletto Cicognani in Washington, D.C. It was also through Archbishop

Zanin's advocacy that the sisters' school in Kaifeng was spared.[75] During the war all communications with the Vatican were conducted through the apostolic delegate's office rather than directly with the Vatican, a restriction which was not lifted until December 1946.

United States Bishops

In Chicago, Archbishop Samuel Stritch had succeeded Cardinal Mundelein in 1939, and in 1946 he was elevated to the rank of Cardinal. On a local level, the relationship between the Congregation and the Indianapolis diocese remained on a strong footing during this time. When Bishop Ritter went to Rome in May 1939, he met with the postulator of Mother Theodore's cause to exert support for her canonization. When he attended national bishops' meetings in Washington, D.C., he stayed at Immaculata. During the years of experimentation with provinces, he continued to provide canonical advice. His appointment of Father Henry Dugan, chaplain and instructor at Ladywood, as chancellor of the diocese in May 1939 solidified the channels of communication through a knowledgeable liaison. In June 1941 Father Emile Goossens was appointed chaplain, beginning eighteen years of devoted service to the community. During the war years, because an accelerated program for seminarians at St. Meinrad Archabbey limited the availability of space for the priests' retreat there, Bishop Ritter requested that it be held at Saint Mary-of-the-Woods, so in 1945 the priests' retreat was held on the campus. Due to travel restrictions, only fifty priests could be accommodated at a time for three consecutive four-day sessions in June, with housing at Le Fer Hall. The clergy loved the location so much that the request was renewed and the annual clergy retreat for the Archdiocese of Indianapolis continued to be held at Saint Mary-of-the-Woods from 1945 to1952.

Provinces

Mother Mary Bernard continued the policies regarding the provinces begun by her predecessor in that she and her council made decisions across the Congregation while relying on the provincial superiors for onsite assistance. Each sister's mission assignment continued to be given from the motherhouse and the names given to postulants in the eastern, western and motherhouse novitiates were not duplicated. Novices who professed vows at Maryhurst were assigned to missions in the East and those at Marywood, Anaheim, were assigned to the California missions, but all these young sisters came to Saint Mary-of-the-Woods for a single second novitiate.

Although the council gave some attention to preparing revisions of the *Constitutions* to bring to the 1944 Chapter, possibly due to the difficulty of consultation with the Sacred Congregation during the war, Bishop Ritter encouraged the continuation of the policy of operating the provinces on an experimental basis. Early in Mother Mary Bernard's second term the council did give some thought to abandoning the idea of provinces in favor of a vicariate structure, as noted in the minutes:

> It was suggested that a study be made of the organization of Vicariates, as used by the Madames of the Sacred Heart. Under this organization, we are told, everything is referred to the Motherhouse. Central government is preserved. Our Sisters want always to feel they belong to St. Mary-of-the-Woods.[76]

As seen in Chapter 5, and to be further examined in detail in Chapter 9, subsequent events made pursuit of an alternate form of government unnecessary. The early postwar period would bring about a more prosperous period for American Catholics which would benefit the sisters as well.

❧ Chapter 8
Postwar Transitions
1944-1949

These students at St. Therese, Alhambra, California, typify the educational ministry which provided a stable environment for children growing up in changing times.

The General Chapter of 1944

Of the thirty-six sisters who assembled for Chapter on June 23, 1944, those who had come from the missions were still experiencing wartime rationing and travel restrictions, and the mood of the gathering reflected the continuing concerns of a country at war. To be sure, Mother Mary Bernard's report showed that growth had continued, though at a gradual pace. Five new missions had been opened, including the totally un-expected gift of a small twenty-five-acre island off the coast of New Hampshire, renamed Lady Isle, and presently in use as the provincial house for the East until alternate property could be purchased to replace Maryhurst. While membership had increased to a total of 1,294 professed sisters, vocations had slowed to the point that only seventeen postulants and forty-four novices were in formation. However, Providence Juniorate had continued to attract girls, enrolling 133 students, of whom forty-eight had entered the novitiate. Information about the Chinese missionaries was worrisomely sketchy though it was known that some of the sisters were being interned. The financial situation was excellent; not only was the budget balanced, but the outstanding debt had been reduced by a third.

Bishop Ritter was most complimentary. He invited Chapter members to express any concerns regarding the provinces if they so desired but no one rose to do so. With no business agenda the delegates proceeded directly to the elections. Mother Mary Bernard was re-elected by an overwhelming majority on the first ballot and, after taking the oath of office, assumed the presidency of the assembly. Rather than re-electing Sister Helen Clare Freiburger as first assistant, the delegates elected Sister Alexis Marie Hoff to that position on the first ballot. Sister Helen Clare was then elected second assistant, but not until the second ballot. Two of the assistants were quickly re-elected to their previous offices with clear majorities on the first ballot: Third Assistant Sister Gertrude Clare Owens for her fourth term, and Fifth Assistant Sister Francis Joseph Elbreg for her third elected term as councilor, which would also mark her twenty-seventh year in the role of directing the Congregation's educational mission.[1]

The results of the elections for fourth and sixth assistants were somewhat of a surprise since neither sister was a member of the Chapter and both were elected on the first ballot. Sister Rose Dolores Thuis, a music teacher, was summoned from Ladywood, Indianapolis, to assume the duties of fourth assistant. Sister Marie Helene Franey, a Latin professor at St. Mary-of-the-Woods College, was elected to the post of sixth assistant and secretary general.

Given the usual exhortations to secrecy and reliance on prayer rather than personal preference, how had all three new assistants been elected on the first ballot? A clue is found in the letter sent to inform each delegate of her election to the Chapter. Dated March 31, 1944, almost three months prior to the elections, it stated, "The sacredness of the trust given to us requires that we use prudence and discretion in pronouncing our election as a delegate."[2]

Doubtless each of the twenty-four sisters who received this letter, eleven of whom had never before been elected to a General Chapter, wondered who else had been chosen to be a Chapter member. The seven ex-officio members who comprised the council had counted the votes and knew who had been elected. Possibly the treasurer and provincials, also ex-officio, knew. But in the absence of a published list of delegates, there was a vacuum of information. However, "prudence and discretion" could certainly have allowed private conversation between and among trusted friends who had proven their ability to keep confidences. The historian can only speculate. In any case, let us meet the newly elected council.

The 1944 Council

Sister Alexis Marie Hoff 1882-1968

Ella Hoff was born in Chicago and became acquainted with the Sisters of Providence as a student at Our Lady of Sorrows. At age twenty she entered the community. During her twelve years of teaching almost every grade, she gained a reputation of being devout and prayerful. At age thirty-four she was appointed superior at Holy Trinity, Washington, D.C., during the final two years of Sister of Providence staffing, 1916-1918. It would seem that she was well suited to the role of local superior, for she went on to serve twenty-six consecutive years in seven different missions. Not only was she widely known, but she was regarded as kind and understanding, undoubtedly a reason for her election for the first time at age sixty-four as a member of the 1944 Chapter and then as first assistant to Mother Mary Bernard. The fact that no photograph of her is available underlines her humility, and indeed it was her observation of Mother's increasingly poor health and her own fear of having to assume the duties of superior general that led her to resign only two years later and return to a classroom.

Sister Rose Dolores Thuis 1899-1969

Born in Vincennes, Mary Henrietta Louise Thuis was the only daughter of four children born to the pioneer Thuis family, Frank and Mary Raban Thuis. She was barely a toddler when her oldest brother left home to become a Benedictine monk, Columban, at nearby St. Meinrad Archabbey, and as she grew up her two other brothers followed him, taking the names John and Stephen. She attended St. Rose Academy where she studied music and entered the Congregation in 1916 at age seventeen. As a music teacher, her first mission of three was Marywood, Evanston, with Sister Gertrude Clare as superior. Immediately after final profession, she was appointed superior, but held this position for only two years before poor health required her to spend two years in the motherhouse infirmary. After another two years as a superior, during which she studied for her graduate

degree in music at Indiana University, she spent fourteen years as music teacher at Ladywood in Indianapolis, and here she found her true calling as a teacher, composer and writer. Several of her teaching materials were published and her articles appeared in the professional magazine *Etude*. In 1944 at age forty-five she was elected fourth councilor. She would go on to serve in that role for four more terms until 1966, when she continued service as supervisor of applied music until her death on November 11, 1969.

Sister Marie Helene Franey 1898-1953

Helena Franey was born in Galesburg, Illinois, in 1898, the first of six children. Her parents, Margaret and Michael, were both natives of Galesburg and had been educated by the Sisters of Providence. Both parents had sisters who had entered the Congregation, and her aunts were known to her as Sister Mary Helena Franey and Sister Louis Joseph Connerton. Since her father worked for the railroad, his promotions required

many moves for the growing family, so Helena learned early how to adapt to changing surroundings. She received her early education in Jackson, Michigan, and Cleveland, Ohio, then graduated from Elkhart High School in Indiana. A good student who enjoyed her studies, she aspired to be a teacher and attended a state normal school in Pennsylvania for her first year of college. Her parents encouraged her to transfer to Saint Mary-of-the-Woods College for her sophomore year in 1917. Here she realized her vocation was to religious life as well as to education and she entered the novitiate the following year at age twenty. After profession, she taught high school at

Marywood in Evanston, Providence High School in Chicago and St. Augustine in Fort Wayne, all schools with highly respected superior-principals. In 1926 she was assigned to the Academy at Saint Mary-of-the-Woods and assisted with its transition to a fully accredited four-year college. After a year at Indiana University, she returned to the College with an MA in Latin and went on to serve in the multi-faceted duties of the time: instructor, dormitory supervisor, sodality adviser, member of the Centenary committee and senior adviser. During these years she had the joy of seeing two of her brothers ordained to the priesthood: Father Louis for the Diocese of Rockford and Father John as a Sulpician. In 1944, when she was elected sixth assistant, she assumed the duties of secretary general.

Superiors' Health Concerns

During her first term, Mother Mary Bernard had written to the Congregation in September of 1940 to tell the news of the death of Mother Mary Raphael, noting that the retired superior's health, "though never robust, had always permitted her to fulfill her duties ... [with] unfaltering trust in the Providence of God in whose care she placed the heavy burdens of her office."[3] At that point in her own life the reference to heavy burdens was undoubtedly influenced by her own experience in the office of superior general. In addition to the normal duties of administration she was closely involved in the many events and appearances of the year-long Centenary celebration. On the final day of the October 1940 events she withdrew to a Terre Haute convent to rest, and by Thanksgiving she was still so weak that she asked to be anointed. She moved to a room in the infirmary from which she continued to conduct business, with the council meeting there during January and February of 1941. The council minutes record that on March 7, 1941, she not only thanked her councilors for their solicitude in recommending a heart specialist but also guided a discussion during which the council decided on the sale of Maryhurst.[4] Within a few months the council was further depleted when Fourth Assistant Sister Mary Rose

Cummings was diagnosed with a tubercular condition and was on leave from June to December of 1941.

Apparently Mother Mary Bernard was sufficiently recovered to the point that the 1944 General Chapter had no hesitation in re-electing her. However, by November she had undergone surgery and again the council met in the infirmary, but once more she rallied and returned to duty. Nonetheless, her condition was closely watched by First Assistant Sister Alexis Marie Hoff, who had had major reservations about accepting her own elected position since she felt totally inadequate to step in as superior general if Mother Mary Bernard faltered. So greatly did this worry afflict her that the doctor advised her to step down, and on December 14, 1945, she asked to be relieved—in effect, resigning her office. By January she was sufficiently recovered to take up the less public duties of classroom teaching at Maternity, Chicago. The council's health troubles were not at an end. In June 1947 Sister Rose Dolores Thuis underwent surgery, but by the end of July she was back on duty.

Changing Council Membership and Responsibilities

As Mother Mary Bernard began her second term, the duties of her assistants changed somewhat. During the six years Sister Francis Joseph had been appointed as supervisor of schools but did not serve on the council (1932-1938), she had been able to devote herself entirely to the work of education. Not only had she observed each sister in her classroom, but she had also developed a detailed file card system of each sister's academic credits in order to arrange the classes needed for certification and degrees. Already, during Mother Mary Bernard's first term, the insights gained from her regular classroom visits had provided valuable input when placement decisions were being considered by the council. However, one area of key importance which had suffered from lack of professional oversight was the supervision of music teachers. Although Sister Mary Lourdes Mackey had visited music classes on a part-time basis, this service was inadequate for the scope of the Congregation's involvement in music education. The 1944 election of Sister Rose Dolores was apparently intended to correct that situation because the council minutes quickly record that she was "officially appointed to take care of matters relative to the music teachers."[5]

As noted above, the resignation of First Assistant Sister Alexis Marie in December 1945 created a vacancy in the council. Mother Mary Bernard wrote to the sisters to announce that Sister was relieved of her position as first assistant and that, "Those who address themselves to Sister Alexis Marie may feel free to correspond with any Council Member of their choice at this time."[6] Such a situation was not without precedent[7] and the Rule directed that the superior general and her council would elect a replacement. However, there was no stipulation regarding the immediacy of such a selection. When Bishop Ritter came to Saint Mary-of-the-Woods for the January 1946 reception and profession ceremonies, he advised an immediate appointment in order to ensure stability. However, it was not until May 19, 1946, that the council unanimously elected Sister Margaret Agnes O'Neill to replace Sister Alexis Marie on the council while continuing her duties as dean of women at the College. To retain continuity, Sisters Helen Clare and Gertrude Clare were moved to the positions of first and second assistants, while Sister Margaret Agnes became third assistant. Mother Mary Bernard announced the arrangement to the community in the June letter circular.

When the sisters came home for the 1946 summer session, the council was once again at full complement

Sister Margaret Agnes O'Neill 1895-1975

When Catherine O'Neill's parents died she and her two sisters were given to the care of their grandparents in Chicago. In 1911 at age sixteen she followed her older sisters to community: Mary (Sister Catherine Gertrude) and Josephine (Sister Teresita, who died at age thirty-two in 1925). As they had done, she completed high school while in the novitiate and after her profession was assigned to teach high school. Apparently she was a most versatile teacher with an amenable disposition because over twenty-five years she taught in fourteen high schools, where she was trained by some of the community's most respected superiors. After earning her MA at Indiana State in 1941 she herself served as principal at several schools before being appointed dean of women at St. Mary-of-the-

Woods College in 1945. She continued part time in this position as she served on the council until the 1949 elections, at which point she returned to high school teaching and administration.

Changes in American Hierarchy

During Mother Mary Bernard's second term, there were numerous changes in the United States Catholic hierarchy in dioceses where the Congregation conducted schools. In 1944, with the creation of the dioceses of Lafayette and Evansville, Indianapolis became an archdiocese. Since Saint Mary-of-the-Woods remained within its territory, the sisters would now address Bishop Ritter as Archbishop. With the many missions in the southwestern corner of the state, the appointment of the scholarly Bishop Henry Grimmelsman as first bishop of Evansville boded well for the educational mission there. The sisters at Assumption parish were delighted to learn that their church would become the cathedral.[8] The Lafayette diocese had been split off from the Fort Wayne Diocese, and newly appointed Bishop John Bennett, a priest of that diocese, was well acquainted with the Sisters of Providence. Only two years later, the transfer of Archbishop Ritter to the Archdiocese of St. Louis brought Archbishop Paul Schulte from Leavenworth, Kansas, to serve as the ordinary of Indianapolis.

Although Washington, D.C., had been created as a diocese in 1939, Archbishop Michael Curley had continued to administer it as a single unit with the Baltimore Diocese until 1948, when Bishop Patrick O'Boyle was appointed to the post. In 1944, Bishop Eugene McGuiness' move from Raleigh, North Carolina, to Oklahoma City was a welcome continuation of his association with the Congregation. Bishop Vincent Waters took his place in Raleigh. In Boston, Archbishop Richard Cushing was appointed in 1944 while Archbishop James McIntyre was named for Los Angeles in 1948. Many of these prelates will appear in subsequent chapters.

The Challenge of Health Care

The Infirmary

By the time Mother Mary Bernard began her administration in 1938, the infirmary had become a well-equipped haven for caring for the sick. In the era before compensation from insurance coverage became a normal benefit, the infirmary was a much-needed investment. Because the primary ministry of the Congregation was education, the very few sisters who were professionally qualified as health care providers not only gave administrative and direct care services, but they also trained the other sisters who were assigned to care of the sick. The four-story building could accommodate sixty patients, and over the years gradual remodeling made it possible to offer additional medical services, until eventually it functioned as a small private hospital. By the thirties it was clear that the range of services provided demanded professional certification.

Sister Mary Bernardo Flaherty had been assigned to the infirmary since the early twenties and had gained the respect of the doctors. In 1939, when she was sent to St. Francis School of Nursing in Chicago, Dr. James F. Spigler sent this recommendation:

> For the past eighteen years I have been working directly with Sister in surgical and general medical cases and have found her most capable. She has more horse sense and general ability than any of our usual run of nurses. I cannot recommend her too highly.[9]

When Sister Dorothy Eileen Howard entered in 1933, she was already certified as a registered nurse and was able to replace Sister Mary Bernardo until she returned with a degree as a graduate nurse in 1940. Contemporary sources provide insight into the workings of the infirmary during this period.[10]

Since her election to the council in 1920, Sister Gertrude Clare Owens had had the responsibility for oversight of the infirmary and was well loved for her attentive care of the sick. Sister Dorothy Eileen provides an appreciative description of her involvement.

> She was our guiding light, really. You could go to Gertrude Clare with anything. She understood human nature more than anybody I have ever met in my life. She really did. ... She was a marvelous woman. And she was so holy ... she would say two words to you and you were a different person ...her sanctity ... her beautiful sense of humor. She was truly selfless. At night she would never go to bed without checking with each nurse to see if there was anybody bad off on the floor, anybody critical. She would go see them ... and if there was somebody seriously ill, she would come over in the middle of the night to see how they were.[11]

The sister-nurses were also very selfless. They wore crisp white uniforms while on duty and each one had charge of an entire floor. For years they had no room of their own, but simply slept on a cot below their buzz station. Each floor had eight to ten rooms with shared baths, and often all were filled. The first floor included a kitchen where a sister cook and her assistants prepared meals. These were transported to diet kitchens on each floor where the novices served the patients their meals on trays. A fully-equipped surgery suite complete with scrub and sanitizing area, doctor's rooms and an operating room was on the third floor. Usually sisters were brought home when surgery was required, and often during the summer as many as seven or eight major operations would begin at 7:00 a.m., with the nurses cleaning and preparing the room for the next patient while the doctors rested. The fourth floor was designated for post-operative care. A house diary of the time even makes reference to "the St. Mary's ambulance," although no such vehicle actually existed, indicating the confidence of the sisters in the efficiency of their health care infrastructure.[12]

Gradually the problem of inadequate staffing was ameliorated as additional sisters were sent to study for RN degrees. One sister was assigned as a night nurse, making it possible for each nurse to have the privacy of her own room at Providence Convent. By 1941 it was possible to assign two sisters to

Infirmary Staff 1955 (left to right) Sisters Ann Gerard (Margaret Ann) Wilson, Henry Butler, Eileen Mary Cunningham, Perpetua Peckham, Dorothy Eileen Howard, Innocentia Ashley, (seated) Mary Bernardo Flaherty.

each floor. With easy walk-through access to the chapel gallery, the sister nurses were able to attend Mass and receive Communion when the priest brought it to the sick before Mass at 6:00 a.m. Already in 1929 Sister Agnes Xavier Olwell had been sent to Purdue University for studies and served as a registered pharmacist until 1942. A small laboratory was equipped to provide routine tests, and when Sister Mary Michael Lager returned with her pharmacy degree from Purdue University in 1953, she staffed the lab until 1990, when the pharmacy was closed. Cleaning in the infirmary was done by canonical novices.[13] During overflow times such as the flu season, novices also had to carry trays to temporary sick rooms in adjacent buildings. When a sister died the Callahan family's funeral services from Terre Haute took care of embalming in the small mortuary on the first floor.

Despite the efficiency of this operation, it became clear that two additional services were greatly needed. First, the number of elderly sisters who were not ill but who needed assistance had increased. Second, more sisters were suffering from mental illness. Fortunately the family of Sister Margaret Alacoque Kerwin provided a large donation in her memory, and the money was designated to add a two-story wing to the infirmary. This addition, dedicated in 1941, was known as Our Lady of Lourdes, and it served several functions. The first floor included not only seven rooms for ambulatory elder sisters but also a completely equipped dental office and a physical therapy room. The second floor added thirteen patient rooms, some of which provided secured access for patients whose condition required close observation. A small chapel on the second floor provided a welcome respite from the busy floor.

Mental Illness

Although mental illness is not a pleasant topic, the need for expanding the infirmary facilities testifies to the fact that the Sisters of Providence were not immune from this condition. Because the council discussed this topic twenty-four times over the time period from 1939-1946, it requires attention. Mother Mary Bernard's report to the 1944 General Chapter includes this statement: "Nine of our Sisters are suffering from mental illness. Seven of these are confined in institutions. We have 2 of these dear afflicted Sisters here at home in our isolation department."[14]

In order to understand how the various situations of sisters suffering from mental illness were handled, a little background regarding contemporary approaches to addressing the problem is helpful.[15] During the early nineteenth century, although little was known about the causes and treatment of mental illness, the presence of afflicted persons whose families were unable to care for them created problems for society at large. In the United States, the philosophy that government had the obligation to care for its citizens led to a public policy of states funding and operating asylums. States often commissioned large hospital buildings on landscaped grounds in order to inspire public trust. The hope was that confinement in a controlled environment would enable patients to take on the values and behavior of normal society. Over the years, it became apparent that most individuals whose condition was so severe as to require their committal were not amenable to treatment. The difficulty of care often led to high staff turnover and abuse. Some Catholic hospitals did offer mental health treatment and could be expected to provide a higher standard of care.

During the Depression and war years, state institutions were a low priority and suffered from lack of government funding. However, several generations of studies and scholarship were bearing fruit in establishing a stronger theoretical basis for treatment. Various therapies such as hydrotherapy, occupational therapy and electric shock therapy were developed to alleviate symptoms of severe psychosis. Biological approaches ranged from drug therapy to lobotomies. The experience of military psychiatrists during World War II opened new avenues, but it would not be until 1952 that the first standardized classification of mental disorders was published.[16] Adherents of behavioral and humanistic psychological approaches favored counseling therapies, but these were not usually effective for persons with true psychoses.[17]

As seen in Chapter 6, a young woman who presented herself for admission was expected to meet certain requirements of suitability for living in community and these were measured in terms of recommendations from the sister who encouraged her and from her pastor. Psychological assessments did not exist during this era and only in cases where some type of hereditary mental illness was known to exist in her family was the possibility of mental illness explored. During the novitiate, when questionable behaviors gave indication of potential psychological anomaly, the individual could be directed to leave.[18] However, once a sister professed vows she became a member of the Congregation and "infirmity" could not be grounds for dismissal.[19] Of course symptoms of mental illness often do not emerge until later in life, and even then the actions of mentally ill sisters could easily be confused with insubordination.

During the late thirties, with more media attention directed to mental illness, it would be likely that a sister exhibiting questionable behaviors would be referred for medical diagnosis. It is clear that such situations caused considerable distress, especially when the sister was deemed "unmanageable." At times the patient would involve her family, and one sister was so adept at gaining sympathy from her caretakers that she persuaded them to call family members on her behalf to intervene in the persecution she imagined she was experiencing from the superiors. To prevent such access, the phone was temporarily removed from the infirmary, causing difficulty in emergencies.

Depending on circumstances, the family was notified and included in care decisions, especially when surgery or shock treatments were recommended. Often the bishop was consulted as a precautionary measure. When possible, sisters were placed in Catholic sanitariums, but at times state institutions proved to be a viable alternative. The need for an intermediate level of care led the council to consider an onsite facility.

> We have considered for a long time to build an addition to our Infirmary for mental cases. The money for this building plan will be furnished by the estate of Sister Margaret Alacoque. The building proposition was put to a vote. Six were in favor, and one opposed. The decision was made to build, but we shall make a further investigation before we build.[20]

The investigation did indeed confirm the need and led to the construction of the Our Lady of Lourdes wing. After 1941, the availability of care at the motherhouse was a great benefit for cases of mild dementia.

Dental Care

During the twenties a dental office was set up in Foley Hall so that a dentist from Terre Haute could come once a week to provide treatment, with various sisters serving as dental assistants. This small office took on a much more professional aspect in the thirties with the arrival of Sister John Francis Troy, who had learned the skills of taking x-rays, cleaning teeth, doing extractions, fillings and lab work during her ten years of employment with a dentist in the Washington, D.C., area prior to her entrance. When plans for the wing to be added to the infirmary were drawn up to include a standard dental office, she selected the equipment and instruments and plied her trade there from 1945 to1980.[21]

Expansion of the Mission

From China to Taiwan

By May 1945, news of the end of the war in Europe came to the sisters in China, all of whom were then under house arrest in Peiping. At that point the Red Cross was not only able to provide relief boxes but also allowed to convey messages from Saint Mary-of-the-Woods. Although Japan surrendered on August 10, 1945, it was not until American pilots dropped leaflets over the city a few days later that the long-imprisoned sisters knew that the war was finally over. Eager to return to their Kaifeng mission, two groups of sisters were able to fly on army planes as far as Sian, where Sister Bernadette Ma enjoyed a visit with her family during their short stay. Railroad and road connections were in shambles but, again, an American C-47 supply plane provided space for them. In spite of the staggering damage to the Catechist house in Nan Kuan on the outskirts of Kaifeng, the missionaries were able to resume their work and even to open in November the long-promised mission of Fu Yu School in Hsinhsiang.

Sister Marie Gratia remained in Peiping with Sister Carmel Baker to establish a hostel to serve as an administrative base and as housing for students. A major concern was money. With no income and no way to receive funds from the motherhouse during the war, the debts they had incurred needed to be paid off. It was a great relief when communications improved and money arrived and she could arrange passage on a navy vessel for two sisters who were to return to the states. It was not until February of 1946 that Sister Marie Gratia was able to return to Kaifeng. Sister Ann Colette Wolf records the welcome she received:

> When Sister Marie Gratia saw the large sign over the arch of the gate, "Welcome home, dear Mother!" she was so touched by that word "Mother" that she could not hold back the tears. Suddenly all the heartaches and worries of the past four years were wiped away, and she found room in her heart only for gratitude to Providence for His all-embracing protection of those who were dear to her.[22]

As events played out, she would indeed earn the title of Mother.

In October, plans went forward for the two sisters in Peiping to return to the states, while four of the missionaries would return from stateside respite, bringing a fifth sister to carry on the mission.[23] These sisters arrived in Shanghai on Christmas Eve 1946, but after enduring a harrowing train journey to Kaifeng, their warm welcome was almost immediately chilled by tragic news. Sister Elizabeth Cecile Harbison, who was to have gone to Peiping to join Sister Carmel and teach music, had been killed when her plane went down in dense fog on January 5, 1947. It was to be a bad year indeed. By May conditions in Hsinhsiang had worsened to the point that the recently opened mission had to be closed. More and more missionaries came to Kaifeng for protection. More tragedy ensued when, amid a blizzard in January 1948, Sister Theodata Haggerty and the sister-catechist who was caring for her in the hospital died accidentally of carbon monoxide poisoning from stove fumes.

War was not yet at an end for the suffering people of China. The cessation of hostilities with the external enemy of Japan reignited the smoldering internal conflict of ideology between the Communists led by Mao Tze Tung and the Nationalists under Chiang Kai Shek. Communist adherents regarded missionaries as foreign spies of western governments and were determined to wipe them out.[24] Stories of atrocities and warnings from the American consulate forced the sisters and a group of the catechists to seek refuge with the Religious of the Sacred Heart in Shanghai. Three of the missionaries went on to the states while the others joined the faculty at the academy. By the summer of 1948, the situation in Peiping had worsened to the point that the two sisters there returned to the States, and by fall it was clear that even Shanghai would fall. In the midst of this chaotic situation the sisters received news that their beloved Mother Mary Bernard had died on October 6, 1948.

Responsibility for the China mission with its commitment to the Chinese Providence Sister-Catechists fell squarely upon Sister Marie Gratia's shoulders. She pursued contacts in Taiwan (then known by the name Formosa),[25] and after an exploratory trip in November, wrote to First Assistant Sister Helen Clare to advise her of the hastily devised plans to move there. A major concern was the future of the catechist community; some of the sister-catechists would also evacuate, while others would remain in Kaifeng or disperse to safer locations. On December 15, 1948, at 3:00 a.m., after an eventful journey by ship and train, four Sisters of Providence with their lay cook, Elizabeth Kuo, and thirteen Providence Sister-Catechists arrived in Taichung, Taiwan. They were joined two days later by the two remaining Sisters of Providence who evacuated by plane.

By February 1949, they had established a convent, and when word went out regarding their plans to establish a school, pupils began coming to them. By May they were able to move to a commodious building large enough for both a convent and a real school, and the five sister-catechists who had been studying in Peiping were able to join them. Despite the unstable political situation, news of the March 1949 election of Mother Marie Helene Franey and her council gave hope for a new era for the China mission.

Saint Mary-of-the-Woods Commercial High School

The motherhouse itself was the scene of another beginning, far more modest in scope, which grew out of the needs of the times. The immediate postwar period saw considerable economic dislocation. The community chronicler records the problem that at the College "it was practically impossible to find girls to take care of the work of serving tables and washing dishes in Foley refectory."[26] This was a problem because the College program included a meal plan designed to foster inter-class relationships. It required assigned seating with meals served family-style. The arrangement of requiring the students to serve one meal a day for a week was temporary and led to a creative solution which advantageously combined two community resources. First, most of the high schools taught by the Sisters of Providence included a well-honed curriculum of commercial offerings. Second, space was available on the fourth floor of Foley Hall. Putting these two facts together, in 1946 the council minutes record a decision to offer room and board and a high school education to "graduates of the eighth grade who will work in the dining room of the college and do work that will be given regular high school credit."[27] The first freshman class was recruited for September, and with the arrival of the next group the following year, the students were designated as "Commercial Class Girls,"[28] which soon was shortened to "commercial girls."

The program was limited to the ninth and tenth grades, with students returning to their homes to complete high school. Transcripts were issued from "Saint Mary's High School" and indicate completion of standard courses such as English, Algebra, General Science and History as well as Typing, Introduction to Business and Art and Design. The faculty was drawn from college students in the College's Education Department and novices who had completed college before entering. The Congregation's Education Office in Foley arranged the classes and supervised instruction. Extra-curricular activities such as dramatic and musical productions with the assistance of the drama department varied from year to year depending on the talents of student-teachers.

The school operated from 1946 to1964, an interesting parallel with the baby boom years. Because students transferred for their junior and senior years, with neither graduates nor alumnae, few records have survived, but clearly the program benefited not only the College but also the girls who enrolled. A 1948-1950 student, Mary Evelyn Bouvier O'Connor, explains the attraction of the program and its success.

> The sisters were looking for help to serve the college girls in the dining room and were offering room and board and $2 a week. We just needed to bring our uniform—white blouses and navy skirts, which I think my mother made for me. I was fourteen and I really wanted to go to a girls' boarding school. I had been to Saint Mary's and had some idea of the beautiful campus. Our eighth grade teacher at St. Charles, Bloomington, encouraged this and three of us decided to go as freshmen. I think

most of the girls came from Indianapolis or Jasper or other places in Indiana.

We lived in Foley Hall on the fourth floor, two to a bedroom. Our schedule was built around our duties in the dining room. After breakfast we set up the tables for lunch and then went to classes until it was time to serve and the same in the afternoon. Sister Theresa Eleanor Blessinger was in charge and taught some of the classes. Some of the college sisters also taught, as well as college girls who were student teachers. I loved Sister Theresa Eleanor—she was like my mother for two years.

We kept busy. We could go to the special programs at the college and used the swimming pool and walked the grounds. On Saturdays we went over to the laundry to pick up our clothes and iron the skirts and blouses. Often on Sundays my parents would take the bus up from Bloomington, bringing treats in a basket to visit in the afternoon after we finished serving. They loved the Woods.

I have very positive memories of my time as a commercial girl. Just being around the sisters with their positive outlook was a good experience. From a later perspective I think my most valuable learning was being able to get along with other girls.[29]

Overseeing the program was an around-the-clock assignment, and much credit must be given to Sister Theresa Eleanor Blessinger, who was assigned to supervise the commercial girls from 1949 to1959 as well as serving on a part-time basis from 1945 to1949 and 1963 to1964. As the oldest of eighteen children growing up in Jasper, Indiana, she was a natural for the role of "house mother." In one respect, her work with the commercial girls was a family affair because when her younger sister also entered, Sister Olivia Blessinger's assignment as cook in the College dining room during 1943-1944 gave the two sisters the opportunity to work together with the girls. Later, from 1948 to 1954, three of their younger sisters, Leona, Mildred and Anna Mae, attended the school.

Secondary Coeducation

On the missions, new establishments followed patterns already in place. In 1945, in the Diocese of Peoria, Illinois, Superintendent Father F. P. Blecke arranged a meeting of Galesburg parents to discuss consolidating the boys' high school, Corpus Christi Lyceum, with St. Joseph Academy. He wrote to Mother Mary Bernard to report that the response had been "enthusiastic." In testament to the cordial relations the sisters at St. Joseph enjoyed with the Fathers of Charity at the Lyceum, he noted that in his subsequent meeting with the priests that they "were all of the opinion that it was best that the Sisters take complete charge of the school."[30] Plans moved forward quickly, and by August 1945 the high school section of St. Joseph Academy was transferred to Corpus Christi Lyceum. It became the coeducational Corpus Christi High School and students were taught by both priests and sisters. The high school sisters continued to live in the St. Joseph Academy convent and to commute from 1945 to 1948, when the private home purchased by Bishop Schlarman was remodeled to serve as their convent. When the nine high school sisters moved in 1948, the nine grade school sisters continued to live and teach at St. Joseph.

Parish Schools: Indianapolis

As the postwar boom got underway and new parishes were established, pastors availed themselves of their connections with the Congregation to request sisters to teach in their schools. While he was at Saint Mary-of-the-Woods to attend the annual clergy retreat in 1947, Father Matthew Herold spoke with Mother Mary Bernard and returned shortly after with blueprints for the school at St. Andrew, Indianapolis, the first of the parish buildings to be constructed. Four sisters were assigned for the opening of school in September 1948, but the enrollment was so large that the first and second grades had to be split and a secular teacher hired.

Meanwhile, the sisters at St. Joan of Arc learned that their parish had grown so much that it was to be divided to form Immaculate Heart Parish. Residents near the intended site were unwilling to have their lovely quiet neighborhood spoiled by traffic and sued to prevent construction. The controversy appeared to take a toll on the agitators because several of them died within months of each other. Not surprisingly, the sisters saw the hand of Providence in these events, noting, "Our Blessed Mother will have her way."[31] Construction went forward on the building, designed with the school on the first floor and the church on the second, but it was not ready until October 1948. The four sisters who were assigned to Immaculate Heart lived at St. John Academy and commuted by taxi until January when the house which had been purchased for the convent was ready, complete with a chapel in the converted garage.

Home Missions in Oklahoma and Texas

When the Ursuline Sisters withdrew from Immaculate Conception, Tulsa, in 1946, the Sisters of Providence were pleased to accept the school, since it was only about a hundred miles from Corpus Christi School in Oklahoma City. Sister Clare Therese Bullock had just completed her term as superior at Corpus Christi and was familiar with the area, so she was named to lead the group of four who arrived in August. Although they inherited a comfortable convent, she recalled that as a way to help the sisters feel welcome the pastor took $11.50 from the votive box with which they purchased fabric to make curtains and cushions for the wicker chairs.[32] Perhaps because only 3 percent of the state's population was Catholic, faith was a strong uniting factor for the parishioners. The sisters were treated like family, often returning from school to find a freshly baked cake or bread or rolls on their kitchen table.[33]

It had been Bishop Kelley of Catholic Extension Society fame who had brought the Sisters of Providence to the home mission field. Another one of the Extension priests who later took advantage of his contacts with the community was Bishop Emmanuel Ledvina, who had been educated by the Sisters of Providence in Evansville. After several posts as priest of the Indianapolis diocese, he served with the Extension Society from 1907-1921. He too went on to become a bishop of missionary territory when he was appointed ordinary of Corpus Christi, Texas, in 1921.[34] His episcopal ordination was held at Saint Mary-of-the-Woods, so it was not surprising that he requested sisters for his mission diocese. The largely rural diocese had attracted immigrants from Czechoslovakia, motivating him to recruit a Czech-speaking priest from the Indianapolis Archdiocese, Father George Scecina, to serve at St. John, Robstown.

Father Scecina had received his elementary education from the Sisters of Providence at Linton, Indiana, and was quick to write to the motherhouse to tell of his plans for a new school and convent. Since he understood that his request had been favorably received, when the sisters did not appear as he expected in August 1945, he called to find out where they were, only to be told none were available. Undeterred, he followed up with a letter stressing his confidence in the prayers of his congregation.[35] His plea was effective and four sisters were sent in January.

They arrived at a newly constructed convent which they described as "just like a picture out of the latest magazine. ... Nothing of the 'wartime' is in our home, only the very best!"[36] Having been reminded by Mother Mary Bernard that a chapel was a very desirable feature, the pastor had engaged a carpenter to build an altar and six prie-dieux in order to convert the dining room for this purpose. St. John School opened with eighty-two pupils on February 1, 1946.

Daily Life

Life on the Missions

Since only a limited understanding of their actual life circumstances can be gleaned through information about the sisters' daily schedule and their standard contract with parishes, this section attempts to fill the gap with a sampling of vignettes gleaned from the archives. Many of the convents owned by the Sisters of Providence had been built in the nineteenth or early twentieth centuries, while the condition of parish-owned convents depended on the attitude of pastors. However, during the postwar period, second-generation Catholics were now better able to show their appreciation of the sisters by providing as convents more suitable houses closer to the schools and usually adapted to provide a chapel with the Blessed Sacrament.

Many of the large Chicago houses dated back to earlier times. St. Mark's in Chicago had opened in 1906 and by the 1920s was a big city parish. It generated unfavorable memories for Sister Loretta Therese O'Leary as she recalled her first mission experience in 1922 when, at age eighteen, she was assigned to teach seventy-two first and second graders.

> My recollections of Saint Mark's are of one of the bleakest places you could ever find. The school was right on the street. You entered right from the street into the school. On the left was the playground. Next door was an apartment, a three floor tenement house, very, very close to ours. They kept their shades down all the time because we could see into their place and they could see into ours if they tried to. No grass any place, no trees and that was such a shock really to me after Saint Mary's and after growing up in a country place.[37]

The parish was actually a single building with the church on the first floor, the school on the second floor and the "convent" on the third floor. This consisted of four classrooms which had been divided to form a community room, dining room, kitchen and two dormitories. The local superior had charge of six classroom teachers, a music teacher and a cook, as well as being school principal and teaching seventh and eighth grades. Lacking a chapel, the sisters went down to the church for morning prayers, but often the priest would not appear at 7:00 a.m. for Mass. Complaints by Mother Mary Cleophas to Cardinal Mundelein about the intransigent pastor were ineffective, so the following year the sisters left at 5:45 a.m. to attend Mass at the Polish church several blocks away. However, visitation from the home superiors did lead to various relief measures. For example, the superior, Sister Mary Lawrence Layden, whose age and arthritis made the frequent trips up and down the stairs difficult, was changed the following year.

Because Sister Loretta Therese suffered from constant colds she also was changed. At St. Athanasius in Evanston she would experience yet another form of convent life at the time, that of an "outsister," the term used to describe those who lived in a Sister of Providence house and commuted to a nearby school. In her case, the five St. Athanasius sisters lived at Marywood, a large Congregation-owned convent with comfortable facilities and took the streetcar each day to the school. This was a relatively common situation, accepted by the Congregation with the understanding that provision of a convent was on the parish's schedule of developments, although life could be difficult in the meanwhile. For example, in Indianapolis, the sisters who taught at St. Ann had commuted from St. John's since 1926, but when additions were made to the school building in 1943, the second floor wing was completely remodeled to serve as quarters for the four sisters on staff.

Often living difficulties were simply a function of the physical plant itself. Many of the convents of the older establishments staffed by the sisters had not kept pace with the growth of the faculty and staff needed to accompany increased enrollment. At Our Lady of Sorrows in Chicago the 1945-1946 enrollment was some 1,324 pupils, so forty-one sisters were assigned for the following year, with residence in the 1866 convent building owned by the Congregation. On Monday,

August 18, 1947, having arrived on the special train to Chicago the previous Saturday, the sisters were enjoying recreation in the large convent yard when they were aroused by the cry of "Fire!" from the fifth floor. Fortunately all the sisters were quickly accounted for and the fire department arrived in time to douse the flames. The rescue was repeated when more fires broke out the following Wednesday and Friday. Water damage made the convent uninhabitable and the sisters had to stay at other convents. Since the school building was unharmed, several classrooms were temporarily converted into dormitory-style bedrooms. The sisters simply had to carry on their usual duties in the midst of the confusion.[38]

When the damaged portion fell to the wrecking ball, the noise and debris of the reconstruction project was exacerbated by the city's construction of the nearby Congress (Eisenhower) expressway. Several sisters suffered illnesses, and the conversion of classrooms to living space curtailed enrollment. These conditions continued through the following year until the completely renovated convent was ready in August 1948. This commodious building then also served during 1948-1964 as a residence for the sisters with summer assignments in Chicago.[39]

Because parish schools formed such a major portion of the Congregation's mission of education, when the superior general and her assistants visited the houses, they always met with the pastors. Frequent references in the council minutes regarding changes warranted by local circumstances indicate efforts to maintain the close ties so necessary for smooth operation of the school. Occasionally situations arose which caused considerable consternation and negotiation, as the following incident illustrates.

For eight years the Sisters of Providence had staffed St. Therese School in Wilson, North Carolina. By 1939 the enrollment had grown from twenty-six to seventy-four as the sisters earned the respect of both Catholic and Protestant parents. However, various personnel shifts occasionally altered the complexion of the working relationships. The energetic and very supportive Bishop Hafey had been replaced by longtime friend of the Congregation Bishop McGuinness in 1937, but at St. Therese differences of opinion had resulted in a turnover of several pastors and superiors.

When first time superior Sister Mary Perpetua Keck arrived in 1939, her first encounter with the pastor was when he greeted her with a tirade on the front porch of the convent. Later, he demanded that she turn over the tuition money, ordered her out of the school on September 28 and told her to take the night train to Washington, D.C. She stood her ground, but did go to nearby Burlington where former Fifth Assistant Sister Eugenia Clare was superior. Letters and telegraphs and phone calls multiplied among Mother Mary Bernard, Bishop McGuinness, Provincial Sister St. Eugenia and the sisters at St. Therese.[40] Once the facts had been laid out, it was clear that the pastor was unstable, and he was removed. Fortunately the new pastor was gradually able to heal the wounds, and by January 1940 the parishioners and school parents were happily joining in the celebration of the Congregation's Centenary. While this situation is certainly extreme, it illustrates the need for clear and mutually understood policies as well for careful choice of pastors and local superior, since a harmonious relationship had a significant impact on daily living.

Another example has a humorous twist but makes the same point. The Sisters of Providence had staffed the school at St. Patrick in Terre Haute since 1882, when they had purchased property and built the school. Over the years the school had expanded to include high school classes, and a large four-bedroom home had been purchased by the parish to serve as a convent. With the 1938 merger with St. Joseph Academy, the faculty of sisters grew to thirteen by 1941, and quarters were not only cramped, but decidedly inadequate. Because there were only two toilets and one bathtub, the bishop was enlisted to put pressure on the pastor to at least put in a second bathtub. When the sisters returned in August, there it stood— a bathtub in the middle of a bedroom. Only after further demands was it enclosed. Even at that, four sisters slept in one bedroom, and it was necessary to dress in the hallway. The sisters could at least take comfort in having their own chapel, since the church was eight blocks away.[41]

At the other end of the cooperative pastor spectrum, many priests exerted themselves to provide well for the sisters. Also in Terre Haute, sisters on the faculty of St. Margaret Mary had commuted daily from the motherhouse across the Wabash River. In 1941 parishioner and philanthropist Anton Hulman donated a residence which was converted into a convent. Knowing the sisters' desire to include a chapel on the premises, the pastor commissioned the building of an altar by workmen at Saint Mary-of-the-Woods. At St. Ann in Washington, D.C., the sisters who had lived at nearby Immaculata in 1940 moved into a large house in which the attic and screened porch had been made into bedrooms. The convenience of proximity came at a price, because the quarters were decidedly cramped, for the residence had to accommodate all fifteen sisters on staff. Fortunately, situations like the one at Corpus Christi in Oklahoma City, where in 1948 the parish constructed an entirely new thirteen-bedroom convent complete with a chapel with stained-glass windows, would more and more become the norm as during the fifties pastors wooed the Congregation for sisters.

Policies and Practices

Concurrently, other signs of the times affected life in the convent. In the late thirties, the liturgical movement which had begun in Europe was finding its way to the United States. It generated interest in the liturgy in the sisters who attended the August 1938 religious conference in Indianapolis to hear Father Virgil Michel, OSB, who had recently returned from studies abroad. Father Stephen Thuis, OSB, from St. Meinrad had also studied in Europe and was invited to give a talk on chant to the sisters.[42] As congregational singing expanded to include the singing of the Proper of the Mass (the prayers of the rite itself rather than accompanying hymns) music teachers attended conferences and workshops to better understand these developments and brought their newfound skills back to the Congregation and schools. In 1944 the November 2 celebration of the Feast of All Souls was the occasion for the congregational singing of the Requiem Mass at Saint Mary-of-the-Woods and the beginning of a longstanding practice.

With sisters stationed in so many dioceses across the country in a variety of circumstances, maintaining uniformity of practices and customs was becoming more difficult, as the Acts of Council show. Whereas a Congregation-owned academy might have a bus which would allow the superior to arrange a picnic outing for her sisters, rather than invite comparisons with parish convents, such excursions were discouraged. Special showings of movies were sometimes offered, even by a diocese, but the opinion that "little good comes either from seeing the movie or from the general assembly which accompanies it"[43] led to refusal of permission, and not only on one occasion. However, renting of selected movies for private viewing was gradually accepted as a legitimate recreation. Even the symphony was insufficient reason to warrant going to a public theater, much to the chagrin of Indianapolis Chancellor Henry Dugan, who pointed out that all the other congregations in Indianapolis had graciously accepted the gift tickets provided.[44] Visits to family required special permission, and decisions at times seemed capricious rather than governed by a consistent policy. Visits of family to sisters at the local convents were gradually becoming more common.

Although the *Constitutions* stipulated that: "The Sisters shall rise, in all seasons, at five o'clock,"[45] gradually custom had allowed for some relaxation of this rule during school vacations to allow for some extra rest with a later rising. The decision about which days later rising could actually be allowed was up to the local superior and naturally became quite variable. To prevent adverse comparisons it was decided to prepare cards listing specific occasions when it could be allowed; these were distributed to each convent to be posted on the bulletin board. Other situations also invited local discretion, prompting sisters to approach superiors who were more lenient with suggestions for adaptation. To address this issue Mother Mary Bernard tried to lay down a guiding principle, as noted by the secretary in the minutes: "Mother urged us to do all we can by counsel to make those who come to us for direction or help religious with a good spirit, strong and able to take No when No is the proper answer."[46]

Changing Transportation Options

Despite curtailments during the war, train transportation continued to be a major means of connecting to the missions, especially when passes were available. Daily train connections to Chicago made trips to the many missions there very convenient, as did the east-west Penn Central route to Washington, D.C. The New York Central route provided convenient service directly from the Saint Mary-of-the-Woods station to Indianapolis Union Station, walking distance from St. John Academy.[47] For many years, the extensive Indiana network of interurban electric trains provided consistent and reliable service, but by the early forties most of these lines ceased operation.[48] Rumors began to circulate that cutbacks in rail service might lead to the closure of the tiny Saint Mary-of-the-Woods station which had been in operation since 1899.[49]

The sisters who were called to open new missions, especially those at a distance, thought themselves fortunate to add adventure to the journey. After a drought of five years with no new missions, the four who traveled in January 1946 to faraway Robstown, Texas, near the Gulf coast, wrote an account that provides a humorous glimpse of train travel of the time.

> We had two sections on the Pullman. The porters were remarkable for their attention to us. Our experiences of sleeping in berths are ones never to be forgotten, especially the upper berth occupants. We thought we would never get undressed. We had to go up fully dressed because there was no place to undress, but in bed! Caps were sitting on our toes, shoes dropping on our heads, and neckerchiefs waving fast enough to flag a train. When lying down, our Habits fanned our faces and everything which has not been mentioned served as anchors to hold down our feet. We never laughed as hard in our lives as when we finally settled, but soon began to worry about getting into everything in the morning. It's a good thing we did not have to make the Morning Prayer bell![50]

At longer stops in St. Louis and Houston the friendly porters vouched for the security of their belongings so they could do a walkabout tour of the station environs, visit nearby churches and enjoy a restaurant meal before returning to their "little home on wheels."

Reliance on cars was more and more evident, especially for trips to Indianapolis. Even when a used seven-passenger Packard was purchased in 1947, the home superiors noted that yet another passenger car was "badly needed."[51] Each of the four priests now had his own car, making it necessary to expand their garage. Although plans to improve highways in the United States had been underway even during the Great Depression years, the war situation highlighted the importance of motorized transport to the country's defense system, with highway construction emerging as a priority. After gas rationing was lifted, the shift to automobile transportation and the decline in rail lines would continue to impact the Congregation's travel arrangements.

Home Improvements

Many of the infrastructure adjustments authorized by the council could easily have gone unnoticed. For example, in October 1939, the purchase of additional electric power from Public Service of Indiana supplemented that supplied by the powerhouse. Who would have known that it was necessary to fire the manager of the chicken farm in 1940 because it was losing money? On the other hand, in all likelihood word probably got around quickly when the trees whose Kentucky coffee beans were used as beads for the large rosary chaplets worn by the sisters no longer produced their harvest. Sister Baptista Courcier recommended the substitution of lily pond pods.[52] By 1948 communication by phone was quickly replacing the wire messages of earlier days, although the difficulty and expense of long distance calls limited regular use.

In the early postwar years, the entire motherhouse operations underwent a much needed overhaul. Without a gardener and lacking proper heating, the greenhouses were losing money, leading to a decision to reduce the number from six to two. A new laundry building was constructed and blessed on May 12, 1948. During 1946, the Inn was vacated to provide for a complete remodeling, and Foley Hall, Guerin Hall, the gymnasium and the bakery underwent major repairs, while in 1948 the plumbing in Providence Convent and the novitiate was replaced. In 1949, after only four years of use, the dental office was provided with updated equipment. Additional interest in investing in technology was evident with the 1948 purchase of an "Executone" sound system which enabled Mother Mary Bernard to deliver the annual summer instructions from her infirmary room to the sisters seated in the Conservatory auditorium.[53]

Death of Mother Mary Bernard

Simply noting the fact that Mother Mary Bernard required technological assistance to speak to the sisters once again calls to mind the ongoing reality of her failing health. By 1948 the strain of administering the affairs of the large and far-flung Congregation was again taking its toll on the seventy-two-year-old superior general. In June Mother Mary Bernard was taken to St. Vincent Hospital in Indianapolis, and in July she was sent to the Mayo Clinic in Rochester, Minnesota. In August she was brought home to the infirmary at Saint Mary-of-the-Woods, where she died on October 6, 1948. Much beloved after her sixteen years of visiting the sisters on mission as part of her service on the council, and highly appreciated both for her truly motherly touch as well as her ability to represent the Congregation in public arenas, her funeral attracted not only mourners but a wide spectrum of media attention.

The close ties between the College and the Congregation, so evident during the Centenary celebration, prompted the dedication of the November 1948 issue of the College magazine, the *Aurora,* to her memory. In "A Tribute," Sister Eugenia Logan commented:

> The memory of our beloved Mother is a benediction. ... Gifted as she was with the tact and capacity for governing, Mother Mary Bernard possessed in an unusual degree the faculty of seeing a problem as a whole and yet being able to grasp its finer details.[54]

Writing for the *Alumnae News*, Sister Ignatia Braheny voiced a more personal view, noting:

> the almost regal dignity of the College President, which could so readily melt into the gracious charm of the Mother, or even the gay banter of the intimate friend. ... Of the Sisters, there are few who cannot recall her witty rejoinders, her apt turns of speech, or her homely, intimate comments. ... She loved to see the Sisters enjoying a hearty, whole-souled recreation, she herself being readiest to laugh at a joke or comic situation.[55]

At the time of her funeral it was decided to change the grave markers for the superiors general in recognition of their unique service to the Congregation. Taking note of this change prompted Sister Eugenia to place Mother Mary Bernard's life in the context of the qualities and spirit so valued by the Sisters of Providence with this tribute:

> Mother Mary Bernard lies at rest near the graves of her predecessors in office, worthy to have her name inscribed with the seven illustrious superiors who came before her. Like them she viewed life with simplicity, with faith, and a deep trust in Divine Providence. She did not fail or falter in conserving the trust given to her even though the complex problems of the present day intruded upon the peace of the religious life, and

the tumult of war in far-off China laid upon her heart a grave anxiety. To the saintly foundress, Mother Theodore, was given the work of founding and establishing the Congregation; to her successors, the work of developing, building and expanding.[56]

In Part II of this volume we will follow the lives of those who took to heart Mother Theodore's advice to ponder old truths, as the signs of the times shed new light on how to continue her legacy. The challenge of a vocation to make God's love, mercy and justice a livening spirit would develop new dimensions as American Catholics faced the demands of demographic explosion and cultural shifts.

❧ Part II:
1949-1966

∾ Chapter 9
New Beginnings
1949-1954

The energy of the 1949 Council is evident as they assemble for the traditional East Door departure for the 1950 Holy Year Pilgrimage. The pilgrims (wearing capes) are Sister Francis Joseph Elbreg and Mother Marie Helene Franey. In the group from left to right are Sisters Rose Genevieve Flaherty, Francis Joseph Elbreg, Loretta Therese O'Leary, Catherine Celine Brocksmith, Mother Marie Helene Franey, Rose Dolores Thuis and Gertrude Clare Owens.

Interim Governance

Despite Mother Mary Bernard's chronic poor health, she had recovered so many times from so many serious illnesses that her council, with its core of long-serving assistants together with the four provincial superiors, had easily carried on the normal governance. However, her long illness in 1948 made it apparent that she would not live to complete her term, so her death on October 6 was not unexpected. One who surely felt the loss most keenly was First Assistant Sister Helen Clare Freiburger. The two had served side by side as first and second assistants on Mother Mary Raphael's 1932-1938 council. Their close partnership had continued during Mother Mary Bernard's 1938-1944 term with Sister Helen Clare in the role of first assistant.

When the 1944 Chapter had chosen Sister Alexis Marie Hoff as first assistant, the apparent demotion to second assistant must have raised questions in Sister Helen Clare's mind. Did the Chapter lack confidence that she was qualified to step in when the superior general was incapacitated, as the Rule designated? Had her reputation for exactitude created the impression that she was unsympathetic? When Sister Alexis Marie resigned, the council had waited six months to re-instate Sister Helen Clare in the role of first assistant. Despite any self-doubt, the need to carry on the governance of the Congregation now fell to her.

In fact, the press of business was urgent. Not only had the council already functioned without a superior since early June and drawn up the usual assignments for the following school year, but they had also dealt with several crises. Mother Mary Bernard's funeral with its many attendant duties was itself a strain. Legal difficulties surrounded the situation in Jasper, where back taxes were demanded. A large debt payment came due. Some matters could be deferred, but other decisions could not wait. Most immediately, since the *Constitutions* stipulated that a General Chapter must be held within six months following the death of the superior general, consultations with canonists and the archbishop determined that the Chapter would be held on March 25, 1949.

The China mission needed constant attention, for the end of World War II had rekindled the smoldering civil war in that huge country. In addition to feeling themselves to be a "lame duck" council, the home superiors were operating in a vacuum of information. Several missionaries had returned to the states for rest, but the situation was in such constant flux that they could not offer current advice. Nonetheless, in the face of ever-changing circumstances, Sister Marie Gratia Luking's many questions needed answers. Should the mission move from

Kaifeng to Nanking? No. Could the Providence Sister-Catechists open a dispensary in Peking? Yes. Could Chinese subjects be admitted? This topic was referred to the upcoming Chapter.

The Chapter of 1949

Sister Helen Clare's December 12, 1948, letter to the sisters provided the usual directions and materials for the process of electing delegates on December 18, 1948. As was the custom, results of the delegate voting came only to the delegates themselves. The February 11, 1949, letter of notification reminded them that "the sacredness of the trust given to us requires that we use prudence and discretion in mentioning our election as delegate."[1] Almost immediately the council received a letter from the much-respected Sister Manetto Quigley, a local superior of many years. Though she was not a delegate herself, she had been one in four previous Chapters. Now she asked that the names of the members of the General Chapter be made known to the sisters. Although the council noted that "She is voicing the wishes of many in making this request," they decided the time was not ripe for change and that the usual custom would be followed.[2]

Certainly everyone knew many of the delegates since the council members and the four provincial superiors were ex-officio. In their careful preparations for the General Chapter the council had gone to the trouble of inviting the noted canonist James O'Connor, SJ, to come to Saint Mary-of-the-Woods to consult with them to make sure that all the arrangements would be proper.[3] Apparently the main concern was making sure the Chapter of Elections occurred within the six months prescribed by the *Constitutions* while ensuring that the usual procedures were followed in the selection of delegates.[4] Since the provincial superiors had participated as delegates in three consecutive Chapters, it seemed perfectly normal for their names to appear on the delegate list as ex-officio members. Once again the agenda would also include discussion of the long-postponed provincial structure, but there is no record of the canonist's recommendation on this point, nor even of any council deliberations or recommendations about provinces.

Although the Rule stated that, "The Sisters shall not inquire curiously among themselves what the Superior General and her Council are about to do or ought to do, in what concerns the government of the Congregation,"[5] after years of stimulating their students' patriotic civic participation it would seem that the sisters had imbibed a democratic spirit. Perhaps a renewed interest in community affairs was a natural by-product of the celebration of the centennial, still fresh in memory, as well as of the optimistic postwar mood of the country, the activities of the fledgling United Nations and the emergence of newly independent countries.

Whatever the reason, when the ballots were counted, of the twenty-four sisters chosen to serve as delegates, half had never before done so. In preparation for their responsibilities as Chapter delegates, surely the new members would not only have read carefully the specific protocols described in the *Constitutions* for the order of Chapter business but also quite possibly sought additional instruction from someone known to have previously served. However, neither experience nor advice would have prepared them for the drama about to unfold.

As the delegates filed into the Chapter room to take their seats on the morning of Friday, March 25, 1949, they must have been aware of the bustle of movement in the adjacent Tile Hall as Archbishop Schulte and his assistant, Father Charles Ross, called Sister Helen Clare into the Bishop's Parlor. Heads surely turned when Sisters St. Eugenia McBarron, Mary Rose Cummings, St. Philomene Cullity and Carita Kiley were tapped on the shoulder and beckoned from the room. Twenty minutes passed. Schooled as they were to silence and recollection, after the lengthy unexplained delay the delegates must have been relieved to stand when the Archbishop, his assistant, and Sister Helen Clare finally stepped into the room. Conspicuously absent were the four provincials.

Archbishop Schulte's announcement that the provincials were ineligible to serve as ex-officio chapter delegates[6] must have prompted muffled gasps. It would have been a special jolt to the council members, who had labored over the details of preparation. The notes from the 1944 Chapter stated that that year Bishop Ritter had given a dispensation allowing the provincials to be ex-officio members on a provisional basis, and they had been present and voting during the 1932, 1938 and 1944 Chapters. Despite their shock, or perhaps because of it, no one raised a question. Indeed, no questions were invited. Requested to remain for the business portion of the meeting, the four provincials quietly filed in, the Archbishop intoned the "Veni Sancte Spiritus" as the opening prayer to the Holy Spirit, and the Chapter was underway.

The immediate routine activity of electing the scrutators, (the two delegates chosen to collect and count the ballots) provided breathing space for the delegates to assimilate the situation. Sister Helen Clare opened her report by paying tribute to Mother Mary Bernard and crediting her with the continued growth of the Congregation, now numbering 1,364 members, with sixty-four novices and twenty-nine postulants, including the six in the East at Maryhurst. Four schools had been opened, with 46,548 students enrolled in ninety-six schools. Two sisters had earned doctoral degrees, fifty had earned master's degrees and 138 had earned bachelor's degrees. The sisters in the China mission were now resettled and active in Taiwan.

Sister Francis Raphael Donlon's financial report showed not only a balanced budget despite considerable investment in motherhouse and college infrastructure, but a significant decrease in debt as well. As this was Archbishop Schulte's first opportunity to receive an overall report of the condition of the Sisters of Providence, the very positive reports dispelled any reservations he might have formed because of the discrepancy regarding the "canonical error" which had resulted in the seating of ineligible delegates, and he commended the reports. An auditing committee was appointed to examine the report, and an undoubtedly very welcome thirty-minute recess ensued.

Following the formal statement of the committee's approval of the reports, the remaining delegates filed from the chapter room to the large crypt chapel below the Church. As presider, Archbishop Schulte emphasized the solemnity of the occasion with an exhortation to put aside personal preferences and think only of following God's guidance in choosing who would bear the burden of office. Kneeling in their assigned places in the dimly lighted crypt, the superiors arrayed in the back row must have been acutely conscious of the vacant places of the four provincials in the pew before them. The senior members with more years in community were in the next two pews beyond, but five of the twelve had never before been Chapter delegates. Of the twelve in the first two pews, seven would ponder their votes for the first time. Because of illness, one delegate, Sister Margaret Donlan, was not present, but the younger of the two scrutators, Sister Rose Genevieve Flaherty, would go to the nearby infirmary to collect each of her ballots. It would be a slow process with plenty of time for each delegate to search for God's guidance.

Who was the best person to be the next superior general? Since 1899 the choice had always fallen to someone with long service in general administration, but the delegates' thinking was clearly divided regarding this advantage. Almost half cast their ballots for long-serving Third Assistant Sister Gertrude Clare Owens, but slightly more than half selected the council secretary, Sixth Assistant Sister Marie Helene Franey. Although the margin was slim, a single ballot sufficed for the election. Doubtless shaken by yet another unexpected turn of events, Sister Marie Helene came forward to take the oath of office and thank the departing clergy. She then assumed the presidency of the assembly for the voting which would determine who would assist her in the office.

Mother Marie Helene Franey

She could count on the experience of Sister Gertrude Clare, as she was immediately elected to serve a sixth term on the council, this time as first assistant. The selection of the second assistant was not so clear. Although Sister Helen Clare received many votes on the first ballot, there was no majority, and Sister Rose Genevieve Flaherty was elected on the second ballot. As in the 1944 Chapter, the remaining choices, all on single ballots, brought two other newcomers "from the ranks," neither of whom was present: Sister Catherine Celine Brocksmith as third assistant and Sister Loretta Therese O'Leary as sixth assistant and secretary. Sisters Rose Dolores Thuis, Francis Joseph Elbreg and Francis Raphael Donlon were resoundingly returned to their positions as fourth and fifth assistants and treasurer.

Based on the archbishop's explanation, Mother Marie Helene and the delegates understood that the Congregation's years of experimentation with a provincial structure had never been confirmed by a Chapter vote, nor had the establishment of provinces been approved by Rome's Congregation for Religious.[7] Realizing that the afternoon session scheduled to discuss the *Constitutions'* sections relative to the provinces was moot, Mother Marie Helene announced that the Chapter was adjourned and that the proclamation of new officers would take place at two o'clock. She and her newly-elected council would now be responsible to reorganize the governmental structure. With this in mind let us meet the new council members.

The 1949 Council

Sister Rose Genevieve Flaherty 1896-1990

Eileen Flaherty was the youngest of six children born to Margaret and Bernard Flaherty in Peru, Indiana. Because of their mother's tragic death from smoke inhalation from a household fire, the oldest, thirteen-year-old Kate, took on the role and most of the duties of mothering her two brothers and three sisters. At age sixteen Eileen entered the novitiate at nearby Saint Mary-of-the-Woods and during this time she completed her high schooling at the Academy and was given the name of Sister Rose Genevieve. A year later, at age twenty-nine, Kate followed, taking the name Sister Mary Bernardo. During her early years Sister Rose Genevieve had a variety of mission experiences teaching middle and upper grades in three large Chicago schools, as well as a year in Huntington, Indiana, and another at St. Joseph in Terre Haute. Following her second novitiate she directed the commercial department at St. Andrew, Chicago, with then Sister Mary Bernard as superior. At age twenty-seven she was appointed superior at St. Sylvester and subsequently served in that role at two other large Chicago schools, St. Mel and St. Agnes. She completed her AB degree during the summers and was known for her skill in mentoring young teachers, actively training them to combine professional standards with personal concern for pupils. As a superior, she took the lead in domestic tasks, putting on an apron to cheerfully assist with household chores and creating a homelike convent atmosphere. Much respected, she was elected as a delegate to the 1938 and 1944 Chapters and again to the 1949 Chapter, when she was elected second assistant at age fifty-two. After two terms on the council she went on to serve as econome and later as director of the shrine of Our Lady of Providence until her retirement.

Sister Catherine Celine Brocksmith 1905-1998

Anna Marie Brocksmith was the second of four girls born to Ethel and Fred Brocksmith in Vincennes, Indiana, all of whom were educated by the Sisters of Providence at the historic St. Rose Academy. Anna Marie looked up to her older sister Margaret who had entered the novitiate at Saint Mary-of-the-Woods in 1922, taking the name of Sister Anna Margaret, so it was natural for her to follow in her footsteps two years later at age nineteen. Her entire mission experience prior to second novitiate was as a primary teacher at St. Francis Xavier in the Chicago suburb of Wilmette, Illinois, and unusually, she returned to the same mission after second novitiate. In 1935 at age thirty she was appointed superior of the six-sister convent in Wilmette. She was appointed the first superior at St. Thomas Aquinas in Indianapolis when it opened in 1941, and she served a six-year term before returning once again to Wilmette in 1947. In addition to her principal's license she earned an MA from Indiana State Teacher's College in 1947. She had been elected as a Chapter delegate in 1944, but was not a delegate in 1949, so she had to be summoned to come to Saint Mary-of-the-Woods when she was elected at age forty-five to the post of third assistant. She would continue in the role of councilor until 1972, assisting three successive superiors general. Upon her retirement she volunteered at the campus Montessori school until her health failed.

Sister Loretta Therese O'Leary 1904-1999

Mary O'Leary was one of two girls and four boys born to Anna and Daniel O'Leary in Everett, Massachusetts. After her initial education by the Sisters of Providence at St. Patrick, Stoneham, she entered the novitiate at age sixteen and com-

pleted high school at the Academy at Saint Mary-of-the-Woods. After five years of teaching primary grades at two Chicago area schools, she returned to the Boston area at St. Rose, Chelsea, where she began teaching high school commercial subjects. She then spent seven years at Providence High School in Chicago, and by 1936 she had completed her AB degree. She had enjoyed excellent mentoring by her superiors, four of whom had also served as provincial superiors. She was named as a novitiate sister with Sister Rose Berchmans Patterson for the 1937-1938 year before returning to high school classrooms at St. Augustine in Fort Wayne, Marywood in Evanston and St. Agnes in Indianapolis. Since she had never served as a superior nor been elected as a Chapter delegate, her election in March 1949 at age forty-five to the post of sixth assistant and secretary undoubtedly came as a complete surprise. Nonetheless, it was a post that fit her talents well, and she went on to serve with four superiors general from 1949-1972. She had completed her studies in history at Marquette University by 1948, and after beginning her duties as secretary, she persevered in writing her master's thesis, receiving her MA in 1951. From 1972-1984 she served in the business office at Immaculata and then returned to the motherhouse where she worked in the Congregation archives.

As always, outgoing councilors were immediately given new assignments. Sister Helen Clare was appointed to replace Sister Catherine Celine as superior of St. Francis Xavier in Wilmette, Illinois. There it soon became apparent to the sisters in her charge that, in her efforts to function as the voice of the administration, she had constructed a "kind of hard shell" that hid her true nature. This shell she quickly shed in favor of the soft-hearted concern for which she is remembered by the sisters at her new assignment.[8] Sister Margaret Agnes O'Neill moved from her brief appointment as third assistant to Immaculata High School in Washington, D.C, where she later served as principal from 1952-1955.

Surely there was a sense of new beginnings when the 1949 council gathered for the first time. The average age of the council members was fifty-one. Two of the new members had not lived at the motherhouse since their formation days, and all three new members came directly from parish schools where families were experiencing a postwar prosperity which had generated grand expectations for the future. Of those who continued on the council, both Mother Marie Helene and Sister Rose Dolores had priest-brothers who kept them in close touch with developments in the Church. Both of the two long-serving councilors, Sister Gertrude Clare and Sister Francis Joseph, brought unique perspectives. Due to her duty of providing the thirty-day retreat during the second novitiate, Sister Gertrude Clare had come to know most of the sisters. Over the almost thirty years Sister Francis Joseph had served as supervisor of education she had observed these same sisters at work on the missions and monitored their higher education. Since the council members were beginning their administration in March, the "CMs" (to use Mother Marie Helene's term of endearment) would have time to get to know each other and their roles before the sisters would come for summer classes and retreat.

The Holy Year of 1950

To a great extent the College journalism department publication *The Bugle Call*, with its articles on the Chinese mission, had long provided Sisters of Providence with personal links to a global worldview. Even from their perspective on the sidelines, the participation of the United States in World War II had considerable impact both on individual sisters whose brothers and fathers were on active duty and on the Congregation's activities.

After war's end international events continued to hover in the background even in the semi-cloistered convents, where some of the sisters had actually watched the January 1949 inauguration of President Truman on television.[9] Stalin's aggressive policy of imposing Communist rule in Eastern Europe, labeled an "iron curtain" by Churchill in 1946, quickly escalated into a Cold War. The 1948 United Nations Declaration of Human Rights set a high moral tone for international relations, while the Truman Doctrine with its inspirational aim of aiding free peoples and its concrete application with the

Marshall Plan and Berlin airlift continued to foster a spirit of patriotism.

No longer could the sisters ignore world happenings as though they were of no concern. Indeed the council decided to take the opposite tack and provide education in current events. The 1948 summer school session included a week-long lecture series on parliamentary procedure, culminating in a model convention to present and debate resolutions on the topic of "The Catholic Teacher's Answer to Secularism," with spirited discussion from the floor.[10] Father Robert Gorman, history professor at Saint-Mary-of-the-Woods College, was invited to present a series of lectures during the 1949 summer session. As the sisters absorbed information on topics such as eastern Europe, NATO and the Far East, they acquired vivid images to enliven their daily prayer for the July 1949 Apostleship of Prayer intention of "the brotherhood of man." That summer a completely unexpected event brought home the fact that the church was providentially connected with evolving world events.

In June 1949, Pope Pius XII proclaimed 1950 a Holy Year: "Let our humble thanks go to divine Providence, which, after formidable events which shattered the earth during the second world conflict and in postwar years, has granted humanity some improvement in general condition."[11] The ancient tradition of inviting the faithful to journey to Rome as pilgrims could not have been more timely for American Catholics, who, as Charles Morris notes, had "benefited disproportionately from the postwar boom, both in population growth and affluence."[12] In October the College Alumnae Association offered to defray the expenses of Mother Marie Helene and a companion to represent the Congregation in the pilgrimage.to Rome. This was exciting news indeed, since this was the first visit to Rome by a superior general since Mother Mary Cleophas' 1922 trip.

Supervisor of Education Sister Francis Joseph Elbreg was named as her companion and arrangements were made for the two to travel with Cardinal Spellman's group, leaving New York on the *SS Atlantic* on February 18, 1950, with stops in Fatima and Malta. In Rome they not only made the Jubilee visits to numerous churches, but also witnessed the impressive ceremony of the beatification of Dominic Savio in St. Peter's.

From the left: Sœur Marie Geneviève Lebreton, Sœur René Joseph Marchand, Mother Marie Helene, Sister Francis Joseph, Soeur Maria Joseph Tribondeau, councilor 1946-1958, superior general 1958-1970.

They attended the pope's Mass in his private chapel and participated in one of his general audiences. They were able to meet with Father Andrew Manescau, the postulator for Mother Theodore's Cause, and Father Francesco Antonelli, OFM, who had been appointed to review all the material already submitted in order to decide whether the work should go ahead.[13]

From Rome the group journeyed to Lourdes by way of Paris, which provided the two sisters with the opportunity to insert a special pilgrimage of their own—a trip to Ruillé. Mother Marguerite Marie welcomed the American Sisters of Providence warmly and with Sister St. George as translator, they enjoyed a tour of the historic grounds. In addition to Benediction in the elegant church, where they heard the beautiful singing of novices who had been sent to Solesmes to be schooled in chant, they prayed at the original "Little Providence" and at Father Dujarié's grave. Despite the language barrier, they enjoyed an evening sharing photos of Saint Mary-of-the-Woods and stories of the founding days. In one of her letters to the other council members, Mother Marie Helene told how in a formal ceremony one of the French sisters, struggling with strongly accented English, paid tribute to Mother Theodore's "robust Breton faith and noble heart. We are the keepers of those sorts of 'Holy Places' where our two Institutes originated. Our prayer of Reunion is now offered in Europe, America and Asia." For the new general superior, "Ruillé was one of the great joys of our visit."[14]

The two sisters rejoined the pilgrimage group at Lourdes and then continued on again to Paris. Feeling herself to be very much a representative of the Congregation, Mother Marie Helene kept a journal of their travels and shared her impressions through letters. Her missives described not only their drive through the beautiful French countryside but also frustrations from trains beset with strikes. In Paris they visited the Church of the Most Holy Trinity, immediately recognizing Mother Mary Cleophas' inspiration for the Church of the Immaculate Conception at Saint Mary-of-the-Woods. En route across the Channel to Dover the effects of bombing were still evident and when a side trip from London took them to the Ruillé Sisters' establishment at Maidstone, the stories of wartime events interwoven in their tour brought home the recent reality of war in that part of the world.

With the comfortable quarters and lively companionship of their fellow pilgrims on the return voyage, there was time to absorb the mind-expanding events of the busy pilgrimage. During the next few months Mother Marie Helene shared the experience with group after group of sisters. Even second-hand, viewing the pilgrimage group's films and hearing her recount the events provided an avenue for the community as a whole to deepen their appreciation of their own participation in a worldwide church mission.[15]

The generosity of friends and relatives made it possible for other Sisters of Providence to enjoy this unusual Holy Year opportunity.[16] Many dioceses had arranged for pilgrimages which included passage on the great steamships of the day, with space where the bishops and priests leading the groups could celebrate Mass for the pilgrims. Often side trips could be arranged, as when on their April pilgrimage with the Archdiocese of Chicago group, Sister Marie Perpetua Hayes' brother, Monsignor Patrick Hayes, included his sister and her companion, Sister Mary Joseph Pomeroy, in an additional week in Ireland. Both sisters also visited Ruillé, renewing the newly re-established ties with the French Sisters of Providence.

During the summer months three more groups of Sisters of Providence combined their pilgrimages with supplementary excursions of great value to their teaching duties. During their time in Rome, Sisters Virginia Murphy and Helen Gertrude Tully witnessed the canonization of Ecuadorian Mother Maria Anne de Paredes. Sisters Teresa Williams, Camille Ostendorf and Mary Viator Sugrue traveled with Cardinal Stritch's Chicago pilgrimage, leaving on the *Queen Elizabeth* on July 6 and returning August 6. In addition to the Rome pilgrimage, Sisters Mary Lourdes Mackey, Esther Newport and Mary Loretta Gaughan attended the performance of the Oberammergau Passion Play. They also took the opportunity to visit the nearby wood carving studio of Mr. Hans Heinzeller, a contact which would later prove of great benefit, as explained in the sidebar on page 272. In Cork, Ireland, Sister Mary Lourdes persuaded the guide of the Protestant church housing the famous "bells of Shandon" to allow her to celebrate the group's pilgrimage theme by playing the Lourdes hymn.[17]

Sister Esther had an additional worrisome responsibility while in Rome. An International Exhibition of Sacred Art had been planned as part of the preparations for the Holy Year. Since Sister Esther was the founding member of the Catholic Art Association, its president had asked her to chair the committee making the arrangements for artists from the United States to participate. Undaunted by the tight timeline and sheer scope of the endeavor, she had embarked on the complex task of soliciting entrants and supplying them with information regarding insurance and shipping. After months of effort and setbacks, including delays in construction of the building which would house the exhibit, she describes her apprehension as she set out to view the results:

> The din and crush of pilgrims in Rome is distressing but there is a living spirit beneath the crudeness which mitigates the discomfort. One feels the pulse of faith – and like any healthy pulse it thumps. [We entered] the winding maze of the exhibit proper. All was quite modern in tone. The setup was rather spectacular and dramatically arranged. The German and Dutch sections were perhaps the best. ... The Spanish section was rich and fresh in color but still very baroque in style. Very little British and a nice blank wall for the United States! Our exhibit just wasn't there.[18]

Delays in shipping prevented her from enjoying the results of her labors.

The travelers returned not only with souvenirs to share, tales to tell and an enriched approach to their interactions with alumnae and students, but also with objects of lasting value. Mother Marie Helene purchased in France a set of Stations of the Cross for the infirmary chapel. In addition to photographs, several of the travelers had made motion pictures which delighted the viewers. Sister Mary Lourdes' purchase of two small wax figures of the Infant Jesus in Lucerne, Switzerland, later prompted the decision to commission an entire nativity set. [19]

Council Activities

The very first decision the new council faced—formal discontinuance of the provinces—jettisoned a structure which

A Legacy of Holy Year Pilgrimages

In 1952 Mr. Hans Heinzeller in Oberammergau was commissioned to carve the three figures of a nativity scene. As an appropriate setting, Sister Immaculee Krafthefer designed a stable in the Bavarian style which was constructed by staff carpenters George and Charles Kerstiens. Preparations for Christmas that year were worrisome when the seventy-pound figures did not arrive on schedule, and relief was great when they were located by New York City's customs office. Just prior to Midnight Mass, the figure of the Infant was carried in procession to the stable in the front of the Church of the Immaculate Conception, where Superior General Mother Marie Helene placed it in the crib. Over the years the colorful figures have developed cracks, but these have recently been repaired, and their simple beauty continues to form a timeless centerpiece as carols are sung during the annual Blessing of the Crib inaugurating the Christmas season.

had limped along for years as a stopgap measure. Their unanimous vote set the stage for a change of approach. Mother Marie Helene seemed to move easily into her new role, drawing upon her natural talent as an organizer and enabler. During her time as council secretary the Tile Hall offices had been renovated by placing a counter in the secretary's office to afford additional storage and workspace. At the same time the small room between the superior general's and secretary's offices became the council meeting room.[20] During the interim before the 1949 Chapter she had proposed a different format for the council's agenda and minutes which called for committee reports and an orderly progression of unfinished and new business.[21] Formal decisions were now carefully recorded with the wording: "The Council voted on the question" with "yes" and "no" votes indicated. Prior to decisions about appointment to offices such as mistress of novices, several weeks were allowed for prayer and reflection. At periodic intervals the minutes were signed by Mother Marie Helene and Secretary Sister Loretta Therese.

Mother Marie Helene's personality and style strongly influenced the work of the council. During her years at the College she had begun a system of typing notes for her talks on four-by-seven inch sheets punched for insertion in small black notebooks, a system which she now used to prepare the talks and instructions she gave to the community. It is from these notes that we get a sense of the woman herself.[22] Examples of her comments to the College seniors in her role as their class adviser reveal a direct and challenging style showing that she herself had internalized the high standards and good habits she encouraged:

> You may insist to yourself, to your friends, that you are indifferent to the law or regulation you are setting aside, but this inner harmony is broken, even though you refuse to admit it.

> Your days will be filled and demands on your time will be many. Be reasonable with yourself. Do not expect the impossible. Take the rest you need. Sleep is one of God's gifts.

Mother Marie Helene used a similar approach in her talks to the sisters, issuing practical challenges based on living out religious ideals, as can be seen in her talks at the motherhouse and during visitations in March 1952:

> We need the strength of soul which comes from our prayer life. Our Holy Rules are arranged to give us this help and our fidel-

ity to these spiritual exercises bring God's blessing. …There
are few things which do greater harm to our spiritual life than
worry, distress over what we cannot change.

The whole of the spiritual life may be summed up as the quest
of the soul for God alone, and progress is measured by the love
with which we work. …When God looks at us, He sees in our
souls the beautiful perfection of which they are capable. His
look is creative; it can create goodness where He finds the will
to become so.

The relative youth of the council members augured well
for carrying this spirit into their work. However, health concerns had some impact on their activities, as when Sister Rose
Dolores required a medical leave of absence during the summer of 1950. Mother Marie Helene herself was hospitalized at
St. Mary's Hospital in Rochester, Minnesota, in December 1952
for surgical resection of the colon, with a flu virus delaying
her return to duty until February 1953.

Legal and business matters required considerable attention
and frequent trips. Sister Francis Raphael proved to be an invaluable asset as business affairs multiplied. In numerous on-
site meetings across the country, Sister Francis Raphael's grasp
of contract details and her quick wit gained the respect of bishops and business professionals alike. In May 1949 she accompanied Mother Marie Helene for a meeting with Archbishop
O'Boyle in Washington, D.C., regarding the sale of Maryhurst
and then remained to finalize the details and see to the disposition of furnishings. When business-like policies on the part
of diocesan chanceries were promoted by the legal department
of the National Catholic Welfare Conference, her research and
advocacy kept the Congregation abreast of these developments.
The Archdiocese of Chicago explored the option of offering
hospital insurance to the sisters but instead in 1953 raised sisters' salaries to sixty dollars a month, as had been done in Los
Angeles. That same year Sister Francis Raphael traveled to
Los Angeles to inaugurate the new bookkeeping designed for
the Archdiocese in the fight against the school tax. The government decided to bring non-profit organizations under the
Social Security plan, and the NCWC's had consequently recommended that religious orders include their employees in the
plan in order to maintain tax exempt status. This entailed learn-

ing new procedures and providing direction for local superiors.[23]

Transition from Provinces

Clearly one of the first challenges the council faced was adapting to the loss of the provincials. As Mother Marie Helene stated in her letter to the sisters informing them of this change:"There is need of considerable adjustment. In the meantime we have delegated to the Provincials the same powers which they have held previously and this will continue at least until the summer"[24]

As we have seen, the "powers" had varied considerably from one province to the next. Distance had been the main factor dictating the extent of the provincials' activities, with those on the East and West Coasts taking a more visible role, while provincial superiors in the Midwest had more contact with home and local superiors than with the sisters themselves. The home superiors had definitely relied on the provincials for assistance with emergency situations.

Train connections to Boston and Washington, D.C., were such that the home superiors could be on the scene within a day, but it was decided to delegate Sister St. Philomene Cullity to be available to the sisters in California.[25] Having served as the first principal at Anaheim and most recently as eastern provincial, she was ideally equipped to assist with the transition. Due to the expense of travel, sisters who were missioned in California stayed there for several years rather than returning to the motherhouse in the summer, so her occasional meetings of the local superiors were valued for the opportunity for discussions among themselves and for close-at-hand support. In the Midwest there are frequent references to former provincials Sisters Carita Kiley and St. Eugenia McBarron filling in with delegated authority in the essential role of companions escorting infirm sisters to the motherhouse or regional hospitals. This indicates continued reliance on such assistance.

Efforts were made to foster close connections with the home superiors by encouraging letters and by the publication of a midyear "Bulletin" which included the names of the sisters making perpetual vows on January 23 and their assignments. Almost immediately after her election, Mother Marie Helene set out to visit missions in Indiana and the East Coast.

The expansion of commercial airlines and the proximity of Hulman Airport in Terre Haute, which had opened in October 1944, prompted the chronicler to note that Mother Marie Helene and her assistants "departed from the customary mode of travel for the Sisters of Providence and made use of the American Airlines for visitation trips."[26]

Key Appointments

As the council members gradually took on the various responsibilities of their offices, within months it became obvious that they would need competent assistance in several key areas.

Mistress of Novices

Already by 1950 the number of applicants to the novitiate had increased to the point that the need for additional help was clear. Since Sister Rose Berchmans had been a novitiate assistant for ten years and then served as mistress of novices for fifteen, the council agreed it was time for a change. On March 4, 1951, the council began with a prayerful reflection on the Rule:

> The welfare of the Congregation and the good it is designed to accomplish depend in great measure upon the manner in which the subjects are formed; therefore, it is essential that the Mistress of Novices be endowed with wisdom, tact, piety, and zeal, and that she have a thorough knowledge of the *Constitutions*. Furthermore, she ought to be remarkable for regularity, modesty, and recollection, in order to teach the practice of these virtues by her example.[27]

Amid the rapidly changing cultural climate, who among the members would fit this description and be able to guide young women aspiring to religious life? During the following days the council members made a novena to the Holy Spirit to ponder the names which were mentioned, as well as to consider others. Mother Marie Helene met with Sister Rose Berchmans during her Lenten retreat to tell her of the upcoming change. In early April, after weighing each possible candidate, the council's formal vote was unanimous in choosing Sister Marie Ambrose McKenna, whose experience had prepared her well for the role.

After graduating from Marywood, Evanston, in 1919, Bessie McKenna had gone on to earn an AB in English and

History at DePaul University in Chicago and had taught for three years
before entering the novitiate in 1926.
During her novitiate years she taught
classes to her companion postulants
and novices and, after two years teaching high school, had returned for a year
as a novitiate sister alongside Sister
Rose Berchmans. After four more years
as a high school teacher, in 1939 she
was appointed mistress of novices in
the western novitiate at Anaheim.
When it was closed in 1942 she re-
turned to a high school classroom at Central Catholic in Fort
Wayne. While she was studying for her MA at Indiana State
College, she was appointed superior at Corpus Christi in Oklahoma City in 1946, where she also taught ninth grade during
the transition to the establishment of a four-year diocesan high
school. Her appointment as mistress of novices was effective
on the feast of Pentecost, May 1951, with Sister Rose Berchmans
immediately taking up duties as local superior at Lady Isle.

Sister Marie Ambrose McKenna

Procuratrix/Econome

The *Constitutions* also provided for the position of
procuratrix, the sister "charged with the care of the temporalities, the cultivation of the land, the supervision of the domes-
tics and workmen, the repairs to be made, and the buying of
provisions."[28] The procuratrix was more commonly referred
to as the econome, and at mid-century the responsibilities of
the office extended not only to the motherhouse and College
buildings and grounds with their extensive farms and outbuildings, but also to consultative services for Congregation-owned
properties in various locations. With so many responsibilities,
the article's further description of the qualifications for this
office seem apt: "She must have a well balanced mind and
ability for business. ...She shall be ... polite, affable, modest,
and prudent." Among several likely candidates, one stood
out—Sister Robert Kiley.

Like her older sister, Sister Annunciata Kiley, Frances Kiley
had waited until she was twenty-two to enter the novitiate in
1928. Of the ten Kiley children, she was the third who entered
the Congregation, the first having been Sister Carita Kiley,

Sister Robert Kiley

whom we have met earlier in these pages. Sister Robert taught for seven years in elementary schools, and then, having completed her BA degree, taught at St. John Academy in Indianapolis for nine years. During those years she was mentored by excellent superiors and principals and had spent her summers studying at Indiana University. Having obtained her MA degree, she had returned as principal at St. John Academy in Indianapolis for two years and, according to the chronicler, seemed "best qualified by training, previous experience and disposition" to take up the demanding duties to which she was appointed on May 30, 1949.

High School Visitor

Sister Eugenia Logan

As the council considered the responsibility of staffing ninety-three schools, it was apparent that, even with Sister Rose Dolores having taken on the supervision of music teachers, the Education Office had been stretched beyond capacity. They agreed that it was time to split the work between the elementary and secondary levels and decided to create the position of high school visitor, a sister who would arrange for the educational program of high-school teachers and supervise them in the field. At mid-century much of the success of Saint Mary-of-the-Woods College was attributable to its extremely capable dean, Sister Eugenia Logan, who had served in that capacity for twenty-seven years and understood well the contribution of higher education to the preparation of teachers. During Mother Marie Helene's tenure at the College, the two had worked closely together, so when Mother approached her with an assignment which would both fulfill a strong community need and also provide new challenges, she readily agreed to pioneer the new post.

Dean of the College

Doubtless this decision was made easier by the availability of someone eminently qualified to replace her as dean, Sister Marie Perpetua Hayes. The oldest of ten children, after finishing the commercial course at Providence High School in Chicago, she had come to Saint-Mary-of-the-Woods where she graduated from the Academy and entered the novitiate in 1922. After eight years as an elementary teacher and the completion of her BA in history in 1933, she taught at St.

Sister Marie Perpetua Hayes

Agnes Academy in Indianapolis for ten years. She was sent to earn an MA in history at Catholic University, with her residence at Immaculata during 1943-1944 also providing the opportunity for close observation of the junior college under Sister Eugenia Clare Cullity's able direction. During her six-year tenure as professor of history at the College, she had gained respect not only for her teaching, but also for her organizational ability. With Mother Marie Helene retaining the title of president, Sister Marie Perpetua was appointed dean in 1950.

Ongoing Formation

As described in Chapter 8, convent conditions could play a large part in each sister's attitude and ability to live out her vows. Situations of non-observance could vary greatly along a spectrum of outright scandal through less stringent attention to community customs. With complaints coming to the council on a regular basis, Mother Marie Helene and her council addressed the issue by direct confrontation with individual sisters, by appealing to the ideals of the majority and by re-visiting long-standing customs in the light of changing times.

During Mother Mary Bernard's 1944-1949 term, the council had had to deal with an unusual number of sisters leaving the Congregation. The name used to describe these departures—defections—indicates the widely held view that once

someone's individual vocation had been confirmed by acceptance for vows only a lack of cooperation with grace could
account for the loss of that vocation. Usually those who left
were sisters under temporary vows who would simply choose
not to continue, but between 1944 and 1946 five sisters who
had been members for twenty-five years or more left. As secretary during this time, Mother Marie Helene had had the responsibility of documenting the circumstances of these
decisions, some of which were quite disheartening to the individuals' convent companions.

On several occasions, sisters who had "given scandal by
their conduct" were called before the council and asked to
sign a statement of what would be required of them in the
future.[29] The canonical procedure for dismissal from perpetual
vows was studied, together with consultations with Bishop
Ritter on the occasion when it was necessary to pursue that
course of action. Other situations called for psychiatric intervention or simply meeting informally with the sister to determine what changes would assist her.

As a positive approach, "Mother's instructions" were a
staple of summer school when the sisters gathered in the auditorium of the Conservatory before the morning classes. In the
summer of 1951 Mother Marie Helene provided another avenue for the sisters' instruction—talks by the sisters for the
sisters. The Community Diary reported:

> The introductory talk of the series on culture scheduled for the
> summer was given this morning by Sister Marie William
> [Hoerner] and proved to be exceptionally fine. Sister developed
> the point that the woman of culture is "something of a lady,
> something of a scholar, and something of a saint."[30]

A relatively young and diverse group of sisters had been
invited to prepare talks for the series. Sister Isabel Storch, a
fourth-year teacher at St. Agnes Academy in Indianapolis,
spoke on "Fundamentals of Convent Courtesy." Sister
Catherine Ursula Hayes, an eighth grade teacher about to
embark on her first appointment as local superior, gave a talk
on "Convent Hospitality." Sister Helen Rose Newland, another
eighth grade teacher, gave suggestions on "The Gentle Art of
Conversation," spicing practical advice on presenting oneself
positively in social situations with humorous anecdotes and
quotes.[31] Sister Clarice Asbury, English professor at the Col-

lege, not only spoke on "Recreational Reading for Religious" but also provided a list of suggested readings. Sister Maureen Therese Brennan, local superior at St. Patrick, Terre Haute, discussed "Religious Spirit and Professional Demands."

Other actions of the council during this time show a growing sympathy with the need to alleviate stress by ameliorating long-standing customs. As an example, Article 90 directed that "The Sisters shall rise, in all seasons, at five o'clock." In recognition of the restorative power of additional sleep, a 5:30 a.m. rising was authorized when school was not in session. During the summer, the senior sisters were allowed to say night prayers privately and retire early. Requests to attend public events such as lectures, the symphony, parish carnivals and prayer rallies received more frequent permissions, but permission was never given for movies or for events at night. Families were expected to visit at the convent, although allowances were occasionally made for very special occasions, such as a siblings' ordination, if it was possible to stay at a nearby convent.

Circumstances often dictated a sister's choice to either visit a dying parent or attend the funeral. Television was generally prohibited, but by 1952 viewing was allowed for very special events. So frequent were requests for clarification of what was considered appropriate and what was not that in September 1952 work began on a revision of the custom book. Rather than a strictly top-down approach, the minutes note that the council members solicited advice from those nearest to real-life situations: "It was decided that we will have a copy mimeographed for each local Superior and ask for their criticisms or suggestions at the end of a year."[32]

When Mother Marie Helene announced to the sisters in July 1953 that they would be allowed to use the college swimming pool, the diarist noted, "The privilege is the more appreciated in that it was unexpected."[33] In February 1954 a sewing pattern for a simple swimsuit was sent out so that "those who are interested may make their own." To this day, stories about the physical and psychological therapeutic effects of this decision continue to entertain those who benefited from it.

New Edition of the Constitutions

Revisions to the *Constitutions* in order to incorporate the experiments in provincial government had been a staple of the council's "old business" for years. Such revisions were no longer necessary, but other changes had been mandated by the 1938 General Chapter and, after twenty years of use, the 1929 editions in the hands of the sisters were quite worn. During her term as secretary, Mother Marie Helene had been responsible for organizing and preparing the material; now Sisters Loretta Therese and Eugenia carried forward this work. Almost at the same time as Archbishop Schulte recommended consultation with a canonist, the council received word of the death of their long-time friend, canonist Father George Sauvage, CSC, in March 1951. A canonical scholar, Father Adam Ellis, SJ, was invited to meet with the council in April 1952 to comment on a draft incorporating the necessary updates. Some of these revisions were carried forward from previous Chapters, and some of them derived from recent council deliberations.

As mandated by the 1938 Chapter, the section on the "the Sisters Coadjutrix" was omitted and a specific statement was added that exempted "the sisters employed in domestic work" from the obligation to recite the Office. The 1929 *Constitutions* clearly placed authority in the hands of the superior general, with the proviso that the authority was shared with the council "in a manner more or less extended, according to the nature and importance of the affairs."[34] To clarify the meaning of "importance," a sentence was added that a matter could be deemed so either by the superior general or by two councilors supported by a majority vote.

Clear recognition of the need to adapt legal stipulations to the realities of life was obvious in the requests for revision. Based on their concurrent experiences of dealing with difficult members, the council members asked that circumstances requiring dismissal be made more specific. Special exemptions regarding wearing of the habit were given for sisters "engaged with the sick" and for those on foreign missions "where this is required by climatic conditions." A relaxation of the horarium was accomplished by changing the hour of rising on Sunday and holydays of obligation from five to six o'clock.

Representation in the General Chapter was a key issue. As seen in Chapter 2, the sisters chosen as delegates exercised the highest authority in the Congregation. However, they only met every six years and then only for a matter of hours to elect the new council. Though one of the Chapter responsibilities was "to transact the more important affairs of the Congregation," the usual arrangements in fact precluded this from happening. Exhortations to secrecy served not only the positive effect of protecting ethical concerns about confidentiality and the reverence due to the acknowledged role of providential guidance, but also the negative effect of disengagement of the members.

Over the years, the number of delegates had varied. Based on a recommendation from the 1920 Chapter, Mother Mary Cleophas had petitioned to fix the number of elected delegates at twenty-four, with the council and general treasurer as ex-officio members making a total of thirty-two. In 1944, the local ordinary, Bishop Ritter, had given a dispensation permitting the four provincial superiors to serve as ex-officio delegates, making a total of thirty-six. Because this arrangement had never received approbation from the Sacred Congregation of Religious, Archbishop Schulte's ruling had peremptorily reduced the 1949 Chapter to thirty-two delegates. Three members of the council, Sisters Gertrude Clare, Francis Joseph and Rose Genevieve, had been delegates to the 1938 Chapter with its spirited discussion of representation, (see Chapter 7) and all the council members were keenly aware of the effect of widening horizons on the sisters' desire for greater participation. With these considerations as their mandate they drafted a revision of Article III, changing the number of sisters each finally professed member could vote for from two to three, only one of whom could be a superior. With three delegates now being elected from twelve geographic sections, the number of elected delegates would become thirty-six, and together with the superior general, her six assistants and the treasurer, the General Chapter would be made up of forty-four members.

The petition for these changes was sent to the Sacred Congregation in 1951. To prepare the sisters for the new edition of the *Constitutions*, during the 1953 summer session Father Ellis was engaged to present a series of ten lectures on canon law pertaining to religious women, utilizing the Sister of Providence *Constitutions* as the basis of his talks.[35] Meanwhile, since no official response had been received from the Sacred Congregation, printing of a new edition was delayed. Perhaps the adage "Rome moves slowly" was operative because the council turned its attention to other agenda items. However, when longtime friend Rev. Raymond Bosler went to Rome in October 1953, he was asked to inquire into the matter. He discovered that approval had been given in March 1952 but that "an unaccountable delay" had prevented proper notification.[36] His cable announcing this news was quickly followed by the official document of approval, and in March 1954 the printing of the new edition was authorized.[37]

As we examine all these internal changes, it is clear that Mother Marie Helene and her energetic council had trimmed the sails for a new course. As we shall see, the sheer size of the ship required a steady course, but the winds of change were blowing and would require "all hands on deck" and careful watch.

❧ Chapter 10
Winds of Change
1949-1953

Senior Teacher Sister Angela Marie Burke accompanies the Class of 1951 of Joliet's Providence High School as they process to the church to receive their diplomas.

Expansion of the Mission

New Parish Elementary Schools

Postwar prosperity and the baby boom led to an unprecedented growth of the Catholic Church in the United States. This brought many letters of requests for sisters to staff the schools which were often the first buildings of a new parish plant. However, by 1949, since the number of entrants had barely kept pace with the number of deaths, departures and those incapacitated by illness, most requests had to be refused. Always the most important priority was maintaining the excellence of existing commitments. Only four small schools had been accepted during Mother Mary Bernard's second term, bringing the total number of establishments to ninety-six. The council was hard put to decide among competing claims for priority, but two factors seemed decisive: historical connections and episcopal pressure.

Some of the earliest missions of the Sisters of Providence had been along the Ohio River across from Louisville, Kentucky, but since the closing of St. Michael in Madison, Indiana, in 1904, Holy Trinity in New Albany had been the lone outpost in the area. When Rev. Paul Gootee was named pastor of St. Paul in nearby Sellersburg, he told Mother Marie Helene that he had thirty-one good reasons to be first on the list for Sisters of Providence—his sibling, Sister Mary Justin, and thirty cousins in the Congregation. No doubt she smiled her agreement. The energetic pastor vacated the rectory and moved to a room in the combination church-school building in order to accommodate the three sisters who arrived in 1949. Constructed of Bedford stone, the newly built school was a forerunner of the many new buildings with modern design and equipment that would be built during the decade, enhancing the learning environment for teachers and students alike.

Another mission of great historical significance for the Congregation was St. Joseph Parish in Indianapolis.[1] The Congregation had purchased property in the city during Mother Anastasie's time but then sold a portion of it to the Little Sisters of the Poor, who in turn had sold it to the diocese. In 1877 two Sisters of Providence had come from St. John Academy to teach in a tiny school for the mission church. A history of the Archdiocese of Indianapolis relates further developments: "In 1879 St. Joseph's Church was constructed and dedicated in 1880. South of it on property they owned the Sisters of Providence built a combination school, convent, and hall."[2] In 1889 Bishop Chatard asked the Congregation to use a building on the property to open a school to house and train adolescent orphan girls. In 1893 the sisters opened St. Joseph Training School for this purpose, closing it in 1924 in favor of alternative opportunities for the girls.

Over the years the parish underwent many changes, with the diocese replacing the school and convent. By 1949 the neighborhood had declined to the point that Archbishop Schulte decided to close the parish, thus ending this seventy-two year mission of the Sisters of Providence. But no! Only months later he opened a new parish at another location and named it St. Joseph, and, of course, invited the Sisters of Providence to staff the school. In the style of the times, a combination church-school building was constructed with a section temporarily partitioned to serve as a convent. As in years gone by, three sisters were assigned to St. Joseph, Indianapolis, arriving at the West Morris Street address in August 1949. Even this would not be the final chapter because five years later freeway construction forced another move of the parish to its present location at 1375 South Mickley Street.

The city of Indianapolis was expanding on the east side as well, where just beyond the city limits at Holy Spirit Parish, Father Francis Early had also incorporated temporary convent quarters in the modern and well-equipped combination church-school building. He was well acquainted with the Sisters of Providence, both because he had been taught by them and also because his sister, Sister Jane de Chantel, was a member. Like other Indianapolis clergy, he had approached Mother Mary Bernard with his request during the priests' retreat and had been promised sisters. With the stipulation that lay teachers would also be part of the faculty, four sisters opened the school in September 1949.

The small nucleus of six schools in southern California had had no new additions for almost a decade despite major population growth during the war years. At St. Teresa of Avila Parish, Father P.J. Beary had been promised sisters, although when four sisters arrived in August 1949, construction was still underway, and they taught in the church basement until the school was completed. However, when Archbishop James McIntyre asked the Congregation to take St. Boniface in Anaheim, Mother Marie Helene had to refuse. In her letter explaining the reasons she noted that due to the large classes younger sisters were needed, and because they would also be expected to teach in the vacation schools, they would be unable to take classes toward their degrees and would be deprived of continuing formation opportunities. She added: "Marywood in itself has become a liability, and at present, is one of the Community's unsolved problems because of the small enrollment and the heavy taxation."[3]

A similar situation existed on the East Coast. There the three Boston-area convents dating to the turn of the century—

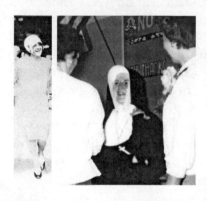

The Life:

Sister Cyril Tobin

"Somerville? We don't even have a mission in Somerville." The thought came quickly to Sister Cyril as she moved from her kneeling position to sit in one of the straight-backed chairs arrayed in the choir loft of the Church of the Immaculate Conception on August 15, 1950. Of this she was sure, since she had grown up in Chelsea and had returned to the Boston area to teach in the nearby town of Malden just two years before. At age thirty-eight her hearing was sharp so she was sure she hadn't been mistaken that Archbishop Schulte had indeed confirmed the rumor that a new mission was being opened at St. Polycarp.

While others around here might be stifling any emotive outbursts beneath their caps, Sister Cyril smiled broadly. Another adventure! Already in the twenty-one years since she had been in the Congregation she had taught primary grades in ten schools in addition to five large Chicago schools and one in Indianapolis, and she had lived in mixed grade/high school convents in Aurora and Fort Wayne. Unlike others in her band, she relished the thought of being in a new place.

Perhaps it was because she had been welcomed into the warm and loving home of Mr. and Mrs. John Tobin when her parents had been forced to give her up for adoption when she was small. She had always thought of them as her parents. Indeed, it was because of them that she had been taught by Sisters of Providence and gone on to enter the novitiate at age seventeen. Perhaps it was that same experience that had contributed to her success as a primary teacher. Highly adaptable, she had been among the first Sisters of Providence to teach kindergarten.

True, it would be hard to leave St. Ann's since being in the nation's capital had been truly special, but after all, she knew plenty of people in Boston.

St. Rose, Chelsea, Sacred Heart, Malden and St. Patrick, Stoneham—had seen only Lady Isle and Rochester in New Hampshire added to the northeast group in 1941 and 1942. The sisters at St. Rose, Chelsea, had been teaching catechism at St. Polycarp in nearby Somerville, and, as the parish grew, the pastor planned to open a school, so of course he put in a request for the Sisters of Providence. The opportunity to cement long-standing ties was welcome, and the council agreed to send four sisters, as noted in the sidebar on page 288. They arrived in 1950 and began teaching in the parish hall and rectory basement until the school was finished the following year. The fact that this was the only school the Congregation opened in 1950 underlines the pressure the council felt in making staffing decisions.

The sisters assigned to St. Mary School in Richmond, Indiana, on the eastern border near Ohio, had since its 1870 foundation been somewhat isolated. As at St. Rose, they were welcomed as teachers of catechism at nearby St. Anne in New Castle. When the parish of St. Anne was able to provide its own small school and a newly renovated house as a convent, three sisters were sent as faculty in 1951. That same year, across the state in Jasper, the Catholic population had outgrown the St. Joseph facilities to the point that a new parish was required. Unlike its publically funded predecessor, the school at Holy Family Parish was a true parochial school built with parish funds, and the people wanted the Sisters of Providence as its teachers. The four sisters who opened the expansive new facilities lived at St. Joseph for two years until a convent was built.

In juggling various requests, the council noted that although the Congregation staffed sixteen schools in Chicago, it had been ten years since any new schools had been accepted in the city. With the urban population moving into new neighborhoods, the pastor of St. Francis Borgia was constructing a large modern building to accommodate the 600 students he expected. As it was the only new establishment opened in 1952, it was possible to send eight sisters to begin operation with six grades.

The needs of the home diocese continued to take precedence, though not without considerable sifting.[4] Because the Sisters of Providence had staffed St. Catherine in Indianapolis since 1910, when the parish was divided to form St. James the

Greater in 1952, some of the sisters there were transferred to form the St. James faculty. The school opened for grades one through six in January 1953, with the sisters continuing residence at St. Catherine until a convent could be built. Across town in suburban Plainfield there was no question of splitting off parishes since there was no Catholic parish at all in semi-rural Hendricks County. The Catholic families who moved to the rapidly growing town became active in a Men's Club and a Women's Club, conducted a survey, obtained the archbishop's permission to purchase a desirable site and petitioned Mother Marie Helene for sisters. The parish took the name St. Susanna in honor of the daughter of the donor of the stone for the combination church-school building. A house on an adjacent lot was purchased for a temporary convent and three sisters opened the school to seventy-six children in six grades in September 1953.

Parish-based Secondary Schools

When two parishes long served by the Congregation wanted to expand to serve the high school population, it was difficult to refuse sisters. One request came from Father George Scecina, who reminded the council of his Indiana roots:

> Greetings from Texas and particularly, Robstown, the home of the only Providence Mission in the state. ... I hope I am not unreasonable in my request [for adding a ninth grade with successive grades added yearly]. Our building plans were started on the strength of additional Sisters. I have not advised His Excellency, Bishop Garriga [also from Indiana] of the improbability of getting the sisters. I never lose hope. ... In conversation with Archbishop Schulte in January he seemed to be pleased with the Providence mission in Robstown. I do hope he will make us an exception.[5]

Father's follow-up letter telling that the result of his prayerful meditation was that "Providence will provide the increase" was rewarded with the news that the necessary faculty would be sent.

Meanwhile the other "home mission" of Oklahoma City faced a similar situation of expansion. A ninth grade had been begun at Corpus Christi while the diocese completed the building of a coeducational Catholic high school to be staffed by sisters from six communities, a priest and lay teachers. In September 1950, two Sisters of Providence began teaching in the commercial department of the new Catholic High School (later named Bishop McGuinness High School) commuting daily from Corpus Christi convent.

Undoubtedly overshadowing all these decisions were ongoing arrangements in cooperation with the Archdiocese of Indianapolis for two major building projects intended to provide coeducational high schools for the New Albany and Terre Haute Deaneries, the regional grouping of parishes within the diocese.

Our Lady of Providence High School, Clarksville, Indiana

In January 1951, Archbishop Schulte came to Mother Marie Helene with his plans for a new coeducational high school in the New Albany Deanery. Having seen the financial report at the March 1949 General Chapter, he was cognizant of the financial workings of the Congregation and had noted that careful management had reduced its debt to a minimal level.[6] He proposed that the archdiocese would purchase the land, the deanery would supply start-up funds and the Congregation would build, own, operate and staff the school. The archbishop's confident assumption that the council would cooperate with his plan was difficult to resist. In addition the Sisters of Providence had a long history in the southeastern portion of the state, which gave the proposal a definite appeal, especially with the recent opening of St. Paul in nearby Sellersburg.[7]

The council's approval of the project set off a whirlwind of activity. The architect and contractor came to the motherhouse the following weekend to go over the preliminary plans. Archbishop Schulte had already purchased a twenty-three-acre site, eight acres of which were designated for a future parish, and he gave over the deed for the high school property. High School Visitor Sister Eugenia and Treasurer Sister Francis Raphael traveled to the site to meet with the architects, the Nolan brothers, who gave them a tour of Bellarmine College in Louisville to illustrate some of the features they planned to include. A February survey of the ten neighboring Catholic grade schools to predict the size of the prospective first class received an enthusiastic response. Ground was broken in March and Sister Eugenia visited deanery schools in April to take registration. Saint Mary-of-the-Woods Superintendent of Grounds Mr. Bernard Bisch and his son Joseph made frequent visits to check progress at the building site. At the June 12, 1951, dedication, Archbishop Schulte congratulated the Sisters of Providence for "providing this splendid opportunity for Catholic secondary education."[8]

During the summer months, Sister Marie Helen Leonard, appointed as the new institution's first principal, went to New Albany to set up the office and instructional program and equipment. Our Lady of Providence High School opened its doors to a freshman class of fifty-seven girls and eighty boys on September 12, 1951, with a faculty of three sisters and a priest. Construction continued during the year with a formal dedication on June 14, 1952. Ground was broken for a convent on May 11, 1953, and it was completed by the following year.

Schulte High School, Terre Haute, Indiana

As seen in Chapter 3, the two girls' academies in Terre Haute merged in 1937 to form Central Catholic High School for Girls, located at St. Patrick Parish. Over the years the enrollment had averaged around one hundred students, but by 1951 local demand was growing to provide Catholic education for boys as well. Monsignor Herbert Winterhalter, pastor of St. Patrick, brought the issue to the attention of Mother Marie Helene and she responded:

> I discussed your project with the Council Members; we would certainly want to help you out, and we feel that our long years in Terre Haute would almost require that we would take charge of the high school which the Reverend Clergy and people of Terre Haute have so long desired.[9]

Parishioners from across the city gathered in the St. Patrick school library on March 24, 1951, where Archbishop Schulte proposed a fund-raising campaign. Monsignor Winterhalter hired a firm to solicit and collect pledges that easily surpassed the goal of $325,000. The young and energetic Father Joseph Beecham was appointed to spearhead the project. As part of the planning phase he built connections with the sisters and parents by teaching religion at the girls' high school during the 1952-53 school year. The Congregation was invited to give recommendations based on their considerable experience, and these were incorporated into the planning schema, along with suggestions from deanery pastors. Local philanthropist Anton

Hulman donated an eleven-and-a-half acre site, and the Wilhelm Company began construction in November 1952. Included in the plans was a convent for the sisters who would be on the faculty. As the spring semester of the 1952-53 school year wound to a close, equipment from the science labs, library and offices was prepared for transfer to the new building. The final commencement of the girls' high school was held at St. Patrick Church on June 1, 1953.

During the summer Father Beecham met with Sister Francis Joseph Elbreg to clarify his responsibilities as priest-principal and supervisor vis-à-vis the superior of the convent, who would also serve as one of the school administrators. Paul Schulte High School opened in September 1953 with 256 students in grades nine and ten and a faculty of six sisters and five lay teachers, with five Terre Haute priests teaching religion classes. As planned, one grade was added each year, so by the 1956-1957 school year the enrollment had increased to 453 students. To accommodate the growth of the sister-faculty the convent garage was partitioned into alcoves, but two sisters still needed to commute.

Taiwan: Refounding the China Mission

Almost without notice or oversight from the council, the educational mission of the Sisters of Providence in the Far East experienced total reinvigoration in a way that can only be considered providential. As seen in Chapter 8, even after Japan's surrender, peace did not return to China. Even during the war, Nationalist leader Chiang Kai-Shek had done little to oust the Japanese occupation and had earned the scorn of American military advisers.[10] Despite a reluctant infusion of American aid, the tide of patriotic fervor was with the Communists. After they returned to Kaifeng to resume their mission, the eruption of the Chinese civil war had forced the Sisters of Providence and Providence Sister-Catechists to leave in April 1948 and take refuge in Shanghai. Five of the group, ill and exhausted from the ordeals of the war, returned to the United States, while the other six took teaching positions at the International School operated by the sisters of the Society of the Sacred Heart.

By October a Communist takeover of Shanghai was imminent. The missionaries did not want to return to the United States and felt a strong obligation to go where the Providence

Sister-Catechists could find work. This crisis occurred shortly after Mother Mary Bernard's death, and Sister Marie Gratia Luking needed to decide immediately on a course of action. Ever resourceful in the face of overwhelming odds, she managed the evacuation and relocation of the China mission to Taichung, Taiwan, in December 1948.

Lying about a hundred miles east of the China mainland, the island, known at that time in the United States by the name Formosa, had been inhabited by Chinese immigrants after they ousted the Portuguese in the seventeenth century, but it had been ruled by the Japanese since 1895. China, having been on the side of the Allies during the war, was now back in charge. But which China? With their backs to the sea, Chiang's Nationalist forces quickly established control of the island, taking advantage of the Japanese-built infrastructure as a strong base, thus ensuring at least temporary breathing space for the fragile Sister of Providence mission. Because Mandarin Chinese was spoken on the island and its written language was the same as the local dialect of Taiwanese, the sisters were able to communicate with relative ease. During the Japanese occupation they had learned to negotiate the unique Chinese-Japanese economic structure and now, at a comfortable distance from "the Reds," and with the support of former students who had resettled there, the refugees were able to establish a base of their own.

Sister St. Francis Schultz provides us with a glimpse of their immediate impressions of their new surroundings:

> The bus fare for forty of the most beautiful miles I have ever traveled [Taipei to Taichung] was 3,000 TWC—something like 7 ½ cents, U.S. It was about the largest money's worth we ever got. ... The food is from a land flowing in milk and honey— bananas, oranges, pineapples—rice is excellent as are also the sweet potatoes. Ducks, geese, turkeys roam about everywhere. Poor Formosa! Japan's 'Treasure Island'—which that country regarded as her richest colony, how she has become the prey of her one-time mother country.[11]

By February 1949, just two months after their arrival, the sisters were operating a boarding school, the sister-catechists had set up an eye clinic, and all of the refugee sisters were learning to speak Taiwanese. When a cable arrived on March 26, 1949, announcing the election of Mother Marie Helene, each missionary wrote to congratulate her. "It was grand to do this," Sister St. Francis wrote. "It rather took the place of kneeling to kiss Mother's hand." [12]

Sister Marie Gratia may have desired to create the impression that all was well, but financial support was minimal, and Mother Marie Helene made it clear that it was impossible to send more sisters. Although the additions to the combination school-convent building and an influx of refugee priests who provided regular Mass in the chapel had made conditions more conducive to convent life, the Taiwan 1949-1950 diary notes the stress of continued conflict and unsettled conditions.

August 17—The U.S. Consul thinks Taiwan will be safe for about six months.

August 22—Rumor today gives Taiwan one month

January 14, 1950–All foreigners are leaving Taipei. We discussed if we should go.

January 19–Few places are open to the Chinese. We have tried Australia, Hawaii, Guam, and the Philippines.

May 4—There are rumors and rumors. We are trying to get visas and passports for [Chinese nationals] Sisters Agnes Joan and Bernadette.

May 17—The newspaper announcement that the Nationalist forces have withdrawn from the Chusan archipelago forced us to announce that we will close school on the 23rd.

May 21—We were able to get the seal on our passports certifying that we are not communists. [Attempts to depart via Hong Kong fail.]

June 21—Much is in the air now. There is talk of MacArthur including this island in his field because of its having been under former Japanese occupation.

June 28—War broke out in Korea on Sunday, an attack on the North. Our position?

June 29—Mr. Coleman says the 7th Division of the U.S. Fleet has arrived to patrol the straits of Formosa; so we should be able to stay. [13]

Stay they did. On the other side of the Pacific another diarist recorded events from the United States perspective:

With everything so peaceful and quiet at our Woodland home, it seems hard to realize that warfare has again started. The

Korean Incident may prove to be insignificant but the President's action would seem to indicate the contrary. The U.S. has reversed its policy on Formosa which may change the plans of our Missionaries there.[14]

The propitious political situation made it possible to send the two Chinese Sisters of Providence, Sisters Agnes Joan Li and Bernadetta Ma, to Saint Mary-of-the-Woods in July 1950. Only three Sisters of Providence remained in the Congregation's lone foreign mission amidst tender beginnings in its new location. A letter from Mother Marie Helene, who had been on the Holy Year pilgrimage to Rome during the escalation of the political crisis, brought comforting assurance to the three that, despite the setbacks, the Taiwan mission was still very much in the forefront of Congregation concerns.

Sister Mary Liguori Hartigan, correspondent to *The Bugle Call*, kept the students in Sister of Providence schools throughout the country apprised of the use of their contributions for the thriving Taichung high school and shared the good news of baptisms through the kindergarten that the Providence Sister-Catechists had recently opened. Frequent visits from the Maryknoll priest, Father William Kupfer, who was appointed bishop of Taichung in March 1951, were accompanied by financial support from the diocese[15] which made it possible to purchase land for expansion. By 1952, sufficient funds were available to purchase an additional house to serve as a dormitory for the high school students. In November they joyfully welcomed the return of their former companion, Sister Carmel Baker, together with Sisters Agnes Joan and Bernadette.

At last the foundation had proved itself sufficiently to receive Congregation funding toward the construction of a brick school building. Sister St. Francis was granted a

Sisters Carmel Baker, Agnes Joan Li, Bernadette Ma and Mother Marie Helene.

five-month leave to travel to the United States, and when she returned in September 1953 she was accompanied by yet another companion from China days, Sister Francis de Sales Russell. For Sister Marie Gratia, who had for so long wished to accept the talented young women who wished to become Sisters of Providence rather than Providence Sister-Catechists, the December 27, 1953, entrance into the postulancy at Saint Mary-of-the-Woods of Madeline Fu,[16] a former student from Ching I in Kaifeng who had reunited with the Sisters of Providence in their refounded mission in Taiwan, was the greatest cause for rejoicing.

Home Improvements

Campus Upgrades

Visitors to Saint Mary-of-the-Woods campus who were impressed with its beauty had little awareness of how its infrastructure constantly clamored for attention. Fortunately the sisters could rely on Mr. Bernard Bisch, who served as superintendent of grounds from 1939 to 1958, for reliable direct supervision of work on projects.[17]

When Sister Robert took up her econome duties as the liaison with the council and treasurer's office, no project proved too big to tackle. Her office was strategically located behind the kitchen by the loading dock with easy access to the nearby support buildings—garage, powerhouse, carpenter shop, laundry, greenhouse and workmen's dining room. The enterprise was enormous in its scope, as these informal notes from the times attest.

> Of the 1350 acre site, 500 acres are under cultivation with corn, wheat, rye, and oats rotated regularly. Fifty acres are covered with apple, peach, pear and cherry orchards, in the midst of which you will find raspberries, strawberries, and grape arbors. Bee hives are located there to pollinate the flowers. The stable houses 15 riding horses and three draft teams. At the dairy farm 55 cows in the herd of 110 cattle provide an average of 180 gallons of milk a day which is pasteurized on site. Approximately 1500 laying hens at the poultry farm provide eggs for the College and motherhouse kitchens. The bakery provides bread and rolls while the cannery supplies fruit and vegetables during the winter months. Six hundred acres are woodland, with almost any tree native to Indiana to be found. Sixty acres comprise the campus with seventeen buildings.[18]

Novices and postulants of the time can also attest to providing seasonal unskilled labor for berry-picking and canning the produce grown on the farm. In the midst of this active farm operation, the relative prosperity of the fifties made possible the planning and execution of several major projects.

Construction of a water plant to process water from the abundant lake systems included a 75,000 gallon steel water tower. When it opened in January 1951 to provide hot water and function as the boiler/heating system, it represented a great savings and supplied better quality water. In August a new switchboard was installed in the Church. On January 13, 1952, the niche over the central west door of the Church, empty since the statue had been moved to the pillar between the church and Foley Hall, received a new occupant—a heroic statue of the Blessed Virgin Mary carved from Vermont granite by Italian artist, Alfonso De Giudice. Hardly had this been accomplished when Sister Robert met with the council to discuss plans for improvements in the carpenter shop, bakery and laundry. She also presented plans for new lavatory facilities to be installed in the two upper floors of the hall connecting Foley Hall with Providence (known as St. Rita and St. Agatha Halls) and a new incinerator for Foley itself. Repairs to the greenhouse were considered too expensive and it was decided to dismantle it and instead build a small one near the gardens.

In cooperation with the program sponsored by the National Catholic Welfare Conference to provide placement for those who escaped the harsh treatment of the Communist regimes in Eastern Europe, in 1951 four of these so-called "D.P.s" (displaced persons) were employed as workmen on the campus. With new government regulations in force, an eight-hour day was adopted to replace the workmen's previous nine-hour shift, with a comparable increase in their wages. Fewer young women were entering the Congregation with a desire to express their dedication through domestic service, making it necessary to employ kitchen workers. To provide on-site housing for these women and girls, construction began in 1954 on an eight-bedroom single-story residence to be named Marian Cottage.

Benefactors were not lacking to assist with a number of these projects. In 1952 the Congregation was the beneficiary of a major gift provided by generous friend Mr. Frank Folsom.[19] As president of RCA, he had access to the latest technology, and he was able to plan and install a speaker system in the chapel and crypt and throughout the infirmary so that each patient could hear at will any service in the church. The community room was also linked with the system so as to permit the sick to hear programs, Retreat Sunday conferences and special announcements.[20]

The College alumnae were also generous in providing for campus improvements. After reconditioning the tennis courts at Guerin in 1952, the following year they commissioned landscaping and flooring at Le Fer Hall and a radio control room at the Conservatory, and they solicited pledges for the new organ in the Church. In 1953 the Board met with Mother Marie Helene to select an Italian artist and to fund the construction of the Fatima statuary group across from Le Fer Hall as a Marian Year offering.

The consistent upkeep and beautification of the campus made it an attractive destination for hosting events for other groups. The clergy of the archdiocese continued to find Saint Mary-of-the-Woods a hospitable location for their annual retreat during the weeks between the College commencement and Homecoming. In June 1952, the chronicler noted that when the priests took part in the Corpus Christi procession, "the rich voices of the priests blended with the lighter ones of the Novices and Postulants in the singing and chanting of the beautiful liturgical hymns to the Blessed Sacrament."[21] In August 1953, the National Council of Catholic Women held their annual meeting at Le Fer Hall.[22] During the 1954 Marian Year, parishioners from Terre Haute made Saint Mary's the destination for their pilgrimage.

Re-interment of Mother Mary Cleophas

Mother Marie Helene's Holy Year pilgrimage with its renewal of ties to Ruillé and her visit with the postulator along with the recent publication of the early history of the Congregation had reinvigorated interest in community history. Very much alive in the minds and hearts of many of the sisters was the memory of Mother Mary Cleophas Foley. This led the council to decide that it would be appropriate to re-inter her remains in the crypt vault beside those of the saintly foundresses, Mother Theodore Guerin, Sister St. Francis Le Fer and Sister Mary Joseph Le Fer. The remains of Mother Mary Cleophas' blood sister, Sister Aloysia Foley, had already been reinterred in the vault in 1911. Mother Marie Helene wrote to the sisters to tell of the plan:

> Because for so many years our dear Mother Mary Cleophas was the guiding force and ruling inspiration of Saint Mary-of-the-Woods, this honor was suggested for her. The spiritual and material growth of the Community which took place under her leadership has led to her being looked upon as a second foundress, carrying on and enlarging the work begun by our venerated Mother Theodore. It seemed fitting, therefore, that these two Mothers be united in this way.[23]

Ecclesiastical permission was obtained, and on April 4, 1951, the disinterment took place with the bones being placed in a small copper coffin. During a formal funeral rite in the crypt the next day the coffin was placed in a cedar box and then placed in the vault below Mother Theodore.

Liturgical Arts and Celebrations

By 1952 it became clear that the old Kilgen organ in the Church of the Immaculate Conception was wearing out. Sisters Mary Lourdes Mackey and Cecilia Clare Bocard, music professors at the College, were designated to search for a suitable instrument. They made trips to different places to see and hear organs of varying makes in order to get ideas of the type, size and specifications suitable for the church. A questionnaire sent to owners of the Canadian Cassavant Company received a very positive response, so it was decided to purchase a three-manual, thirty-stop organ. Though much of the $28,400 cost was covered by donations, fireproofing of the tower and strengthening of the spiral stairway to the organ loft added to the expense. Installation took several weeks since the intricate combination of keyboard, pedalboard and pipes required "voicing" to give the organ a unique sound within the acoustics of the church. The new organ was blessed on December 8, 1953, with a program inaugurating the celebration of the Marian Year that included a composition by Sister Cecilia Clare, appropriately titled "Te Deum Laudamus." Father Edwin Sahm's lecture on the arts that day, together with two dedicatory recitals by visiting artist Mr. Raymond Keldermans in March and July of 1954, provided opportunity to reaffirm the Congregation's long-standing commitment to liturgical arts.

The celebration of liturgy, augmented with popular devotions, was an integral element in the spirituality of the Sisters of Providence. Shrines were regularly a destination for processions, such as the annual summer processions to the Sacred Heart Shrine and St. Anne Chapel. World-wide events such as the Holy Year of 1950 and the Marian Year of 1954 became occasions for special events at the motherhouse, as we see from a contemporary account.

> A candlelight procession to the Grotto followed Benediction at 7:45 p.m. Dusk had fallen and the long line of lights was beautiful to see. The choir sang the Litany en route across the bridge and through the path in Providence Park. The junior Sisters grouped about the grotto and the senior Sisters and Superiors on the road immediately opposite the grotto. [Chaplain] Father Goossens gave out the Rosary which all answered. On the return, down the road to the Inn and up the avenue to Foley, and across to the Church, organ music was broadcast through amplifiers, and the Lourdes' hymn—Immaculate Mother—was sung by the Sisters. When the group came to the Church, the Sisters came up in a massed body to the west door of the Church and sang the Plain Chant CREDO. At its conclusion, candles were extinguished and the Sisters quietly dispersed after a brief private visit to the Blessed Sacrament since night prayers had been said at 7:30. The effect of the procession was touching and indescribably beautiful. It seemed like a tremendous profession of faith.[24]

Major changes in Catholic liturgy announced for 1953 would have an impact on convent schedules. The strict regulation of complete fast from midnight before receiving communion the next day was mitigated to allow drinking of water, and evening Masses were now allowed. The biggest change was felt during Holy Week, with the restoration of the Easter Vigil service on Holy Saturday morning. Like many Catholics, the sisters had formed a strong emotional attachment to Good Friday's *Tre Ore*, a three-hour service with unique chants and readings, and many found it difficult to relinquish this cherished time of meditation. The sisters on some of the missions who had become accustomed to having the Holy Week services in their chapel were disturbed to discover that they would now be expected to participate with the parish congregation. The Marywood, Anaheim, diarist noted their reaction when the pastor of nearby St. Boniface Church told them of the new arrangement.

> 'In spite of your immemorial custom'— he would send a priest for Mass on Holy Thursday and that would be all. We had a Low Mass. Father had said it was not rubrical for us to have the services. We have *always* had the services. On Holy Saturday no one went to the church as some were recovering from colds and others did not care to go, thinking if we once started it we would be expected to continue.[25]

Winds of Change

National Conference at Notre Dame

Amid all the activities of the 1950 Holy Year was an event that despite its low-key internal nature would soon have a ripple effect not only on the Sisters of Providence but on the sisterhoods of the entire world. Pope Pius XII convoked a gathering of religious men and women in Rome to discuss renewal of spirit and adaptation to the needs of the times. He had appointed a Spanish Claretian, Bishop Arcadio Larraona, as secretary of the Sacred Congregation for Religious, a man whose experience as canonist, professor and superior within his own congregation lent itself to moving from lofty rhetoric into concrete goals and criteria. The new secretary's first step was to organize another conference the following year focused on the formation of young sisters in congregations devoted to the educational apostolate. Through the apostolic delegate, superiors were invited to contribute suggestions based on their experience.[26]

The idea was not new. Superiors in the United States would have had numerous suggestions to send based on years of efforts to provide a strong grounding in the spirit of religious life at the same time as making sure their newer members would be qualified to meet state accrediting standards. A decade earlier, as part of her doctoral dissertation, later published as *The Education of Sisters*, Sister Bertrande Meyers, SC, had conducted an extensive survey of sixty congregations from all geographic regions, visiting and interviewing superiors at motherhouses and colleges.[27] Recognizing that infrequent contact and lack of cross-fertilization of ideas between religious congregations prevented joint planning, she nonetheless identified a universal desire for programs in which "adequate synthesis of the religious and social, the cultural and the professional ideals of the Community" could be realized.[28]

She bemoaned the temporary expedients of summer school and Saturday classes which stretched over many years. Feeling this had led to the goal of credits rather than "genuine learning"[29] or "the real pleasure and stimulus of educational activity,"[30] she pleaded for a truly Catholic education for those who would themselves later offer it to others. Her rigorous research demonstrated that the best results were achieved when the postulancy and novitiate were strictly devoted to religious formation, and two or three additional years of college and professional study in a supportive formation atmosphere were completed before the young sister was sent to teach. Several congregations had successfully incorporated lay teachers into their faculty to allow for deferring the first assignments of the young sisters. As she conducted her on-site interviews she discovered that "one Community was quite uninformed as to what policy another pursued."[31] A major difficulty for many congregations was the location of the motherhouse at a distance from a Catholic college. For all, the constant demand for more teachers created great pressure for maintaining the status quo.

With the goals of the Vatican and those of the United States sisterhoods so clearly aligned, Secretary Larraona's announcement that the First National Congress of the Religious of the United States would be held at Notre Dame in August 1952 was a welcome next step. Even more welcome was the news that the sisters themselves would constitute the planning committee for the first-ever event. Most welcome news of all to the Sisters of Providence was the invitation for Mother Marie Helene to be a member of the planning committee. She and Sister Eugenia Logan traveled to Notre Dame in May 1952 to participate in the planning, which included sorting through the suggestions sent from many congregations and matching these with the topics suggested by the Sacred Congregation. They decided on a threefold process whereby a speaker would present a paper, another speaker would respond and the floor would be opened to discussion.[32] Speakers were asked to organize their ideas around three themes: the founding spirit, adaptation to the times and unity with the universal church.

*Planning committee members, left to right: Mother M. Joan of Arc Cronin,
OSU, Mother Mary Killian Corbett, CSC, Sister M. Madeleva Wolff, CSC,
(Publicity), Mother Mary Gerald Barry, OP, (Chair), Mother M. Catherine
Sullivan, DC, Mother Marie Helene Franey, SP, Mother M. Rose Elizabeth,
CSC.*

Although the National Catholic Education Association had
provided opportunity for discussion of educational issues, this
was the first time superiors had been asked to share their
thoughts and experiences about religious life itself. As they
talked, they realized that despite superficial differences they
had much in common. Three issues emerged as major concerns: the vows, formation and cooperation with the hierarchy in exercising the mission of education.

Mother Marie Helene was one of eight sisters and five priests
invited to present one of the papers, and in July she took the
occasion of the usual summer instructions as a dress rehearsal
of sorts to share with her own sisters her reflections on "The
Spiritual Possibilities of Teaching as a Vocation."[33] Stressing
"the art of teaching," she used the example of foundress Mother
Theodore Guerin to stress that "a teacher educates more
through what she is than what she says,"[34] and that each
sister's daily efforts to become such an inspirational person
was her "vocation within a vocation."[35] She quoted the Rule's
admonition that "they shall try to gain the hearts of their pupils,"[36] but in typical fashion she added a dose of reality: "We
cannot afford to take all the so-called hard things from our

children."[37] Sounding a note which would have crescendoing echoes in the conference, she put the sisters on notice about changes to come by declaring publicly: "The preparation of our sisters in the secular and religious fields of instruction is now the great preoccupation of major superiors of communities."[38]

Nine Sisters of Providence accompanied Mother Marie Helene to join the more than 600 priests and 1,300 sisters and brothers who attended the Congress at Notre Dame on August 9-13 in 1952. In addition to Sisters Francis Joseph and Eugenia from the Education Office, Mistress of Novices Sister Marie Ambrose McKenna and six superiors of Congregation high schools had the opportunity to mingle with their peers, participate in the religious women's sections of conferences, and attend daily Mass and Benediction. Inevitably the ideas planted in the seed bed of the Congress would take root in the consciousness of these relatively young superiors. They themselves would be called upon to play leading roles in the near future, when such ideas would take on increased urgency. [39] To understand the growing shift in consciousness among women religious we will take the time to examine the content of the papers presented at the Congress.

Central to religious life are the three vows of poverty, chastity and obedience. After talks by two priests on theological and canonical aspects of the vows, the sisters themselves took the floor to discuss practical applications. Mother Mary Josita Baschnagel, BVM, didn't hesitate to talk about the "Special Problems of Religious Obedience in Modern Times," noting that young women were being educated to raise questions about what they were told to do and simply didn't understand the concept of "blind obedience."[40] Regarding the vow of poverty, a panel of four superiors spoke about how the spirit of their founders (Saints Benedict, Francis, Dominic and Vincent de Paul) would motivate them to address issues of "Modern Convenience and Comfort in their Relation to the Religious Spirit." One speaker pointed out that "Comforts and conveniences are creatures of God, and the recommendations of St. Ignatius on indifference, developed in the *Spiritual Exercises*, can safely be followed in their use."[41]

Formation was very much on the minds of the religious leaders. Mother Joan of Arc, OSU, described how the New

York Ursulines had developed "Ways and Means of Prolonging the Formation Initiated in the Novitiate" by establishing a house of studies so that their young religious were able to complete their degree prior to their first teaching assignment. Sister Madeleva Wolff, CSC, gave a spirited talk on the importance of including the study of theology in formation programs. Sister Madeleva was well known to the assembly not only as a member of the organizing committee and president of adjacent St. Mary's College, but also as an outspoken advocate in the NCEA's College Committee. The paper she had presented at the April 1949 NCEA convention, "The Education of Sister Lucy," was already gaining strong support for the type of program Mother Joan of Arc described.[42]

Detroit Superintendent of Schools Rev. Carroll Deady lauded "The Role of the Religious Teacher in America," pointing to current demands for expansion as a tribute to their success. He likely drew applause when he warned that expecting an individual sister to teach larger and larger classes would "lay the perfect foundation for a nervous breakdown for herself."[43] He was followed on the platform by Sister Mary Patrick Riley, IHM, whose Monroe, Michigan, motherhouse was in the Detroit Archdiocese and whose words would draw no applause from him. Noting that all the superiors had to refuse taking additional schools due to insufficient numbers, she issued a call to adopt the "Share the Sisters" plan proposed by an NCEA committee. "Specifically, it is a plea to share the sisters on a national scale; more specifically, it is a plan to extend Catholic education by replacing at least twenty per cent of the teaching sisters with lay teachers."[44]

She went on to present the role of the lay teacher as a form of Catholic Action and also provided a detailed addenda calling for paying them a living wage. She then suggested available sources of persons who were already qualified to step into this role.[45]

With its hard-hitting facts based on returns from a national survey, this speech must have come as a shock to the assembly made up of superiors used to dealing one on one with the hierarchy. For days they had heard wonderful and appealing ideas regarding how to strengthen their formation programs. Were such idealistic goals merely pie in the sky? As they looked around, the thought of presenting a united front with an actual plan to relieve the pressure of staffing made the goal not only desirable but actually possible. Walking shoulder to shoulder as the candlelight procession wound its way to the Grotto for the solemn closing ceremony, they could not but share a sense of solidarity and inspiration. As we shall see, the ideas shared not only in the formal conferences but also in informal conversation with other religious women would give strong impetus to their planning in the next few years.

As we leave with a mental image of the storied campus crowded with so many talented women in so very many varieties of traditional attire, it is interesting to note that a topic of great interest was not addressed in the formal speeches—the habit. Because the planning committee had sounded the theme of adapting to modern conditions, it was not surprising that they received numerous questions on this topic. The *Proceedings* contain a brief note of how the situation was handled:

> Not a few [of the suggestions] concerned the advisability of modifying some of the religious habits which, having originated centuries ago, are not suited to present-day conditions of living nor to the work expected of religious in our day. Announcement was made at the Congress that the Sacred Congregation would give sympathetic attention to any request on the part of communities which feel that such modification would be desirable.[46]

This muted invitation for each congregation to address such a prickly issue according to its own timeline did not go unnoticed, as we shall see.

Committees of Religious Women

The momentum for reform was building. Even as the Congress met, Secretary Larraona had sent out a letter announcing the creation of an international Central Consultative Commission with a section for religious women made up of the twenty congregations who had residences in Rome. Following this Commission's recommendation, all superiors, not only those with Roman headquarters, were invited to attend a meeting in September 1952 to discuss the establishment of a university level school for sisters in Rome. This invitation was seconded by a letter from Apostolic Delegate Cicognani, but due to the lateness of the notice, Mother Marie Helene asked

Mother Mary Gerald Barry, OP, to represent the Sisters of Providence at the Rome meeting.

The following April Mother Marie Helene received word that the Congress's organizing committee was to be kept in existence as a permanent national committee. In August 1953, she was notified that she had been appointed a member of the Commission of Forty Superiors General that had been recently established to represent the superiors general of the world. A major objective of this Commission was the establishment of the projected house of studies in Rome, with each congregation asked to send a donation. In mid-August Mother Marie Helene flew to Washington, D.C., to attend a meeting with Mother Gerald and Mother Bernardine, RSM, the two other U.S. members of the Commission. Sadly, due to Mother Marie Helene's untimely death the following November, the involvement of her lively mind and energetic spirit were not part of the designs of Providence for this Commission. We will follow the Commission's plans and Mother Gertrude Clare's involvement in Chapter 11.

Death of Mother Marie Helene

Mother Marie Helene had been a fifty-year-old in the prime of life when she was elected. She had suffered a bout of pneumonia in December 1951 and recovered, but the following December she was so ill that nurse Sister Mary Bernardo accompanied her to St. Mary's Hospital in Rochester, Minnesota. The diagnosis of a mild malignancy in the large intestine was treated with surgery on January 6, 1953. Despite contracting the flu during the recuperation period, she had regained her health and resumed her duties with her usual energy. While she was in Washington, D.C., for the August 1953 meeting of superiors general, a physical checkup diagnosed a heart condition, but after a period of rest she resumed normal duties. Following her attendance at the November 15, 1953, centenary celebration of Assumption Parish in Evansville, despite a heavy cold, she went on to a visitation in New Albany. There she was overcome with abdominal pain and advised to either enter the hospital or return by ambulance to Saint Mary-of-the-Woods. She chose the latter, and after an examination indicated possible heart damage, was advised to take absolute rest for six weeks.

On November 23, when head nurse Sister Dorothy Eileen Howard checked Mother Marie Helene's room, she found her slumped over from a heart attack. After alerting the other nurses she went immediately to Tile Hall to notify Sister Gertrude Clare who was giving a retreat conference to the aspirants. By the time they reached the infirmary and Chaplain Emile Goossens arrived to anoint the fifty-five-year-old Mother, she breathed her last. The diarist recorded that as the word went out, "everywhere the response was the same— deep grief for the loss of the dearly loved Mother who had gone so quickly from our midst."[47] Writing from the infirmary to a friend regarding her death, Sister Mary Borromeo Brown expressed the feelings of many:

> What a shock we have had. ... Our dear Mother Marie Helene is gone and gone so soon it seems. Her administration has left a definite mark on the community, a reflection of her own upright soul with its unwavering trend to God. We have reason to thank God for having given her to us. She certainly did her duty to the last ounce of her strength.[48]

As was the custom, when the bell tolled the news, Father Goossens went to the church to lead the Stations of the Cross. Later he commented, "Towards the end, we began to realize that the cross that she had carried and that she had now put down at the command of her Divine Master was the sign of her victory."[49] As it was Thanksgiving week, the funeral was delayed until Friday, and her body lay in state in the church with groups of sisters keeping watch. Archbishop Ritter came from St. Louis to assist Archbishop Schulte and Mother's two brothers, Rev. John Franey and Rt. Rev. Louis J. Franey, in celebrating the Requiem Mass sung a capella by the novices' choir. Among the mourners was her mother, Margaret, flanked by her own brother and two sisters. Because of the prominence Mother Marie Helene had attained through her recent appointments and involvement in renewal work, condolences poured in from across the country.

The January 1954 memorial issue of the College magazine, *The Aurora,* was filled with tributes. Former student Mary Louise Keefe Jordan recalled, "Her whole attitude toward life was sane and wholesome—she understood our weaknesses and sympathized with us, yet never did she encourage us in them."[50] Dean Sister Marie Perpetua lauded Mother's rich background as student, faculty member and member of the board of directors which "enabled her to view the College as a whole [with] a calm, undisturbed intelligence that looks reality squarely in the face."[51]

Twice in the short space of five years the Congregation had lost its superior general to death. Once again the sisters were called to "lean with all their weight on Providence," as Mother Theodore had enjoined. Once again it seemed that the designs of Providence would be announced in the demands of the times. The winds of change continued to blow. The watch must be kept and the sails trimmed.

❧ Chapter 11 Adapting to Changing Times 1954-1960

Mother Gertrude Clare places items in the cornerstone of the novitiate building during the blessing ceremony on July 25, 1959.

Interim Governance

Sister Gertrude Clare's long tenure on the council provided a sure anchor when the grief-stricken members assembled on November 29, 1953, for the first time after Mother Marie Helene's funeral. Several council members had been in Chicago when they learned of her death, while others had spent hours calling the various houses to break the news as gently as possible. The Franey family had been frequent visitors to Saint Mary-of-thhe-Woods, and the need to comfort the young Mother's elderly mother made the arrangements especially poignant, even more so because it was a Thanksgiving weekend. Providentially, a letter from the Vatican announcing the celebration of 1954 as a Marian Year provided a focus for honoring her memory by carrying forward several projects she had set in motion, one at the national level and three others closer to home.

Two bishops closely associated with the Congregation were active as chairs of the committee for building the National Shrine of the Immaculate Conception in Washington, D.C. When Bishop Noll of Fort Wayne suffered a stroke in 1954, Archbishop Ritter, now in St. Louis, succeeded him as chair and led the drive to complete the shrine during the Marian Year.[1] To meet the request for funds being solicited for the shrine, the council decided to ask the sisters to send to the motherhouse any donations received at Christmas for this purpose. On the campus itself, a proposal by the College Alumnae Association to erect a shrine to Our Lady of Fatima across from Le Fer Hall in honor of Mother Marie Helene was well on its way to completion.[2] Its May 30, 1954, dedication would serve as a local focus of celebration for the Marian Year. When the just-completed residence for the women and girls working in the kitchen was dedicated on June 5, 1954, it was given the name Marian Cottage.

The need for new books for use in praying the Little Office of the Blessed Virgin Mary also coincided with the Marian Year. The daily recitation of Lauds, Vespers and Compline of the Little Office of the Blessed Virgin Mary, a heritage from the French foundation, formed a portion of the daily prayer of the community. In 1937 a small booklet with commentaries on the psalms and antiphons was composed and published internally to be kept in the prie-dieux as an aid to devotional recitation.[3] By 1954 the need for replacing the office books had become a priority due to the sad state of the books available for use. However, the decision was complicated by the fact that the translation of the psalms in the new edition from Benziger Press was quite different than the one the community had used since its approval by Bishop Chatard in 1879. Because the Little Office enabled the community to participate in the liturgical prayer of the church, there was a question as to whether the translation itself required official approval. Assured by inquiries that the traditional version was still approved, the council decided to simply order a reprint in order to retain the familiar cadences of communal recitation. To commemorate the timing, the reprinted edition, with parallel Latin-English columns, was approved by Archbishop Schulte with the phrasing, "Given at Indianapolis in this Marian Year, January 11, 1954."[4]

Preparations for a General Chapter in June 1954 were already underway in accordance with the normal six-year schedule called for in the *Constitutions*. After consultation with the archbishop, to comply with the requirement for the replacement of a Superior General within six months of her death, the date was simply advanced to May 5, 1954. The council's previous discussions of the changes in the *Constitutions* relative to expanding the number of delegates from twelve superiors and twelve private sisters to twelve superiors and twenty-four private sisters had set the stage for a smooth preparation. In January Sister Gertrude Clare sent a letter to the sisters explaining the changes, the council's rationale, and the approbation from the Sacred Congregation.[5] Since the printing of the revised *Constitutions* was already underway, small inserts of the sections explaining the Chapter membership were sent to each sister.

In addition to the usual topics which routinely made up the council agenda, some items were cause for rejoicing, such as reports from Taiwan indicating that the refounding of the China mission was flourishing and funds contributed through the schools were being put to good use. Ongoing concern regarding train service was exacerbated with the visit of the New York Central supervisor, who raised hopes that the station building might not need to be dismantled and advised sending a written request to this effect. By February, Sister Francis Joseph Elbreg's broken arm and Sister Loretta Therese

O'Leary's emergency appendectomy caused a certain amount of stress. However, discussion of the pattern for the recently authorized bathing suits surely brought a light moment, while reports from the council members who attended the dedication of the new convent in Clarksville augured well for the future.

The 1954 Chapter

The council members' involvement in national committees had an effect on their preparations for the upcoming General Chapter. Sister Catherine Celine Brocksmith had attended the second Notre Dame conference for major superiors in August 1953, while Sisters Francis Raphael Donlon and Robert Kiley had participated in a conference for treasurers that summer. Articles explaining ways in which religious congregations could implement the suggestions emerging from such exchanges were appearing on a regular basis. The impact of these ideas on the council's deliberations is evident in the January 30, 1954, circular letter convoking the Chapter. In addition to the announcement of the date and manner of voting for delegates, Sister Gertrude Clare included two quotes from recent articles in the *Review for Religious* by canonist Rev. Joseph F. Gallen, SJ. The first quote noted that after prayer, sisters would be well advised to seek information about the qualifications of potential delegates. The second quote cautioned against using such information to tell the delegates whom to vote for, but rather to have confidence in the delegates themselves.[6]

Given the directions for electing the delegates that were enclosed with the letter, one wonders about the point of the recommendation to seek information prior to voting. The first time those eligible to vote had access to the names of the sisters for whom they might cast a ballot would be when they gathered in silence on February 5, 1954, and opened their envelopes. All sisters professed with perpetual vows for at least five years were eligible to be elected, but this large pool had been divided into twelve sections of at least sixty sisters. A sister living in the Indianapolis or Chicago Archdiocese could only vote for the sisters in her section, and she might look in vain for the person she favored as a delegate since that sister might be listed in another section. Two other factors were at play. The large number of sisters at Saint Mary-of-the-Woods, many of whom were well known throughout the Congregation, were dispersed among three sections. In addition, "superior" referred to the sister appointed to head a convent, whereas sisters appointed to responsible offices such as principal or dean were considered "private" sisters.

In former elections the second caution about refraining from telling delegates to vote for certain sisters would have been unnecessary since no official list of delegates had ever been published to the community. At last this long-sought change in procedure was implemented. At the end of March, Sister Gertrude Clare sent a letter to the houses which included a list of the names of the delegates elected in each section. Still, the letter was sent only to the superiors, asking them to read it to the sisters, "but not to post it or the list on the bulletin board."[7] The delegates themselves were advised not to advertise their election but, "if you are questioned, you may of course say that you are a Delegate."[8]

And who were the delegates? Not surprisingly the six "private" sisters from the three Indiana sections with Saint Mary-of-the-Woods sisters included High School Visitor Sister Eugenia Logan, Econome Sister Robert, Mistress of Novices Sister Marie Ambrose McKenna, her assistant Sister Mary Dominica Adamson and from the College, Dean of Women Sister Mary Joan Kirchner and Dean of Admissions Sister Rose Angela Horan. Despite this concentration of administrators, delegates chosen were indeed much more representative of the Congregation membership than in previous Chapters. The superiors chosen were divided almost equally between eight from high schools and seven from grade schools; there were three high school teachers and eight grade school teachers, with a single music teacher in the mix. The median age of the thirty-six elected delegates was fifty-six.

The council's implicit blessings on a cautious loosening of tongues did not go unheeded. At the request of several delegates the Chapter was scheduled over two days, with elections to take place on May 5, and an additional session to take place the following morning. Delegates were invited to submit topics for discussion with the understanding that this exchange would provide helpful information as the newly elected superior general and her council began their new administration. In addition, the diarist reported that on the day before the official opening of the Chapter, "The delegates of the General

Chapter have been meeting in groups in sessions throughout the day," although there is no record of an agenda or process for these deliberations.[9]

Thus when Archbishop Schulte and Father Ross walked into the chapter room at 9:00 a.m. on May 5, 1954, to call upon the Holy Spirit to guide the deliberations of the General Chapter, they must have sensed a completely different atmosphere than that of five years earlier. The loss of their brief-ruling and much beloved superior appeared to have given the community strength and confidence, together with a readiness to carry forward the work she had left unfinished. Despite her diminutive frame, Sister Gertrude Clare's voice was clear and strong as she opened her report with a tribute to Mother Marie Helene that found obvious resonance in the group of forty-three Sisters of Providence who made up the assembly.

The Chapter report itself showed a membership of 1,396 professed sisters teaching in 110 schools, ten of which had been opened during the previous five years. Since1949 eighty-two sisters had died, ten had withdrawn and one had been dismissed, while nine were suffering from mental illness. There were sixty-one novices and twenty-seven postulants in formation. The number of degrees earned was impressive: forty-nine master's and 188 bachelor's, as well as 198 teacher's certificates of varying kinds. The enrollment in the elementary schools was 45,000, in the high schools 6,360 and in the colleges 390. In addition, 293 sisters taught Confraternity of Christian Doctrine classes to more than 8,100 children annually. The missionary sisters were now well established in Taiwan, with a flourishing high school and a preschool staffed by the Providence Sister-Catechists.

Sister Francis Raphael's treasurer's report showed considerable expenditures for improvements at the motherhouse and Lady Isle, as well as the construction of additional buildings at Immaculata and the new high school at Clarksville, with a small balance of cash on hand. Although debt had been incurred due to loans for financing Clarksville, the overall debt of the Congregation was less than it had been five years previously. Archbishop Schulte took the occasion to note the fact that the increase in the number of novices boded well for the future, since the great increase in enrollment of first and second graders indicated a need for more teachers in the coming years in order to provide a Catholic education for all.

Three minor revisions of the Rule were presented. Rather than the requirement that the sisters should wear a "crucifix of white bone," the text would simply read "a white crucifix." The duties to be assigned by superiors of houses were designated in a generic list rather than identified specifically. Dropped altogether was the article referring to the duties of the evening visitor charged with extinguishing the lights in the house. These revisions were passed unanimously. A committee was elected to examine the report and the chapter adjourned for a half hour. Upon the delegates' return, scrutators were elected to count the ballots and the Chapter moved to the crypt of the church for the elections.

Mother Gertrude Clare

Archbishop Schulte's opening remark that he was sure each delegate had spent much time in prayer to seek guidance was immediately affirmed when the delegates elected Sister Gertrude Clare superior general by a wide margin on the first ballot. During six previous Chapters she had heard her name read out as the choice of the delegates to serve as an assistant to the superior general, but never before had she been the one to come forward to take the oath of the highest office. After thirty-four years of service as assistant, now, at age sixty-seven, she found herself presiding as she awaited the elections of the sisters who would assist her.

The first decision was somewhat of a surprise. The delegates did not turn to a seasoned councilor to serve as first assistant, but rather cast their votes for seven different sisters. Twenty-three of the twenty-two required votes went to Sister Rose Angela Horan. The reinstatement of each of the assistants and the treasurer general on single ballots by strong majorities gave a resounding vote of confidence to the previous council. After a silent noon meal the community gathered in the chapel at 1:30 p.m. for the proclamation of results. Secretary Sister Eugenia describes the occasion:

> The Ceremonial calls it an "impressive ceremony," but it was more than that. The exhibition of loyal obedience and submis-

sion given by young and old, well and infirm, strong and crippled, as they passed by saluting the new Superior-General and her Council was indeed very touching. The childlike simplicity and the faith thus shown is a happy augury for the future.[10]

The next day, as scheduled, the delegates assembled at 9:00 a.m. for the special session. Mother Gertrude Clare greeted the delegates and assured them that "frankness will be appreciated." She began the proceedings with two announcements. Since the council had learned that a separation of the role of the superior general and that of the president of the College was advisable, this was an opportune time to appoint Sister Francis Joseph to the role of president of Saint Mary-of-the-Woods College and Sister Eugenia as vice-president.[11] The second announcement advised the delegates about the forthcoming reprint of the *Little Office of the Blessed Virgin*.

Following an agenda of five items drawn up from items submitted previously by the delegates, together with three addenda submitted later, the delegates were invited to comment. During the hour-and- a-half session, twelve elected delegates and three ex-officio delegates took the floor. Most of the issues raised had to do with the Congregation's mission of education. Continuing education was needed to provide intellectual stimulation and professional excellence for those who completed their degrees. High schools were suffering both in comparison with central high schools and also because the requirement of an advanced degree excluded younger sisters from high school assignments. Handbooks prepared by committees to foster excellence needed better utilization and even publication to wider audiences. Frequent supervision was desired both to show interest and support and to improve teaching.

Two items revealed the effects of the discontinuation of provinces. Visitation was a sore point for the East since superiors' visits were short. Sisters who did not return to the motherhouse on a regular basis were losing touch with the other sisters and avoiding professional development. In the West, the decision to appoint a "community representative," a superior with delegated authority who could gather local superiors for discussion, was lauded as an effective means of maintaining unity. The opinion was voiced that the home superiors were too preoccupied with temporal matters at home.

Another item of concern was the health of the home superiors, who were urged to make it a practice to take periodic rest opportunities. Larger houses were reminded that the Rule provided for the possibility of sharing responsibility through the use of a local council. An additional item of more uniform application of the horarium was referred to summer instructions for local superiors. As we shall see in the next chapter, the frankness with which the delegates expressed their concerns made a strong impression on the new council. The lone new member of the council was well-positioned to assure that these matters would receive regular attention.

Sister Rose Angela Horan 1895-1985

Mary Cecilia Horan, born in 1895 in Vincennes, Indiana, was the first child of Michael and Mary Horan. She enjoyed playing the role of oldest as five brothers and two sisters gradually formed the family, growing up in the Cathedral Parish and attending St. Rose Academy. After graduating in 1913 she entered the novitiate at St. Mary-of-the-Woods. An avid student herself, she enjoyed excellent mentoring by fine superior/principals during her early mission experience as a high school teacher at St. Joseph in Galesburg, Marywood in Evanston and Providence High School in Chicago, where she spent fifteen years in two separate assignments. She completed her studies during summers, earning a BA in 1926 and an MA at Indiana State Teacher's College in 1937, with a thesis entitled "An Investigation of the Ideals of Present-day Adolescents." In addition to the requirements for her principal's license she managed to take additional courses in her beloved field of English literature and composition at Loyola University in Chicago and Indiana University. Eager to share her enthusiasm for teaching, she was active on curriculum committees and conferences during summers. She also composed poetry, wrote the words to the Congregation's traditional hymn, "Our Lady of Providence," and piloted the publication of the *Woodland Echoes* newspaper. In 1934, at age 39, she began a series of appointments as principal, first at St. Agnes, Indianapolis, then St. Simon, Washington, for a year. After two years as fourth-year teacher at St. John, Indianapolis, she returned to her home parish as principal of St. Rose Academy in Vincennes, where she also served as superior for eight years. After a six-year term as superior and principal at Marywood, Evanston, in 1953 she was appointed secretary to the dean at Saint Mary-of-the-Woods College. Apparently this impressive background of scholarship and experience made her an ideal choice for the 1954 Chapter to elect her at age fifty-nine as first assistant to Mother Gertrude Clare.

Committees of Women Religious Continue

As noted earlier, during the 1950 Holy Year Pope Pius XII had inaugurated a movement of renewal for congregations of religious women by convening the International Congress of the States of Perfection in Rome. A series of initiatives followed in rapid succession. The very next year, Apostolic Delegate Archbishop Amleto Giovanni Cicognani invited American superiors to send suggestions for the agenda of the 1951 conference arranged by the Sacred Congregation for Religious to discuss the formation of young sisters.[12] In 1952 Congregation Secretary P. Arcadio Larraona set up a Central Consultative Commission of superiors to coordinate the apostolate of religious women and to provide an ecclesiastical university for women religious.[13] All three of these papal objectives—the formation of young sisters, a Roman university and a conference of major superiors—would have repercussions for the Sisters of Providence.

Sister Formation

Secretary Larraona had worked with a committee of superiors to bring the Sister Formation movement to the United States through the 1952 Notre Dame Congress. In addition to serving as a member of this committee, Mother Marie Helene had been appointed as one of three American members of the Commission of Forty Superiors General. The minutes of the August 1953 meeting of the three superiors provide a clue to Rome's evolving plans for a national organizational structure to coordinate the apostolates of the numerous American congregations. The minutes include this paragraph:

> A letter from Father Heston, CSC, from Rome, on April 17, 1953, states that Father Larraona wishes the same committee which

organized the Notre Dame Meeting to remain in order to be available for similar needs. It would be a permanent committee and provide a "front" for regional, local, or national meetings. These meetings would not be publicized and would be held discreetly. The committee has no power to impose any measures on any community, but would act as an advisory committee from which the right information and the right guidance could be obtained when needed.[14]

During the Notre Dame Congress Secretary Larraona learned that the papal objective of providing more in-depth formation for sisters was already underway in the United States. His contacts convinced him that his best course of action was to utilize the existing structure of the National Catholic Educational Association rather than waiting until the major superiors would be organized. We will follow that development in a later section of this chapter.

University in Rome

Meanwhile, the immediate agenda of the small superiors' committee would be to provide input for the projected university in Rome. The Holy Cross Procurator General in Rome, Father Edward Heston, CSC, had been appointed as a liaison between the Sacred Congregation and the superiors' committee. In June 1954, Mother Gerald Barry, OP, chair of the superiors' committee, wrote to him with some questions about the arrangements for the recruitment of American sister-students. In August Mother Gertrude Clare, replacing Mother Marie Helene, attended a meeting at Adrian, Michigan, to discuss concerns regarding the curriculum, instructors, accreditation, language of instruction and housing. Soon after this meeting, with the appointment of a French Ursuline, Mother Marie de St. Jean Martin, as secretary to the Executive Committee of Mothers General, the role of American superiors regarding the university project shifted to financial support. A Sister of Providence would be among the early students at Regina Mundi, the name given to this university.

A Permanent Conference: CMSW

With two major papal objectives being handled in other venues, what was the future of the committee? Apparently the time had come to formally introduce a national organizational structure for all major superiors. The prefect of the Sacred Congregation for Religious, Cardinal Valerio Valeri, took up direct supervision of the project by notifying Mother Gerald that his representative, Father Bernard Ransing, CSC, would come to the United States to meet with the committee.[15] In place of Mother Gertrude Clare, First Assistant Sister Rose Angela traveled to Adrian for the April 9, 1956 meeting. Only three of the original committee were in attendance, as three of the original superiors were replaced by their successors.[16] Father Ransing provided an explanation of the proposed organization with analogies to similar groups in other countries, as well as information regarding the setting up of a conference for men's religious congregations. Encouraged to express a frank reaction, the superiors noted that they were already actively involved in existing organizations such as the National Catholic Educational Association (with its subsidiary, the Sister Formation Conference), the Catholic Hospital Association, and others connected with the National Catholic Welfare Conference.[17] Since they had become accustomed to activities sponsored on a national basis not only by the NCEA but also by various committees of the National Catholic Welfare Conference, they were not yet persuaded of the need for such a conference, but they agreed to meet again.

Meanwhile, Mother Gerald provided new information to the committee by circulating a talk given by Father Elio Gambari of the Sacred Congregation in August 1956 and copies of by-laws proposed for the men's group. Father Gambari emphasized that in such conferences each congregation retained its independence; he stressed the advantages of collaboration not only with others involved in similar works but also with the hierarchy. A lengthy list of the countries where such conferences had already been established during the five years since the first Congress in Rome, together with initiatives they had sponsored, was described by Father Gambari as "this excellent and most fruitful movement of renewal in the states of perfection."[18] When the same group of superiors, including Sister Rose Angela, gathered at Notre Dame on September 9, 1956, they agreed that the United States should certainly follow through on the recommendation of the Sacred Congregation. After drawing up a summary of the caveats raised in their discussion, plans were made for a meeting of all major superiors in order to present the proposal and obtain approval for the conference.

In order to consolidate travel arrangements, Mother Gerald scheduled the inaugural gathering of United States major superiors in Chicago on November 26, 1956, so those who wished could easily go on to attend the previously scheduled meeting of the NCEA-sponsored Sister Formation Conference in Milwaukee a few days later.[19] Mother Gertrude Clare was among the 238 superiors in attendance at the Conrad Hilton Hotel as Cardinal Stritch welcomed them. Three sisters from the organizing committee explained the rationale for establishing such a conference, the projected regional structure and the statutes proposed for governing its operation. In a momentous unanimous vote the assembled superiors affirmed their desire to establish a unified structure for their apostolic efforts. After decades of dealing one-on-one with the Sacred Congregation for Religious they would now have a forum through which they could coordinate their efforts. Not only that, but this had been achieved at the invitation of the hierarchy and with the blessing of the Holy Father himself.[20]

The organization was now officially underway as the Conference of Major Superiors of Women (CMSW).[21] The forum immediately displayed a uniquely American characteristic of democratic discussion with a motion to bring the Sister Formation Conference under its auspices. However, this move was considered premature until the conference itself was up and running. The sheer numbers of religious congregations in the United States had dictated a regional structure and the planning committee had recruited six able superiors to head each region during the first year. As one of the 160 congregations in the Midwest region, the Sisters of Providence would be looking to Sister Mary Benedicta Larkin, OP, a Sinsinawa, Wisconsin, Dominican, to assist them in the transition. Smaller regional meetings would pave the way for the establishment of a national executive committee with a secretariat office in Washington, D.C.

An April 1957 notation in the Diary provides notice from Mother Gerald of official closure to the role played by the Sisters of Providence in the formation of the CMSW. "The Committee formed by Rome, of which Mother Gertrude Clare is a member, will be dissolved with the election of permanent officers of the Conference of Major Superiors of Religious Institutes of Women in the United States."[22] With their contribution to the pioneering work of the steering committee behind them, the council now turned its attention to a new chapter in the formation of its own members.

The Sister Formation Initiative

The Sister Formation Conference

As noted in Chapter 10, the National Catholic Educational Association had provided leadership for improving the educational formation of young sisters.[23] With a long history of cooperation between the hierarchy and religious institutes of women, the NCEA was ideal for implementing papal pronouncements on improving the preparation of young sisters by providing coursework comparable to that required for seminaries. In 1952 the organization had sponsored a survey of Catholic women's colleges which provided a data base of approaches used by various congregations for preparing their young sisters to meet accreditation standards. In 1954 the NCEA Executive Board established the Sister Formation Conference (SFC) as part of its College and University Department. Sisters Mary Emil Penet, IHM, and Rosemary Bradley, CHM, were released by their congregations to plan and implement regional conferences to inform superiors of possible modes of implementation. In 1955 the SFC began publication of a quarterly newsletter, the *Sister Formation Bulletin*, with timely articles from scholars and thinkers.

During the years in which these activities gained momentum, although Sister Francis Joseph Elbreg continued active NCEA membership, the council was occupied with other matters. Mother Marie Helene's involvement in the superior's committee was cut short by her sudden death, an event which required a complete resetting of the Congregation agenda. Ever on the minds of each council member was the optimal placement of sisters both to maintain staffing of existing and new schools and also to ensure convents conducive to strong religious life. Because 1956 was the centenary of Mother Theodore's death and the sesquicentennial of the foundation in France, plans were underway for special celebrations during the summer. Nonetheless, the council members' contacts with other congregations at meetings and through publications brought news of developments which created more and more pressure to alter the formation program. Inevitably the council members began to wonder if the Congregation was being left behind.

Samplings from the autumn 1956 issue of the *Sister Formation Bulletin* provide a glimpse of such pressures. A vocation survey of 15,000 students across the country indicated that many young women felt that the sisters "have so withdrawn themselves from contact with life that they do not know the students or the world in which they are living."[24] Analysis of the data indicated that

> Only 25 per cent of our students believe that Sisters think for themselves. But our Sisters cannot form opinions on issues of the day because they do not have time to read. It takes time to keep informed. … Crowded horariums produce strain, but students think that it is the religious life itself that does this.[25]

An analysis of a typical horarium led to the conclusion that "something has to give."[26] The astute editor did not leave this question hanging. Immediately following was an article by BVM Superior General Mother Consolatrice Wright describing their congregation's experiment with more relaxed horariums. Both topics likely provided food for each council member's thought.

A major section of this same issue of the newsletter was devoted to "The Everett Report." To provide a high standard for congregations developing a full four-year educational curriculum for their young sisters, Sister Mary Emil Penet, IHM, had obtained a grant from the Ford Foundation and arranged a three-month summer workshop at Everett, Washington.[27] Fifteen sisters from different congregations, all professors in different academic fields, developed goals for a well-rounded formation and a sequence of courses to meet them. Sister Esther Newport, professor of art at Saint Mary-of-the-Woods College, was one of three sister consultants to give presentations during the workshop. The article provided a summary of the recommendations developed at the Everett conference. These were to appear in a separate publication being sent to superiors and bishops throughout the country.

Adapting the Formation Program

Discussion of articles and papers given at the Sister Formation meetings they had attended became a staple of council meeting agendas. In recalling their deliberations, Secretary General Sister Loretta Therese reflected:

> Having the newly professed Sisters remain at St. Mary-of-the-Woods for the completion of their scholastic work was due more to Mother Gertrude Clare's efforts and determination than to any other individual. She presented various plans to the Councilors for this project and wrote to Pastors explaining the desirability and benefits which would result. Support and opposition she accepted calmly and went on her determined way. Sister Eugenia Logan said of Mother: "At times seemingly insurmountable opposition had some waiting and wondering what to do, only to find that Mother had bypassed the obstacle and moved on." Mother did not act precipitously, but after consultation, prayer and study of all angles of a problem or need, she acted.[28]

Although in May 1956 it was decided to postpone participation, by November, the council minutes state the plan which was adopted: "It was suggested that we keep home for study the Sisters who take Final Vows on January 23, 1957, and in August 1957 keep home the newly professed for the Formation Plan as desired by our Holy Father."[29] To understand this plan we need to recall the two-part structure of the formation program—the novitiate for new entrants and a second novitiate for the aspirants, those preparing for final vows. Each year one group (known as a "band") entered the novitiate in January and a second group entered in July. After a six-month postulancy, these sisters spent a year as canonical novices and then a second year as scholastic novices. At the end of the scholastic year, either in January or August, they professed vows and were sent "on mission" to teach. Thus the novitiate building always held five groups: a band of postulants, two bands of canonical novices learning the elements of religious life and two bands of scholastic novices enrolled in college classes.

Mother Gertrude Clare welcomes sisters making their second novitiate to the thirty-day retreat in preparation for perpetual vows.

The second phase of the formation program was the second novitiate. The *Constitutions* required that after five years each sister would return to the motherhouse for a second novitiate of five months during which she would make a thirty-day retreat. In keeping with the semi-annual arrangement, one group came for second novitiate in February in order to take final vows on August 15, while the next group remained at the motherhouse after the summer session to make their second novitiate and take final vows in January. During her long tenure on the council, one of Mother Gertrude Clare's highly appreciated assignments had been to give the thirty-day retreat. Now she suggested an alternative plan. By arranging overlapping times for both groups, only one retreat would be needed.

The challenge now facing the council was to alter both phases of this deeply embedded structure to comply with the emerging sister formation norms. The advantages for maintaining high educational standards were clear. With one year of the two-and-a-half year novitiate devoted to spiritual formation, entrants arriving directly from high school were given their teaching assignments when they had completed only about half of their college credits. The plan to keep them home for an additional two years would enable them to earn a bachelor's degree and a teaching certificate. Unlike many congregations, the Sisters of Providence enjoyed the major advantage of a four-year college on the same campus as the motherhouse. Sister Francis Joseph's education office could readily be expanded to weave the newly professed sisters into the existing college curriculum rather than into only the summer sessions designed for the sisters themselves. In fact, the College was enjoying a spurt in enrollment and a concomitant growth of programs, ensuring strong curriculum offerings.[30]

The advantages of these decisions were many, but there were no illusions about the difficulties involved in beginning the Sister Formation Program. The chronicler summarizes the rationale for the decision: "Having no young sisters for placement in 1957 and 1958 will create many problems, but in the end the Community should be the gainer by participation in the program recommended by Our Holy Father and the Sacred Congregation."[31] How would the schools continue to be staffed? The pastors were notified that implementing the program was required by the hierarchy and would eventually benefit their parish schools with better trained faculty. In addition, they were reminded of the earlier notice from diocesan offices about the "Share the Sisters" plan to distribute sister personnel in proportion to lay teachers.[32] Who could be entrusted to supervise the "juniorate," as this new phase of formation would be called? For this responsibility, former Mistress of Novices Sister Rose Berchmans Patterson was recalled to take charge of the practical organization of the program and the spiritual formation of the junior sisters.

To acquaint the Congregation at large with the new requirements, copies of the address given by Father Gambari of the Sacred Congregation of Religious to the regional Sister Formation meetings were sent to each mission. Mother Gertrude Clare explained the newly adopted terminology to the community:

> Beginning with Pentecost of this year, we shall use the following terms to designate the respective periods:
>
> Our preparatory school previously known as the Juniorate and the members as candidates, hereafter will be known as the *Aspirancy* and the members as *Aspirants;* that is, young persons aspiring to enter religious life.
>
> The time of temporary profession will be known as the period of the *Juniorate*, two years of which will be spent in the House of Studies at Saint Mary's and the remaining years of temporary profession in the work of the apostolate on the missions.
>
> The second novitiate will be known as the *Tertianship*, and the members as *Tertians*, preparing for perpetual profession.[33]

Considering the breadth and diversity of Congregation activities, these changes had little effect on the daily lives of most sisters. Superiors in most houses had already adapted to a faculty composed of lay teachers as well as sisters. In houses with sisters eligible for second novitiate, now to be called tertianship, local superiors had to negotiate between the pastor and the motherhouse to arrange a several-month replacement. As for the tertians themselves, while they enjoyed re-connecting with their band members for recreation and instructions, the thirty-day retreat was the central feature of the second novitiate experience as they examined their choice to live as a Sister of Providence for the rest of their lives.[34]

One of the most pressing questions was how to find space at the motherhouse for these stay-at-home sisters. Two solutions were devised, one a stop-gap measure, and the other a major investment. Projections regarding those eligible for tertianship showed that even with the overlapping groups, the usual arrangement of housing them in a dormitory in Providence Convent with a room in Tile Hall dedicated for their use would be adequate. As for the "juniorate," creative thinking led to the stop-gap adaptations needed for accommodating them in the 1890 Providence Convent building. A large space in the basement was furnished with tables and chairs to serve as a combination community room/study hall, with additional study space in Foley Hall. With the installation of heaters on the sun porches off second and third Tile Halls, temporary dormitories were created. The group of junior sisters would continue to grow for two years and then become stable in January 1959 as the newly degreed sisters left for their teaching assignments.

A New Novitiate Building

By 1957, when the first group of newly professed sisters moved from the novitiate building over to Providence alongside those staying for their second novitiate, it was obvious that a long-range solution was needed to accommodate the groups that would follow. Mother Gertrude Clare had quietly suggested building a new novitiate some months previously, and now the council realized the urgency of the need. With a separate structure for the novitiate to house the postulants and novices, the still sturdy 1904 novitiate building could then be used for the junior sisters. In writing to the sisters to announce the plan, Mother Gertrude Clare noted that the establishment of the Sister Formation Program was in response to the Holy Father's wishes:

> The creation of this new educational and spiritual project has increased our material problems, and we find ourselves faced with the necessity of providing accommodation and adequate space for those who will take part in this work. ... It is our feeling then that the wisest course would be to build a new Novitiate. ... I tell you this so that you will see what a problem we have to meet, and will realize that it is for the benefit of our loved Community that we do it.[35]

In December 1957 the council met with Superintendent of Grounds Bernard Bisch and architect Robert Bohlen to discuss possibilities. The D.A. Bohlen and Son Company of Indianapolis had served the Sisters of Providence for more than a century, beginning with the founder, Diedrich Bohlen, and then his son Oscar, by designing all the major edifices on the campus.[36] When Mr. Bohlen presented sketches of several building shapes which could blend into the campus plan, they chose a site north of the Shrine Path bordering the grove, across the road from the old novitiate.

Because in 1958 the feast of Our Lady of Lourdes on February 11 marked the one-hundredth anniversary of the apparition at Lourdes, that date was chosen for the blessing of the site. The plan of the building was marked off with flag-topped stakes, and during the ceremony a container with several sacred objects was placed in a hole where the altar would be placed. Because of recent very large expenditures for the new buildings at Immaculata, financial arrangements took time, so it was already September when bids were opened, with the contract awarded to the Wilhelm Construction Company of Indianapolis. The official groundbreaking ceremony took place on September 24, 1958, and the very next day large steam shovels appeared and work began in earnest. Almost immediately it became apparent that the ground was too unstable to support the weight of the building. The news was a blow, but old-timers recalled that the same situation had held back the construction of Foley and Le Fer Halls; in fact before Le Fer could be built it had been necessary to drive 580 concrete piles into the soil to ensure a firm foundation. The Raymond Foundation Company of St. Louis was called in to do a soil study and it confirmed the need for driving piles ranging in depth from 6-20 feet, estimating the need for about 526 piles.[37]

There was no doubt about the need for stability since the building, with four floors and a total floor area of about 100,000 square feet, was designed to accommodate 150, with possible expansion to 200. The need for the piles not only greatly delayed the actual construction but also dramatically increased the cost of the project. Whereas the original estimate of approximately a million dollars had seemed manageable in view of debts already incurred for construction of Providence High School, a convent in Clarksville, Marian Cottage and buildings at Immaculata in Washington, D.C., strengthening the foundation doubled the cost.[38] As the work progressed, it was necessary to authorize the sale of some stocks to meet the bills, and a large gift from the Hulman family was most welcome, even as the debt was refinanced.

The entire community was enthusiastically behind the project, with grass-roots efforts designed to help defray the costs. A popular marketing tool of the times, giving trading stamps as a premium for purchases, was adopted as a fund-raising effort. Stamps were saved and pasted into books which could be traded in for items such as furniture or appliances. Families of children enrolled in Sister of Providence schools were asked to donate some of their stamp books to help furnish the novitiate, with a goal of ten filled books per forty-pupil classroom. Sisters Mark Schwartz and Virginia Cecile McCarthy at St. Athanasius School in Evanston, Illinois, volunteered to be a central clearing house, distributing mimeographed posters declaring, "This is the house that stamps can fill!" With the aim of helping "our dear Mother" save thousands of dollars, their pleas for stamps were magnificently rewarded. Their goal of providing one hundred mattresses was surpassed when they were able to order one hundred and forty. In addition, they were able to procure sheets, bedspreads, dishes, tablecloths, irons and kitchen items, as well as tables and chairs.

Another opportunity for fund-raising came knocking in the form of a letter from Mr. H. Douglas Cotton, president of Barton-Cotton, Inc., publisher of fine color work greeting cards, inviting the submission of original designs for Christmas cards.[39] In 1959 cards with designs by the sisters were sold so successfully through the schools, with the Congregation receiving ten cents per card, that the following year the project was repeated. For the sisters at the motherhouse, the daily sight of the workmen laboring at the many jobs such a large construction entailed was a reminder that sales alone seemed insufficient as a way to contribute. So they asked that the money usually spent for small gifts for them at Christmas be used instead for the building fund. In January 1960 Mother Gertrude Clare was able to report that, "The financial returns from your activities during the past four months, culminating in your Christmas offerings, are almost incredible." She was able to report a total, "between the Christmas cards and donations, amounting to $63,775.38."[40]

While the construction progressed, the council members were active in planning other aspects of the building. Through the Rigali company Sister Rose Dolores researched the type of organ most suitable for the chapel, eventually deciding on a Wicks pipe organ.[41] It was agreed that the air system for heating and ventilating needed to allow for possible later installation of air conditioning in assembly areas. Glazed tile was chosen for the ground floor with a special pattern for the chapel floor. The lobby would be enhanced with Bottichino marble with the Congregation seal worked into the terrazzo floor.[42] Sisters working in the sewing room and sacristy were consulted regarding those rooms. The arrival of a notice that typewriters and desks were available as "government surplus" at Camp Atterbury led to an impromptu shopping trip. Lest the purpose of the building be lost, it was decided to place an aluminum plaque to the right of the main entrance with the Biblical quote which had introduced the 1904 textbook explaining the educational methods used by the Sisters of Providence: "Those who instruct many unto justice shall shine as stars for all eternity" (Daniel 12:13).[43]

On July 25, 1959, as the chimes played a fifteen minute concert, the entire community attending the summer session together with the architect, representatives of the construction company and trustees of the College assembled near the construction site for the blessing and laying of the cornerstone. Following a drum and bugle fanfare, all sang "Bless this House, O Lord," and Archbishop Schulte conducted the formal blessing. The sisters then formed into ranks on the nearby Shrine Path for the annual St. Anne procession.

With the exterior completed, attention turned to the interior. The chapel, just inside the main entrance, was a focal point. Its green botticino marble altars were set off by cherry wood paneling which provided a backdrop for the Daprato Company's Way of the Cross with white figures on red botticino marble. In October Sisters Rose Genevieve and Francis Raphael made a special trip to nearby Effingham, Illinois, to order matching cherry-stained pews. In January, most of council traveled by car to Jasper, Indiana, to visit several of the furniture factories. In January 1960, Archbishop Schulte notified Mother of his intention of appointing Reverand William Stineman to the dual post of novitiate chaplain and College faculty as soon as he completed his doctoral studies, with residence in the chaplain's quarters behind the sacristy of the novitiate chapel.

In February there came the cruel blow of news that Mother Gertrude Clare was critically ill, yet work on the interior continued, with the dedication of the chapel taking place on April 19, 1960. In his sermon, Rev. Joseph Brokhage, former faculty member of the College and now rector of the Latin School, highlighted the many sacrifices which had made the building possible and praised the Congregation for establishing the Sister Formation Program. The May 22 Open House afforded those in the area the opportunity to inspect the building, and a week later the diarist wrote: "The novitiate moved to their new quarters today. The beautiful new building which had been for so long a need, is now a dream fulfilled."[44]

Regina Mundi and European Studies

As noted in earlier sections, one of the initiatives being pushed by the Sacred Congregation for Religious was the creation of a university for sisters in Rome comparable to those for preparing men for the priesthood. Because of the participation of Mothers Marie Helene and Gertrude Clare on the original committee, this topic had been on the council agenda from the first notification of the pope's desires. In July 1954 Archbishop Larroana announced the opening that fall of "Regina Mundi," an Institute to provide "religious thoroughly well trained in sacred studies and therefore better prepared both for the work of government and the guidance of others within their religious institutes."[45]

Admission standards were high, with prospective students being expected to have a good knowledge of philosophy and the ability to read reference books in Latin. Students could enroll for a one-year course, which was offered every year, or they could remain two more years to achieve the certificate offered. The academic program was overseen by the former rector of the Pontifical Gregorian University, while arrangements for sister students were handled by the dean, a French Ursuline, Sister Mary Magdalen Bellasin.[46] Although the Congregation's subscription donation of $1,000 would cover tuition,[47] the council's deliberations regarding placements for the 1954-1955 school year were already underway, making it impossible to send anyone that year. However, several other congregations did respond, and in October Mother Mary Gerald, OP, forwarded a booklet indicating that forty sisters were enrolled in the English section of the four-language program (Italian, English, French and Spanish).

Additional hierarchal pressure was felt the following year when Archbishop Larraona reminded the Sisters' Committee about "this undertaking which is so dear to the heart of the Holy Father."[48] When Mother Gertrude Clare compared notes with Mother Mary Gerald, OP, her reply stated that she also had received this letter, but a larger number of sisters than usual had died and that, "I doubt that he has any idea of what teacher shortage means for any Superior General of today."[49] The council did suggest several names with the intention of sending two sisters in the fall, but as placements continued, all of them received other appointments. The September 1955 Regina Mundi report indicated an enrollment of fifty-eight congregations from twenty-two nations in the four language sections and was accompanied by letters not only from the Sacred Congregation for Religious but also from Archbishop Schulte urging support. At last the time had come. Sister Alexa Suelzer was named to study at Regina Mundi during the 1956-1957 academic year.

Unanticipated events from another quarter were to make this year of study even more memorable. Industrialist and philanthropist Myron C. Taylor, who had served as President Roosevelt's personal envoy to Pope Pius XII, had in 1941 deeded to the pope the family home, Villa Schifanoia in Florence, to be a graduate school of fine arts for American women under the direction of the Dominican Sisters of Sinsinawa, Wisconsin. Opened in 1948, the school advertised in its brochure a staff of "professors of international repute from the University of Florence, the Accademia Delle Belle Arti and the music conservatory, Luigi Cherubini."[50] A longtime benefactor of the Congregation, Mr. Frank Folsom, had used his influence to recommend that one of the four scholarships given annually through Cardinal Spellman would be awarded to a professor of art at Saint Mary-of-the-Woods College, Sister Immaculee Krafthefer, for the 1956-1957 term.[51] Sister Cecilia Ann Miller, another member of the College faculty, was assigned for a year of piano study at the music conservatory of the Villa.

The three sister students began their year with a six-week tour of sites renowned for music and art, including stops in London, Dublin, Edinburgh, Stockholm, Copenhagen, Amsterdam, Brussels and Paris, with a side trip to Ruillé, then on to Cologne, Frankfurt, Geneva and Genoa, finally arriving at Florence and Rome. Once in Rome, Sister Alexa settled into her somewhat Spartan *pensione*, a short walk from Regina Mundi. She was delighted to learn that Wednesdays were free, providing opportunity for her and her sister companions to explore Rome's churches and places of interest. In addition, Signora Guila Sartori, a longtime friend of College faculty member Sister Gertrude Smith from her own study days in Rome, took Sister Alexa under her wing and used her connections to arrange behind-the-scenes tours.

In addition to their academic studies, supplementary tours during the year and at its end rounded out their educational experience. Sisters Immaculee and Cecilia Ann returned to the College while Sister Alexa spent a year at Corpus Christi High School in Galesburg before being sent the following year to study for a doctorate at Catholic University. Later, in comparing the two educational experiences, she commented, "The instruction that I subsequently experienced here in the States was better, but nothing could have replaced the cultural influence of that year."[52] Because opportunities for higher theological studies were increasingly available in the United States, no other Sisters of Providence attended Regina Mundi but the university continued to educate women religious from all over the world until it closed in 2005.

Canonization Efforts

Concurrent with all these events was another project most dear to Mother Gertrude Clare and indeed, all the Sisters of Providence. With the Holy Year pilgrimages and Pope Pius XII's initiatives regarding the renewal of religious congregations centered on the work of the founders, attention to the Cause of Mother Theodore's canonization took on new vigor. During the thirties when Mother Mary Raphael had enlisted the support of the hierarchy, Bishop Ritter had appointed Father Thomas Kilfoil as postulator, and he had gone to France to begin a collection of material regarding her early life. With the on-site assistance of Ruillé superior, Mother Marie Armelle, many original documents had been made available, but after 1940 the Nazi occupation prevented further contact. The publication of Mother Theodore's *Journals and Letters* in 1937 and of volume one of the Congregation history in 1949 had made her story beloved to the sisters and to some extent brought her biography before the public. During her 1950 visit to Rome, Mother Marie Helene had met with the postulator, Father Andrew Manescau, to discuss the progress of the Cause.

Councilors Go to Rome

Almost immediately after her election, Mother Gertrude Clare initiated efforts to encourage the canonization process. When she learned through Holy Cross Procurator Rev. Edward Heston in October 1954 that Father Manescau had died two years earlier, it became glaringly clear that personal onsite contact was needed. Accordingly, First Assistant Sister Rose Angela and Secretary General Sister Loretta Therese were commissioned to go to Rome in November 1954 to arrange a replacement. It would seem that Mother Theodore herself was smiling on these two because the assistance of so many friends on their journey would later prompt Mother Gertrude Clare to write to the sisters with the comment, "We have no doubt that the contacts so providentially arranged were the result of the loving and fervent prayers of all of you, dear sisters."[53]

In New York, Mother's brother, Ed Owens, and his wife met the travelers. A former student of the Sisters of Providence, Herbert Lynn, president of Trans World Airlines, provided travel assistance. Longtime benefactor Frank Folsom arranged to have the two emissaries met in Rome by an American priest, Father Bede MacEachen, secretary to Cardinal Nicola Canali, a good friend of Mr. Folsom. The cardinal arranged for them to stay in Vatican City itself and provided Father Bede's services as chauffeur and interpreter.[54]

A preliminary meeting with Cardinal Protector Pietro Fumasoni-Biondi not only re-established ties begun when he had blessed Le Fer Hall in 1923 while serving as apostolic delegate to the United States, but also provided insight into the role of the postulator, since he had also been the first to perform those duties on behalf of Mother Theodore. After meeting with Cardinal Canali, they followed up on his recommendation to secure the services of Monsignor Emidio

Federici as postulator, as he had served as vice-postulator for the cause of St. Thèrése of Lisieux.[55] The other key individual selected to carry the process forward was the lawyer Signor Guilio Dante. Several meetings with Msgr. Federici to go through the material already available assured them that it would be possible to move the case forward to the next level, where Signor Dante could begin preparation of his brief.

Their time in Rome included a trip to Castel Gandolfo, where they were part of a large audience with Pope Pius XII, prohibited by his long illness from speaking, but able to give blessings to all in the courtyard. They visited the newly opened Regina Mundi University, met the director, Mother Mary Magdalene Bellism, OSU, and enjoyed a visit with Sister Gertrude's friend, Signora Sartori. The convenience of their quarters in Vatican City made it possible to slip into St. Peter's for visits and services, including the canonization of Blessed Martin Maye, a private tour of several receptions rooms in the Vatican Palace, the Vatican Gardens and the Sistine Chapel and a visit to the new Holy Cross Generalate.

Their return route included a stop in Paris where the American Consul, Jean Mary Wilkowski, an alumna of Saint Mary-of-the-Woods College, provided able assistance. A weekend trip to Ruillé enabled the resumption of filial ties toward the canonization of Mother Theodore. "The feast of the Immaculate Conception itself brought the European visit to a providential and fitting climax with the participation of the two sisters in the closing ceremonies of the Marian Year at our Lady's shrine at Lourdes."[56] The fruits of this journey would soon be apparent. Meanwhile Mother Gertrude Clare urged the sisters to "build up with renewed hope our own confidence in the Cause,"[57] not only with prayer and sacrifice, but also with efforts to propagate devotion with the hope of receiving favors which would substantiate Mother Theodore's heroic virtue.

Work of the Rome Officials

Monsignor Federici and Signor Dante energetically circulated what Monsignor described as "a large, beautiful Italian biography"[58] to Cardinal Adeodato Giovanni Piazza, the Ponente and the other cardinals, prelates and officials of the Consistorial Congregation. When the Consistory gathered for an audience with the pope on February 19, 1956, Cardinal Prefect Gaetano Cicognani presented the summary document to Pope Pius XII. Monsignor Federici's went on to describe Cardinal Piazza's "marvelous and most efficacious presentation of Mother Theodore before all the cardinals."[59] The consistory voted in favor of the cardinal's request and the Holy Father gave his approbation for the Introduction of the Cause with the Apostolic Process.

Ciotti portrayed Mother Theodore in her role as teacher.

Monsignor Federici lost no time in utilizing the event to advance the Cause. He had a special ring made as a gift to Cardinal Piazza. When newspaper accounts prompted requests for information about Mother Theodore, he had pamphlets prepared in several languages and commissioned an artist, Professor Guiseppe Ciotti, to prepare a small oil painting of her which could be printed within the pamphlets.[60] The following year the painting was purchased by the Congregation and sent to Saint Mary-of-the-Woods. An item more immediately significant for the community was the preparation of a large display-board printing of the *Decretum*, the decree authorizing the Introduction of the Cause, which arrived in time for the May 14, 1956, commemoration of the one-hundredth anniversary of Mother Theodore's death. Noting that the *Decretum* had been placed prominently in the sanctuary of the Church and honored during the day's High Mass, the diarist wrote: "One hundred years ago our beloved Foundress came to the end of her way of sorrow and entered into her hoped-for reward."[61]

Celebrating Mother Theodore and the Foundation

During the summer session of 1956 the entire community celebrated two significant anniversaries, the 1806 foundation in France and the 1856 death of their foundress. During their summer of study in Europe the previous year, two of the College faculty, Sisters Georgiana Terstegge and Mary Olive O'Connell, had visited Ruillé and extended an invitation to the French sisters to visit Saint Mary-of-the-Woods during the celebration planned for the following summer. Anticipating the joyousness their presence would add to the festivities, the council was delighted to second the invitation. Two of the French Congregation's councilors, Sister Gabriel Marie, secretary general, and Sister Maria Joseph, the visitator, arrived by plane in Indianapolis. Although they had just that year adopted a modernized habit, they obligingly donned the former habit in honor of the historical nature of their visit.

The Book of Important Events provides a glimpse of the celebration:

> At breakfast on Thursday morning, July 26, each Sister tied a blue and white tag bearing her name to her cross string, and the three-day celebration of the Centenary of Mother Theodore's death and the 150th anniversary of the Founding of the Community began. The program was planned so as to combine the spiritual with the artistic.[62]

The annual St. Ann Procession was accompanied by the presentation by the postulants of a play on the life of Mother Theodore written by Sister Mary Roger Madden. In an evening concert, the sisters' and novices' choir sang "In the Providence of God, A Cycle of Psalms" written by Sister Cecilia Clare Bocard. The composition featured psalms selected to epitomize various phases in the history of the community from the founding days in France, with the choirs and various soloists concluding the ten selections with an antiphonal chorus of "Praise Ye the Lord." Archbishop Schulte was the celebrant for the solemn closing Pontifical High Mass, with Sister Rose Dolores' brother, Abbot Columban Thuis, OSB, delivering a sermon that highlighted significant historical events.

To acquaint the French sisters with the American foundation, a flurry of brief tours was packed into their short stay: the founding mission of Vincennes, the Holy Cross foundation of Notre Dame, contemporary missions in Chicago, the new Schulte High School in Terre Haute and even an American grocery store, Kroger. When the time came for their departure the sisters' band came to the east door to play French national airs and American selections. En route back to Paris, the two French sisters included a stopover at Immaculata in Washington, D.C.

Gathering Testimony for the Cause

The next major step in the canonization process, declaring Mother Theodore to be "Venerable," was in place by November. Father Joseph Kempf, professor of history at the College, was named as vice-postulator. Advocate for the Cause Signor Guilio Dante came to Indianapolis with the necessary documents to establish the tribunal which would hear witnesses to the heroicity of virtue of Mother Theodore. At Saint Mary-of-the-Woods he worked in the archives to examine original documents and then went to Indianapolis to work in the diocesan chancery. In a formal public ceremony held in Cecilian Auditorium on November 5, 1956, the archbishop and nine priests were sworn in as judges and the apostolic process was officially begun.

During subsequent months those named as witnesses were interrogated. Who were the witnesses? As Mother Gertrude Clare explained,

> The Sisters called as witnesses were thought to have a more or less specialized knowledge of the life and virtues of Mother Theodore through their intensive study of the early history of the community and through their acquaintance with much of her correspondence relative to the affairs of her times.[63]

Of particular interest were those who could provide testimony regarding Sister Mary Theodosia Mug's cure from cancer, which appeared to have definite potential for being declared miraculous. Although most of the interrogatory sessions were held at the chancery in Indianapolis when the judges were available, special sessions on this topic were held at the motherhouse during August and September 1958.

The final work of the tribunal was the "Recognition of the Remains of the Servant of God" which took place in the crypt on September 13, 1958. The archbishop and five priests came from the chancery, together with three priests from Saint Mary-of-the-Woods, Father Kempf, the vice-postulator, Father Gorman, the diocesan historian and Father Goossens, the chaplain. Also in attendance were Mother Gertrude Clare and the council, those sisters involved with the process and two doctors. Two superintendents of grounds assisted two senior workmen with the removal of the small coffin from the vault where it had been placed in 1907. After the remains were examined, several bones were placed in a steel box to be placed in the archives while the other remains were re-interred in a new copper box lined with linen. An identifying parchment was added, the box was soldered and it was then placed in a red cedar box which was sealed and returned to the vault.

Two of the tribunal judges were charged with taking the tribunal's report to Rome. Fathers Joseph Brokhage and Charles Koster came to Saint Mary-of-the-Woods on October 22, 1958, to show the community the box holding the twelve bound volumes of 7,221 handwritten pages of testimony. As they departed for the train station, Sisters Carol Ann Belucci, Charles Ann Belucci and Cecilia Ann Miller expressed the jubilation of the sisters with bugle and drum.[64] More rejoicing was in order when the postulator, Monsignor Federici, cabled on November 11 to inform Mother Gertrude Clare that the testimony had been presented to the Congregation of Rites, and again on their return when the two priests visited to provide in-person accounts of their visits with the postulator.

Promotional Efforts for the Cause

It is clear from the numerous and detailed letters to the sisters during this time that the entire Congregation was intensely interested in the progress of the Cause. There were frequent requests for prayers and for efforts to promote devotion to Mother Theodore with the hope that heartfelt intercession on the part of the faithful would be rewarded with a cure which could be deemed miraculous. Since it was apparent that the process involved considerable expense, Mother Gertrude Clare did not hesitate to point out that the translation and copying of the testimony, while expensive, would provide income for the Italian sisters charged with this task. Once again she designated any Christmas donations for this purpose. Equally touching to the generous response to this directive was the prayer initiative devised by Sister Mary Viola Burke. Not only did she mail out thousands of pamphlets to hospitals, parishes and motherhouses, but she invited retired and infirm sisters to become members of a group who promised to spend an hour of prayer each day for the success of the Cause.[65]

The council realized the need for a popular biography which would enable the Catholic public to appreciate Mother Theodore's life and works. Several council members were familiar with the popularized biographies written by Katherine

Burton, a prominent Catholic journalist and author. In March 1955, they contracted with her to write Mother Theodore's biography. Over the 1956 Christmas holidays she came to Saint Mary-of-the-Woods and spent several days reading almost continuously during several sessions each day. The draft she submitted in March 1957 proved unsatisfactory, prompting Sisters Rose Angela and Eugenia to meet with her while they were in New York attending a canon law conference. Publication was further delayed so that the book would appear at the same time as the completion of the Apostolic Process. Great was the excitement when the first copies of *Faith Is the Substance* were received from the St. Louis publisher, Herder, on Foundation Day, October 22, 1957. The favorable reviews which soon followed assured that Mother Theodore's story would soon become widely known in the land she had adopted as her own.

Certainly the significant events described in this chapter signaled that the Congregation had entered a new era. The major growth of the American Catholic church during the fifties would have significant effects on the educational mission of the Congregation.

❧ Chapter 12
The Educational Mission in Changing Times 1954-1960

Members of the first class at Providence High School, Clarksville, Indiana, confer with Sister Marian Thomas Kinney about an upcoming project. The student to Sister's right is Ann Margaret O'Hara, who entered the Congregation after graduation in 1955 and became the seventeenth general superior in 2001. From left to right, the other seated students are Walter Kahl and John McCloud; standing are Daniel Burke, JoAnn Cottingham, Mary Ann Trindeitmar and James Hartlage.

Signs of Changing Times

Mother Gertrude Clare's administration occurred at a unique period in the United States, as described by Charles Morris:

The Catholic impulse was perfectly in accord with powerful forces that were transforming American society and culture in the 1940s and 1950s. ... Average family size rose right along with wages. ... Women had been entering the labor force in greater numbers for decades, but in the 1950s, they quit their

TABLE 7: *Growth of educational apostolate, 1949-1966*

Chapter year	U.S Catholic population	U.S. Sisters	U.S. Parish schools	SP membership	SP staffed schools
1949	26,718,343	not available	7,777	1,364	96
1954	31,648,424	154,055	8,493	1,396	110
1960	40,871,302	168,527	10,372	1,444	124
1966	46,246,175	181,421	10,962	1,488	136

Source: http://www.npg.org/facts/us_historical_pops.htm; *The Official Catholic Directory.* New York: P.J. Kenedy & Sons. Annual editions as indicated. SP data from General Chapter reports.

jobs, stayed home, and had more children. … From about 1948, three generations of women began having children at the same time—the younger members of the Depression-era cohort who were still of childbearing age; the women who had come of age during the war and postponed childbearing until the fighting ended; and younger women just entering their childbearing years. The result was the famous 1950s baby boom. …

Catholics were younger than other Americans, had larger families, and benefited disproportionately from the postwar boom. For one thing, the Catholic population was growing very fast, doubling just between 1940 and 1960. … The Catholic share of the nation's population increased from 19 percent to 23 percent, and its share of the Church-affiliated population from 33 percent to 37 percent. … The Catholic Church grew very rich [and] … built virtually brand-new infrastructures two separate times in a single decade—once immediately after the war, when urban Catholics made the jump from center cities to the first ring of new suburbs, and then a second time later in the 1950s, when newly affluent Catholics moved out to the second and third suburban rings.[1]

As can be seen from Table 7, these trends would have a great impact on the decisions of the Sisters of Providence whose mission of education had become deeply embedded in the Catholic school system.

Sisters' Views on Adaptation

With the background of major events described in Chapter 11, we turn our attention to multiple concurrent events within the Congregation. As he had done five years previously, in 1954 Archbishop Schulte delegated Rev. Charles Ross to conduct the canonical visitation required by canon law. With papal emphasis being placed on the renewal of religious life, the new council took the opportunity to use the information gleaned from the visitation questionnaires to gain insight into how they might foster such renewal. They met with Father Ross on July 15, 1954, and invited him to present a report to the entire community on the evening of July 19. The council minutes' list of the report's responses to the question, "What do you consider the greatest need for the Community?" reveals a range of issues:

1) Charity and union—this was the *number 1* recommendation of the sisters.

2) A lessening of the burden for Reverend Mother and the Council.

3) Kindness and understanding in superiors; competence in spiritual direction; spirituality plus ability to manage. Uniformity in matter of permissions granted or refused.

4) Greater love for silence and practice of poverty, with simplicity of living.

5) Recreation and relaxation—a need for these because of the increased tension, etc. Work at recreation should not be school work.

6) A little more time for meals; less rush.

7) Visiting of homes. Permission to make visits for serious illness of other members of the family in addition to parents.

8) School and study—wish of the Sisters to work better in the sharing of help with others, etc.

9) Question of the change of the cap—cost of laundering, etc.

10) Air conditioning of chapel.

11) Improved attitude toward the racial question.

12) Expression of opinion that we should have provinces.[2]

Growth of the Catholic Church

Changes in the Hierarchy

The fifties were a proud time to be a Catholic. In the United States, all religions were enjoying a period of revitalization so that by the end of the decade sixty-three percent of the nation's population belonged to a church.[3] Jay Dolan chronicles the numerical impact of this growth on the church's infrastructure:

> Across the country four to five new churches opened each week. By 1959 more than four million children attended Catholic elementary schools, more than twice the number in 1945. The archdiocese of Chicago alone built 75 new elementary schools at the cost of $85 million over the course of eighteen years, 1939-58. The number of Catholic high schools was also on the rise. The 1950s was also a decade of intense interest in religious life. More than 21,000 women entered the convent in the 1950s. Seminaries were forced to expand as record numbers of young men chose to study for the priesthood. The number of priests increased 25 percent, reaching an all-time high of 53,746 in 1960.[4]

Such growth demanded strong leadership from the hierarchy and Dolan acknowledges that it was available. "A new breed of bishops emerged to guide the church in the post-war period. ... Educated and articulate, they became spokesmen for the church in their city and region."[5] During a time of rapid turnover of bishops in the dioceses in which the Sisters of Providence operated schools, they had the good fortune to work with several such bishops. In St. Louis, Archbishop Ritter (elevated to Cardinal in 1960) not only recruited the Congregation to staff two new schools, but occasionally stopped by to visit. In Chicago, when Cardinal Samuel Stritch was appointed the first American prelate to serve in the Curia, the scholarly Archbishop Albert Meyer succeeded him in September 1958 and was elevated to the rank of Cardinal in December 1959.

The church in the Midwest saw many changes during the fifties. The growth of the Chicago metropolitan area had been so explosive that in 1948 the seven-county area to the west and south was split off to form the Diocese of Joliet. Rev. Martin McNamara, pastor of Sister of Providence-staffed St. Francis Xavier in Wilmette, was named its first bishop. In 1956 upon the death of the long-serving and much revered Bishop John

Francis Noll, his auxiliary, Bishop Leo Pursley, was named Bishop of Fort Wayne and was installed February 26, 1957. At that same time the growth of the church in the northwest corner of Indiana led to the splitting off of the four industrial counties on the outskirts of Chicago from the Fort Wayne Diocese to create the diocese of Gary on December 29, 1956, with Bishop Andrew Grutka as its first bishop. Upon the 1957 death of Bishop John Bennett in Lafayette, his multi-talented auxiliary, Bishop John Carberry, began nine years of active leadership in that diocese.[6] With the August 1959 installation of the energetic Bishop John Baptist Franz to the diocese of Peoria, Illinois, the historic Galesburg mission could expect changes.

Beyond the American episcopacy, recent events had drawn the council's attention to the Roman hierarchy. Following the December 1957 death of Cardinal Piazza, the Cardinal Ponente for Mother Theodore's canonization cause, Mother Gertrude Clare received notification the following April that Cardinal A. Gaetano Cicognani, prefect of the Sacred Congregation of Rites, would replace him in that role. Pope Pius XII had become beloved for his initiatives to support religious women, and his poor health became a cause of concern when a long period of illness began in 1954. The ringing of the toll announced the news of his death to the campus on October 9, 1958. The entire community, including the College students in caps and gowns, mourned his passing at a solemn funeral Mass, and the toll was rung after the Angelus for nine days. On October 28 the conclave elected the Cardinal Patriarch of Venice, Angelo Roncalli, to succeed him as Pope John XXIII. Only three months later the seventy-seven-year-old new pope amazed the world by calling an ecumenical council, an event which would have profound effects on the Congregation.

While the sisters were simply spectators of these events on the world stage, their pontifical status required sending a statistical report of Congregation affairs to the Sacred Congregation for Religious every five years. After review of the 1950-1955 report, officials from that office wrote to suggest that the superior general and council should "consider the division of the Community into Provinces and that this matter be taken up with the Congregation of Religious."[7] The recommendation was regarded as "a matter for prayer," but was tabled in favor of more pressing events until the next General Chapter.

Visit of the Apostolic Delegate

Although a congregation located in a tiny Indiana village would not normally have much contact with the hierarchy in Rome, 1954 would prove an exception to that supposition. When Mother Gertrude Clare learned that the apostolic delegate to the United States, Archbishop Amleto Giovanni Cicognani, planned to visit St. Meinrad Archabbey on the occasion of its centenary, she extended an invitation to him through Archbishop Schulte to visit Saint Mary-of-the-Woods as well. The party arrived in the evening of October 14, 1954, and were welcomed by the postulants in the novitiate. Then, as the council minutes record, "Mother and the Superiors enjoyed a delightful informal visit with the two Archbishops."[8] After visiting the Church and the Blessed Sacrament Chapel, the archbishops and their two priest-secretaries retired to the priests' house.

Archbishop Cicognani celebrated the 6:30 a.m. community Mass the following morning, with the College girls in caps and gowns joining the sisters, novices, postulants and candidates as the novices' choir sang. At nine o'clock the novices welcomed the visitors with song to a brief program in the community room while Sister Mary Ruth Lucey recorded the event with a movie camera. Sister Rose Angela had composed an address which was read by Sister Mary Joseph Pomeroy. This was followed by a musical program with a violin and harp ensemble and a soloist, and the program was closed with a group of novices and postulants singing the "Ave Maria." Archbishop Cicognani then spoke, commending the contributions of the Congregation to education, noting the participation of the College students at Mass that morning. Having inquired about the bell rung at 9:00 a.m. and learning of the prayer of Reunion said then, he invited the sisters to join with the Holy Father in praying for the reunion of the whole world in Christ. He next went to the Conservatory to meet the College student body, then toured the campus and won the hearts of all by declaring a free day from classes.

Adapting the Educational Mission

Immaculata Improvements

One of the first items to be considered by the newly elected council was carrying out major improvements at Immaculata in Washington, D.C. Built in 1905 with a chapel added in 1918, the school had established an excellent reputation not only as a girls' academy but also as a private school for younger girls at Dunblane Hall on the same property. Over the years the curriculum was expanded to include college level courses to the point that, in 1937, the post-secondary section was accredited as a junior college.[9]

Over the years the convent had provided hospitality for sister-students at Catholic University, and, after Maryhurst was sold in 1949, it became the gathering place for the sisters in the Mideast. With the increase in population during the war years and the District being given its own bishop, Most Rev. Patrick O'Boyle, in 1948, the time was ripe for expansion. In September 1954 Sisters Rose Genevieve Flaherty and Francis Raphael Donlon flew to Washington to confer about plans for new buildings to include classrooms, dormitory, dining hall, gymnasium and auditorium. Motherhouse Superintendent of Grounds Bernard Bisch made several trips to confer and make recommendations.

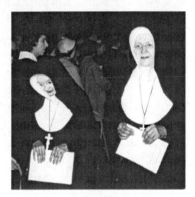

Mother Gertrude Clare and Sister Mary Joan at the Immaculata celebration.

By April 1955 loans had been negotiated and ground was broken, and in December Mother Gertrude Clare attended the laying of the cornerstone presided over by the apostolic delegate, Archbishop A.G. Cicognani. The dedication of the new buildings on October 7, 1956, was a gala affair with newly appointed superior Sister Mary Joan Kirchner hosting alumnae and dignitaries celebrating the golden anniversary of the school as well. Commenting on the new additions, Marian Hall (the college classroom and residence hall), Loretto Hall (the dining hall, kitchen, science laboratories, library and art department), and Regina Hall's auditorium and gymnasium, Mother Gertrude Clare declared that "they far surpass our expectations."[10]

Nearby properties would also require attention since the house across from Immaculata, formerly called Loretto, was no longer needed. Over subsequent years appraisals and offers culminated in the March 1960 sale of the property. A 1959 routine fire department inspection of the Dunblane building revealed that it had deteriorated to the point that it was unsuitable for residential occupation. Because the cost of renovation was prohibitive, it was decided to retain the small grade school for day students only.

A Music Education Initiative

When Sister Mary Lourdes Mackey had been appointed supervisor of music in 1938, she had drawn on her own experience as a teacher in the Chicago public schools prior to entering the Congregation, as well as her own musical studies. Over the years it had become apparent that classroom teachers needed better teaching materials in order to provide more than mere rote singing. During her school visits and summer session courses she was able to identify music teachers with a special gift for classroom music. Through her attendance and participation in national music organizations she realized that Catholic schools throughout the country would benefit from

Sisters Mary Canice (Beatrice) Hoberg, Brendan Harvey and Mary Lourdes Mackey work on the To God Through Music *course.*

music books which incorporated liturgical music. The Gregorian Institute of America was willing to publish such a course of study.

With encouragement and support from the council, Sister Mary Lourdes drew up a master plan to include not only hymns, chants and songs, but also ear training, music theory, rhythm and music appreciation. Sisters Mary Canice (Beatrice) Hoberg and Brendan Harvey were named to assist her by writing songs and testing them in their classrooms, giving up their vacations to come to the motherhouse to work on the series. Other sisters contributed artwork and musical pieces. In addition to student books, teacher editions were supplemented with a piano book, recordings and filmstrips. The grade one materials were published in 1953, with other grades following until the grade eight materials completed the entire course of study in 1959. The series, entitled *To God Through Music*, proved extremely popular, and it was adopted by many dioceses. Throughout the decade and into the sixties Sister of Providence music teachers were invited to present workshops all over the country.

Secondary Schools

A major topic of discussion at the 1954 General Chapter had been the situation of the secondary schools. Several schools had been in operation for more than one hundred years, with others having been merged to form diocesan high schools. Staffing was an ongoing challenge since teachers in the small high schools needed to be able to teach across several disciplines and would be sharing convent life with sisters in attached grade schools. Table 8 on the following pages illustrates the situation faced by the council as they prepared the annual Obedience List, the assignment for each of the approximately 1,400 sisters under their charge. As they gathered around the council table almost daily during the hot summer days to exchange information and suggestions regarding each sister's placement, the recommendation regarding a possible subdivision into provinces likely had a strong appeal.

Demographic Changes at Older Institutions

As the council members conducted their visitations, several realities became apparent. While new parishes were opening in the suburbs, at the same time parishes in the central city

TABLE 8: *High schools staffed by Sisters of Providence in 1954*

City	State	Institution	Founded (merged)	Type[a]	Enrollment[b]	SP faculty[c]	
						High school only	Grade school combination
Vincennes	IN	St. Rose Academy	1843	SP girls	136		18
Terre Haute	IN	Schulte	1843 (1953)	D co-ed	390	8	
Fort Wayne	IN	Central Catholic	1846 (1938)	D co-ed	1268	28	
Evansville	IN	Reitz Memorial	1853 (1925)	D co-inst	700	13	
Washington	IN	St. Simon Academy	1857	SP girls	—		24
Indiana-polis	IN	St. John Academy	1859	SP girls	187		17
Galesburg	IL	Corpus Christi	1878 (1945)	D co-ed	166	8	
Chelsea	MA	St. Rose Academy	1889	P girls	—		29
Indiana-polis	IN	St. Agnes Academy	1893	SP girls	361		28
Chicago	IL	St. Columbkille	1899	SP girls	—	17	
Washington	DC	Immaculata	1905	SP girls	125		24
Evanston	IL	Marywood	1915	SP girls	376	27	

City	State	Institution	Founded (merged)	Type	Enrollment	SP faculty	
						High school only	Grade school combination
Joliet	IL	Providence High School	1918	P girls	150	11	
Indiana-polis	IN	Ladywood	1926	SP girls	55	12	
Chicago	IL	Providence High School	1929	SP girls	1183	51	
SMW	IN	Aspirancy	1930	SP girls	60	7	
Anaheim	CA	Marywood	1934	SP girls	119	9	
Oklahoma City	OK	Bishop McGuiness	1950	D co-ed	—	2	
Clarksville	IN	Providence High School	1951	SP/D co-ed	450	14	
Robstown	TX	St. John High School	1951	P co-ed	60		8

ᵃ D = Diocese, P = Parish, SP = Sisters of Providence.
ᵇ Dash indicates enrollment figures are not available.
ᶜ Approximate, due to multiple duties of resident Sisters of Providence.

were losing population and enrollment. Several of the oldest schools staffed by the Sisters of Providence were acutely affected, both from the changing conditions of the neighborhood and also from the deteriorating conditions of the once proud buildings. The importance of the second factor riveted the attention of the entire nation on December 1, 1958, with news that ninety-two children and three Sisters of Charity of the Blessed Virgin Mary had perished in a tragic fire at Our Lady of the Angels School in Chicago.[11] As would be expected, this heartbreaking event motivated both school administrators and fire departments to immediately increase their scrutiny of school building safety.

After Sister Frances Alma McManus, principal and superior at Marywood, Anaheim, came to the motherhouse in March 1959 to discuss the situation there, the council summarized the current state of affairs:

> As in the case of our high schools in Vincennes, Joliet, and St. John's, Indianapolis, also Providence High School, Chicago, expensive and extensive repairs and changes are called for at Anaheim by fire officials. At the same time, these high schools (with the exception of St. Rose) are in neighborhoods that have changed radically in the past twenty years.[12]

Let us consider each of these situations.

St. John, Indianapolis

Over the years since its establishment in 1859 the location of St. John Academy in downtown Indianapolis near the train station had provided a convenient hub of transfer for the comings and goings of the community. The school was known for making available a stream of qualified graduates to serve area businesses, while many graduates followed a vocation to the sisterhood. However, when Archbishop Schulte met with Mother Gertrude Clare in May 1958, he brought up the sad fact that the neighborhood had changed significantly and that he favored the closing of St. John in favor of building a coeducational high school to serve a wider area. She could only agree. The diarist records the situation:

> But now, alas, time and residential problems have brought to the Sisters of Providence and to the reverend administrators of the archdiocese the sad conviction that the work of the present building has been finished and that it must close. Economic reasons are cruel and unanswerable, but they must be faced.

The steady decline in the number of families in St. John's parish, and the consequent falling off of enrollment in the school have made it impossible to maintain Saint John's Academy and grade school any longer.[13]

Negotiations went forward, and on April 14, 1959, Mother Gertrude Clare went by car to Indianapolis to meet with the sisters and give in person the news that the school would close in June.

Providence High School, Chicago

A similar situation existed in Chicago where several long-established Sister of Providence schools were greatly affected by changing circumstances. When she was appointed principal at Our Lady of Sorrows in 1958, Sister Regina Cecile Ryan was carrying on a seventy-one year tradition of partnering with the Servite community to provide Catholic education in the neighborhood. Providence High School had its beginnings at this site, and it was located there until 1929 when the Congregation cooperated with the Archdiocese of Chicago to construct a state-of-the-art building to serve the area as a regional high school. Little did Sister Regina Cecile realize the sweeping changes she would soon witness, as she later recalled in the parlance of the day:

> During the first scholastic year, 1958-59, all progressed rather normally. In the Spring, however, rumbles of change were heard in the pressure, and scare-tactics, put upon long time homeowners by Real Estate agents, "to sell for cash," or get nothing later—literally driving them from their life-long homes, and devoted ties to their Parish. The agents in turn sold them to the Colored and Puerto Ricans for double the price they paid for the properties.

> The following year, 1959-60, saw the beginning of the influx of Colored and Puerto Rican residents. This necessitated immediate curriculum and discipline adjustments. During the following year every effort was made to meet the challenge of these adjustments, using apostolic means to promote moral standards; and the use of efficient academic methods geared to the spiritual and mental needs of these newly integrated races.[14]

Because Providence High School was such a short distance from Our Lady of Sorrows, the trickling away of the solid Catholic families together with the unwillingness of parents to allow their daughters to ride the bus to school sent enrollment into an alarmingly downward trend. In April 1959 Sisters Francis Joseph Elbreg and Rose Genevieve met with Archbishop Meyer to discuss the future status of Providence as a regional high school and also to reiterate an earlier request for a new high school in a suburban area.

Mindful of the longstanding contribution of the Congregation, Chicago's superintendent of schools, Msgr. William McManus, followed up by coming to Saint Mary-of-the-Woods to meet with the council and High School Visitor Sister Mary Corona Sullivan on February 14, 1960, to discuss plans for the educational system in the Catholic schools of the archdiocese.[15] Adjustments to the regional system would allocate grade schools as feeder schools to specific high schools, thus benefiting Providence. To care for those families moving to the suburbs, plans were underway to construct new high schools, including one for girls at 8000 Belmont Avenue in suburban River Grove. The council regarded this idea as favorable and agreed to accept the offer, along with the staffing of two grade schools.[16] While the plan provided welcome relief regarding the future, the sisters at Providence were not surprised at the negative reaction from parents in the city. Many whose daughters could not be accommodated at their preferred school were recommended to Providence, but instead they choose to enroll in another Catholic school or a public school. After a peak enrollment of 1,171 during the 1955-1956 school year, a steady decline in applicants prompted superior Sister Marie Clarice Toomey to express to the council in 1959 the need of attention to the needs of Providence High School.[17] We will return to the subsequent fortunes of both these schools in chapter 14.

St. Rose, Vincennes

A much more stable neighborhood situation existed in Vincennes in the Diocese of Evansville, where the second-oldest of the Sister of Providence schools, St. Rose Academy, had been cooperating with the Christian Brothers who in 1947 had come to re-open a diocesan boys' school nearby. Repairs were badly needed in the 1884 building. However, the financial situation was complicated by the fact that, while parents had to pay tuition for their girls at St. Rose, parents of boys did not have to pay tuition because parishes of the vicariate supported the boys' Central Catholic School. On March 2, 1958, two Vincennes pastors came to Saint Mary-of-the-Woods to meet with Mother Gertrude Clare, and, although she was willing to assist with the cost of upgrading the building, she made the point that a more equitable policy was needed. In March of the following year Sisters Francis Joseph and Francis Raphael went to Evansville for a special meeting with Bishop Henry Joseph Grimmelsman to discuss the situation. Bishop Grimmelsman was not in favor of coeducation and decided the best course of action would be to purchase a parcel of adjacent land and build a new wing, with only absolutely necessary repairs being made to the old building.[18] With many different points of view about the best solution, planning and discussion would continue until 1962.

Providence High School, Joliet

By the mid-fifties, the small parish-based Providence High School in the city of Joliet was no longer adequate due to both the increased population of the area and the extreme deterioration of the old building. Considering the safety of the sisters, the council considered withdrawing from the school, and matters came to a head when the fire department condemned the building in 1959. Sisters Francis Joseph and Catherine Celine Brocksmith went to Joliet to meet with Bishop McNamara, and plans were worked out for a temporary location at the elementary school building in St. Mary Nativity Parish until such time as a new diocesan co-institutional high school could be financed and constructed, with the Sisters of Providence invited to form part of the faculty.

Marywood, Anaheim

In 1958 principal Sister Frances Alma McManus notified Mother Gertrude Clare that due to the southward sprawl of Los Angeles, the consequent need for regional planning had prompted the archdiocesan school office to offer assistance in relocating and expanding Marywood, Anaheim. She flew to the motherhouse in March 1959 to explain the somewhat desperate state of affairs posed by the deteriorating conditions in the aging building. Following a visitation of the California schools and a study of the situation, in the following October Sisters Rose Angela and Francis Raphael visited the chancery to discuss the possibility of obtaining financial assistance for relocating to another property and building an entire new facility.

Other High Schools

When Providence High School in Clarksville had opened in 1951, it was with the understanding that, depending on enrollment and financing, additional construction would be necessary. In April 1958, Sisters Francis Raphael and Robert Kiley, together with Superintendent of Grounds Bernard Bisch, made several trips to consult with the architects about an addition, and they in turn met with the council. Meanwhile Archbishop Schulte consulted with the priests of the deanery to arrange partial financing, and on June 24, 1958, ground was broken for ten classrooms as well as shops for the boys. Meanwhile the Diocese of Peoria had plans underway to provide new facilities for Corpus Christi High School in Galesburg.

Parish Elementary Schools

As bishops and priests from the dioceses with long-established ties to the Sisters of Providence broke ground for new parishes to accommodate their upwardly mobile Catholic population, it was usually a combination church/school building that was first erected. Naturally they turned to the sisters they knew to staff those schools. The pattern of accepting new schools during Mother Marie Helene's term as described in Chapter 9 would continue unabated. Staffing in combination with lay teachers was rapidly becoming the norm as bishops accepted the ratio concept. However, the standard adopted in 1955 by the Archdiocese of Indianapolis of a ratio of six sisters to one lay teacher would soon prove unworkable and would require considerable one-on-one negotiation with individual pastors. Because the new houses could be opened with fewer sisters, more schools could be accepted. Since each house was governed by a local superior, more young sisters with fewer years of experience were appointed to that role, and they found themselves having to adapt the horarium to the makeshift convents and suburban parish schedules.

Indianapolis Archdiocese

The growth which took place in the Archdiocese of Indianapolis could serve as a textbook example of the national demographic, with new parishes being established in a ring around the existing city limits while a long-time establishment in the city center was abandoned. We have seen that the downtown St. John Academy had been closed in 1959. In suburban areas, construction typically began with combination church/school buildings and small enrollments likely to grow. Three or four sisters were sufficient for the new establishments since lay teachers would be expected to round out the faculty. As the annual clergy retreat was held at Saint Mary-of-the-Woods, priests assigned to these new parishes often took the opportunity to visit Mother Gertrude Clare's office in Tile Hall and describe their plans in glowing terms as they put in their request for sisters. During the fifties a ring of small Sister of Providence missions soon formed around the city.

Rev. Daniel Nolan, formerly an assistant chaplain and college instructor at Saint Mary-of-the-Woods, was assigned to open St. Michael in Greenfield, a rural area northeast of Indianapolis with a relatively small percentage of Catholics, but with easy access from neighboring towns. Three sisters were welcomed in a well-provisioned convent and opened school in September 1954 with an enrollment of 109 pupils in grades one through eight. The following year, on the west side in the town of Brownsburg, Rev. Edward Bauer, brother of Sister Gertrude Marian, welcomed three sisters to St. Malachy, even vacating his residence and renovating it as a convent. Also in 1955, south of the city in the town of Greenwood in Johnson County, three sisters opened Our Lady of the Greenwood. Since many of the children were not Catholic, the sisters felt they were in missionary territory. This impression was reinforced by the fact that they had to commute from St. John Academy for several weeks. Even after they were able to move to Our Lady of Greenwood, their pupils made do with folding chairs until their desks arrived, while the sisters quarters consisted of an office converted to serve as a kitchen with a classroom subdivided to form a community room and bedrooms.

By 1955, at the extreme east of the city, the relatively new Holy Spirit Parish was already being subdivided. Because the parishioners living in the area designated for the new parish used a renovated stable for their first church, it was appropriately named Nativity of Our Lord Jesus Christ. Pastor Rev. Louis Gootee had promised Mother Gertrude Clare he would retrofit his home for the convent and did indeed live in a trailer until the rectory could be built. Three sisters opened the very modern school in September 1955. Similarly, St. Jude Parish was created as an offshoot from several rapidly growing parishes, requiring four sisters when the school opened in September 1959 with 340 pupils. A home was purchased to serve as a convent on a temporary basis, since the large property was also the site of construction for the new coeducational Chartrand High School, but until it was available, the sisters lived at St. Patrick for a short while. Another new parish, St. Matthew, did not have a convent when the school opened in September 1958, but it was sufficiently proximate to Ladywood that the five sisters were able to commute.

In the southern part of the archdiocese, the New Albany area across the Ohio River from Louisville was experiencing continued growth so Mother Marie Helene had promised sisters to staff Holy Family Parish. A portion of the combination church/school building was designed as a temporary convent, and four sisters welcomed 188 students when it opened on September 7, 1954.

Evansville Diocese

Further south along the winding Ohio River in the Diocese of Evansville, the Congregation opened schools in three newly created parishes. In the city of Evansville three sisters took up their residence in two classrooms when Corpus Christi School opened in 1957. Two years later, by reassigning one sister from each of the other three Evansville schools, the Congregation was able to open Good Shepherd School to 224 pupils, with three sisters and three lay teachers forming the faculty. The sisters commuted from St. John, Newburgh, until temporary quarters in three classrooms could be fitted out as a temporary convent. The city of Jasper had grown to the point that yet another parish was needed, but construction of Precious Blood School lagged, so when the school opened in September 1957 classes began in the basement. By October the pupils could move upstairs and the three sisters commuting from St. Joseph moved to their own convent.

Archdiocese of St. Louis

One of the first requests to come to Mother Gertrude Clare after her election came not from a pastor but from the former ordinary of Indianapolis, Archbishop Joseph Ritter, now heading the neighboring Archdiocese of St. Louis. Although previous requests had been refused, congratulating his old friend of many years on her election as superior general was the perfect occasion for him to renew the invitation. Perhaps Mother Gertrude Clare recalled the adventure of her own early mission experience as the train passed through St. Louis en route to Omaha and felt it was once again time to look westward, but certainly the fact that the new parish was to be named Our Lady of Providence was a major inducement. Clearly the pastor and parishioners were delighted, bringing the plans for the school and convent to Saint Mary-of-the-Woods for council approval and while there, ordering pictures of Our Lady of Providence for every home in the parish. When the four sisters arrived at the train station in August 1955, they were met by a delegation of alumnae from Saint Mary-of-the-Woods College as an escort to their new home in the lovely residential section of Grantwood. Their arrival prompted an immediate request from nearby Annunziata Parish, but it could not be accepted until two years later when the requisite number of three sisters for a local community arrived. Two were assigned for the fifty-nine-pupil, grades one-through-four school, while the third sister, a music teacher, divided her time between Our Lady of Providence and Annunziata.

Peoria Diocese

The Congregation had strong ties to Galesburg, having staffed St. Joseph since 1878, and having had two superiors general who were born there: Mothers Mary Raphael and the recently deceased and much loved Mother Marie Helene. When Immaculate Heart Parish was created in 1956, the school was accepted for the following year, with the plan to take some sisters from St. Joseph School. Three sisters and five lay teachers were required for the large enrollment in the new building situated on a large thirty-acre tract donated for the plant. Superintendent of Schools Father Logan had long-range plans for additional use of the tract, and in April 1960 he invited the local superiors to accompany him to the motherhouse to explain to the council the diocese's intention to construct a new high school on the site to replace Corpus Christi High School, as well as a convent for the sisters.

Improved Facilities

Meanwhile, growth in various parts of the country led to developments which benefited Sisters of Providence. In November 1956, St. John in Whiting, Indiana, completed a new parish unit which included new schoolrooms and a gym. In January 1958, the parishioners at St. Charles in Bloomington, Indiana, proudly dedicated their new school and convent. With the 1957 completion of a new bridge linking Lady Isle with the New Hampshire mainland, access was greatly improved. The Ladywood property in Indianapolis was a frequent topic on the council agenda due to negotiations with Marion County for purchase of fifteen acres in order to put a road through the property, with a welcome payment to the Congregation of $90,500 concluded in 1958. Additional income was realized with rental of a portion of the land to a farmer in 1960.

Continuing Efforts at Racial Integration

When Bishop Vincent Waters, ordinary of the Raleigh Diocese in North Carolina, approached Mother in January 1955 with a request to open another school in his sprawling statewide diocese, the pressure of honoring promises for opening six other establishments in two years prompted an immediate refusal. However, Bishop Waters had already gained considerable attention for his 1953 order to integrate all the parishes and schools of the diocese and for his willingness to face down resistant congregations. In Fayetteville he saw a unique opportunity to firmly establish a policy of integration.

In 1939 The Oblates of Mary Immaculate had responded to the invitation of several black Catholic families to establish St. Ann Parish in Fayetteville, saying Mass in a barbershop until, with the sponsorship of Cardinal Cushing, the people of a Boston parish provided funds to build a church in 1940.[19] Coming from nearby Sister-of-Providence-staffed St. Patrick's, the sisters helped train the choir and prepare children for the sacraments. With the growth of neighboring Fort Bragg and the gradual desegregation of the army following President Truman's executive order in 1948, the parish had grown to the point that a school was needed. The sisters encouraged the pastor, Father William Ryan, to ask for Sisters of Providence. Meanwhile, the 1954 unanimous decision of the Supreme Court declaring that separate educational facilities are inherently unequal gave added impetus to Bishop Water's determination to use this opportunity to establish the first integrated Catholic school in North Carolina.

The bishop pressed his case persuasively, pointing out that with a lay teacher, three sisters would suffice and the sisters could live at the nearby St. Patrick Convent. The council agreed, and three sisters arrived in September 1956 to team with a lay teacher, black parishioner Alice McAllister. Overcrowding at St. Patrick guaranteed that white families who valued Catholic education would send their children to an integrated school, especially since a bus brought those from Fort Bragg. Enrollment in grades one to six started with 102 students but by year's end had risen to 142, with seventh and eighth grades added the next two years.[20] Sister Joann (Joan Margaret) Quinkert recalls those early days:

> Since the convent was 2-3 miles from St. Ann and we did not drive, the pastor or a mother who dropped off her children at St. Patrick's provided transportation. Occasionally we had to ride the bus with the children from Fort Bragg. We took our lunches and ate standing up in the very small kitchen, as we had to hurry out to supervise the children on the playground. ... The bishop was so proud of the school that it was nothing to see him pull up in his car and drop in just to see how things were going and encourage us as he was passing through town.
>
> Of all my teaching experiences, St. Ann's was my favorite. In the Civil Rights Era St. Ann's had a spirit of peace. It was like integration in reverse where an all black parish opened its doors and welcomed all. In the school the children didn't seem to see color. The smallness in the beginning made for a family-like feeling and spirit.[21]

The College

The growth and economic advancement of the Catholic population was reflected in an increased enrollment at Saint Mary-of-the-Woods College. As early as 1947 more than 400 young women had applied, with 147 freshmen and seven upper class students being accepted.[22] To ensure continued strong leadership, the first item of business taken up by the newly elected council was the need for a more independent administration of the College. As explained in Chapter 3, the general superior held the title of president of the College but the Congregation actually exercised its oversight of the College through the Board of Trustees (composed of council members and College administrators). One aspect of Mother Gertrude Clare's duties during her years as assistant had been to make decisions regarding the College in her capacity as a member of the College Board of Trustees. Now, as general superior, it seemed opportune for her to relinquish the title of president in favor of someone with more educational experience, a move which took place at the very first meeting of her new council on May 6, 1954.[23] Sister Francis Joseph Elbreg, director of education, was named president of the College and Sister Eugenia Logan, high school visitor and longtime dean, was named vice-president.[24] In practice, these titles were honorific since the actual day-to-day administration continued to be the responsibility of the dean with the assistance of sisters whose faculty appointments included administrative duties. In her history of the College, Tracy Schier remarks:

> With Sister Marie Perpetua as dean, and Sister Mary Joan in the position of dean of women, the administration was in place for several more years of College growth. As in past years, the person who held the office of dean was the most visible administrator. ... In contrast to the many years when the Superior General held the title of president and was essentially invisible in that office, Sister Marie Perpetua set a tone that assisted Saint Mary-of-the-Woods in its efforts to achieve visibility and to be in the forefront in the Catholic higher education of women.[25]

The position of College secretary included responsibility for admissions and public relations, and with Sister Rose Angela's election to the council, Sister Catherine Joseph Wilcox was named to this office.[26] By September 1957 the roster reported an upward-trending enrollment of 69 juniors, 108 sophomores and 155 freshmen.[27] To provide funds for improvements which would relieve pressure on the existing facilities, Sister Mary Joseph Pomeroy was appointed director of development. To assist with this increasingly significant role, a change was made in a long-standing advisory group, as noted on October 4, 1958, in the community Diary:

> The first meeting of the reorganized Board of Lay Trustees of the College met today in the college library. The board increased its numbers to 20 lay and 4 ex-officio members. The latter are: Reverend Mother, Sisters Francis Joseph [president of the College], Francis Raphael [treasurer general] and Mary Joseph. In

the years since 1926 this Board of Lay Trustees has given counsel regarding investments and helped to administer the College Endowment Fund. The members and their wives were guests of the Community at a luncheon preceding the meeting.[28]

The curriculum continued to adapt to prepare graduates for careers. As early as 1928 the College had been the first Catholic women's college to establish a journalism department, using its range of publications to provide hands-on experience and cooperating with the speech and drama department to work with Terre Haute radio stations to produce shows. The art and music departments offered tracks leading to teaching certificates in those fields, and English and history majors could also qualify for secondary teaching certificates. Schier notes a significant addition for career preparation:

> Another addition during these years, one that instituted what was to be one of the College's most popular majors, was elementary education. For many years the sequence of courses leading to elementary teaching certificates had been available for the novices and Sisters in the Juniorate. Because of many requests from lay students, it was decided in 1949 to open these classes to young women wishing to prepare for elementary teaching.[29]

In 1957 the Alumnae Association was active in providing funding for two major improvements. Auditorium seating in the Conservatory was completely replaced with "self-rising seats of nylon pile, bisque in color with a touch of gold thread,"[30] expanding the auditorium's capacity to 724. A $25,000 gift from Eileen O'Shaughnessy, Class of 1935, and a member of the Association's Board of Directors, made possible a complete makeover for the dining room, including new tables and chairs as well as chinaware and draperies. Now able to accommodate 500 diners, the spacious room was renamed in her honor. Newly available government grants made possible the installation of a language lab in Guerin Hall in 1959.

The Taiwan Mission

Despite the sea changes in Catholic education underway in the United States, it was in the foreign mission where the most amazing transformations were taking place as the former China mission sank new roots in Taiwan. In December 1948,

Sister Marie Gratia Luking had been the first American missionary to simply pick up and move the mission from soon-to-be Communist China and establish a Catholic educational presence on the island in the city of Taichung.[31] When Nationalist leader Chiang Kai-Chek evacuated China and moved his government to Taipei a year later, more than a million refugees followed him from mainland China. Their arrival greatly increased tensions between the native Taiwanese, who were ready for independence after Japanese occupation and the newcomers who expected to set up a China-in-exile government. By now accustomed to governing in a dictatorial mode, Chiang suppressed all political opposition from the native Taiwanese populace.[32] Among the refugees were many other Catholic missionaries fleeing the Communists, so the gradual establishment of a church hierarchy along with other new missions and schools lessened the sisters' isolation and enabled Sister Marie Gratia to slowly build up the Taichung compound.

Due to this ongoing political unrest, Sister Marie Gratia had advised the council that the conditions in Taiwan were still too unsettled for the superiors to visit. Instead she sent films showing the new buildings at Taichung: the school building called Providence Hall and the dormitory building and sisters' quarters called Franey Hall, both of which had been in use since February 1954. Nonetheless, the council felt it was important to have first-hand information to guide their decisions regarding the fledgling mission's future. Sisters Marie Gratia, Mary Liguori Hartigan and Ann Colette Wolf had not been home for years, and Sister St. Francis Schultz had returned to Taiwan in 1953 after a year in the States, as had Sisters Carmel Baker, Agnes Joan Li and Bernadette Ma in 1952 after a four-year hiatus. With regular air transportation now available, a fixed term of five years seemed advisable.

A novice, Sister Donna Marie Fu, the first Chinese sister accepted into the novitiate since 1931, had arrived at the motherhouse in 1953 to begin her formation. In addition, there were the Providence Sister-Catechists to consider. What was the responsibility for them? After consulting with the apostolic delegate and being advised that new candidates should be accepted, it seemed more important than ever to visit before establishing a novitiate for them on the island. By 1954 the situation had stabilized to the point that a visitation was possible.

Sisters Francis Joseph and Eugenia were delegated to visit and made the trip via plane, arriving on November 19, 1954, in Taipei where they were met by Sisters Marie Gratia and Carmel. They had arranged a visit with the exiled internuncio, Archbishop Anthony Ribera, who expressed warm appreciation for Sister Marie Gratia's pioneering education efforts on the island. The train trip to Taichung afforded views of the beautiful countryside, and their first view of the school compound inspired even more admiration for Sister Marie Gratia's careful planning and collaboration with the hierarchy. Despite the overcrowded conditions in Franey Hall, with not only ninety-six boarders but also eight Sisters of Providence and five Providence Sister-Catechists in "convent" quarters in the attic, the visitors noted that, "Almost immediately we found ourselves in community routine."[33]

The next day, when they began their visitation at Providence School and observed more than 200 day students join the boarders, the visitors described how they were introduced to a completely different educational experience: "It was quite a sight to see Sister St. Francis addressing the school gathered on the plaza, first in Chinese, and then in English, giving out the 'orders for the day.'"[34] As they visited the classes, they learned much about how the teaching methods employed in Chinese schools differed from those to which they were accustomed. It became apparent that the sisters were seriously overextended. In addition to classes taught in English for the high school and junior college sections, they also staffed a small elementary school for American children of the United States Military Advisory and Assistance Group (MAAG). Each of the visitors held meetings with the teachers to discuss their methods and teaching load. They also visited the kindergarten conducted by the Providence Sister-Catechists and their Morning Star Eye Clinic, noting: "We admired these Sisters very much. They are quiet, gentle, and well-trained in the religious life."[35]

Bishop-elect William Kupfer, MM,[36] who had provided funds to finance purchase of part of the land for the compound, paid a visit, explaining that he came often to consult Sister Marie Gratia because, "She has almost thirty-five years of suffering and service to her credit."[37]

During their visit, in addition to stops at the new bishop's house, the Ministry of Foreign Affairs and the Jesuit house, they were treated to an excursion to scenic Sun Moon Lake. The visit certainly yielded the desired twofold effect of having the missionaries feel less isolated and the superiors much more informed about the circumstances of daily life on the Chinese mission. The following July a second Chinese postulant, Mary Lee, who had come into contact with the Sisters of Providence while attending Providence English College, arrived at the motherhouse to begin formation. She was one of a large family that had converted to Catholicism in China and come to Taiwan in 1948.

The growth of the school had been such that advanced junior college level courses were begun. Discussions ensued as to whether or not to register with the government to accredit the program so students who completed the course of study would be able to continue in government schools. Certainly this would be an advantage to their students, but adopting this course of action would mean that the school could no longer offer religion as a course. Another major change would be the government's requirement of naming a qualified native Chinese to the office of president. Consultation with Bishop Kupfer, who agreed to appoint Father Joseph Kung as president, led to the decision to discontinue as a secondary school and instead register the school as Providence English College. The sisters would offer inquiry classes outside of regular school hours for girls who wished to study religion. With these changes in place, the official government recognition was given on September 17, 1956. This was truly a banner year for the school, for when Sister Marie Gratia had come to the United States for her Golden Jubilee that summer she had been given a $10,000 donation collected from all the Sister of Providence schools across the country. She used these funds to construct a separate convent building for the sisters.

The following year Sister Marie Gratia Luking requested additional funds to finance building of a second dormitory, Raphael Hall, to house the overflow of boarding students. By 1958 Sister Donna Marie had finished her BS degree and returned to replace Sister Bernadette at Providence English College. At that point the enterprising superior, affectionately nicknamed Kai Hsia (successful builder),[38] wanted to proceed with construction of a novitiate for the Providence Sister-Cat-echists, but due to the debt being incurred for construction of the new novitiate at Saint Mary-of-the-Woods, funds were not available. Again she was advised to seek local funding. Because the Providence Sister-Catechists were attracting vocations, one of their number, Sister Mary Loyola Wen, was appointed mistress of novices. Encouraged by the nuncio, Sister Marie Gratia was successful in raising sufficient money so that by 1959 the novices had a new home.

Cultural Changes

The shifts in American society brought on by prosperity as well as the shifts within the church inevitably brought pressure to bear on the lives of Sisters of Providence. Mother Gertrude Clare's subtle guidance can be detected as the council dealt with decisions regarding longstanding customs. Realizing the pressures felt by local superiors, in September of 1958 she had a private phone installed near her bedroom so that they would be able to reach her at any time.[39] She had the ability to link the concerns of the day to the spiritual underpinnings that had attracted the sisters to their vocation, as we see in her 1956 Christmas circular letter to the community:

> We, like Our Lord in His day, live in the midst of a very worldly world. On all sides, allurements tend to entice us, consciously or unconsciously, to seek self in easy living and in exterior distractions. Many things that a few years ago were practically unknown to us or at least were regarded as luxurious and superfluous, now appear to be almost necessary for our general well-being. In certain respects, and to a certain extent, we must make adaptations to the needs of the times; even our Holy Father has advised us to do so; but in all these adaptations, let us be careful not to lose the spirit of Bethlehem and the spirit of religious life.[40]

Perhaps such exhortations had a special impact because as they were read by the sisters on the missions, the words reawakened memories of the personal bond established during their thirty-day retreat when they had meditated over the conferences Sister Gertrude Clare had so faithfully given. Certainly her own devotion to duty and her gracious demeanor softened the sacrifices often demanded. She was known for her mild manner, and one can almost see her eyes twinkling

as she conveyed to the council the advice received from canonist Rev, Adam Ellis regarding the custom of the sisters placing
their hands within their wide sleeves while receiving communion: "Since there is no rule, why make one?"[41]

Relaxation Of Customs

Father Ellis was one of a core group of Jesuits who had in
1942 launched the publication of the periodical *Review for Religious* with a twofold purpose: "first, to aid religious in their
personal sanctification; and secondly, to be of some service to
them in carrying on their respective apostolic works."[42] In addition to articles, which gradually came from sisters as well as
male religious, each issue included regular sections on "Book
Reviews," "Questions and Answers," (largely on canonical
topics) and "Decisions of the Holy See of Interest to Religious."
From time to time, a series of articles would follow a single
topic, such as "The Negro Apostolate" in 1944-1945 and
"Founders" in the fifties, which included Sister Eugenia
Logan's piece on Mother Theodore in July 1956. Articles applying knowledge from the emerging field of psychology to
spirituality and religious life became more frequent. Information formerly only of interest to superiors was now widely dis-
seminated as convent subscriptions made copies available to
many sisters. It was inevitable that customs which had been
accepted without question would now come under scrutiny.

Little by little the advantage to educators of more interaction with the world around them was recognized with relaxation of customary strictures. Permission was given to listen to
radio broadcasts of the opera and sports games on Saturday
mornings. Access to television was more restricted but allowed
on special occasions such as President Eisenhower's 1957 inauguration, when a portable set was placed in Providence library, where "reception was splendid and many availed
themselves of the privilege."[43] Long prohibited from eating with
"seculars," the sisters were told that occasions such as faculty
meetings and conventions might be exceptions to this rule. Sisters were more frequently allowed to attend parish functions,
school games and public concerts and to chaperon students,
although chaperoning senior trips was given over to lay teachers. Supervision of CYO-sponsored recreation in the Chicago
parks became a regular summer assignment for sisters who
had completed their studies. Family visits were more frequent

and permissions to travel long distances for events such as parents' golden wedding anniversaries or even a nephew's ordination became more readily available when, as the diarist noted: "The fact was brought up that privileges given to some cannot be refused to others."[44]

Soliciting Sisters' Wishes Regarding the Habit

As we have seen, adaptation of the religious habit was one of the issues which had been raised at the 1952 Notre Dame Congress, with Archbishop Larraona opening the door to petitioning the Congregation for Religious for changes to the religious habit. Due to heat and humidity the sisters in Taiwan had already been dispensed from wearing the cap. Such developments did not escape notice among the Sisters of Providence, as the Diary notes in describing Mother Gertrude Clare's remarks to the sisters during the August 1957 retreat:

> Mother announced that the Sisters would find a slip in their prie-dieux on which after prayerful thought they were to express their opinion as to a change in the cap and neckerchief. Many had spoken to M on this subject, anonymous notes had been left at her place in chapel, her office, etc., and it was decided we would get a community vote in the matter.[45]

In the January 1958 letter circular Mother Gertrude Clare announced that the survey indicated that most favored a change of cap but only a minority felt the neckerchief needed adaptation.[46]

Other areas regarding clothing showed practical adaptation to circumstances. Permission was given for the use of kimono-style bathrobes. At Lady Isle permission was given for roping off a secluded section of beach where sisters could wear swimsuits as a preferable alternative to having them "wade out in a strange assortment of old clothes."[47] Mirrors were allowed in the postulants' and novices' lavatories and a more comfortable collar was adopted for the postulants. The black mantles worn by the two professed sisters and two novices assigned to "the Hour" in the Blessed Sacrament Chapel were dispensed with.

Liturgical Renewal

Another periodical which was influential among the members, particularly those with musical backgrounds, was *Orate Fratres* (later renamed *Worship*), published by the Benedictines at St. John's, Collegeville, to promote liturgical renewal. Because council member Sister Rose Dolores Thuis' three brothers were all Benedictine monks at St. Meinrad, expert advice was readily at hand as various innovations in liturgical practice were introduced. Even more immediately at hand were the highly educated musicians who divided their time between the College and community liturgy. All three, Sisters Cecilia Clare Bocard, Francis Angela Kolb, and Mary Lourdes Mackey, had a deep and abiding interest in liturgy. The 1956 promulgation of new rubrics for the celebration of Holy Week required adaptation of the traditional horarium and were soon followed by other changes.

Since the motherhouse community was long accustomed to devotional processions, the addition of the Palm Sunday procession was not a difficulty. However, arranging for evening services—Holy Thursday Mass at 5:00 p.m., Good Friday liturgy at 3:00 p.m. and the lengthy Easter Vigil celebration at 8:00 p.m.—was indeed challenging. In parishes where the convent was near the church, sisters were given permission to attend the night-time Easter Vigil. That same year Sister Cecilia Clare's request to prepare an English version of the sung Christmas Office was approved. Beginning in Advent 1958, the entire motherhouse community began use of the *Missa Recitata*, responding in English to the prayers of the Mass. Longstanding devotional community practices also underwent revision with the discontinuance of the singing of the Litany of Our Lady prior to High Mass on Sunday and shortening of the time devoted to religious exercises on Retreat Sunday.

Chaplain Rev. Emile J. Goossens was active in promoting the implementation of liturgical directives by incorporating explanatory notes as a part of the services. The 1959 summer session included a "Liturgical Day" with keynote speaker Rev. Stephen Thuis, OSB, giving an address based on Pope Pius XII's Instruction on the Liturgy. The highlight of the day was a pageant-style Mass of the Seventh Century written by liturgical scholar Josef Jungman, SJ. Students from the Cathedral Latin School formed the cast, with the choir directed by Rev. Bernard Head. The program showed the beginnings of present-day ceremonies through a re-enactment of the ancient Roman stational Mass. It was sung entirely in English and included the offertory procession and Communion under both species.[48]

Travel

Like most Americans, the Congregation, with its nation-wide system of schools, found itself gradually adapting to changing patterns of transportation. With increased prosperity, more and more people were choosing the automobile as their preferred choice of transportation not only because of its convenience but also because rationing of tires and gasoline had ended. The prospect of easier inter-city travel only whetted the appetite for owning a car. As early as 1939 studies had been conducted regarding ways to link major metropolitan areas, but when President Eisenhower, drawing from his military experience and appreciation of the German autobahn system, argued forcefully for an interstate highway system, in 1954 Congress enacted the Federal-Aid Highway Act.[49]

Car sales in the decade of the fifties would reach 6,665,800.[50] Two of those cars came into the possession of the Sisters of Providence. In 1955 the pastor at St. Anthony in Gardena, California, purchased a station wagon for the sisters with an offer for the priest to drive them, but this wasn't considered an acceptable arrangement.[51] The Diary records that in May 1957, "Mr. Hartigan of Chicago gave a new Chevrolet to Mother. Later Sister Robert drove it into the garage."[52] Since the habit cap prevented side vision, the sisters did not drive but relied on volunteer parents in parishes or employees in the larger houses where the houses owned cars. Perhaps the potential of increased independence following increased range of vision influenced the sisters' vote on the cap.

Ever since Mother Theodore had negotiated the placement of train connections at Saint Mary-of-the-Woods, the sisters, students and visitors had enjoyed relatively easy access to destinations near and far. In 1899 the New York Central Railroad and the Congregation had jointly financed the construction of the tiny station building just outside the gate. East-west connections were available via the New York Central, which operated the station. The short trip to Terre Haute provided a link to the far-flung Indiana interurban railroad system which had for many years afforded excellent connections to many of the missions, but the interurbans dwindled over the years and completely closed in 1941. For north-south connections, the C and EI (Chicago and Eastern Illinois Railroad) was so familiar that comings and goings were described as "on the Georgian," or "on the Hummingbird."

In the course of time, the Saint Mary-of-the-Woods station had become a "Stops on signal" station.[53] Rumors of the demolition of the station had circulated for some time, causing great concern especially at the College, where Sister Helen Agatha Bourke frequently arranged to have railroad agents set up ticketing desks on the main floor of Le Fer just before Christmas and summer vacations.[54] In May 1953 these fears were confirmed by a visit from an official from the New York Central, prompting the council to engage the Congregation's lawyer to accompany Sisters Francis Raphael and Helen Agatha to appear at a hearing regarding the continuance of the station. The following January a NYC supervisor visited the council to advise writing to the railroad president to preserve the station.[55] The last effort to maintain service took place when Sister Francis Raphael registered a protest in another hearing in June 1957, but in 1958 the service was ended.

One of the responsibilities of the treasurer general was to make the arrangements for large groups of sisters to travel to Saint Mary-of-the-Woods for the summer session, so Sister Francis Raphael turned her attention to the possibility of bus transportation, and in May 1958 the council decided that "the Community will use bus transportation from Chicago for the first time."[56] To complicate travel arrangements even more, on September 28, 1958, different parts of Indiana adopted two different time zones, some moving to Eastern time with others remaining on Central time.

Plane transportation was becoming more common not only for superiors for visitation trips but also for sisters at a distance traveling for family emergencies or even educational conferences. By 1957 it was cheaper for two sisters to fly from Boston than to come by train.[57] In July 1957 Sisters Francis Raphael and Mary Virginia Petty were the first Sisters of Providence to experience jet plane travel to California.[58]

Events at the Motherhouse

Honoring Sister Marie Gratia

The annual Golden Jubilee celebration took on a special significance in 1956 since Sister Marie Gratia was among the celebrants. She had been one of the six original missionaries to depart from Saint Mary-of-the-Woods on September 29, 1920, and this would be the first time she had returned to the motherhouse. Her courage and tenacity in maintaining that mission by managing the strategic exodus of both the Sisters of Providence and the Providence Sister-Catechists and re-founding the China mission in Taiwan had made her somewhat of a celebrity. Hundreds of sisters gathered at the east door of Providence Convent to welcome her and Sister Ann Colette Wolf. The Jubilee Mass had a special solemnity due to the presence of two exiled Chinese bishops—Thomas Cardinal Tien, Archbishop of Peking, and Bishop Joseph Yuen, of Chu-ma-tien, Honan—as well as the recently named bishop of Taichung, Formosa, Most Rev. William Kupfer, MM, who was in the United States to attend the Maryknoll General Chapter.

Because this was the summer for celebrating the French foundation and Mother Theodore's death, Sister Marie Gratia had the opportunity to deepen her community roots, but, like Mother Theodore before her, she had adopted her mission country. During a special mission program in the Conservatory auditorium on July 29, the audience was deeply moved as she and Sister Ann Colette spoke eloquently and personally about their work. They were touched in turn when Sister Mary Joseph announced that the students in the Sister of Providence schools throughout the country had collected a total of $10,000 to support that work. After Sister Marie Gratia enjoyed several weeks of rest and relaxation, a large group accompanied her and Sister Mary Liguori to the Terre Haute airport. In comparison with the very lengthy journeys of old, the trip by plane through St. Louis, Los Angeles, Honolulu, Wake and Guam must have seemed astonishingly rapid, but it was not without drama, as the two barely escaped a typhoon.

Fire at Rosary Hill

An unexpected tragedy occurred on March 18, 1955, when the house on the Congregation property at Rosary Hill, just beyond Saint Mary-of-the-Woods Village, caught fire. The house was the one which had been used briefly as a residence for senior sisters in the twenties and, after being used by workmen for some years, had been completely reconditioned in 1951 before being rented out to two families, the Tevlins and the McKays. Fortunately the children were in school and Mrs.

Fire destroys Rosary Hill residence, March 1955.

Tevlin was outside with the baby when the fire broke out in the early afternoon. She was able to rouse the man who was asleep inside and the fire departments from West Terre Haute and Terre Haute responded quickly. Mother Gertrude Clare and the superiors rushed to the scene only to see the firemen's efforts defeated by the flames. Mother immediately made arrangements for the homeless families to be placed at the residence at the nearby chicken farm and in the Woodland Inn until they could find homes.

As the ruins were examined by the insurance adjusters, it was thought that a curtain had caught fire as it blew over a flame from the gas stove in the kitchen. The damage was so great that there was no thought of rebuilding, and the site was simply cleared. The site itself, purchased in 1908 with an adjacent parcel needed for right-of-way purchased some years later, was extremely valuable to the motherhouse because of the wells there which supplied drinking water.

Training Claretian Sisters as Cooks

An unusual opportunity presented itself to the Congregation in 1956 when the Claretian Sisters of the Immaculate Heart asked if the Sisters of Providence would undertake to train several of their sisters from Argentina, Colombia and Cuba in American ways of cooking. Their congregation had thirty-three houses world-wide, but were only just then establishing a house in the United States. Three sisters arrived at Saint Mary-of-the-Woods on February 16, 1956, with bilingual Sister Mary Christina Cockrell serving as hostess as they settled into their rooms in Foley Hall. One of the sisters worked with Sister Rose

Sister Zita Kidwell demonstrates a coffee service.

Patricia Ward in the College dining room, one with Sister Mary Rosita Thewes in the infirmary and one with Sister Zita Kidwell (pictured) in Providence. In between their work hours, Sister Eugenia provided English lessons during their several months' stay.

Loss of Significant Colleagues

Within two months in 1958 the community lost two long-time and greatly valued employees at the motherhouse. Joseph Sauer, Sr., head of transportation facilities, suffered a heart attack on Easter Sunday, April 6, 1958, while stopping at the garage after Mass for a brief inspection. Superintendent of Grounds Bernard Bisch died of a heart attack on May 4, 1958. With two aunts and a sister (Sister Marion Celeste) as members of the community, he had been especially close to motherhouse operations. In expressing the community's grief Mother Gertrude Clare offered this tribute: "No one knew Saint Mary-of-the-Woods as he did, through its buildings, its lay-out, its possibilities, and no one was more faithful to carry out the directions of Superiors, and to advance ideas that would promote the interests of the place."[59] Fortunately, Bernard's son, Joseph L. Bisch, was well prepared to take on the super-intendent duties.

The following year another great loss occurred with the death of Chaplain Emile J. Goossens. The long-serving chaplain suffered a heart attack in the sacristy while preparing to

Chaplain Rev. Emile Goossens at the novitiate groundbreaking.

distribute Communion to the sick in the infirmary at 6:00 a.m. on September 22, 1959. Father Goossens had an extended association with the Sisters of Providence. He received his early education from them at St. Francis Xavier parish school in Vincennes and, after his ordination, serving at four parishes with Sister-of-Providence-staffed schools in the archdiocese before studying for an MA in history at the Catholic University. When he had been appointed chaplain in 1941, his reputation as "possessed of a hasty and aggressive temperament"[60] preceded him, but over the eighteen years in that capacity, "his punctuality . . . patience, tolerance, cheerful manner, and devotion to the sick brought their own reward."[61] As he frequently substituted in the village church, he became involved in the affairs of the small community and was instrumental in organizing a volunteer fire department for the village. So popular was he among his fellow priests that 109 of them attended his funeral; at his request, he was buried in the community cemetery. Rev. Francis Dooley was appointed to replace him as chaplain and took up his duties on October 4, 1959.

Home Improvements

The Infirmary

By 1955 water from heavy rains had seeped through the uncompleted sun porch section of the fourth floor of the infirmary. Since this floor's original purpose of care for tuberculosis patients was obsolete, architects recommended renovating the space into eight bedrooms to be used for post-operative and very ill patients. Impetus to the plan was provided by the use of a legacy from the family of Sister Mary Alexandrina Heinmann which would offset the major cost of the project.

During the spring and summer the work progressed rapidly and the renovated area was blessed on September 8, 1955. Improvements in the third floor operating room followed.

The following year, when Sister Virginia Ann Worden received her RN, she was assigned to the fourth floor, freeing Sister Dorothy Eileen Howard, RN, to take on more supervisory duties, including the daily check with patients and nurses and making doctors' appointments. She also piloted a project of requiring local superiors to maintain basic health records for the sisters on mission. With Mother Gertrude Clare's election, the council's oversight of the infirmary had shifted from her to First Assistant Sister Rose Angela. In this role, a frequent responsibility was arranging to have sister-nurses serve as companions for sisters going for specialized care at the Mayo Clinic or for sisters whose mental health condition required hospitalization at off-campus institutions.

The Shrine of Our Lady of Providence

For many years a statue of Our Lady of Providence had stood in a simple niche in first north hall of Providence Convent. For Sister Mary Providentia Grussi, director of the Confraternity of Our Lady of Providence, this location seemed too humble for a true shrine and she was instrumental in obtaining donations from benefactors. By 1955 she persuaded the council to consider a more fitting setting, and in February a consultation with the architect Robert Bohlen and Superintendent of Grounds Bernard Bisch led to the decision to erect a shrine at the end of the corridor linking Providence Convent to Foley Hall. In April the Daprato Studios of Chicago were engaged to construct the shrine (described in the sidebar on page 380) and the work was completed in time for a dedication on the feast of the Immaculate Conception, December 8, 1956.

Various Improvements

Management of the 1,350-acre motherhouse grounds with their highly diversified activities was an unending

Original simple Our Lady of Providence Shrine.

challenge, as a sampling of the many other projects underway at this time makes clear. The coal mine, in operation since 1894 and employing thirteen men in order to fuel on-site production of electricity, was practically mined out and was actually becoming dangerous. In August 1954 the mine was closed, with the entire College and motherhouse operations switching to purchase electricity from a public utility. Two major and expensive projects of replacing the plumbing of Le Fer

---

Our Lady of Providence Shrine

The Book of Important Events describes the shrine: "Arches of Pavanazzo marble outline the new shrine. Wrought iron inlaid with gold-leafed rosettes frame the Madonna and Child. Above this centerpiece, a circular stained-glass window portrays Murillo's 'Heavenly Father,' and represents the Providence of God. In the south wall of the shrine, a window pictures the  *miracle of Cana. A third window in the north wall depicts Mary lighting the lamp in her home while the Infant sleeps in His crib and Joseph works. Hence, she received her title, Queen of the Home. Beneath the Pavanazzo console supporting the picture, a group of 'lilies of the field' again represent the Providence of God. On either side of the entrance are wrought iron grills ending in marble pillars. The portrait of Our Lady of Providence is a copy of the original made by Pompeii Coccia in 1927 at the request of Mother Mary Cleophas. Mater Divinae Providentiae, the original painting, is the masterpiece of the Italian artist, Scipione Pulzone (1550-1588)." These materials were reconfigured when the shrine moved to its present location in Providence Center in 1990.*

Hall and the infirmary were accomplished that year. The financial aspect of management had increased to the point that additional space for the treasurer's office was provided by partitioning off a portion of the second floor Tile Hall.

Improved campus lighting and repairs to the power house smokestack were the major maintenance efforts during 1955, but by the following year it was necessary to purchase new laundry equipment and make urgent repairs to the windows of Providence Convent and to undertake a complete renovation of Providence Convent kitchen. More on public view and also in need of attention was the Blessed Sacrament Chapel. The Daprato Studios were engaged to carry out a complete cleaning and repainting of the chapel, and adoration was temporarily moved to the crypt of the church. A quieter atmosphere in Providence Convent was achieved by replacing the linoleum in the west hall with cork flooring.

The chimes, a beloved feature of so many events at Saint Mary-of-the-Woods, had suffered over the years due to wear and tear and even lightning strikes. Sister Mary Lourdes was charged with studying their current condition and engaging a consultant to plan for an upgrade which would make it possible to play the chimes from a keyboard or console rather than by pulling levers in the bell tower. The McShane Company was hired and began work in April 1957. By June 1958 the diarist was able to record: "The present value of the chimes is very great. A set of chimes such as we have—eleven bells ranging from low D to high E, with G-sharp, C-natural—is now worth $23,000 or more."[62]

Less exciting but equally necessary that year were repairs to the Foley Hall scullery where pots and pans were scrubbed and a major overhaul of the carpenter shop. By 1960 it was necessary to increase the telephone capacity on the campus with the installation of two completely separate switchboards, one in Providence Convent and one in Le Fer Hall.

Shortly after the fire at Rosary Hill, Father Goossens had organized a volunteer fire department in Saint Mary-of-the-Woods Village. The council had readily agreed to his request to lease a plot of land there for the construction of a new concrete-block fire station built by the volunteers themselves to house its all-purpose fire truck. On July 12, 1958, when a sudden fire broke out in one of the generators in the power house on campus, the volunteers quickly extinguished the blaze. An open house to show off the new fire station had been scheduled for the very next day, prompting double congratulations from villagers and sisters alike.

With the College enrollment growing, the novitiate filled to capacity and the juniorate overflowing Providence Convent, the strain was showing on the sisters who so faithfully tended to the infrastructure. Sister Cecile Morse, who had operated the small but extremely active Print Shop on campus for forty-one years, was in need of a rest. Now the decision was made to restrict Print Shop operations to community business and to send the College printing to a commercial shop in Terre Haute.

Sister Rose Patricia Ward, director of food operations in Foley Hall kitchen, suffered a heart attack in 1959. She had learned the skills of kitchen management and food preparation for large groups in the infirmary kitchen and then took over Foley kitchen where she was responsible for meals for the College girls, the juniorate/aspirancy girls, the commercial girls, the sisters during the summer and for special groups such as the diocesan priests' retreats. During twenty-nine years, she was both admired for her artistic presentation of tasty food and loved for her kindness and sense of humor. With the decline in candidates wishing to follow the coadjutrix path, there were no sisters qualified to carry on this work, leading to the decision to contract with the SAGA food service to handle College meals.

The health of the home superiors also suffered during this time. After thirty years as director of education requiring constant traveling to visit classes and intensive office and committee work, at age sixty-one, Sister Francis Joseph was sent to St. Joseph Sanitarium in Mt. Clemens, Michigan, for a month's rest and treatment at the mineral baths there. In March 1958 Sister Rose Dolores benefited from treatment at the same institution.

Illness and Incapacitation of Mother Gertrude Clare

Mother Gertrude Clare had always been frail in appearance, but her energy was unflagging in the midst of an extremely demanding schedule. From the beginning of her term as superior general travel had been the most difficult aspect of her duties. When she journeyed by plane to Adrian, Michigan, for a meeting in August 1954, the diarist commented: "Our dear Mother stood the trip very well. On her return a large group of Sisters greeted her and welcomed her. This was her first overnight visit away from St. Mary's in many years."[63] Since long car trips were the most difficult for her, over the years she restricted her visitations to the Terre Haute houses, delegating other visits to her council members as provided by Rule,[64] but ensuring that local superiors could consult with her at any time by phone. To keep her consistently aware of the situations on the missions, small groups of local superiors often came to Saint Mary-of-the-Woods to meet with her on Saturdays.

On the day after Christmas in 1959, she went to the infirmary to recover from a heavy cold. As had often been done during short illnesses of superiors general, the first council meeting of 1960, convened to count the ballots for the election of Chapter delegates and discuss plans for the Chapter, was held in her sickroom. In February when she returned from visiting the new convent at Schulte High School in Terre Haute, her depleted condition was such that she again returned to the infirmary. So critical was her condition that on February 11, Sister Rose Angela sent a letter to the sisters advising them of her illness and asking for prayers. She was anointed the next day, when the diarist penned this alarming notation: "Mother appears to be unaware of her surroundings due to extreme nervous exhaustion although at times she is alert for a minute or so. Now and then she has tried to say something, at times understandable and again not."[65]

A few days later Sister Rose Angela again notified the sisters of Mother's condition with details which presaged a protracted illness:

> Since our last letter we have tried to reach you through various relayed telephone messages or telegrams to keep you informed, dear Sisters, at least in a general way of the condition of our precious Mother. ...

> During the past week the initial causes of alarm, a lung congestion and also a kidney infection, have both cleared up; but the state of coma, or at times semi-coma, that has marked Mother's illness from its early stages, has been diagnosed as the effect of

a deep-seated virus which has attacked the central nervous system.

We know, dear Sisters, that it will grieve you as it does us to know that Mother is suffering from a virus-produced encephalitis, which often proves fatal but from which it is possible to recover. The next few days probably will be decisive in dear Mother's condition. If she does rally, however, her period of convalescence will be slow and more or less prolonged.[66]

As her condition did not improve, her brother Ed Owens, his wife, a niece and a cousin came to see her, and prayers for the dying were recited, but she rallied somewhat. A spinal tap ruled out the possibility of a brain tumor and a diagnosis of virus encephalitis was given. Over the course of the next weeks there was a cycle of improvement, during which she showed signs of awareness in recognition of persons by her bedside, followed by relapse into a coma. In early March Archbishop Schulte visited, and by May 1960 Sister Rose Angela wrote to the sisters to advise them that Mother was definitely failing. She had suffered convulsions and been anointed, after which "she lay utterly depleted and limp, apparently asleep or unconscious, just too weak to react in any way. ... This morning she seems somewhat better ... smiled a number of times ... it is amazing to see that she has revived even as much as she has."[67]

Once it became apparent to the council that they must carry on the affairs of the Congregation without their superior and beloved colleague, First Assistant Sister Rose Angela and the council rallied to carry forward the ambitious administrative tasks they had begun, as well as to cope with the unrelenting demands of daily life. The campus was no longer able to accommodate the entire community for the summer session, so a system was devised to identify those who for various reasons had been deprived of this opportunity.[68] Due to requests from several dioceses asking to be advised by the end of April as to the number of sisters to be assigned to each school and the grades they would teach, Sister Rose Angela also made an unprecedented request, "that any Sister who feels in conscience that she wishes to be changed from her present mission will make this known to her Home Superior before March 31st."[69] With preparations for the General Chapter of 1960 looming, one can only imagine the pressure this put upon the council 's annual responsibility of preparing the Obedience List.

As yet the sisters did not know where the obedience they would receive on August 15, 1960, would place them, but already there was a sense of change in the air. Although the Supreme Court had ruled in 1954 that separate educational facilities were inherently unequal, the need to call out National Guard troops in Little Rock, Arkansas, only three years later to enforce this decision indicated a long struggle ahead. The Soviet's successful launch in 1957 of Sputnik, the world's first orbiting satellite, had challenged the country's educational system and intensified the Cold War. The determination to strengthen the teaching of math and science through the passage of the National Defense Education Act the following year was already opening additional opportunities for sisters to apply for scholarships. Pope John XXIII had surprised the world with his January 25, 1959, announcement of an ecumenical council, giving notice that the church itself was poised for reform. The thirty-six sisters arriving on campus as delegates on June 16, 1960, inaugurated this new era for the Sisters of Providence with a remarkably different model for the General Chapter.

❧ Chapter 13
An Emerging Model
of Participative
Governance

This photo at a 1963 meeting of high school principals illustrates the increasingly frequent occasions for discussion and consultation as policies were adapted. Standing left to right: Sisters Joseph Eleanor Ryan, Mary Xavier Coppersmith, Mary Raymond Schelkopf, Dorothy Mary Noe, Mary Ellen Kilday, Miriam Joseph Cahill and Catherine Ursula Hayes. Seated are Director of Education Sister Mary Joan Kirchner and Mother Rose Angela Horan.

Even prior to Mother Gertrude Clare's illness, the regular six-year cycle of General Chapters had once again put the topic of planning for the 1960 General Chapter on the 1954 council agenda. A number of factors contributed to a significant in- crease of attention on the part of all the sisters on what had traditionally been a very limited engagement in Congregation government. The building of the new novitiate had become a project that had galvanized community effort. Fourteen new missions had opened during the 1954-1959 period, all in new parishes with founding energies. Younger superiors had been appointed to head new missions where only three or four sisters made up the house and formed a faculty together with lay teachers. Although their access to press and television coverage was limited, sisters could not help but be aware of the political campaign underway with the first Catholic candidate for president since 1928. Following Pope John XXIII's January 25, 1959, announcement of an upcoming ecumenical council, Catholic newspapers featured regular articles on the planning activities. Such events were beyond their field of influence, but not so the upcoming General Chapter.

A New Style of General Chapter

As first assistant, Sister Rose Angela had attended a series of workshops sponsored by the Conference of Major Superiors of Women on the topic of canon law. Such gatherings of superiors of other congregations stimulated the attendees to encourage the involvement of the entire membership in Chapter preparations. The ideas she brought to the council would contribute to the emergence of a considerably more participative style of General Chapter.

Suggestions for the Agenda

Still very much alive in community discussions was the memory of the 1954 Chapter, which had included not only the elections but an additional day devoted to discussion of topics suggested ahead of time by the delegates. The positive response to this innovation prompted Mother Gertrude Clare to extend the scope of such participation for the 1960 Chapter. She announced that not only the delegates, but any sister who had been in community for twenty-five years or more was invited to submit topics. This invitation reflected her recognition that it was increasingly true that many sisters had opportunities similar to those of the superiors in gaining a broader perspective on issues pertaining to religious life. The letter Mother Gertrude Clare received from Sister Helen Rose Newland indicates that her confidence in the membership was well-placed:

> For the past several years I have been keeping up with every article in the Sister Formation Bulletin; articles in the Review for Religious; articles in other magazines, both secular and educational. I learned to my great relief that hundreds of other

Sisters in all parts of the country have pretty much the same attitudes of mind as I have. In addition, my being at Notre Dame for the past few summers, and my getting acquainted with so many Sisters of numerous Orders have given me much food for thought and for personal benefit.[1]

Emboldened both by her experiences and the invitation, Sister Helen Rose went on to write three and a half single-spaced pages of suggestions. Regarding the habit, she was unequivocal: "Let us get rid of the cap and neckerchief—and may it be soon!" In order to relieve the "rush, rush, rush, and strain" of life, she recommended changing the horarium (the daily schedule prescribed in the Rule), eliminating parish responsibilities such as teaching catechism and giving "obediences" or mission assignments in the spring rather than on August 15. Acknowledging that some of her points might sound overly critical, she ended by saying: "I do want to thank you for letting me say it. Here again, is one more thing you're doing: allowing us democratically to express our views."[2] She was not alone in expressing her views. Suggestions were submitted by 132 sisters, resulting in a large number of items for consideration.

Election of Delegates

An English major familiar with literature stressing democratic ideals, Sister Helen Rose also raised an oft-heard complaint in the same context: "Could we not have a more democratic method for voting when it comes to sending delegates to the Chapter? Once and only once did I vote for people I *wanted* to send."[3] Surely the irony of this plea was not lost on her when in March she received a letter notifying her that she herself was a delegate. The elections had been held on December 21, 1959, in the usual manner, grouping those eligible to vote into twelve geographical sections, thus limiting the choices of the sisters eligible to vote to only those sisters in their geographic section.

As in the 1954 Chapter, thirty-six delegates were elected to serve alongside the six ex-officio councilors and treasurer. Of this number, six of the elected delegates had served in this capacity two or more times and ten had been in one previous chapter, while twenty had been elected for the first time. Their median age was fifty-six, with about a third of the members drawn from grade school teachers and principals, a third from the high schools and a third from various administrative posts.

Chapter Preparations

As had been true for preparations for the 1949 and 1954 Chapters, it would fall to the first assistant to carry through the planning, for it was obvious that Mother Gertrude Clare was incapacitated. In this regard, Sister Rose Angela's administrative talents proved well-suited to build on the experience of the 1954 Chapter as she organized and implemented procedures for a completely new Chapter format. In contrast to previous secrecy, the names of the delegates were published to the entire community on the same day as the delegates themselves received notice. At the same time a preliminary agenda of topics for discussion drawn from the suggestions already received was circulated as well.

The scheduled dates revealed for the first time a distinction between a Chapter of Elections and a Chapter of Affairs. Included in the June 17-23, 1960, schedule were three days of preparatory activities: first, a day of recollection and then two days for meetings and discussion. These days of preparation were followed by a day for the Chapter of Elections and three days for the Chapter of Affairs. A sheet of quotations from recent articles in the *Review for Religious* provided the context and rationale for what was clearly a major change of the Chapter process. These included quotes from papal documents encouraging adaptation according to the spirit of the founder. Recent changes in liturgical practice were cited in Sister Rose Angela's letter as the example indicating that, "our times demand that religious have the courage to make changes in their mode of life ... to achieve greater success in bringing Christ's message to the modern world."[4]

Based on the large number of suggestions sent for the Chapter agenda, it was obvious that the entire membership was already actively discussing the issues of the day. When the council met to go over the points, they realized that even with the overlap of comments the sheer scope of the issues demanded preliminary consideration. Five major topics were designated to be assigned to committees: 1) the method of electing delegates, 2) the annual announcements of mission assignments, 3) spiritual renewal, 4) provinces, and 5) "facing our educational problems." Delegates were given their choice of committees. The council members felt it was important for the Chapter delegates to have complete freedom to offer their own ideas, so they did not participate in the committees but rather served as a resource group.

One of the council's first actions had been to arrange a consultation with a canonist from the Congregation for Religious, Father Bernard Ransing, CSC, to take advantage of his expertise regarding the new Chapter procedures.[5] Some of the anticipated decisions, such as lengthening the period of postulancy from six to ten months, would require changes in the *Constitutions*. Background papers drawn from articles in *Review for Religious* and canon law were sent to the delegates. In addition, they were provided with six sample horariums which would modify the daily program and prayers said in common along with a summary of the changes in prayers throughout the years. The topics of adaptation of clothing and the horarium were not assigned to committees because, "so much interest, attention, and suggested material have already been directed toward these matters."[6]

Preliminary Meetings

Off-campus delegates had arrived on the feast of Corpus Christi, Thursday, June 16, 1960. The forty-three delegates spent a significant portion of the next day in the crypt chapel listening to four conferences by Father Neil Parsons, CSSP. Then, on Saturday and Sunday they met with their committees to organize the assigned material for discussion by the entire body. Their time together had provided the opportunity not only to engender a unanimity of purpose but also time to assess the next steps and discuss who among the membership would be most capable to carry forward the decisions they would make.

The official opening of Chapter took place on June 20, 1960, in the library of Providence Convent with Archbishop Schulte leading the prayer to the Holy Spirit and calling the roll. This formal opening inevitably emphasized the absence of Mother Gertrude Clare, who would normally have been at his side. Although six months of news from her sickbed had accustomed the sisters to her absence, the moment brought to mind the fact that she had been among the delegates seven times in the previous forty years. Sister Rose Angela paid fitting tribute to her as she began the report of the previous administration, noting that "her absence from this group today will give an opportunity to speak freely of her rare qualities of spiritual leadership, her unfaltering trust in God, and her untiring activity in His service."[7]

Sister Rose Angela's report began with the Council's acknowledgment that regular visitations had indicated that "many factors in present-day life and activities militate against regular observance."[8] The statistical data indicated a membership of 1,462 professed sisters teaching in 120 schools. In the previous six years, 113 sisters had died, three perpetually professed sisters had received dispensations and fifteen had left after temporary vows expired, while six were receiving care in mental institutions. Seventy-four novices and ten postulants had recently moved into the new novitiate building. Between 1957 and 1959 the beginning of the Sister Formation Program had kept all newly professed sisters home but regular replacements were now being sent out much better prepared, and seventy-six sisters were currently in the formation group.

Major construction included not only on-campus projects but also new buildings at Immaculata Junior College. All of the fourteen new schools accepted were elementary parish schools, while both St. Joseph in Terre Haute and St. John in Indianapolis had closed. Of the 998 teaching sisters, 763 served in elementary schools with the others active in twenty high schools, the College, and two junior colleges in Washington, D.C., and Taiwan. The growth of the Taiwan mission was notable. The number of sisters receiving degrees and certificates was the largest ever, with 109 master's degrees and 216 bachelor's degrees, as well as numerous certificates: 45 principal's, 245 general teaching, 38 music and 43 critic teachers certificates earned. Seven sisters were studying toward PhD degrees, while during the two previous summers thirty-eight sisters had financed their study by qualifying for grants and scholarships.

Due to the scope of the major construction projects, the financial report must have been of great interest. Indeed, the new buildings at Immaculata had cost $1,786,130 and the new novitiate came in at $2,232,270. Nonetheless, receipts had been strong, so only about one million dollars, or 12 percent of the $9,157,450 income, had come from loans. Because the

Congregation's assets in terms of land, buildings and equipment could be listed at almost $15 million, the liabilities in terms of outstanding debt of approximately $1,367,000 was deemed manageable. However, in accordance with the mood of openness, one sheet of the report was devoted to a brief summary of the debt, where a comparison with the mere $109,191 owed at the time of the 1954 Chapter provided a different perspective.

The Chapter of Elections

A committee of three was given thirty minutes to compare the report to the books in the Treasurer's office; following this review, the delegates reassembled to receive the committee's statement that the report was approved. At 10:40 a.m. the entire group moved to the crypt of the Church for the elections. Among them as a first-time delegate was Sister Mary Pius Regnier (later Mother Mary Pius), who recalled that the delegates had enjoyed frequent opportunities to talk with each other during the preceding days. Many related that after the list of delegates had been posted, other sisters had taken time to speak with them or write to them about their concerns. Some had felt that Sister Rose Angela was so different from Mother Marie Helene and Mother Gertrude Clare, less approachable and very straightforward, that they couldn't see her as superior general. By then Sister Mary Pius had formed her own opinion: "When we got into the Chapter, I saw nobody to vote for except Rose Angela. She was just head and shoulders above everybody with her understanding of it all."[9] Apparently others had come to the same conclusion. With Archbishop Schulte presiding, thirty-five of the forty-three delegates cast their votes for Sister Rose Angela as superior general, electing her on the first ballot.

As always, the newly elected superior came forward to take the oath of office. At this point the usual procedure called for the archbishop to leave but, much to the dismay of those who had been in previous Chapters, he remained and presided over the election of the assistants.[10] Despite the meticulous care in the preparation of so many documents for the Chapter, the ceremonial booklet given to the archbishop did in fact include the direction for him to continue the proceedings. A single ballot was sufficient to elect Sister Catherine Celine Brocksmith as first assistant. For second assistant, with a scattering of votes for three sisters not on the council and only a few votes for incumbent Sister Rose Genevieve Flaherty, Sister Mary Pius was the choice of the assembly on a single ballot.

As the delegates pondered the makeup of a new council, the voting for third assistant showed a continuation of the preference for new blood. On the first ballot the votes were scattered, with only four votes for Sister Rose Genevieve and other votes spread over eight sisters. However, a second ballot was sufficient to identify Sister Rose Loretto Wagner as the somewhat surprising choice since, not being a delegate, she was not even present. For fourth assistant, Sister Rose Dolores Thuis was returned to office for a fourth term with forty-one votes on the first ballot. As had been true during several previous Chapters, the role of fifth assistant/director of education had once again become a subject of varying opinions. Although long-serving incumbent Sister Francis Joseph Elbreg received fifteen votes, the twenty-two votes cast for Sister Mary Joan Kirchner indicated a desire for change, and she was elected on the first ballot. As for sixth assistant/secretary general, with thirty-eight votes, Sister Loretta Therese O'Leary was clearly approved to continue in that role for a third term. The same was true for Treasurer General Sister Francis Raphael Donlon, who was returned to office for a fifth term with forty-one votes.

After the newly elected officers came forward to take their oath of office, the Chapter adjourned until one thirty when the entire community gathered in the Church for the proclamation. Sister Rose Loretto, then superior at St. Charles in Bloomington, Indiana, received the news of her election by phone. The remainder of the day was given over to celebration.

The Chapter of Affairs

The first of the three days scheduled for the Chapter of Affairs was devoted to "adaptation"—discussion of changes to time-honored policies and practices in the areas of formation, the horarium, the giving of obediences (assignments), clothing and customs. In order to manage the large number of topics in a timely manner, each delegate received a sheet specifying the vote that would authorize a change. For example, the council's decision to keep the newly professed sisters home to participate in the Sister Formation Program had been in operation since 1957. Now the delegates were advised of their responsibility as the highest governing body of the Congregation with the statement: "The vote will be to authorize the permanent adoption of the Juniorate and to incorporate in the Rule this period of formation."[11] In like manner the Chapter voted to lengthen the postulancy from six to eleven months and to shorten the tertianship to three months, as well as to modify the schedule of prayers.

Mother Rose Angela served as chair, using parliamentary procedure to announce a topic, ask for discussion for or against each statement, call for ayes and nays and formally announce the result. In recalling the proceedings, newly elected Second Assistant Sister Mary Pius, experiencing her first chapter, described the atmosphere with a touch of humor as she recalled the discussion of one of the lighter topics of the day:

> When we got into the chapter, we met in the library and we had our chairs all in a big circle around there. We talked about the possibility of doing away with the cloak, with the mantle. And I can remember we were to have a show of hands, and then we had to stand so everybody could be counted and (laughing) there sat Colette (Sister Colette Garrity) at the end. She sat when everybody stood, and everybody laughed. And then, "Those not in favor," and the only one was Colette.[12]

Even on more serious matters there was an obvious openness as the delegates pondered the many and varied matters before them. Regarding the modification of the habit, since the entire community had already expressed the desire to change the cap and neckerchief, the delegates simply approved procedures for the sisters to view sample alternatives during the summer session prior to a final decision.

On the second and third days, the agenda was devoted to subjects that because of their complexity had been given to committees. Following the presentation of each report, the question, "What is your pleasure?" brought comments, questions and suggestions for amendments before being referred to a committee or brought to a vote. As they considered the reports regarding spiritual renewal, the election of Chapter delegates and the formation of provinces, council members shared information from their own experiences. As committee chair, when Sister Mary Joan introduced the multi-faceted topic of "Facing our Educational Problems," she provided a

TABLE 9: *Increase of missions and sisters assigned by decade, 1890-1959*

Year	Number of Missions	Number of sisters staffing	Increase over decade		Number of houses by size	
			Missions added	Sisters added	12 or more sisters	11 or fewer sisters
1890	47	411			11	36
1900	50	534	3	123	15	35
1910	54	653	4	119	22	32
1920	62	843	8	190	30	32
1930	78	994	16	151	36	42
1940	87	1,103	9	109	39	48
1950	101	1,212	14	109	39	62
1959	120	1,252	19	40	37	83

statistical analysis of the numerical growth of the Congregation's educational mission. As shown in Table 9, the study emphasized the need for future planning.

The difference between the current total membership (1,462) and the sisters available for 1959 staffing (1,252) was a silent acknowledgment of the fact that increasing numbers of sisters were incapacitated by age. The gain of only forty sisters during the 1950-1959 decade was explained by the decision to keep newly professed sisters home to complete their degrees. However, with the acceptance of nineteen additional schools during that decade, it had been necessary to take sisters from other missions to meet all the commitments. Since this was a temporary situation, it was not overly alarming, yet the numbers emphasized the need for more vocations in order to maintain growth. The great increase in smaller houses during the two previous decades—from forty-eight in 1940 to eighty-three in 1959—called attention to the acceptance of many parish elementary schools that were now usually staffed with only four or five sisters in conjunction with lay teachers.

Careful consideration of these realities led to a decision to impose a moratorium on accepting any new elementary schools except for commitments already made. Emphasis would be placed on the high schools and a director of vocations would be appointed. The committee's recommendation that a standing "Board of Education" be established to widen the oversight of the educational work of the Congregation received enthusiastic support. Integral to this move was a shift in the role of the fifth assistant from supervisor of schools to director of education, as Sister Mary Joan described: "We felt that the person in that position was doing a great deal more than supervising schools and that this term did not cover everything that she was doing and the term Director of Education was presented to the Chapter and it was passed as the official title for that office."[13]

As the work of the Chapter drew to a close, there was a sense that their time together marked a watershed moment for the Congregation. During the closing session Sister Mary Corona Sullivan rose to state: "I think I speak for the group when I say each one of us feels highly privileged to have been here for these days."[14] Indeed, the entire Chapter process had established the precedent of inviting the sisters at large to participate in government. It would now be the responsibility of the new council to carry that process forward. With this in mind, let us meet the new members.

The 1960 Council

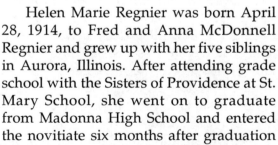

Sister Mary Pius Regnier 1914-2005

Helen Marie Regnier was born April 28, 1914, to Fred and Anna McDonnell Regnier and grew up with her five siblings in Aurora, Illinois. After attending grade school with the Sisters of Providence at St. Mary School, she went on to graduate from Madonna High School and entered the novitiate six months after graduation on January 23, 1932. She served in five different missions before second novitiate and final profession in 1939 and then taught at Providence High School for seven years. She taught at St. Simon in Washington, Indiana, for four years and was then appointed principal and superior there from 1952-1958. During this time she earned an MA in Education at St. Louis University in 1955. After a year teaching at Ladywood, Indianapolis, she was named principal and superior at Reitz Memorial High School in Evansville. It was from this position at age forty-six that she was elected to the council as second assistant.

Sister Rose Loretto Wagner 1910-1992

Helen Wagner was born to Joseph and Helen Mayworm Wagner on October 1, 1910, in Chicago. She and her six siblings received their early education from the Sisters of Providence at St. Angela School, and she attended Providence High School. She entered the novitiate in February 1930, and her sister Vera followed her two years later, taking the name Sister Marie Cyril. After a year at St. Philip Neri in Indianapolis she moved across the city to St. Joan of Arc where she remained for twelve years under five different superiors. In 1945 she returned to her home neighborhood to teach eighth-grade boys at St. Mel, Chicago for eleven years. These two somewhat unusual long-term assignments can be explained by later testimonials describing her as one who "not only taught but also charmed a roomful of obstreperous young boys." She was also remembered as a "wonderful person who in a quiet and gentle way challenged all of us to an appreciation of learning and study."[15] She was made superior at St. Charles, Bloomington, in 1956 and had completed her studies for an MS degree at Indiana University in 1959 when she was called home the following year to serve as third assistant at age forty-nine.

Sister Mary Joan Kirchner 1901-2000

Marguerite Kirchner was the first child born to Peter and Mary Haring Kirchner on February 24, 1901, in Terre Haute, Indiana. Over the succeeding years the family came to include four brothers and two sisters. After her early education at St. Benedict School, she continued with the Sisters of Providence at St. Joseph Academy and then in 1919 went on to pursue a

teaching credential at Indiana State Normal School before entering the novitiate in 1922. In her first years on mission she moved frequently, enjoying the tutelage of excellent superiors while teaching at St. Agnes, Indianapolis, St. Augustine, Fort Wayne, Immaculata in Washington, D.C., and nine years at Providence High School in Chicago. Her natural talents were recognized and she was one of the first sisters sent to earn an MA in educational administration. In 1934 she had barely completed her thesis, "The Biological Terminology Required for the Intelligent Reading of High School Classics," when she was appointed principal at Marywood, Anaheim, at age thirty-five. She was then appointed principal/superior for a three-year term at St. John, Indianapolis, a six-year term at Central Catholic in Fort Wayne and a three-year term at St. Agnes, Indianapolis. In 1949 she was named dean of women at Saint Mary-of-the-Woods College, a position she held for seven years before being appointed superior at Immaculata in Washington, D.C. Over the years she had been active on the Congregation's education committees and had published several articles in professional journals. Her recent experience at the college level had familiarized her with certification requirements and enabled her to utilize her Sister Formation contacts to adapt the summer session to provide required courses. Her election to the position of fifth assistant and director of education at age fifty-nine was a tribute to the respect she had earned.

The transition to the new council was not without difficulty. It was immediately apparent to Mother Rose Angela that the two members of the 1954 council who had not been re-elected had not expected this outcome. Sisters Rose Genevieve and Francis Joseph had been council members long before she had, and this fact created an awkward situation. Moreover, replacing Sister Mary Joan as superior of the complex Immaculata establishment would not be easy. Because Sister Robert Kiley, econome at the motherhouse, was well-qualified by education and experience to fill the multiple duties of Immaculata superior, she was assigned to fill that post. Her vacated position was an excellent fit for Sister Rose Genevieve's talents and she assumed the duties of supervising motherhouse operations.

The situation regarding Sister Francis Joseph proved more difficult. Since the council had met separately while the Chapter committees held their meetings, she had heard nothing of the informal discussions as to who would be the best person to carry forward the recommendations being proposed by the education committee. She had spent the thirty-six years since her 1924 appointment in the role of supervisor of education and had lived at the motherhouse and traveled to Europe and Taiwan as well as all over the United States. Now at age sixty-five she seemed at a loss. To complicate matters, it had been she who had identified the talents of the others in her age cohort (including both Mother Rose Angela and Sister Mary Joan) and prepared them for senior positions by sending them at an early age to study for master's degrees. Now, of the various positions suggested by them to take advantage of her experience, she accepted the position of instructor of education classes for the junior sisters, gradually vacating her offices in Tile Hall and Foley Hall.

The treasurer's office was another concern for Mother Rose Angela. Before the Chapter, Sister Francis Raphael Donlon had expressed the wish that she not be asked to continue in this role. She, like Sister Francis Joseph, had served at the motherhouse since 1924, first as an assistant and then, beginning in 1938, in the office of treasurer general for four terms for a total of twenty-two years. Her policy had always been to handle matters on her own as much as possible so as not to worry the council, but at age sixty-six, the accumulated stress of negotiating the financial arrangements for the building projects at Clarksville, Immaculata and the new novitiate building had taken a toll. However, one of the Chapter committees had suggested changes to relieve her of two time-consuming responsibilities. Rather than a top-down system of the general administration arranging for summer travel to and from the missions, this would be done by local superiors. They were also provided with simplified forms for reporting convent financial reports to expedite tasks at the generalate level. With the Congregation's large debt, the subject of money would

never be far from the 1960 council's thoughts and deliberations, and they were grateful indeed to know that they need
only call upstairs to have her expertise at the table.

Implementing the Chapter

Sharing the Decisions

On July 8, 1960, scarcely two weeks after the close of the
General Chapter, Mother Rose Angela addressed the entire
community of sisters attending the summer session from the
stage of the auditorium to explain in detail the decisions of the
General Chapter. As she emphasized the need for approval
by Rome of the points relative to the Rule, she sounded the
note which would characterize her administration, quoting
from the Foreword to the 1954 *Constitutions*: "With the sense
of security that comes from the faithful observance of the rule,
there comes for the religious a peace of soul which brings with
it possibly the greatest measure of happiness that can be experienced in this vale of tears."[16]

Even as Mother Rose Angela emphasized fidelity to the
Rule, three of the items she went on to explain would certainly have lightened the tone of her remarks and created a
lively buzz among the assembled sisters. The first, a change
which reinforced each sister's sense of personal responsibility,
was the decision that the prayer schedule could now be arranged so each one could do the half hour of spiritual reading
in the privacy of her room or even outdoors rather than being
required to sit in chapel. Mother Rose Angela's accompanying
exhortation expressed confidence that each sister understood
her obligation: "Give our Lord and your own soul the full
time."[17] The second change would not be felt immediately, but
the decision to give each sister her assignment for the following scholastic year on the first Sunday of May instead of on
August 15 would require considerable adjustment. The third
item, expanding the use of television, would receive almost
immediate implementation due to the Democratic convention
being held later that week.

Many of the decisions were future-oriented, with little immediate impact, such as the announcement of research into a
program of spiritual renewal and of a study of the method of
electing delegates. Several items were stated in such definite

terms that they stood out: the moratorium on the opening of elementary schools, the authorization of the superior general and her council to proceed with whatever help is necessary toward the establishment of provinces and the news that since "Home" could no longer accommodate everyone, each sister would be expected to remain on mission during every fourth or fifth summer.

Changes in the Habit

Definitely eclipsing these notices as the most immediate topic of interest within the community was the announcement that several sisters had submitted designs for new styles of cap and neckerchief and would be seen in the coming days modeling their creations on the campus. Doubtless the rule of silence suffered many infractions as those chosen to model the novel headdresses struggled to maintain decorum when the inquiring minds of their companions wanted to know the details of construction. To ensure an objective opinion, the council arranged a consultation with Dr. Carlton I. Calkin, director of the Art and Design Department at Purdue University, who had done a design for the Franciscan Sisters of Mishawaka. Sisters Mechtilde Schaaf, home economics instructor at the College, and Mary Loyola Bender, motherhouse seamstress and sacristan, accompanied Sister Loretta Therese to meet with him. They brought pictures of eight of the Sister of Providence designs, and also modeled them for his observation. The Book of Important Events chronicles the decision:

> Mother Rose Angela met the community in the auditorium at 1:10 on July 14, 1960 and commented on the various styles of caps. ...Ten were shown on the stage and Mother read the comment which had been made on each one. The design which was chosen as the more practical and harmonious was the cap by Sister Consuelo, and the neckerchief designed by Sister Edith. This practical demonstration convinced the Community of the excellence of having an outside opinion and the choice was unanimously approved.[18]

Sister Consuelo Burtschi was known not only for her ability to run the Woodland Inn as a sort of bed-and-breakfast, but also as a seamstress who created hand-made gifts for the gift shop. Sister Edith Pfau, in addition to teaching art at Ladywood, was also an artist in her own right. Sister Consuelo's cap was chosen for both practicality and artistry because "the

Mother Rose Angela Horan

variations of curves give a sense of balance," while Sister Edith's small neckerchief with a subtle point drew attention to the cross.[19]

To inform the sisters on the missions that summer in a timely manner, Mother Rose Angela simultaneously sent a letter to explain the decision-making process, noting that, "We really do not feel free *not* to change, in view of the repeated recommendations by ecclesiastical authorities that the face would be unimprisoned, the vision unimpeded, and the starch problems solved."[20] Arrangements were made with a company to manufacture the new caps and neckerchiefs. December 27, 1960, was set as the date for the change, with press releases including photos sent to the various diocesan newspapers in November. On the designated Sunday, following prayers at one thirty in the afternoon, each sister made the change, then returned to the chapel at four o'clock for Benediction and renewal of vows. After this a period of recreation provided an emotional outlet.[21] With several days of Christmas vacation to get used to the new attire, the sisters were ready to face their classes in the new year.

The Influence of Vatican Council II

In a sense, the change of the cap was a metaphor for the activities of the 1960 council. Like their habit, the basic mission and lifestyle of the sisters remained unchanged, but the "vision unimpeded" that Mother Rose Angela described would make it possible to see the world in new ways. And, indeed for many of the sisters, the world seemed to be changing right before their eyes, both within convent walls and beyond. To do justice to the veritable avalanche of Congregation activities during these 1960-1966 years, we will necessarily skip from topic to topic, although in fact many of the situations demanded attention at the same time and were experienced against the backdrop of major world events. Undoubtedly the most influential of such events for the Sisters of Providence was the Second Vatican Council. In fact, when the editors of *Time* magazine bypassed the Cuban missile crisis, men in space, and European unification to name Pope John XXIII as 1962's "man of the year," they explained that their choice was guided by the long view. "By launching singlehanded a revolution whose sweep and loftiness have caused it to outrank the secular concerns of the year, Pope John created history in a different dimension."[22]

Elevation of Cardinal Ritter

One of Pope John's earliest decisions, the 1961 elevation of their longtime friend, Archbishop Joseph Ritter, to the rank of cardinal, had provided an immediate occasion for the community to feel connected to the historic events taking place in Rome. Sisters Rose Dolores and Eugenia Logan were designated to represent the Congregation, traveling by plane with a Saint Mary-of-the-Woods College Alumnae group to Rome on January 14, 1961. The event included colorful ceremonies over several days; first, the bringing of the letter of announcement to the North American College, then the conferring of the red biretta by Pope John XXIII at the Vatican Hall of Benedictions, followed by the Great Consistory in St. Peter's Basilica where the red hat was conferred and finally culminating with a private audience with the Holy Father for Cardinal Ritter's party.

In addition to the festivities, their time in Rome provided the occasion for renewing acquaintance with the Congregation's Cardinal Protector, A. Gaetano Cicognani, and recalling his visit to Saint Mary-of-the-Woods, as well as a visit with Monsignor Emilio Federici, postulator for Mother Theodore's Cause. In addition to sight-seeing tours, Countess Guila Sartori, who had befriended Sisters Gertrude Smith and Alexa Suelzer during their study times in Rome, gave them a driving tour of the environs. After visiting Assisi, they went on to Paris and Lourdes, finishing the trip with a visit to Ruillé before returning home. The following summer the entire community had the opportunity to congratulate the new cardinal when he visited Saint Mary-of-the-Woods on July 1, 1961. After being greeted by sisters waving flags along the Avenue as the chimes rang, he visited Mother Gertrude Clare in the infirmary and was feted in a program at the Conservatory that evening.

With his elevation taking place during the preparations for the Second Vatican Council, the sisters took special interest in following Cardinal Ritter's activities during the next few years as he emerged as a leader of the American hierarchy. He was appointed to serve on the Pontifical Preparatory Commission, and he was among the first to criticize the schema on the Church which was presented by the Theological Commission and was instrumental in having the document completely reworked.[23] Having quickly gained the respect of other prelates, he continued to play an influential role in the Council's deliberations.

Events on Campus

A series of eminent speakers came to the Saint Mary-of-the-Woods campus to provide background and personal observations of the events unfolding in Rome, including scripture scholar Rev. Roland Murphy, OC, and the Rev. Gustave Weigel, SJ. A more local perspective was provided through Rev. Raymond T. Bosler, who had been appointed as Archbishop Schulte's *peritus*, or "expert" with advanced theological training, and who came to share with the sisters his experience of attending the Council meetings. In addition, there were persons from the Terre Haute area with a special interest in the talks going on in Rome regarding the goal of Christian unity and relations among the religions. Largely due to the energy of history professor Sister Mary Jean Mark, they came together for dialogue at Saint Mary-of-the-Woods College on a regular basis.

The most newsworthy of these efforts was the meeting she arranged between Archbishop Paul Schulte and Orthodox Metropolitan Antony Bashir on April 6, 1964. The *Terre Haute Star* described the carefully staged meeting:

> A brilliant late afternoon sun flooded the campus of St. Mary-of-the-Woods College Wednesday, adding warmth and splendor to the 'fraternal spirit of ecumenism' symbolized in an historic meeting. ... The two prelates were kept in separate area of the campus until the time for the meeting. Then shortly after 4 p.m., two black automobiles rolled to a halt in front of Le Fer. The first one carried Archbishop Schulte, who stepped out of the auto and slowly mounted the steps to the first landing. When he had assumed his position, the doors of the second car swung open, allowing Archbishop Bashir to alight from the auto and make his way to the landing.

The two religious leaders shook hands, and the crowd joined in polite applause as both men were escorted into the foyer of the hall where photographers snapped pictures and shot newsfilm against a backdrop painting of a similar meeting between Pope Paul VI and Ecumenical Patriarch Athenagoras I, world leader of Orthodoxy.[24]

After a brief meeting with the College Board of Trustees and a formal reception, the dignitaries were feted at a dinner during which the College chorale entertained them. The guests then moved to Cecilian Auditorium to join the audience of Catholic and Orthodox priests, student representatives and religious, educational and civic leaders of the area. Following hymns sung by the choir of Terre Haute's St. George Orthodox Church, where Archbishop Bashir had served as pastor from 1927-1929, he delivered an address in which he applauded the overtures toward reunion.

Sifting Various Interpretations

Among the sisters at large, articles in Catholic periodicals such as *America, Worship, Review for Religious* and the *Sister Formation Bulletin* were avidly followed and enthusiastically discussed. One of the most influential publications of the time was the small paperback book *The Nun in the World* by Belgian Cardinal Josef Suenens. Because of his strong academic background as professor and later rector of the University of Louvain and his practical experience as archbishop of Malines-Brussels, his views had strong appeal. First published in English in December 1963, the book quickly went through three additional printings the following year.

When Suenens was announced as the speaker for the conference for major superiors to be held at Mundelein College in Chicago in May 1963, Mother Rose Angela encouraged the council members to read the book. She, together with Director of Education Sister Mary Joan and Mistress of Novices Sister Marie Ambrose, attended the conference and included a discussion of Suenens' ideas during a subsequent council meeting. Afterwards she wrote to the sisters, "A reading of the book will throw light on the thought of true apostolic activity."[25] Mother Rose Angela clearly interpreted Cardinal Suenens' message as an endorsement of how she herself had characterized each sister's apostolate in an earlier letter: "To 'go on mission' must mean for each sister to go as one sent by

God to carry His message of love and redemption to the children or the persons entrusted to her care."[26]

Cardinal Suenen's central thesis of identifying the role of religious women in the church's mission of evangelization flowed from his Catholic Action understanding of "the apostolate [as] activities of the Christian sent by virtue of his baptismal vows to bring Christ to the world."[27] He minced no words in making his point.

> As a general rule the life of a religious is dedicated to children, to the sick, or to the elderly. ...Nevertheless it is grown-ups who run the world, create the climate of opinion and the atmosphere we all breathe. ...One does not see [religious women] playing any part among adult lay-women whom the Church calls to the apostolate but who often lack anyone to stimulate and sustain them.[28]

Noting that there was increased recognition of the role of women in society, he flatly declared, "A religious is a woman of her times,"[29] and went on to ask, "Why should their voices not be heard in councils where pastoral work is planned, as is the case already in many parishes?"[30] After citing examples from the Acts of the Apostles and foundresses, as well as quoting previous popes, he called for a reappraisal of Rules, customs and schedules which prevented "the nun, that high-powered Christian,"[31] from working directly with adult lay women, since in his view this was the place of the nun in the world.

His views gained additional authority the following year when Pope Paul VI appointed Sister Mary Luke Tobin, SL, then president of the Conference of Major Superiors of Women, as one of fifteen women auditors at the Vatican Council and the only American. Articles by other theologians, such as the 1963-1964 series in *Review for Religious* by French Dominican Jean-Marie Roger Tillard, OP, provided timely updating of the place of religious life in the overarching theology of the church. The *Sister Formation Bulletin* published numerous "articles appearing in English translation for the first time"[32] by theologians such as Bernard Haring, CSSR, Karl Rahner, SJ, and Godfrey Diekmann, OSB. With the closing of the Council and the publication of its sixteen documents, the March 1966 symposium at Notre Dame, featuring not only Rahner and Haring, but also Henri de Lubac, SJ, Charles Davis, SJ, Barnabas Mary

Ahern, CP, and John Courtney Murray, SJ, drew an enthusiastic group of Sisters of Providence.[33]

Implementing Liturgical Directives

Long at the forefront of liturgical developments, the Congregation was well-prepared to implement the Constitution
on the Sacred Liturgy. Already the 1960 General Chapter had
acted on preliminary directives to change some liturgical practices. Rather than the somewhat monastic posture of placing
their hands in their sleeves as they approached the communion rail, sisters now contented themselves with clasping their
hands as did lay people. Frequently recited prayers now required more attention in order to address the third person of
the Trinity as Holy Spirit rather than Holy Ghost and the *Pater
Noster* at Mass was now simply "Our Father" since English
was allowed. Pleased by an early instruction that pipe organs
should replace electronic organs, the Congregation purchased
a pipe organ for the novitiate chapel and it was blessed on
December 18, 1960.[34]

After the liturgy document was officially promulgated on
December 4, 1963, the council encouraged purchase of copies
of study editions and gave permission to use the time allotted
for spiritual reading for discussion of the document. At the
motherhouse, sisters on the College faculty led panel discussions and groups traveled to Indianapolis to attend liturgical
conferences in December and April. By July 21, 1963, a temporary altar in the Church of the Immaculate Conception made
it possible for Chaplain Francis Dooley to celebrate a Mass
facing the congregation for the first time, and by May 1964 a
permanent altar was in place.[35]

In preparation for the 1964 summer session the College
music teachers prepared a selection of hymns from the newly
published hymnal *Our Parish Prays and Sings* in order to acquaint the sisters with the emerging repertoire of new music.
Each house was asked to purchase copies of the hymnal for
the sisters who would be attending the summer session. Also
introduced that summer during the Masses were a sung litany
of petitions and an offertory procession. By the first Sunday in
Advent the choir sang parts of the Mass in English. By 1965
the news that a sister was being anointed no longer meant
imminent death but rather prayer for spiritual strength in time
of sickness, especially when the service was conducted for a

small group. The first funeral using white vestments and resurrection themes was celebrated for Sister Marie Athanasius Matthews on December 5, 1963, and by September 18, 1965, the English Requiem Mass composed by Sister Cecilia Clare was sung for the funeral of Sister Marie Genevieve Clark.[36]

The importance of scripture in the liturgy was increasingly evident with encouragement of bible vigils and scripture services, as well as the use of scripture passages for the devotional Way of the Cross.[37] The 1966 decision to use the Divine Office or Liturgy of the Hours for Lauds, Vespers and Compline as community prayer required the purchase of the new office book, *Lauds, Vespers and Compline in English*.[38] To further the gradual implementation of such a major change from the Little Office of the Blessed Virgin Mary to the Divine Office, scripture scholar Roland Murphy, ODC, gave a series of three talks on the Psalms.

Papal Visit to the United States

The announcement that Pope Paul VI would visit New York City in October 1965 to address the United Nations Assembly, only weeks before the opening of the fourth and final session of the Council, was stirring news for American Catholics. Since tickets to a pontifical Mass at Yankee Stadium were available through the Conference of Major Superiors of Women, Mother Rose Angela and Sister Mary Pius made arrangements to attend. By that time regional government was in place, making it possible for the superiors of the eastern region, Sisters Anna Rose Harrington and Robert to come from Washington, D.C. Sister Mary Pius recalled the excitement of being close to the events:

> We sat watching television the day the Holy Father came and then all of a sudden Mother said, "Let's get up and go down there." So we went down to Fifth Avenue where the Holy Father was coming along and we stood there and saw the Holy Father pass us by. It was really thrilling—the atmosphere of the crowd.[39]

Indeed, the significance of the event was such that a general permission was given for all the sisters to share in the excitement by watching on television. As Mother Rose Angela later described the experience of the pontifical Mass,

> The spirit of jubilation, good will, spiritual uplift, kindness, and consideration for everyone else was indescribable. Above

all, however, reverence for His Holiness, a sense of unity of heart, purpose, and prayer pervaded everywhere. If only we could preserve that spirit always, what a world of peace, harmony, good will, and charity would exist.[40]

Adapting the Style of Governance

The governance of the Congregation during the 1960s presented some daunting challenges. As a pontifical congregation, its basic governance structure was dictated by canonical regulation. However, as the detailed description of the 1960 General Chapter illustrated, increased interaction among major superiors through the Conference of Major Superiors of Women injected a new vitality into observance of the required norms. The traditional government structure described in Chapter 2 no longer sufficed, and other areas required adjustment.

Working with the Hierarchy

Relationships with U.S. bishops

Cordial relations with Archbishop Schulte continued, with regular consultations and visits. Sister Mary Pius recalled that Mother Rose Angela would send the councilors to the diocesan offices when papers needed to be signed. "I remember going up with Loretta Therese right after the Vatican Council in Rome and the Archbishop was so excited about it and he had pictures of the whole thing and told us exactly where he was sitting."[41] In addition to his help with fund-raising activities for building projects at the College and at Ladywood in Indianapolis, Archbishop Schulte demonstrated support for education by conferring the diplomas at summer commencement ceremonies for sisters and by appointing Rev. Bernard Riegal as professor at the College when Father Robert Gorman died in 1963. In preparation for the celebration of the archbishop's golden jubilee of ordination, four sisters were commissioned to prepare a set of pontifical vestments. After accompanying Sister Rose Dolores to St. Meinrad Archabbey to research suitable samples, Sisters Mary Loyola Bender, Francis Pierre Pagels, Lourdes Kline and Inez Marie Kruse created a mitre, cope, chasuble, dalmatics and veil.[42] The vestments were displayed in the Tile Hall parlors and then presented to Archbishop Schulte on June 7, 1965, during a celebratory program in his honor.

Due to the intense fundraising efforts on behalf of the College, Mother Rose Angela and her council had occasion for many visits with the bishops in the dioceses where the Congregation staffed schools. In the final year of Mother Rose Angela's administration, several changes occurred within this group of prelates. In April 1965 Bishop Romeo Blanchette succeeded Bishop McNamara in the Diocese of Joliet. Since the new appointee had assisted Bishop McNamara in establishing the chancery when the diocese was created in 1949, he was well-acquainted with the Congregation. Two additional changes occurred in August of that year: Bishop Raymond J. Gallagher succeeded Bishop Carberry in the Diocese of Lafayette and when Cardinal Meyer died in April 1965, Archbishop John P. Cody was named to head the Archdiocese of Chicago.

Mother Theodore's Cause

During their January 1961 visit to Rome, Sisters Rose Dolores and Eugenia had visited with postulator Msgr. Federici, who had shown them the twelve bound volumes of testimony which he had arranged to have translated into Italian. He explained that although the testimony indicated that the cure of Sister Mary Theodosia Mug had the potential to be considered miraculous, this topic could not be introduced until the full consideration of Mother Theodore's life and virtue had been concluded. He also noted that about a thousand other causes were pending. In March 1962 he wrote to inform Mother Rose Angela that Cardinal Arcadio Larraona (formerly secretary of the Congregation of Religious), "a very affable person, an expert jurist, a great worker,"[43] had been appointed the new prefect of the Congregation of Rites. When Cardinal Larraona visited Chicago, Mother Rose Angela and Sister Loretta Therese met with him in May 1962 to request his continued assistance on behalf of the Cause.

In May 1963 Msgr. Federici sent word that additional documentation of the original sources was needed. A Franciscan priest who had been expelled from Yugoslavia by the Communist government, Father Bruno Koroshak, was engaged for this work. He wrote to request that Mother Theodore's extensive correspondence be transcribed prior to his arrival. Since the letters were numerous and their condition made them difficult to read, archivist Sister Eugenia enlisted the assistance of a large group of College sisters, junior sisters and novices to prepare the translations, typescripts and copies. Additional correspondence used by Sister Mary Borromeo Brown for Volume I of the Congregation history but still located in the Notre Dame archives was also included.

When Father Bruno arrived at Saint Mary-of-the-Woods on August 14, 1963, he had already done research at Ruillé, Rennes, Le Mans and Paris. The large "Bishop's Parlor" in Tile Hall was given over to his use since the archives room was quite small, and documents and photostats were brought as needed. As the chronicler of this project noted,

> His work was most exhaustive and perhaps one should say exhausting, as he worked steadily from after Mass until dinner in the evening, taking only a short time out for lunch. ...

> It would be very difficult to list everything asked for, but the investigation was most thorough. We have considered it a great blessing that Father Bruno came, as in drawing up various facts to be presented one would have no idea of the importance of surrounding data nor of the interrelation between the letters Mother Theodore had received from other clerics and her answers. ...

> Other legal documents, such as her parents' marriage license, the registration of birth and decease of various members of the family, were also obtained by Father Bruno [44]

Father Bruno departed on September 22, 1963, to take up his regular teaching duties in Rome but left instructions for sending further material as needed. By the time the project was completed, it had required six reams of specially printed paper to make up three copies of the set of four volumes bound in black buckram, the contents of which were sworn to be conformable to the originals.

National Influences

Conference of Major Superiors of Women (CMSW)

Due to her participation in the transitional committee of major superiors which had spearheaded the founding of the Conference of Major Superiors of Women (CMSW), Mother Rose Angela had a strong interest in the development of the Conference and regularly attended its annual meetings. As mentioned in Chapter 11, immediately after the major superiors voted to form the conference in 1956, some had wished to bring the Sister Formation Conference (SFC) into the CMSW. The move had seemed premature until the CMSW had established itself more firmly. The SFC, through its position as a committee of the National Catholic Educational Association's College and University Department, continued to sponsor workshops and publish its popular and often controversial *Sister Formation Bulletin.* Gradually tension sharpened between the SFC ideal of "a woman who can think for herself" and the CMSW's desire that formation should engender the attitude that obedience required viewing a superior's decisions as the will of God.

By 1962, CMSW Chair Mother Consolatrice Wright, BVM, had convinced Vatican official Rev. Bernard Ransing that the time was right for bringing the SFC under the auspices of the CMSW. He wrote to give his approval: "The principle is only too clear. If anything should be in the hands of the Major Superiors, it is the formation of the young subjects."[45] He and Archbishop Philippe of the Sacred Congregation for Religious attended the August 1963 CMSW meeting and announced the change. However, both officials expressed support for the work of the SFC and after a somewhat difficult transition to its new position as a committee of the CMSW, the SFC took on momentum in implementing the decrees of the Second Vatican Council.[46]

Meanwhile the CMSW established a dues structure and began the sponsorship of an annual Institute. Although the meetings were usually restricted to the major superiors themselves, the Conference also sponsored special meetings open to councilors, such as the May 1963 lecture by Cardinal Suenens and the series of workshops on canon law mentioned earlier. The Conference also drew on the expertise of members of its constitutive congregations, and at the 1964 CMSW meeting in Cincinnati, two Sisters of Providence, Sisters Alexa Suelzer and Ruth Eileen Dwyer, were invited to participate in a panel presentation. That same year the Conference began another phase of activity when the secretariat sent out a request to all member communities to write to their congressional representatives in support of the Civil Rights Bill.

The organization drew national attention when Conference Chair Mother Mary Luke Tobin, SL, toured the country sharing her experience as the only American woman appointed as an auditor at the Vatican Council. In another significant move, each CMSW congregation was asked to submit suggestions for the revision of canon law which would follow the conclusion of the Council. Due to her participation in the CMSW-sponsored workshops, Mother Rose Angela felt well-prepared to complete the Vatican's questionnaire shortly before the end of her term in January 1966.

Contemporary Movements

Pope John XXIII's exhortation to "read the signs of the times" had caught the attention of council member Sister Catherine Celine. She was interested in exploring how the Sisters of Providence could incorporate contemporary movements into their spirituality and ministry. The work of Father Joseph Cardjin, dubbed the "worker-priest" for his efforts to organize the laity as Young Christian Workers, had become popular in the United States, especially in Chicago through Msgr. Reynold Hillenbrand's influence at the seminary. Cardjin's vision of Catholic social action meshed well with the ideas in Pope John XXIII's encyclicals and the documents emerging from the Council. Cardjin's relatively simple system of "See, Judge, Act" had been adopted by the Young Christian Student (YCS) organization, and Sister Catherine Celine saw the potential for this system as a vehicle for group discussions in the 1964 summer session. Many of the sisters were already familiar with YCS due to its popularity in Chicago schools.[47] In 1965 Sister Catherine Celine not only attended a meeting at Notre Dame on the topic, but in December she also participated in a Cursillo retreat. Inevitably such regular contacts of council members with sisters in comparable positions in other congregations affected their approach to internal administration.

Adapting Internal Administration Structures

Home Superiors and Visitation

The topics and decisions of the 1960 council flowed directly from their participation in the General Chapter which had elected them. The seven members of the council were responsible for 1,462 professed sisters living in 120 missions scattered among ten states, the District of Columbia and Taiwan. When the Chapter discussed reinstating the provincial structure to delegate this responsibility to an intermediate level, a key question arose. Would councilors at the generalate level continue to relate to individual sisters as "home superiors?" The concern was to assure that the sisters would have the ear of a superior who would fulfill the time-honored role of "someone who could offer spiritual direction or simply someone to whom the sisters could express their feelings."[48] Since not only Mother Rose Angela, but also Sisters Mary Joan (director of education) and Loretta Therese (secretary) were mostly exempt from this duty, until an intermediate level was implemented this responsibility fell to the other four sisters on the council.

Another major responsibility of the council was visitation of the houses in order to understand the life situations of the sisters. Although this was primarily a responsibility of the superior general, in practice all the council members were delegated to assist with this key duty. Formerly these visits could be scheduled in the fall and spring, but now with the obediences (mission assignments) set to be given on the first Sunday of May, this time was greatly curtailed. The importance of visitation in helping the superiors understand the circumstances on the missions can be illustrated with two examples. Although the Chapter had specifically tabled the issue of driving, word came that the sisters at Lady Isle were using the car there to drive the sisters to Mass. Mother Rose Angela immediately wrote to say she didn't recall having given this permission, but later, after visiting and seeing the practicality of the arrangement, she brought the matter to the council, who voted to make an exception to the restriction on driving.[49]

Another Chapter discussion had been on the regulation that sisters could not take meals with seculars. Since no rule could fit every circumstance, the members determined that decisions regarding eating with seculars were to be guided by the principle that it was allowed but not encouraged. When Mother Rose Angela visited the recently established mission in Arequipa, Peru, in January 1965 she noted that the sisters not only offered refreshments to visitors who stopped in but also joined their guests. At first she chided superior Sister Kathleen Therese O'Connor. However, when Sister Kathleen Therese returned from a short trip to the Juliaca mission, she was delighted to see that Mother, having adopted the custom of the

missionaries, was herself the first to serve and join the returning visitors and their drivers.[50]

In an effort to alleviate the stress on the councilors, Mother
suggested that each take an afternoon out of her office, setting
the example by designating Wednesday as her own free day.
The usual meeting time for the council was Sunday after Mass,
but midway through their term they began to meet instead on
Thursdays. Nonetheless, Mother Rose Angela's own health
suffered from the relentless press of business, with periodic
bouts of strep throat and heavy colds requiring her to follow
doctor's orders for bed rest in the infirmary or even short respite times at a convent. Sister Rose Dolores suffered major
health setbacks during this term, with several hospitalizations
or stays in the infirmary, and she spent the summer of 1963
resting at Lady Isle.

Local Superiors

Because the success or failure of the mission was largely in
the hands of the local superior, whose spirituality and natural
ability were so influential for those entrusted to her care, careful consideration had always gone into selecting individuals
capable of exercising authority well. To prepare for this office,
future superiors were given responsibilities in assistance to
competent superiors. After a new superior's appointment, she
conferred with the home superiors in person or via phone or
letter and attended Mother's instructions in the summer.
Mother Gertrude Clare had begun the practice of providing
opportunities for several local superiors to meet together with
her on weekends and had instituted an interactive style of summer instructions. With the rapid expansion of the number of
missions and the need for more sisters to fill the role of local
superior, greater attention was now given to both selection
and training.

Plans for the 1960 summer session took the form of a "Workshop in Ascetical Principles and Administrative Procedures
for Local Superiors." Participants worked in groups led by
moderators, all experienced local superiors themselves. As a
follow-up, newly elected Mother Rose Angela continued with
weekly workshops. One of the situations brought up as a recent concern was attendance at evening PTA meetings and at
student games. Rather than rendering an immediate top-down

decision, the council decided to conduct a survey to see how widespread the problem was. As they discussed this situation, they decided to explore other emerging topics and developed an entire questionnaire. Based on the results and also on the fact that many local superiors were studying at different universities during the summer and were unable to attend the usual summer session workshops, the decision was made to schedule a superiors' Institute during the 1963 Christmas vacation.

Meanwhile, in August 1962 twenty-five superiors attended the Institute for Spirituality at Notre Dame and the following July it was this group who conducted panel discussions for local superiors. In another attempt to assist superiors, that summer Mother Rose Angela stayed overnight at a residence hall at Indiana State University in Terre Haute in order to meet individually with local superiors who were studying there.

One hundred twenty-five local superiors arrived at Foley Hall on Friday evening, December 27, 1963, to attend the superiors' Institute. Following the opening Mass, Mother Rose Angela welcomed them as the "backbone of the community."[51] Emphasizing that they had authority of office, she spoke of the common sense principles that would enable them to exercise their responsibilities with wisdom and tact. The sessions included information and guidelines on the topics of the common fund, medical reports, health costs and possible insurance plans. Vocations and formation received in-depth treatment so that superiors might understand the characteristics of suitable candidates and develop techniques and attitudes for dealing with the young sisters coming new to the missions. The sisters in charge of each level of formation explained details of her program: Sisters Margaret Maureen Verdyn the high school program, Ann Bernice Kuper the postulancy, Marie Ambrose McKenna the novitiate and Louise Beverly the juniorate.

Sister Ann Patrick McNulty, superior at St. Charles, Bloomington, described the practice of allowing sisters once a week to choose to use discussion formats for "collective meditations" on assigned spiritual readings. As they had in the summer workshops, the local superiors engaged in open discussion of questions of interest. There were suggestions regarding books and articles which could be pursued as follow-up. When they departed to return to their missions on December 31, they had much to digest.

Local Councils

As she attended the series of summer workshops on canon law, Mother Rose Angela became familiar with the notion of appointing a local council to assist superiors of larger houses. Not only would the formal appointment of two sisters to this role relieve the burden of the local superior, but it would allow increased participation in decisions affecting the local community. Directives for local council meetings were distributed to the houses in 1962, and the Obedience Lists included the appointment of two local councilors in the larger houses.

Giving of Assignments

The council met regularly during the spring of 1961 to work on placements for the 1961-1962 school year. Following their decisions came the extensive secretarial work of preparing a slip for each sister designating her mission, grade assignment and superior. The slip was placed in an envelope with the sister's name, and the envelopes were grouped according to the current year's list for distribution to the houses. The typed alphabetical list of the almost 1,500 members of the community became the essential organizing document—the official Obedience List. In addition to this work, the summer assignments had to be prepared at the same time since those who would be remaining on mission or studying during the summer received this assignment in the same envelope.

The protocol developed for the new method of receiving notice of the next assignment was designed to foster each sister's sense that it was truly an "obedience"—a spiritual acceptance of God's will for her. Special prayers were recommended for the three days before May 7, the first Sunday in May 1961. The superior was to arrive early in chapel and place each sister's envelope in her prie-dieu. After reciting morning prayers, each sister was to open her envelope, as described in the sidebar on page 418. The meditation period immediately following provided time for an internal acceptance of her next assignment. Despite the religious solemnity of the moment, the directives made allowance for human nature: "In spite of the fact that it is retreat Sunday, those who wish may assemble in the community room for a half hour and share the news

The Life: Sister Ann Bernardine Dunne

As usual, on Sunday, May 7, 1961, Sister Ann Bernardine slipped into her place in chapel at St. Charles Convent, Peru five minutes early. As she expected, a small white envelope rested on the top of her prie-dieu. Unlike the five other sisters taking their places, she already knew its contents. The day before she had received a call from her home superior to prepare her for the news that, she would be taking on the duties of superior of the house and principal of the school in August.

She had to acknowledge that the appointment came as a surprise. At age forty-nine she had noticed that younger sisters were being named superiors and had been content that she wouldn't have the extra worries that went with the post. On the other hand, she had plenty of experience during her twenty-eight years of mission life. After starting out as a boys' teacher at St. Mel, Chicago, with Sister Rose Genevieve as her superior, she had felt prepared for anything. Over the years she had seen more of the country than most sisters. She had especially enjoyed her time at her home parish, St. Rose, Chelsea, with its opportunities to visit with her family, where her two priest brothers made the Dunne name well-known. Last year's move from suburban Maryland to the cornfields of north central Indiana where the "convent" was simply remodeled rooms on the second floor of the school had certainly been a major change. She definitely had never been any place where her pupils were looking forward to spending their summer as circus performers! Who could have known that John Ringling had set up circus headquarters in Peru the same year she came to the novitiate in Terre Haute, and Peru still claimed the title of Circus City.

As morning prayers concluded, the sound of envelopes being slit and the crackle of papers barely broke the stillness. With relief she saw that three names on her list were the same as this year's group. With the new cap, she could even see smiles on their faces as they saw her name. She too smiled. It would be a good year ahead.

with one another."[52] After this the strict silence of retreat was resumed until dinner; the entire Obedience List could be opened during noon recreation to satisfy everyone's curiosity regarding the placement of those in other houses.

The directives included a veritable nosegay of caveats regarding behaviors appropriate for the new system. As for spreading the news with family and friends, "a well-balanced and womanly way" was offered as the norm. Telephones should not be in constant demand. Charity was enjoined and gossip should be shunned. Gracious notes of welcome on the part of the new superior to her charges, and on their part to her, were recommended. The fact that the current superior's term would be in effect until the following August 15 was emphasized. The Book of Important Events noted the historic nature of the day: "After 120 years of hearing the Obedience list read, on May 7, 1961, the Community was notified of appointments by a new method." Nonetheless, once the excitement died down, normal routines demanded attention. Pleased or disappointed, sisters found that the additional time to adjust to the next year's assignment proved the value of the revised approach and additional procedures were gradually added to handle situations when changes needed to be made during the summer.

Regular Updates

Another adaptation of internal government procedures was subtle yet noteworthy. Rather than the quiet behind-the-scenes work of the council, which had an aura of secrecy, frequent communication became the new norm. Echoes of the comfortable conversational tone Mother Rose Angela had used in her presiding style during the Chapter could be heard in the style of her frequent newsy letters to the sisters. Clearly she had adopted the mindset that the free flow of information would engender a strong community spirit. She was a prolific writer, and her comment that a letter was becoming too long would often be followed by an additional page. Topics in a single letter could range over a variety of subjects: an update on the Cause of Mother Theodore; plans for the new mission in Arequipa; descriptions of the new work of staffing a home for retired persons; the announcement that long-serving College professor and assistant chaplain Father Joseph Kempf had been given the rank of Monsignor.[53] Directives on policies, updates regarding Mother Gertrude Clare's condition, information about the progress towards regional reorganization and news of changes at "Home" were staples of these letters.

The traditional format of the twice yearly "letters circular" provided a suitable vehicle for her literary skills as she conveyed her desire for a deep spiritual grounding during rapidly changing times. This is exemplified in an excerpt in which she builds upon Jesus' Easter message of peace:

> This peace, however, is not a tranquility which seeps into our hearts un-won. Abiding peace of soul is a blessing we must strive for; it is one we can attain only at the price of steadfast effort and of growing strength in Christ. ...
>
> In these days of transition and change in almost every phase of life, we all need an open mind, firm convictions, a Christ-centered heart, and a reasonable balance to know what to accept and what to decline accepting wholly or in part.[54]

Changing Customs

Mother Rose Angela's missives during this time show how she conveyed the council's encouragement of several changes in the physical arrangements of the houses, changes that fostered a gradual change in convent culture. A series of suggestions for adjustments to the formal environment of the convents indicated a recognition both of the need for a more relaxed environment and for decision-making at the local level. Although the use of television had been authorized, its placement was a problem both to allow for aerial connection and also to prevent interference with the relaxed give and take of recreation. How should this be decided? Mother Rose Angela offered this suggestion:

> If there is any question as to where the TV may be best located with a view to the common good, perhaps the Local Superior and the Sisters could have a little round-table discussion as to the best arrangement and then place the TV accordingly. We wish only to have great confidence in the mature and religious judgment of all of you, and in the wholehearted response to whatever contributes to the good spirit of your convent.[55]

The standard U-shape arrangement of dining tables in the refectory could now be changed so sisters could converse more easily "if the members of your household will find it helpful,"[56] At the motherhouse Mother Rose Angela asked for suggestions toward altering the tables and straight backed chairs in the community room, leading to what the diarist described as "smaller tables, sets of wicker furniture with covered cushions."[57] In all the houses some Saturdays could be considered "no bell" days when prayers and meals could be scheduled individually rather than at designated times.

Since it was acceptable not only to have a television but also to use a portion of the recreation period to watch the news, clearly the sisters were much more aware of events in the world around them.

Due to the tension surrounding the Cuban missile crisis and the increased threat of nuclear war, school and church buildings were often designated as shelters, so a good number of sisters received civil defense training, and superiors were entrusted with transistor radios for emergencies.

Managing Home Improvements

The normal ebb and flow of internal government required ongoing oversight of motherhouse operations. Given the enduring interest in all things "Home," several of the happenings at the motherhouse recorded in the Diary and Book of Important Events deserve mention. Health care expanded during this time, with the addition of a physical therapy room to the infirmary in May 1962. That same year members enrolled in a blood bank in Terre Haute, donating blood in exchange for eligibility for transfusions as needed. Head nurse Sister Dorothy Eileen Howard prepared data cards for each sister to record and update health records.

The infrastructure required regular attention, beginning with investing $95,000 in a new boiler in 1962, repairing the laundry building due to considerable fire damage in 1961 and changing over the entire complex to AC electric current. In March 1962 the entire motherhouse community moved to the Church crypt for spiritual exercises while the Church was painted and redecorated. Later that year the reliquaries were moved from the small room by the Blessed Sacrament Chapel staircase to the crypt. In 1961 the political situation was such that inspectors visited the campus to check on readiness for civil defense. In 1966 the people living in the areas surrounding the campus formed the Marion Heights Conservancy in order to assure sufficient water supply. The Congregation gave a land easement for the construction of a water tower and agreed to support the project by monthly purchases of water to supplement the Rosary Hill well.

In 1963 the cemetery was enlarged, with a Marian shrine forming a focal point at the southeast end. Above a limestone altar stood a white stone statue of Our Lady of Providence against a red brick background. The shrine was the gift of an anonymous donor in honor of the two former superintendents of grounds and buildings who served a total of sixty-five years—Joseph Bisch, Sr. (1893-1939), and Bernard Bisch (1939-1958). When Father Robert Gorman, assistant chaplain and professor of history at the College, died in 1963, he was buried in the chaplain's circle. Practices to honor the deceased sisters also underwent alteration. The small parlor at the east end of Providence Tile Hall began to be used for wake services. The retirement of Charles Kerstiens, who had made the coffins for many years, made it necessary to use caskets purchased from the Callahan Funeral Home.

Various occasions for honoring Sisters of Providence during this period included an invitation from the Catholic Hospital Association to attend their June 1961 annual meeting in Detroit, where the fifteen congregations whose sisters had served as nurses during the Civil War were presented with copper plaques engraved with the cross surmounting the crossed flags of the Union and Confederate states. Mother Rose Angela and Sister Eugenia accompanied infirmary staff nurses Sisters Dorothy Eileen and Eileen Mary Cunningham for the occasion. In 1962 the group of thirty Golden Jubilarians was the largest ever. Because they wished to honor Jubilarian Sister Helen Agatha Bourke, the College Alumnae arranged to have a Terre Haute caterer serve dinner to all the guests at Le Fer Hall. With this as a sort of precedent, and since Mother Rose Angela celebrated her Golden Jubilee the following year, the same practice was followed in 1963 and continued through 1965.

Death of Mother Gertrude Clare

After a protracted illness, Mother Gertrude Clare died on November 18, 1963. Mother Rose Angela's November 23, 1963, letter circular to the sisters was in one sense, a letter she had long expected to write, and in another sense, a means of expressing feelings of shock and grief about another death.

> Who of us can ever forget the momentous events of yesterday, November 22,—events which drew together in an even deeper and more sacred union of prayer and devotedness the hearts of our Community and the hearts of our nation! In the morning we laid to rest the precious body of our beloved Mother Gertrude Clare, with hearts uplifted by the beautiful ceremonies of the Church and by the deep conviction that dear Mother had seen God and had entered into the peace of eternity won by her humble and holy life. Then came the message of the tragedy that had befallen our nation in the assassination of our great and noble President. How truly do these two memorable events exemplify the fact of life's alternations of joy and sorrow as well as of God's mysterious ways of calling home His faithful servants.[58]

She then went on to tell of Mother Gertrude Clare's final hours during which many sisters came to pray at her bedside. They then kept watch day and night near the casket in Providence parlor until the pontifical funeral Mass on Friday. As Archbishop Schulte was in Rome for the Council, Vicar General Msgr. Cornelius Sweeney was the celebrant, with Father Joseph Brokhage delivering the sermon. His eulogy compared her to Pope John XXIII, in that both had been given a charism, a "special gift to do something extraordinary for God."[59]

Mother Gertrude Clare was indeed unusual in that all but the newest members of the Congregation would have had some personal remembrances of her. Because the months of her illness had stretched to almost three years, many of the sisters' conversations contrasted her diminished state with memories of encounters during her forty-three years of service on the council. As Sister Georgiana Terstegge had commented in her address during the 1957 summer celebration of Mother's feast,

> Surely each Sister has her own story to tell of our Mother's personal interest. How well she has learned from that Providence of God which is "the inexhaustible source of all good" to be herself an asylum of the afflicted and a refuge for the needy. ...This unhurrying little Mother of ours, who has never been seen in haste or flurry or excitement, has never, on the other hand, been even a minute behind schedule. How unexpectedly she can turn up at corners, as if she foresaw some special need. And that precious sense of humor which never fails even amid

stress and strain—how we love it! Untiring, courageous, confident, she will undertake tremendous projects with ease and quietness. To watch her is to take heart for one's own tasks; to look into her eyes is to feel close to God.[60]

To mark the departure of their beloved Mother and indeed of a significant period of the community's life, a small memorial booklet was sent to each sister on the next Foundation Day, October 22, 1964. They were no longer able to make their accustomed visits to her bedside, but one can easily imagine the sorrowing members of the council taking time to visit her grave near the circle where the Celtic cross bore the comforting words bequeathed by Mother Theodore, "I sleep, but my heart watches over this house which I have built." The new cap may have provided for unimpeded vision, but to govern well in a fast-changing world as Mother Theodore had done in her day, they too would need to cultivate a heart's vision.

❧ Chapter 14
Building for the
Future

When the 1960 Council met for the first time on June 26, 1960, the three new members quickly learned that in addition to the considerable new business given to them by the General Chapter just concluded they had inherited a great deal of old business from the previous administration. Of course, prior to their election, all the council members had been actively engaged in the educational apostolate and it was from this perspective that they took up the work of providing facilities and personnel to serve the growing Catholic population.

Workers are attentive to instructions from artist Sister Immaculee Krafthefer as they place mosaic tiles on the façade of Mother Theodore Guerin High School in River Grove, Illinois. High School Supervisor Sister Mary Corona Sullivan holds the drawing of the design depicting Our Lady of River Grove.

Parish Grade Schools

During the final year of Mother Gertrude Clare's administration it had become apparent that the needs of the high schools would require serious attention. The 1960 General Chapter had given a ringing endorsement to this policy by declaring a moratorium on accepting any more grade schools, with the understanding that previous commitments would be honored. As we have seen, the demographic growth outward to the suburbs, together with the baby boom, had led to the opening of many new parishes. Consequently, in addition to the fourteen schools opened during Mother Gertrude Clare's administration, the 1954 council had accepted three more parish schools which were already scheduled to open within the next two years.

St. Alexander, Palos Heights, Illinois

In June 1959, Cardinal Meyer appointed Father Joseph Hanton as pastor of the new parish to be opened in the Chicago suburb of Palos Heights. Since Father Hanton had received his early education from the Sisters of Providence at St. Anselm and his sister was now Sister Marie James, his request for sisters was kindly received. Due to the activity of eager parishioners, ground had already been broken for the church and school in December 1959. Typical of the times, a portion of the school building was temporarily fitted out to serve as living quarters for the sisters until a convent could be built. In September 1960 four sisters and two lay teachers opened the school with 247 pupils, and by the time of the October 4, 1960, dedication, the enrollment had already reached 350.

St. Luke, Indianapolis, Indiana

Although the Archdiocese of Indianapolis had purchased a site in the suburban Meridian Hills area in 1948, it was not until 1958 that St. Luke Parish was officially established there. Even then, development was delayed until February 1961 because the town zoning commission refused to issue a building permit. When a judge reversed this decision, the town took the case to the Indiana Supreme Court which settled the issue in favor of construction with its ruling that, "churches and schools promote the common welfare and the general public interest."[1] Two nearby residences were purchased for a rectory and a convent, and ground was broken in April. St. Luke School opened to 179 pupils that September with a faculty of three sisters and four lay teachers, and a formal dedication was held on October 22, 1961.

St. Simon, Indianapolis, Indiana

A little farther north, matters had gone more smoothly when Archbishop Schulte established St. Simon Parish in October 1960. Construction began on a school and auditorium/church building in December and was completed in time for dedication on July 16, 1961. The four sisters who formed the first faculty lived at Holy Spirit Convent and commuted until the convent was completed. These two 1961 school openings marked the end of a significant period of expansion in the staffing of parish schools, seventeen in eight years. Given the unceasing flow of requests, the moratorium was a very difficult policy to implement. Over the six years of Mother Rose Angela's administration, the council refused sixty-six requests to staff elementary schools in twenty-three states and seven foreign countries.[2] However, as explained in Chapter 12, plans were already underway to revitalize and expand the high school apostolate.

Major High School Construction Projects

Mother Theodore Guerin High School, River Grove, Illinois

Under the leadership of Superintendent Msgr. William McManus, during the 1950s the Archdiocese of Chicago had developed long-range plans to expand the regional high school system. The Archdiocese would partner with religious congregations to locate sites, purchase land and provide up to a million dollars toward construction costs. During his February 14, 1960, meeting with the council, Msgr. McManus suggested that the site proposed at the River Grove location would "twin" with the boys' high school being constructed by the Holy Cross Brothers on the same property. Although the council was favorable to this plan, it was not until January 1961 that a formal acceptance letter was sent.

Almost immediately Msgr. McManus replied that Holy Cross was scheduled to open with a freshman class in September 1961 and that the projected enrollment figures for girls' high schools in the archdiocese were well over capacity. He felt it was urgent to open the new girls' school in September 1962 in a wing of Holy Cross while the new school was being constructed.[3] This plan was accepted, and in early May Cardinal Meyer approved the name of the new school, Mother Theodore Guerin High School. In August the council met with architect Gerald Barry, Jr., and visited schools which his firm had designed. There were subsequent meetings with the council and Superintendent of Buildings Joseph Bisch at Saint Mary-of-the-Woods to go over plans. Sister Mary Corona Sullivan was named community consultant for the project to supervise construction and recruit students. Further consultations with Brother Donatus, CSC, principal at Holy Cross, ensured cooperation between the two schools. Following the signing of a formal agreement with the archdiocese, bids were awarded in April 1962, with groundbreaking taking place on April 15, 1962.[4]

May 6, 1962, was an exciting day for all Sisters of Providence. For only the second time they would learn of their assignment for the following year in the spring rather than on August 15. Six of those sisters opened their envelopes to discover that they would form the first faculty at Mother Theodore Guerin High School in River Grove, with residence at nearby Saint Francis Borgia convent. Named as principal was Sister Frances Alma McManus. She had taught for a year at Ladywood, Indianapolis, after completing a six-year term as principal at Marywood, Anaheim, where her duties had included a search for a new site for that school. She would now draw on her experience to bring the Sister of Providence approach to a new institution. On September 4, 1962, the sisters and nine lay teachers welcomed 398 freshmen girls to classrooms in a wing of Holy Cross High School.

Principal Sister Frances Alma McManus and High School Supervisor Sister Mary Corona Sullivan greet visitors in the lobby of Mother Theodore Guerin High School.

Each day the six sisters passed the construction site of what would become their school and convent. There were frequent shopping expeditions to purchase furniture and equipment for their new abode. A special distraction was watching the creation of the twenty-foot tall mosaic of *Our Lady of River Grove*, designed and executed by Sister Immaculee Krafthefer for the exterior wall above the front entrance.[5] Although construction lagged behind schedule at times, progress was steady. The convent was ready for occupancy on August 12, 1963, and when the cornerstone was laid on August 24, 1963, officiating Bishop Cletus O'Donnell also consecrated the altar in the convent chapel, which was beautifully illuminated with stained glass windows designed by Sister Adelaide Ortegel. In September classes began in the $3,200,000 building for 796 freshmen and sophomores, with a formal dedication by Cardinal Meyer on April 11, 1964.[6] By the 1966 General Chapter, the school, built for 1,200 girls, enrolled 1,298.

Chartrand High School, Indianapolis, Indiana

Archbishop Schulte had adopted the coeducational model for secondary education. He first persuaded the Congregation to not only supply staffing but to actually finance the building of Providence High School in Clarksville in 1951. Deanery-wide fundraising made possible the 1953 opening of both Schulte High School in Terre Haute and Scecina High School on Indianapolis' east side. The success of this model led to the decision to launch a $5 million campaign to construct three more deanery-wide high schools in Indianapolis, with invitations to religious congregations to provide faculty. The prospect of Sisters of Providence staffing one of these schools had softened the blow of the decision to close St. John Academy in 1959. Shortly after the first of the three schools, Chatard High School, opened on the north side of the city in 1961, ground was broken in April 1962 for Chartrand High School on the south side. Construction included a large convent intended to accommodate not only the high school faculty but also the sisters teaching at St. Jude Elementary School on the adjacent property. Three sisters were assigned to teach at Chartrand alongside the priests and lay teachers who welcomed the first class of freshmen in September 1962.[7] The archdiocese's long-range project reached completion two years later when Cardinal Ritter High School opened its doors to serve the western deanery.

Ladywood, Indianapolis, Indiana

Meanwhile the northeasterly expansion of Indianapolis which had led to the acceptance of St. Luke and St. Simon also affected Ladywood. Over the years, small portions of the original acreage had been sold, and by 1956 development near Ladywood had continued to the point that a lease was signed with the city for sewer extension. The following year the con-

Mother Rose Angela at the Ladywood groundbreaking in a pose which would characterize her administration.

struction of a bridge on Emerson Street over Fall Creek cut off thirteen acres and made it necessary to build a new entrance to the property. By 1960 a new highway was planned for the area, with adjacent land to be laid out in city lots. With the other archdiocesan high schools under construction, together with plans for a new Jesuit boys' high school, Archbishop Schulte recommended enlarging Ladywood. The remodeled country estate with the 1927 classroom building could only accommodate a 1960 enrollment of fifty-two day students and fifty-six residents, many from foreign countries. In July 1961 he also asked to purchase a portion of the property in order to build a retreat house.

Prior to the close of her six-year term, Ladywood principal Sister Maureen Therese Brennan added yet more urgency to the situation with her March 1961 report that a visit from the health department had confirmed some of the safety concerns she had already presented to the council. Clearly a new building was needed. Follow-up visits by Sisters Rose Dolores and Francis Raphael led to a consultation with architect William Bohlen and the appointment in May of Sister Dorothy Mary Noe as principal.

During her terms as principal of Marywood, Evanston, and as dean of women at the College, Mother Rose Angela had worked alongside Sister Dorothy Mary and had come to appreciate not only her business acumen but also her forthright personality. After graduating from Providence High School in Chicago, Dorothy Noe had attended DePaul University and joined the work force before entering the novitiate at age twenty-two in 1939. After final vows she taught commercial subjects for six years at Marywood, Evanston, and earned an MA in Business Education at Indiana State College in 1951.

From there she joined the College faculty. Describing this period in Sister Dorothy Mary's life, her eulogist notes:

> When it was time to build a new building for Ladywood School, she carried out this task in the style of [her father], Frank P. Noe. She worked with the workers; she knew every jot and every tittle of the plans AND every cent that would be spent. Sister Dorothy Mary and the sisters lived and breathed the construction of that building for months.[8]

During July the council met to discuss the financing of loans for several construction projects, including the plans submitted by Mr. Bohlen for Ladywood. In August sales of 12.7 acres of the Ladywood property for Fatima Retreat House and two additional parcels were finalized, providing additional cash. In May 1962 the F. A. Wilhelm Company was awarded the bid and construction began immediately with a groundbreaking ceremony following the May 28 commencement. Construction proceeded rapidly throughout the summer on the building, which included classrooms, science, home economics and language laboratories, an auditorium, chapel, library, administrative offices and a cafeteria.[9] A dedication ceremony on September 1, 1963, preceded the first day of classes in the new buildings on September 4, with a new bus bringing day-students to the campus. A bustle of fund-raising activities and open houses marked the 1963-1964 school year, resulting in a gradually increasing enrollment of 178 in 1964, 242 in 1965 and 304 by 1966.

Marywood, Anaheim, California

During this period the Congregation was fortunate to have very capable principals to carry out the on-site responsibilities of the building projects. Prior to her appointment as principal at Mother Theodore Guerin High School, Sister Frances Alma had held the same position at Marywood, Anaheim, where she had begun the negotiations for its relocation to another site. Asked why the move was necessary, she replied simply, "Mr. Disney came to Anaheim."[10] In addition to the 1954 construction of the famed amusement park, the concurrent completion of Interstate 5 and the enormous increase in population following the Second World War had changed the landscape of Orange County from semi-rural to rapid development. With more and more girls applying to Marywood, Sister Frances Alma had asked for and received preliminary approval from the council to begin planning for expansion. However, after meeting with Cardinal McIntyre in July 1959 she had to change her request because he insisted that rather than building on to the Anaheim property the Congregation should sell the property and build elsewhere. For the next two years she spent considerable time visiting numerous possible sites in relation to population projections and city permits with no success, while the limitations of the Anaheim property became ever more apparent.

The principal appointed for the next six-year term, Sister Marie Helen Leonard, was well-suited for taking up this work. Having entered the Congregation in 1918 from Cheverus High School in Massachusetts, after a series of high school teaching assignments, she had returned there as superior and principal and then taught at Marywood, Anaheim. She served as principal at Marywood during the war years of 1938-1942, completing an MA from Notre Dame during the summers. She had been the founding principal at Providence High School in Clarksville during the organizational and building years of 1951-1957. Though she was only midway through a term as principal at Central Catholic in Fort Wayne in 1961, she was not surprised to find herself returning to California for a new challenge. At age sixty-one her experience and talent for public relations would prove invaluable.

Almost immediately a constant stream of letters from Sister Marie Helen began arriving in the mailbox of the already beleaguered Mother Rose Angela. When it was discovered that the architect who had been doing preliminary drawings for the project was not certified, an architect from a San Francisco firm, Mr. Vincent Raney, was recommended. The brother of two Sisters of Providence, Sisters Angelina and Marguerite Raney, his acquaintance with the Congregation buttressed his interest in the project. After meeting him, Sister Marie Helen, who had dealt with several other architects, wrote to recommend him: "From the start Mr. Raney impressed us. What a relief to talk with one who knows his business so very well!"[11] In October he came to the motherhouse and met with the council and High School Supervisor Sister Mary Corona, real estate adviser Paul Pfister, and Superintendent of Buildings Joseph Bisch. Meanwhile Sister Marie Helen pursued leads and visited a number of promising sites. In November Sisters Mary

Pius and Francis Raphael visited with Bishop Timothy Manning (Cardinal McIntyre was attending the Council in Rome) only to learn that the Tustin site which Mr. Pfister had placed in escrow was not approved by the archdiocese. Sister Marie Helen's contacts with several priests echoed the lack of support she felt from the archdiocese, as she wrote to Mother Rose Angela after the meeting with Cardinal McIntyre and then speaking with Father Sammon, the pastor of St. Cecilia in Tustin.

> We had experience of what one meant when [Father Sammon] said, "The Cardinal fires detailed questions. If they aren't answered immediately he sends the priests home to get all the answers."... and so on. It seems strange even to be writing this. ...The Cardinal felt that he should have been informed all along the way. All I say is that it is a good thing that we saw him when we did.[12]

Her experience was not unique. Cardinal McIntyre's autocratic managerial style was legendary, as described by social historian Charles Morris:

> When McIntyre took over the diocese, ... his first official act was to scrap plans to build a new cathedral in favor of building an infrastructure for his exploding Catholic population. ... He opened more than 100 parishes, built almost 200 schools, a seminary, 6 hospitals, and brought in 68 new religious orders. Like Philadelphia's Cardinal Dougherty, a generation earlier, he financed a substantial portion of his construction program by speculating in a rising real-estate market—picking up land in advance of new housing development, then selling off the excess to pay for schools and churches.[13]

Sister Marie Helen's discouragement at what she regarded as an endurance test would soon be alleviated when in December one of the students' mothers drove her to view a site which prompted another letter. "Really beautiful! Hills atop level ground! The hills could be just cut off and buildings placed there. The site overlooks the city of Orange . . . an ideal place for us since we have so many girls from there."[14] Contacts with the very active Marywood lay board led to meetings with City of Orange Mayor White and real estate developer Mr. Louis Nohl, after which the Chancery sent Bishop Manning to inspect the site. A short while later, Sister Marie Helen wrote to assure Mother Rose Angela that, "the Cardinal and Bishop seem quite impressed."[15]

In February 1962 Sisters Catherine Celine Brocksmith and Loretta Therese O'Leary went to California to consult in person with Sister Marie Helen, Mr. Nohl and Mr. Raney, and then to visit with Cardinal McIntyre. Following their visit, clergy representatives of the Archdiocesan Building Commission visited the site and recommended purchase. Some months were required to update the articles of the California nonprofit corporation which had been formed at the time of the purchase of the Anaheim property and to negotiate the purchase of the thirty-one acre site. Since the property was situated on a ridge, in consultation with a soil engineer it was decided that thirteen acres would be leveled. The surrounding land would ensure privacy, and there was the option of selling small marginal parcels to persons judged as potential good neighbors.

In April 1962 Mr. Raney met with the council to go over sketches for a complex to include a forty-room residence hall and a thirty-room convent with a large chapel, all connected to the school with its auditorium and gymnasium. During this time the Congregation was moving toward the establishment of regions, so one fortunate byproduct of the extended site

Following the dedication, sisters gather in the courtyard in front of the school auditorium at Marywood, Orange.

search was the incorporation of potential living quarters for a yet-to-be announced regional superior. Meanwhile, Sister Marie Helen's attention turned to both publicity and fund-raising for the new facility and also to the search for a buyer for the Anaheim property, utilizing the well-established network of Marywood parents and alumnae. During her December 1962 visitation, Mother Rose Angela met with the local community to assist them in planning for the final three semesters at Anaheim and a smooth transition to the new facility. In February 1963 the sale was finalized and all during the 1963-1964 year construction went forward at the Orange site.[16] In the final phase of planning for the move, Sister Catherine Celine joined Sister Marie Helen at a meeting with Cardinal McIntyre, Bishop Manning, and Chancellor Hawkes. June 30, 1964, was moving day as the sisters' sorrow at leaving the much-loved property which had served the Congregation for thirty years was ameliorated by their joy at occupying such a spacious and beautiful new home. Surely even Cardinal McIntyre had to smile as he arrived for the dedication on December 5, 1964. Built for 600 students including seventy-three residents, within the first year the school was filled to capacity.

St. Rose, Vincennes, Indiana

As we saw in Chapter 12, although St. Rose Academy in Vincennes had been one of the high schools included in earlier planning, its situation followed a completely different trajectory from the construction projects for Ladywood and Marywood. It was originally known as St. Mary's Female Academy and Bishop de la Hailandiére had transferred its administration from the Emmitsburg Sisters of Charity to the Sisters of Providence in 1843 during Mother Theodore's absence in France. It was renamed St. Rose Academy in 1865, and a combined school/convent building had been constructed in the historic district near St. Francis Xavier Cathedral in 1884. The convent housed both the high school and parish grade school sisters. The fact that two members of the 1954 council, Sisters Rose Dolores Thuis and Rose Angela, had graduated from St. Rose, the latter having returned as principal from 1941-1946, only strengthened historic ties with this establishment.

Vincennes became one of the vicariates of the newly established Diocese of Evansville in 1944, and in 1947 Bishop Grimmelsman recruited the Christian Brothers to staff a diocesan high school for boys, Central Catholic, also near the cathedral. Discussions had begun in March 1959 between Vicar General Msgr. Paul Deery, pastor of St. Francis Xavier, and Mother Gertrude Clare to upgrade the St. Rose Academy building. In August Sister Sheila O'Brien was appointed principal, but due to Mother Gertrude Clare's illness there had been no follow-up for these plans. Sister Sheila was well-prepared for the circumstances at St. Rose. She had graduated from St. Agnes Academy in Indianapolis in 1932 and entered the novitiate the following February. During her twenty-four years of teaching music she had been at only five missions but had fourteen superiors. One of those missions was St. John in nearby Logootee, another parish in the diocese with a similar combined academy/grade school arrangement. She had also spent a year at the co-institutional Reitz Memorial in Evansville, and her most recent appointment had been as superior at St. John, Indianapolis, during its 1958-1959 closing year.

By the spring of 1961 the council was once again ready to address the situation at St. Rose and they invited Sister Sheila to come to Saint Mary-of-the-Woods to present possible plans for expansion. Following this consultation, Mother Rose Angela wrote to Evansville Bishop Henry J. Grimmelsman to apprise him of the council's thinking about possible plans for expansion, including in her letter a discreet query: "On the other hand, has there been any thought that the school for the girls should be on parish or diocesan property as is the case with Central Catholic for the boys?"[17] Her letter prompted action. Not only did the bishop invite further suggestions, but he also convened a meeting of the Vincennes Deanery priests, leading to the decision to launch a fund-rising drive for both the boys' Central Catholic and the girls' St. Rose high schools. Clearly in his mind there was no thought of adapting the co-institutional model to the coeducational form used by the Archdiocese of Indianapolis.[18]

In July 1961 Mother Rose Angela, together with Sisters Mary Joan Kirchner, Loretta Therese, Francis Raphael Donlon and Sheila went to St. Rose to meet with Msgr. Deery. As vicar-general of the diocese and pastor of the old cathedral, since both St. Rose and Central Catholic were on blocks adjoining the cathedral, he would head the fund-raising drive and combined expansion. As a St. Rose contribution to the public relations effort, senior teacher Sister Catherine Ursula Hayes drew up a design for the yearbook featuring a dedication to the local pastors together with pictures of their churches. She hoped to project "the image of Saint Rose Academy as 'the school that has educated the young women of your parish.'"[19] The success of the drive led to an increase in enrollment the following year, which added momentum to the plans for a new building for St. Rose to include classrooms, science and home economics laboratories, a library and a combination gymnasium/auditorium, as well as a new wing at Central Catholic.

Given the large expenditures for the four concurrent building programs in Chicago, Indianapolis, Orange and on the college campus at Saint Mary-of-the-Woods, the council was relieved that the diocese had taken responsibility for the new St. Rose. Nonetheless, they felt it was only right to contribute to the project. In consideration of the fact that the St. Rose property had originally belonged to the diocese and that the diocese had sustained the expense of the purchase of adjacent land, in March 1962 they decided to offer to return the deed to the diocese, an offer which was quickly accepted.[20] Relying on Sister Sheila to relay Msgr. Deery's reactions to the ongoing discussions, Mother Rose Angela took care to state her understanding of the pending agreement between the diocese and the Congregation in her letters. Pointing out that never during the 119 years of service to the Catholic people of Vincennes had the Sisters of Providence requested financial assistance, she summarized the new arrangements.

> We will deed to the Diocese the present property ... which has recently been appraised at the value of $20,000. Moreover, we will make a loan for $50,000 as a contribution toward the new convent. ...

> We are assuming that the Sisters will receive a monthly salary comparable to that given to the Christian Brothers of the boys' department, that this salary will be adequate to help them maintain themselves in a reasonable manner, and help us to pay off over a period of years the interest and principal due on this loan which we are making. ...

> We are grateful ... to continue our teaching program even though it will not be a private institution under our Community's responsibility alone, but rather as a part of the parochial and diocesan system.[21]

By March 1963 contracts were let, with groundbreaking taking place on March 25, 1963, and construction continuing through the next year. The St. Rose house diary described February 28, 1964, as follows:

> "The Day of Days," for on that day and within one hour and fifteen minutes the transference of the school—student, faculty, and properties—was happily completed. Beyond our expectations, the moving proved most interesting and enjoyable. The spirit of the faculty with that of the students proved to be the means by which a burden became a delight.[22]

A week later on March 8 the dedication took place, with an open house for the public and donors.

Costa High School, Galesburg, Illinois

During this time, two other historic Sister of Providence foundations were also cooperating with the Christian Brothers to implement the co-institutional model. St. Joseph Academy in Galesburg, Illinois, had gone through a similar transition when, in cooperation with the Rosminians, it became Corpus Christi High School in 1948. At that point, the original St. Joseph Academy continued as a grade school for the two Galesburg parishes, St. Patrick and Corpus Christi. In 1957 Bishop John B. Franz took advantage of the gift of a large parcel of land on the northeast corner of the growing city to establish Immaculate Heart Parish, with long-range plans to build a new high school on the same property to replace Corpus Christi High School. Priests from the vicariate negotiated with the Christian Brothers of the St. Louis Province to staff the new high school. The school would be named for Father Joseph Costa from the Order of Charity (also known as the Rosminians after their founder), who had come to the Diocese of Peoria in 1877 at the request of Bishop John Lancaster Spalding. Costa had not only invited the Sisters of Providence to staff St. Joseph Academy in 1879 but had also arranged for his congregation to open Corpus Christi Lyceum for the high school boys in 1895.

In 1962 Bishop Franz launched a fund drive whose success led to a ground-breaking in October 1963. The new convent constructed for the sisters at Immaculate Heart in 1960 was now halfway between the parish church and the new high school, and during the summer of 1964 it was expanded to house the sisters on the high school faculty. In June the diarist at the faculty house for Corpus Christi High School recorded the last graduation of forty-four seniors and noted yet another transition taking place at that time: "Providence Convent as a home for the high school faculty is no more. It has become a regional house. Amen."[23] In August 1964 sisters from both schools took up residence in the convent, and in September Costa High School opened with Brother John Joseph Johnston, FSC, and Sister Marie Monica Slingsly as principals.

Providence Catholic High School, New Lenox, Illinois

As explained in Chapter 12, the building housing Providence High School in Joliet, Illinois, had been condemned in 1959. With long-range plans still in flux, Bishop McNamara arranged with the pastor of nearby St. Mary Nativity Parish for the students in the four-year commercial high school to continue classes in their facilities. Since the convent had been part of the razed building, two small houses were purchased and renovated for the sisters staffing St. Mary Carmelite grade school and the sisters staffing the high school. In March 1961, Mother Rose Angela met with Vice Provincial Brother Joel Damian Wilhelm, FSC, and Bishop McNamara to plan for co-staffing the new co-institutional Providence High School, to be constructed on a completely new campus in the nearby suburb of New Lenox. In September 1962, Brother J. Edmund Burke, FSC, welcomed seventy-eight freshmen boys to Providence High School, and Sister Marie Loretta (Julia) Shea welcomed 150 girls, both returning students and freshmen.

Saint Mary-of-the-Woods College

Reorganization of the Administrative Structure

Almost the first act of the 1960 council was to strengthen the position of the College. Although in 1954 the title of president had been transferred from the superior general to the fifth assistant since as supervisor of schools she was more academically qualified, it was time to bestow the chief administrative titles on the ones who actually served in these roles. On June 26, 1960, Sister Marie Perpetua Hayes was named president of Saint Mary-of-the-Woods College and Sister Mary Joseph Pomeroy was named vice-president for development; Sister Marie Agatha Vonderheide was appointed dean. As explained in Chapter 3, the Board of Trustees which had been established in 1928 to oversee the affairs of the College was composed of both council members and College administrators. During their tenure as College administrators working under Sister Marie Perpetua's leadership as dean, both Mother Rose Angela and Sister Mary Joan had been ex-officio members of the Board of Trustees.[24] Since they were very familiar with the situation of the College, when they began to serve on the Board as council members they saw the advantage of utilizing the expertise of the College members of the Board to greater advantage. Not only was the College the Congregation's first foundation, it was integral to the Sister Formation Program. In order to position the institution for the new decade, the council supported the Board of Trustees' recommendation to employ an outside consultant to analyze current needs and priorities and to develop a long-range plan for development. Ever active in support of their alma mater, the Alumnae Association agreed to fund the $12,000 annual cost of the services of the consultant chosen, the Financial Planning Association of the Fund Fulfillment Corporation.[25]

Separation of Motherhouse and College Finances

The ambitious plan immediately stumbled on a major difficulty—the need to report the finances of the College in standard form. Until this could be done, the College would not be eligible for federal grants and loans. Although the Congregation and the College had established two separate civil corporations in 1928,[26] the finances of both entities were completely intertwined.

In her position of College treasurer, Sister Marie Armelle Connors declared herself insufficiently trained to provide the required information. Sister Myra Ann (Hallie) McMahon was appointed to this very difficult task, assisted by an outside auditor. Basic to the construction of two separate accounting systems were the Articles of Agreement dating back to 1928.

> These articles indicated that the buildings and estate remained the property of the Congregation and were leased to the College—the equipment was the property of the College, while maintenance costs, labor charges, etc. were charged to the College by the Congregation, which provided the labor, etc.[27]

Topics brought to the council over the early months of 1961 point up the sensitivity needed to identify expenditures and allocate them equitably. For example, the food service for the students in Foley Dining Hall during the academic year was only possible because the Congregation sponsored the two-year commercial high school whose boarders served the meals. On the other hand, during the summer session the sisters' use of the dining room included use of the College-owned dishes. As for maintenance, all requests for electrical and plumbing services for the College buildings were handled through the econome's office, making it very difficult for Superintendent of Grounds Joseph Bisch to provide cost estimates. The salaries paid to the sisters on the faculty were minimal since the differential between a comparable lay salary was considered as contributed service, and this amount was booked as an endowment. However, the Congregation supplied basic living expenses since the sisters on the faculty took their meals at Providence and received their clothing from the Habit Room there, costs which were simply subsumed in the sisters' common fund.

Once the preliminary work of identifying various costs had been done, a special business meeting to revise the Articles of Agreement took place on August 6, 1961. Participants included the council with Treasurer Sister Francis Raphael, Econome Sister Rose Genevieve and College administrators Sister Marie Perpetua, Mary Joseph, Mary Josephine Suelzer, Marie Agatha, Catherine Joseph Wilcox and Myra Ann. A small 1947 study of College funds for the purpose of establishing tuition amounts had provided a useful baseline for research. This study, together with regular audits of the endowment income by the Board of Lay Trustees and records of both expenditures and income from tuition, board and fees, had made it possible to construct a reporting scheme. The original Articles of Agreement were examined and modified.

Major discrepancies became clear. No tuition was being paid by the Congregation for the scholastic novices and junior sisters attending classes. On the other hand, although the previous articles required the College to pay an annual rent to the Congregation, in order to meet the requirement of maintaining cash reserves this amount was never paid in full. A new and significant cost was the need to hire an outside food concession to replace the in-house kitchen staff; in this case it seemed equitable that food expenses would be charged to the

Congregation for one semester and to the College for the other.[28] Since the Congregation was responsible for overall financial oversight, it also assumed all indebtedness, but with no budget and no audit a true statement of assets and liabilities was not yet possible. As Mother Mary Pius later recalled, "All the books were laid open. It had to be done, but that was a very difficult meeting."[29] Nonetheless, a major step forward had been made.

Assessment of Needs

Meanwhile, in April 1961 two representatives of the North Central accrediting team met with the council and Sisters Marie Perpetua and Mary Joseph to explain areas which must be improved in order to maintain accreditation standards. The major need addressed was the improvement of the library, for the fact that its collection was scattered among various locations in Foley Hall made it a substandard element of the overall college program. It was also evident that the lay faculty needed to be more closely integrated into operations and that the College should make provisions for in-service opportunities, for sabbaticals and for housing for the lay women faculty. Offering of so many majors had led to a multiplication of courses in which very few students were enrolled. Separation of finances would ensure eligibility for government funding. After hearing the recommendations, the council acknowledged that the criticisms were fair, and it was decided to give immediate priority to building a new library and providing a faculty house.

Rev. Edward V. Stanford, OSA, former president of Villanova University and a consultant for the American Association of Colleges and Universities, was invited to study the way the College was structured and make recommendations. Through the Lilly Endowment he was funded to engage in this work for some forty similar colleges. On September 10, 1961, he met with the council and Sisters Marie Perpetua and Francis Raphael and suggested a more definite separation of the Congregation and the College by setting up a completely separate Board of Trustees for the College and by deeding the College buildings and land over to the College.[30] He provided specific suggestions for establishing a cash exchange to show the College paying salaries for sister faculty and the Congregation paying tuition and fees for sister students. In addition, rather than the Congregation assuming all indebtedness, he advised that it would be better for the College to show a deficit when asking for help. He also provided suggestions for modifying the membership and operations of the board.

By December 1963 Director of Education Sister Mary Joan was able to present specific proposals regarding salaries for the sisters on the College faculty together with a method for recording the tuition for the novices and junior sisters. After approval by the council on behalf of the Congregation and Sister Marie Perpetua on the part of the College, the revised Articles of Agreement replaced the earlier version.

Fund-Raising Efforts

When the College's long-supportive Board of Lay Trustees (also known as the Endowment Board) met in May 1962 they formulated plans for a ten-year development program, with construction of a new library to be completed in time for the celebration of the 125th anniversary celebration in 1965 as the focus for the first phase of the fund-raising efforts. Sister Camilla Troy, librarian at the College since 1931, was appointed to work with Sister Mary Joseph Pomeroy, vice-president for development, to head up the committee planning for a building to house 250,000 volumes and to cost approximately $1,500,000. The minimum goal of the campaign would be $2,500,000 to include additional construction of a science building and faculty residence as well as student aid and an administrative fund.

The Alumnae Association was instrumental in arranging to hire Community Consulting Services (CCS) of New York, a firm that specialized in working with Catholic institutions. Representatives met with the council in May, and in July they made a presentation to the sisters attending the summer session to explain that the sisters' involvement in solicitation was a key aspect of their approach. The first step was to have the chief officers—their term for Mother Rose Angela and Sister Marie Perpetua as heads of the Congregation and the College—meet individually with the bishops of the dioceses where the sisters staffed schools. The objective was to acquaint the bishops with the needs of the College relative to the education of the sisters teaching in their dioceses and to enlist their support. Thus Mother Rose Angela and Sister Marie Perpetua embarked on a grueling round of trips to Indianapolis, Fort

Wayne, Gary, Joliet, Rockford, Peoria, Evansville, Chicago and St. Louis. Sisters Marie Perpetua and Mary Joseph traveled east to meet with Cardinal Cushing in Boston and Archbishop O'Boyle in Washington, D.C., as well as with the sisters in those areas. The Community Diary reported that the emissaries met with "a kindly and gracious reception from each."[31]

The actual fund drive was set to launch in the fall after all the bishops had been contacted. Frank M. Folsom, Chairman of the Board of the Radio Corporation of America and long-time member of the advisory College Board of Lay Trustees, accepted the appointment as national chairman of the campaign and met with Cardinal Spellman to interest him in the project. Meanwhile alumnae coordinator Sister Estelle Scully was setting up campaign headquarters and arranging for sisters to chair boards in different areas of the country. Mr. O'Brien of CCS met several times with the council to update them on the project and explain the plan of having the sisters visit their families to solicit. This plan was not acceptable, but it was decided to have some sisters receive training from CCS and visit selected families in teams of two. Mr. O'Brien also made follow-up visits to several bishops. In California, Cardinal McIntyre did not approve of such solicitations but arranged through Bishop Manning to have the pastors of the schools staffed by Sisters of Providence contribute $1,700 per sister for the Congregation in general rather than for a specific building.

During the spring the well-organized campaign gained momentum. Prominent businessmen such as William P. Flynn, chairman of the board of the Indiana National Bank, whose six daughters had been taught by the sisters, served as chairmen of regional committees which numbered some 500 men throughout Indiana.[32] In addition to assisting Sister Marie Perpetua with visitation of major donors, Mother Rose Angela appointed sisters to serve as coordinators for ten regions throughout the country. The sisters themselves visited families with considerable success, as noted in a community diary description of the busload of sisters from Saint Mary-of-the-Woods who returned from the nearby town of Brazil "with more than five thousand in pledges and enjoyable experiences to relate."[33] The campaign newsletter noted that this unprecedented outreach effort had a welcome side effect: "The manner in which the Sisters are conducting solicitation is breaking down a common opinion that the Sisters of Providence are aloof and withdrawn."[34] Even the community chronicle allowed that "Many contributions have been made by very poor people who were anxious to do something for the Sisters. Many pleasant contacts were made and much good will created just by the visit of the Sisters whether it was productive of any financial results or not."[35]

When the council and college administrators met with the CCS Company in June to evaluate the progress of the fund-raising effort, 70 percent of the money pledged at that point had come from the sisters' efforts. The campaign was already over budget, but to maintain the follow-up with College alumnae who had yet to be contacted and to complete the redemption of pledges the drive was extended through December 1963. Meanwhile tangible results of these concerted efforts were visible on the campus. After architects Bohlen and Burns of Indianapolis had completed the design for the library building, the contract had been awarded to the J. L. Simmons Company of Indianapolis and construction had begun. In October 1963, chaplain Father Francis Dooley conducted a small ceremony blessing the cornerstone.

Funding Further Building

In January 1964, the second phase of the development began with plans for a new science building and a residence for lay faculty. The passage of the Higher Education Facilities Act opened up the possibility of obtaining government loans to private colleges, but in order to be eligible to receive such loans or grants from foundations, the College had to own the land on which any building would be placed. The previous spring, in the midst of the fund-raising, when the Congregation negotiated an additional twenty-year, two and a half million dollar loan with the B. C. Ziegler Company, questions arose regarding the provisions of the College Charter.[36] Within the council itself, "the difference between the 'Board of Directors' and 'Administrators of the College Board' was discussed at length."[37] Once again, both legal research and the presentation of separate financial reports needed to be provided in order to establish the separate responsibilities of the Congregation and the College.[38] The interdependence of the two entities would continue to require negotiation. For example, it was necessary to provide a tunnel from the Power Plant on the Congregation side of the property to the library on the College side. However, the advantage of receiving outside funding greatly increased the pressure to complete the final step in the definitive separation of the two entities.

In May the council received a legal opinion that "it is considered permissible for a parent corporation to transfer property to a subsidiary corporation; [that is] the Motherhouse may transfer property to the college."[39] In September Supervisor of Grounds Joseph Bisch prepared for the council's consideration a plot map of the campus showing the buildings and surroundings with suggested lines of demarcation for the College and Congregation. During a business meeting with Sister Francis Raphael, Mr. Bisch and three of the Congregation lawyers, it was agreed that the deed should include descriptions of each building with the land surrounding it, noting the community's right to use the buildings in the summer and mutual perpetual easements for the use of all needed roads. The gymnasium and Foley Hall with its dining area were to be leased to the College, which would supply maintenance.[40] At the same time as this deed was being drawn up, deeds for two of the houses owned by the Congregation on adjacent property were also drawn up, with careful provision regarding stipulations for future disposition.[41] In her April 1965 letter circular, Mother

In the children's section are (left to right) Sister Francis Angela Kolb, Superintendent of Grounds Joseph Bisch with his wife, Mary, Mrs. and Mr. Kelly, parents of sophomore, Kathy. The seated sister is unidentified.

Rose Angela informed the sisters of the new arrangement and the rationale for its execution.[42]

Several sites were suggested for the location of the science building, but a decision was postponed until the College faculty and the architect, Mr. Bohlen, could be consulted. Once the site to the east of Le Fer Hall was decided on, the college administrators immediately applied for government funding, with hope that one-fourth of the cost would be in the form of a grant and the remaining three-fourths would be covered through a government loan. Meanwhile, in March 1964, with the promise of a grant from the Ford Foundation, the council had authorized the College to proceed with plans to construct the faculty residence (now known as the Goodwin Guest House). Construction proceeded rapidly to the point that on February 14, 1965, a blessing and open house took place.

By June library construction was complete. One can only imagine the feelings of Sister Camilla Troy as she stood in the lobby of the beautiful modern air-conditioned building to supervise the distribution of box after box of the extensive collection. She had come to the campus in 1926 at the invitation of Sister Gertrude Smith at the time of the closing of the Academy when the College collection in Guerin Hall was to be combined with the Academy collection in Foley Hall. She was well qualified for this task, having received a library diploma from the University of Wisconsin in 1913 and worked for the Chicago Public Library from 1913 to 1926. During her time there she visited libraries throughout Europe, and her work included the devising of a catalog system for the fifty-nine branches of the Chicago library.[43] In 1928 she entered the novitiate at age thirty-four and embarked on her life's work of developing the Saint Mary-of-the-Woods College collection to augment the academic program. From the first 1930 library move, when she gratefully accepted books carried from Guerin by sisters on their way from class to dinner in Foley Hall, through the years of shelving new acquisitions in her beloved children's room or rare book room, till the 1964 move, there was scarcely a volume that had not passed through her hands.

Celebrating Success

The events of October 22, 1965, were the culmination of these efforts to provide a twentieth-century face to the tiny foundation begun with the arrival of Mother Theodore and her pioneer band one hundred twenty-five years before. Following a Pontifical High Mass and luncheon in Foley, delegates from approximately fifty colleges and universities joined the Saint Mary-of-the-Woods College faculty and administration in an academic procession in the Cecilian Auditorium of the Conservatory. As they toured the new building which formed a gracious link with its storied companions, Le Fer Hall, Guerin Hall, the Conservatory of Music and Foley Hall, Mother Rose Angela's comments rang true.

> A building is not merely a structure of steel and stone, for scarcely has a building begun to function and serve its purpose when it becomes an embodiment of the life that is lived within its walls, of the ideals that are engendered there, of the truth that is promoted, the culture that is fostered, and the spirit which knowledge and virtue combine to produce. ...

> Each generation has erected new buildings to meet new needs, and each building has come to be identified with the fundamental purpose for which this motherhouse and educational institution of Saint Mary's exists.[44]

Key to the entire building program was the intention to continue the tradition of excellence in education which had always characterized the Congregation's apostolic activity. Concurrent with the brick and mortar external evidence of that commitment was a shift in focus in the preparation of the young women who came with the desire to share in that mission. The move to the new novitiate had taken place on May 27, 1960, just days before the General Chapter began. During

Constructed of Bedford stone and adorned with the carving of Our Lady of the Woods *designed by Sister Esther Newport and executed by Adolph Walter, the library represented a renewed dedication to learning.*

that Chapter, the careful analysis of the distribution of the Congregation's personnel called attention to the need to encourage vocations. This impetus, in combination with the availability of the old novitiate building as a stable center for the juniorate, set the direction for a more explicit incorporation of the national Sister Formation program.

Focus on Sister Formation

Vocations

In accordance with Chapter decisions, by April 1961 the Providence Vocations Center was set up as a small office in Third Tile Hall where newly appointed Vocation Director Sister Marie Armelle Connors coordinated a variety of activities. She created exhibits and flyers featuring the Sisters of Providence for display at events such as diocesan vocation rallies and arranged for the participation of students and sisters from local high schools. Another activity was arranging for overnight visits featuring tours of the novitiate and campus when houses brought groups of students from high schools to Saint Mary-of-the-Woods. Panel presentations featuring the junior sisters themselves were scheduled in Indianapolis and Chicago. In 1962 the College journalism class, under the direction of instructor Sister Mary Gregory (Jeanne) Knoerle, filmed an entire day at the novitiate to produce a film that aired on a Terre Haute television station and could be used as a centerpiece for talks in various locations.

The topic of vocations was also very much in the minds of diocesan officials at this time as they contemplated the seemingly "never enough" of their schools and turned to the superiors of religious congregations to continue the flow of sister-teachers. When Msgr. McManus, superintendent of schools for the Archdiocese of Chicago, sent a questionnaire regarding staffing projections to superiors in 1963, his attitude clearly hit a raw nerve, as shown by Mother Rose Angela's reply:

> In conclusion, though, may I venture to say, Monsignor, that the last sentence of the second paragraph of your letter would be enough to chill the blood in the veins and arteries of any Major Superior of Sisters if she really took it to heart and believed that it means what it seems to mean, namely: "… that to a large extent the destiny of our Catholic Schools is in the hands of the Superiors of Religious Communities."

Monsignor, the issues at stake in the present school crisis are
beyond the control of Religious Superiors, and definitely we do
not have the solution. In fact, I do not think anyone has the
solution except God; so we will all probably have to keep on
doing the best we can until He raises up people to solve the
crucial problems of society of which our schools are but a cross-
section.

You know that Superiors cannot produce Sisters by magic; we
cannot buy them, nor rent them, nor hire them. They must come
to us from the homes of our Catholic people. Thus it certainly
seems as though the destiny of our schools lies in great part in
the homes of our Catholic families. I have yet to see this point
stressed in Catholic publications or to hear it emphasized from
the pulpit that if Catholic people want Sisters in the schools,
they themselves must provide them from their own households.[45]

In response to a question as to whether or not the vocation
situation was improving, Mother Rose Angela provided a table
showing that, despite the fact that the number of students in
Sister of Providence schools had increased since 1903, the number of vocations had remained relatively constant. She attributed this both to the increasing pace of life and also to the
move toward coeducation, thanking the Chicago archdiocese
for its policy of single-sex high schools.

Screening of Candidates

In addition to the outreach efforts of the Vocation Center,
efforts were made to help the sisters on the missions to identify and encourage girls who might truly be called to the life of
a teaching sister. When the local superiors gathered for the
December 1963 workshop, talks by the formation directors were
a major component of the program. As the superiors listened
to descriptions of current practices and approaches in the
aspirancy, novitiate and juniorate, their discussion enabled
them to develop updated criteria. In her letter circular the following spring, Mother Rose Angela expressed the need to encourage likely subjects and articulated specific criteria but also
sounded a note of caution:

Wholesome personalities, solidity of character, qualities of faith,
spirituality, and emotional maturity consistent with chronological age are all necessary for wholesome adjustment and are
foundation stones upon which divine grace can be effective in
the subsequent years of their life in Religion .... In this important and sacred work of encouraging vocations to religious life,

however, let us take care to give pre-eminence to the work of the Holy Spirit and not let ourselves become possessive in any way of those whom we may have the privilege of helping.[46]

In addition to the recommendations of the sisters themselves, new consideration was being given to a candidate's psychological readiness. The publication of numerous theories of human development during the 1950s had spawned a variety of psychological studies and measurement instruments. In January 1961 novitiate chaplain Father William F. Stineman, whose recent PhD in psychology had led to his dual appointment as novitiate chaplain and college instructor, was invited to participate in a study of the psychiatric readiness of novices and college freshmen. With expert advice readily at hand, that year's applicants were included in the study. By 1962 the use of psychological tests was required of novices for vow approval and by the following year the policy of requiring applicants to submit results from psychological tests and also from the College Board examinations was adopted.[47]

By the time of her report to the 1966 General Chapter, Mother Rose Angela was able to provide statistical information to illustrate the effort to encourage vocations. Even prior to entrance, the application process had proved effective in helping prospective candidates decide whether or not to follow through on an initial desire to be a sister.

TABLE 10: *Discernment through the application process, 1963-1965*

Year	Number of applicants	Number interviewed	Cancellations	Number not accepted	Number accepted
1963	81	59	10	11	60
1964	72	43	14	8	50
1965	72	52	10	9	53

SOURCE: *Report of Mother Rose Angela to the 1966 General Chapter, Chart VI, SMWA.*

Changing Approaches to Formation

As noted in Chapter 13, at the time the major superiors of the United States voted to form their congregations into the overarching national organization of the Conference of Major Superiors of Women (CMSW), one of the very first motions to come to the floor had been to move the Sister Formation Conference (SFC) from the National Catholic Education Association (NCEA) to their newly formed group. Since the superiors had the ultimate responsibility for formation, yet the SFC had already established an effective structure, there was no clear agreement about the better course of action. Gradually the philosophical divide behind the organizational dispute became more obvious. The clash of viewpoints is well expressed by Sister Margaret Brennan, OP, who had been appointed novice director in 1962 by her congregation, the Dominicans at Adrian, Michigan: "Another tension that arose was the content of the intellectual formation the young sisters were receiving. Teaching young religious to become critical thinkers at a time when spiritual formation did not tend in this direction was bound to provoke some tensions."[48]

Within the Sisters of Providence the question came to the surface through the choice of formation personnel. Always the aim had been to select sisters who had gained respect for their ability to blend spiritual grounding with personal capabilities. Two factors now called the effectiveness of the time-honored approaches to formation into question. In her retrospective on the era, Benedictine Sister Joan Chittister comments on one of the factors, the change in the candidates themselves:

> The young woman who entered religious life in the late 1950s, therefore, found herself caught between her formation in the values of her parents' generation and the emerging expectations of her own. The erosion of those values that had given unqualified support to the very notion of religious life itself had already begun. Developments in the life sciences, theories of human sexuality, the changing role of women in society, and the emergence of globalism with its awareness that there are unlimited other ways to be holy, to be human, struck quietly but deeply at the traditional theological foundations of religious life. The assault came silently but not without impact.[49]

For the Sisters of Providence, a second factor was the freeing up of space at the motherhouse to house the juniorate in its own building (the old novitiate). When the program began in 1957 the initial focus had been to keep the newly professed sisters on the campus for the additional two years needed to complete a bachelor's degree. When the newly constituted Board of Education met for the first time in August 1960, plans were put in motion to follow more fully the entire formation approach. As president of the College, Sister Marie Perpetua was delegated to visit other campuses with juniorates and to invite others to visit Saint Mary-of-the-Woods. As Mother Rose Angela and members of her council attended regional Sister Formation Conference meetings, the need to integrate an updated theological formation component into the formation program became increasingly clear. In order to provide for this, several sisters were sent to study.

Theological Formation

One of the potential theology instructors, Sister Alexa Suelzer, was already well into her studies. During her sophomore year at Saint Mary-of-the-Woods College, Alexa Suelzer decided to follow two of her older sisters, Sisters Mary Josephine and David, to the community. After professing vows in 1940, she taught fourteen years in a variety of high school settings, ranging from urban Chicago to rural Indiana, studying at Marquette University during summer sessions to earn an MA in English in 1956. As noted in Chapter 11, it was that very summer that she was named to study at the Regina Mundi Institute in Rome during the 1956-1957 year. The following year she was assigned to teach at Corpus Christi High School in Galesburg, Illinois, after which she was sent to study for a PhD in religious studies at Catholic University in 1958. It was a time during which fresh approaches to analysis and interpretation of scripture were developing, approaches still very controversial among bishops who had been educated in earlier methods. Graduate theological education was mostly conducted in seminaries rather than in Catholic universities, and few women were encouraged to pursue study in the specialized field of scripture. Fortunately she had the assistance of supportive professors, who sagely advised her to avoid controversy by entitling her dissertation, "The Utilization of the Pentateuch in the Teaching of College Scripture."[50] After earn-

Sister Alexa Suelzer

ing her degree in Sacred Doctrine in 1962, she was assigned to the College faculty, including teaching scripture in the juniorate.

Her 1962-1965 appointment at the College coincided with the Second Vatican Council, making it convenient for the council to call upon her to provide lectures and study groups for the sisters at the motherhouse. Since the establishment of an official Catholic approach to scripture study was a lively topic at the Council, in 1963 her dissertation was published under the title, *The Pentateuch: A Study in Salvation History.* The positive response to these activities made her a natural choice to be appointed to direct the juniorate program in 1965. Meanwhile, to supply the formal theological training expected in the Sister Formation Program, two other sisters were sent to study.

After graduating from Providence High School in Chicago, Barbara Doherty entered the novitiate in February 1951 and professed vows as Sister Vincent Ferrer in 1953. During her seven years as an upper-grade teacher she earned a BA degree in Latin and then taught one year at St. Agnes Academy in Indianapolis. Despite her youth, during 1962-1963 she was sent to study for an MA in Sacred Doctrine at the Graduate School of Sacred Theology founded at Saint Mary's, Notre Dame, by Sister Mary Madeleva Wolff, CSC, in 1941. Aware that she was being prepared to instruct the new members, she wrote her master's thesis as a way to "chart a program for undertaking a more vital study of Scripture in the formational years."[51] The thesis included a survey of the preparation of formation directors across congregations. Studying responses from thirty-two congregations, she noted the concerns of superiors: "No one envies the task of the Major Superior, for responsibilities and cares surround her like Joel's locusts." Nonetheless, she unhesitatingly asserted, "To these questions this paper gives but one answer. Found and form the Sisters on the Word of God."[52] In other words, don't hesitate to use the latest methods of scripture study, no matter how controversial. Having completed her degree she came to the novitiate in the fall of 1963 as a teacher and the following year was appointed Mistress of Postulants.

The other potential instructor was also relatively young but had additional experience of mission life. After graduating from the Academy of Our Lady in Chicago, Eileen Dwyer chose to join the community which had taught her in grade school at St. Leo, enter-

Sister Vincent Ferrer (Barbara) Doherty

ing the novitiate in February 1944. After professing vows as Sister Ruth Eileen in 1946 and teaching at grade schools in Washington, D.C., Chicago and California, she was appointed at age thirty to be superior/principal at Holy Spirit in Indianapolis. At the conclusion of her six-year term she began summer studies toward an MA in Theology at St. Xavier in Chicago. She then taught at St. Joseph in Hammond for a year before moving to high school as one of the founding faculty at Guerin High School in River Grove. She had only completed a year and a half on that faculty when she was assigned to the novitiate in January 1964.

As Sister Ruth Eileen continued her graduate studies during the summers, she applied them to her role as instructor by writing a thesis entitled "Rationale and curriculum plan for the religious education program for sisters in a congregation whose principal service is education." She developed course descriptions for a comprehensive series to be taught during the six semesters of the novitiate and the four semesters of the juniorate. By the time she completed her MA in Theology in 1966,

Sister Ruth Eileen Dwyer

the Vatican Council had concluded, allowing her to make liberal use of its published documents in her courses. She also
drew on the work of contemporary writers to stress her belief
that "besides the knowledge of the role of religious communities, there must be at the center of the instruction program a
knowledge of the individual as a woman who is essential in
her own individuality to the formation of the community and
its successful activity."[53] Although the idealized curriculum
was never fully implemented, the influence of these three relatively young sisters with degrees in a theology which was still
evolving would be profound.

The Novitiate

Following the move to the new novitiate in May 1960, Sister Marie Ambrose with her eighty-nine novices and Sister
Isabel Storch with her eleven postulants, together with their
assistants, Sisters Joan Marie (Eleanor) McAuliffe and Mary
Alma Murphy, devoted themselves to adapting the practices
and routines of novitiate life to their new surroundings. In
fact, several sisters who lived in the new structure for only
three months before making their first vows on August 15 recall that summer as a time of constant cleaning, with the novice diarist recording, "This house is big—when you have to
clean it!"[54] Novitiate life did undergo significant change. Even
before the move, in order to better align with the College academic year, the council had settled on a single entrance date
of September 12, 1960, rather than the twice yearly arrivals in
February and July. The fifty-three young women who arrived
that September were the first to embark on the eleven-month
postulancy that had been established by the General Chapter.
Whereas formerly a smaller group of postulants could easily
be absorbed into a much larger novice group and would have
had the example of attending prayers with the professed sisters in the motherhouse chapel, now they constituted a full
third of the completely segregated novitiate group. Not only
that, but those who had just graduated from high school in
June began their freshman year of college work immediately,
while creative scheduling was needed for those who were farther along the educational path. Indeed, the very act of setting
aside her individuality to put on uniform dress and fall in the
long black line in an era when uniqueness was prized and
new opportunities for women were opening up was an act of

faith on the part of each young woman who entered during these years.

The adaptations required in the postulant program at this time pointed to the need for a change of personnel. With this in mind, the council looked ahead with their 1960 appointment of Sister Ann Bernice (Bernice) Kuper to teach at Reitz Memorial High School in Evansville.

Novices and postulants assemble for prayer in the new novitiate chapel.

Growing up in Jasper, Indiana, Anna Bernice Kuper had come to Providence Juniorate for high school and entered the Congregation in 1940, professing vows in 1943 as Sister Ann Bernice. After eleven years as a middle-grade teacher at three Chicago schools, she served a six-year term as local superior and principal at St. Patrick, Terre Haute. During her 1959-1960 year at Nativity, Indianapolis, she began her studies for a MA in Education at Notre Dame University. In order to prepare her for a role in the novitiate, she was given a year of experience with high-school students at Reitz Memorial High School, and in 1961 she was assigned to the post of novitiate sister. She replaced Sister Isabel as mistress of postulants the following year and in January 1964 she was named mistress of novices.

Sister Ann Bernice Kuper

To augment her ability to provide example and instruction for the new members, Sister Ann Bernice asked to change her graduate major to counseling, and she returned to Notre Dame each summer in order to complete her degree by 1964. She also relied on the Sister Formation Conference's workshops and publications to stay up-to-date on emerging developments. She recalled that it was from one of these many articles that she adopted the maxim she used with her young charges: "Freedom with responsibility."[55] Since there was no standard book of instructions, rather than simply relying on the motto of, "Keep the Rule and the Rule will keep you," as she taught Congregation practices such as silence and reading at meals she drew on the spiritual formation she had received from her home superior of many years, Sister Rose Dolores, and strove to explain these practices in a context meaningful to the ideals of the young women.[56]

Sister Robert Ellen Brophy

In 1964 when Sister Vincent Ferrer was assigned to the College faculty, the council looked to someone with experiences similar to Sister Ann Bernice's to fill the position of mistress of postulants, deciding on Sister Robert Ellen (Joyce) Brophy. After graduating from Providence High School in Joliet, Joyce entered the novitiate in July 1947 and then taught fifth grade for four years in Chicago. After final vows she returned to Chicago for a semester as an eighth-grade teacher, and then she spent four years teaching eighth grade in California. At age thirty Sister Robert Ellen was appointed superior/principal for a six-year term at Immaculate Heart in Galesburg and was then named mistress of postulants. She too completed her graduate studies during the summers, earning a MS in Education from Indiana State University in 1966.

These sisters who had charge of formation during the early 1960s were facing new challenges. A quick survey of novitiate life at this time shows both similarities to and differences from the descriptions of Chapter 6. From the point of view of the postulants and novices themselves, although the academic schedule was a significant determiner of their activities, it was the ceremonies of August 15 that marked key turning points. It was then that postulants received the habit and white veil and a "canonical employment" as they began in-depth instructions in spirituality with the mistress of novices. Canonical novices became scholastic novices and received their full-time class schedules with the assurance that they would be able to keep up with assignments since they were now allowed to study until 10:00 p.m.

The next month would be a time of transition during which, as the novitiate diarist observed, "Now we are all 'white'—no postulants!"[57] As they prepared to welcome "our cherished little sisters," (as a traditional novitiate song described the postulants) by sewing numbers on clothes, they also looked forward to being a formation community. As others had done for them, they would gradually introduce the incoming group to recreational activities such as gym night, softball games and hikes as well as to infirmary service and congregational singing. Those with a more creative bent were always in demand for preparing special feast day programs, and during 1966-1967 the talent was such that a literary magazine, *The Reed*, was published.[58]

In fact, the diversity of ages and previous education among each new group of postulants required ongoing efforts to accommodate the program to individual needs. Each young woman responded in her own way as she matured in her vocation so that by the end of scholastic year, she was ready to pronounce her vows. Now wearing the black veil, she moved across the road to the juniorate building where she would begin the next phase of formation

The Juniorate

The recently established juniorate program had itself matured. Once the old novitiate building became available with offices, study hall, recreation room and dormitories in a single building, the program itself took on a more professional air. Sister Rose Berchmans continued in her role as juniorate mistress during the transitional year of 1960-1961. Sister Francis Joseph was now available to provide both scheduling and teaching duties, as well as supervision of student teaching for the junior sisters who were assigned to teach in Terre Haute. As plans went forward to implement the program more fully, Sister Louise Beverley was appointed mistress of the junior sisters in August 1961.

A graduate of Providence High School in Chicago, Victoria Beverley entered the novitiate in July 1936. After professing vows as Sister Louise, she taught middle grades until her final profession, when she went to the Boston area and taught high school in Stoneham and Malden, then at Central Catholic in Fort Wayne. A year as a teacher in Providence Juniorate (later called the aspirancy) was followed by a year as a novitiate sister assisting Sister Marie Ambrose. She then taught at Providence, Clarksville, for a year. In 1955 she returned to Chicago as superior and principal at St. Columbkille, studying for an MA in Education at Indiana State during the summers. When she was appointed juniorate mistress in 1961, since she had not yet completed her graduate studies, as part of her duties she modeled the role of student for her charges by continuing to take classes both in Terre Haute and during the summers at St. Mary's College, Notre Dame.

During her four years in the juniorate, Sister Louise did much to improve the program. During the 1962 summer session, the juniorate played host to Sister Annette Walters, CSJ, chair of Sister Formation, who gave two lectures to the novitiate, juniorate and local superiors on the topics of "Mental Health and the Spiritual Life" and "The Role of the Emotions in the Religious Life." In 1964, "Project Mission," the practice of sending the junior sisters to spend a week on the missions to assist with preparations for the school year, was begun.

Although she herself bemoaned her lack of theological preparation, Sister Louise's instruction notes display a careful blending of contemporary movements such as the urban apostolate with traditional religious virtue. In reflecting on a daily reading of the prodigal son, she noted: "The father desired the conversion of both sons. This is the movement for a Better World. . . . We cannot afford to be mediocre."[59] Instructions were now centered on a deeper living out of the vows, taking advantage of the young sisters' scripture studies to prepare discussion materials which applied the passage to situa-

Sister Louise Beverley

tions of daily life. For example, in considering 1 Thess. 5:1-28, the phrase in verse 14: "support the weak," served to call attention to community life because at different times "the weak" could be "those members of the community (including ourselves) who for whatever reason especially need the help of others," while verse 12, " to respect those who are laboring among you and who are over you in the Lord and who admonish you,"[60] easily lent itself to the topic of obeying superiors. The junior sisters themselves were encouraged to research topics in order to present panels of talks to their companions or to lead group discussions and bible services.

The turnover of formation personnel during these years speaks to the difficulty of formation work. Individual sisters at the motherhouse and College felt free to complain to home superiors, the council members, about what they felt were deteriorating standards. With a significant investment in five years of intensive formation, the home superiors were sensitive to such criticism, and their efforts to sustain legitimate expectations added additional stress to the work of the three formation mistresses, who were trained to allow for gradual growth. With a backdrop of press reports of disputes and factions among the bishops holding differing viewpoints and the heated debates about scripture interpretation at the Second Vatican Council's four sessions during 1962-1965, disagreement among community members was not surprising, Sister Ann Bernice recalls:

> Being in formation ministry at the time of Vatican II was an unusual experience! You have to realize that as the Council progressed and word about the bishops' decisions and excerpts from the documents reached us, there was an anticipation in the air. It was such a chaotic time. Mother Rose Angela was the general superior for most of my time in formation. I think the thing that made it possible for me to continue through those years was the fact that I knew she trusted me.[61]

The "anticipation in the air" fueled considerable discussion. Surrounded by young women looking to the future reinforced Sister Vincent Ferrer's opinion that "to offer young women of today the poorly transliterated 'spiritual works' of yesteryear is to frustrate within them the newness that the Holy Spirit is creating in our civilization."[62] On the other hand, in her peer group of major superiors Mother Rose Angela was among those who welcomed the September 1965 announcement that the Sister Formation Conference would become a committee of the CMSW. As superior general, she was often caught in the middle between responding to regular reports from sisters at the motherhouse and College regarding alleged infractions of religious decorum by the novices and junior sisters and her desire to defend formation efforts, a position which did not lend itself to peaceful coexistence. Nonetheless, the change of the title "Mistress" to "Director" in 1966 indicated the recognition that new times needed new approaches.

Vocation Discernment

During the five-year period of novitiate and juniorate formation, each entrant engaged in a mutual process of discernment to decide if she was truly called to live her life as a Sister of Providence. Sister Ann Bernice described the process in this way:

> My sense is that women in those years came to the novitiate because they wanted to do something good for God. Options for women in those years were not that plentiful. As they came to realize that they could find God in other walks of life, some chose to leave. These decisions were not made precipitously. They prayed, thought about it and in the midst of this is when they would come to talk with me and make a decision to stay or leave.[63]

Of course it was also her responsibility to make recommendations to the council, and prior to approval for professing vows, Mother Rose Angela took the time to interview each novice. By the time of the 1966 General chapter, her report included the summary in Table 11.

Ceremonies of Reception and Profession

Due to the change to a single entrance date, the January profession of vows ceremony was held for the last time on January 23, 1964. As of August 15, 1961, the ceremonies themselves became the focus of the celebration since the reading of the Obedience List was no longer added to the service. With a single large entrance group, the 1962 ceremony included fifty-two postulants receiving the habit, with the earlier smaller group of ten making first vows, thirty-one renewing vows and fifteen professing perpetual vows. The following year saw forty-two postulants receiving the habit and thirty-six professing first vows, with thirty-three for perpetual vows. By 1963 the Book of Important Events recorded a major change in the ceremony:

> A long-standing custom will be set aside in 1964, according to Mother Rose Angela's announcement to the Community. The postulants to be vested will not wear bridal outfits at reception, beginning in August 1964, but will wear instead the regular

TABLE 11: *Preserverance during stages of formation, 1960-1965*

Entrance year	Number of entrants	Withdrew during novitate	Professed status as of 1966	Withdrew after profession	Perservering to date
1960	53	17 (32%)	36 (68%)	5	On mission 31 (59%)
1961	66	31 (47%)	35 (53%)	4	Older juniors 31 (47%)
1962	47	18 (38%)	30 (62%)	0	Younger juniors 30 (64%)
1963	58	24 (41%)			Scholastic novices 34 (59%)
1964	52	12 (23%)			Canonical novices 40 (77%)
1965	57	10 (17.5%)			Postulants 47 (82.5%)
Totals	333	112	101	9	92 professed 121 in novitate

SOURCE: *Report of the Superior General to the 1966 General Chapter, SMWA.*

postulant dress. The decision was arrived at too late to make the change this year. A heavy financial outlay has been made in the past for this occasion merely for a symbol. In the endeavor to spare parents extra expense, this display will be done away with.[64]

By 1965 the same journal noted that changes made to the Church's liturgy by the Second Vatican Council led to further adaptations of the ceremony: "New beauty and meaning were given to the age-old religious ceremonies of reception and profession at St. Mary-of-the-Woods Sunday morning when they were conducted for the first time in the vernacular during the celebration of the Mass."[65] All those participating in the ceremony, the forty-two postulants receiving the habit, the thirty novices making first vows and the twenty-six for perpetual vows, preceded the clergy in the entrance procession, with the ceremonies incorporated into the liturgy immediately following the homily.

Tertianship

The tertian program, long the high point of formation, was caught in the middle of the many alterations in the overall initial formation program. As always tertianship was the normal time for discerning the decision to make a lifetime commitment, with some making the decision to leave. The traditional thirty-day retreat in preparation for final vows continued to be a feature of the five-month tertianship, but in June 1961 it was given for the first time by a Jesuit priest, Rev. W. J. Young. However, this change was not well-received and over the next few years the tertianship was shortened to three months with a concomitant shortening of the retreat. It would not be until 1970 that a completely reworked program was instituted, and even then additional adaptations were made to meet the needs of the various groups of sisters preparing for permanent commitment.

Departures

Both the continuing formation of day-to-day community life as well as exposure to the changes in church and society affected the entire membership. Inevitably some sisters decided to leave the Congregation. However, their departure ceased being labeled a "defection," but was simply noted as "receiving a dispensation." The self-reports of several sisters who departed at this time indicate that they had gained greater psychological insight through counseling as they made the decision that they did not have a religious vocation. Too, superiors were better able to offer a sympathetic ear. In some circumstances, rather than an outright dispensation, the option of an "indult of exclaustration" was used, as described by the community diarist:

She had applied for a dispensation but this was given instead, no doubt because of her age and the number of years she had been in religious life. During the Year she is still bound by her Vows but her obedience is under Msgr. Hillenbrand, V.G. of Chicago.[66]

In such cases, as the year of discernment came to a close, the individual was free to return to the community and again wear the habit, or she could ask to be dispensed from her vows. Many of those who left continued to be motivated by the ideals that had been nurtured and developed in their lives as Sisters of Providence, and they put to good use the education and training they had received with the Congregation in service to the Church and society.

Special Formation Events
Sisters from India Join Juniorate

In November 1960 the council received a request from the Sister Formation Conference to assist congregations from mission lands with the education of their younger sisters and agreed to accept two sisters from India for the fall term. On August 31, 1961, Sisters Littishia and Jessy Maria, members of the Congregation of the Sacred Heart at Palai from Kerala State in South India, arrived and took up residence as part of the juniorate community. During their four-year stay, they majored in biology with a view to working in the hospitals staffed by their congregation, and they won the hearts of the sisters with their joyful participation in community events. When they completed their studies, July 18, 1965, was declared "Indian Day," with a lawn party to mark their farewell. They presented the council members and juniorate mistress Sister Louise with rosaries made from elephant tusks. Although the original intention had been to accept eight sisters over several years, the financial strain experienced by the College during this period prevented the funding of additional scholarships and the council felt that the Congregation was already supporting the church's mission effort in Taiwan and Peru.

Performances of the "Angel Choir"

As a way to support the fund-raising efforts of the College, the music department under the leadership of Sister Marie Brendan Harvey organized a choir of selected junior sisters, novices and postulants. Through the cooperation of one of the

The "Angel Choir" rehearses under the direction of Sister Marie Brendan Harvey in the choir loft of the Church of the Immaculate Conception, with Sister Cecilia Clare Bocard at the organ console.

fund raising committees, two concerts were arranged, one at the Chicago Civic Opera House on January 10, 1965, and a second at Clowes Hall at Butler University in Indianapolis on March 28, 1965. The Book of Important Events reported not only that "the overwhelming response in the purchase of tickets surprised everyone," clearing $75,000, but, "the monetary returns were not the only benefit derived. Our choir was given the most complimentary notices possible."[67] In gratitude, the organizing committee was feted with a dinner at Saint Mary-of-the-Woods on March 25. The concert was later recorded and released commercially on the Delta label as the recording, "In God's Providence."

Without doubt, BUILDING was the hallmark of the 1960 council. But certainly in the minds of Mother Rose Angela and her council, the brick and mortar buildings were simply the means for accomplishing the mission of education. It was this mission that attracted the young women who entered the Congregation. The roots of the mission were deep and it is those roots we next explore.

ᔰ Chapter 15 Education as a Mission

Sister Elizabeth Clare Vrabely questions her 1965 religion class at Providence High School, Chicago.

In 1965 Indiana State University was accredited as a full university and noted the occasion at its June Commencement exercises by conferring honorary degrees on the leaders of the two other historic educational institutions in the area—Dr. John Logan, president of Rose Polytechnic Institute, and Mother Rose Angela of Saint Mary-of-the-Woods, which that year celebrated its 125th anniversary. The citation bestowing the honorary LLD degree read in part, "As Superior General, Mother Rose Angela serves as administrative head of all projects, programs, and activities of the Sisters. This responsibility includes supervision of more than 1,500 Sisters who teach 65,763 students in 113 grade schools, 23 high schools, and three colleges in 11 states and one foreign country."[1] The commendation went on to list the major achievements of her administration, both the construction of new high schools and also the encouragement of continuing education of the sisters. Having focused on construction in the previous chapter, we now turn our attention to the preparation of the sisters for their mission of education.

The invigoration of the Congregation's educational apostolate during the 1960s was the culmination of decades of effort. The 1960 General Chapter had created the Board of Education as a means of providing a unified focus for the multi-faceted activities described in the preceding chapters. The mere listing of schools and programs does not do justice to the underlying spirit that motivated the desire to influence society through education. A host of scientific breakthroughs in the early 1960s—the discovery of quasars and the molecular structure of DNA, the launching of weather satellites and human space flight, the use of laser devices and even artificial hearts—had completely altered the educational landscape. In order to introduce the work of the Board of Education and its efforts to address these challenges, we will first step back to attempt to capture the spirit of zeal that drove the mission. Indeed, it was the way in which each sister internalized the animating spirit that made the Sisters of Providence work of education truly a mission.

The Animating Spirit

The over-arching model for every Sister of Providence's approach to teaching was the legacy of Mother Theodore. Her maxim, "Love the children, then teach them,"[2] was the basis for the student-teacher relationship. Over the years, as stories of Mother Theodore's early teaching experiences in France were told and retold, newer members unconsciously caught the flavor of the philosophy developed by St. John Baptist De La Salle in his foundational work, *The Conduct of Christian Schools*, a philosophy adopted by the French Sisters of Providence.[3] In an effort to carry forward these ideals, in 1899 Sister Basilissa Heiner and her Board of Examiners had written a small book, *The Teacher's Guide*, later republished in 1914.[4] In order to "love, then teach" her pupils, each sister's task was clear:

> She is to educate heart and mind, to instill, at one and the same
> time, principles of knowledge and virtue. To effect this noble

purpose, she must constantly give her attention to the means best adapted to its accomplishment, remembering that her work is internal—the development of the mind in the pursuit of truth, and the guidance of the heart in the love of virtue. Therefore, the teacher should closely observe her pupils, that, knowing their difficulties and tendencies, she may be able to direct them intelligently and secure their individual co-operation and progress.[5]

By the 1960s few would have seen a copy of this work, but the emphasis on mind and heart, knowledge and virtue was clearly evident in the motto *Virtus cum Scientia* adapted from the original Academy seal's "Knowledge and Virtue United," attributed to Mother Theodore.[6] Since the cohort of sisters educated through the *Guide* went on to become the superior/principals who mentored the next generation, its directives became the standard for Sister of Providence schools. As each band of newly professed sisters entered the classroom, their in-service training would take place in an environment where good order and discipline prevailed.

Over the years, the commonsense approach to classroom management so well articulated in the *Guide* survived in teacher education handouts that distilled much of its wisdom, as illustrated by these sample quotes:

- Stand or sit where you can see each pupil. Move around. Teach from all parts of the room.

- Merely through her vocal usage a teacher can make of herself a despot, a friend, or a completely indifferent person.

- Encourage your pupils frequently.

An early 1950s class at Our Lady of Sorrows School in Chicago is introduced to library etiquette and resources.

- Lessons should not be too long. Do not talk at your class. (10 min. limit)

- Be blind when not sure who the offender is. This is very necessary with younger children.

- Quietness is not order. The hum of industry is no sign of weak control, nor is the stillness of unnatural constraint a sign of good discipline. Noise is no sin.

- Refuse to talk unless all are listening. Superior teachers stimulate pupils to self-activity. 80%—pupil activity; 20%—teacher activity.[7]

The pointed brevity of these directives might cause the reader to question the type of certification training these future teachers received. As the reader has probably noticed from the brief biographies in the preceding pages, most of the women who entered the Congregation came from Sister of Providence schools. It was the cultivation of this very atmosphere by animated teachers that had attracted them. They had already caught the spirit of zeal exemplified by their teachers and sought to imitate it when the time came for them to step to the front of the classroom. It was to prepare them for the profession of teaching that a complete system of oversight had evolved.

The Professional Spirit

Preparation and Experience

As we have seen in earlier chapters, it is Sister Francis Joseph Elbreg who deserves the credit for developing a system for teacher education and supervision. She had been instrumental in establishing the Office of Education with its highly organized system of ensuring the needed certification of teachers and principals. The anchor of the system—a precursor to today's database—was the specially designed cumulative record to track each sister's courses taken toward a degree. Prior to each postulant's arrival, her transcripts were examined and the courses and credits from previous schools were typed directly on the form. The records of those who came with previous college courses would show the name of the institution, courses taken, dates and grades. With a quick scan of the cards of each new band, Sister Francis Joseph was able to prepare the lists of which classes would be needed and then proceed to identify sisters qualified to teach them. Sisters on

In her capacity as Director of Education, Sister Francis Joseph Elbreg (seated at desk, right) benefited from a devoted corps of volunteers. Here are pictured (standing left to right) Sisters Marie Perpetua Hayes, Helene Black, Amelia Hickey, Agnes Loyola Wolf, (seated) Mary Joanita Walsh, Marie Elvire Marc.

the novitiate staff then prepared class lists and individual schedules for each postulant and novice. For the professed sisters, the Education Office cooperated with the College to plan the program for the summer session courses. Specially trained sisters came early from the missions to prepare the class lists and individual slips for each sister. Following the completion of the summer session, teachers submitted grades which were then added to the cumulative record.

Over the years the experience record section of each sister's cumulative card tracked not only the mission location and grade or subjects she taught, but also her superior. Usually the superior was the principal who would be responsible for assisting new teachers with the actual work of teaching, especially lesson preparation and classroom management. Through her regular classroom visitations, Sister Francis Joseph was able to add supplemental notes and her reports were key to placing sisters with appropriate qualifications in each school, as well as to identifying those in line for higher studies. Although the frequent supplemental assignments of teaching catechism to public school pupils on Sundays were not included on these records, the careful records of these assignments kept separately illustrate the importance attached to this weekend service to the parish. Totals of all the teaching activities of the sisters were included in the reports given at each General Chapter and also used for the report which was sent to Rome every five years (the mandatory Quinquennial Report) to supply information about how many children of each grade had received religious instruction from the sisters.

Teaching Methods

In addition to the "career guidance" provided by the Office of Education, Sister Francis Joseph was responsible for gathering committees to work on a variety of projects to develop the curriculum for Sister of Providence schools. To supply full faculties for so many schools it was frequently necessary for sisters to change grades. The transition was eased since for many years the entire Congregation used the same lesson plan format; this included a yearly schedule with weekly plans, the aim of the lesson, study questions and tests. These lesson plans were available for the subjects of religion and history for both grade and high school teachers. The quality of these plans was such that one of the resulting curriculum guides had been published in 1937 by Benziger Brothers under the title *Our Government and our Civic Duties: A Text for the Upper Grades of Catholic Elementary Schools Showing How We Are Governed and How Civil Authority Depends upon the Divine Law.*

Children who attended Sister of Providence schools might at times be surprised to look up and see a new face inside the cap and veil in the front of the classroom, but they could count on the fact that "Sister" would pick up where her predecessor had left off. Why? In addition to access to common curriculum guides, all had been well-trained in the same methods. Almost without knowing how it happened, indifferent pupils became serious students. With the daily "Drill, review, teach, assign," any pupil who studied would be able to pass the inevitable Friday test. If their deportment corresponded, a good report at the end of the term was assured.

Summer School

A major responsibility of the Office of Education was the summer school. A dedicated group of trained sisters came home during Easter vacation to study each sister's card and draw up an individual schedule of classes she would take that summer as she worked toward a teacher's certificate and eventually, a bachelor's degree. Special arrangements were made for those on the East and West Coasts, with classes at Immaculata or Marywood, Anaheim, being supplemented by individual study or attendance at nearby colleges. In order to understand the reason why far and away most Sisters of Providence looked forward to a summer at "Home," we need to describe the activities that complemented the pleasure of reconnecting with sister-friends. A sampling of press coverage done by the *Terre Haute Tribune-Star* during the late 1940s and 1950s provides a glimpse of why summers were so attractive to Sisters of Providence.

The newspaper ran a regular summer feature with photos in its rotogravure section depicting campus activities, even going so far as to describe the presence of eleven hundred sisters present for the college summer session as "perhaps the largest educational activity of its kind in the nation."[8] With a seventy-five member liberal arts faculty and twenty-two staffing the music department, perhaps the boast had some justification. The liberal arts curriculum included a conversational approach to French set in *L'Aterlier francais*, the spacious ground floor of Le Fer Hall converted into a six-room apartment furnished with everything French, where students pledged to speak only French. Other sisters could make puppets in art class as a take-home project to spice up their own classroom instruction. They could practice the use of audiovisual and science lab equipment or develop journalism skills by contributing to the weekly publication, *Woodland Echoes*, sent to all the convents open during the summer.

Music majors followed a specialized curriculum, but any sister who played an instrument was welcome to play in the orchestra, which offered a summer "Pops" concert on Guerin Hall's terrace or in the auditorium of the Conservatory building. Sisters who organized the marching band were not above putting a clarinet into the hands of someone who was known to play in order to swell the ranks of the Fourth of July parade. The entire congregation at the opening Mass of the Holy Spirit

The 1954 orchestra prepares to perform.

and Sunday's High Mass was schooled to sing Gregorian chant. Special observances such as the 1955 commemoration of Our Lady's apparition at Lourdes were celebrated with both an outdoor Mass at the Lourdes shrine and a performance of the two-act opera, *The Cleft in the Rock*, written by Sister Cecilia Clare Bocard.

Outside speakers were brought in to provide lectures and workshops on a variety of current topics, ranging from Christopher Dawson's contribution to Christian Culture in 1955 to the lay apostolate of the Cana Conference movement in 1957 to the Christian approach to interracial justice in 1962. Sisters who had enjoyed the opportunity of travel or to pursue special studies in Europe presented talks illustrated with photos and artifacts. As early as 1948 the summer session included a week's course on parliamentary procedure, culminating in a model "convention" featuring vigorous discussion of resolutions to utilize the sisters' role as Catholic educators to combat secularism.[9]

Two of the leading lights of the Sister Formation Conference, Sister Mary Emil Penet, IHM, in 1955 and Annette Walters, CSJ, in 1962, spoke to the assembly of summer session students to explain current trends in sister education.

Professional Milestones

For many years, often the first a sister knew that she had completed her degree or teacher's license was when she was notified that she was to begin studies for a graduate degree and/or a principal's license. When she completed her master's degree, others would know of her achievement when she was assigned to teach one of the summer session classes, as illustrated in the sidebar on page 475. With the beginning of the

The Life: Sister Mary Regis

"Oh dear!" exclaimed Sister Mary Regis as she entered St. Patrick Convent in Terre Haute on a crisp November afternoon in 1960. "What's going on?" About to rush down the hall to silence the chattering in the community room, she paused as realization dawned. After-school recreation was now a normal feature of the horarium. Yes, she was the superior, but no longer was there a rule of silence to enforce. Rather, she could contribute to the enjoyment.

While it was true that she had been among the assembly in the auditorium last summer when Mother Rose Angela had explained the decisions of the just-concluded General Chapter, Sister Mary Regis would be the first to admit that her mind had been more occupied that day with the class on curriculum development that she would be teaching that afternoon. With all the buzz on campus about who was wearing which experimental cap, it was hard enough to keep the attention of her sister students. Besides, at that point it had only been days since she had finished her first year as superior.

As her thoughts drifted back, she was amazed at how much her life had changed in recent years. Having entered the Congregation in 1929 at sixteen, she had managed to earn a Normal Diploma and teaching certificate by 1934, but it had taken seventeen years of summer sessions at the motherhouse to earn her BS in Education. After she learned in 1956 that she was to begin study for a master's at Indiana University, she spent four summers at the Bloomington campus. She could still remember coming home for retreat in August 1959, exhausted after taking her comprehensive exams, only to be sent for by Sister Rose Genevieve to prepare her for the fact that she would be called as superior/principal at St. Patrick's on August 15. However, at age forty-seven, she had twenty-seven years of successful teaching experience at eleven missions under sixteen superiors, so felt far better prepared than others who were being made superiors after only one or two missions.

Sister Formation Program in 1957 and the desire to highlight the sisters' professional preparation, for the first time those who had completed their degrees came to the campus to receive their diplomas in the June 1960 graduation ceremony. Beginning on August 5, 1961, a summer commencement ceremony was inaugurated as a public recognition of those who completed their bachelor's degree either through the Sister Formation Program or over a number of years of summer study. That year, during a morning ceremony at the Conservatory, Archbishop Schulte conferred diplomas on seventy-two candidates with a variety of majors: fifty-seven bachelors of science in Education, six bachelors of science in Music Education, one bachelor of science in Music, six bachelors of arts and two other bachelors of science. Sisters who preferred a private ceremony received their diplomas from Mother Rose Angela in the parlor. Little by little, those who had had to spread their courses over many years had the satisfaction of reaching their goal. By August 1965, with all but a very few having completed college, the Congregation diarist was able to note that: "One hundred thirteen Sisters received their undergraduate degrees today, the largest number at any one time and the largest we shall ever have."[10]

The Board of Education

Much of the invigoration of the Congregation's educational apostolate during the 1960s was due to the collaborative energies of the exceptionally qualified group of educators who gathered on July 27, 1961, for the first meeting of the Board of Education established by the 1960 Chapter. The nine members whose appointed offices included membership on the Board all belonged to a cohort that had entered between 1913 and 1931, and all would have been formed with the spirit of zeal articulated in *The Teacher's Guide*. As can be seen, each member of the Board had a unique perspective on the overall educational mission of the Congregation:

> *Mother Rose Angela—ex officio-Superior General*
>
> *Sister Mary Joan Kirchner—Director of Office of Education*
>
> *Sister Mary Josephine Suelzer—Academic Dean of College*
>
> *Sister Esther Newport—Art education*
>
> *Sister Mary Lourdes Mackey—Classroom music education*

Sister Rose Dolores Thuis—Applied music education

Sister Mary Corona Sullivan—High School Supervisor

Sister Irma Therese Lyon—Grade School Supervisor

Sister Teresa Aloyse Mount—Immaculata Junior College President

As each member is introduced, we will focus on the impact of two major contributors to the Sisters of Providence mission of education—the College and the Office of Education.

Contributions of the College

As noted above, *The Teacher's Guide* described the core of each sister's mission as instilling principles of knowledge and virtue in her pupils. As a consequence, the aim of each sister's formation was to deepen virtue and acquire knowledge. Over the years, the College had served as the fountainhead of intellectual formation. In fact, eight of the nine members of the Board had at one time served on the College faculty. At the Board's first meeting the newly appointed academic dean, Sister Mary Josephine, represented the College. She had been a student at the College when she entered in 1931 and, after five years of teaching high school, had been sent to study for an MA at Indiana University to prepare her to join the College faculty, and she did so in 1939. Three years later she was released for doctoral studies in Latin and Greek at Catholic University and then returned to the College. Her career was emblematic of the faculty she represented.

Sisters who had demonstrated academic proficiency with advanced studies or degrees prior to entrance were periodically sent to leading universities to acquire the higher degrees needed for leadership in different areas of learning. Not long after Sister Eugenia Logan was named dean in 1927, four sisters were sent to study for doctorates. Although two had died by 1960,[11] the other two had gone on to join the dedicated core of tenured College faculty. After graduating from the College, Sister Mary Joseph Pomeroy had earned a PhD in English from Catholic University and then joined the faculty. Her warm personality made her an ideal person to foster connections with the alumnae through the active Alumnae Association and the alumnae section of the College magazine, *Aurora*. In the words of one alumna, "Her zealous, enthusiastic work

MADE the association."[12] Sister Gertrude Smith, a native French speaker from Montreal, who had also entered from the College and had been sent to Indiana University, became the second Sister of Providence to join the faculty with a PhD in English. She went on to head the Foreign Language Department, where she mentored a generation of high school language teachers. Over the years she also provided extensive translation services for Mother Theodore's Cause of canonization.

Once the financial situation of the Depression-era improved, three more sisters were sent to Catholic University. The first to be sent, Sister Mary Ruth Lucey, who had joined the faculty in 1933, returned with a PhD in biochemistry/biology in 1942. The second was Sister Mary Josephine in 1944, and the third was Sister Georgianna Terstegge, who became a member of the faculty in 1946. She returned to her position in 1949 with a PhD in French, Spanish and philology. Three sisters who entered during this same period came well prepared with professional experience and degrees that greatly expanded the breadth of College offerings. Sister Mechtilde Schaaf entered in 1929 at age twenty-three with a BS in home economics and chemistry from the University of Nebraska and an dietetic internship from the Mayo Clinic; she joined the faculty in 1932 and went on to earn a MS in chemistry at Indiana University in 1937. Sister Catherine Joseph Wilcox entered in 1939 with a BA from Mundelein College and three years of experience at the *Chicago Daily News*; she joined the journalism faculty in 1945 and was sent to Marquette University for a master's degree in 1948. In1954 she was named director of public relations. At her entrance in 1940, Sister Mary Olive O'Connell had a degree from Trinity College in Washington, D.C., and after joining the faculty in 1944, she went on to become the first graduate of the Catholic University Graduate School of Speech and Drama. In cooperation with her colleagues, her efforts greatly enhanced the College's visibility through its stage and radio productions.[13]

Alongside these tenured faculty, outstanding high school teachers were often assigned to teach at the College for relatively short terms, while others found a secure niche for their talents. A noteworthy example is Sister Mary Jean Mark, who entered in 1927 at age eighteen, and after teaching grade and high school for twenty-five years, joined the faculty in 1955 when she completed her MA at Marquette University. It was during this time that a particular course, "Christian Civilization," became an anchor of the curriculum, as noted by historian Karen Kennelly:

> Humanities, the social sciences, and fine arts fields were developed in ways that set the Catholic women's colleges apart from other single-sex as well as coeducational undergraduate institutions. Faculty at two Indiana colleges, Saint Mary's and Saint Mary-of-the-Woods, used British historian Christopher Dawson's concept of Christianity as the basis for Western civilization to design and teach courses on Christian culture and civilization that transformed the educational experience of students.[14]

And as a later chronicler noted, "'Christian Civ' became synonymous with the name of Sister Mary Jean for every junior at the College. *Her* tests and *their* term papers formed a tradition!"[15]

As we consider the contributions of the College faculty to the preparation of sister teachers, it must be remembered that even during the academic year, instruction was but one part of the duties of the sisters on the College faculty. Many of them lived in the College residences and were responsible for making the rounds and student supervision, but they also walked across campus to Providence Convent for meals and prayers. At a time when students did not have cars, student activities were very much campus-centered with sisters serving as faculty advisers for each class and for the various clubs. The cycle of traditional annual events such as Ring Day, when juniors received the cherished College ring, Christmas caroling, Twelfth Night, drama productions, proms, May crowning and graduation needed constant attention. Close proximity to the students was demanding, but also fostered mutual admiration and lasting ties that carried over after graduation, as evidenced by the alumnae support for various projects noted in previous chapters. As was true of sisters who staffed the boarding school/academies, the need to be available round-the-clock certainly made their experience of community life different from that of most other sisters. Nonetheless, the enjoyment of working with other sisters who shared their goals was itself its own reward since the informal setting made it possible to "get things done without red tape."[16]

Together with the humanities, Saint Mary-of-the-Woods College could certainly boast of its arts programs, represented on the Board of Education by Sister Esther from the College Art Department and Sister Mary Lourdes from the Music Department. These two, along with Sister Rose Dolores, council member and supervisor of applied music, had entered the Congregation at a time when the strong belief so succinctly stated in *The Teacher's Guide* that "All educated teachers realize that the arts, music and drawing, aid greatly in the development and culture of their pupils"[17] was woven into the Congregation's approach to education. Each was well-prepared to ensure that this tradition was observed with excellence.

Art Education

Sister Esther entered the Congregation in 1918 after graduating from St. Joseph Academy in Terre Haute. Following a series of eight assignments in grade and high school teaching and a year of study at the Chicago Art Institute, where she earned a BA in Art Education, she joined the College faculty in 1931. Historian Karen Kennelly comments on the perspective Sister Esther brought to the curriculum during her thirty-three years as director of the art department:

> Colleges founded by women religious also led the way in applying ideas generated by the Catholic revival to art departments that had an influence far beyond college campuses. Sister artists at Saint Mary-of-the-Woods followed the inspiration of noted Catholic art critic Graham Carey in the 1920s by establishing a unique program emphasizing Christian art and craftsmanship. Sister Esther Newport from the art faculty there took the lead in forming the National Catholic Art Association in 1937 and publishing the *Christian Social Art Quarterly.*[18]

In addition to her instructional role, Sister Esther earned a reputation as an artist in her own right as her art works garnered awards at exhibitions. Her illustrations for a widely used 1931 Bible study textbook brought scripture to life for children in an era in which scripture study was not the norm. In addition to teaching the sisters during the summer session she also taught at Catholic University, gave workshops across the country and wrote numerous articles. Over the years a number of talented sisters joined her on the faculty, while others developed their talents through further study and created art works in addition to their teaching responsibilities.

Since art education had not enjoyed the emphasis given to music education, Sister Esther had been asked to develop the art curriculum in the schools. Now she was eager to expand her influence through her membership on the recently created Board. Especially important in Sister Esther's mind was the need for art

Sister Esther Newport uses two of her works to illustrate a point to students.

appreciation in both the elementary and secondary levels in order to augment the cultural formation of students. Regarding the elementary level, she was able to report:

> In general there has been a great improvement in the last four years in the quality of the work being done. This seems to be the result of intensive workshops, both here and on the missions, summer school classes, and the providing of well defined teaching plans for the teacher. Another strong influence has been the energetic example of a small group of Sisters who have taught their own classes successfully and have given generously of their time and art knowledge to help others on their mission to do the same. ... Last summer we published a three book set of ART TEACHING PLANS for the elementary teacher. They contain an adequate art program and complete directions for use in the self-contained classroom.[19]

Music Education

Pride of place among the College departments surely belonged to the Music Department, largely due to the vision of Sister Marion Cecile Spencer, whose unusual talent was such that she had been named department head in 1893 at age twenty-six. After a year of study in Berlin and Paris in 1909, she earned a bachelor's degree from Bush Conservatory in 1918, returning for an MM in 1928. Meanwhile, the decision to devote an entire building to the music program with the 1911 construction of the Conservatory of Music provided an elegant location for music instruction. In the reorganization following Sister Eugenia's appointment as dean in 1927, the Conservatory of Music was given the status of a department in 1929. It was during this era that an extraordinarily talented group of women entered the Congregation and joined a College music faculty that in turn educated an entire generation of music teachers. Three in particular deserve special mention for the impact their teaching had in preparing sisters to teach applied music. Sister Florence Therese Fitzgerald entered in 1913 and after a number of years of teaching in several high schools, earned an MS in composition at Northwestern University in 1931. She then joined the music faculty with a specialty in violin and harp, winning many awards for her compositions.

Sister Cecilia Clare Bocard entered in 1916. She first taught piano at the College while pursuing her other studies, then at Marywood, Evanston, while studying for bachelor's and master's degrees from the Bush Conservatory. In addition to her duties as professor of theory, composition, piano, organ

Sister Cecilia Clare Bocard edits one of her many compositions.

and history of music, she became a prolific composer of sacred choral works and piano compositions. She also oversaw the liturgical music program at the motherhouse, in which capacity she is frequently mentioned in these pages.

Sister Francis Angela Kolb entered in 1921 at age twenty-three after studying for several years at the Hammond Conservatory of music. For many years she taught in both high schools and the College, but after earning a MM from Northwestern University in 1940, she was named professor of music education at the College and given the responsibility of directing the novices' choir and training the sisters in Gregorian chant, with the Solesmes tradition as her specialty.

Classroom Music Education

To ensure that music was well taught, Sister Mary Lourdes had been appointed supervisor of classroom music in 1938. She was ideally prepared for this role. When she entered in 1929 she had already earned her degree at Chicago Teachers' College and had taught in the public schools. After several years of teaching in high schools, she earned a MM from Northwestern University in 1931 and joined the College music faculty that year. She later divided her time between teaching and supervision in the schools. In 1950 she founded the National Catholic Music Honor Society, Delta Mu Theta, for undergraduates. During the 1950s she became the dynamic organizer of the *To God through Music* textbook series published by Gregorian Press. She attended the first meeting of the Board of Education in 1961, although her supervisory duties would be interrupted since she was beginning a leave to study for a PhD at Catholic University. She reported that while primary and intermediate grades were making good use of the music textbooks, despite the availability of supplementary recordings and filmstrips, music in the upper grades was not well taught.

As a follow-up from this first meeting of the Board of Education, efforts were made to identify interested and qualified teachers who could teach art and music classes throughout the school and be named as consultants to assist sisters in their geographic areas.

Applied Music Education

The adage "No piano, no pupils!"[20] coined by Mother Theodore when she first visited American schools reveals the importance given to preparing qualified sisters to teach applied music. This can scarcely be overemphasized. It was expected that every house would have a music teacher whose income from private lessons supplemented the meager stipends of the classroom teachers. What was it like to be a music teacher? How did you become one?[21] Uppermost in the mind of each young woman who entered the Congregation was the desire to follow her vocation, leaving the decision to her supe-

Sister Theophane Faulstich demonstrates the group method of piano instruction with her 1950 pupils at St. Patrick School, Terre Haute.

riors as to the work she would be assigned. Those who had been music pupils in Sister of Providence schools were usually recommended by their piano teacher as likely candidates for this path.[22] They could be sure that in addition to the classes taken by their band members they would be taking courses in harmony and composition, as well as participating is special workshops. Many signed up for the sisters' choir and special performances during the summer session simply for the enjoyment engendered by performing with other talented sisters.

Since, as one music teacher remarked, teaching single pupils could be "deadly dull," they welcomed Sister Rose Dolores' encouragement to organize the pupils into small groups. Although this method increased the number of pupils (and thus the income), in an article describing ten years of supervising such instruction, Sister Rose Dolores explained that the primary purpose was the benefit to the children themselves:

> They loved the social contact afforded by group lessons, and the challenge of competition that brought out the best in them. Moreover, the pupils were becoming less self-conscious and were advancing easily as fast as they would have done in private lessons—in some cases they even progressed more rapidly! Too, they were afforded the additional advantages of

keeping time with others, of hearing enriched harmonies or accompaniments, and of comparing their progress with that of the other members of the class. The general interest was contagious[23].

Often the music teachers in parish schools trained children's choirs and prepared better students as church organists. Some remember using the evening study hour to open the small envelopes brought by each child to his or her lesson, removing the money and preparing an account for the superior. Since the superior was usually also a school principal who taught in the classroom, she was pleased to welcome the music teacher for a period of classroom music while she attended to office duties. In addition to recitals, special occasions such as Christmas or the pastor's feast provided an incentive for creative programs that might even feature folk dancing and costumes. During the years when baton twirling was all the rage, despite the challenge of "all the yardage" of the habit, such instruction became part of many sisters' activities.

The specific outline of work throughout Sister of Providence schools was designed to enable pupils to achieve a certificate at each level by successfully performing the required pieces for another teacher using the program. In the high schools, music teachers often remained for longer assignments, building up a reputation for the awards won by their students and chorales in area-wide competitions. Many of these exceptional musicians were also composers who inspired their sister students as they taught courses during the summer.

Classroom Supervision

Longstanding tradition dictated that one of the superior general's assistants would be in charge of supervision of the schools, a duty that required visiting the houses and examining the classes. We have seen that when the job became too big for a single individual, the position of supervisor of secondary schools was created in 1954 with the appointment of Sister Eugenia, with Sister Mary Corona succeeding her in this capacity five years later. The complementary position of supervisor of elementary schools was created in 1960 with the appointment of Sister Irma Therese. When Sister Mary Joan was elected in 1960 the vibrant personalities and years of experience in the field provided by her two assistants greatly

Sisters Irma Therese Lyon, Mary Corona Sullivan and Mary Joan Kirchner confer about classroom instruction.

increased the effectiveness of the Office of Education when they served as members of the Board.

Sister Mary Corona had honored her father's wishes and postponed her entrance for a year after high school. When she entered at age twenty in 1919, her year of work experience prompted the decision to assign her to studies so that she could complete a BA in 1924 while teaching part-time. She then taught at Marywood, Evanston, and her alma mater Providence High School for ten years before returning to Marywood at age thirty-six as principal/superior. After earning her MA from Indiana State in 1937 she was given successive appointments as principal at Ladywood in Indianapolis, Providence High School in Chicago and Reitz Memorial in Evansville before being named dean of women at the College from 1956-1959 and then high school supervisor in 1959. Sister Irma Therese entered in 1919 and after teaching for one year at each of four schools in Indiana and one year in Malden, Massachusetts, she began a long series of teaching assignments in the Chicago area, first at St. Athanasius, Evanston, then at St. Andrew and then at her home parish, St. Leo. She then returned to each of these schools as superior between 1933-1955, completing her BA in 1942 and her MS in Education at Indiana State in 1948. Following a year at St. Mark in Chicago and another term as superior/principal at St. Sylvester, in 1960 she was appointed to supervise the elementary schools.

Immaculata Junior College

Sister Theresa Aloyse Mount

Rounding out the membership of the Board was Sister Teresa Aloyse, the dean of the Congregation's only junior college, Immaculata in Washington, D.C. After graduating from St. Rose Academy, Vincennes, she entered in 1922 and completed her BA degree in 1930. She taught for fourteen years at Marywood, Evanston, studying at Notre Dame during the summers to earn an MA in journalism in 1938. In 1937 she joined the College faculty, becoming known not only for the articles and poetry she published but also for collaborating with her musical colleagues to produce chorale presentations. She then taught three years at Central Catholic in Fort Wayne before being appointed dean of Immaculata Junior College in 1948; after ten years in that position she spent the 1958-1959 year at Providence High School in Chicago before returning to the position of dean in 1959. Because the junior college was in line for renewal of accreditation by the Middle States Association of Schools and Colleges, her experience would be a valuable asset.

Immaculata had been founded as an academy for young ladies in 1905[24] but, as noted in the college catalog, in subsequent years,

> Parents and graduates began asking for instruction beyond the high school level. In the years between 1910 and 1920 the curriculum was gradually brought into line with the requirements of the first and second years of the standard four-year college. Gradually the program of instruction was expanded to include courses in keeping with the concept of the American junior or community college.[25]

The curriculum was designed to address the needs of three groups of students: those who wanted a "finishing school" prior to marriage, those who aspired to office and business careers and those who intended to transfer to four year institutions. In addition to the sisters, professors and priests from nearby Georgetown University and Catholic University often taught specialized courses. An array of activities, including sports teams and a children's theater program augmented the academic offerings. As in 1944 when Monsignor Fulton J. Sheen graced the rostrum, well-known priests often gave the annual retreat.[26] Half of the student body were residents and half were day students from the Washington, D.C., area, and over the years, many graduates went on to distinguished careers.

Due to its location in the heart of the nation's capital, an assignment at Immaculata in either the secondary or college programs greatly enriched the teaching careers of many Sisters of Providence. For example, Sister Francis Helen McBarron served on first lady Eleanor Roosevelt's committee for the celebration of George Washington's 200th birthday. Not only did the sisters accompany the students on field trips to federal government offices, but proximity to major events allowed personal access to what most could only view on television.[27]

The report prepared by Father Edward Stanford, OSA, prior to the accreditation visit provides a useful framework for understanding the unique configuration of the institution during this time:

> On a campus of approximately eight acres the Sisters of Providence operate three more or less separate institutions. These are: Dunblane Hall, an elementary school with 325 day students; Immaculata High School with 400 day students; and Immaculata Junior College with 250 students, half of whom are resident students.[28]

This very description points to the prickly problem of overlapping responsibilities on the part of the several administrators.

Prior to her election as director of education, Sister Mary Joan had served from 1956-1960 as superior at Immaculata. In this capacity she held the title of president of Immaculata Junior College, although the day-to-day administration was handled by the dean. While there she had overseen the construction of new buildings, so was well aware of the interrelating aspects of the three institutions. Consequently, as the Board of Education continued to meet in subsequent years, attention would continue to be given to the Immaculata situation.

By 1962 the council felt the time was right to clarify the duties of the superior vis-à-vis the dean, as explained by Mother Rose Angela in her letter to Immaculata superior Sister Robert Kiley:

> We are assigning Sister Teresa Aloyse to the combined offices of President and Dean [of the junior college]. You likewise, are the Superior of the entire institution and are Comptroller of the College as well as finance manager of the other departments. No changes in the physical plant and no changes of any significance are to be made without your full approval. I am writing the same to Sister Teresa Aloyse and telling her of our decision regarding this transfer of authority, due in great part to the coming evaluation program, and because you will have enough responsibility without acting as president of the college.[29]

Sister Teresa Aloyse was formally installed as president on October 7, 1962.

As they had done at Saint Mary-of-the-Woods College, the council took advantage of the services of Father Stanford to prepare a preliminary report prior to the accreditation visit. His recommendations for Immaculata were similar to those for the College in terms of setting up a Board of Trustees and separate financial reporting with an audit. Because of its unique situation, he recommended that at Immaculata each of the three institutions be separately incorporated under distinctive names and that administrative space be more efficiently organized. The first three of these recommendations were acted upon immediately and by 1965 three separate corporations were formed for Immaculata College of Washington, Immaculata Preparatory School and Immaculata-Dunblane Hall. The fourth recommendation proved more troublesome. Correspondence at this time had made Mother Rose Angela aware that the views of the very capable sisters appointed to positions of responsibility often clashed due to shared facilities.[30] Although accreditation was granted, as Sister Teresa Aloyse had anticipated, it was provisional. Because of the previous consultation, steps were already underway to address the recommendations. In May 1963 Sister Anna Rose Harrington was appointed to the high school faculty, so when she was named regional superior for the East in March 1964, she was well acquainted with the situation. After taking up residence in the Dunblane building in August 1964 she would be near at hand to assist with implementation of the recommendations and the subsequent growth of Immaculata's three institutions.

The Changing Role of the Office of Education

When Sister Mary Joan called the meeting of the Board of Education to order at 9:00 a.m. on July 27, 1961, a glance around the table gave her reason for confidence in the renewed vigor each of these very competent individuals was bringing to the mission of education. She had lived with and worked alongside many of them and knew that she could count on not only the very impressive credentials and experience described above but also on the obvious enthusiasm they were able to communicate to those they supervised.

Coordinating Supervisory Efforts

Sister Mary Joan believed in the power of publicizing success to stimulate success. One of her first actions after her election as Director of Education was the publication of a newsletter, *PEN—Providence Educational News,* that made its debut in September 1960. Her purpose was to encourage innovation and excellence by informing members of the many activities of their sisters across the country. Each issue's lead article related details of current projects, such as the 1961 summer adventures of Sisters Cecilia Clare and Frances Angela as they attended the International Congress on Catholic Church Music in Cologne, traveled through Europe, studied with Nadia Boulanger in Paris and with Dom Gajard, OSB, director of the Solesmes choir and visited the Ruillé motherhouse. The sampling below of the activities announced in the 1960-1966 issues reveals the variety of ways Sisters of Providence were participating in the events of the day.

Sisters at St. Athanasius, Evanston, and Immaculate Heart in Indianapolis were able to utilize televised segments to supplement their classes through their participation in the Midwest Program on Airborne Television Instruction, sponsored by the Ford Foundation. Two members of the Chicago Catholic Science Teachers Association, Sisters Ann Carolyn (Carolyn) Kessler and Mary Magdalene Schwartz were part of a group that traveled on a U.S. Air Force plane to Fort McClellan, Alabama, to meet the men and learn the methods behind the U.S. Army's Chemical Corps Training School. Sister Marceline Mattingly, after a 1961 summer research project with the National Science Foundation's Institute in Modern Biology Perspectives at Howard University, where enrollment included "both Negroes and white students,"[31] was invited to return as a staff member for the 1962 and 1963 sessions.

Sister Marie Caroline Carroll was named to set up one of the first Project Head Start centers at Chicago's St. Mel-Holy Ghost School with funding from the Office of Economic Opportunity. Sister Adelaide Ortegel was using her puppet clown, Oki-Doke, to teach catechism on a Sunday morning television show. The junior sisters were learning the skills of the urban apostolate as they visited families in Dresser, a small community in a depressed area near West Terre Haute. Sister Mary Olive O'Connell was a charter member of the newly formed National Catholic Theatre Conference.

Accounts of the work being done at Providence English College in Taiwan and Sister Michael (Loretta) Schafer's attendance at a conference in Stockholm brought a global perspective, while notice of students who had won awards and descriptions of the work of vocation committees showcased events closer to home. The "Have you seen?" section provided information about how to obtain free and inexpensive teaching materials. Excerpts from a variety of conference speakers provided a seed bed of current ideas. Attendees shared notes from Rev. Richard Lombardi, SJ, of the Better World Movement, Rev. Roland Murphy on scripture study and Msgr. Agostino Casaroli's talk to the major superiors at Notre Dame explaining the need for missionaries to South America. Reflecting her conviction that higher education was the avenue for each sister to develop her own individual ability, Sister Mary Joan devoted considerable space in *PEN* to lists of sisters studying on university campuses throughout the country.

Revisions to Teacher Preparation

Without doubt, the times were changing, with the concomitant need to update the system of teacher preparation that had the served the Congregation so well for many years. Though the College was the envy of many congregations that lacked such a resource, to ensure expertise in the rapidly emerging fields of theology and scripture sisters were sent to study for advanced degrees in those fields. With fewer sisters needing undergraduate courses, Sister Mary Joan took up the challenge of reorganizing the summer session program. Recalling her own frustration at not having been assigned to the courses she needed to prepare her for the subjects she was asked to teach, she revised the system to allow for personal choice. "I just took what I was told to take. I felt it was time for the sisters to do that choosing. They were going into graduate school and someone wasn't going to take care of this for them."[32]

There were now three groups of sisters to require her guidance: those still needing bachelor's degree, those studying for master's degrees on other campuses and those registering for continuing education. Based on her study of who needed which courses, as well as classes that would appeal as continuing education options to those who had completed their degree, she contacted prospective teachers and set up the schedule of courses to be offered. In January, lists of these classes were sent to each mission, together with instructions for registration. In this manner, there was a steep decline in the number of sisters who completed their undergraduate degree through the "fifteen year" program, while there was a small but steady number of sisters able to complete it through the Sister Formation Program.[33] By the 1966 Chapter it was possible to report that 91.9 per cent of the 876 active elementary school teachers had earned bachelor's degrees, while eighty-two also had completed master's degrees and 135 were enrolled in master's programs. As for the secondary teachers, all 267 had bachelor's and 61.4 per cent had master's, with fifty-nine enrolled in master's programs. In addition, fourteen

Sister Charlotte Bruck tries out her guidance steps with a group of eighth grade boys. The program she authored was later published for use in elementary schools as SEARCH: Discovery through Guidance.

sisters were studying for doctorates, as those named for study in the 1950s were gradually followed by others.[34]

After the 1965 passage of the Elementary and Secondary Education Act and the Higher Education Act, sisters were encouraged to apply for grants for the summer institutes being underwritten by the National Science Foundation. The notice to be placed on the bulletin appears quaint by today's standards: "A national listing of colleges and universities offering such Summer Institutes is issued annually by the Foundation. For this listing send a postcard to: National Science Foundation, Washington 25, D.C."[35] Posted on the community room bulletin board, the flyer clearly caught the attention of a good number of adventurous sisters. The number who obtained grants or fellowships grew from twelve in 1961 to sixty-five in 1966. This opportunity also greatly expanded the range of college and university campuses where sisters studied, many of them "on their own" rather than with companions. Between 1961-1966, Sisters of Providence were enrolled in some ninety-seven institutions of higher learning across the country.[36]

The timeliness of these efforts to increase the professional proficiency of the sisters cannot be overestimated. Given the rapid acceleration of social change in the 1960s, no matter where their assignments might take them, sisters walking into classrooms faced a different type of student. Television had created a mass culture. Images of political confrontations about racial integration on college campuses became images of the March on Washington in 1963 and race riots in the Watts area of Los Angeles in 1965. Protests about the country's involvement in the war in Vietnam popularized the slogan, "Question authority." As countercultural ideas gained acceptance, changing standards of taste and behavior eroded support for traditional teachings of morality and conduct. For Catholics, the excitement generated by the solemn closing of the Second Vatican Council on December 8, 1965, would lead to questions of how to interpret the wave of documents that issued from its deliberations. Already Mary Perkins Ryan's 1964 book, *Are parochial schools the answer? Catholic education in the light of the Council*, called into question the whole purpose of the Congregation's mission. Nonetheless, those who took the time to read her analysis of the history and trends of religious education in the United States could surely notice the similarity of the Sister of Providence "spirit of zeal" to her message that "the central aim of the renewal is the formation of a Catholic people so open to the formation given by Christ and the Holy Spirit in the Church that they are continually enabled more fully to 'practice the truth in love.'"[37] Indeed, in order to accomplish the very core of its mission, the Congregation faced challenging new horizons.

❧ Chapter 16
New Horizons

*With the 1964 adoption of a regional form of government, four regional
superiors joined the council, forming what would be come to be known as the
Congregation Council. Seated are the newly appointed regional superiors:
(from left) Sister Marie Clarice Toomey (West), Anna Rose Harrington (East),
Mother Rose Angela Horan, Mary Raymond Schelkopf (Indiana), and
Edwardine McNulty (Illinois). Standing are the 1960 council members: (from
left) Sisters Mary Joan Kirchner, Rose Loretto Wagner, Loretta Therese Leary,
Catherine Celine Brocksmith, Mary Pius Regnier and Rose Dolores Thuis.*

The sheer volume of activities which occupied the attention of the 1960 council emphasizes the high tide lifting the
bark of Peter during these years. The waves certainly lapped
high on America's shores on November 9, 1960, when Catholics woke to the news that the United States had elected its
first Catholic president, John F. Kennedy. That very day
Mother Rose Angela sent a telegram to the president-elect as-
suring him of the prayers of the sisters.[1] Important though this
change in federal government might be, it was Congregation
government that required her attention.

Institution of Regional Government

Planning for an Intermediate Level of Government

Even prior to Pope John XXIII's announcement of the Second Vatican Council, the Sacred Congregation for Religious had advised Mother Gertrude Clare that the size of the Congregation was such that an intermediate level of government was needed. Consequently, one of the topics discussed by the 1954 council during the committee days which preceded the 1960 Chapter was the re-instatement of provinces. As they studied a summary report of the experiment with provinces during the 1930s and 1940s, the chronicler noted two significant items: "Perhaps the most important one was the fact that the duties and work of the Sisters named as Provincials were not sufficiently clear. Too, the Provincials did not have sufficient authority."[2] When the 1960 council took up the planning for re-introducing an intermediate level of government they were concerned to avoid repeating the errors of the past. Like their predecessors, they sought sound canonical advice from Rev. James O'Connor, SJ, and consulted with the Holy Cross Brothers regarding finances.

Father Bernard Ransing, CSC, also proved to be both friend and adviser. After earning a doctorate at the Gregorian University in Rome, he had taught at Holy Cross College from 1939-1952 while simultaneously serving in congregation administration. In 1962 he was appointed Consultor for the Sacred Congregation for Religious, and in this capacity he had begun the practice of attending the annual meetings of the Conference of Major Superiors of Women to make himself readily available. A councilor at the time, Sister Mary Pius later recalled that his advice helped solve one of the most pressing difficulties faced by the council as they began to plan—how to provide qualified teachers for the various curriculum subjects in high schools across the country. "He said to us, 'Why don't you talk about regions? Then you don't have to worry. The sister belongs to the region but she can be moved from region to region.' So we set up regions."[3] A regional system would also make it possible to maintain a centralized financial structure during the transitional period.

As had been the case in the earlier plan, there would be four regions: Indiana, Illinois, the East and the West. All states were included with a view to future growth. In order to decide on the geographical distribution of the regions, the council used a jigsaw map of the United States, observing Mother Rose Angela's suggestion that each region would be bordered by water.[4] They drew names to commend each region to the care of a heavenly patron; three were given to the care of archangels—Indiana to St. Gabriel, the West to St. Michael and the East to St. Raphael—while Illinois was placed under the patronage of beloved Congregation patron St. Joseph. With the locations of existing missions stretching from Maine to South Carolina along the eastern seaboard, St. Raphael enjoyed a diversity of mission opportunities. Though concentrated in Chicago, St. Joseph spanned the midwest states along the western banks of the Mississippi and included missions in St. Louis and Oklahoma. St. Gabriel's existing missions were entirely in Indiana but future possibilities reached from Michigan to Florida. St. Michael was tiny in terms of existing missions in California and Texas but vast in terms of the size of the western states. The constant stream of requests for sisters to staff schools across the country gave promise of continued growth for each region.

During the summer of 1963 Mother Rose Angela's instructions to the sisters included an explanation of the general plan for the regions. Each sister was asked to choose the region to which she would "belong." As yet the full implications of this choice were not clear, but the option of being assigned to a mission closer to family was the determining factor for most sisters as they filled out their forms. A glance at the map on the following pages with statistics given to the delegates of the 1966 Chapter shows the very unequal distribution which ensued.[5]

The sisters were also asked to fill in another form that generated excitement. The council invited each sister to think about who should be named as their regional superiors. After first pondering and listing the qualities needed for the office, each sister could then suggest names of sisters who should be considered for appointment. Within the council much thought and discussion went into the actual appointments. With the regions set to begin in August 1964, after prayerful consideration of the suggested names, decisions were made prior to the 1963-1964 assignments. The plan was to wait until March 1964 to announce the appointments. At that point, the regional

ST MICHAEL (W)

STATES	12
CONVENTS	8
SCHOOLS	9
SISTERS	82

ST JOSEPH (IL)

STATES	22
CONVENTS	33
SCHOOLS	34
SISTERS	408

NO. FOR ST MICHAEL
AS FIRST CHOICE 88

NO. FOR ST. JOSEPH
AS FIRST CHOICE 482

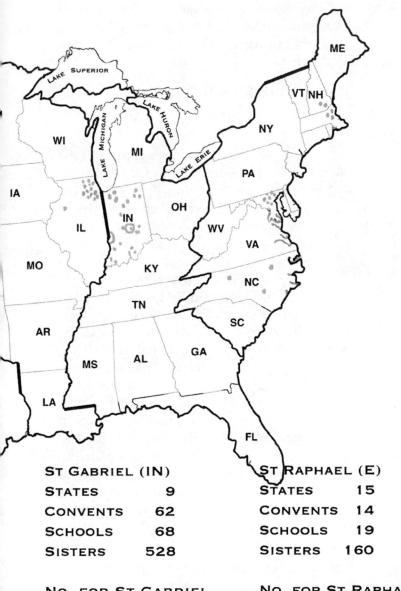

St Gabriel (IN)

States	9
Convents	62
Schools	68
Sisters	528

No. for St Gabriel
as first choice 679

St Raphael (E)

States	15
Convents	14
Schools	19
Sisters	160

No. for St Raphael
as first choice 178

superiors would come to the motherhouse to prepare for their duties by participating in making the assignments for the 1964-1965 year. As can be seen below, the four sisters who were chosen were well-qualified for the task ahead.

The Regional Superiors

Sister Anna Rose Harrington 1906-1993

Eileen Harrington was born in 1906 to Michael and Hannah Driscoll Harrington, growing up in Chelsea, Massachusetts, with her four sisters. Her teachers at St. Rose made such an impression that in 1923 she took the train westward to enter the novitiate at age sixteen. Her first teaching assignment was as a middle-grade teacher at St. Francis Xavier in Wilmette and after final vows she returned to the Chicago area for three years at St. Angela. In 1932 she returned to her home parish to teach high school at St. Rose, where in 1943 she took on the duties of principal and superior. After a year at Central Catholic in Fort Wayne she again went to Chicago as superior/principal at St. Sylvester for a six-year term, during which time she completed her MA in Education at Indiana State University. She then returned to the East Coast to teach eighth grade at St. Patrick, Stoneham, before being assigned to another six-year term as superior at Lady Isle. Her 1963 appointment to Immaculata in Washington, D.C., was interrupted in March with her appointment at age fifty-seven as regional superior for the East.

Sister Edwardine McNulty 1918-

Veronica McNulty was born to Edward and Veronica Cassidy McNulty on March 15, 1918, in Chicago where she grew up with her three brothers in St. Frances of Rome Parish. From there she went on to attend Providence High School. She entered the novitiate in 1936 at age eighteen. Her first teaching assignment as a middle-grade teacher was at Holy Cross, Indianapolis, and after second novitiate she was sent to St. Ann in Washington, D.C. In 1950 at age thirty-two she was appointed superior/principal for a six-year term at St. Anthony in Indianapolis. After a year teaching four grades at tiny St. Peter School in Linton, Indiana, she returned to Chicago as principal/superior at St. Angela, Chicago, completing an MA in Education in 1959. Since high school experience was considered a prerequisite for understanding regional organization, in 1963 she was assigned to Providence High School, Clarksville, and from there in March 1964 at age forty-six she was appointed regional superior for Illinois.

Sister Mary Raymond Schelkopf
1899-1991

Cecilia Schelkopf was born to John and Elizabeth Megan Schelkopf on October 20, 1899, in Brinfield, Illinois. She and her brother attended public grade school. She went on to attend St. Joseph Academy in Galesburg. It was not until 1924 that she entered the novitiate at age twenty-four. After only a year in the Midwest, she was sent to teach grade school at St. Rose, Chelsea, for four years. She then taught at St. Benedict in Terre Haute for five years before being named principal/ superior there in 1936 at age thirty-five. In 1941 she was sent to California as superior at St. Ambrose, Hollywood, for a six-year term. In 1947 she returned to her home town to teach at St. Joseph for a year. She then taught at St. Agnes in Indianapolis for three years and in 1951 began a six-year term as superior at Providence High School, Joliet. During these years she began graduate studies, attending Boston College and Immaculate Heart College in Los Angeles before completing her MS in Education at Indiana University in 1953. After returning to grade school for a year at St. John in Fort Wayne she was appointed superior/principal at St. Agnes in Indianapolis. In March of the final year of her six-year term there she was appointed regional superior for Indiana at age sixty-four.

Sister Marie Clarice Toomey
1909-1997

Agnes Clarice Toomey was born to Cornelius and Marie Mulhern Toomey on November 25, 1909, in Chicago. She and her brother Dan received their early education from the Sisters of Providence at Maternity. She went on to graduate from Providence High School and entered the novitiate on February 3, 1929, at age nineteen. During her first years of teaching she had five different superiors in five years at St. Sylvester in Chicago, and after two years at St. Agnes in Indianapolis was herself at age thirty named as superior/principal at Holy Cross, Indianapolis. After a year at Our Lady of Sorrows in Chicago she taught high school for a year at Central Catholic in Fort Wayne. During this time she earned an MA in Education from Indiana State University. In 1947 she was again named superior/principal at Assumption in Evansville for three years. She was then sent to St. Elizabeth in Van Nuys, California, for a full six-year term. She returned to her alma mater in 1956 to teach at Providence High School in Chicago, where two years later she was appointed superior during the four troubled years of a rapidly changing neighborhood. It was from there that she was appointed regional superior for the West at age fifty-four.

Preliminary Implementation

The long-anticipated announcement of the appointments was made by letter on March 12, 1964. The four sisters had previously received the news by personal letter in order to prepare them for their impending change. Sister Edwardine recalls that her superior, Sister Mary Xavier Coppersmith, brought the letter to her classroom door; since both suspected its contents, Sister Edwardine asked Sister Mary Xavier to remain with her while she read it. She found the news, "not only shocking, but frightening with the thought, 'I'm not sure I can do it!' [but deciding that], if the superiors had so much confidence in me I felt I had to respond positively."[6] On March 19, she found herself with the other newly appointed regional superiors seated at the council table where Mother Rose Angela assured them that, "We shall respect the decisions they make, that we know they will conform to community customs and practices."[7] As they became familiar with the plan it was clear that each region would have unique problems based on the very unequal number of sisters constituting each region.

The expanded group of superiors got down to business immediately, with a great deal to be decided. Each regional superior was to serve a four-year term, but in order to avoid having to replace all at the same time, a rotational scheme was arranged by a drawing to determine the length of each one's first term, with eligibility for reappointment. Sister Marie Clarice's term would be for one year, Sister Anna Rose's for two years, Sister Edwardine's for three years and Sister Mary Raymond's for four years. Each regional superior would be given two councilors. Due to their large size, Indiana and Illinois would be given one full-time councilor with another who would function on a part-time basis in addition to her main assignment. In the East and West, both councilors would assist the regional superior on a part-time basis.

As the discussions for the 1964-1965 obediences went forward, the decisions regarding councilors were made. In Illinois, Sister Mary Carina Connors would be named as full-time councilor, with Sister Charlotte Wohlhieter assisting part-time in addition to her duties as assistant principal at Guerin High School. In Indiana, Sister Rose Louise Schafer would be full time with Sister Helene Wernsing assisting part-time in addition to teaching at Reitz Memorial in Evansville. In the East, Sister Adrian Hickey would teach at Dunblane while assisting Sister Anna Rose part-time and Sister Robert Kiley would be second councilor in addition to her responsibilities as superior at Immaculata. In the West, first councilor Sister Mary Francisca Bowes would continue as superior and eighth grade teacher at St. Ambrose while second councilor Sister Marie Helen Leonard would continue her duties as superior at Marywood, Orange.

A major challenge was the establishment of a viable infrastructure for the regions. In order to be viewed as a true intermediate level of government, the regional superiors needed to be in independent houses rather than to simply have an office in one of the large established houses. However, given the Congregation's indebtedness and ongoing fund-raising efforts to finance the current building program, no money was available to provide for this need. When Mother Rose Angela wrote to the bishops to announce the change, she included a plea for them to provide assistance toward the establishment of suitable headquarters for the venture. Bishop Franz of Peoria responded that with the opening of Costa High School in Galesburg, the high school sisters would be moving to the large nearby convent at Immaculate Heart Parish and their vacated house would be available for the St. Joseph regional headquarters.

Arrangements for the other three regions were intended to be temporary. For the East, the former dormitory of Dunblane Hall on the Immaculata campus was remodeled for this purpose, while in the West, a wing of the newly constructed Marywood, Orange, building was designated as office and living quarters. Likewise the Indiana region made its initial home in a wing of the newly opened Providence Retirement Home in New Albany. To provide a start-up bank account, the amount of "a nickel a head," was set. Using the ten-month stipend as a base period, at five cents for each of the 303 days, each mission would contribute $15.15 for each sister.[8] While equitable, the amounts generated were obviously unworkable, but at least provided a starting point pending necessary subsidies.

During their four-month "in-service training" period at the motherhouse, in addition to participating in the placement decisions for the following year and arranging for their housing, the regional superiors participated in various workshops for superiors. Together with the council they prepared the revisions to the Rule which defined their responsibilities and which would be distributed to the sisters in leaflet form. With the long-standing practice of each sister having a "home superior," uncertainty as to how the personal connection with the motherhouse "Home" would be maintained was a concern which could only be resolved over time. The Book of Important Events describes the goal of the regional government structure:

> It is hoped that the new arrangements which doubtless will develop into provinces will bring relief to the overtaxed general administration, and make a closer connection between the Sisters and their respective superiors. While the duties of the re-

spective officers have been defined, there is no separation of the Community from the administration. The Sisters may have recourse to Mother and the Home Superiors according to the methods outlined for this purpose.[9]

Formal Inauguration of Regions

In a simple ceremony during the summer retreat, on August 12, 1964, the regional organization was formally inaugurated by promises of fidelity to the Superior General, first by the four regional superiors and then by the five regional councilors who were present. The leaflets with the revisions to the Rule detailing the mutual obligations of the superiors and sisters were then given to each sister present. During the remaining two years of Mother Rose Angela's administration, as they set up their offices, visited the houses and attended workshops in their geographical areas, the regional superiors continued to work closely with the council. Little by little they were able to relieve the home superiors of subsidiary responsibilities. One can only imagine the joy felt by Sister Francis Raphael Donlon at the announcement that: "The Regional Superiors will arrange with the houses of their respective areas about travel plans for homecoming in June as well as for travel back to their respective missions August 16."[10] The regional superiors participated in the deliberations of the regular meetings of the Board of Education and in the placement of sister personnel in the spring. As plans for the 1966 General Chapter moved forward, Mother Rose Angela wrote to the Congregation for Religious to assure that the regional superiors would be admitted as ex-officio delegates. Inevitably, situations arose in which there was confusion as to who was in charge of what, but gradually both superiors and sisters adjusted to the new structure.

The previous chapters recounted the multiple activities through which the 1960 council systematically addressed their agenda of adapting the governance structure and everyday convent life to better carry out the Congregation's educational mission. Already they seemed to be stretching the boundaries well beyond the confines of the time-honored Rule. Nonetheless, this was "the sixties," when the youth culture sparked by the maturing of the baby boom generation and the volatile social changes of the era had repercussions within the convent. Though they might have missed performances of Peter,

Paul and Mary or Ed Sullivan's introduction of the Beatles to American television audiences on February 9, 1964, music teachers were receiving more requests for guitar instruction. High school teachers found it necessary to use yardsticks to measure hemlines' inches from the floor as miniskirts became the fashion. Their students' mothers found themselves heeding Betty Friedan's advice that they were perfectly capable of pursuing post-domestic careers. Serious students had a new role model as they watched Rachel Carson testify to Congress in support of her research that pesticides were producing the effects described in her 1962 book, *Silent Spring*. New ideas and the rapid pace of life of contemporary culture found a parallel in the circumstances through which Providence invited the council to explore new directions.

Foreign Missions

Invitation to Arequipa, Peru

August 16, 1961, at Saint Mary-of-the-Woods had a decidedly different atmosphere from previous years. Rather than the emotional greetings and goodbyes of sisters who had only learned the previous day that they were changed to a different mission, since all had three months to absorb such news there was a firmness of step as the sisters gathered with those who would companion them during the year ahead. Joining the relatively calm exodus from the motherhouse campus that day were four council members, Mother Rose Angela with Sisters Catherine Celine Brocksmith, Mary Pius Regnier, and Loretta Therese O'Leary, who were on their way to the National Congress for Major Religious Superiors at Notre Dame. Anticipating respite from the press of council business relative to plans for four high school building projects and the difficult details of separating Congregation and College finances, they were soon to be surprised by yet another challenge.

Among the Congress sessions was a presentation restricted to only the general superiors of the men's and women's congregations. Even years later Mother Rose Angela's comment to her councilors when she returned from the session was still clear in Sister Mary Pius' recollection: "I think we are going to have to rethink some decisions we have made."[11] When Jesuit provincial Father John Connery had written to inquire if the Sisters of Providence would consider staffing a school in

Arequipa, Peru, the council had responded negatively. Not only were they following the 1960 Chapter's decision to place a moratorium on the acceptance of grade schools, but they felt that support of the Taiwan mission and the agreement to offer scholarships in their Sister Formation Program to sisters from India were already a strong contribution to worldwide missionary activity.

That evening the other council members joined Mother for Cardinal Valeri's address to the entire assembly in which he presented Pope John XXIII's request that the religious congregations in the United States contribute ten percent of their personnel to South America. Sister Mary Pius recalled, "I can remember writing down 140 and showing it to the nun next to me. How could we send 140 sisters to South America? I remember the people just gasping, and Cardinal Valeri trying to smooth everybody's feathers afterwards."[12] Clearly that number was not realistic, but the need could not be denied. In March 1961 President Kennedy had highlighted the United States' efforts to resist communist advances in Latin America by calling for an "Alliance for Progress" to provide developmental aid to South American countries. Certainly the Pope too had concerns for his flock. When Mother wrote to Father Connery asking if sisters were still needed, he replied that he too had been at the meeting and had been waiting for her letter.

A month later Mother Rose Angela and Sisters Catherine Celine, Rose Loretto Wagner and Loretta Therese attended the Mission Secretariat meeting in Washington, D.C., as recorded in the Book of Important Events:

> Here they learned that the Holy Father imposes on the Sisters of the United States the duty of establishing missions in South America. His Holiness feels that this is the only way the faith can be saved there. ... The Holy Father's wishes leave her no choice, and consequently, Mother immediately made plans to inform herself of the needs, and even to visit South America if she could do so.[13]

Planning for the New Foreign Mission

In preparation for Mother's trip, Father Ernest McClear, SJ, came to Saint Mary-of-the-Woods to give information about Colegio San Jose in Arequipa, Peru. The Chicago Jesuit province had arranged to take over the operations of the Spanish

Jesuits in the Lima Archdiocese and wanted to establish a grade school for boys which would feed into their high school there. Eventually the establishment could expand to include a school for girls, the primary apostolate of the Congregation. Another visitor to the council at that time was Maryknoll Father John Considine, whose extensive missionary experience enabled him to recommend appropriate cultural as well as language preparation for those who volunteered for mission assignments. He noted that Arequipa would not be a hardship mission in the same sense as some locations, but that education was in high demand and would address the need to provide a strong Catholic grounding for children of the upper class who would later enter decision-making positions, as well as become a source of potential vocations.

Not content with these conversations, Mother Rose Angela wanted to assure herself of the on-site situations. Commercial jet travel had already become commonplace, and since the expense could be mitigated by combining visitation to Taiwan with an added trip to Arequipa, arrangements were made for Mother and Sister Mary Joan Kirchner to visit Arequipa in person. Even at that, the trip took two weeks. They left Taipei on Sunday, January 7, 1962, with an overnight stop in Tokyo before continuing with stops in Honolulu, Los Angeles and Miami. They stayed overnight in the capital city of Lima in order to meet with the apostolic nuncio, Bishop Romulo Carboni, before reaching Arequipa on Wednesday, January 10. Arequipa is the regional capital and second-largest city in Peru, situated between volcanic peaks and some seven thousand feet above sea level. The combination of the Spanish charm of Arequipa's colonial buildings and its sunny summer warmth presented an attractive prospect for the new establishment. The two sisters stayed at a hotel during the three days of the visit, meeting with members of the Jesuit community and inspecting the site of the proposed convent and school. Having satisfied themselves of the possibilities and of what would be needed by way of preparation, they made a Saturday-Monday return trip via Lima, Miami and St. Louis. Any exhaustion they might have felt was amply rewarded by a warm welcome on January 15 from a group of sisters at the Terre Haute airport, by the novices singing the Magnificat in Tile Hall, the presentation of leis and a festive meal.

With plans for opening Colegio San Jose for the Fall term in March 1963, a major consideration was the appointment of sisters to begin the new work. Excited at the prospect of being part of the second foreign mission of the Congregation, many sisters volunteered. Because the superiors' return flight included a layover in St. Louis, the travelers stayed overnight there, giving Mother Rose Angela the opportunity to speak with one of the volunteers, Sister Kathleen Therese O'Connor. Upon graduating from Providence High School, she had entered the Congregation in 1935 and after teaching at four schools in eleven years, at age thirty-three Sister Kathleen Therese had been named as superior/principal to open Holy Spirit in Indianapolis. Upon completion of her term there, she taught at three different schools during the next three years and was then appointed superior/principal at Our Lady of Providence, St. Louis, in 1958, completing her MA in Education at Indiana State University the following year. Although she acknowledged that she had volunteered "out of guilt,"[14] she agreed to lead the mission.

Two other volunteers were named to inaugurate the mission. Sister Agnes Miriam Leissler had served in China and wanted to be part of the new venture, but when she attended a missiology course at the University of Dayton, she realized her knowledge of Chinese conflicted with the need to learn Spanish, so she asked to be relieved. Sister Patricia Ann (Monica) Withem was pleased to replace her. A graduate of St. Agnes Academy, she had entered the novitiate in 1933 and gone on to teach middle and upper grades at eleven schools in twenty-eight years. Since she was about to complete her MA at Marquette University, she was eager to explore a new field. Sister Agnes Veronica Hester, a graduate of Providence High School in Joliet, had worked for several years before entering in 1937. She had taught primary and middle grades at five schools over a period of nineteen years before returning to St. John, Newburgh, Indiana, as superior/principal in 1959 and was also ready to take on a new challenge.

The three fledging missionaries prepared for their work with a 1962 summer course in missiology at the University of Dayton and then intensive Spanish language courses at Georgetown University. With advice from the Precious Blood sisters already in the Peruvian mission field, a gray fabric was selected as more ideal for the climate and setting, so special habits were made for them of that material. Final preparations included the reception of mission crosses from Archbishop Schulte. To assist with start-up on-site arrangements, Sisters Catherine Celine and Francis Raphael Donlon were designated to accompany the missionaries.

South American Mission Beginnings

On departure day, March 1, 1963, the missionaries were surprised not only by a snowstorm but by the appearance at the Indianapolis airport of Jesuit provincial Father Connerly who braved the storm to see them off. During their layover in Miami, Mother Gertrude Clare's brother and his wife met the group and took them to dinner. They had planned several days in Peru's coastal capital of Lima, where they stayed with the Immaculate Heart sisters, who provided tours of the city, including shrines of the city's beloved saints, St. Rose and St. Martin de Porres. During their time there they visited with the papal nuncio and shopped for items for the mission before flying the final six hundred miles southwest to Arequipa.

As had become customary among the United States missionaries, they were met and welcomed by a delegation of sisters and priests of several congregations from "the States." Because the convent was still under construction, the missionaries stayed with the Sisters of the Holy Names while the superiors stayed with the sisters at the hospital.[15] The Jesuit rector, Father Robert Beckman, and the prefect of the high school, Father Jerry Bowman, provided transportation to acquaint them with the business district and convents of other communities in the vicinity. Sister Catherine Celine was pleased to report that "the convent is a dream and modern in every way."[16] The as-yet-unfinished building was across the street from the Jesuits' house and school with a retreat house in the same compound. All of the buildings were surrounded by fields under cultivation with various crops, both for the produce and to prevent encroachment by squatters.

The sisters noted that "the American Jesuit touch is beginning to be more visible."[17] There were many scholastics (young men in formation prior to ordination) whose services could be put to good use, and some of the priests had received their early education from the Sisters of Providence, making it possible for Sister Kathleen Therese to refer to Father Mulhern as "one of our boys from St. Sylvester's."[18] In addition to their teaching duties, the priests said Mass and taught catechism in the barriadas, the poorer neighborhoods. After becoming more proficient in Spanish, the sisters would be able to assist them by taking on the catechetical work. The missionaries began their duties both by participating in matriculation (enrollment for the upcoming term,) and arranging their schedules. In addition to continuing their own Spanish studies, the three American sisters would be teaching English and religion to all the boys, while the Spanish sisters (and later lay teachers) would teach the other subjects

Meanwhile Sisters Catherine Celine and Francis Raphael arranged for a bank account, health certificates, visas and the purchase of furniture. All five sisters became acquainted with the other North American missionaries through visits and hospitality. A highlight was a picnic in the Andes, which involved a drive on dusty roads which passed over steep canyons on very narrow bridges without rails on either side.

As the mention of so many other religious congregations indicates, the new Sisters of Providence foreign mission was part of a broad effort from the United States which had begun even prior to Pope John's appeal. Already by 1960 the National Catholic Welfare Conference had opened a Latin American Bureau.[19] In fact, the November 1961 visit of Father John Considine, MM, to Saint Mary-of-the-Woods as a consultant was part of his work as head of this bureau. With the backing of Boston's longtime mission-minded Cardinal Richard Cushing, he had worked to heighten awareness of conditions

The 1965 Arequipa missionaries: (left to right) Sisters Patricia Ann Withem, Agnes Veronica Hester, Kathleen Therese O'Connor, Marie Jean Dawson and Marie Michele (Marikay) Duffy show off local artifacts.

in Latin America among United States Catholics. Msgr. William Quinn, long active in Chicago's Christian Family Movement and migrant worker causes, had toured Latin America and advocated the idea that what was needed was a forum through which Latin American bishops could speak for themselves, a plan which evolved into the Catholic Inter-American Cooperation Program, or CICOP. The intermingling of hierarchy across continents during the first and second sessions of the Second Vatican Council set the stage for the first of several annual meetings of this group in Chicago on January 20, 1964.

By May 1964 the personnel situation was such that two additional sisters were released to study in preparation for their assignment as missionaries to Peru. Sister Marie Michele (Marikay) Duffy had entered from Providence Juniorate in 1953 and had taught primary grades in four schools in Chicago and California for nine years. Sister Marie Jean Dawson, also from Providence Juniorate, had entered in 1954 and taught in three schools in Indiana and California for eight years. Both of these relatively young sisters traveled to Ponce, Puerto Rico, to study Spanish for a semester in an immersion program prior to joining the other three at Colegio San Jose in Arequipa in December 1964.

Life on the Arequipa Mission

When Mother Rose Angela and Sister Loretta Therese visited in January 1965, the effectiveness of the Arequipa mission was already apparent as the missionaries expanded their activities outward from their base at Colegio San Jose. A sense of their everyday life can be gleaned from Sister Agnes Veronica's letter to her younger sister, Sister Loretta Eileen, telling of winter in May when the classroom curtains on one side of the building had to be drawn against the sun's heat while across the hall she felt as though she were freezing. She described how their small boy pupils were enjoying skipping up from the bus stop on planks placed over an unfinished asphalt road and also mentioned that their local community was hosting a Franciscan sister on a month's altitude leave from the *altiplano* in Yunguo.[20] In another missive, newcomer Sister Marie Jean describes efforts she and Sister Marie Michele made to begin catechism classes in the barriadas:

We are surrounded here at the school by little clusters of houses scattered in and around cultivated fields. In an effort to gather a class of girls we asked our little neighbor girl to invite the little girls who came for water at the public "tap" near us, telling her where and when we'd hold classes. Several times we questioned her and always her answer encouraged us to ready two classrooms, so many friends of hers would be coming.

The day arrived, teachers were ready and waiting for the eager crowd. To our utter shock, not one girl appeared, not even our scout. She was home baby-sitting. The message was never passed on! So there we were, feeling like the man in the Gospel, feast ready—and without guests. We quickly decided to do our own scouting that very afternoon.

Our first target was a set of single-room housing units provided by the railroad for its poor employees. From door to door we went announcing our class, and from each family we received promises of pupils. Next we crossed the road and started into the fields beyond the *colegio*. We went along the foot paths, climbed up and down rock-studded hills, and jumped water-filled irrigation ditches, all the time announcing our proposed class to all we met. Great fortune came, however, in that finally we met a man working his onion crop. He directed us to continue to a hilltop village known as Bellevista. He assured us of finding many girls there. Feeling somewhat like Cyril and Methodius, we climbed up into the street, or better, dirt road that led to the village. We rehearsed again our story, the whole time aware of the handful of people who were standing outside their houses watching our ascent.

As it turned out, the people had never seen Madres in their streets and shyly but gladly welcomed us.[21]

The result? The teachers went to where the pupils were, Bellevista. Forty girls came from the area around Bellevista for catechism classes, with older girls serving as assistants so individual attention could be provided for the different age groups. Not only that, but the sisters were able to assist the Carmelite priest who said Mass by providing instructions for the congregation on the meaning of the Sunday afternoon Mass, now being said in Spanish rather than Latin

In November 1965 Sisters Catherine Celine and Mary Joan arrived for visitation. At that point the five sisters were sufficiently competent in Spanish to teach a half day with one group, exchanging with five lay teachers for the other half day with another class. Sister Mary Joan wrote that in the upper division the Jesuits were giving scholarships to poor Indian boys with the aim of contributing to the development of a middle class in the two-tiered Peruvian society.[22] She not only enjoyed the English lessons given to first-grade boys but also visited the weekend catechism classes in the barriadas. Unfortunately a revolutionary uprising in the settlement of Juliaca in the 12,500 foot elevation of the *altiplano*, eight hours away on a slow train, both prevented her visit to a site where there were plans for the next Sister of Providence mission to be established and also served notice that this was indeed a missionary land.

By June 1966, Mother Rose Angela was able to report to the General Chapter that after three years the South American mission was well-established, with 310 boys enrolled in the primary department of Colegio San Jose.[23]

Growth in Taiwan

Honoring the Foundress of the China Mission

As we have seen, the school the sisters established when they arrived in Taichung in 1949 had prospered to the point that in 1956 it had become Providence English College, an accredited three-year junior college, with Father Joseph Kung as first president. In 1960 the Taiwan Ministry of Education honored the school with an invitation to become a four-year institution empowered to grant bachelor's degrees. The new president, Father Mark Tsai, wrote to Mother Rose Angela listing weighty reasons why this move was timely. The council readily approved the decision but with a strong caveat that neither additional personnel nor money was available in the way of assistance.

Nonetheless the council was well aware of the magnificent contribution Sister Marie Gratia Luking had made with her adroit negotiations to obtain property and building permits and her diligent supervision of the buildings which made up the campus. The fortieth anniversary of the foundation of the China mission was marked in Taichung on November 24, 1960, not only with a High Mass and dinner, but with a program during which the Ministry of Education presented Sister Marie Gratia with an elaborately worked and bound citation in recognition of her dedication to the education of the Chinese people. The council minutes record plans for the Congregation's mode of recognition: "Mother Rose Angela suggested that the title of 'Mother' be given to Sister Marie Gratia in view of her foundation of the Kaifeng and Taichung missions and her forty years engaged in this missionary work."[24] The formal conferring of the title was dated March 12, 1961, Laetare Sunday. The following year a new campus library building was named Luking Library.

Mother Marie Gratia continued as superior for three more years, but due to her failing health, Sister Ann Colette Wolf was appointed to this role in 1964. When Mother Marie Gratia, the much beloved and revered "Summer Builder,"[25] died on October 29, 1964, an elaborate funeral procession formed to walk for a mile to the church. Students marched four abreast; a band, banners, floral arrangements, and a pedicab with a large picture of Mother Marie Gratia were interspersed with groups of faculty, sister catechists, her own Sisters of Providence and thirty-five priests.

Providence College

When the school, now renamed Providence College, opened for the 1962 fall term, it had expanded to include both a day school and a night school, enrolling 260 freshmen divided among five departments: Mathematics, Business Administration, Chinese, Western Languages and Science.[26] While Father Tsai served as president, Sister St. Francis Schultz as dean was responsible for the day-to-day administration during the rapid period of growth which followed. In addition to the five other veteran missionaries, Sisters Carmel Baker, Mary Liguori Hartigan, Agnes Joan Li, Bernadette Ma and Ann Colette Wolf, two young Chinese sisters had returned from formation at Saint Mary-of-the-Woods, Sister Donna Marie Fu in 1958 and Sister Marie Pius Lee in 1961. Sister Donna Marie fondly recalls her first assignment:

> The youngest in those days was given all kinds of little jobs besides teaching classes. I was given four classes: three math classes at the American high school for dependents of the American military families, and one New Testament class at the college. I was in charge of one of the college student dormitories, the student dining room, directed three student clubs, two Legion of Mary groups, and was giving private instructions for

knowing about the Catholic religion. ....I was pretty busy but extremely happy. ...

[The other sisters] were really so proud of me for being such an addition to our convent life and that I was good with the students. Then when Sister Marie Pius came back to Providence College, Oh, to have a peer group, a real good companionship, we were very happy to work and live together.[27]

With the addition of Sister Angelica Raney in 1959, ten Sisters of Providence, seven priests and twenty-two lay teachers formed the faculty of the college.[28] Due to the college's new status as a four-year institution and also to Mother Marie Gratia's gradually failing health, the burden of administration fell to Sister St. Francis. Her correspondence to her niece Valentine conveys a sense of the pressure she felt. In a handwritten addenda (with many abbreviations) to a typed letter, she describes her role vis-à-vis that of the president: "I am only acting pres. here. The real must be Chinese. Father Tsai comes once a week or once in two weeks. We work well together. He was 4 years in Rome & 14 in the U.S.—Ph.D. in Educ—Fordham. His M.A. in Educ. is Columbia."[29] In 1960 and 1965 Father Tsai included visits to Saint Mary-of-the-Woods during his time in the United States.

Another aspect of Sister St. Francis' role was developing the curriculum, as she relates:

I have been unutterably occupied, but next summer things will be easier, for the series of our English textbooks will be finished. Last summer I prepared a new Freshman College Readings—took all summer getting material together, editing and assembling. A Survey of English Literature, for which I did

Sister St. Francis Schultz confers with an unidentified faculty member.

most of a preface and edited a first book of Our Survey of American Literature, and almost from scratch a new edition of Introduction to International Organizations and Relations. This last and a new English Conversation Book were mimeographed.[30]

Mother Rose Angela's visit to Arequipa described earlier was an extension of her Taiwan visitation. This journey that she and Sister Mary Joan made in December 1961 greatly expanded the superiors' vision of the global character of the Church. During their layover in Honolulu, the two were treated to a tour of the island by Navy chaplain Father Costa, who introduced himself as a friend of the Sisters of Providence at Lady Isle, New Hampshire, from the time of his posting at the naval base in Portsmouth. Their overnight stop in Tokyo with Benedictine sisters who during the war had been interned in the concentration camp in China with the Sisters of Providence provided a unique history lesson. After being welcomed by a large group of Providence English College alumnae in Taipei, they were greeted in Taichung with crackling firecrackers and 200 resident students waving American flags. In the travelogue they wrote to send to the sisters, they expressed their amazement and satisfaction.

> I assure you, dear Sisters, that S. Mary Joan and I are in admiration of the zeal and devotedness of the Sisters here and the growth and expansion from nothing here, since this was a rice field and swamp when they started anew after their exile from the mainland only 14 years ago. ... We cannot express our admiration and amazement over the atmosphere that surrounds the school and the attitude of the students as "real Sisters' girls," whether they are Catholic or unbaptized.[31]

For Sister St. Francis, the January 1962 visit of Mother Rose Angela and Sister Mary Joan was splendid indeed: "[Mother] enjoyed everything. She found, both did, our recreations exhilarating. Sometimes Mother laughed till she cried. She was so understanding, so enthusiastic, so charmed with the students."[32] The letters Mother Rose Angela wrote to the sisters describing their visit apparently sparked a renewed interest in the Taiwan mission because during the next few years several sisters volunteered for relatively short postings as members of the college faculty.[33]

The Providence Sister-Catechist Society

A major purpose of the superior's visit was to follow up on Mother Marie Gratia's desire to have the Providence Sister-Catechists firmly established. Because the foundation had been made in the Diocese of Kaifeng, where the bishop had been forced into exile, authority for the diocesan congregation had been transferred to Bishop Joseph Kuo of Taipei. He generously assisted with the purchase of land for a novitiate in Hsintien in 1956. In 1959 Sister Mary Loyola Wen was appointed novice mistress and welcomed six aspirants on September 21, 1959. Permission was sought to change the Providence Sister-Catechist Rule so that members who wished could opt to take perpetual vows rather than renewing them each year.

The next step would be for the Catechist Society to become completely independent of the Sisters of Providence by electing its own superiors. During her visit Mother Rose Angela worked out an agreement for the Sisters of Providence to provide ten years of financial support. Later, she wrote to the sisters to describe the moment of transition:

> Because of dear Mother Marie Gratia's many long years of devoted care, training, and position as their foundress and Superior, good Cardinal Tien urgently requested that she be present at Taipei for the momentous event that now gives them in the Church their own rightful place as a self-governing Congregation. [She attended] not as a member of their Chapter but to be present to receive, welcome, and aid in whatever way seemed necessary.[34]

Mother Mary Loyola Wen

In these August 14, 1962, elections, Sister Mary Loyola Wen was chosen as superior general. As Madeline Wen, she had attended Ching-I school in Honan and joined the Sister-Catechist Society in 1940. Although she was eligible for profession in 1942, because the Providence sisters were interned in the concentration camp she stayed steadfast in the novitiate until they returned in 1945 and she was able to make her first vows. She was among the Providence Sister-Catechists who accompanied the Sisters of Providence when they left China for Taiwan in 1949. To provide training for her new role, Mother Rose Angela arranged for her to accompany councilors Sisters Mary Pius and Loretta Therese when they returned from visitation in January 1965, as described in the Book of Important Events:

> Reverend Mother Rose Angela felt that Mother Mary Loyola would benefit greatly by seeing American schools and methods, but more particularly, by having an informal training in administration of a community. For this purpose, as soon as the Sisters arrived on January 13, 1965, this training was begun. Records, archives, and accounts were shown to Mother Mary Loyola, and she was instructed in the best methods of organizing her community. ...

> During her three-month stay in this country, Mother Mary Loyola visited Columbus, Ohio, to negotiate a loan for the Catechist Society, appeared on WTHI Radio and TV in Terre Haute where she made an excellent impression, visited Vincennes, and also the Illinois missions, and on March 4, left for California with Sister Dorothy Eileen to interview some priests interested in the Chinese missions. From there she took her departure about the middle of the month.[35]

Upon her return, Mother Mary Loyola was able to use the loan money she had managed to obtain to purchase property adjacent to the Providence Sister-Catechist Society's novitiate in Hsintien, where they built Chuan Kuang Middle School, which opened in 1966.

In 1964 word was received from the Mission Secretariat in Washington, D.C., that it was possible to file claims to receive reimbursement for property lost in China due to the forced evacuation of the Kaifeng mission. The sisters in Taiwan who had lived in Kaifeng prepared notarized testimony to accompany copies of the deeds to the school and novitiate properties. In July 1964 Sisters Francis Raphael and Eugenia Logan went to Washington to meet with the representative of the Foreign Claims Commission; the result of this meeting was a payment of $4,500.[36]

With the acceptance of the mission to Arequipa, Peru, and the focus on the worldwide vision of church fostered by the Second Vatican Council, the council sought the advice of Maryknoll Father Considine in November 1961. "Father spoke of the need of cross-cultural orientation, use of a language in the cultural frame or habitat."[37] Both to foster a global outlook among parishioners and to raise funds, Sisters Rose Loretto and Marie Pius conducted a mission appeal collection at St. John, Indianapolis.

During these years, several promising young women had come from Taiwan to enter the novitiate, but none had persevered, while others who had expressed interest were not proficient in English. Sister Donna Marie, who had herself weathered this transition, pointed out that, "when we came to the States for religious formation, it was really a triple adjustment—the culture, the language, and the religious life itself."[38] Consequently, prior to the 1966 General Chapter the sisters in Taichung developed a proposal for a pre-novitiate program and its approval paved the way for the later establishment of a novitiate in Taiwan in 1967.

Providence Retirement Home

In 1959 the sisters in the New Albany, Indiana, area heard the news that St. Edward Hospital was scheduled to close because the sponsoring congregation, the Poor Sisters of St. Francis, had neither sufficient personnel to adequately staff it nor sufficient money for the improvements which were necessary at the time. By the 1960s life expectancy in the United States was increasing, making health care for the elderly a concern for Archbishop Schulte. With this concern in view, he purchased the property with plans to remodel it to serve as a retirement home for seniors similar to the recently opened St. Paul's Hermitage in the Indianapolis suburb of Beech Grove. He envisioned accommodations for eighty to ninety persons, both men and women, in single or double rooms, with a chapel, dining room, lounge and snack room. The Sisters of Providence had staffed Holy Trinity Parish in New Albany since 1857 and had recently increased their presence in the southeastern portion of the archdiocese with the construction of Providence High School in Clarksville and the opening of a school at Holy Family in New Albany in 1954. Therefore the archbishop asked them to consider the administration of this project.

Since withdrawing from Providence Hospital in Terre Haute in 1875, the Congregation had restricted its establishments to schools. Attempting to discern if this request should be heeded as a "sign of the times," Mother Rose Angela visited the facility in early 1962. Sister Mary Pius later recalled the deliberations of the council: "We thought about it a long time. Mother Rose Angela paged through the Rule looking for passages that would justify our taking it on. There was no doubt in any councilor's mind and we knew that the pastor, Msgr Jensen, would be a good adviser."[39] Indeed, the Rule gave great latitude to the council in describing "The works of charity to be performed by the sisters," as not only, "(a) The instruction and education of children," but also as "(b) The care of the sick, whether at their homes or in hospitals, (c) The relief of the unfortunate, whether in prisons or in charitable institutions."[40] Mother Rose Angela wrote to the archbishop that the council had agreed to "undertaking a new type of work in the interests of the church."[41] The new venture was given the name Providence Retirement Home.

With an eye to her considerable experience, Sister Catherine Loretto Maguire was appointed in August 1962 to head up the still-evolving project with the goal of opening in the spring of 1963. Born in Ireland in 1889, young Josephine Maguire had immigrated with her family to Chicago, where she attended Providence High School, entering the novitiate in 1907. As a commercial and eighth grade teacher, she had proved highly adaptable, with assignments in nine schools in twelve years before being made superior at age thirty-one. Between 1920 and 1951 she had alternated between the roles of superior/principal and teacher in fourteen missions. Immediately after her appointment as administrator of Providence Retirement Home, she and Sister Francis Raphael went to Chicago to visit retirement homes in order to acquaint themselves with various aspects of the work. Sister Margaret Kern, who was teaching at Providence High School in nearby Clarksville and studying for an MBA at Notre Dame during the summers, was commissioned to draw up an accounting system suitable

Sister Catherine Loretto answers a call in Providence Retirement Home.

for this type of institution. Through Msgr. Jensen, contracts were let to renovate the 1902 building to provide for eighty-one residents in sixty-three double and nine single rooms on three residential floors, a dining room, recreation areas, administrative offices and furnishings for the rooms and common areas.

A number of former employees took staff positions and a public relations agent was hired to advertise the new facility. By April the home was ready for state inspection and the deed was transferred to the Congregation with a clause that if the sisters withdrew the home would revert to the archdiocese. Five persons had already taken up residence when the home was dedicated on May 28, 1963. Following a Mass in the chapel, Archbishop Schulte went through the home to bless it; after this a lunch was served for the clergy and sisters. As an estimated crowd of 2,000 people thronged through the building during the afternoon Open House on June 2, 1963, it was obvious that interest was high. The number of residents gradually increased, numbering seventy by 1966, with five sisters on staff.

Providence Speech and Hearing Center

The willingness of the council to entertain the possibility of accepting charge of a retirement home extended to yet another innovative venture at this time in a completely unexpected way. As we saw in Chapter 15, a great many sisters were taking advantage of federal grants for summer study; one of these sisters was Sister Ann Monica Inman. After graduating from the College in 1936, Margaret Ann Inman had taught for a year and then entered the Congregation at age twenty-two. Diminutive in size, her lively personality made her a welcome member of six varied high school faculties ranging from the huge Providence High School in Chicago to the small St. Rose in Vincennes. However, she greatly enjoyed teaching boys and after receiving her MS in biology at Marquette University, she returned to coeducational Central Catholic High School in Fort Wayne in 1953 and then taught science at the two coeducational high schools begun during the 1950s, Providence in Clarksville and Schulte in Terre Haute. In 1962 she was named as one of the founding faculty for the coeducational archdiocesan Chartrand High School in Indianapolis.

She was always an avid student, and the grant she received that summer introduced her to speech pathology. Her intuitive ability in clinical work with children with communication disorders so impressed the director of the speech therapy program, Dr. Alfred J. Sokolnicki, PhD, that he contacted the superiors at Saint Mary-of-the-Woods to recommend her for a grant to study for a MA in speech pathology during 1964-1965.[42] In addition to completing her graduate degree in 1965, Sister Ann Monica met requirements for certification as a speech pathologist with the American Speech-Language-Hearing Association. Dr. Sokolnicki recommended her to Dr. Merl (Kit) Carson, a pediatrician at St. Joseph Hospital in Orange, California, where the children's department was expanding to become Children's Hospital of Orange County (CHOC). Soon afterward, Dr. Carson was appointed the first medical director at CHOC.

Because Marywood had moved from Anaheim to Orange that summer, it was possible for Sister Ann Monica to reside at Marywood. While CHOC was in the final stages of construction, she began evaluating children referred by hospital-affiliated staff physicians in a room at Marywood Convent. The other new resident at Marywood in 1964 was Sister Marie Clarice Toomey, who was beginning her term as regional superior and in whom Sister Ann Monica found a strong advocate for her unique ministry. Once she was established in rooms at the hospital itself, the influx of referrals both confirmed her desire to assist her tiny charges to develop the ability to communicate and spawned a vision of what could be accomplished with additional facilities.

Dr. Carson convinced her of the need to establish a separate clinic with comprehensive services. Well aware that the Congregation was in no position to supply funds for such a venture, she approached Carl N. Karcher, the father of one of her patients and a generous philanthropist. Together with insurance agent William J. Reilly and other individuals committed to Sister Ann Monica's vision, Karcher worked to raise funds to purchase a site for Providence Speech and Hearing Center. By 1966 she was able to explain the project to the Congregation through *Providence Educational News (PEN)*:

The clinic opened on November 15, 1965. ... Although the ultimate goal is to accept pre-school children (age three with a cut-off at seven) who present minimal neurological damage which overtly manifests itself in no speech or very little speech, while the clinic is in initial stages it is necessary to take any child whose speech involvement warrants therapy and whose emotional overlay is not too great.[43]

She went on to tell about three of her small clients, two with brain injuries and one severely hard-of hearing. She was pleased to report that because the clinic was affiliated with Loyola University, this provided a degree of prestige for the new venture. In addition she reported that she had been able to assemble a board of directors that would aid with incorporating the clinic as a non-profit organization. Clearly she had come into her own not only as a speech therapist but as a dynamic organizer and advocate for disabled children.[44]

Continuing Efforts toward Civil Rights

St. Mel-Holy Ghost School

Demographic changes in Chicago's West Garfield Park neighborhood during these years would have a profound effect on several of the oldest Sister of Providence schools. St. Mel Parish had undergone significant alteration from the days when the 1887 parish's "one hundred and fifty families were scattered hither and yon"[45] across the prairie grass of a Central Park suburb. While most Chicagoans were cheering the December 15, 1955, opening of the first segment of the Eisenhower freeway, parishioners along the south boundary of St. Mel Parish stared in disbelief at the cars whizzing past on the expressway below their porches. Some could recall the war years when the Catholic population had grown to the point that in 1941 the parish had been split to form a second parish several blocks away, known as St. Mel-Holy Ghost, with the Congregation taking on the staffing of that parish school as well.[46]

When auxiliary bishop Raymond P. Hillenger was named pastor of St. Mel-Holy Ghost in 1959, he found parishioners who were determined to maintain the Catholic character of the working-class neighborhood. Indeed, enrollment at St. Mel-Holy Ghost peaked at 1,735 students that year. The following year, when he proposed a drive to build a gymnasium/auditorium style parish hall as a recreation and community center for youth and adults, the parishioners enthusiastically rallied to the cause. Despite the setback of a fire that did serious damage to St. Mel Church on April 10, 1961, when Purcell Hall was dedicated on September 8, 1962, its supporters proudly declared that "this building will permit various organizations to instill and develop cultural and civic progress in the groups that comprise our community."[47] The groups that comprised the community were indeed increasingly diverse, as is indicated by a description provided by a later parish chronicler:

> Between 1962 and 1963, St. Mel-Holy Ghost parish underwent rapid racial change. As white families moved away from the West Garfield Park neighborhood, enrollment in the parish grammar school declined from a record 1,919 students in 1961 to 1,067 in 1966.[48]

The Sisters of Providence felt themselves very much a part of this diverse community and were in a far different position than when they had left St. Anselm in 1934.[49] Widespread attention to the civil rights issue included efforts to educate sisters on how to respond to the changing social landscape. During the summer of 1962 Mr. Alan J. Nolan came to Saint Mary-of-the-Woods from Indianapolis to moderate a seminar on the role of the Catholic school in the Christian approach to interracial justice.[50] In January 1964 the council minutes indicate that Sister Catherine Celine was absent due to attending a meeting on urban renewal in Chicago.

Just as the increase in the neighborhood's population had led to the splitting of St. Mel Parish in 1941, the decrease in Catholic population twenty years later resulted in a reverse move when the two parishes of St. Mel and St. Mel-Holy Ghost were reunited in 1965. Even prior to the May 1964 assignments, Mother Rose Angela wrote to Bishop Hillenger to explain that Superintendent of Schools Msgr. McManus had "presented to us the advisability and possibility of combining St. Mel's School and St. Mel-Holy Ghost and also the personnel. He stated, however, that it would have to be done most cautiously and prudently because of the nature of the neighborhood; also without publicity."[51]

The two sisters named as superior/principals during these troubled times were well-suited to the task. Appointed as principal at St. Mel-Holy Ghost in 1958, Sister Marie Bernardine Swygman, had entered in 1922 and begun her teaching career in Chicago, including two years at St. Mel-Holy Ghost.

She went on to teach at three schools in California and two in Indianapolis before being named superior/principal at age fifty-three. At St. Mel, Sister Jean de Lourdes (Rose Marie) Ruffle, had been superior/principal for only a year. Having graduated from Marywood, Evanston, before entering the Congregation in 1948, she was familiar with the Chicago archdiocese. Her seven years of teaching grade school in four Indiana schools had included the experience of being among the sisters who had closed St. John, Indianapolis, due to its location in a changing neighborhood. Her return from a four-year assignment in California coincided with her completion of her BS degree in 1963, when she was appointed superior/principal at St. Mel at age thirty-three.

The St. Mel-Holy Ghost convent diary provides background for the careful negotiations underway for combining the parishes. When St. Mel-Holy Ghost School closed for summer vacation in 1961, it counted 796 pupils and remedial reading classes were held that summer. Each of the following years the enrollment declined further, with 758 pupils enrolling in September 1961 and only 636 in 1962. The convent diary relates that by the following September, of the 554 pupils, 63 percent were black, 38 percent were non-Catholic and the first black teacher was hired. The following year the ratio had become 85 percent black with 50 percent non-Catholic.[52] The vacated classrooms in the school building of St. Mel-Holy Ghost were seen as an opportunity for alternate educational programs. Several were used for a school program for the deaf operated by Catholic Charities. Taking advantage of federal funds, the sisters initiated a Head Start program, as explained by primary teacher Sister Marie Caroline Carroll in a letter to Mother Rose Angela:

> Thank you for allowing me to be a part of President Johnson's War on Poverty. The Chicago Commission on Urban Opportunity will handle the federal funds for 45 Pre-Kindergarten Centers which will be operated by the Catholic and Public School Boards.[53]

The personnel solution for the 1964-1965 assignments was to keep both schools open but to combine the two convents at St. Mel, appointing Sister Mary Augusta (Marguerite) McCauley as principal at St. Mel-Holy Ghost, taking advantage of her experience during the two previous years at St.

Mel and enabling her to work closely with the superior/principal at St. Mel, Sister Jean de Lourdes.[54] Nonetheless, on July 25, 1965, the St. Mel parish bulletin ran the inevitable announcement:

> It is with much regret and keen sorrow that we announce the closing of Holy Ghost Chapel and School. The operation of the two churches and schools has always been expensive, but now and for some time before, it has become an expenditure that is financially impossible to carry. There was no alternative but to consolidate our entire parish program at St. Mel.[55]

Fortunately, all the children were able to be accommodated at St. Mel School and the facility was expanded. The Holy Ghost school building was sold to the Chicago Board of Education, and it reopened as Nathan Goldblatt Elementary School in September 1965, continuing to house the Head Start program.

Two other announcements in the July 25, 1965, St. Mel bulletin shed further light on the contemporary situation. The first item stated that Dr. Martin Luther King would hold a rally that afternoon in a nearby location, and the second was in reference to what the bulletin simply described as "what happened last weekend." Sister Janet (Janet Marie) Gilligan has a vivid memory of the circumstances to which the bulletin alludes:

> Sister Diane [Martin Therese] Ris and I were living at St. Mel that summer. As we walked back from the public library one Saturday we noticed that the streets were unusually quiet and empty. Then a number of young black men wearing bandanas around their heads came hurrying toward us, politely saying "Good afternoon, sisters," as they rushed by. At the convent door we were met by our anxious summer superior. The sisters had already heard about a disturbance at the fire station in Garfield Park that afternoon. Apparently a protest about the lack of black representation among the firemen had escalated into a riot. There was a strong police presence near the church and convent for a few days and the sisters were told not to leave the convent.[56]

What had started as a neighborhood protest was the beginning of what eventually escalated into the Chicago race riots. Apparently it was this incident that prompted the following comment in the St. Mel parish bulletin:

> It is absolutely necessary to realize the rightness of the civil rights cause and not be deterred by the indiscretions of any individual or group. Rather than point the finger of blame, all of us must extend the hand of friendship and cooperative effort to erase the evils that hurt not just some of us, but all of us.[57]

Within two years the sisters at St. Mel would experience further changes, as the parish chronicler summarizes:

> In November 1967, the Christian Action Ministry (CAM), an ecumenical group of nine Protestant and Catholic institutions, moved into the former Apollo bank building at 3932 W. Madison Street. The West Garfield Park neighborhood was emerging as a Black community, and St. Mel-Holy Ghost was taking on a new identity as a Black parish.[58]

These events serve both to highlight the leadership of Bishop Hillenger and also to buttress the analysis of historian James Sanders:

> The great majority of Blacks remained Protestant or unchurched and attended the public schools. Their invasion of a Catholic parish left its school largely unfilled. Catholic authorities had to face both the burden of preventing depopulated parishes and schools from going under financially and of providing facilities for displaced white Catholics migrating to the suburbs. They also had to deal with the problem of enforcing the Church's official racial policy on a largely unwilling constituency.[59]

Providence High School

Sanders also put his finger on the root of the difficult situation facing the Sister of Providence flagship secondary institution, Providence High School, one of the many high schools owned and operated by religious congregations as part of Chicago's regional Catholic high school system. "For the most part, even the older schools in what had now become the heart of the Black Belt remained almost totally white by drawing their students from outside the neighborhood."[60] As we saw in chapter 12, after the enrollment at Providence peaked at 1,171 during the 1955-1956 year, it had steadily declined. Sister Marie Clarice Toomey had joined the faculty the following year and when she was appointed superior of the house four years later, she alerted the council to the situation. When Msgr. McManus visited with the council in February 1960 to discuss the possibility of a new high school in suburban River Grove, he also strove to reassure them that new archdiocesan enrollment policies were intended to alleviate the situation.[61] However, the large freshmen classes enrolling at suburban Mother Theodore Guerin High School in 1962 and 1963 made it clear that the trend was irreversible. With Sister Marie Clarice's appointment as regional superior for the West in March 1964 and the ebbing energy of Providence principal Sister Miriam Gunning, new blood was needed. Fortunately, a number of qualified sisters were available to fill the breach.

Sister Marcella O'Malley had entered the Congregation in 1932 and after teaching junior high school for many years was appointed a superior at age thirty-three. She had gone on to serve as superior/principal at two other schools, meanwhile earning a MS in Education from Indiana University. Most recently, she had been among the first faculty at the new Guerin High School, so when she was named as superior of Providence at age fifty-one, she needed only to move across town.[62] As principal the council chose Sister Lucy Yenn, who had entered in 1932 and taught both junior high and high school; having earned her MS in Education from St. Louis University in 1960, she had most recently served as principal of Corpus Christi High School in Galesburg, which was closing in June 1964 in order to re-open as the co-institutional Costa High School the following September.

Since an increasing number of Providence High School students were black, it was necessary to address the changing social mix of students. The council had a unique resource in the person of Sister Pauline Marie (Ruth) Sondhaus. She had grown up in a Protestant home, but after graduating in 1938 from the University of California at Berkeley with a degree in social work, her experience working among the Mexican poor in Los Angeles prompted her to take instructions to become a Catholic. During World War II she joined the United States Navy and as a WAVE officer served with an intelligence unit in Washington, D.C. She then entered the Congregation at age thirty. After a few years of teaching in grade schools, she taught in four high schools from 1952 to 1964. Sister Mary Joan wrote to her to prepare her for her 1964 assignment:

> You probably know that Providence High School is feeling the effects of the changes that are taking place in "the inner city." The percentage of negroes in the incoming class is increasing

each year. With them they bring problems of inadequate preparation for high school work, emotional and moral problems,
etc. This is a real missionary activity to serve these people and
to do what we can to help them. Certainly in a situation like
this there is no end of opportunities to do apostolic work. It is
with this in mind, Sister, that we are assigning you to do social
work with these girls and their parents, when needed.[63]

At the same time Sister Mary Joan wrote to Superintendent McManus to tell him of the Congregation's new administrators at Providence and soon received a grateful reply:

Your gracious letter of May 2 is convincing evidence that contrary to a number of unfortunate and somewhat malicious rumors, the Sisters of Providence, far from considering the
abandonment of Providence High School, are resolved to continue it and to adjust its program to the changing condition of
the neighborhood and the changing needs of its students.[64]

That summer Sister Pauline Marie studied at Notre Dame
to update her social work credentials. There she had the opportunity to make contacts with others from the Chicago area.
From them she learned techniques for adapting youth groups
such as the Sodality and Young Christian Students to introduce students to interracial activities. She also met members
of the Catholic Interracial Council who were working to make
scholarships available to black students. By the following May
she sent a lengthy letter to Sister Mary Joan reporting on her
work the previous year, a major part of which had been to
take advantage of a government work-training project by interviewing and placing girls and completing the necessary
forms for them to participate.

The Sisters have done a wonderful job in giving of their time to
this work and it has worked wonders in the personalities of the
girls. It has convinced them as nothing else could that they
have value, are learning something worthwhile in terms of getting a good job after they leave school, and that they have
achieved a measure of independence financially, which to them
spells maturity and adulthood.[65]

While she was forthright in explaining the difficulties experienced by sisters who had become accustomed to working
with high achievers, she stressed the positive effects of training seniors to welcome incoming freshmen "to become
'Provites.' The emphasis was on 'Prov relations,' not 'race relations,' yet the same effect was obtained but by the positive

approach of emphasizing what all share in common."[66] Despite these efforts, the transition to becoming an integrated school in a black neighborhood was fraught with difficulty and would become explosive within a few years.[67]

An Activist Role in the South

The struggle for civil rights during the 1960s took on great intensity during the summer of 1964 with riots in Philadelphia and other cities. In January 1965, when council members heard the story of one of the speakers for the College's annual series, author of *Black Like Me* John Howard Griffin, they agreed that "the facts were appalling and terrifying!"[68] A journalist from Texas who wanted to document the difficulties faced by blacks in the South, Griffin was assisted by a doctor in darkening his skin so he could pass as a black man. He then traveled for six weeks hitchhiking and taking buses through the racially segregated states of Louisiana, Mississippi, Alabama and Georgia. In 1961 he published the journal of his 1959 adventure as a memoir and his story was made into a movie in 1964. With his words fresh in their memories, when Sister Marie Perpetua informed the council in February that as College president she had received a letter from civil rights leader Martin Luther King, Jr. asking colleges to recruit faculty and students to assist that summer with his education program SCOPE (Summer Community Organization and Political Education), the council gave the College permission to participate.

Two sisters on the faculty volunteered for the project. The first to step forward was a surprise to no one. Sister Mary Jean Mark, a professor of history who had been active in sponsoring a series of interfaith dialogue sessions at the College during the Second Vatican Council, was an outspoken advocate of the social justice themes she saw emerging from papal and Vatican II documents. She would later explain her reason for volunteering as "we used to pray, pray all the time. Now, we want to be counted with the doers."[69] The second volunteer was professor of biology Sister Alma Louise Mescher. She had entered the novitiate at Anaheim in 1937, received her initial formation in California, and then gone on to teach high school for fifteen years. At that point she had been assigned to study for a PhD in biology at Notre Dame and had joined the College faculty in 1963.The two sisters recruited student volunteers, three from Saint Mary-of-the-Woods College and three from Indiana State University in Terre Haute, and then solicited donations to support the combined Terre Haute delegation.

In later years Sister Mary Jean explained that the delegation received a week of preliminary training at King's headquarters of the Southern Christian Leadership Conference.

> It was a common-sense, practical briefing. Our particular mission in Albany was to upgrade the education of the underprivileged Negro children. ...Stressed repeatedly was the major theme of non-violence. Emphasis was on our role of fostering education. In the late summer, however, we were directed by King's headquarters to go to Americus, Ga., for a peaceful march.[70]

Sister Alma Louise's letter to Mother Rose Angela tells how their orientation training helped them adapt their teaching style.

> There is the dearest elderly lady, Mrs. Septima Clark, who has been teaching adult illiterates and organizing classes all over the South for years and years. She explained her methods to us. We have had negro history, organizations, enactments affecting negroes, etc.[71]

In later years, she described the events which followed when they arrived in Albany, Georgia.

> We lived in an empty four family flat in the black section of town with no hot water. When I took our clothes to the Laundromat I got acquainted with the ladies down there that way. And as soon as school was over, we'd go around to the houses and collect people to go and get registered to vote. Our students would take them to the polls because otherwise they would have been intimidated. And at night, we taught people to read. We had all kinds of help. We stayed there ten weeks. At night we went to a little café that charged $1.00 for a meal. And then I would buy enough for us to eat for breakfast and lunch in our house. Yes, we got a pretty good meal for $1.00.[72]

Sister Mary Jean provides additional details:

> Our first week in Albany generated in us a sense of apartness, of alienation, and we were very conscious that we were white people living in all-Negro ghetto. They hate hypocrisy and they detect it every time. Nevertheless, we remained hopeful. One morning about ten days after our arrival—classes had begun— we were on our way to early Mass. "Seesta Lisa, Seesta Jean"— it was a child's voice that broke the silence of the early morning,

Sisters Alma Louise Mescher and Mary Jean Mark set out to register voters in Albany, Georgia.

and we turned to wave back at a child whose mother was smiling approvingly at the child's excitement. The ice was broken.

Mutually we won the Negroes in our area and they won us. No longer did we see black. Negro children had built bridges and only children could do that.[73]

Although a number of Catholic colleges were represented, as the only nuns who participated, the two Sisters of Providence gained national attention with a five-page spread in *Look* magazine, which told how two sisters were able to: "transform a rickety frame house on a dirt road into a Freedom Center. ... The nuns slept in the basement of the Center and attended 7:30 a.m. mass at a nearby Negro church. Neither the heat, nor the dirt—red dust that cakes floors and skin—could spoil their spirit."[74] Photographer Vernon Merritt captured the unique contribution of the sisters with the caption under his photo of an encounter between Sister Mary Jean and Roy Shields, Jr., head of the Student Nonviolent Coordinating Committee: "They clashed, but she won his respect."[75]

Changing Financial Structures

The process of separating Congregation and College finances and the need to present the financial picture in an accepted accounting format highlighted the need to update the operations of the Treasurer's office. By 1964 dioceses across the country began to raise their stipends, as noted in the council minutes:

Cardinal Meyer of Chicago announces salary to be raised to $1000 so that communities might take care of their elderly and also the education of the young Sisters. Mother spoke at length of the meager amount paid to the Sisters throughout the country as compared with the salary paid to pastors and assistants.[76]

Mother Rose Angela's frustration can be easily understood in view of the fact that salaries were paid only for the ten months of the school year, so even with convent housing provided, the $1000 salary would be equivalent to $6930 in 2011 terms.[77] Although Mother Rose Angela had begun her administration with a debt of $1,367,000, the need to borrow large sums to pay for the new high school construction projects had ballooned the Congregation's indebtedness to $5,100,000. Even as the council agreed that they could not afford a new car, the minutes note that Mother Rose Angela, keenly aware of her responsibility for oversight of both the spiritual and temporal needs of the Congregation, "felt that would be well if the Sisters could be given a 'sense of saving' without antagonizing them, but rather 'a spirit of poverty, and 'contentment of spirit.'"[78]

Sister Francis Raphael had held the non-council office of treasurer general since 1938, working from a philosophy that it was her responsibility to make sure the bills would be paid without worrying the council. Trusting her proven expertise, the council had based its approval of loans to finance the construction of three new high schools on the philosophy of furthering the educational mission despite the significant cost. Sister Margaret had assisted in the treasurer's office during 1954-1960 while she was also teaching at the College, but her assignment to teach at Providence, Clarksville, took her away at the same time that Sister Francis Raphael's health declined.[79] Because Sister Margaret was already a familiar figure in Tile Hall, when she began her MBA studies at Notre Dame in 1960, she felt comfortable in dropping by Mother Rose Angela's office to offer advice. In later years she recalled her Notre Dame summers:

It was a very fine program. I had professors that were really dedicated to women religious and their preparation so that they would understand that field thoroughly and be prepared to do a good job for their hospitals or their schools or whatever in the congregation. They were mentors for me ... [Later], when

I wanted some information I could call any one those men ... So
it was a wonderful contact and a resource for us to have that.[80]

At this time the sisters' desires regarding their majors were
more likely to be honored, with the fortunate outcome that
two other sisters also pursued MBAs at Notre Dame and, in
consultation with the council and their academic directors,
each of their theses would greatly contribute to the financial
resources of the Congregation. Sister Margaret developed an
integrated congregational accounting system to include the
general administration, the regions, the high schools and the
local houses. Sister Marie Robert (Anne) Krause did her master's
thesis on budgeting and Sister Mary Maxine Teipen did hers
on management and personnel. On the part of the council,
Sister Rose Loretto was designated to attend several finance
meetings sponsored by the Congregation of Major Superiors.

Given the financial straits of the time, Mother Rose Angela
was resistant when Superintendent of Grounds Joseph Bisch
spoke to her about getting health insurance for the employees.
Sister Margaret also brought the topic to her attention with
the argument that such benefits were not only a way to practice the virtue of justice, but also a way to keep good employees. She also pointed out that each of the congregation-owned
high schools would need to adopt the same policy. Thus apprised of the need, the council authorized her to seek information regarding companies which could be asked to bid on a
contract and in 1962 the Congregation took on the expense of
providing this benefit.[81]

However, health insurance for the sisters was another
matter. When a representative of the Metropolitan Life Insurance Company came to present a plan for group insurance for
community members, the council regretfully noted that the
$132.84 per month per sister was prohibitive.[82] Fortunately,
by the following year, dioceses were coming forward to offer
health insurance coverage as an adjunct to the stipend. As the
country's elderly population approached nine percent, the
decades-old debate about providing health coverage through
the social security system finally bore fruit with the passage of
Medicare in July 1965. Mother Rose Angela must have been
delighted to write to the sisters shortly before she left office:

> The purpose of this letter is to call your attention to the *Medicare*
> program which within recent months has been approved by

Congress and which is available to persons, including Religious, who are now 65 years old or who will reach 65 by January, 1968.[83]

Included with the letter was a sheet explaining that during the transitional period the program would cover even those not enrolled in Social Security, which was certainly the case for most Sisters of Providence. Thereafter, a good number of sisters would become eligible for hospitalization and extended care simply by obtaining a Social Security number and enrollment form.[84]

Preparations for the 1966 General Chapter

When the 1960 council turned its attention to preparing for the 1966 General Chapter, they built upon the now well-established pattern of the two previous Chapters to include even more participation on the part of the membership. As they petitioned the Sacred Congregation to authorize including the regional superiors as ex-officio members, they also requested that twelve additional members could be elected, thus swelling the membership to sixty. Other seemingly minor changes of procedure accented the role of the sisters at large. Rather than adding to the secretary general's duties with the tedious task of drawing up a list of sisters eligible to be voted for and those eligible to vote, each house was asked to prepare and submit their list. On the day designated for electing delegates, the entire prayer hour was allowed for a quiet consideration of names before marking the ballot.

Since all the sisters were invited to submit proposals, a carefully thought-out system was devised to deal with the anticipated onslaught of ideas. A sheet explaining the type of suggestions appropriate for Chapter consideration was sent to each house. To provide a future-oriented context, sisters were urged to study the *Constitutions* in light of scripture and the recently promulgated Vatican Council's documents on the Church and on Religious Life. Forms were provided with the suggestion that the local community should discuss each suggestion and prepare a summary before sending the forms on to the regional superior. Convents with fewer sisters were encouraged to get together with other small houses. The four regional superiors were designated to categorize and collate the proposals. A preliminary sifting of the proposals inevitably brought to the surface items of custom such as clothing and daily prayers which could be taken care of by council decisions rather than requiring Chapter attention. Regarding further changes in the habit, Mother Rose Angela simply pointed out that "your wishes are still too undefined for us to know what is the consensus of opinion in regard to changes in the Religious habit. In due time each one will have an opportunity to indicate her wishes."[85]

With the regional level of government still in transition, Congregational membership was divided into the usual twelve sections, with Indiana missions accounting for six sections, Illinois missions for three, the East for two and the West for one. Given the increased number of elected delegates, when the list was circulated on February 11, 1966, not surprisingly, only thirteen of those chosen as delegates had previously been members of a General Chapter. Only seven held appointed office, while those serving in high schools and grade schools were evenly divided at eighteen each, with four from the College and one music teacher making up the remainder. In order to prepare the proposals for discussion at the Chapter of Affairs, delegates were assigned to four committees: 1. Religious government and temporalities; 2. Apostolate and immediate revision of the *Constitutions*; 3. Formation and spiritual renewal; and 4. Community living, clothing and miscellaneous. Once again, the views of the entire community were solicited and those who wished to participate were invited to join the delegates when they held committee meetings in the four regions.

Another innovation in the preparatory process was the preliminary gathering of the full General Chapter membership at Saint Mary-of-the-Woods on the weekend of April 1-4, 1966, when Rev. Edward Stokes, "an authority on General Chapters, lectured, discussed problems, and answered questions."[86] The Chapter itself was scheduled over a two-week period, June 16-25, in three phases of committee meetings, the Chapter of Elections and the Chapter of Affairs.

On a rainy spring morning that April, as Sister Eugenia Logan was on her way to the long narrow room off second Tile Hall in Providence Convent at the motherhouse which served as her archives office, she paused at the community room bulletin board. "Hmpf!" sniffed the elderly sister already scanning the array of papers before her. "All these official-looking papers just for the Chapter! In the old days the delegates just came home and did their duty and we found out who would be Mother and that was it."

Sister Eugenia's memories of "the old days" of Chapters stretched back to 1920 when the community had waited in suspense for a week before learning that the determined effort of the Chapter to re-elect Mother Mary Cleophas, despite her protests, for an unprecedented sixth term had been reluctantly approved by Rome. In 1926 she had been teaching at Immaculata in Washington, D.C., when Mother Mary Raphael was elected, but for the five subsequent Chapters she herself had been a delegate. She had to admit that her companion's assessment was not far off the mark for most of those 1932-1954 years. True, in 1938 she and her friend and colleague Sister Eugenia Clare Cullity had helped prepare an agenda for a small Chapter of Affairs, but it had not been until the 1954 Chapter that the concept of the Chapter as the highest authority in the Congregation had been truly operational. And now in 1966 it had come to the point where she didn't even need to be a delegate to have her say.

"Wait!' she called to her departing companion as she pointed to one of the sheets. "One thing is the same. Homecoming will be on June 27th!"

❧ End of an Era

As Mother Rose Angela labored over the preparation of her report for the 1966 General Chapter, she had much to ponder. Due to the incapacity of Mother Gertrude Clare it had fallen to her to prepare the report for the 1960 Chapter, but she had done so from the perspective of first assistant. Now she was mindful of her responsibilities as described in the *Constitutions*:

> All affairs of administration are under the authority of the Superior General assisted by her Council, in conformity with the present *Constitutions*. She makes all the regulations concerning the temporal welfare of the entire Congregation, sees to the observance of the *Constitutions*, makes the appointments for the various employments throughout the Congregation, and recalls or replaces the Sisters when she judges it necessary, without being obliged to give an account of her reasons.[1]

During Mother Rose Angela's fifty-three years of membership, three editions of the Rule had all contained this wording, but each of the five superiors general under whom she had lived that Rule had carried out the designated powers in a different manner. In fact, her own style had varied as her perspective was altered by the many experiences of her twelve years of generalate administration that were never available to her predecessors. Her travels had taken her to the center of Catholicism, Rome, and to the historical birthplace of the Sisters of Providence, Ruillé. She had crossed the Pacific Ocean to Asia to visit the Taiwan mission and had twice gone to South America. Within the United States she had traveled from coast to coast not only to visit with the sisters in their missions but also to meet with her counterparts in other religious congregations and with bishops in their dioceses. She had read widely from the increasing array of spiritual books and commentaries and media reports, as well as sampling television news and programs.

Discussions with her Council, the formation directors, the regional superiors, many local superiors and individual sisters had inevitably modified her views. Known for her strong belief in the adage, "Keep the Rule and the Rule will keep you," it was the phrase "sees to the observance of the *Constitutions*" that she felt was her most important responsibility. Nonetheless, since she herself had encouraged so many changes in observance, she now felt obliged to explain her reasons. The overarching rationale was a close adherence to the mind of the church. Citing the spirit of aggiornamento fostered by the Second Vatican Council, she began the report by stating that she and the Council and the regional superiors "have tried to update the Community in so far as reliable norms have been available and in so far as updating has seemed prudent and possible during these years of rapid and unprecedented change."[2]

Rather than the simple enumeration of facts characteristic of previous General Chapter reports, her analysis noted the disparity between the spirit of the times and the requirements of the Rule.

> The ferment of change, the emphasis upon personal freedom and the highly publicized criticism of religious life in general in recent years tend to produce unrest and insecurity. At the same time the increased stress laid upon the need for greater contact with the laity, the need for vacations and greater relaxation for Sisters, the importance of more and more activity as a means of "meeting the needs of the times," make the government of a religious community and of local houses difficult in this transitional era when reliable norms for change in the structure and discipline of religious life are still so unclear.[3]

Two areas discussed at length in the earlier chapters of this book, formation and governance, were now in need of major overhauls. Speaking of vocations, Mother Rose Angela pointed out factors that now inhibited the spirit of piety characteristic of earlier times:

> The spirit of restlessness, emotional instability, and weakness of faith in our age ... parental objection, together with the worldly atmosphere and loosely structured family life in which children are now reared. ... Attraction of careers and opportunities

for doing good in such organizations as the Peace Corps, Papal Volunteers, Extension Lay Volunteers, positions as lay teachers in Catholic schools.[4]

As for governance, considerable effort had gone into the selection and training of local superiors. Having studied the weaknesses of the earlier attempt to form provinces, the Council's gradual implementation of an intermediate level of government through close cooperation with the four regional superiors had been met with strong support. The veritable avalanche of proposals for the Chapter together with lively discussions across the Congregation bore witness to the effectiveness of the policy of sending sisters to other campuses for graduate study. Evidence that already the sisters at large were becoming independent thinkers appeared in the returns sent to the Chapter's clothing committee. Aware that the Second Vatican Council's recently published *Decree on the Up-to-Date Renewal of Religious Life* (*Perfectae Caritatis*) stated that the religious habit "must be in keeping with the requirements of health and must be suited to the time and place and to the needs of the apostolate,"[5] the committee had sought the opinion of the sisters regarding the habit. The remarkable return of 1,413 questionnaires revealed that 375 sisters were satisfied with the habit, 175 favored a complete change and 865 recommended one or more modifications. The clothing committee's recommendation that the Chapter refer the matter to a committee for further study was a clear indication that the practice of governing by committee was well established in the Congregation.

As Mother Rose Angela studied *Perfectae Caritatis*, it was clear to her that the movement begun by Pope Pius XII and furthered by Mother Marie Helene's participation in the 1952 Notre Dame Congress was alive and well in the words of the decree. Having been among the superiors who had planned the meeting at which the Conference of Major Superiors of Women had been adopted for the United States, she was pleased to see the statement that "conferences or councils of major superiors, erected by the Holy See, are to be welcomed."[6] As had been true for the 1920 General Chapter, major adjustments in the overall governance structure of the Congregation would be affected by the changes in canon law which would inevitably follow upon the Vatican Council's work. But just as *Perfectae Caritas* counseled superiors to listen to their members, Rome was now inviting advice from superiors. Only a month after the Vatican Council's conclusion the Conference of Major Superiors of Women had sent a questionnaire to its members inviting them to send suggestions for changes in the sections of canon law pertaining to religious. The much-publicized principle of subsidiarity was already being implemented by including input from those most affected.

The very setting of the 1966 Chapter presaged the transition to a new era. When the sixty delegates gathered at 7:00 p.m. on June 19, 1966, for the opening session of the General Chapter, they assembled in the new College library rather than in Providence library. Surely the words spoken by Pope John XXIII on October 11, 1962, as he opened the Second Vatican Council would have seemed pertinent to this occasion as well.

> We feel we must disagree with those prophets of gloom, who are always forecasting disaster, as though the end of the world was at hand. In the present order of things, Divine Providence is leading us to a new order of human relations which, by men's own efforts and even beyond their very expectations, are directed toward the fulfillment of God's superior and inscrutable designs. And everything, even human differences, leads to the greater good of the Church.[7]

The twelve ex-officio and forty-eight elected delegates had been primed by their discussions and committee work to appreciate that Providence was indeed leading them.

Each one was able to follow attentively in her own spiral-bound copy as Mother Rose Angela presented her fourteen-page report with its eleven supplementary statistical charts. Likewise, the sobering information presented in Sister Francis

The delegates to the 1966 General Chapter.

Raphael Donlon's twelve pages of financial exhibits reminded the delegates that during their time together the affairs of the Congregation were their responsibility. As the long evening session ended, a fitting tribute listing Mother Rose Angela's many outstanding contributions brought the delegates to their feet in applause.

The next morning the elections were conducted in the traditional manner as the delegates assembled in Providence library and then adjourned to the church crypt. A clear sense of direction was apparent when by 11:00 a.m. the tower bell summoned the local community to come to the church for the announcement. Not surprisingly the delegates had chosen First Assistant Sister Mary Pius Regnier to take on the responsibilities of superior general as Mother Mary Pius. As the newly elected officers appeared one by one in the front of the church, the sisters recognized familiar faces. Sister Loretta Therese O'Leary would move from the secretary's office to that of First Assistant, while Sisters Catherine Celine Brocksmith, Rose Loretto Wagner and Mary Joan Kirchner would also continue on the Council.

Sister Agnes Virginia Arvin

Even the newest assistants were familiar. As fourth assistant, Sister Agnes Virginia (Agnes) Arvin had followed a path similar to that of her predecessors. She had become widely known during eleven years at five schools in Chicago and Indiana before being appointed superior/principal of St. John in Fort Wayne at age thirty-one and later as the founding superior/principal when St. Jude, Indianapolis, opened in 1959. One of the early graduates from Providence Juniorate, she had begun her postulancy midway through her senior year in January 1939 and completed her BA over the summers before earning an MS in Education from Indiana University in 1964. At age forty-four, she was clearly well prepared by experience and education to bring a fresh voice to the Council.

Neither of the two other newly elected sisters was a delegate but both were well-known to the delegates. The new

Sister Ann Kathleen Brawley

Sister Margaret Kern

secretary general, Sister Ann Kathleen Brawley, was clearly capable of stepping into the council position because she had been assisting Sister Loretta Therese in the secretary's office since 1955. After graduating from Providence High School in Chicago, she had entered the Congregation in 1939 and taught in three schools in Indiana, Texas and Chicago before returning to the motherhouse in 1949 as principal of the small school in St. Mary-of-the-Woods Village.

The new treasurer general, Sister Margaret Kern, also had much experience to offer. After graduating from Saint Mary-of-the-Woods College in 1948, she had honored her father's wishes to delay entrance for three years, meanwhile enrolling in law school at Indiana University and working in law offices and as an intern for United States Senators William E. Jenner and Homer E. Capehart before entering the Congregation in 1951. During her novitiate years and then while teaching business administration at the College she had assisted Sister Francis Raphael in the treasurer's office. As we have seen, during the summers of her three 1962-1966 teaching assignments she had developed accounting systems for the Congregation as part of her studies for an MBA from Notre Dame University. Her expertise had already been apparent to the delegates due to her assistance in preparing a more in-depth financial report for the Chapter. During the business section of the Chapter they would approve a motion that she be given "every encouragement and assistance" with the implementation of the comprehensive financial structure designed for her graduate thesis.[8]

The work of the pre-chapter committees became the agenda as the delegates heard the reports and discussed the pros and cons of the motions proposed. The many adaptations already in practice which required changes in the Rule were delineated for approval in order to publish them to the sisters pending a final rewrite prior to referring them to Rome. Cognizant of the seal of approval given by the Vatican Council to such changes with *Perfectae Caritatis'* directive that "the manner of life, of prayer and of work should be suited to the physical and psychological conditions of today's religious,"[9] the delegates approved a series of revolutionary modifications. Not only would the sisters discontinue wearing the chaplet, but they could select shoes of a style they preferred, purchase a ready-made swim suit, wear a wrist watch, eat with seculars, travel without a companion when necessary and have more flexibility regarding the curfew hour of returning to the convent. They were now free to phone and write without supervision and could look forward to both a three-day visit with their families and a week's vacation each year. Most transformative of all was the permission to drive cars, though finances and license requirements would ensure that this adjustment would be gradual.

As for the apostolate, the Chapter cautiously ruled "that the goals and values of this entire apostolate of education be studied and implemented according to the thought of conciliar decrees."[10] The stirring summons in the most recent of the Vatican Council's constitutions, *The Church in the Modern World* (*Gaudium et Spes*), was already generating a strong response.

> The joys and hopes, the grief and anguish of the people of our time, especially of those who are poor or afflicted, are the joys and hopes, the grief and anguish of the followers of Christ as well. Nothing that is genuinely human fails to find an echo in their hearts.[11]

The desire for a time of spiritual renewal was evident not only in the thoughtful commentaries on topics such as silence and poverty, but also in a motion calling for an entire summer of renewal. The need to tailor the formation program to individual needs included a recommendation to establish a postulancy in Taiwan. The need for specialized care of sisters during their retirement years was recognized by recommending professional geriatric preparation for someone to take on this responsibility. For the delegates, the experience of the Chapter had been but one step in an ongoing process of fostering "our religious spirit—that of our Holy Foundress—in tune with new life situations that we confront today through gradual changes in outlook and attitude."[12]

The June 26, 1966, High Mass in the Church of the Immaculate Conception provided fitting liturgical rituals to solemnize the closing of the Chapter as the delegates formed the entrance procession, and the former and new councilors and treasurers made up the offertory procession. The words of the community chronicler depict a poignant moment as Reverend Mother Mary Pius and Mother Rose Angela returned to their seats after presenting the gifts. "Mother Rose Angela has taken her place among the Sisters in such a way as to be the admiration of all and to the edification of all. It is many years since the Community has had a 'retired' Mother."[13] In the following days, as the two exchanged greetings with "Good morning, Mother," they would have much to discuss. But that is a story for another day.

❧ Endnotes

Prologue

[1] The song was first performed at Saint Mary-of-the-Woods Novitiate in 1917, pairing a LaFarge "Cantata to honor Saint Therese" with verses attributed to Sister Loretta Therese Biermann, SP.

[2] Sister Mary Theodosia Mug's chronologically edited *Journals and Letters of Mother Theodore Guérin* (Saint Mary-of-the-Woods, IN: Sisters of Providence, 1937) provides not only insight into her spirituality, but also her detailed contemporary observations of the 1840-1856 period of American history. Direct quotes from Saint Mother Theodore will be cited as *Journals,* while biographical narrative will be cited as Mug, *Journals.* Biographies of Saint Mother Theodore include: Sister Mary Theodosia Mug , *Life and Life-Work of Mother Theodore Guérin* (New York: Benziger, 1904); Katherine Burton, *The Eighth American Saint* (Chicago: ACTA Publications, 2006); Penny Blaker Mitchell, *Mother Theodore Guérin—Saint of God: A Woman for All Time* (Saint Mary-of-the-Woods, IN: Office of Congregational Advancement—Sisters of Providence, 2006); Sisters Diane Ris, SP, and Joseph Eleanor Ryan, SP, *Saint Mother Theodore Guérin, Woman of Providence* (Bloomington, IN: AuthorHouse, 2011). A video *Saint Mother Theodore Guérin: A Woman for All Time* (2007) is available from Providence Center, Saint Mary-of-the-Woods, IN 47876. Biographical information is also available at the Sisters of Providence Archives at Saint Mary-of-the-Woods, www.spsmw.org (SMWA).

[3] Sister Mary Borromeo Brown, *The History of the Sisters of Providence of Saint Mary-of-the-Woods,* vol.1 (New York: Benziger, 1949); Sister Eugenia Logan, SP, *History of the Sisters of Providence of Saint Mary-of-the-Woods,* vol. 2 (1856-1894) (Terre Haute, IN: Moore-Langen Printing Company, 1978); Sister Mary Roger Madden, SP, *The Path Marked Out: History of the Sisters of Providence of Saint Mary-of-the-Woods,* vol. 3 (Saint Mary-of-the-Woods, IN: Office of Congregational Advancement—Sisters of Providence, 1991); (See also Sister Mary Roger Madden, SP, ed., *A Journey in Love, Mercy, and Justice: A Pictorial History of the Sisters of Providence of Saint Mary-of-the-Woods celebrating 150 years of service among the people of God* (Saint Mary-of-the-Woods, IN: Sisters of Providence, 1989).

[4] Section summary based on Brown, and Mug, *Journals*.

[5] Brown, 18.

[6] Ibid., 19.

[7] Brown, 19, describes the 1835 Rule, citing this passage: "the spirit of the Congregation was great zeal for the glory of God and an ardent desire to acquire perfection and contribute to the sanctification of the neighbor."

[8] See Carol K. Coburn and Martha Smith, *Spirited Lives: How Nuns Shaped Catholic Culture and American Life, 1836-1920* (Chapel Hill: University of North Carolina Press, 1999), Chapter 1, "The French Connection," for an account of the roots of the St. Joseph congregation during this era.

[9] Mug, *Journals*, xxiff., provides brief biographies of the founding sisters.

[10] Mug, *Journals*, 6, quoting Mother Theodore.

[11] Mug, *Journals*, 122. Brown describes the discussion in terms of Mother Theodore's "eleven fundamental questions" which clarify "the American Community's character of an independent, self-governing body with no claims upon the French house," but with the understanding that it would be governed by the Ruillé Rule, with any necessary adaptive changes to be made by the sisters' council in consultation with the Bishop of Vincennes (378). Later this is noted as a definitive separation (270). In her April 24, 1848, letter to Bishop Bouvier, Mother Theodore refers to her letter of Obedience appointing her as "Superior of the establishment and Superior of all the houses which should be formed later on" (*Journals*, 258).

[12] Brown, 402. In the Ruillé congregation's account of the American foundation, *The Providence of Ruillé-sur-Loir*, we find this assessment: "A wall of incomprehension separated the prelate and the Sisters" (14).

[13] Ibid., 479.

[14] In her letters, Mother Theodore often comments on pupils who ask for baptism or whose positive experience of the Catholic Church changes the opinion of anti-Catholic sentiment. Cf. *Journals*, 297-8, 332, 325.

[15] In a paper, "Immigrant Among Immigrants," delivered at the 2006 Conference of the History of Women Religious, Sister Mary Roger Madden states that of the 135 young women who entered during Mother Theodore's time in office, 54 (40%) were foreign-born, 24 being from Ireland. Readers interested in genealogical research can access the Entrance Book which shows the chronological entrance date of each sister, together with her baptismal name, birth date and place of birth, her parents' names, her religious name, and date of

death or departure, as the case may be, in the Sisters of Providence Archives at Saint Mary-of-the-Woods, at http://spsmw.org/2011/09/01/entrance-book-digitally-preserved/ (accessed February21, 2013).

[16] Brown, 647; *Journals*, 87.

[17] In her July 10, 1851, letter to Bishop Bouvier, she asks his intercession for the Ruillé community to send some who are qualified. "It is not necessary that they have great talents and a brilliant education; a solid and enlightened piety, a good head and sound judgment, joined to a good will—that is what we want" (*Journals*, 319).

[18] In her December 4, 1847, letter to Bishop Bouvier, Mother Theodore praises, "the admirable union that exists between persons of different nationalities, of dispositions so opposite, some well informed, others without education" (*Journals*, 249).

[19] Brown, 703, describes the content of these instructions, noting "Usually it took the form of an informal instruction on the Rule."

[20] In her July 10, 1851, letter to Bishop Bouvier, Mother Theodore comments: "But it becomes absolutely necessary to build. We are literally piled upon one another, which is not only inconvenient, but very unhealthy during the extreme heat of the summer"(*Journals*, 320).

[21] Brown, 668, quotes Mother Theodore's words as recorded in the Community Diary.

[22] The summary of this section is based on Logan. Additional biographical information about Mother Mary Cecilia may be found in *In God's Acre*, "Mother Mary Cecilia Bailly," by Sister Anita Cotter, 1-36, SMWA.

[23] The title "econome" refers to the person charged with practical responsibility for the infrastructure of the motherhouse: supervision of lay staff, purchasing, maintenance, the farm, etc.

[24] It is unfortunate that the only picture we have of Mother Anastasie was taken late in life. She is described as "very tall and powerful. She was masterly in eloquent expression, yet gentle and benign" (Mug, *Journals*, 273). Additional biographical information about Mother Anastasie may be found in *In God's Acre*, "Mother Anastasie Brown," by Sister Francis Cecile Miller, 37-66, SMWA.

[25] Madden, *The Path Marked Out*, 11, quotes Sister Camilla Morrison's recollections of the time: "Many a night Mother Anastasie spent in tears—it was a terrible time to live through. Mother Anastasie could never have battled through without Sister Mary Joseph; she, the latter, was the rock of defense and support."

[26] Additional biographical information about Mother Mary Ephrem may be found in *In God's Acre*, "Mother Mary Ephrem Glenn," by Sister Anita Cotter, 67-88, SMWA.

²⁷ Additional biographical information about Mother Euphrasie may be found in *In God's Acre*, "Mother Euphrasie Hinkle," by Sister St. Cosmas Gallagher, 89-112, SMWA.

²⁸ The summary of this section is based on Madden, *The Path Marked Out*.

²⁹ Ibid, 556

³⁰ Ibid, 167 ff., for the change of policy.

³¹ For the history of this mission, see *Against All Odds: Sisters of Providence Mission to the Chinese, 1920-1990* by Sister Ann Colette Wolf (Saint Mary-of-the-Woods, IN: Office of Communications—Sisters of Providence, 1990). The present volume will summarize its progress as needed.

³² Mother Mary Cleophas' 1926 circular letter, quoted in Madden, 546.

³³ Madden, 51.

Chapter 1

¹ Photograph found in the Saint Mary-of-the-Woods Archives, with "*The Boston Globe* July 24, 1929 South Station/5 Chelsea Girls Enter Convent" written on the back. The July 24, 1929, issue of *The Daily Boston Globe* does have an article entitled "Five Chelsea Girls Going to Novitiate" on page 32, but this photograph does not appear in the paper. The article begins "Five Chelsea girls will leave the South Station this afternoon for Saint Mary-of-the-Woods, Indiana, where they are to enter the novitiates of the Sisters of Providence." Within months the young women received these religious names (left to right): Sisters Mary Regis O'Kane, Anne Bernardine Dunne, Cyril Tobin, Philip Conlin and Mary Patricia Carroll.

² Brown, *History*, 688, quotes Mother Theodore's words as recorded in the Community Diary.

³ Sydney E. Ahlstrom, *A Religious History of the American People* (New Haven and London: Yale University Press, 1972), 895.

⁴ David Kyvig, *Daily Life in the United States, 1920-1939: Decades of Promise and Pain* (Westport, Conn.: Greenwood Press, 2002) provides excellent background for the period.

⁵ Dorothy M. Brown, *Setting a Course: American Women in the 1920s* (Boston: Twayne Publishers, 1987), 6.

⁶ Kyvig, 8

⁷ Charles Morris, *American Catholic: The Saints and Sinners Who Built America's Most Powerful Church* (New York: Random House, 1997), 113.

⁸ Ahlstrom, 901.

⁹ Ibid. The author characterizes the twenties as "the critical epoch when the Puritan heritage lost its hold on the leaders of public life, and when the mainstream denominations grew increasingly out of touch with the classic Protestant witness" (899). He notes: "The vast promotional campaigns of the churches also supported the nation's anti-Red hysteria. Over and over they depicted religion as a valuable bulwark against radicalism" (900).

¹⁰ Council Diary, November 4, 1924, SMWA.

¹¹ Ibid., November 6, 1924, SMWA.

¹² Morris, 160.

¹³ Ibid., 177. Carol K Coburn and Martha Smith, *Spirited Lives: How Nuns Shaped Catholic Culture and American Life, 1836-1920* (Chapel Hill: University of North Carolina Press, 1999) claim that "Nineteenth and early twentieth century American Catholic life revolved around the ethnic parish, and the parochial school provided the focal point" (90). The 2008 movie *Doubt* dramatically juxtaposes the lifestyles of priests and sisters in the parish during this era.

¹⁴ Necrology files of Sisters Ann Bernardine Dunne and Mary Regis O'Kane, SMWA.

¹⁵ Morris, 195.

¹⁶ Ibid., 164.

¹⁷ Dolan, *American Catholic Experience,* 349-50. See also Morris, 136.

¹⁸ Joshua Zeitz, *Flapper: A Madcap Story of Sex, Style, Celebrity, and the Women Who Made America Modern* (New York: Crown Publishers, 2006), 5-6.

¹⁹ Kathleen Sprows Cummings, *New Women of the Old Faith: Gender and American Catholicism in the Progressive Era* (Chapel Hill: The University of North Carolina Press, 2009), 5. See also Jay P. Dolan, *In Search of an American Catholicism: A History of Religion and Culture in Tension* (New York: Oxford University Press, 2002), 117ff.

²⁰ "Religious Life through the Generations: Interview with Sister Marceline Mattingly," SMWA. See Sisters of Providence Archives at Saint Mary-of-the-Woods: http://spsmw.org/2009/01/05/religious-life-through-the-generations/ (accessed February 21, 2013)

²¹ Ibid.

²² Sister Mary Theodosia Mug, *Life and Life-Work of Mother Theodore Guérin, Foundress of the Sisters of Providence at St.-Mary-of-the-Woods, Vigo County, Indiana* (New York: Benziger, 1904), 183.

²³ Ibid., 181.

²⁴ Sister Mary Borromeo Brown, *The History of the Sisters of Providence of Saint Mary-of-the-Woods, vol. 1* (New York: Benziger, 1949), 20. Her reference is to the 1929 edition of the *Constitutions.*

[25] *Constitutions* (1929), Article 3.

[26] *Love, Mercy, Justice: A Book of Practices of the Sisters of Providence* (Saint Mary-of-the-Woods, Indiana: Sisters of Providence, 2006), i. This collection of essays examining seventeen practices of the Sisters of Providence is a rich resource for capturing the essence of the spirit of the Congregation across historical contexts.

[27] See Sister Mary Roger Madden, S.P. *The Path Marked Out*, vol. 3 (Saint Mary-of-the-Woods: Office of Congregational Advancement, 1991), 269ff., "The Spirit of the Life," for details.

[28] *Constitutions* (1929), Article 2.

[29] Ibid., Article 70.

[30] Ibid., Article 292. Chapter XLIV, Duties of Teachers, Articles 292-298.

[31] Testimonial letter from Frances Hayes Rubit recalling the extra help given in 1922. Necrology file of Sister Francis Joseph Elbreg, SMWA.

[32] Bailly, Mother Mary Cecilia, *Life of Mother Theodore, Foundress of the Congregation of the Sisters of Providence in America* (1873), 2. SMWA.

[33] *Prayer Book for Our Times*, (Paterson, N.J.: St. Anthony Guild Press, no date), 27. This is a 2 ½ x 4" paperback pamphlet. Similar in size but hard bound and thicker were *The Catholic's Guide: A Manual of Devotions for the Use of Catholics*, revised by a Jesuit Father (New York: The Regina Press, 1938) and *Rosary Novenas to Our Lady* by Charles V. Lacey (New York: Benziger, 1926).

[34] Rev. F.X. Lasance, *My Prayer-Book: Happiness in Goodness, Reflections, Counsels, Prayers, and Devotions* (New York: Benziger, 1923), 17. The book was originally published in 1908 and later editions appeared in 1936 and 1944. Part I contained reflections, Part II prayers and devotions.

[35] The introduction to the wartime edition aligns religious and patriotic themes: "May the pleading words of Pope Pius X never be forgotten! 'Active participation in the sacred mysteries is the primary source of the true Christian spirit.' 'Active participation,' the oft-repeated call to patriotic duty for every citizen in days of war! How necessary, though that every Christian hearken to his Baptismal duty of 'active participation' in the 'primary source' of all peace, the Holy Mass!" *My Sunday Missal* (Brooklyn: Confraternity of the Precious Blood, 1942), 7.

[36] Angelyn Dries, OSF, "The Americanization of Religious Life: Women Religious, 1872-1922," *U.S. Catholic Historian* 7, nos. 1-2 (1992): 15.

[37] In *Love, Mercy, Justice*, see "The Practice of Hospitality to One Another and to the Stranger," 13-22.

[38] In an informal interview, asked to describe her favorite memory of life as a Sisters of Providence, Sister Dorothy Karier replied it was

walking up the Avenue on a hot June Homecoming day, suitcase in hand. Summer memory stories are a staple of similar interviews.

[39] The Volume I, Number 1, August 4, 1932, issue lists as editor-in-chief Sister Rose Angela, then a teacher at Providence High School in Chicago and later to become superior general. The staff is listed as the "News Writing and Editing Class," but apparently the newsletter was so well received that it continued publication through 1965.

[40] For this section I am indebted to the sisters who gathered on April 23, 2009, for "A Walk Down Memory Lane": Sisters Francis Joan Baker, Rita Clare Gerardot, Sheila FitzSimons, Laurine Haley, Brendan Harvey, Annette Cecile Holmes, Helen Dolores Losleban, Mary Roger Madden, Adele Mann, Marceline Mattingly and Edwardine McNulty.

[41] This prayer had been given to the early French community by Father Dujarié in 1822 and was traditionally recited every three hours as a means of uniting in the Sacred Heart of Jesus. See Brown, 13.

Chapter 2

[1] Proceedings of the 1926 General Chapter, SMWA.

[2] Angelyn Dries, OSF, "The Americanization of Religious Life: Women Religious, 1872-1922," *U.S. Catholic Historian* 10, nos. 1-2 (1992), notes the tendency to mirror the style of American businesses: "Rather than looking to a person of 'vision' as the major superior, communities began to choose persons with business skills" (17-18).

[3] Elizabeth Rapley, *The Lord as Their Portion: The Story of the Religious Orders and How Thy Shaped Our World* (Grand Rapids: Eerdmans, 2011), 177.

[4] Ibid., 197.

[5] Lynn Jarrell, OSU, in "The Development of Legal Structures for Women Religious Between 1500 and 1900: A Study of Selected Institutes of Religious Life for Women" (Ph.D. diss., The Catholic University of America, 1984), demonstrates how the "fruitfulness of the works," (274) of four groups of religious women who chose to live without strict enclosure in order to devote themselves to service of God's people "extended the universal law of the church" (291).

[6] Rapley, 209.

[7] Ibid., 285. See also Chapter 1, "The French Connection," in Carol Coburn and Martha Smith, *Spirited Lives: How Nuns Shaped Catholic Culture and American Life, 1836-1920* (Chapel Hill: University of North Carolina Press, 1999), for the historical background of the founding of the Sisters of St. Joseph at Le Puy during the same era.

[8] See Sister Mary Borromeo Brown, *The History of the Sisters of Providence of Saint Mary-of-the-Woods*, vol. 1 (New York: Benziger, 1949), 19-21, for details.

⁹ Ibid. Brown notes that Bishop Bouvier chided Bishop de la Hailandière about his interference in elections (299), and his handling of funds from the Propagation of the Faith (305), and he continued to advise the American community on matters such as establishing contracts with pastors (657).

¹⁰ Ibid. See 730ff. for an account of the consideration given to Bishop Bouvier on his trip to Rome for the promulgation of the doctrine of the Immaculate Conception in 1854, including a personal interview with Pope Pius IX.

¹¹ Jarrell, 287.

¹² Sister Eugenia Logan, *History of the Sisters of Providence of Saint Mary-of-the-Woods*, *vol. 2* (Terre Haute, Ind.: Moore-Langen Printing Company, 1978), 311-12.

¹³ See Sister Mary Roger Madden, *The Path Marked Out*, (Saint Mary-of-the-Woods, IN: Sisters of Providence—Office of Congregational Advancement, 1991), 76-82, for additional detail on the approbation process.

¹⁴ To appreciate the importance of papal approbation in the face of the "divide and conquer" tactics of many American bishops, see Coburn and Smith, 57ff., on the situation of the Sisters of St. Joseph of Carondelet. Kathleen Sprows Cummings, *New Women of the Old Faith: Gender and American Catholicism in the Progressive Era* (Chapel Hill: The University of North Carolina Press, 2009), states the dilemma well: "to make a choice: report to a female general superior in St. Louis or to a male bishop in their own diocese who would have complete control over their community" (107).

¹⁵ Jarrell, 287.

¹⁶ Brown, 20.

¹⁷ *Constitutions* (1929), Article 69, SMWA.

¹⁸ Ibid., Article 125.

¹⁹ Ibid., Articles 252-55.

²⁰ Ibid., Article 240.

²¹ Acts of Council, May 8, 1932, SMWA.

²² *Constitutions* (1929), Article 90, SMWA.

²³ Sister Rosarie Hussey's memoir of her first assignment at St. David, Chicago, 1917-19, SMWA.

²⁴ Undated 3x5 loose-leaf notebook of handwritten admonitions, SMWA.

²⁵ Madden, 51.

²⁶ *Constitutions* (1929), Article 203, SMWA.

²⁷ Ibid., Article 187.

[28] Joseph Creusen, SJ, and Adam C. Ellis, SJ, in *Religious Men and Women in Church Law*, 6th ed. (Milwaukee: Bruce, 1958) point out that "the professed religious in all religious institutes have, by their act of profession, given to superiors the free disposal of their person; they have freely submitted their will to their superiors. . . . When this personal authority is brought to bear directly on the will of the subjects, and when the persons themselves depend entirely on the superiors, this authority is called dominative power" (42).

[29] *Constitutions* (1929), Article 202, SMWA.

[30] Ibid., Article 195.

[31] Ibid., Article 1.

[32] Ibid., Article 14.

[33] Due to various closings and openings of houses, the 1920 Chapter was composed of *only* seventy-two members, still an unwieldy number.

[34] Lynn Jarrell, OSU, in "The Development of Legal Structures for Women Religious Between 1500 and 1900: A Study of Selected Institutes of Religious Life for Women," *U.S. Catholic Historian* 10, nos. 1-2 (1992), notes, "Both dialogue and the support of influential persons are indispensible" (28).

[35] Edward N. Peters, Curator, *The 1917 or Pio-Benedictine Code of Canon Law* (San Francisco: Ignatius Press, 2001), explains that each religious institute had the services of a ranking member of the hierarchy in Rome to "promote by his counsel and patronage the good of the religious institute," (C. 499, 1917 Code), although he had no jurisdiction over its affairs (194-95).

[36] See Madden, 527ff., for the cooperative efforts regarding devotion to Our Lady of Providence.

[37] Book of Important Events, September 30, 1919, SMWA.

[38] Mother Mary Cleophas' Letter Circular, March 29, 1926, SMWA.

[39] Documents listing the procedures for voting use the French word *billet* (a note, a ticket) for the slip on which sisters were to write the names of their choices.

[40] It was not until 1949 that a request was made to publish a list of delegates to the community, "voicing the wishes of many in making this request," and even then, "since this custom has been followed in the past, no change will be made at this time." Acts of Council, February 16, 1949, SMWA.

[41] C. 506 §4 of the 1917 Code states: "The Ordinary of the place in which the election is conducted presides, personally or through another, over the general election of the Superioress in Congregations of women if it concerns a Congregation of diocesan right, [and it is for him] to confirm the election results or to rescind it as an

action of conscience" (Peters, 197). Although as of 1887 the Sisters of Providence were constituted as a congregation of pontifical right rather than diocesan, this practice had been retained in the Rule.

[42] House diary of St. Elisabeth, Van Nuys, June, 1938, SMWA.

[43] Community Diary, June 27, 1926, SMWA.

[44] A 1910 record by Sister Mary Clarissa Paquette of a conversation with Mother Gertrude Clare's mother provides an intriguing perspective on her life. After her mother attended the funeral of her other daughter, Sister Genevieve Therese, she then stopped at St. Joseph, Indianapolis, to visit Sister Gertrude Clare. While there she told two of the sisters that during the previous night she had experienced a visit from Mother Theodore. In her dream Mrs. Owens had seen the foundress standing by her bed. Mother Theodore had assured her that her other daughter would not follow her sister quickly in death but rather "live and do great things for the Community." Sister Mary Clarissa, together with the local superior at St. Joseph, Sister Mary Theodata O'Grady, visited with Mrs. Owens and documented this conversation, describing Mrs. Owens as "a very sensible, well-balanced woman who was not given to imagining unusual occurrences." Signed memoir of Sister Mary Clarissa Paquette, Necrology file of Mother Gertrude Clare Owens, SMWA.

[45] See Madden, "Evolution of a Liberal Arts College for Women," 377-399.

Chapter 3

[1] See Sister Mary Roger Madden, *The Path Marked Out: History of the Sisters of Providence of Saint Mary-of-the-Woods, Indiana, vol. 3* (Saint Mary-of-the-Woods, IN: Sisters of Providence—Office of Congregational Advancement, 1991), 454ff., for details of the plan to strengthen the identity of Saint Mary-of-the-Woods College by gradually relocating Mother Theodore's first educational institution. This involved phasing out the high school classes on campus and simultaneously opening Ladywood School for Girls in Indianapolis.

[2] *Constitutions* (1929) Article 292, SMWA.

[3] Jay P. Dolan, *The American Catholic Experience: A History from Colonial Times to the Present* (New York: Doubleday and Company, 1985), 244.

[4] Dolan, 268-269, states that the 1858 Second Provincial Council of Cincinnati had decreed that every pastor build a school under pain of mortal sin. Because the Diocese of Vincennes (later Indianapolis) was one of the suffragan dioceses of Cincinnati, the Sisters of Providence also enjoyed strong support for their mission of education due to the leadership of Catholic school advocate, Cincinnati's Bishop Purcell,

[5] Cummings cites these statistics: In 1840 approximately 900 sisters from 15 orders staffed fewer than 200 Catholic schools; by 1900, 46,583 sisters from 170 congregations were available, most of them teachers (109). See Carol K. Coburn and Martha Smith, *Spirited Lives: How Nuns Shaped Catholic Culture and American Life, 1836-1920* (Chapel Hill: University of North Carolina Press, 1999), 129ff., for exploration of how class, ethnicity and gender issues were intertwined in the implementation of the policy requiring parishes to have schools.

[6] Undated contract form, SMWA. After the Archdiocese of Chicago set up a school board, the office had its own contract form which contained similar stipulations. In addition, the written consent of the archbishop was required to "assume or abandon charge of a parochial school," and the pastor's wishes regarding the appointment of teachers was to be taken into consideration by the Congregation. Contract form in St. Anselm documents, SMWA.

[7] Coburn and Smith, 144. Catholic teaching justified such discrimination on the basis of the man as breadwinner for the family, with the woman as wife, mother and unpaid head of the domestic household. As an example of the male/female discrepancy within Catholic schools, the authors cite this situation: "At St. Mary's Institute in Amsterdam, New York, the two male teachers each earned $600 for the year, the lay female teacher earned $300, and each CSJ earned $250, even though three of the six CSJs had thirteen to nineteen years of experience and one of the male teachers had taught for only one year" (145).

[8] Sister Agnella Hyde, Oral History, SMWA.

[9] Report of the Archdiocese of Chicago School Board to Superintendent Msgr. Bona on Housing Conditions for Sisters, June 24, 1927. Three Sister of Providence convents were included: St. Angela, St. Genevieve and St. Leo. St. Angela is described as a private house a half block from the school, with eighteen sisters accommodated in two porches with four beds in each, four rooms with two beds in each and two private rooms; the recommendation was for a new convent. SMWA.

[10] Much of this section is based on Philip Gleason, *Contending with Modernity: Catholic Higher Education in the Twentieth Century* (New York: Oxford University Press, 1995).

[11] Ibid., 46. James W. Sanders, *The Education of an Urban Minority: Catholics in Chicago, 1833-1965* (New York: Oxford University Press, 1977), quotes the 1904 recommendation of the Catholic Education Association that "in cities where there are several Catholic parishes there should be a central high school connected with the parochial schools of the several parishes" (166).

[12] Father Damen had been influential in persuading Bishop Saint-Palais to authorize extending the educational mission of the Sisters of Providence beyond the Diocese of Vincennes. See Madden, 105-106.

[13] Sanders, 143.

[14] Ibid., 145.

[15] Information in this section is drawn from a variety of documents and descriptive material in the Ladywood box of SMWA.

[16] Reitz Memorial Convent 1947 Diary, SMWA.

[17] St. Simon House Diary, SMWA.

[18] Letter of Mother Mary Raphael to Rev. John O'Hara (pastor of St. Simon), July 30, 1934, SMWA.

[19] See Sister Mary Borromeo Brown, *The History of the Sisters of Providence of Saint Mary-of-the-Woods, vol.1* (New York: Benziger, 1949), 576ff., for the founding story.

[20] Sister Eugenia Logan, *History of the Sisters of Providence of Saint Mary-of-the-Woods, vol.2* (Terre Haute, IN: Moore-Langen, 1978), 151-54, provides an account of the ill-fated attempt at providing a comparable boys' academy in 1872 when St. Vincent Academy moved to another location while the original building was retrofitted as St. Bonaventure Lyceum. Neither school did well, so when the Franciscan fathers closed the boys' academy, the Sisters of Providence returned in 1876 to the original building where the girls' school continued under the title of St. Joseph Academy.

[21] See Logan, 267-68.

[22] Bishop Ritter to Mother Mary Raphael, July 3, 1937.

[23] Book of Important Events, August 19, 1937, SMWA. At the end of the 1936-1937 term St. Joseph counted 13 graduates while St. Patrick had 48 in its graduating class. The combined enrollment at St. Patrick for the 1938-1939 school year was 305 while the newly merged girls' high school enrolled 96. The St. Patrick Diary notes: "Much excellent biology equipment was brought from St. Joseph Academy, now closed."

[24] See Brown, 345ff., for the unusual founding story and Logan, 81-87, for the somewhat confusing details of adapting the educational program over the years.

[25] Memorial booklet, "A Century of Service of the Sisters of Providence, Vincennes, Indiana: 1843-1943," 24-25, SMWA.

[26] See previous volumes in this History of the Sisters of Providence series: Brown, 555-56 and Madden, 322. The author of volume 2, Sister Eugenia Logan, was herself a graduate of St. Augustine and two superiors general, Mother Euphrasie Hinkle and Mother Mary Bernard Laughlin, were graduates of the Fort Wayne academies.

[27] Biographical data on Bishop Noll is taken from <http://www.osv.com/>.

[28] Acts of Council, October 6, 1938, SMWA.

[29] Community Diary, 1937, SMWA.

[30] Sanders, 167.

[31] See Madden, 451ff., for the details of the transfer of this school from the Ladies of Loretto of Toronto, Ontario.

[32] Ibid., 448.

[33] See Sanders, 165ff., for a description of Cardinal Mundelein's consolidating efforts.

[34] See Logan, 303ff., for the very interesting tale of this foundation.

[35] The vacated building was immediately converted into classrooms and a convent to accommodate the grade school faculty of Our Lady of Sorrows.

[36] Providence High School Jubilee Program, SMWA.

[37] 50th Anniversary Book of Our Lady of Sorrows, 1924. Courtesy of Sister Rosemary Borntrager, SP.

[38] Sanders, 169.

[39] The Book of Important Events notes that in the two-year period 1926-28, missions in Nebraska, California, Texas, Illinois (six in Chicago and its suburbs), Michigan, Milwaukie, Oklahoma and Maryland were refused. SMWA.

[40] Acts of Council, August 18, 1926, SMWA.

[41] Rev. Fr. Jacobi, SJ, to Mother Mary Cleophas, August 3, 1901. Several follow up letters invite a visit to see the possibilities of situating a house for infirm sisters in an area "very picturesque and is planted in vineyards, and in prunes, oranges, English walnuts, apricots, peaches, olives, and almonds." SMWA.

[42] See Madden, 440-442, for details of the 1916 trip by Mother Mary Cleophas and Sister Mary Alma.

[43] Mother Mary Cleophas to Bishop Cantwell, November 9, 1921, SMWA.

[44] Bishop Cantwell to Sister Mary Ignatia Hanson, October 18, 1921, SMWA.

[45] In an interview by St. Joseph's parish historian, Mary Vandal, Sister Marie Dolores Walta recalls: "Father Ford, our pastor, delighted in repeating, 'I went to St. Mary's myself to get the Sisters of Providence.'" He had been taught by Sisters of Providence and then worked with the sisters as a young assistant at St. Sylvester Parish in Chicago. Gassed as a soldier in World War II, he had been shot in a Chicago gang war and had gone to California for his health. "History of St. Joseph Parish," SMWA.

[46] In her memoir, S. Alma Clare Lauer recalls: "We were privileged to travel in compartments, getting off at the Harvey Houses for meals along the line. During the day, we opened the door of the compartment and used it as a community room. We had complete privacy all the way to California." After a two-night, day-and-a-half trip, their warm welcome by parishioners was accentuated by rapid growth of the school from 60 pupils at opening to 120 by October 1928 and within a few years, 900, with 800 on the waiting list. Sister Alma Clare Lauer, Memoir regarding founding of St. Elisabeth, Van Nuys, SMWA.

[47] Ibid. SMWA.

[48] Sister Marie Dolores Walta, Memoir re early days at St. Joseph, Hawthorne, SMWA.

[49] The Van Nuys house diary notes her arrival on February 15, 1929, and departure on September 16, 1929, with side trips to Santa Barbara and visits from First Assistant Sister Berchmans in April.

[50] This account is based on Acts of Council, May-December, 1934, and Marywood House Diary, SMWA.

[51] The Marywood diary lists six sisters with this summer catechetical assignment: Sisters Rita Cecile Egan, Mary Loretta Gaughan, Josephine Therese Heindl, Edna Marie Hugenard, Mary Adele Miller and Florence O'Connor. In addition, the memoir relates that "the Marywood Lincoln" transported eight sisters to attend the procession on retreat Sunday and the novices and postulants prepared little "First-Communion Booklets," and that Sisters Margaret Mary Ryan and Sister Rose de Lourdes Durment "an excellent primary teacher, helped out with the little ones." SMWA.

[52] Sister Mary Adele Miller Memoir, "First Experiences in a Mexican Vacation School," SMWA.

[53] Miller Memoir, SMWA.

[54] See Madden, 498.

[55] Periodical, "The North Carolina Apostolate," February, 1936, 5, SMWA.

[56] House Diary of Blessed Sacrament, Burlington, August 19, 1937, SMWA.

[57] Sister Mary Charles Campbell recalled: "When you live in a missionary country like that, the Bishop [McGuinness] would walk in, maybe bringing with him the sisters keeping house for him, bringing them over, come for dinner, come out in the kitchen and help me with dishes or something. A wonderfully simple man!" Oral History, SMWA.

[58] See Madden, 476ff., for an account of the various phases of the early development of this property.

[59] Book of Important Events, October 7, 1916, SMWA.

[60] David M. Kennedy, *Freedom from Fear: The American People in Depression and War, 1929-45* (New York: Oxford University Press, 1999), 131.

[61] Book of Establishments, 1927, 49, SMWA.

[62] Ibid., 49.

[63] See Madden, 448-451 for the interesting account of this foundation.

[64] Book of Establishments, 48, SMWA.

[65] Ibid., SMWA.

[66] See Sanders, 114ff. for an excellent analysis of early efforts at racial integration in Chicago.

[67] Dolan, 365. Dolan provides several examples of how integration of parishes was handled in various dioceses and of black Catholics' organized efforts by to address such inequality.

[68] Sanders, 208.

[69] In 1995 the Chicago Historic Resources Survey rated the church as possessing "some architectural feature or historical association that made it potentially significant in the context of the surrounding community." http://st_anselm1.tripod.com/id2.html

[70] St. Anselm house diary, 1919. One of the girls had taken home a gold medal in the same contest. James T. Farrell, noted author of the Chicago Irish-American Washington Park neighborhood, attributed his beginnings as a writer to his teacher at St. Anselm, Sister Mary Magdalen Miller. Article in her necrology file by Ron Ebest, "The Irish Catholic Schooling of James T. Farrell, 1914-1923." SMWA.

[71] Father Gilmartin to Mother Mary Cleophas, January 20, 1911, SMWA.

[72] St. Anselm house diary, 1932. The "special missionary work" of the Sisters of the Blessed Sacrament had already proved itself at St. Elizabeth, since 60 percent of the children enrolled were non-Catholic, but 95 percent graduated as Catholics (Sanders, 214).

[73] Book of Establishments, 20, SMWA. God's designs certainly seemed to favor Archbishop Mundelein's evangelizing policies as by 1936, 500 children attended the all black school. With the continued exodus of white parishioners, the "one parish" policy was revised to fit the territorial parish boundary model, with neighboring 2,000 member Corpus Christi Parish enrolling 800 black pupils in its school (Sanders, 214).

[74] Even as late as 1939 the council refused a school for "colored children in Pensacola because we are not prepared for this work." Acts of Council, May 18, 1939, SMWA.

[75] In his letter to the superior, Sister Clare Mitchell, he stated, "Eventually, I think we should direct the colored children to St. Bridget's,

and whatever money the diocese will have for the development of the negro cause should be expended there." Bishop Ritter to Sister Clare Mitchell, September 4, 1935, SMWA.

[76] Father Strange to Mother Mary Raphael, August 31, 1936, SMWA. Father Strange was to devote many years to the parish, building a new school in 1954, a new church in 1959, and hosting youth and community events as the Martindale neighborhood was split by interstate highway construction. http://www.polis.iupui.edu/ruc/neighborhoods/martindalebrightwood/mbnarrative.htm; http://stritachurchindy.org/about-us/ (Accessed March 2013).

[77] Sister Clare Mitchell to Mother Mary Raphael, September 14, 1936, SMWA.

[78] Father Strange's position was a prophetic stance for the times. Segregated Catholic parochial schools were not uncommon but integration of white and black students was unheard of. A few years earlier, Mother Grace Damman, RSCJ, had led a study of interracial relations by students at Manhattanville College in New York which resulted in the publication of the "Manhattanville Resolutions." These eight resolutions, as quoted in R. Bentley Anderson, *Black, White, and Catholic: New Orleans Interracialism, 1947-1956* (Nashville, TN: Vanderbilt University Press, 2005), were prefaced by this statement: "Whereas I am enjoying the privilege of a Catholic higher education, I recognize that I have certain duties and obligations toward my fellow man, among which I must consider my conduct and attitude toward the American Negro"(201). However, as noted by Philip Gleason in *Contending with Modernity: Catholic Higher Education in the Twentieth Century* (New York: Oxford University Press, 1995), it would not be until 1938 that Manhattanville College would admit an African-American student, and even then a group of alumnae raised objections (156).

[79] Memoir, Sister Mary Joan Kirchner. Sister goes on to speculate that not all the clergy were in favor of accepting black students since they felt it would hurt enrollment. Yet, while in 1937 there were forty-some freshmen including the five black girls, in the fall of 1938 they enrolled eighty-five, the largest freshman class in the city. Only one of the five black students, Marjorie Graham, went on to graduate, leading her class in Latin.

[80] Helen O'Gara to Bishop Ritter, October 14, 1937, SMWA.

[81] Helen O'Gara to Mother Mary Raphael, October 29, 1937, SMWA.

[82] Memoir, Mother Rose Angela Horan, SMWA. At the time she was Sister Rose Angela, one of the homeroom teachers. SMWA.

[83] Diary of St. Agnes Academy, 1938-39. "St. Agnes this year graduated the first colored student to finish from a Catholic girls' high school in Indianapolis. The name of this student was Marion Lenchman. She made a very good scholastic record." SMWA.

[84] Sister Mary Joan Kirchner's oral history. SMWA.

[85] See Madden, 522ff., for an account of this project, noting that the reason for its lack of success once again demonstrates the sisters' deep-seated attachment to Saint Mary-of-the-Woods: "Despite the many positive aspects of the home, few sisters could be reconciled to being separated from the Motherhouse environs. This isolation only exacerbated the distress many felt at being retired from active duty" (523).

[86] Community Diary, 1927. SMWA.

[87] The following section is drawn from an account Sister Rose Louise Schafer gave to Sister Mary Roger Madden to accompany her Oral History interview, from an article in *Community* and from the Oral History interview with Sister Rose Louise by the author. The congregation is deeply indebted to Sister Rose Louise for her efforts not only to chronicle accurately the initial foundation of the Juniorate but also to maintain contacts with its alumnae through the years.

[88] Memoir, Sister Rose Louise Schafer, SMWA.

[89] Book of Important Events, September, 1930, SMWA

[90] Sister Rose Louise was the first of 142 candidates who became Sisters of Providence. Oral History, SMWA.

[91] See Madden, 172 and Chapter 12, "Evolution of a Liberal Arts College for Women," 377-399, for details of this development.

[92] See Madden, 396, for a list of the accrediting institutions.

[93] See Cummings, Chapter 2, "Enlarging Our Lives: Higher Education, Americanism, and Trinity College for Catholic Women," for a fascinating account of the School Sisters of Notre Dame's establishment of Trinity College in Washington, D.C., which opened in 1900. Like Saint Mary-of-the-Woods College, most other women's colleges evolved from existing academies. Examples include the College of St. Catherine in St. Paul in 1905, the College of St. Angela in New Rochelle, New York, in 1904, and Marymount College in Tarrytown, New York, in 1918, and probably of most interest to the Sisters of Providence due to its proximity and potential for competition, Saint Mary's, Notre Dame, in 1906. Gleason also traces this development (89-91).

[94] Gleason, 93-94.

[95] Gleason, 145.

[96] Gleason notes that, among the women's colleges on the CEA's 1918 list of accredited institutions, although "St. Mary-of-the-Woods in Terre Haute, Indiana, was handicapped by an out-of-the-way location, it had an excellent reputation and drew students from Chicago where the Sisters of Providence were also active" (90).

[97] Acts of Council, November 27, 1927, SMWA.

[98] Acts of Council, February 19, 1928, SMWA.

[99] The goal of this fund-raising effort was extraordinarily ambitious, equivalent to $12,300,000 in the year 2010. http://www.measuringworth.com

[100] Much of this section is based on H. Tracy Schier, "History of Higher Education for Women at Saint Mary-of-the-Woods: 1840-1980" (PhD diss. Boston College, 1987), 118-129.

[101] Acts of Council, March 17, 1929.

[102] See Madden, 593 for a complete list. The Book of Important Events, September 1919, notes: "As nearly all sisters have their degree from St. Mary-of-the-Woods and the Catholic University, and one of the requirements of a successful College is that its faculty be composed of instructors having degrees from various high class schools." SMWA.

[103] Schier lists the universities from which this faculty had earned degrees: The University of Chicago, Fordham University, Roman College, Indiana University, University of Illinois, Catholic University, University of Notre Dame, University of Minnesota, Northwestern University, The University of Iowa, Bryn Mawr, University of California, University of Wisconsin, Stanford University, Pennsylvania State University, Kansas State University, Harvard University and Columbia University.

Chapter 4

[1] David E. Kyvic, *Daily Life in the United States, 1920-1939: Decades of Promise and Pain* (Westport, Conn.: Greenwood Press, 2002), 8.

[2] Sister Mary Adele Miller, "First Experiences in a Mexican Vacation School," Memoir, SMWA.

[3] Acts of Council, May 21, 1933, SMWA.

[4] Newsletter to sisters remaining on mission during the summer, June 29, 1933, SMWA.

[5] Sister Mary Roger Madden in *The Path Marked Out* (Saint Mary-of-the-Woods, IN: Office of Congregational Advancement—Sisters of Providence, 1991), 533-534, lists construction of the Bakery/Cannery in 1910, the Greenhouse in 1919, and the Dairy Barn in 1923.

[6] Jay P. Dolan, *The American Catholic Experience: A History from Colonial Times to the Present* (New York: Doubleday & Company, Inc., 1985), 384-85.

[7] David M. Kennedy, *Freedom from Fear: The American People in Depression and War, 1929-45* (New York: Oxford University Press, 1999), 227ff.

[8] Charles R. Morris, *American Catholic: The Saints and Sinners Who Built America's Most Powerful Church* (New York: Random House, 1997), 145ff. and Dolan, 403ff.

[9] Sydney E. Ahlstrom, *A Religious History of the American People* (New Haven and London: Yale University Press, 1972), 1,009.

[10] See Morris, 196ff., for an in-depth analysis of Catholics and the film industry.

[11] Morris notes several instances: In 1933 Cardinal Mundelein didn't hesitate to use his White House connections with his friends Franklin and Eleanor Roosevelt to garner praise for Catholic efforts to regulate films (204). In 1935 the cardinal brokered an honorary degree from Notre Dame for President Roosevelt (231). In 1938 the cardinal's visit to Rome was abetted by the U.S. Navy and diplomatic corps (224). Dolan, *In Search of an American Catholicism*, describes the furor created when in 1939 President Roosevelt named Myron C. Taylor as his personal representative at the Vatican (166).

[12] Much of this section is based on Sister Ann Colette Wolf, *Against All odds: Sisters of Providence Mission to the Chinese 1920-1990* (Saint Mary-of-the-Woods, IN: Office of Communications—Sisters of Providence, 1990), which chronicles in absorbing detail what can here only be summarized. As that volume utilizes the Wade-Giles Romanization of Chinese names, it is used here as well rather than the Pin Yin spelling.

[13] Distance and slow communication were significant factors not only for the Sisters of Providence, but for other congregations who sent missionaries to China. Regina Siegfried, ASC, *"Missionaries More and More": The History of the China Mission of the Adorers of the Blood of Christ, 1933-1945* (Bloomington, Ind.: Authorhouse, 2005), 225, chronicles parallel experiences of internal disagreements among the group with conflicting reports sent in letters to superiors at home. Like Sister Marie Gratia, Sister Sophie Gartner, ASC, "began the bridging process" of adapting the strict religious rule and customs to the needs of the Chinese culture and lifestyle sooner than some of the other Adorers.

[14] Apparently Mother Mary Raphael's conversation with Bishop Tacconi had influenced this decision. The October 22, 1927 Acts of Council note: "The Rt. Rev. Bishop of Kaifeng ... is very pleased with the Sisters, who are 'good religious.' ... Sr. Joseph Henry is not a business woman . . . and we need to pray regarding who is to succeed Sr. Joseph Henry." The council had already decided to bring Sister Joseph Henry back to the motherhouse for consultation, but the combination of the conflicting reports in the letters from the missionaries, the terrible stresses of the ongoing civil war on their very doorstep and the concurrent sick leave of Mother Mary Raphael made it impossible to reach a timely decision. It was not until January 20, 1929, that the council made the appointment. SMWA

[15] See Ahlstrom, 858-67, for a description of this aspect of "Crusading Protestantism." One such student who went on to become a Presby-

terian minister in China was Absalom Sydenstricker, father of 1938 Nobel prize winning author Pearl S. Buck, who grew up in China during the Chinese civil wars and whose popular 1931 book *The Good Earth*, followed by many other works, provided a humanitarian view of the Chinese people.

[16] Wolf, 63-64, describes how during the 1920s Chinese civil war, Father King's mission in Sinyangfu was overrun by soldiers and he stopped at Kaifeng to warn the Sisters of Providence.

[17] Acts of Council, January 15, 1933, SMWA.

[18] Sister Agnes Joan Li, Oral History, SMWA.

[19] The overarching rationale for encouraging Chinese vocations was Pope Benedict XV's 1919 apostolic letter *Maximum Illud* calling for the establishment of native hierarchy in missionary countries. Wolf notes that Sister Marie Gratia was quick to understand that "the American sisters would always be just a few drops in the great ocean of souls in China"(44). She was constantly on the alert to foster vocations among the Chinese women with whom she came in contact. However, this was a time when racist discrimination was on the rise, with the Immigration Act of 1924 intensifying restrictions against Asians entering the United States. The Chinese postulants entered under study visas since they needed higher education. To meet the need for Catholic higher education in China, the apostolic delegate worked with the Benedictines to establish a Catholic University in Peking in 1925.

[20] *Constitutions* (1929), Article 20, "The Superior General," SMWA.

[21] Angelyn Dries, OSF, "The Americanization of Religious Life: Women Religious, 1872-1922," *U.S. Catholic Historian* 10, nos. 1-2 (1992):17.

[22] Immaculata 1926 House Diary, SMWA.

[23] *Constitutions* (1929), Article 21, SMWA.

[24] Ibid. Article 25.

[25] Acts of Council, September 19, 1926, SMWA.

[26] These include the decisions to accept the mission at St. Therese, Alhambra, on May 25, 1930, with a 6-1 vote in favor; to accept St. Joseph, Downers Grove, Illinois, on April 8, 1932 with a 5-2 vote. Acts of Council, SMWA.

[27] See Acts of Council, June 5, 1927, and August 21, 1927. SMWA

[28] Kennedy, 38, 41.

[29] Kennedy notes that the majority of banks at that time were independently owned and operated and "could only look to their own resources in the event of a panic. ... Disaster first flared in November 1930 at Louisville's National Bank of Kentucky, and then spread virulently to groups of affiliated banks in neighboring Indiana, Illi-

nois, Missouri, and eventually Iowa, Arkansas, and North Carolina" (66).

[30] Ibid., 67. In assessing the situation of the times, the author notes: "A singular event, the Depression has thus far resisted comprehensive explanation by analysts applying supposedly universal theories of economic behavior" (71).

[31] This description is based on Sister Margaret Kern's Oral History, Transcript #1, SMWA. In 1952 as a novice, she was assigned to help Treasurer General Sister Francis Raphael Donlon, who told her she used the system Sister Mary Raphael had set up when she was treasurer in the 1920s. Plans for the building's vaults were developed in accord with Article 74, "Depository," of the *Constitutions*, while the procedures of the treasurer's office follow the directives of Chapter XVI, "The Temporalities Belonging to the General Administration."

[32] The intricate Elbreg Cabinet Secretary desk designed to hold precisely folded invoices in alphabetical order is displayed in the Heritage Museum at Saint Mary-of-the-Woods. It was built by Henry H. Elbreg of Greenfield, Indiana, the grandfather of Sister Francis Joseph Elbreg.

[33] Sister Margaret Kern recalls dusting the mantel and "bills would fall off of it because there were so many behind St. Joseph." Oral History, Transcript #1, SMWA.

[34] http://www.measuringworth.com/calculators/uscompare/index.

[35] In her oral history account, Mother Mary Pius Regnier recalls a conversation with Sister Mary Neil Gleason who quoted her father as saying, "I'll never have enough money to give a million dollars to the Church, but I think I know enough to save the Church several million dollars." He also donated his financial services to his home Archdiocese of Milwaukee. The story was often told that when he came to Saint Mary-of-the-Woods, as part of his tour he was given a view of the campus from the roof of Foley Hall, thus gaining a visual picture of the brick and mortar investment structure of the Congregation finances. SMWA.

[36] Letter, February 3, 1929, SMWA.

[37] http://search.time.com/results.html. December 21, 1931.

[38] Minutes of the 1932 Chapter, SMWA.

[39] See Madden, 363 ff.

[40] The August 21, 1932 Acts of Council state, "Mother is going for a rest and hopes not to be known where she is." SMWA.

[41] Commenting on Canons 499 and 500 CIC, Joseph Creusen, SJ and Adam C. Ellis, *Religious Men and Women in Church Law: Sixth English Edition* (Milwaukee: The Bruce Publishing Company, 1958) note:

"These faculties deal with such matters as the alienation of property, loans, dowries required by the constitutions, leaving the cloister, celebration of certain offices such as those of Holy Week, etc"
(46).

[42] The August 5, 1932, Acts of Council records the result of Mother
Mary Raphael's interview with Bishop Chartrand: "The Bishop was
determined that we would take over the school, and no argument
that Mother advanced was accepted. It was decided that we would
take the school for one year." This was in spite of the council's
previous discussion of the question on July 8, when "it was unanimously condemned." However, Mother had just refused assuming
full control of Reitz Central High School in Evansville "because we
have not taught the older boys." The November 8, 1931, minutes
record that "The Bishop decided also that the lay Sisters should be
permitted to vote for the delegates to the General Chapter." Since the
council had been discussing revisions of the section of the *Constitutions* pertinent to the coadjutrix sisters, this advice was apparently
taken as a dispensation. SMWA.

[43] The December 17, 1933, Acts of Council note that some banks were
refusing to honor the notes signed by the recently deceased Bishop
Chartrand and that a nearby congregation had defaulted. "Thank
God we have been spared." SMWA.

[44] Mother Mary Raphael to pastors, September 15, 1933, SMWA.

[45] Nicholas A. Schneider, *Joseph Elmer Cardinal Ritter: His Life and
Times* (Liguori, MO.: Liguori Press, 2008), 48. Biographical information regarding Bishop Ritter is drawn from this work.

[46] Ibid., 52.

[47] Letter from Bishop Ritter to Mother Mary Raphael, November 13,
1934, SMWA.

[48] Acts of Council, December 8, 1934, SMWA.

[49] In a September 9, 1937, letter to Mother Mary Raphael, Bishop Ritter
urges reconsideration of a sister: "I can easily see that she would be
a little difficult in any house, however, she has many splendid qualities and I think an effort should be made to place her properly."
SMWA

[50] Bishop Ritter to Mother Mary Raphael, April 7, 1936, SMWA.

[51] Bishop Ritter to Mother Mary Raphael, March 30, 1937, SMWA.

[52] Copy of letter to Bishop Ritter with signature and date deleted,
forwarded by him to Mother Mary Raphael and Sister Francis Joseph on September 9, 1937, SMWA.

[53] Bishop Ritter to Sister Francis Joseph, September 9, 1937, SMWA.

[54] Acts of Council, September 26, 1937, SMWA.

[55] See Kathleen Sprows Cummings, *New Women of the Old Faith: Gender and American Catholicism in the Progressive Era* (Chapel Hill: The University of North Carolina Press, 2009), 107ff., for a discussion of this movement, as well as a detailed description of the relationship in the Philadelphia Archdiocese's Superintendent Father Philip McDevitt with Sister Assisium McEvoy, CSJ, as an example of how the cooperation of teaching orders with the hierarchy evolved to create the vast American Catholic school system.

[56] *Constitutions* (1929), Articles 256-258 , SMWA.

[57] Four page single-spaced letter dated June 29, 1933, and signed "Your Sisters at Home," SMWA.

[58] See Sister Mary Borromeo Brown, *The History of the Sisters of Providence of Saint Mary-of-the-Woods, vol. 1* (New York: Benziger 1949), 179ff., for interesting details of this foundation.

[59] The St. Joseph house diary contains an historical account of the foundation and development of St. Joseph School, later named Tenth Street School. SMWA.

[60] Summary account, "Vincennes Parochial Public Schools, 1933-1941," in St. Francis Xavier Convent Diary, SMWA.

[61] An undated newspaper clipping in the Vincennes House Diary lists the characteristics which defined the school as "Catholic" as: "1. Teachers were hired from the Sisters of Providence in Terre Haute and the Benedictine Sisters in Ferdinand and these teachers taught in no other public schools; 2. Children were assigned by religious preference; and 3. Children were marched to a nearby edifice for religious services." SMWA.

[62] "City School Board to Take over St. John School," *The Martin County Tribune*, January 14, 1932.

[63] *History Book of St. John's Catholic Church, Loogootee, Indiana*, 26, SMWA.

[64] "St. John School History," SMWA.

[65] House diary, St. Simon, Washington, Indiana, 1935-36, SMWA.

[66] In order to foster equality among the members, under the title of "Humility" the *Constitutions* required that: "They shall avoid speaking of themselves, of their family, and of anything of a nature to flatter their vanity." Article 133.

[67] Necrology of Sister Rose Genevieve Flaherty, SMWA.

[68] Memoir of Sister St. Francis Schultz, "Missionary in China," SMWA.

[69] See Madden, 407-415, for a biography of this exceptionally talented woman. Details of the early history of the Cause are also gleaned from this source.

[70] The Book of Important Events, June 14, 1921 notes: "Never would we have known of the existence of this correspondence had not Divine Providence, who orders all things sweetly, made the occasion an extraordinary means of bringing to our knowledge these important documents and placing them at our disposal for advancement of the Cause." SMWA.

[71] Acts of Council, January 23, 1927, SMWA.

[72] Acts of Council, November 10, 1932, SMWA.

[73] The Book of Important Events, November 5, 1934, states: "Letters were then prepared according to the three forms required and presented for signature to the members of the Hierarchy who attended the Cardinal's Jubilee in October." SMWA

[74] "Letter of Mother Mary Raphael," in *In God's Acre: Biographical Sketches* (Saint Mary-of-the-Woods, IN: 1940). The letter was first published as *Biographical Sketches, Volume I*, for the sisters only in 1937. SMWA.

[75] *Woodland Echoes*, Volume 1, Number 1, SMWA.

Chapter 5

[1] See Sister Mary Roger Madden, *The Path Marked Out: History of the Sisters of Providence of Saint Mary-of-the-Woods, Indiana, vol. 3* (Saint Mary-of-the-Woods, IN: Office of Congregational Advancement—Sisters of Providence,1991), "Romanization," 429-38, for additional discussion of this issue.

[2] Angelyn Dries, OSF, in "The Americanization of Religious Life: Women Religious, 1872-1922," *U.S. Catholic Historian* 10, nos. 1-2 (1992) notes that after 1872, due to immigration, there was a "notable increase in the foundation of new congregations . . . and the formation of provinces" (14).

[3] See Madden, 311, for detail regarding the Washington, D.C., foundations.

[4] 1914 Chapter minutes, SMWA.

[5] Book of Important Events, 51, SMWA.

[6] Biographical information courtesy of Notre Dame Archives.

[7] Father Sauvage to Mother Mary Raphael, August 24, 1927, SMWA.

[8] *Constitutions* (1929), Article 2.

[9] Acts of Council, January 1, 1929, SMWA.

[10] Mother Mary Raphael to Cardinal Lèpicier, May 14, 1930, SMWA.

[11] Mother Mary Raphael to Bishop Chartrand, August 10, 1931, SMWA.

[12] Mother Mary Raphael to Cardinal Lèpicier, August 21, 1931 , SMWA.

[13] Letter of Bishop Chartrand to Mother Mary Raphael, July 22, 1932, SMWA.

[14] The Acts of Council for May 21, 1933, state that secretary general Sister Eileen Walker showed a clipping sent by one of the sisters, noting, "The good Bishop Cantwell must be responsible for the publication." SMWA.

[15] Letter Circular, June 15, 1932, SMWA.

[16] Edward N. Peters, Curator, *The 1917 or Pio-Benedictine Code of Canon Law* (San Francisco: Ignatius Press, 2001) quotes the 1917 Code, Canon 488's listing of major superiors "the supreme moderator of a religious institute, a provincial superior, and their vicars having power like a provincial" (190).

[17] Acts of Council, July 16, 1933, SMWA.

[18] Leaflet, "Rules for Provincial Superiors," SMWA.

[19] Mother Mary Raphael to the sisters, September 12, 1933, SMWA.

[20] Ibid.

[21] To understand the egalitarian nature of the Sister of Providence hierarchy, it is interesting to note that when the author was assigned her first teaching appointment at St. Andrew, Indianapolis, she had no idea that one of the sisters with whom she lived, Sister Mary Rose Cummings, who taught fourth grade, had formerly held such influential positions in the Congregation.

[22] Marywood, Evanston house diary, August, 1933, SMWA.

[23] Maryhurst house diary, September 23, 1933, SMWA.

[24] Undated typescript: probably prepared by Sister Eugenia Logan, "An Account of the Beginning, the Progress, and the Discontinuance of the Provinces of the Sisters of Providence," 7, SMWA.

[25] See Chapter 3 for details of this establishment.

[26] Acts of Council, May 3, 1936, SMWA.

[27] Mother Mary Raphael to Bishop Ritter, October 9, 1937, SMWA.

[28] Bishop Ritter to Mother Mary Raphael, October 11, 1937, SMWA.

[29] Bishop Ritter to Mother Mary Raphael, July 1, 1936, SMWA.

[30] Father Sauvage to Mother Mary Raphael, January 22, 1937, SMWA.

[31] Mother Vincentia, CSC, to Mother Mary Raphael, June 26, 1938, SMWA.

[32] Attached to the minutes are a sheet listing specifics for provincial chapters, a sheet explaining representation at the General Chapter, a two-page memorandum listing exact page numbers of the *Constitutions* which would be affected by the proposed changes and a nine-page typescript of the revised articles.

[33] Handwritten letter from Bishop Ritter to Mother Mary Raphael, July 23, 1938, SMWA.

[34] Ibid.

[35] Acts of Council, August 10th, 1938, SMWA.

[36] Annotated typescript. However, this copy has many strikeouts of "provincial council," substituting "under the control of Mother General and her council." SMWA.

[37] Acts of Council March 16, 1941 and May 31, 1941, SMWA.

[38] Sister Berchmans had gone from the position of second assistant to three appointments as local superior at Chelsea in Massachusetts, Berwyn in Maryland and Chicago before her appointment as Indiana provincial at age sixty-seven.

[39] Undated typescript on history of provinces, 12, SMWA.

[40] Ibid., 12.

[41] Acts of Council, June 29, 1945, SMWA. At Immaculata, Sister St. Philomene had worked closely with her blood sister, Sister Eugenia Clare, who was superior of the house and principal of Immaculata High School. As Provincial of the East, she was able to be with her when she died on January 16, 1948.

[42] Joseph Creusen, SJ, and Adam C. Ellis, SJ, *Religious Men and Women in Church Law: Sixth English Edition* (Milwaukee: The Bruce Publishing Company, 1958). Earlier edition not available for citation.

[43] In a conversation with the author, Sister Agnes Farrell related that she had been on duty in the phone room while at Saint Mary-of-the-Woods during her second novitiate and had placed the call.

[44] Minutes of 1949 Chapter, SMWA.

[45] Sister Francis Joseph was absent, having gone to Chicago to fulfill a schools appointment.

[46] Acts of Council, March 26, 1949, SMWA.

[47] Mother Marie Helene Franey to the sisters, April 1, 1949, SMWA.

[48] Maryhurst house diary, August 1949, SMWA.

Chapter 6

[1] Wendy Kaminer, *Women Volunteering: The Pleasure, Pain, and Politics of Unpaid Work from 1830 to the Present* (New York: Doubleday & Company, Inc., 1984), 24.

[2] Suellen Hoy, *Good Hearts: Catholic Sisters in Chicago's Past* (Chicago: University of Illinois Press, 2006), 43.

[3] Ibid., 45. Here she quotes Joseph G. Mannard, "Converts in Convents: Protestant Women and the Social Appeal of Catholic Religious Life in Antebellum America," *Records* [of the American Catholic Historical Society], 104 (Winter-Spring 1993): 90.

[4] Charles M. Morris, *American Catholic: The Saints and Sinners Who Built America's Most Powerful Church* (New York: Random House, 1997), 180. In addition to this rather cynical assessment, he also states: "In truth, there were few lay positions open to women that carried the prestige of a Catholic nun, and none with the authority and independence of a mother superior. Nuns ran hospitals, orphanages, schools, and colleges, jobs that in the lay world were reserved for men" (116).

[5] Chapter reports of Mother Mary Raphael, 1938, and Mother Mary Bernard, 1944, SMWA.

[6] Kathleen Sprows Cummings, *New Women of the Old Faith: Gender and American Catholicism in the Progressive Era* (Chapel Hill: The University of North Carolina Press, 2009), 112.

[7] Oral history, Sister Marie William Hoerner, SMWA

[8] Decades after her 1939 entrance, when her mother was in difficult straits, Sister Bernadette Mary Carroll offered to investigate the possibility of a temporary exclaustration to help out. Her mother wrote to refuse any such move, saying: "Dear Daughter: You make me feel very bad to think that you ever thought of leaving. You have been my inspiration and my only chance for heaven. ...God wanted you and still wants you. ...I have been so happy about you giving your life to God and it would make me very unhappy if you thought of anything else." Copy of this June 1, 1961, letter courtesy of Sister Bernadette Mary.

[9] *Constitutions* (1929), Article 33, SMWA.

[10] Ibid., Article 38.

[11] Mary Pipher, *In Another Country: Navigating the Emotional Terrain of our Elders* (New York: Riverhead Books, 1999), 78. The author goes on to say: "In 1974, the same question was asked, and the list was exactly reversed. What modern parents most desired for their children was autonomy and independence."

[12] Oral history, Sister Doris Healy, SMWA. She speaks of the tender care she and her younger sister received from the sisters as a child at Dunblane after the death of her father, of the excellent educational opportunities afforded her and of the assistance of her "sponsor," Sister Mary Borromeo Brown, niece of Mother Anastasia Brown, who had just finished her PhD, yet was "so relaxed and welcoming that you could go in and sit on her bed and talk."

[13] *Constitutions* (1929), Article 35.

[14] Consider the ages of the 1929 band: Six were 15, four were 16, ten were 17, six were 18, three were 19, four were 20, three were 21, one was 22, three were 23, three were 24, two were 25, one was 28, one was 35. In addition, some of these candidates entered not to teach,

but rather to provide domestic support as coadjutrix sisters, thus needing a different curriculum altogether.

[15] Sister Marie William Hoerner, oral history, SMWA.

[16] *Community,* Nov.-Dec., 1990, 9. The newsletter article goes on to cite a 1965 survey indicating that from 1930-1965, 686 of the 889 young women who enrolled went on to graduate and of them, 37.6 percent entered the novitiate, with 75 percent of that number eventually becoming professed sisters. As will be seen in later chapters, changing circumstances caused the school to close in 1966. SMWA.

[17] See Sister Mary Roger Madden, Chapter 9, "The Spirit of the Life," in *The Path Marked Out, History of the Sisters of Providence of Saint Mary-of-the-Woods, vol. 3* (Saint Mary-of-the-Woods, IN: Office of Congregational Advancement—Sisters of Providence,1991), 269ff. for additional detail of the historical evolution of the religious practices undergirding the formation process. See also *Love, Mercy, Justice: A Book of Practices of the Sisters of Providence* (Saint Mary-of-the-Woods, IN: Sisters of Providence, 2006).

[18] *Constitutions* (1929), Article 261, SMWA.

[19] Clipping of the article from *Extension Magazine,* February 1947, in Sister Rose Berchmans' necrology file, SMWA.

[20] *Constitutions* (1929), Article 41.

[21] "Novitiate Instructions," undated notes. SMWA.

[22] The term "Examen" is derived from the Ignatian *Spiritual Exercises* and encompasses much more than a simple examination of conscience. In the *Exercises* particular examen is a means of focusing on a specific fault by pausing three times during the day to review and record failures.

[23] Acts of Council, April 16, 1927, and December 7, 1930, SMWA.

[24] Joseph Creusen, SJ, and Adam C. Ellis, SJ, *Religious Men and Women in Church Law: Sixth English Edition* (Milwaukee: Bruce, 1958), 150, clarifies that the purpose of the canonical examination was to ensure that the postulant was acting with full liberty and that it was up to the superiors to make a decision as to admission. A letter from the chancery, such as that of June 24, 1941, from Chancellor Dugan, served as a reminder to schedule these interviews. SMWA

[25] Ibid., Canon 208, 160.

[26] Quotes in this paragraph are taken from novitiate instruction notes, SMWA.

[27] *Constitutions,* (1929), Article 49.

[28] Acts of Council, December 1, 1929, SMWA.

[29] Sister Mary Borromeo Brown, *The History of the Sisters of Providence of Saint Mary-of-the-Woods, vol. 1* (New York: Benziger, 1949), 56.

[30] Hoy, 19. Here she describes the motivation of nineteenth-century poor Irish women, but it quite likely would apply to the daughters of early immigrants to the United States.

[31] Brown, 150.

[32] *Constitutions* (1887), 94; also in the 1897 and 1915 editions.

[33] Ibid.

[34] Bishop Dwenger to Mother Euphrasie, January 13, 1887, SMWA.

[35] Mother Mary Raphael to Father Sauvage, October 4, 1927, SMWA.

[36] Minutes of the 1938 General Chapter, SMWA.

[37] David M. Kennedy, *Freedom from Fear: The American People in Depression and War, 1929-45* (New York: Oxford University Press, 1999), comments on the rise of labor, noting: "A heightened sense of class consciousness did indeed emerge in the United States in the Depression years, but it was of a stubbornly characteristic American type. It did not frontally challenge existing institutions, but asked— demanded—a larger measure of participation in them" (322).

[38] Four of the thirty sisters who made the August retreat in 1844 were given coadjutrix assignments. "In accordance with the custom prevalent in Europe, Sister Ann Walter continued as Sister Olypiade's assistant in the care of the domestic animals; Sister Lucy Doyle, Sister Philomene's sister, was in training under Mother Theodore as pharmacist and infirmarian, and Pére Michel's two elder daughters, Sister Therese and Sister Martha Guthneck, were already excellent cooks. All these Sisters were retained at the motherhouse for many years" (Brown, 359-60).

[39] The June 22, 1930, entry in the Community Diary includes this notation: "Rev. Mother and the members of her Council decide to give the co-adjutor sisters a course in domestic science." SMWA.

[40] The author is deeply indebted to Saint Mary-of-the-Woods Archives assistant Sister Donna Butler for her meticulous research in identifying all the coadjutrix sisters by name and date in order to compile these statistics, as well as for her research of the early editions of the *Constitutions* and the attempts to modernize the sections referring to the coadjutrix sisters. Sister Donna was responsible for preparing a presentation honoring the remaining living coadjutrix sisters at the June 2009 Annual Meeting: Sisters Mary Eymard Campeggio, Michael Ellen Green, Catherine Alberta Kunkler and Rosalie Marie Weller.

[41] The presentation mentioned in the previous note brought tears to the eyes of many sisters and prompted a great deal of storytelling on the part of those who remembered living with these sisters.

[42] Sister Alma Louise Meschner recalled that in 1938 she had just finished three years of college and landed a very good job, so she wouldn't have considered entering if the option hadn't been local. Oral history, SMWA.

[43] Maryhurst House Diary, September 25, 1934. In March, 1935, the diarist notes that in preparation for the next reception ceremony, "S. Ann Marie's bridal dress was fitted. It was bought at May's in Baltimore, price $14.50, less 10% discount. It is entirely satisfactory." SMWA.

[44] Maryhurst Diary, 1943, SMWA.

[45] The December 23, 1929, Acts of Council state: "A special meeting of the Council is called at 11 o'clock. The object of the meeting is to decide on establishing a catechist society in Kaifeng, China. After the decision is given, it is agreed to request Sister Marie Gratia, superior at Kaifeng, to draw up an agreement with Bishop Tacconi for the support of the catechists." SMWA.

[46] The November 9, 1930 Acts of Council state: "Reverend Mother Mary Raphael offered for consideration an important proposition: namely the future status of the Chinese catechists. Are these catechists to be affiliated to the Sisters of Providence at Saint Mary-of-the-Woods, Indiana, or are they to remain a diocesan organization? After much discussion and deliberation, it was decided that the catechist organization should be strictly diocesan." The decision was to be referred to the local ordinary, Bishop Chartrand. Nonetheless, the council committed the Congregation to support the formation of the new institute by appointing Sister Marie Patricia Shortall to the post of Mistress of Catechists.

[47] Sister Marie Gratia to Mother Mary Raphael, July 16, 1931, SMWA.

[48] Sister Mary Liguori Hartigan, Memoir, SMWA. Being of a more practical bent than Sister Monica Marie, she also relates that her duties at the relatively rural location of the novitiate came to include supervising not only the novices' recitation of noon beads but also the man hired to care for the cows.

[49] Sister Marie Gratia Luking, "The First Profession at Kaifeng," *The Bugle Call,* December, 1932, 7. Photos of the novices wearing the gray Chinese-style uniform with white veil gave concrete witness to the swiftness with which the program had taken hold.

[50] Music by Sister Genevieve Cecile Tuberty, words by Sister Marie Armelle Connors, first sung December 8, 1934, SMWA.

[51] Diary of the Novitiate, 1936-1941, SMWA.

[52] Reception ceremonial. (undated). The quotes which follow are from this ceremonial. SMWA.

[53] *Constitutions* (1929) Article 3.

[54] In her oral history, Sister Robert Kiley recalls, "Our first year or two on mission we wrote monthly to the mistress. After our three-year vows, we were transferred to a council member for direction." SMWA.

[55] Sister Rose Dolores Thuis,. "Letters and Spiritual Reading Papers, 1949-1966." Collection prepared by Sister Catherine Joseph Wilcox, 1995. Sister Bernice Kuper recalls Sister's influence: "Because Rose Dolores had a brother who was a Benedictine monk she had been influenced by Dom Marmion. One of the books that I remember reading was *Christ, the Life of the Soul.* It introduced me to what in those days we would have called the doctrine of the Divine Indwelling. Rose Dolores taught me how to become aware of and to acknowledge and trust the presence of God within myself. She used to correspond with us and she would give us information that would guide us in this way of thinking." Oral History, SMWA. Other home superiors were doubtless equally influential, but such information is not available in the Archives.

[56] Necrology file of Sister Eugenia Clare Cullity, SMWA.

[57] *Constitutions* (1929), Article 118.

[58] Retreat notes of Rev. James F. Walsh, SJ, August, 1935, SMWA.

[59] *Constitutions* (1929), Article 121.

[60] "Monthly Retreat and Preparation for Death," undated, but with an Imprimatur by Bishop Joseph Chartrand, SMWA.

[61] *Constitutions* (1929), Article 284.

[62] Edward N. Peters, Curator, *The 1917 or Pio-Benedictine Code of Canon Law* (San Francisco: Ignatius Press, 2001), C. 574, CIC, 222.

[63] Letter to the Sacred Congregation, July 20, 1923, signed by Bishop Chatard in addition to Mother Mary Cleophas and her assistants, SMWA.

[64] Quotes selected from Acts of Council from this period, SMWA.

[65] Acts of Council, December 5, 1927, SMWA.

[66] Acts of Council, January 25, 1930, SMWA.

[67] Acts of Council, June 19, 1927, SMWA.

[68] Book of Important Events, April 1930, SMWA.

[69] Community Diary, January 23, 1941, SMWA.

[70] Acts of Council, August 18, 1944, SMWA.

Chapter 7

[1] In a June 8, 1937, letter to Mother Mary Raphael, Chancellor Dugan cited Pope Pius XII's four encyclicals on atheistic communism and the Church in Germany, Spain and Mexico, inquiring on behalf of Bishop Ritter "as to what plan you have followed to acquaint the religious of your community with the recent pronouncements of the

Holy See given to the world." He concludes: "Awaiting your answer." SMWA.

[2] It is interesting to note that Sister Eugenia Logan, who was consistently elected as a delegate and as Chapter Secretary for the Chapters from 1932 to 1954, makes no note of this discrepancy, even though in 1949 she is at pains to explain that there are only thirty-one delegates rather than the thirty-two called for by the Rule due to the death of Mother Mary Bernard, SMWA.

[3] The minutes of the 1944 and 1949 Chapter include the statement: "In 1938, a dispensation was obtained from His Excellency the Most Reverend Joseph E. Ritter, D.D., Bishop of Indianapolis, to permit the four Provincials and the Supervisor of Schools to be admitted 'ex-officio.'" However Mother Mary Raphael's October 9, 1937, letter written to Bishop Ritter from Anaheim requesting the dispensation refers only to the provincials. The original copy of his response is not on file, only an annotated copy, apparently an excerpt forwarded to her. No documentation of the dispensation is included with the 1938 Chapter materials. SMWA.

[4] Minutes of 1938 General Chapter, SMWA.

[5] David M. Kennedy, *Freedom from Fear: The American People in Depression and War, 1929-45* (New York: Oxford University Press, 1999) suggests that the shifting demographics of the times that likely contributed to changing attitudes within the community. (See note 37, Chapter 6.)

[6] Summary of committee minutes, 1932-36, SMWA. One of the committee members, Sister Laurence Gonner, had recently completed a master's thesis, "History of the First 50 Years of the Sisters of Providence in America."

[7] Sister Mary Theodosia Mug. *Life and Life-Work of Mother Theodore Guérin, Foundress of the Sisters of Providence at St.-Mary-of-the-Woods, Vigo County, Indiana* (New York: Benziger, 1904).

[8] Sister Mary Theodosia Mug, Ed. *Journals and Letters of Mother Theodore Guérin* (Saint Mary-of-the-Woods, Indiana, 1937). In 1940 Sister Mary Borromeo Brown succeeded Sister Mary Theodosia in this work while writing a history of the Congregation covering Mother Theodore's lifetime. It should be noted that in addition to the historical documents, a concurrent collection of ongoing Congregation diaries, correspondence, etc. was maintained through the sixth assistant/secretary's office. It would not be until 1976 that Sister Ann Kathleen Brawley would organize all the materials according to recognized archival principles and procedures and move them to their present location in Owens Hall.

[9] Mr. Kamke was remunerated with room and board at the Woodland Inn and a payment of $100 on the first of every month, $2000 total,

with the stipulation that the dioramas were to be erected by June 1, 1940. Acts of Council, October 2, 1939, SMWA.

[10] Book of Important Events, March 16, 1938, SMWA.

[11] Currently buried in this section are the Reverends John Corbe, John B. Chasse, John Guéguen, Augustine Rawlinson, Vincent Dwyer, Robert Gorman, Emile Goossens, James Galvin and Joseph Kempf.

[12] This description is based on the accounts in *Woodland Echoes*, February 15, 1940, SMWA.

[13] A sheet of assignments for the sister faculty "reception committee" includes duties of greeting the guests, arranging the tables, assisting the head cook, Sister Rose Patricia Ward, supervising the students and musical accompaniment. The directives note: "We hope everyone will be able to hear the speeches. The program will be given in the Auditorium afterwards. Everybody please be available and stay till the end of the evening." Doubtless they were also expected to be on time to teach their classes the next day.

[14] Concert program, SMWA. The program reveals an astonishing amount of talent with original compositions by Sisters Marion Cecile Spencer, Florence Therese Fitzgerald, Regina Cecile Carlos, Rose Dolores Thuis, Angelita Morgan, Brigid Boyle, Mary Lourdes Mackey, Mary Basiline Booker, Bernadette Cecile Egan, Loretto Cecile Murphy, Maurelia O'Brien, Cecilia Berry, Francis Cecile Miller, Francis Angela Kolb and Cecilia Clare Bocard, not to mention the vocal, choral, orchestral and instrumental performers.

[15] Book of Important Events, 1940, SMWA.

[16] Acts of Council, October 4, 1940, SMWA. It was decided that in addition to the usual bishop's throne, because Archbishop McNicholas of Cincinnati, as the metropolitan, outranked the bishop of Indianapolis, Bishop Ritter, that two thrones would be needed in the sanctuary.

[17] The chronicler describes the practices and spirituality of the times: "The holy Masses begin in the church at 6:00. All seven altars are occupied. As soon as one priest finishes his Mass, another takes his place. This continues up until 8:45. The community Mass is said at 6:30. In the Crypt, the Masses begin at 6:30 and continue until 9:00. At Le Fer, Guerin and in the Infirmary, one Mass after another is celebrated. At 7:00, the holy Sacrifice is celebrated in Sacred Heart Chapel for the students and Alumnae, other Masses follow here, too. Every visiting and local priest has the opportunity of celebrating. The Angels must have counted reverently the down pourings of the Precious Blood." SMWA.

[18] This description is drawn from the detailed account in the Book of Important Events, 1940. SMWA.

[19] Ibid.

[20] See Sister Mary Roger Madden, *The Path Marked Out: History of the Sisters of Providence of Saint Mary-of-the-Woods, Indiana, vol. 3* (Saint Mary-of-the-Woods, IN: Office of Congregational Advancement—Sisters of Providence, 1991), 386-392, for an account of his tenure.

[21] Book of Important Events, 1940, SMWA.

[22] Book of Establishments, September, 1940, SMWA.

[23] Kathleen Sprows Cummings, *New Women of the Old Faith: Gender and American Catholicism in the Progressive Era* (Chapel Hill: The University of North Carolina Press, 2009), 109, describes this trend.

[24] Book of Important Events, December, 1951.

[25] Notes provided by a former resident of Cathedral Convent, Sister Rosemary Borntrager.

[26] Michael Walsh in "Great Expectations," *Smithsonian* (June, 2010), states: "By the end of the [1900-10] decade, black Americans had begun the Great Migration northward, leaving the old Confederacy for the industrial cities of the North. Between 1910 and 1940, an estimated 1.75 million black Southerners would uproot themselves and settle not only in New York, Philadelphia and Chicago, but also in such smaller cities as Dayton, Toledo and Newark" (53).

[27] Money for the construction of the church and school had been donated by John H. Fendrich, whose daughter, Mrs. Anton Hulman, Jr., had been educated at Saint Mary-of-the-Woods College; his granddaughter graduated from Ladywood School in Indianapolis. Mr. Hendrich continued to be a strong support to the parish. Letter of Mr. Hendrich to Mother Marie Helene Franey, July 28, 1952, SMWA.

[28] The minutes of the 1944 General Chapter note that in his remarks Bishop Ritter "thanked Reverend Mother and her council for the cooperation of the Sisters throughout the diocese, especially the work among the colored children. The progress at Saint Rita's school was especially praised. His Excellency pointed out that all communities were not generous in taking up this work. In lighter vein, he mentioned that some day perhaps a negro girl might ask admission to the novitiate! He urged the full Catholicity of this work among the colored." SMWA.

[29] Book of Establishments, September, 1940, SMWA.

[30] Ibid. 1941, SMWA.

[31] Sister Eugenia Logan, *History of the Sisters of Providence of Saint Mary-of-the-Woods, vol. 2* (Terre Haute, Indiana: Moore-Langen, 1978), 300.

[32] James W. Sanders, *The Education of an Urban Minority: Catholics in Chicago, 1883-1965* (New York: Oxford University Press, 1977), 95. Here he quotes the description in *The New World*, February 6, 1931.

[33] The Book of Establishments, 1941, SMWA.

[34] *The St. Mel's Grade School Centennial, 1886-1986.* Memorial publication, SMWA.

[35] The December 15, 1955, edition of the Chicago Tribune reported: "To build the $183 million expressway, hundreds of buildings had to be razed, 3,000 graves in two cemeteries had to be relocated and a tunnel had to be knocked through the base of the main post office near Canal Street." http://www.chicagotribune.com/

[36] Information supplied by Fr. Conrad Borntrager, OSM, archivist and historian.

[37] The biographical information is based on an undated clipping from *The Saginaw News*, Necrology of Sister Marie Besner, SMWA.

[38] Sister Marie Besner taught at St. John Academy from 1886 to 1931 and again from 1933-42, fifty-four years in all!

[39] Bessie Marable Brennan to Reverend Mother Mary Raphael, February 17, 1934, SMWA.

[40] Book of Establishments, 1941, SMWA. A newspaper clipping, presumably from the *Portsmouth Herald*, dated November 14, 1949, provides a description of the property: "Lady Isle consists of a 13-acre island in Little Harbor and 12 acres on the mainland connected by a bridge of concrete and steel. The residential part of the property is on the island, completely surrounded by tidewater, but a channel on one side permits keeping a motor boat afloat and a tender for same. Little Harbor connects directly with Portsmouth Main Harbor and with the ocean about half a mile away. It is just 10 minutes from the railroad station and the shopping center of Portsmouth." SMWA.

[41] Sister St. Eugenia McBarron's memoir, SMWA. The two other pioneer residents were Sisters Magdalena Fitzpatrick and Francis Aloyse Dalton. The fear of the sisters was not unfounded. Kennedy describes the "Battle of the Atlantic" in which German submarines sank hundreds of merchant ships (565-72). "A single U-boat prowling off New York harbor in January 1942 sank eight ships, including three tankers, in just twelve hours" (566).

[42] Letter of Sister St. Eugenia McBarron to retreatants, September, 1942.

[43] Acts of Council, January 15, 1945, SMWA.

[44] Oral history, Sister Mary Joseph Pomeroy. She notes that Sister Helen Agatha Bourke took on this duty as part of her unofficial public relations activities. SMWA.

[45] Book of Important Events, SMWA.

[46] H. Tracy Schier, "History of Higher Education for Women at Saint Mary-of-the-Woods: 1840-1980" (PhD diss., Boston College, 1987), 140.

[47] The 1940 Faculty list includes Sister Marion Cecile Spencer, M.Mus., as Director, Conservatory of Music, Sisters Mary Cecilia Summers,

M. Mus., Florence Therese Fitzgerald, M.Mus. , and Cecilia Clare Bocard, M. Mus. Theory and Composition, Sister Bernadette Cecile Schweikert, BS in Mus., Vocal Music, and Sister Mary Basiline Booker, BS in Mus.Ed., Public School Music.

[48] Schier, 140.

[49] Acts of Council, September, 1946, SMWA.

[50] Book of Important Events, December, 1948. SMWA.

[51] Chancellor Henry Dugan to Mother Mary Bernard, June 8, 1939. The letter announces the appointments of Father Robert Gorman, PhD, for history, Rev. George Saum for philosophy and Rev. Daniel Nolan as religion instructor and assistant chaplain. Father Joseph Kempf, PhD, had previously been appointed for sociology. SMWA.

[52] Book of Important Events, December 8, 1941, SMWA.

[53] Sister Ann Colette Wolf, *Against All Odds: Sisters of Providence Mission to the Chinese, 1920-1990* (Saint Mary-of-the-Woods, IN: Office of Communications—Sisters of Providence, 1990). Once again, we are indebted to her account for this summary.

[54] Sadly, Bishop Barosi's tenure was cut short. Within the month he and several of the Italian priests were captured by bandits disguised as Chinese soldiers and killed. (Wolf, 146).

[55] Acts of Council, April 25, 1941, SMWA.

[56] See Wolf, Chapter Seven, 167-193, for the very interesting story of the events of their internment.

[57] Acts of Council, September 9, 1944, SMWA.

[58] Oral history, Sister Agnes Joan Li, SMWA.

[59] Acts of Council, January 1, 1939, SMWA.

[60] Sister Marie Gratia Luking to Mother Mary Bernard Laughlin, "Council Notes" 1945, SMWA.

[61] Mother Mary Bernard Laughlin to "the Sisters of Providence," January 6, 1942, SMWA.

[62] The size of the winter box was specified in inches as 28 x 16 x 19 and notice was given that at the time of transfer from one mission to another superiors were authorized to ship only this one box.

[63] Maryhurst 1941 Diary, SMWA.

[64] Mother Mary Bernard Laughlin to Local Superiors, May 24, 1943, SMWA.

[65] Ibid.

[66] Bishop Riitter to Reverend Pastors, Military Chaplains and Superiors of Religious Communities, June 24, 1943, SMWA.

[67] Oral history, Sister Agnes Farrell. Sister Agnes and another novice who later left were the two who traveled by train from Anaheim to

complete their novitiate at Saint Mary-of-the-Woods in January. Novice Mistress Sister Mary Stanislaus Graffe was most apologetic that she had not opened the letter earlier and arranged for Sister Agnes to call her mother in San Diego. Fortunately during the attack her father was in the hospital at the Pearl Harbor base recovering from an automobile accident and her brother had leave from his destroyer to visit him at this time.

[68] Oral history, Sister Charles Ellen Turk, SMWA.

[69] 1943 Maryhurst Diary, SMWA.

[70] Oral history, Sister Agnella Hyde, SMWA.

[71] Lest there be any confusion on this point, mimeographed lists of requested items were sent to the superiors of large houses. Acts of Council, May 3, 1945, SMWA.

[72] Book of Important events, May-September, 1945, SMWA.

[73] Maryhurst Diary, 1944, SMWA.

[74] Community Diary, March 1, 1939, SMWA. A later entry notes that in April the sisters viewed a film of the five hour coronation ceremony.

[75] Wolf, 181, 186, 201. Letter of Archbishop Cicognani to Bishop Ritter, September 26, 1943, SMWA.

[76] Acts of Council, September 17, 1944, SMWA.

Chapter 8

[1] Sister Francis Joseph had previously been elected to the council in 1926 and 1938. However her supervision of education had begun when Sister Basilissa Heiner became ill in 1923, as recorded in the Book of Important Events, July 20, 1923: "After mature deliberation it was decided to appoint S. Francis Joseph for the remainder of the term. She is particularly fitted to supervise the schools." SMWA. She continued in that role during her 1926-1932 term as fifth assistant, then was appointed supervisor of schools during Mother Mary Bernard's 1932-1938 term, and retained this title and duties during 1938-1944 after her election as fifth assistant by the 1938 Chapter.

[2] Mother Mary Bernard to Chapter delegates, March 31, 1944, SMWA.

[3] Mother Mary Bernard to the sisters, September 9, 1940, SMWA.

[4] Acts of Council, March 7, 1941, SMWA.

[5] Acts of Council, June 25, 1944, SMWA.

[6] Mother Mary Bernard to the sisters, December 18, 1945, SMWA.

[7] In addition to Sister Francis Joseph being appointed to replace Fourth Assistant Sister Basilissa in 1923, Fifth Assistant Sister Saint Margaret Foohey had resigned in 1911 and was replaced by Sister Mary Ernestine Sullivan, who, after being elected first assistant by the

1914 Chapter, resigned in 1918 and was replaced by Sister Angela Therese Brillon. See Madden, 354, 440, for the circumstances.

[8] 1944-45 Assumption Convent Diary, SMWA.

[9] O.R. Spigler, M.D. to Sister Gertrude, February 21, 1939. Necrology file of Sister Mary Bernardo Flaherty, SMWA.

[10] Much of this description is drawn from Sister Dorothy Eileen Howard's oral history. Physical descriptions are based on an undated *Bugle Call* article by Sister Catherine Ursula Hayes, "In His Providential Care," and scale drawings of the floor layout of the building. SMWA.

[11] Oral history of Sister Dorothy Eileen Howard, SMWA.

[12] The Our Lady of Sorrows 1947 House Diary includes this item: "After two weeks Sister Mary Bernardo and Sister Mary Dorothy took Sister Louis Joseph Home in St. Mary's ambulance."

[13] Sister Dorothy Eileen proudly noted that during all those years there was never a staph infection. SMWA.

[14] The Diary provides more detailed descriptions of difficult incidents. SMWA.

[15] This truncated treatment is based on Gerald N. Grob, *The Mad Among Us: A history of the Care of America's Mentally Ill* (New York: The Free Press, 1994).

[16] *The Diagnostic and Statistical Manual of Mental Disorders (DSM)* has been published by the American Psychiatric Association in successive editions as more research becomes available.

[17] It should be noted that exposés of institutional mistreatment during the forties led to calls for reform and created a movement toward community-based treatment, but mental health is still an emerging profession with no firm consensus as to best practices.

[18] The Acts of Council indicate that from time to time this course of action was indeed followed.

[19] Canon 637 specifically prohibits exclusion from vows on the basis of infirmity, unless it has been certainly proved that this was intentionally withheld prior to profession. "Hysteria, notwithstanding its regrettable consequences in religious life, is not, therefore a reason for dismissal. The sick person will frequently find, however, that this disease is a sufficient reason for asking to leave religion and to try, in the world, to strive after the ideal which she was pursuing in religion." Joseph Creusen, S.J. and Adam C. Ellis, S.J., *Religious Men and Women in Church Law*, 6th ed. (Milwaukee: Bruce, 1958), 270.

[20] Acts of Council, March 21, 1940. SMWA

[21] Sister John Francis Troy, Oral History, SMWA. Sister John Francis

and her twin sister, Sister James Marie, entered the novitiate at the same time, having been among the first children to be educated by the Sisters of Providence when they began the school at Maryhurst that was later moved to Berwyn, Maryland.

[22] Sister Ann Colette Wolf, *Against All Odds: Sisters of Providence Mission to the Chinese 1920-1990* (Saint Mary-of-the-Woods: Office of Communications—Sisters of Providence, 1990), 202-03.

[23] The two departing sisters were Sisters Monica Marie Rigoni and Marie Patricia Shorthall. The returning missionaries were Sisters Elizabeth Cecile Harbison and Mary Evangela O'Neill, Mary Liguori Hartigan and Theodata Haggerty. The newest missionary was Sister Ann Colette Wolf, who would be joining her sibling, Sister Agnes Loyola Wolf, whom she had not seen for ten years. She would go on to serve for many years and would later be the chronicler of the China mission in *Against All Odds,* often quoted in these pages.

[24] Wolf, 217ff.

[25] The Portuguese name Formosa meaning beautiful island was used at the time but it is now known by its Chinese name, Taiwan.

[26] Community Diary, September 15, 1945, SMWA.

[27] Acts of Council April 28, 1946, SMWA.

[28] Acts of Council, September 14, 1947, SMWA.

[29] Oral history of Mary Evelyn Bouvier O'Connor, SMWA.

[30] Rev. F. P. Blecke to Mother Mary Bernard, June 9, 1945, SMWA.

[31] Book of Establishments, SMWA.

[32] Oral history of Sister Clare Therese Bullock, SMWA.

[33] Ibid. Also, Book of Establishments, SMWA.

[34] Dolan in *American Catholic Experience*, 375, comments on the influence of the *Extension* magazine in raising "close to a million dollars for the church in Texas" by 1930.

[35] Bishop Ledvina and Father Scecina had asked for sisters in 1944 and expressed great disappointment when Mother Mary Bernard wrote to say that none were available, but she had hoped to have them the following year. Apparently they understood "hope" as a promise and unwilling to take no for an answer, devised a strategy for acquiring sisters. On November 15, 1945, Father Scecina wrote to Mother Mary Bernard: "In our telephone conversation of August 17, 1945, you asked me to communicate with you on this matter in November. I have informed His Excellency, Bishop Ledvina, and also my Parishioners that Sisters of Providence will arrive in January, 1946. It was not boldness on my part, because I am convinced and the members of the Parish are also convinced that our prayers have been heard." He went on to describe the newly constructed school

and convent. It was too much. Four sisters were named on the Obedience List following the normal January vow ceremonies. Bishop Ledvina to Mother Mary Bernard, October 2, 1944, and Rev. G.S. Scecina to Mother Mary Bernard, November 15, 1945, SMWA.

[36] Book of Establishments, 1946, SMWA. As the Abbott family had moved from Buffalo, New York, to Robstown the previous month, the author was one of the original student body.

[37] Oral history of Sister Loretta Therese O'Leary, SMWA.

[38] Our Lady of Sorrows House Diary provides a detailed account of the event of the fire and the extremely harsh living conditions which followed, SMWA.

[39] Sister Rosemary Borntrager supplied information regarding Our Lady of Sorrows gleaned from correspondence between her brother, Fr. Conrad Borntrager, OSM, Servite archivist and historian and Sister Eugenia Logan, SP, historian.

[40] It was not until Sister Eugenia Clare urged the very shaken Sister Mary Perpetua to write a full account to Bishop McGuinness that he was able to understand the aberrant behavior of the pastor. She had not written because "I thought I would do better to leave the matter for my Superior to communicate to you, since she knew the place and its difficulties better than I, I being a newcomer." In the absence of specific documentation of procedures regarding tuition, she "expected to handle it as I had in other schools. . . . Your Excellency, permit me to say this for myself. Father's requirement to hand in the tuition with the personal account of the children each Friday seemed impossible to me." Sister Mary Perpetua Keck to Bishop E.J. McGuinness, October 25, 1939. It is not surprising that after her one year experience as a local superior, Sister Mary Perpetua returned to teaching music.

[41] Oral history of Sister Alexa Suelzer and Book of Establishments, SMWA.

[42] Acts of Council, August 26, 1938, September 9, 1938, SMWA.

[43] Acts of Council, March 24, 1945.

[44] Letter of Rev. Henry Dugan to Mother Mary Bernard, November 14, 1938, SMWA.

[45] *Constitutions* (1929), Article 90.

[46] Acts of Council, February 3, 1945, SMWA.

[47] The map and schedule in the February, 1949, edition of *The Official Guide of the Railways* shows the tiny St. Mary-of-the-Woods station as one of three "stops on signal" stations between Paris, Illinois, and Terre Haute, Indiana. My thanks go to John Lloyd Bluntzer, brother of Sister Barbara, for supplying a copy of this publication.

[48] The Community Diary entry for June 26, 1936, describes the arrival

of the sisters from the missions for summer school: "The Interurban that conveyed Indianapolis, Fort Wayne, New Albany, Richmond and Lafayette, and also Brazil arrives at four; the Chicago train is in before 4:30." SMWA. Dorothy J. Clark describes the electric railways, stating that in Indiana by 1914 "over 1,600 cars were shuttled about the state on 2,300 miles of trackage" and that the Indianapolis terminal, largest in the world, handled seven million passengers that year. Although they carried mail baggage and freight in addition to passengers, they were overbuilt and a strike in 1937, together with a Securities and Exchange Commission ruling which separated utility companies from electric trains, forced most lines to close. *Historically Speaking* (Evansville, Indiana: Whipporwill Publications, 1981), 279, 288.

[49] The last mention of the New York Central stopping at the Saint Mary-of-the-Woods train station occurs in the Community Diary on June 26, 1957, SMWA.

[50] Typescript signed as "a joint letter of the four sisters," who were: Sister Loretta Clare Gehring, superior, and Sisters Ann Kathleen Brawley, Helene Marie Kelly and Mary Ethel Ringe.

[51] Acts of Council, June 19, 1947, SMWA.

[52] Acts of Council, February 26, 1940, SMWA.

[53] These "home improvements" are described in the Book of Important Events, various dates, SMWA.

[54] Sister Eugenia Logan, *The Mother Mary Bernard Memorial Supplement to The Aurora*, November, 1948, 174, SMWA.

[55] Sister Ignatia Braheny, *The Saint Mary-of-the-Woods Alumnae News*, Autumn, 1948, 73-74, SMWA.

[56] Logan, "A Tribute," 175.

Chapter 9

[1] February 11, 1949, letter of Sister Helen Clare Freiburger to the delegates, SMWA.

[2] Acts of Council, February 16, 1949, SMWA.

[3] In his October 20, 1948, letter to Sister Helen Clare, Father O'Connor summarizes his opinion regarding setting the date of the Chapter. SMWA.

[4] See Chapter 2 to understand this somewhat complicated process.

[5] *Constitutions* (1929), Article 195.

[6] See Chapter 5, page 158, for the minutes of the 1949 Chapter.

[7] The secretary for the 1949 Chapter, Sister Eugenia Logan, later wrote an addendum to the Chapter minutes which records Archbishop Schulte's statements to the Chapter members. SMWA.

588 • Endnotes—Chapter Nine

[8] Oral history of Sister Bernice Kuper, who was missioned with Sister Helen Clare for four years at St. Francis Xavier. SMWA.

[9] The 1949 Maryhurst Diary states: "On January 20, Inauguration Day, Sister Provincial and S. Angela Therese went to St. Ann's to see all of the program over their television. It was excellent! The first time in history the inauguration was televised!" SMWA.

[10] "Providence Teachers Discuss Secularism," in *The Indiana Catholic and Record*, August 6, 1948.

[11] *Time*, June 6, 1949. http://www.time.com/time/magazine/article/

[12] Charles Morris, *American Catholic: The Saints and Sinners Who Built America's Most Powerful Church* (New York: Random House, 1997) notes that the Catholic share of the population had increased from 19 percent to 23 percent, making up 37 percent of the church-affiliated population (223).

[13] Diary, April 16, 1950, SMWA.

[14] Mother Marie Helene to the Council, March 13, 1950, SMWA.

[15] On October 7, 1950, the Anaheim, California, house diary recorded: "This is reunion day in honor of Rev. Mother. . . . 59 of us saw the films Mother brought of her pilgrimage to Rome, Ruille, & Lourdes." SMWA.

[16] Both the Book of Important Events and the Diary provide details of these pilgrimages. SMWA.

[17] Diary, July 1950, SMWA.

[18] Sister Esther Newport, "Journal of a Holy Year Pilgrimage," SMWA.

[19] Notes regarding the Christmas crib courtesy of clippings of articles supplied by Sister Rosemary Borntrager: "Story of the crib emphasizes the spirit of Christmas," *Companions* (Winter 1996) and "Away in a Manger," *Terre Haute Tribune-Star*, December 24, 2002.

[20] Book of Important Events, October 2, 1944, SMWA.

[21] Acts of Council, September 1948, SMWA.

[22] The quotes which follow are taken from Mother Marie Helene's typed notes. SMWA.

[23] Mother Marie Helene to superiors, December 18, 1950, SMWA.

[24] Mother Marie Helene to the sisters, April 1, 1949, SMWA.

[25] Mother Marie Helene to the sisters in California, September 1, 1949. SMWA.

[26] Book of Important Events, May 2, 1952., SMWA.

[27] 1929 *Constitutions*, Article XL, SMWA.

[28] Ibid., Article XXXV, SMWA.

[29] The Acts of Council record such formal accountability sessions on August 14, 1950, May 8, 1951, and January 12, 1952, SMWA.

[30] Diary, June 30, 1951. Subsequent entries describe the other talks. SMWA.

[31] A copy of Sister Helen Rose's speech was prepared to submit for publication, but there is no record that this occurred.

[32] Acts of Council, September 9, 1951, SMWA.

[33] Diary, June 29, 1953, SMWA.

[34] 1929 *Constitutions*, Article 20, SMWA.

[35] Book of Important Events, April 7, 1952 and July 14-19, 1952.

[36] Undated memo, "Changes in the Rule." SMWA. The style and scope of the memo make it likely that Sister Eugenia Logan prepared this summary to assist Mother Gertrude Clare in informing the sisters about the changes in the number of delegates to the General Chapter.

[37] Each sister had to hand in her 1929 copy of the *Constitutions*, and today it is almost impossible to find a copy outside of the Archives.

Chapter 10

[1] See Sister Eugenia Logan, *History of the Sisters of Providence of Saint Mary-of-the-Woods, vol.2* (Terre Haute, Indiana: Moore-Langen, 1978), 246, for the history of the purchase of the property and Sister Mary Roger Madden,*The Path Marked Out: History of the Sisters of Providence of Saint Mary-of-the Woods, Indiana, vol. 3* (Saint Mary-of-the-Woods, IN: Office of Congregational Advancement, 1991), 153-165, for its use as St. Joseph Training School for orphan girls.

[2] Thomas C. Widner, ed., *Our Family Album A Journey of Faith Sketches of the People and Parishes of the Archdiocese of Indianapolis in celebration of her 150th Anniversary* (Indianapolis: The Criterion Press, Inc., 1984), 163.

[3] Mother Marie Helene to Archbishop McIntyre, March 6, 1952. SMWA. Sister Francis Joseph and Sister St. Philomene had visited with the archbishop in person the previous February to explain that the sisters were overextended. At that time California taxed Catholic schools.

[4] The May 10, 1953, council minutes note: "Mother stated that she had considered writing to His Excellency to tell him of these requests as she found it difficult to say yes to one and no to another." Acts of Council, SMWA.

[5] Rev. G. S. Scecina to Mother Marie Helene, July 13, 1950, SMWA.

[6] The report indicated a positive balance sheet with the June 1, 1944, debt of $1,551,000 reduced to $276,500 by January 1949. SMWA.

[7] During the early years when the Ohio River was a major avenue of transportation, the sisters had accepted schools in many towns along the river, including St. Michael in Madison (1844-1904) and St. Au-

gustine in Jeffersonville (1869-1925) as well as shorter commitments in Madison, Lanesville, Cannelton and Frenchtown.

[8] Book of Important Events, June 12, 1951, SMWA.

[9] Mother Marie Helene to Rev. Herbert Winterhalter, February 20, 1951, SMWA.

[10] James T Patterson, *Grand Expectations: The United States, 1945-1974* (New York: Oxford University Press, 1996), 170.

[11] Sister St. Francis Schultz was told to keep a chronology of the mission and embellished it with insightful comments. This excerpt is taken from December 1948 entries. During her retirement years she typed and organized an impressive account of the Taiwan mission. SMWA.

[12] Ibid

[13] Schultz diary, SMWA.

[14] St. Mary-of-the-Woods Diary, July 3, 1950, SMWA.

[15] Strictly speaking, Taichung was designated as an apostolic prefecture in 1950, not being elevated to diocesan status until 1962

[16] Madeleine Fu's name in the Congregation is Sister Donna Marie, SP.

[17] The name Bisch appears often in these pages, and for good reason. Three of the Bisch girls entered the Congregation, Anna in 1881, taking the name Sister St. Ignatius, Frances in 1882, taking the name Sister St. Bernardine, and Mary in 1883, taking the name Sister Mary Anthony. They influenced their brother, Joseph N. Bisch to take a job at the motherhouse, where he went on to serve as superintendent of grounds from 1893-1939. Upon his death, he was succeeded by his son, Bernard, whose sister Madeleine had entered in 1921, taking the name of Sister Marian Celeste. In 1958, Bernard's son, Joseph L. took over the duties of superintendent until 1988. During 1984-1988, his son Stephen worked beside him.

[18] Notes kept by Sister Margaret Patrice Foley, courtesy of Sister Rosemary Borntrager, SMWA.

[19] Mr. Folsom, a graduate of Fordham and the University of San Francisco, had married a Saint-Mary-of-the-Woods graduate and their daughter Betty graduated from the College in 1941. His name appears in several references at this time for kind deeds such as arrangements for Holy Year pilgrimages.

[20] Book of Important Events, June 1952, SMWA.

[21] Ibid., June 23, 1952, SMWA.

[22] The Book of Important Events indicates that the topics chosen showed attention to the issues of the day: "the tensions which have arisen in the negro problem, the inter-group lack of understanding, migrant workers and housing problems." August, 1953, SMWA.

[23] Mother Marie Helene to the sisters, April 6, 1951, SMWA.

[24] Book of Important Events, July 30, 1954, SMWA.

[25] Marywood House Diary, April 5, 1954, SMWA.

[26] Archbishop A. J. Cicognani to Mother Marie Helene, August 17, 1951, SMWA.

[27] Sister Bertrande Meyers, *The Education of Sisters: A Plan for Integrating the Religious, Social, Cultural and Professional Training of Sisters* (New York: Sheed and Ward, 1941).

[28] Ibid., xxx.

[29] Ibid., 39.

[30] Ibid., 40.

[31] Ibid., 93.

[32] This section is drawn from *Religious Community Life in the United States: Proceedings of the Sisters' Section of the First National Congress of Religious of the United States* (New York: Paulist Press, 1952).

[33] Ibid., 117-125.

[34] Ibid., 118.

[35] Ibid., 123.

[36] Ibid., 119.

[37] Ibid, 122.

[38] Ibid.

[39] Sister Rose Angela Horan, then superior of Marywood, Evanston, would be elected as first assistant in 1954 and superior general in 1960. In these roles she would have able assistance from Sister Marie Perpetua Hayes as dean and later president of Saint Mary-of-the-Woods College, as well as two attendees who took leading roles in the Education Department, Sisters Mary Corona Sullivan (then superior at Providence High School, Chicago) and Mary Carina Connors (then superior at St. Angela, Chicago).

[40] Highlights of the conferences are taken from the *Proceedings*.

[41] Mother Mary Berchmans Reed, SC, in *Proceedings*, 97.

[42] See M. Loretta Petit, OP, "Sister M. Madeleva Wolff, C.S.C." *Catholic Education: A Journal of Inquiry and Practice,* http://ejournals.bc.edu/ojs/index.php/catholic/article/view/703/690 March, 2006, and Karen M. Kennelly, *The Religious Formation Conference, 1954-2004* (Silver Spring, MD: Religious Formation Conference, 2009) for more on the influence of this work. This talk must have made a strong

impression on the Sisters of Providence. Although the council had declined Sister Madeleva's two previous invitations to send sisters to the summer theology courses offered at the Holy Cross St. Mary's College, she was approved as a speaker the following November. Acts of Council, May 15, 1944, March 2, 1945, and November 11, 1949, SMWA.

[43] *Proceedings*, 130.

[44] Ibid., 184.

[45] An interesting sidebar to this on-stage encounter is the story told in Kennelly, 11, as she recounts the parlor encounter between Father Deady and Sister Mary Patrick when the latter asked for financial assistance from the archdiocese in implementing their plan for keeping the young sisters at home until they had completed their degrees. "Deady glanced around the tastefully appointed parlor, coughed a few times, and said it seemed to him that the sisters weren't in need of help as they appeared to have 'done pretty well for themselves.' [whereas from Sister Mary Patrick's point of view] It would have been more accurate had Deady claimed the Sisters had done pretty well *by* themselves."

[46] *Proceedings*, 186.

[47] Diary, November 23, 1953, SMWA.

[48] Sister Mary Borromeo Brown to Sister M.T., Thanksgiving Day, 1953. Letter in Mother Marie Helene's necrology file, SMWA.

[49] Book of Important Events,"Funeral Sermon," November 27, 1953, SMWA.

[50] *The Aurora*, (January, 1954), 15.

[51] Ibid. 17. In her role as superior general, Mother Marie Helene was the president of the College and chair of the College Board of Trustees consisting of members of the council and faculty in administrative positions.

Chapter 11

[1] Nicholas A. Schneider, *Cardinal Ritter: His Life and Times* (Ligouri, Mo.: Ligouri Press, 2008), 75.

[2] In discussing the longstanding impact of Marian piety among American Catholics, Jay Dolan notes: "Inspired by the Marian apparition in Fatima in 1917, the cult of Fatima received a papal endorsement in 1942. The message of Fatima was one of prayer and repentance, with a specific request of Mary reportedly being prayers for the conversion of Russia. In the Cold War atmosphere of the late 1940s and 1950s, devotion to Our Lady of Fatima took on a very strong anti-Communist quality." *The American Catholic Experience: A History from Colonial Times to the Present* (New York: Doubleday & Com-

pany, Inc., 1985), 385-386.

[3] *Explanation and Reflection on the Little Office of the Blessed Virgin.* In keeping with the practice of the times, no author is listed. SMWA.

[4] 1954 Office Book, SMWA.

[5] Sister Gertrude Clare to the sisters, January 15, 1954. Acts of Council, January 15, 1954, SMWA.

[6] Letter circular, January 30, 1954, SMWA.

[7] Sister Gertrude Clare to the sisters, March 31, 1954, SMWA.

[8] Sister Gertrude Clare to the delegates, March 19, 1954, SMWA.

[9] Diary, May 4, 1954. In reference to the May 6 session, the Diary notes that it took place "since a third meeting had been requested by the delegates to discuss points relative to educational matters." The several items added to the previously circulated agenda may have been generated by the discussion on May 4. SMWA.

[10] Minutes of the 1954 General Chapter, SMWA.

[11] The change of title had first been put forward by Mother Mary Raphael, who noted that the title of president had been passed from Mother Mary Cleophas to her, but that new needs required "one equipped scholastically with the proper degrees." She went on to suggest that Sister Eugenia's title of dean be changed to president, but for whatever reason, this suggestion was not pursued at the time. Acts of Council, June 4, 1937, SMWA.

[12] Archbishop A. G. Cicognani to Mother Marie Helene, August 17, 1951, SMWA.

[13] P. Arcadio Larraona to Reverend Mother General, August 12, 1952, SMWA.

[14] "Proceedings of the Washington Meeting" of Mothers Mary Gerald, OP, Marie Helene, SP, and Mary Bernadine, RSM, at the Dominican House of Studies, Washington, D.C., August 18, 1953, SMWA.

[15] Cardinal Valeri to Mother Mary Gerald, December 21, 1955. DLCW SCR LCWR 1955, Archives of the University of Notre Dame.

[16] Minutes of the Meeting of the National Executive Committee for Women Religious of the United States, April 9, 1956, Archives of the Adrian Dominican Sisters.

[17] Dolan points out that: "The trend toward a national organization was typical of everything Catholic in the twentieth century ... and most often the national organizations were affiliated with the National Catholic Welfare Conference in a committee type of arrangement. This had the obvious effect of turning the Conference into a super church agency at the national level" (380).

[18] "The Organization of Religious throughout the World," by Father

Elio Gambari, Archives of the Adrian Dominican Sisters.

[19] Mother Mary Gerald to Cardinal Valeri, September 17, 1956. DLCW SCR LCWR 1956, Archives of the University of Notre Dame.

[20] In his December 20, 1956, letter to Mother Gerald, Cardinal Valeri gave praise to the committee's "efficient and energetic activity, and to the striking success it has achieved," and told of his private audience with Pope Pius XII who extended an apostolic blessing to the conference. Ibid.

[21] See https://lcwr.org/about/history for a timeline summary of the organization's activities.

[22] Diary, April 27, 1957, SMWA. Seventeen years later, in 1971, the name of the Conference was changed to the Leadership Conference of Women Religious (LCWR), and in 1995 a portion of the member congregations sought papal approval to organize separately as the Conference of Major Superiors of Women Religious (CMSWR).

[23] See Chapters 10 and 15 for the influence of Sister Bertrande Meyers, SC, and 18 for the influence of Sister Madeleva Wolff, CSC, on these developments. The following section is based on Karen M. Kennelly, CSJ, *The Religious Formation Conference: 1954-2004* (Silver Spring, MD: Religious Formation Conference, 2009).

[24] *Sister Formation Bulletin*, 3, no. 1, (Autumn, 1956): 2-3.

[25] Ibid., 4.

[26] Ibid., 7.

[27] See Kennelly, 23-39, for details on this groundbreaking endeavor.

[28] Sister Loretta Therese O'Leary, Memoir, SMWA.

[29] The May 1956 Acts of Council acknowledge: "Various suggestions were presented, but first of all the needs of the schools were presented by Mother. It was decided we will have to postpone our participation." The quote stating the plan appears in the minutes for November 1956. SMWA.

[30] Tracy Schier, "History of Higher Education for Women at Saint Mary-of-the-Woods: 1840-1980" (PhD diss., Boston College, 1987) reports that: " by 1957-58 the freshman, sophomore and junior classes were the largest ever, with 155, 108, and 69; in 1959, 69 seniors graduated, the largest ever" (182).

[31] Diary, August 15, 1957, SMWA.

[32] Acts of Council, February 1955, SMWA.

[33] Mother Gertrude Clare to the sisters, May 5, 1958, SMWA.

[34] The author is grateful to several sisters who responded to questions regarding their experience of "second novitiate in changing times": Sisters Rosemary Borntrager, Jackie Hoffman, Mary Ann Leahy, Marie Grace Malloy, Marie Esther Sivertsen, Emily Walsh.

[35] Mother Gertrude Clare to the sisters, undated letter, SMWA.

[36] Over the years they had designed the Woodland Inn, Foley Hall, the Church of the Immaculate Conception, Providence Convent, Guerin Hall, the Conservatory, Le Fer Hall, the Novitiate and the Blessed Sacrament Chapel. See Sister Mary Roger Madden, *The Path Marked Out: History of the Sisters of Providence of Saint Mary-of-the Woods, Indiana, vol. 3* (Saint Mary-of-the-Woods, IN: Office of Congregational Advancement—Sisters of Providence, 1991), 383, 396.

[37] Diary, October 2, 1959, SMWA.

[38] In reviewing the financial records from the times, former treasurer general Sister Margaret Kern listed the 1955 debt as $1.6 million and the final cost of the novitiate building as $2,674,000. Oral history, February 13, 2007, SMWA.

[39] Mr. H. Douglas Cotton to Mother Gertrude Clare, March 17, 1959, SMWA.

[40] Mother Gertrude Clare to the sisters, January 14, 1960, SMWA.

[41] A two-manual four rank Wicks pipe organ with a full pedal board of thirty-two pedals was installed Dec. 13, 1960, in Owens Chapel. "History of Organs at Saint Mary-of-the-Woods," compiled by Sister Regina Marie McIntyre. SMWA.

[42] The opinion that the seal should not be stepped on led to its removal to its present place in Providence Center. See Madden, 381-382, for a description of the seal and an account of its adoption.

[43] The quote appears on the frontispiece of *The Teacher's Guide or Educational Methods of the Special Use of the Sisters of Providence of Saint Mary-of the-Woods* (Saint Mary-of-the-Woods, Indiana, 1914). SMWA.

[44] Diary, May 27, 1960, SMWA.

[45] Archbishop Larroana to United States superiors'committee, July 28, 1954, SMWA.

[46] Sister Mary Magdalen Bellasin, OSU, to Mother Gertrude Clare welcoming Sister Alexa, July 27, 1956. Sister Alexa notes that the sister-students referred to her as "Mother Mag" but that "she kept order in the place." Oral history, SMWA.

[47] Descriptive materials sent with the letters of invitation, SMWA.

[48] Archbishop Larraona to United States superiors' committee, June 27, 1955, SMWA.

[49] Mother Mary Gerald to Mother Gertrude Clare, September 5, 1955, SMWA.

[50] Brochure of "The Institute Pius XII, Villa Schifanoia." File of Sister Cecilia Ann Miller, SMWA.

[51] Cardinal Spellman to Sister Immaculee, October 8, 1955, SMWA.

[52] Oral history of Sister Alexa Suelzer, SMWA.

[53] Mother Gertrude Clare to the sisters, December 21, 1954, SMWA.

[54] Cardinal Canali was President of the Pontifical Commission for the Government of the Vatican City. The Diary notes: "Residence at Santa Marta entitled the visitors to the use of the Vatican City bank and post office and to walks in the Vatican Gardens. The words, 'Santa Marta,' the Sisters found, provided a satisfactory password whenever they needed identification in passing Swiss Guards." Later, a representative of Mr. Folsom's company, RCA, arranged a trip to Castel Gandolfo for a public audience and blessing from Pope Pius XII. Diary, November 13, 1954, SMWA.

[55] Sister Loretta Therese O'Leary's "Travel Diary" provides the details of their stay in Rome. SMWA.

[56] Diary, December 10, 1954, SMWA.

[57] Mother Gertrude Clare to the sisters, December 21, 1954, SMWA.

[58] Monsignor Federici to Mother Gertrude Clare, October 26, 1955. In his letter he apologized for the cost, explaining, "But I pray you to consider that the book has come out much greater than was foreseen, both in size and beauty, with its large number of illustrations; so that in the end its cost is very moderate." He assured her that he had arranged to have reviews of the book widely published. SMWA.

[59] Monsignor Federici to Mother Gertrude Clare, February 24, 1956, SMWA. It should be noted that the Cardinal Prefect was not the former apostolic delegate who had visited Saint Mary-of-the-Woods, Amleto Giovanni Cicognani, but rather his brother, Gaetano, who was then prefect of the Sacred Congregation of Rites.

[60] Letter of Monsignor Federici to Mother Gertrude Clare, February 24, 1956. The entire letter was printed as part of Mother Gertrude Clare's March 2, 1956, letter to the sisters. SMWA. In his subtle manner of letting Mother understand the way things were done in Rome, he later offered her the opportunity to purchase the original painting for $1,800, to which the council agreed, noting, "We can hardly refuse." Acts of Council, May 2, 1957, SMWA.

[61] Book of Important Events, May 14, 1956, SMWA.

[62] Book of Important Events, July 30, 1956, SMWA.

[63] Mother Gertrude Clare to the sisters, undated letter, SMWA.

[64] Diary, October 22, 1958, SMWA.

[65] Book of Important Events, January 1958, SMWA.

Chapter 12

[1] Charles Morris, *American Catholic: The Saints and Sinners Who Built America's Most Powerful Church* (New York: Random House, 1997), 221-223.

[2] Acts of Council, July 15, 1954, SMWA.

[3] Jay Dolan, *In Search of an American Catholicism* (New York: Oxford University Press, 2002), 180.

[4] Ibid., 181.

[5] Ibid., 181.

[6] With doctoral degrees in philosophy and theology from Rome and a canon law doctorate from Catholic University, Carberry had served as chancellor in Trenton, NJ, and after a stint as a seminary professor returned to Brooklyn where he became known as "the radio priest." In 1965 he was appointed bishop of Columbus, Ohio. http: http://www.colsdioc.org/AboutUs/TheBishopsofColumbus.aspx.

[7] Acts of Council, January 7, 1958, SMWA.

[8] Book of Important Events, October 15, 1954, SMWA.

[9] *Immaculata College of Washington Catalogue, 1974-1976*, 10, SMWA.

[10] Book of Important Events, October 7, 1956, SMWA.

[11] Kathryn Lawlor, BVM, in *From There to Here: The Sisters of Charity of the Blessed Virgin Mary from 1942-1972* (Dubuque: Mount Carmel Press, 2010) states that, "The elementary school on Chicago's west side had an enrollment of nearly 1,400 children and a faculty of twenty-four sisters. The three sisters and their students who died were in classrooms on the second floor where the flames and smoke quickly spread and where escape was nearly impossible" (84). Our Lady of the Angels was a feeder school for Providence High School and Sister Suzanne Smith, SP, recalls that girls who had been in the building during the fire and had lost siblings were enrolled in her classes when she taught at Providence High School in the early sixties.

[12] Acts of Council, March 26, 1959, SMWA.

[13] Book of Important Events, November 30, 1959, SMWA.

[14] Memoir of Sister Regina Cecile Ryan, SMWA.

[15] Mother Gertrude Clare had arranged for this meeting, but it occurred just when she fell ill. Mother Mary Pius recalls visiting Saint Mary-of-the-Woods while Monsignor McManus was there in Tile Hall and hearing the sisters comment, "Why are *they* doing this when *she* is in the Infirmary?" Clearly the extremely serious nature of Mother's illness was not yet apparent. Oral history, SMWA.

[16] Acts of Council, February 14, 1959, SMWA.

[17] Acts of Council, March 1959, SMWA.

[18] Diary, March 15, 1959, SMWA.

[19] Oral history of Sister Mary Charles Spalding, SMWA.

[20] http://www.stanncatholicchurch.org/history.htm.

[21] Memoir of Sister Joann Quinkert, SMWA.

22 Tracy Schier, "History of Higher Education for Women at Saint Mary-of-the-Woods: 1840-1980" (PhD diss., Boston College, 1987), 181.

23 Acts of Council, May 6, 1954. SMWA.

24 Book of Important Events, May 12, 1954.

25 Schier, 191-192.

26 Diary, June 20, 1954, SMWA.

27 Schier, 182

28 Community Diary, October 4, 1958. SMWA.

29 Ibid., 184

30 Book of Important Events, February 1957, SMWA.

31 Sister Regina Siegfried, ASC, summarizes her congregation's decision to leave: "Some missionaries, like the Adorers, withdrew all their members from China at the close of World War II. Others, like the Sisters of Providence of St. Mary-of-the-Woods, moved their work to Taiwan in 1948. All missionaries were expelled from mainland China in 1953. The Chinese Catholic Church, for all intents and purposes, went underground." *Missionaries More and More: The History of the China Mission of the Adorers of the Blood of Christ, 1933-1945* (Bloomington, Ind.: Authorhouse, 2005), 213.

32 http://iml.jou.ufl.edu/projects/students/tung/mainhistory.htm Accounts of this period of Taiwan's history vary considerably due to differing political viewpoints.

33 Book of Important Events, November 1954, SMWA.

34 Ibid.

35 Ibid.

36 Strictly speaking, Taichung operated as a Prefecture Apostolic under William Kupfer, MM, from August 1950 until June 1986 when it was elevated to diocesan status with Bishop Joseph Wang Yu-jung as first bishop.

37 Book of Important Events, SMWA.

38 Sister Ann Colette Wolf tells us that the faculty of Ching I in Kaifeng had felt this was an appropriate designation for someone so able to find the resources and organize the construction of the buildings which made the education of Chinese women possible. *Against All Odds: Sisters of Providence Mission to the Chinese, 1920-1990* (Saint Mary-of-the-Woods, IN: Office of Communications—Sisters of Providence, 1990), 286.

39 Letter to superiors, September 30, 1958, SMWA.

40 Letter circular of Mother Gertrude Clare to the sisters, December 12, 1956, SMWA.

[41] Rev. Adam Ellis, SJ, to Mother Gertrude Clare, April 21, 1955, SMWA.

[42] *Review for Religious* 1, no. 1 (January 15, 1942): 6.

[43] Diary, January 21, 1957, SMWA.

[44] Diary May 26, 1957, SMWA.

[45] Diary, August 13, 1957, SMWA.

[46] Circular letter, January 1958, SMWA.

[47] Acts of Council, March 5, 1955, SMWA.

[48] Description based on the Diary entry of July 4, 1959, SMWA.

[49] Richard F. Weingroff. "Federal-Aid Highway Act of 1956: Creating the Interstate System." http://www.fhwa.dot.gov/publications/ publicroads/96summer/p96su10.cfm.

[50] Bradley, Becky, "1950-1959," *American Cultural History*. Lone Star College-Kingwood Library. Last modified July 2010. http:// wwwappskc.lonestar.edu/popculture/decade50.html.

[51] Acts of Council, January 1955, SMWA.

[52] Diary, May 29, 1957, SMWA.

[53] In the January 30, 1949, copy of the schedule for the New York Central System serving St. Louis, Terre Haute, Indianapolis and Cleveland, Saint Mary-of-the-Woods is shown at Milepost 176.5 with St. Louis being Milepost zero and Cleveland being at Milepost 535.6. This information courtesy of train buff John Lloyd Bluntzer, brother of Sister Barbara Bluntzer.

[54] Donna Forill McKeon, *This Is Sister* (Saint Mary-of-the-Woods: Saint Mary-of-the-Woods Alumnae Association, 1968), 12.

[55] Acts of Council, January 10, 1954, SMWA.

[56] Acts of Council, May 27, 1958.

[57] Diary, July 15, 1957, SMWA.

[58] Diary, July 5, 1957, SMWA.

[59] Mother Gertrude Clare to the sisters, May 5, 1958, SMWA.

[60] The biographical information is drawn from the Diary, September 22, 1959. SMWA

[61] Ibid.

[62] Diary, June 1958, SMWA.

[63] Diary, August 9, 1954, SMWA

[64] Article 20 of the 1954 *Constitutions* (exactly replicating the 1929 edition) included among the responsibilities of the Superior General, "She visits all the houses of the Congregation at least once every two years, or, if legitimately prevented, has them visited by a member of her Council."

[65] Diary, February 12, 1960, SMWA.

⁶⁶ Sister Rose Angela to the sisters, February 16, 1960, SMWA.

⁶⁷ Sister Rose Angela to the sisters, May 19, 1960, SMWA.

⁶⁸ With her February 29, 1960 letter to the sisters Sister Rose Angela sent sample 3x5 cards asking the sisters to list the "summers away" in order to identify the four hundred who must remain on the missions to prevent overcrowding. SMWA.

⁶⁹ Ibid.

Chapter 13

¹ Sister Helen Rose Newland to Mother Gertrude Clare, January 24, 1960. Necrology, SMWA. Note that it was not till mid-February of 1960 that Mother Gertrude Clare became seriously ill.

² Ibid.

³ Ibid.

⁴ Background sheet sent to the delegates, "Adaptation," quoting *Review for Religious* 17 (1958): 344, SMWA.

⁵ Father Ransing later used Pope John XXIII's famous "opening the windows" image to advocate for encouraging discussion. Describing his speech to the Conference of Major Superior of Women in August 1963, Sister Kathryn Lawlor, BVM, relates that: "He said that perhaps the time has come to open the windows of communities and invite the sisters to have open discussions." *From There to Here: The Sisters of Charity of the Blessed Virgin Mary, From 1942-1972* (Dubuque: Mount Carmel Press, 2010), 77.

⁶ Sister Rose Angela to Chapter delegates, May 21, 1960, SMWA.

⁷ Report of the State of the Congregation of the Sisters of Providence, June 20, 1960, SMWA.

⁸ Ibid.

⁹ Mother Mary Pius Regnier's oral history, SMWA.

¹⁰ The Chapter secretary, Sister Mary Corona Sullivan, recorded in the minutes that, "Though the Ceremonial calls for the chairmanship of the newly elected Superior General at the other elections, His Excellency resumed the chair and presided for the remainder of the elections." Given the great attention of the council to all the other preparations, this change is curious indeed.

¹¹ General Chapter of 1960 discussion materials, SMWA.

¹² Mother Mary Pius Regnier's oral history, SMWA.

¹³ Sister Mary Joan Kirchner's oral history, SMWA.

¹⁴ Transcript of sessions of the 1960 Chapter of Affairs, SMWA.

¹⁵ The first comment was penned by J. Peter Smith, one of her students in 1938 at St. Joan of Arc in a January 24, 1992, letter to Sister Marie William Hoerner. The second quote is taken from a column written

by Archbishop Thomas Murphy in the June 1992 issue of the Seattle archdiocesan newspaper, *The Progress*, describing his 1945 eighth grade teacher at St. Mel.

[16] 1954 *Constitutions*, 6, SMWA.

[17] "Report on the General Chapter, July 8, 1960," SMWA.

[18] Book of Important Events, July 1960, SMWA.

[19] Brief descriptions sent with photos to the missions to inform sisters unable to attend the assembly, SMWA.

[20] Mother Rose Angela to the sisters, July 23, 1960, SMWA.

[21] Interestingly, the Diary records that two sisters died that day. SMWA.

[22] *Time*, Friday, January 4, 1963. http://www.time.com.

[23] Nicholas A. Schneider, *Joseph Elmer Cardinal Ritter: His Life and Times* (Ligouri, MO.: Ligouri Press, 2008). See 123-160 for accounts of Cardinal Ritter's interventions in the aula, as well as samples of his behind-the-scenes correspondence with American prelates.

[24] Quoted in the Book of Important Events, April 1964, SMWA.

[25] Mother Rose Angela to the sisters, May 24, 1963, SMWA.

[26] Mother Rose Angela to the sisters, Feast of Our Lady of Providence, November 1961, SMWA.

[27] Leon Joseph Cardinal Suenens, *The Nun in the World: Religious and the Apostolate* (London: Burns & Oates, 1962), 23-25.

[28] Ibid., 27.

[29] Ibid., 9.

[30] Ibid., 114.

[31] Ibid., 97.

[32] Karen M. Kennelly, CSC, *The Religious Formation Conference, 1954-2004* (Silver Spring, MD: Religious Formation Conference, 2009), 74.

[33] Community Diary, March 28, 1966, SMWA.

[34] Book of Important Events, December, 1960. By teaching extra lessons after school and on Saturdays, the music teachers "realized over $7000 over a period of three years" to enable Sisters Rose Dolores, Cecilia Clare Bocard and Frances Angela Kolb to select and purchase the organ from the Wicks Organ Co. at Highland, Illinois. SMWA.

[35] Ibid., July 1963, SMWA.

[36] Book of Important Events, December 1963 and September 1965, SMWA.

[37] Book of Important Events: December 1663, "Bible Vigils are encouraged"; November 1964, "Scripture Service to be held on the Eve of Thanksgiving"; February 1966: "Sister Alexa's Way of the Cross." SMWA.

[38] The Congregation had been using *Officium Parvum Beatae Mariae Virginis: Little Office Of the Blessed Virgin Mary According to the Roman Ritual for the use of the Sisters of Providence of Saint Mary-of-the-Woods Archdiocese of Indianapolis* reprinted in 1954. The new text was *Lauds, Vespers, Compline in English Reprinted from The Hours of the Divine Office In English And Latin*, an officially approved edition of the Roman Breviary prepared by the staff of The Liturgical Press (Collegeville, MN: 1965).

[39] Mother Mary Pius Regnier's oral history, SMWA.

[40] Mother Rose Angela to the sisters, October 12, 1965, SMWA. Only ten days later Saint Mary-of-the-Woods would host its own Pontifical High Mass to celebrate the Congregation's 125th anniversary in conjunction with the dedication of the new College library building.

[41] Mother Mary Pius Regnier's oral history, SMWA.

[42] Community Diary, January 29, 1964, SMWA.

[43] Postulator Emilio Federici to Mother Rose Angela, March 3, 1963. SMWA.

[44] Book of Important Events, August 1963, 185-192, SMWA. The description of the project is quite detailed and lists the names of all the sisters who contributed to the effort.

[45] Rev. Ransing to Mother Consolotrice Wright, April 11, 1962. Quoted in Lawlor, *Sisters of Charity*, 76.

[46] See Lawlor, 74-79, and Karen M. Kennelly, CSC, *The Religious Formation Conference, 1954-2004* (Silver Spring, MD: Religious Formation Conference, 2009), 69-74, for two differing and complementary accounts of this situation.

[47] See Jay P. Dolan, *The American Catholic Experience: A History from Colonial Times to the Present* (New York: Doubleday & Company, Inc., 1985), 415-416, for an explanation of the link between the European brand of Catholic Action and its American offspring.

[48] 1960 Chapter transcript, SMWA.

[49] Acts of Council, December 18, 1960 and October 29, 1961, SMWA. However, in August 1961, permission for the sisters at Joliet to drive was refused because there were too many other factors involved.

[50] Sister Kathleen Therese O'Connor's oral history. In one of her many newsy letters to the sisters, Mother Rose Angela blithely commented, "Sometimes we would have 15 or 20 for a meal and every time they came, out came the coffee or tea or supplies, and everybody helped prepare and clean afterward." Mother Rose Angela to the sisters, January 9, 1965, SMWA.

[51] "Notes: Local Superiors' Workshop, December, 1953," SMWA. This forty-one page mimeographed booklet summarizing the talks and

topics was marked with the notice that it was to be kept in each house for reference.

[52] "Recommendations for the Giving of the Obediences" enclosed in Mother Rose Angela's April 26, 1961, letter circular, SMWA.

[53] Undated (est. 1962) "Items of Interest." Monsignor Kempf was first assigned to Saint Mary-of-the-Woods from 1923-1925 and then returned in 1930, serving until his 1968 retirement, remaining on campus until his death in 1978. SMWA.

[54] Mother Rose Angela to the sisters, April 22, 1965, SMWA.

[55] Mother Rose Angela to the sisters, November 30, 1963, SMWA.

[56] Ibid.

[57] Community Diary, October 22, 1964, SMWA.

[58] Mother Rose Angela to the sisters, November 23, 1963, SMWA.

[59] Rev. Joseph Brokhage's funeral sermon, November 22, 1963, SMWA.

[60] Mother Gertrude Clare's necrology file, SMWA.

Chapter 14

[1] *The Indianapolis Star*, February 8, 1961, SMWA.

[2] Report of Superior General to 1966 General Chapter, SMWA.

[3] Msgr. McManus to Mother Rose Angela, January 25, 1961, SMWA.

[4] The financial report for the 1966 General Chapter included the statement: "A site in River Grove, Illinois, valued at $150,000 was given to the Institute in December, 1961, by the Archdiocese of Chicago, together with $1,000,000 to apply towards construction costs of the school plant. The aforesaid land was acquired by gratuitous title. Part of the construction costs were paid with funds of the Institute, but chiefly through borrowed money. …[Total Sister of Providence costs for] classroom building, gymnasium, auditorium, convent, and equipment = $1,668,543.86." SMWA.

[5] Sister Catherine Joseph Wilcox in her monograph, "For the Record: An Account of Significant Happenings at Mother Theodore Guerin High School, 1962-2001," notes that the eyes of the Virgin were made from pieces from a fifth century mosaic at the Vatican which had been given to Sister Immaculee while she was studying in Florence. SMWA.

[6] Constructions costs amounted to $2.6 million with a $650,000 outlay for furniture. Interestingly, the architect, Mr. Gerald Barry, was the nephew of Sister Mary Gerald Barry, OP, who had chaired the planning committee for the 1952 Notre Dame Congress.

[7] During this same period the 1914 Sacred Heart High School was renamed Kennedy High School in 1966 and in 1969 Chartrand and Kennedy merged operations under the name Roncalli High School.

[8] Necrology, SMWA. The eulogy was delivered by Sister Dorothy Mary's niece, Sister Barbara (Vincent Ferrer) Doherty. Sister Dorothy Mary was so successful that when her six-year term was up, members of the Ladywood Lay Advisory Board petitioned to have her term extended. This did not happen but her considerable talents were used in her role as the director of development for Immaculata Junior College in Washington, D.C.

[9] The financial section of the 1966 General Chapter report stated the total cost as $2,528,696.27. The school could now accommodate 600 students. SMWA.)

[10] Sister Frances Alma McManus's oral history, SMWA.

[11] Sister Marie Helen Leonard to Mother Rose Angela, September 15, 1961, SMWA.

[12] Sister Marie Helen Leonard to Mother Rose Angela, October 31, 1961, SMWA.

[13] Charles R. Morris, *American Catholic: The Saints and Sinners Who Built America's Most Powerful Church* (New York: Random House, 1997), 259.

[14] Sister Marie Helen to Mother Rose Angela, December 16, 1961, SMWA.

[15] Sister Marie Helen to Mother Rose Angela, January 24, 1962, SMWA.

[16] The financial section of the 1966 General Chapter report included the income from the sale of the 2.5 acre Anaheim site as $373,991, which was applied to construction costs of $2,884,708.02. SMWA.

[17] Mother Rose Angela to Bishop Grimmelsman, May 8, 1961, SMWA.

[18] In his November 11, 1961, letter to Msgr. Deery, Bishop Grimmelsman praised him for the fund-raising effort, adding: "God will reward you, too, for your wisdom in conducting separate high schools for the boys and for the girls. This, too, is the will of the Church." SMWA. In 1970, under Bishop Francis Shea, the two schools merged as co-educational Rivet High School.

[19] Memo of Sister Catherine Ursula Hayes to Mother Rose Angela, July 14, 1961, SMWA.

[20] Mother Rose Angela subsequently wrote on March 21, 1962 to Apostolic Delegate Egidio Vagnozzi for the permission to transfer the deed and also to Archbishop Schulte to inform him of the arrangement. SMWA.

[21] Mother Rose Angela to Msgr. Deery, May 4, 1962.

[22] St. Rose 1963-1964 House Diary. Apparently the writer referred only to the moving of books from the library in the old building to that of the new since an undated newspaper clipping mentions alternate moving operations. SMWA.

[23] House Diary of Providence Convent, Galesburg, June 25, 1964, SMWA. As will be described in Chapter 16, the house would become the home office of the newly established St. Joseph Region.

[24] Both had moved from the position of superior/principal at a private girls' academy to positions at the College: Mother Rose Angela from Marywood, Evanston, to serving as secretary (in charge of admissions and public relations) from 1953-1954, and Sister Mary Joan from St. Agnes, Indianapolis, to dean of women from 1949-1956. Sister Marie Perpetua had succeeded Sister Eugenia as dean in 1950.

[25] Acts of Council, October 11, 1960, SMWA.

[26] See Chapter 3, page 94.

[27] Summary sheet as part of Acts of Council: "Relationship of Saint Mary-of-the-Woods College to the Congregation of the Sisters of Providence," Undated, SMWA.

[28] Acts of Council, August 6, 1961, SMWA.

[29] Mother Mary Pius Regnier's oral history, SMWA.

[30] Acts of Council, September 10, 1961, SMWA.

[31] Diary, July 23, 1962, SMWA.

[32] *The Indianapolis Star*, March 24, 1963. Clipping in SMWA.

[33] Diary, April 28, 1963, SMWA.

[34] *Campaign News*, April, 1963, SMWA.

[35] Book of Important Events, August, 1963, SMWA.

[36] In 1909 the Charter had been amended to remove the $30,000 limit to the College holdings. Sister Mary Roger Madden, *The Path Marked Out: History of the Sisters of Providence of Saint Mary-of-the Woods, Indiana, vol. 3* (Saint Mary-of-the-Woods, IN: Office of Congregational Advancement—Sisters of Providence, 1991), 381.

[37] Acts of Council, February 18, 1963.

[38] Acts of Council, January 31, 1963, February 15, 17, 18, 1963, SMWA.

[39] Acts of Council, May 8, 1964, SMWA.

[40] Acts of Council, May 5, 1965.

[41] Two employees of the College, Mr. Tim O'Dwyer and Mr. James Sullivan, asked to purchase the homes they were renting from the Congregation. Acts of Council, January 1966.

[42] The July 26, 1965, Quit Claim Deed that effected this transfer specifically states "that the Sisters of Providence of St. Mary's-of-the-Woods, [sic] Indiana, a corporation, of Vigo County, State of Indiana, convey and quit claim to St. Mary-of the-Woods College, a corporation, of Vigo County State of Indiana, for and in consideration of the sum of One ($1.00) dollar and other good and valuable consideration, the receipt thereof, is hereby acknowledged." Sister of Providence

Secretary's Office. The financial section of the report to the 1966 General Chapter lists the value of the approximately sixty-acre property as $66,000 and the value of buildings and equipment as $10,268,884 but carefully notes that actions of the College require "due authorization of the Board of Trustees (the Superior General and the General Council.)" SMWA.

[43] Biographical information from a talk given by Sister Emily Walsh on the occasion of the dedication of a plaque in the College library on October 22, 1978, and from Sister Camilla's necrology file, SMWA.

[44] Mother Rose Angela's comments had been delivered on the occasion of the June 2, 1962, groundbreaking, SMWA.

[45] Mother Rose Angela to Rt. Rev. William E. McManus, February 6, 1963, SMWA.

[46] Letter circular, April 26, 1964, SMWA.

[47] Acts of Council, June 1961 and December 1962, SMWA.

[48] Margaret R. Brennan, *What Was There for Me Once: A Memoir* (Toronto: Novalis Publishing Inc., 2009), 47.

[49] Joan Chittister, *The Way We Were: A Story of Conversion and Renewal* (Maryknoll, New York: Orbis Books, 2005), 35.

[50] Sister Alexa recalled that the head of her department, Father Gerald Sloyan, advised her that the theology faculty had been severely criticized for teaching modern criticism and had told her to be careful how she entitled the dissertation, so she had made the title pedagogical. Sister Alexa Suelzer, Oral history, SMWA.

[51] Sister Vincent Ferrer, "The use of scripture in the formation of religious women" (master's thesis, St. Mary's College, Notre Dame, 1962), 2, SMWA.

[52] Ibid.

[53] Sister Ruth Eileen Dwyer, "Rationale and curriculum plan for the religious education program for sisters in a congregation whose principal service is education" 10, SMWA.

[54] Interview by the author with Sisters Patricia Fillenwarth and Katherine Manley; quote from Novitiate Diary, August 16, 1960, SMWA.

[55] Sister Bernice Kuper's oral history, SMWA.

[56] Ibid.

[57] Novitiate Diary, August 17, 1961.

[58] Following her term as dean and later president of Immaculata Junior College, Sister Teresa Aloyse Mount, well-known in the community for her writing and speaking, was appointed assistant and instructor in the novitiate from 1965-1967 and served as adviser to novice editor Sister Gilchrist Conway and the several talented novices who contributed to this short-lived journal.

[59] Sister Louise Beverley's undated handwritten notes in small loose-leaf binder. "Better World" was the title of a contemporary movement stressing social justice. SMWA.

[60] "Juniorate Materials, 1962-65," (A Binder of hectographed hand-outs), SMWA.

[61] Sister Bernice Kuper's oral history, SMWA.

[62] Sister Vincent Ferrer, "Use of Scripture" 1, SMWA.

[63] Sister Bernice Kuper's oral history, SMWA.

[64] Book of Important Events, July 22, 1963, SMWA.

[65] Ibid, August 15, 1965, SMWA.

[66] Community Diary, January 26, 1962, SMWA.

[67] Book of Important Events, March 28, 1965, SMWA.

Chapter 15

[1] Book of Important Events, June 7, 1965. SMWA.

[2] Notes from Mother Theodore's Instructions, n.d. SMWA.

[3] Maria (Carol) Scatena in her dissertation, "Educational movements that have influenced the sister teacher education program of the Congregation of the Sisters of Providence, 1840-1940" (PhD diss., Loyola University of Chicago, 1987) does an admirable job of describing the aspects of this work and others that contributed to the educational formation of Congregation members.

[4] See Sister Mary Roger Madden, *The Path Marked Out: History of the Sisters of Providence of Saint Mary-of-the Woods, Indiana, vol. 3* (Saint Mary-of-the-Woods, IN: Office of Congregational Advancement— Sisters of Providence, 1991), Chapter 11 for treatment of the preparation of sisters for teaching during earlier times. The Board of Examiners was eventually supplanted by the supervisor of schools and the Education Office, so the 1961 Board of Education in one sense restored the wider oversight of the original group.

[5] *The Teacher's Guide: or Educational Methods for the Special Use of the Sisters of Providence of Saint-Mary-of-the-Woods* (Saint Mary-of-the-Woods, Indiana, 1914), 11-12.

[6] The college seal was designed by Sister Agnes Clare Cassidy. See Madden, 401.

[7] Handout found among Sister Cecilia Clare Bocard's papers. Such maxims might not have been as significant for applied music teachers such as herself, but after her retirement her painstaking work in archives to document the Congregation's music program made her very aware of the value of this type of training. SMWA.

[8] *Terre Haute Tribune Star*, July 30, 1950. SMWA.

[9] Newspaper clipping from *The Indiana Catholic and Record*, August 6, 1948. SMWA.

[10] Community Diary, August 6, 1965. SMWA.

[11] Sister Amata McGlynn had only taught for two years after earning her PhD in Chemistry from Indiana University before her career was cut short by an early death. Sister Ignatius Ward had taught at the College for ten years before being sent to Catholic University for a PhD in English; she then taught for ten years as well as serving as academic dean.

[12] Necrology. SMWA.

[13] In 1960 when Sister Mary Olive was suffering from rheumatoid arthritis, Sisters Marie Perpetua and Mary Gregory accompanied the U.S.O. drama group to New York. The group then went on to Iceland to entertain U.S. troops with the play *I Remember Mama*. Book of Important Events, SMWA.

[14] Karen Kennelly, "Faculties and What They Taught," in Tracy Schier and Cynthia Russett. *Catholic Women's Colleges in America* (Baltimore: The Johns Hopkins University Press, 2002), 115-116.

[15] Necrology, SMWA.

[16] This section is based on several informal conversations with long-time College faculty members Sisters Laurette Bellamy, Jean Fuqua, William Eyke, Jeanne Knoerle and Alma Louise Mescher.

[17] *Op. cit.* 124.

[18] Kennelly, "Faculties and What They Taught," in Schier, *Catholic Women's Colleges*, 116-117.

[19] "Report – Art in the Community, July 1961," SMWA.

[20] Sister Mary Theodosia Mug, ed., *Journals and Letters of Mother Theodore Guérin* (Saint Mary-of-the-Woods, IN: Sisters of Providence, 1942), 43. After arriving in New York on September 4, 1840, as they journeyed to Indiana Mother Theodore and her five companions had the opportunity to visit the Academy of the Sisters of Charity in Frederick, Maryland. A fuller quote reveals the impact of this visit: "They teach the various sciences scarcely known in our French schools, but they excel in music, which is an indispensable thing in this country, even for the poor. No piano, no pupils! Such is the spirit of this country—Music and Steam!"

[21] The author is grateful to this group of music teachers who gathered to reminisce about "Life as a music teacher in the 50s and 60s": Sisters Laurette Bellamy, Marie Paul Haas, Jackie Hoffman, Mary Catherine Keene, Joan Matthews, Carol Nolan and Lucy Nolan.

[22] Regardless of an individual sister's natural talent or who might recommend her, the Rule dictated that "the Superior General shall designate those who are to pursue and teach the higher studies or particular subjects; also the ornamental branches, music and art,

and no one may apply herself to them without her permission." *Constitutions* (1954) Article 143.

[23] Sister Rose Dolores, SP, "Ten Years of Group Piano Work," *Musart* (September-October, 1958). The periodical was the official publication of the National Catholic Music Educators Association. Sister Rose Dolores included a reference to the series of three workbooks, *Musical Speed Drills*, that she had published under the pen name of Mary Raben; these contained a collection of devices to teach the three fundamentals of note-reading, chord-building and scale-playing.

[24] See Madden, 311, for the very interesting account of the foundation.

[25] *The Immaculata College of Washington Catalogue*, 1974-76, quoted by Scatena, "Educational Movements," 10.

[26] In her memoir, Sister Marian Brady recalls that as a graduate of the high school then enrolled at nearby Trinity College, she was invited to attend the retreat and did so. Sister Marian later went on to become President of Immaculata College of Washington. SMWA.

[27] Sister Eileen Ann Kelley, who was principal at Dunblane from 1963-1967, tells of how a friendly gentleman assisted Sister Anna Rose and her to gain a place in the line of mourners who crossed the Capitol Rotunda to view the coffin of President John F. Kennedy after his assassination on November 22, 1963. Sister Eileen Ann's oral history, SMWA.

[28] Memorandum Report for Sister Teresa Aloyse following Father Stanford's January 9-11, 1963, consultation at Immaculata. SMWA.

[29] Mother Rose Angela to Sister Robert, March 3, 1962, SMWA.

[30] Within the week of January 20-February 4 she received letters from the superior, Sister Robert Kiley, the dean of students, Sister Marian Thomas Kinney, and the president, Sister Teresa Aloyse Mount. In August 1963 Sister Teresa Aloyse attended two meetings of the council to negotiate further details of administrative arrangements. Acts of Council, August 11 and 13, 1963. SMWA.

[31] *Providence Educational News* (November 7, 1963), SMWA.

[32] Sister Mary Joan Kirchner's oral history, SMWA.

[33] The ratios of sisters completing degrees in the "fifteen-year" program as compared to those finishing in the Sister Formation Program were: 1961: 28-43; 1962: 64-30; 1963: 77-15; 1964: 73-25; 1965: 110-30; 1966: 36-25; 1967: 15-29.

[34] "General Report of the State of the Congregation," June, 1966, SMWA.

[35] Education Office flyer, December 3, 1961, SMWA.

[36] "General Report of the State of the Congregation," June, 1966, SMWA

[37] Mary Perkins Ryan, *Are Parochial Schools the Answer?* (New York: Holt, 1964), 27.

Chapter 16

[1] Community Diary, November 9, 1960, SMWA.

[2] Acts of Council, June 19, 1960, SMWA.

[3] Mother Mary Pius Regnier's oral history, SMWA.

[4] Ibid.

[5] While it is obvious that the number of sisters in each region is very unequally distributed, the careful reader will notice that 1,427 sisters indicated a preference for belonging to a certain province, but the actual total of sisters in all four provinces is only 1,178. The other 249 sisters resided at Saint Mary-of-the-Woods and in the foreign missions. Within the two-year 1964-1966 period, it was already clear how unworkable this arrangement was. When the move was made from regions to provinces in 1973, a fifth province, Sacred Heart Province, was formed from the Saint Mary-of-the-Woods and Terre Haute houses. Taiwan was governed through the central administration until 1973 when it was made a region.

[6] Sister Edwardine McNulty's oral history, SMWA.

[7] Acts of Council, March 19, 1964, SMWA.

[8] Oral histories of Mother Mary Pius Regnier and Sister Margaret Kern. SMWA.

[9] Book of Important Events, August 1964, SMWA.

[10] Mother Rose Angela's Letter Circular, April 22, 1965, SMWA.

[11] Mother Mary Pius Regnier's oral history, SMWA.

[12] Ibid.

[13] Book of Important Events, September 1961, SMWA.

[14] Sister Kathleen Therese O'Connor's oral history, SMWA.

[15] Although the travelogue provides names of the many congregations of sisters in Arequipa at the time, this group is consistently referred to simply as the hospital sisters.

[16] Typescript of the travelogue, "Madres de la Providencia, Colegio San José, Apartado 60, Arequipa, Peru," written by Sisters Catherine Celine and Kathleen Therese, SMWA.

[17] Transcript of the travelogue.

[18] Sister Kathleen Therese O'Connor's oral history, SMWA.

[19] This brief summary is based on Gerald M. Costello, "The End of 'The Missions' in Latin America," *America* (January 13, 1979). The article goes on to chronicle the increasingly political involvement of the organization, which led to its early demise in 1973.

[20] Sister Agnes Veronica Hester to Sister Loretta Eileen Hester (addressed as "Dear Topsy"), May 16, 1965. Necrology, SMWA.

[21] Excerpts from an undated (likely May 1965) and unaddressed letter from Sister Marie Jean in the Arequipa file, SMWA.

[22] Sister Mary Joan Kirchner's hectographed letter to "Sister," November 27, 1965, SMWA.

[23] The Juliaca mission, El Cristo Rey, opened in 1968 and closed in 1971. Between 1962 and 1976, twelve Sisters of Providence pursued cultural and language training and went on to work in Arequipa and Juliaca. In December 1975 the Congregation withdrew from Colegio San Jose because of the strongly nationalistic ethos of "Peru for the Peruvians." In subsequent appointments, the returning missionaries built upon their Spanish language proficiency and experience to be of service to various Hispanic communities in the United States.

[24] Acts of Council, December, 1960, SMWA.

[25] Sister Ann Colette Wolf, *Against All Odds: Sisters of Providence Mission to the Chinese, 1920-1980* (Saint Mary-of-the-Woods, IN: Office of Communications—Sisters of Providence, 1990), 286, explains that the Chinese name Kai Hsia (pronounced Guy Shia), given to Sister Marie Gratia in Kaifeng because it sounded like Gratia, had the literal meaning of "Summer Builder," which can also be interpreted as "Successful Builder."

[26] Ibid., 263.

[27] Sister Donna Marie Fu's memoir, SMWA.

[28] Wolf, 264.

[29] Sister St. Francis Schultz to Valentine Schultz, July 28, 1963, SMWA.

[30] Sister St. Francis Schultz to Valentine E. Schultz, April 24, 1963, SMWA.

[31] "Excerpts from letters from our dear Mother and Sister Mary Joan," January 1962, SMWA.

[32] Sister St. Francis Schultz to Valentine Schultz, January 14, 1962, SMWA.

[33] These included Sisters Loretta Francis Ryan and Joseph Angela (Rita) Faucher, 1962-1964, Sister Marie Blanche (Margaret) Gallagher, 1965-1969, Sister Mary Gregory (Jeanne) Knoerle, 1966-67, and Sister Michael (Loretta) Schafer, 1967-1968, who later served as general superior, 1976-1981.

[34] Mother Rose Angela to the sisters, September 1, 1962, SMWA.

[35] Book of Important Events, May 1965, SMWA.

[36] Wolf, *Against All Odds*, 342. Sister Ann Colette goes on in this section to discuss further negotiations between China and the United

States regarding the claims-assets issue in 1979.

[37] Acts of Council, November 1961, SMWA.

[38] Sister Donna Marie Fu's memoir, SMWA.

[39] Mother Mary Pius' oral history, SMWA. Monsignor James Jensen was pastor of St. Mary's Church, in the same block as St. Edward Hospital, and was the dean of the area parishes.

[40] *Constitutions* (1959), Article 71.

[41] Mother Rose Angela to Archbishop Schulte, April 24, 1963, SMWA.

[42] The author is grateful to Margaret McElroy, who, as novice Sister Sara, was a speech pathologist staff member at the clinic. Although she later discerned that she was not called to follow a vocation as a Sister of Providence, she maintained strong ties with the Congregation and the clinic, pursuing further graduate work and becoming the clinic's first audiologist. She was able to research and provide accurate information to supplement archival material.

[43] "Providence Clinic for Speech-Handicapped Children," in *Providence Educational News*, March 21, 1966, SMWA.

[44] The rapid development of the center occurred in the years after 1966, when this book ends, but a few brief items round out this account. Interestingly, prior to her entrance, novice Sister Sara McElroy had completed her certification as a speech and hearing therapist, so in 1967 during her scholastic year, Director of Novices Sister Ann Bernice Kuper arranged to place her at the center with residence at Marywood. Two years later Sister Catherine Therese (Kay) Manley joined the staff as teacher and coordinator of school programs. Sister Ann Monica went on to earn a doctorate in special education from the University of Beverly Hills. The center did not receive financial support from the Congregation, but rather functioned as a non-profit under the direction of its Board with Sister Ann Monica as executive director. So all-consuming did this effort become that in 1971 she made the painful decision to leave the Congregation and to devote herself completely to the work as Dr. Margaret Anne Inman. Providence Speech and Hearing Center continued to flourish and today serves as an exemplary national model for service delivery in communication disorders.

[45] Sister Eugenia Logan, *History of the Sisters of Providence of Saint Mary-of-the-Woods vol. 2* (Terre Haute, Indiana: Moore-Langen, 1978), 300.

[46] See Chapter 7 for the story of the formation of St.Mel-Holy Ghost parish and school.

[47] Memorial book, a souvenir program at the September 8, 1962, dedication of Purcell Hall. The building was named for the founding pastor, Monsignor Purcell.

[48] "St. Mel's Grade School Centennial, 1886-1986," memorial book, 34, SMWA.

[49] See Chapter 3 for the story of the withdrawal from St. Anselm School.

[50] Community Diary, July 2, 1962.

[51] Mother Rose Angela to Bishop Hillenger, April 27, 1964, SMWA.

[52] St. Mel-Holy Ghost convent diary, 1960-65, SMWA.

[53] Sister Marie Caroline Carroll to Mother Rose Angela, March 7, 1965, SMWA.

[54] Interestingly, as a consequence of her summer graduate studies during this time, Sister Jeanne de Lourdes (Rose Marie) Ruffle received a teaching fellowship at the English Language Institute in Cairo, Egypt, the following year, 1966-1967.

[55] St. Mel Parish Bulletin, July 25, 1965. Reproduced in the centennial memorial book, 35, SMWA.

[56] Interview with the author.

[57] St. Mel Parish Bulletin.

[58] St. Mel's Grade School Centennial, 1886-1986," Memorial Book, 34, SMWA.

[59] James W. Sanders, *The Education of an Urban Minority: Catholics in Chicago, 1883-1965* (New York: Oxford University Press, 1977), 223. He points out that Cardinal Stritch "had taken a strong stand on the Negro question, stronger than much of his white flock and some of his pastors were ready to accept" (218-219). As a result, "By 1960, 13,730 Negro pupils attended parochial schools, and by 1965, over 21,000, one-third of them non-Catholics" (219).

[60] Ibid., 220.

[61] Ibid., 199. Sanders states that in 1959 the superintendent's office required high schools to administer common entrance examinations. Since the archdiocese had begun to provide supplemental funding to the religious orders for building high schools, this policy enabled better overall planning by encouraging acceptance of all ability levels rather than recruitment of gifted students from across the city.

[62] Sadly, Sister Marcella would live only five more years. The outpouring of grief at her untimely death was a testimony to the excellent work she did to lift morale during difficult years.

[63] Sister Mary Joan to Sister Pauline Marie, May 3, 1964, SMWA.

[64] Msgr. William McManus to Sister Mary Joan, May 13, 1964, SMWA.

[65] Sister Pauline Marie to Sister Mary Joan, May 18, 1965, SMWA.

[66] Ibid.

[67] As the racial change in the neighborhood continued, despite the efforts to modify the curriculum, enrollment continued to decline to

well below capacity. In order to keep the school open, the archdiocese agreed to subsidize operations. A similar pattern affected nearby St. Mel High School, operated by the Christian Brothers. In May 1968 the two schools merged as a co-institutional archdiocesan high school, renting the Providence facility for $1 per year. However, by March 1969 the unrest in the neighborhood spilled over into the school, requiring police intervention to counteract vandalism, with militant student demands leading to complete consolidation and a new administration. Gradually the enrollment stabilized with a strong academic program but by 1978 the archdiocese could no longer sustain the subsidy and announced the school would close in 1978. Charging racial motivation, principal Paul Adams announced that the school would not close but would remain open as a private, independent, Catholic high school and launched a vigorous media campaign to gain support. On June 28, 1978, Superior General Sister Loretta Schafer wrote to the sisters to inform them that to "continue their pursuit of a viable form of education for black students" the storied building was being sold to the newly incorporated Providence-St. Mel High School for $100,000, noting, "As Mr. Paul Adams, the principal, put it: 'It's a gift.'" Sisters of Providence continued to serve as faculty and staff from 1969-1971 and again from 1980-1998. As documented in the 2009 film documentary, "The Providence Effect," the school has continued to thrive.

[68] Acts of Council, January 19, 1965, SMWA.

[69] "Two Nuns in Georgia: Gentle Crusaders," *Look* (November 2, 1965): 11-15. Photographed by Vernon Merritt, III.

[70] Sister Mary Jean Mark, "Martin Luther King, Jr. – and memories of a summer," *Canticle* 1968.

[71] Sister Alma Louise Mescher to Mother Rose Angela and Sisters, June 17, 1965, SMWA.

[72] Sister Alma Louise Mescher's oral history, SMWA.

[73] Sister Mary Jean Mark, op. cit.

[74] Op. cit. 12.

[75] Ibid.

[76] Acts of Council, December 1964, SMWA.

[77] According to http://www.measuringworth.com/uscompare, in terms of the consumer price index, $1,000 (for ten months) would be equivalent to $6,930 in 2011.

[78] Acts of Council, November 1962, SMWA.

[79] Sister Margaret Kern's oral history, SMWA.

[80] Ibid.

[81] Ibid. To her recounting of this episode, Sister Margaret adds the comment, "I remember she said later, 'When you come the next time, don't bring me any more ideas.'"

[82] Acts of Council, November 1964, SMWA.

[83] Mother Rose Angela to the sisters, January 27, 1966, SMWA.

[84] In 1972 the Congregation took advantage of Congressional legislation allowing religious congregations of men and women to buy into the Social Security system.

[85] Mother Rose Angela to the sisters, February 11, 1966.

[86] Book of Important Events, June, 1966, SMWA.

End of an Era

[1] *Constitutions* (1954), Article 20, SMWA.

[2] 1966 Chapter Report, 1, SMWA.

[3] Ibid., 11.

[4] Ibid., 4.

[5] Austin Flannery, OP, ed. *Perfectae Caritatis* in *Vatican Council II: Constitutions, Decrees, Declarations* (Northport, New York: Costello Publishing Company, 1996), Article 17, 398.

[6] Ibid., Article 23, 400.

[7] Pope John XXIII, "Opening Address," in Michael R. Prendergast and M.D. Ridge, *Voices from the Council* (Portland, Oregon: Pastoral Press, 2004), xii.

[8] "Decisions of the General Chapter on Religious Government and Temporalities." Interestingly the report also recommended professional training of sisters for internal administration positions. SMWA.

[9] *Perfectae Caritata,* Article 2, 387.

[10] 1966 Chapter decisions. SMWA.

[11] Flannery, *Gaudium et Spes,* in *Vatican Council II*, Article 1, 163. Joan Chittister, OP, in *The Way We Were: A Story of Conversion and Renewal* (Maryknoll, New York: Orbis Books, 2005) notes, "The sixteen major documents that came out of Vatican II ... completely reframed both the role and the definition of church. ... The lives of religious were affected by every one of them" (78-79).

[12] "Concluding remarks," in 1966 Chapter Decisions, SMWA.

[13] Community Diary, June 26, 1996, SMWA.

❧ Appendix A

Superiors General and Councils, 1926-1966

1926

Mother Mary Raphael Slattery—Superior General

1st Assistant—Sister Mary Bernard Laughlin

2nd Assistant—Sister Berchmans Collins

3rd Assistant—Sister Gertrude Clare Owens

4th Assistant—Sister Mary Ignatia Hanson

5th Assistant—Sister Francis Joseph Elbreg (Supervisor of Schools)

6th Assistant—Sister Geraldine Mullen (Secretary)

Appointed Treasurer General—Sister Adelaide O'Brien

1932

Mother Mary Raphael Slattery—Superior General

1st Assistant—Sister Mary Bernard Laughlin

2nd Assistant—Sister Helen Clare Freiburger

3rd Assistant—Sister Gertrude Clare Owens

4th Assistant—Sister Eileen Walker

5th Assistant—Sister Eugenia Clare Cullity (Supervisor of Schools)

6th Assistant—Sister Marie Stanislaus Curran (Secretary)

Elected Treasurer General, but not a member of Council—Sister Adelaide O'Brien

Appointed Supervisor of Schools, but not a member of the Council—Sister Francis Joseph Elbreg

1938

Mother Mary Bernard Laughlin—Superior General

1st Assistant—Sister Alexis Marie Hoff (resigned December 1945)

2nd Assistant—Sister Helen Clare Freiburger

3rd Assistant—Sister Gertrude Clare Owens

4th Assistant—Sister Rose Dolores Thuis

5th Assistant—Sister Francis Joseph Elbreg (Supervisor of Schools)

6th Assistant—Sister Marie Stanislaus Curran (Secretary)

Elected Treasurer, but not a member of Council—Sister Francis Raphael Donlon

1944

Mother Mary Bernard Laughlin—Superior General (died October 6, 1948)

1st Assistant—Sister Helen Clare Freiburger

2nd Assistant—Sister Eileen Walker

3rd Assistant—Sister Gertrude Clare Owens

4th Assistant—Sister Rose Dolores Thuis

5th Assistant—Sister Francis Joseph Elbreg (Supervisor of Schools)

6th Assistant—Sister Marie Helene Franey (Secretary)

Elected Treasurer, but not a member of Council—Sister Francis Raphael Donlon

1949

Mother Marie Helene Franey—Superior General (died November 23, 1953)

1st Assistant—Sister Gertrude Clare Owens

2nd Assistant—Sister Rose Genevieve Flaherty

3rd Assistant—Sister Catherine Celine Brocksmith

4th Assistant—Sister Rose Dolores Thuis

5th Assistant—Sister Francis Joseph Elbreg (Supervisor of Schools)

6th Assistant—Sister Loretta Therese O'Leary (Secretary)

Elected Treasurer, but not a member of Council—Sister Francis Raphael Donlon

1954

Mother Gertrude Clare Owens—Superior General (incapacitated February 1960)

1st Assistant—Sister Rose Angela Horan

2nd Assistant—Sister Rose Genevieve Flaherty

3rd Assistant—Sister Catherine Celine Brocksmith

4th Assistant—Sister Rose Dolores Thuis

5th Assistant—Sister Francis Joseph Elbreg (Supervisor of Schools)

6th Assistant—Sister Loretta Therese O'Leary (Secretary)

Elected Treasurer, but not a member of Council—Sister Francis Raphael Donlon

1960

Mother Rose Angela Horan—Superior General

1st Assistant—Sister Catherine Celine Brocksmith

2nd Assistant—Sister Mary Pius Regnier

3rd Assistant—Sister Rose Loretto Wagner

4th Assistant—Sister Rose Dolores Thuis

5th Assistant—Sister Mary Joan Kirchner (Director of Education)

6th Assistant—Sister Loretta Therese O'Leary (Secretary)

Elected Treasurer, but not a member of Council—Sister Francis Raphael Donlon

⮞ Appendix B

Timeline of Major Events 1926-1966

Mother Mary Raphael Slattery

1926   **General Chapter** – June 27, 1926
       Ladywood, Indianapolis, opened

1927   College incorporated, Dean appointed
       Maryland expansion: two missions opened near Maryhurst

1928   California beginnings: two missions opened
       Oklahoma City mission opened

1929   *Constitutions* approved
       Mother Mary Raphael's sick leave
       Sister Marie Gratia opens Chinese novitiate.
       Providence High School, Chicago, opened

1930   Catechist society established
       Providence Juniorate opened at Saint Mary-of-the-Woods

1931   Sister Berchmans visits China
       North Carolina mission opened

1932   **General Chapter** – June 23, 1932

1933   Provinces begin; four provincial superiors appointed
       Novitiates opened in East (Hyattsville), West (Anaheim)
       Financial situation worsens during Depression.

1934   Marywood, Anaheim, opened
       Bishop Joseph Ritter consecrated for Indianapolis

1935

1936

1937   *Journals and Letters* published
        Japanese occupation of China

Mother Mary Bernard Laughlin (1938)

1938   **General Chapter** – June 24, 1938
        Fort Wayne academies become Central Catholic High School

1939

1940   Centenary celebrations: January, Summer, October

1941   New Hampshire: Lady Isle and Rochester opened
        New wing of infirmary: Our Lady of Lourdes
        United States declares war on Japan

1942

1943   No homecoming due to war

1944   **General Chapter** – June 24, 1938
        Indianapolis made an archdiocese
        Creation of dioceses of Evansville and Lafayette

1945   Allies victorious; VE day in May, VJ day in August
        Commercial high school at Saint Mary-of-the-Woods

1946   Bishop Paul Schulte appointed Archbishop of Indianapolis
        Texas mission opened in Robstown

1947

1948   Diocese of Joliet created from Chicago
        Death of Mother Mary Bernard, October 6, 1948
        Evacuation of China mission to Taiwan

1949   **General Chapter –** March 25, 1949
          Provinces discontinued

Mother Marie Helene Franey (1949)

1949   Reorganization to central government

1950   Holy Year pilgrimages

1951   Our Lady of Providence, Clarksville, opens

1952   National Congress of Religious at Notre Dame

1953   First books of *To God through Music* series published
          Death of Mother Marie Helene, November 23, 1953

1954   **General Chapter**—May 5, 1954
          New edition of *Constitutions*

Mother Gertrude Clare Owens (1954)

1954   NCEA Sister Formation Committee
          President of College title given to Dean Sister Marie Perpetua Hayes
          Councilors visit Rome re Mother Theodore's cause

1955   St. Louis, Missouri: Our Lady of Providence opened
          Sisters Francis Joseph and Eugenia visit Taiwan
          Apostolic process for Mother Theodore's canonization Cause

1956   Conference of Major Superiors of Women instituted
          Hearings re Mother Theodore's Cause
          Diocese of Gary created from Fort Wayne
          Construction of new buildings at Immaculata
          Holy Week liturgical changes

1957   Formation changes: establishment of tertian and juniorate
          programs

1958   Rome recommends creating provinces.
Plans for new novitiate building
Death of Pope Pius XII; election of Pope John XXIII

1959   *Faith Is the Substance,* biography of Mother Theodore, published
Pope John XXIII announces ecumenical council.
December: Mother Gertrude Clare's illness

1960   Invitation of suggestions and planning for General Chapter
Move to new novitiate building, juniorate to old novitiate
Providence English College, Taichung accredited
General Chapter—June 16-20, 1960
Moratorium on acceptance of grade schools

Mother Rose Angela Horan (1960)

1960   Change of habit cap
Major high school construction projects underway

1961   Councilors visit Rome for Cardinal Ritter's elevation
Mission assignments given in May

1962   Mother Theodore Guerin High School, River Grove, opened
Chartrand High School, Indianapolis
Providence High School, Joliet, opened
College fund-raising drive begins.
Providence Catechist Society receives independent status.
October 22: Opening of Second Vatican Council

1963   Intensive research for Mother Theodore's Cause
Sister Formation Program moves from NCEA to CMSW.
March: Arequipa mission begins.
May: Providence Retirement Home opens.
September: Ladywood School dedicates enlarged facilities.
November 18, 1963: Death of Mother Gertrude Clare
December : local superiors' workshop
December: Vatican II *Constitution on the Liturgy*

1964   November: Vatican II *Dogmatic Constitution on the Church*

1965   Legal separation of Congregation and College
College faculty house built
Providence Speech and Hearing Center established
Sisters participate in civil rights action in Albany, Georgia
October: Pope Paul VI visits New York
Vatican II *Decree on Renewal of Religious Life*
Performances of "Angel Choir" in Indianapolis, Chicago

1966   **General Chapter** – June 19-26, 1966

❧ Appendix C

Biographical sketches of the 1929 Boston entrants

Sister Mary Patricia Carroll

Eileen Moira Carroll was born to Irish immigrants John J. and Delia Lennon Carroll on November 14, 1908, in Revere, Massachusetts. The family included two brothers, Brendan and Bill (later Father Carroll), and a sister Beatrice. After teaching middle grades for thirty-six years, a heart condition with associated palsy led to her early retirement in 1974 at Saint Mary-of-the-Woods, where she died on December 18, 1983.

Sister Philip Conlin

Frances Elizabeth Conlin was born to Edward and Elizabeth Houghton Conlin on March 3, 1908, and grew up with her brother Philip and sister Barbara in Chelsea, Massachusetts. After she spent twenty-seven years as a primary teacher, her health declined. Although she recovered from heart surgery in 1957 and returned to the classroom, in 1978 she retired in the Boston area. She died at Massachusetts General Hospital on February 22, 1985, and is buried at Holy Cross Cemetery in Malden.

Note: The habit in this photo was adopted in 1968.

Sister Ann Bernardine Dunne

Catherine Dunne was born to James and Ellen Coppinger Dunne on August 3, 1910, in Chelsea, Massachusetts, becoming the youngest of three girls and four boys. After she spent thirty-six years in teaching and administration, in 1968 her poor health forced an early retirement in the Boston area. In 1984 she returned to Saint Mary-of-the-Woods, where she died on July 30, 1990.

Note: In 1969 sisters were given the option of wearing contemporary clothing with the distinctive Sister of Providence cross.

Sister Cyril Tobin

Bertha Tobin was born to Canadian immigrants James and Alexanderine Chavenelle Paradis on August 28, 1911, in Cambridge, Massachusetts. As her parents were unable to afford to raise all their children, following the custom of the time they gave two daughters up for adoption to two families from St. Rose, Chelsea, Bertha to Mr. and Mrs. Tobin and Gertrude to the Canterbury family. After teaching primary grades for thirty-nine years, she earned a library certificate and served as school librarian in four schools before retiring to the motherhouse in 1985. In her later years she had the joy of reconnecting with her other sisters, Elise and Frances. She died at the motherhouse on November 3, 1998.

Sister Mary Regis O'Kane

Marie Eva was born to James and Zilda Gion O'Kane on October 14, 1912 in Dudley, Massachusetts, their only child. After forty-four years of teaching and administration in fifteen schools, including three assignments in her home state of Massachusetts, she returned to Saint Mary-of-the-Woods where she coordinated the activities of Our Lady of Providence Shrine from 1980 until her 1985 retirement. She died on January 16, 2005.

❧ Bibliography

Sister of Providence Publications

A Journey in Love, Mercy, and Justice: A pictorial history of the Sisters of Providence of Saint Mary-of-the-Woods celebrating 150 years of service among the people of God. Saint Mary-of the-Woods, IN: Sisters of Providence, 1989.

Bailly, Mother Mary Cecilia. *Life of Mother Theodore, Foundress of the Congregation of the Sisters of Providence in America.* 1873.

Brown, Sister Mary Borromeo. *The History of the Sisters of Providence of Saint Mary-of-the-Woods.* Vol. 1. New York: Benziger, 1949.

Constitutions of the Sisters of Providence of St. Mary-of-the-Woods. 1929.

Cullity, Sister St. Philomene. "Educational Work of the Sisters of Providence in Indiana." MA thesis. Loyola University, Chicago, 1933.

Elbreg, Sister Francis Joseph, ed. *Our Government and Our Civic Duties: A Text for the Upper Grades of Catholic Elementary Schools Showing How We Are Governed and How Civil Authority Depends upon the Divine Law.* New York: Benziger, 1938.

In God's Acre: Biographical Sketches. Series One and Two. Saint Mary-of-the-Woods, IN: Sisters of Providence, 1940.

Little Office of the Blessed Virgin Mary according to the Roman Ritual for the Use of the Sisters of Providence of Saint Mary-of-the-Woods. 1954.

Love, Mercy, Justice: A Book of Practices of the Sisters of Providence. Saint Mary-of-the-Woods, IN: Sisters of Providence, 2006.

Logan, Sister Eugenia. *History of the Sisters of Providence of Saint Mary-of-the-Woods.* Vol. 2. Terre Haute, IN: Moore-Langen, 1978.

Madden, Sister Mary Roger. *The Path Marked Out: History of the Sisters of Providence of Saint Mary-of-the Woods, Indiana.* Vol. 3. Saint Mary-of-the-Woods, IN: Office of Congregational Advancement—Sisters of Providence, 1991.

Manual of the Sisters of Providence. Saint Mary-of-the-Woods, IN: Sisters of Providence, 1950.

Mug, Sister Mary Theodosia, Ed. *Journals and Letters of Mother Theodore Guérin.* Saint Mary-of-the-Woods, IN: Sisters of Providence, 1937.

Mug, Sister Mary Theodosia. *Life and Life-Work of Mother Theodore Guérin, Foundress of the Sisters of Providence at St.-Mary-of-the-Woods, Vigo County, Indiana.* New York: Benziger, 1904.

Ryan, Sister Joseph Eleanor. *Call to Courage: A Story of Mother Theodore Guérin.* Notre Dame: Dujarie Press, 1968.

Wolf, Sister Ann Colette. *Against All Odds: Sisters of Providence Mission to the Chinese, 1920-1990.* Saint Mary-of-the-Woods, IN: Office of Communications: Sisters of Providence, 1990.

The Teacher's Guide: or Educational Methods for the Special Use of the Sisters of Providence of Saint-Mary-of-the-Woods. Saint Mary-of-the-Woods, IN: Sisters of Providence, 1914.

Woodland Echoes. Summer newsletter of the Sisters of Providence, published 1932-1965.

Secondary Sources

Ahlstrom, Sydney E. *A Religious History of the American People.* New Haven and London: Yale University Press, 1972

Brennan, I.H.M., Margaret R. *What Was There for Me Once: A Memoir.* Toronto: Novalis, 2009.

Briggs, Kenneth. *Double Crossed: Uncovering the Catholic Church's Betrayal of American Nuns.* New York: Doubleday, 2006.

Brown, Dorothy M. *Setting a Course: American Women in the 1920s.* Boston: Twayne Publishers, 1987.

Campbell, D'Ann. *Women at War with America: Private Lives in a Patriotic Era.* Cambridge, Mass.: Harvard University Press, 1984.

Chittister, Joan. *The Way We Were: A Story of Conversion and Renewal.* Maryknoll, New York: Orbis Books, 2005.

Coburn, Carol K., and Martha Smith. *Spirited Lives: How Nuns Shaped Catholic Culture and American Life, 1836-1920.* Chapel Hill: University of North Carolina Press, 1999.

Creusen, S.J., Joseph and Adam C. Ellis, S.J. *Religious Men and Women in Church Law: Sixth English Edition.* Milwaukee: Bruce Publishing Company, 1958.

Cummings, Kathleen Sprows. *New Women of the Old Faith: Gender and American Catholicism in the Progressive Era.* Chapel Hill: University of North Carolina Press, 2009.

Dolan, Jay P. *The American Catholic Experience: A History from Colonial Times to the Present.* New York: Doubleday & Company, 1985.

_____. *In Search of an American Catholicism.* New York: Oxford University Press, 2002.

Dries, Angelyn, OSF. "The Americanization of Religious Life: Women Religious, 1872-1922." *U.S. Catholic Historian* 10, nos. 1-2 (1992): 13-23.

Flannery, Austin, OP, ed. *Vatican Council II: Constitutions, Decrees, Declarations.* Northport, New York: Costello Publishing Company, 1996.

Friedan, Betty. *The Feminine Mystique.* New York: W.W. Norton & Company, 1997.

Fornero, George V. "The Expansion and Decline of Enrollment and Facilities of Secondary Schools in the Archdiocese of Chicago, 1955-1980: A Historical Study." Ed.D. Diss. Loyola University of Chicago, 1990.

Gleason, Philip. *Contending with Modernity: Catholic Higher Education in the Twentieth Century.* New York: Oxford University Press, 1995.

Gourley, Catherine. *Rosie and Mrs. America: Perceptions of Women in the 1930s and 1940s.* Minneapolis, Minn.: Twenty-First Century Books, 2008.

Grob, Gerald N. *The Mad Among Us: A History of the Care of America's Mentally Ill.* New York: The Free Press, Macmillan, Inc., 1994.

Hoy, Suellen. *Good Hearts: Catholic Sisters in Chicago's Past.* Chicago: University of Illinois Press, 2006.

Jarrell, Lynn, OSU. "The Development of Legal Structures for Women Religious Between 1500 and 1900: A Study of Selected Institutes of Religious Life for Women." *U.S.Catholic Historian* 10, nos. 1-2 (1992): 25-34.

_____. "The Development of Legal Structures for Women Religious Between 1500 and 1900: A Study of Selected Institutes of Religious Life for Women." Ph.D. diss. The Catholic University of America, 1984.

Kaledin, Eugenia. *Daily Life in the United States, 1940-1959; Shifting Worlds.* Westport, CT: Greenwood Press, 2000.

Kaminer, Wendy. *Women volunteering: The Pleasure, Pain, and Politics of Unpaid Work from 1830 to the present.* New York: Doubleday, 1984.

Kennelly, Karen M. *The Religious Formation Conference, 1954-2004.* Silver Spring, MD: Religious Formation Conference, 2009.

Kennedy, David M. *Freedom from Fear: The American People in Depression and War, 1929-45.* New York: Oxford University Press, 1999.

Kyvig, David. *Daily Life in the United States, 1920-1939: Decades of Promise and Pain.* Westport, CT: Greenwood Press, 2002.

Lawlor, Kathryn. *From There to Here: The Sisters of Charity of the Blessed Virgin Mary from 1942-1972.* Dubuque: Mount Carmel Press, 2010.

Marty, Myron A. *Daily Life in the United States, 1960-1990: Decades of Discord.* Westport, CT: Greenwood Press, 1997.

McKeon, Donna Forill. *This Is Sister.* Saint Mary-of-the-Woods, IN: Saint Mary-of-the-Woods Alumnae Associatein, 1968.

Meyers, Sister Bertrande. DC. *The Education of Sisters: A Plan for Integrating the Religious, Social, Cultural and Professional Training of Sisters.* New York: Sheed and Ward, 1941.

Morris, Charles R. *American Catholic: The Saints and Sinners Who Built America's Most Powerful Church.* New York: Random House, 1997.

Patterson, James T. *Grand Expectations: The United States, 1945-1974.* New York: Oxford University Press, 1996.

Peters, Edward N., ed. *The 1917 or Pio-Benedictine Code of Canon Law.* San Francisco: Ignatius Press, 2001.

Pettit, M. Loretta, OP. "Sister M. Madeleva Wolff, CSC." *Catholic Education: A Journal of Inquiry and Practice.* http://ejournals.bc.edu/ojs/index.php/catholic/article/view/703/690, March 2006.

Rapley, Elizabeth. *The Lord as Their Portion: The Story of the Religious Orders and How Thy Shaped Our World.* Grand Rapids: William B. Eerdmans, 2011.

Religious Community Life in the United States: Proceedings of the Sisters' Section of the First National Congress of Religious of the United States. New York: Paulist Press, 1952.

Ryan, Mary Perkins. *Are Parochial Schools the Answer? Catholic Education in the Light of the Council.* New York: Holt, Rinehart and Winston, 1964.

Sanders, James W. *The Education of an Urban Minority: Catholics in Chicago, 1883-1965.* New York: Oxford University Press, 1977.

Scatena, Maria (Carol). "Educational movements that have influenced the sister teacher education program of the Congregation of the Sisters of Providence, 1840-1940." PhD Diss., Loyola University of Chicago, 1987.

Schneider, Nicholas A. *Joseph Elmer Cardinal Ritter: His Life and Times.* Ligouri, MO: Ligouri Press, 2008.

Schier, Tracy. *History of Higher Education for Women at Saint Mary-of-the-Woods: 1840-1980.* PhD Diss. Boston College, 1987.

Schier, Tracy and Cynthia Russett. *Catholic Women's Colleges in America.* Baltimore: The Johns Hopkins University Press, 2002.

Schmidley, A. Dianne, *Profile of the Foreign-Born Population in the United States: 2000.* U.S. Census Bureau, Current Population Reports, Series P23-206. Washington, DC: U.S. Government Printing Office, 2001.

Siegfried, Regina, ASC. *"Missionaries More and More": The History of the China Mission of the Adorers of the Blood of Christ, 1933-1945.* Bloomington, Ind.: Authorhouse, 2005.

Sister Formation Bulletin 3, no. 1 (Autumn, 1956).

The Official Catholic Directory. New York: P.J. Kenedy & Sons, 1920 et.al. (Annual editions as indicated.)

Weatherford, Doris. *American Women and World War II.* New York: Facts on File, Inc., 1990.

Zeitz, Joshua. *Flapper: A Madcap Story of Sex, Style, Celebrity, and the Women Who Made America Modern.* New York: Crown Publishers, 2006.

Sources from Saint Mary-of-the-Woods Archives

Book of Establishments

Book of Important Events

Entrance Book

Community Diaries

Council Diary

Necrology

Acts of Council

Oral Histories (unless otherwise noted, interviews by
Sister Mary Roger Madden)

Farrell, Sister Agnes (interview by author)

Healy, Sister Doris

Hoerner, Sister Marie William

Howard, Sister Dorothy Eileen

Hyde, Sister Agnella

Kern, Sister Margaret

Kiley, Sister Robert

Kirchner, Sister Mary Joan

Knoerle, Sister Jeanne

McManus, Sister Frances Alma

McNulty, Sister Edwardine

Mescher, Sister Alma Louise

O'Connor, Mary Evelyn Bouvier (interview by author)

O'Connor, Sister Kathleen Therese

O'Leary, Sister Loretta Therese

Pomeroy, Sister Mary Joseph

Regnier, Mother Mary Pius

Schaefer, Sister Rose Louise (interview by author)

Suelzer, Sister Alexa

Troy, Sister John Francis

Turk, Sister Mary Charles

Memoirs

    Brady, Sister Marian

    Brawley, Sister Ann Kathleen

    Fu, Sister Donna Marie

    Hartigan, Sister Mary Liguori

    Horan, Mother Rose Angela

    Hussey, Sister Rosarie

    Kirchner, Sister Mary Joan

    Lauer, Sister Alma Clare

    Li, Sister Agnes Joan

    McBarron, Sister St. Eugenia

    Miller, Sister Mary Adele

    Newport, Sister Esther

    O'Leary, Sister Loretta Therese

    Quinkert, Sister Joann

    Schafer, Sister Rose Louise

    Schultz, Sister St. Francis

    Walta, Sister Marie Dolores

House Diaries

Correspondence of Superiors General

Pamphlets

    Monthly Retreat and Preparation for Death

Typescripts

    Anonymous (probably Sister Eugenia Logan). "An Account of the Beginning, the Progress, and the Discontinuance of the Provinces of the Sisters of Providence."

    Krafthefer, Sister Immaculee. Collection of letters from 1955-1956 study at The Institute Pius XII in Florence.

Suelzer, Sister Alexa. Collection of 20 letters describing 1955-1956 European travels in conjunction with a year of study in Rome.

Thuis, Sister Rose Dolores. "Letters and Spiritual Reading Papers, 1949-1966." Collection prepared by Sister Catherine Joseph Wilcox, 1995.

❧ Indices

Index of Sisters of Providence

Sisters are listed by first name.
Bold page numbers indicate photos.

Index of Subjects

Bold page numbers indicate photos.

❧ About the Author

Maureen Abbott, SP, has lived a biography similar to many in this book. Inspired by the example of the sisters at St. John, Robstown, Texas, who provided her early education to follow their path, she was among the first to enjoy the benefits of the Sister Formation Program. She earned a BA degree in history and English from Saint Mary-of-the-Woods College, then went on to serve as teacher and administrator in Sister of Providence schools in Indiana, Illinois and California. Master's degrees in educational administration from the University of Washington and theology from the University of Notre Dame enriched her later ministries as provincial superior and diocesan service. A previous book, Paulist Press's *With Love Beyond All Telling*, is based on the curriculum she developed for parish lay ministers for the Diocese of Corpus Christi, Texas. She currently ministers at the Tribunal of the Archdiocese of Portland.